math expressions

Dr. Karen C. Fuson

Watch the moose come alive in its snowy environment as you discover and solve math challenges.

Download the *Math Worlds AR* app available on Android or iOS devices.

Grade 3

Volume 1

This material is based upon work supported by the
National Science Foundation
under Grant Numbers
ESI-9816320, REC-9806020, and RED-935373.

Any opinions, findings, and conclusions, or recommendations expressed in this material are those of the author and do not necessarily reflect the views of the National Science Foundation.

Cover Illustration: ©Josh Brill

Printed in the U.S.A.

ISBN 978-1-328-74382-4

7 8 9 10 0928 26 25 24 23 22 21 20

4500817361 C D E F G

Unit 1 Multiplication and Division with 0–5, 9, and 10

BIG IDEA 1 - Meanings of Multiplication and Division: 5s and 2s

BIG IDEA 2 - Patterns and Strategies: 9s and 10s

BIG IDEA 3 - Strategies for Factors and Products: 3s and 4s

Unit 2 Multiplication and Division with 6s, 7s, and 8s and Multiply with Multiples of 10

BIG IDEA 1 - The Remaining Multiplications

BIG IDEA 2 - Problem Solving and Multiples of 10

Unit 3 | Multidigit Addition, Subtraction, and Multiplication

BIG IDEA 1 - Understand Place Value and Rounding

BIG IDEA 2 - Addition and Subtraction Strategies and Group to Add

BIG IDEA 3 - Ungroup to Subtract

Student Resources

Dear Family:

In this unit and the next, your child will be practicing basic multiplications and divisions. *Math Expressions* uses studying, practicing, and testing of the basic multiplications and divisions in class. Your child also should practice at home.

Homework Helper Your child will have math homework almost every day. He or she needs a Homework Helper. The helper may be anyone — you, an older brother or sister (or other family member), a neighbor, or a friend. Please decide who the main Homework Helper will be and ask your child to tell the teacher tomorrow. Make a specific time for homework and give your child a quiet place to work.

Study Plans Each day your child will fill out a study plan, indicating which basic multiplications and divisions he or she will study that evening. When your child has finished studying (practicing), his or her Homework Helper should sign the study plan.

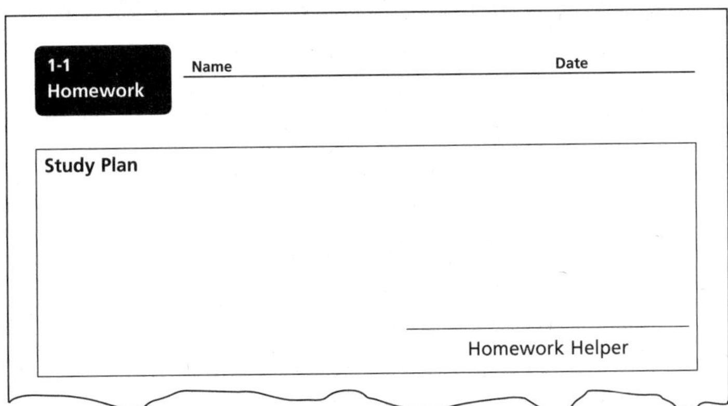
1-1
Homework
Name
Date
Study Plan
Homework Helper

Practice Charts Each time a new number is introduced, students' homework will include a practice chart. To practice, students can cover the products with a finger or pencil. They will say the multiplications, sliding the finger or pencil down the column to see each product after saying it. Students can also start with the last problem in a column and slide up. It is important that your child studies count-bys and multiplications at least 5 minutes every night. Your child should study each division on the Mixed Up column by covering the first factor.

Keep all materials in a special place.

	In Order	Mixed Up
5s	1 × 5 = 5	9 × 5 = 45
	2 × 5 = 10	5 × 5 = 25
	3 × 5 = 15	2 × 5 = 10
	4 × 5 = 20	7 × 5 = 35
	5 × 5 = 25	4 × 5 = 20
	6 × 5 = 30	6 × 5 = 30
	7 × 5 = 35	10 × 5 = 50
	8 × 5 = 40	8 × 5 = 40
	9 × 5 = 45	1 × 5 = 5
	10 × 5 = 50	3 × 5 = 15

To help students understand the concept of multiplication, the *Math Expressions* program presents three ways to think about multiplication.

- **Repeated groups**: Multiplication can be used to find the total in repeated groups of the same size. In early lessons, students circle the group size in repeated-groups equations to help keep track of which factor is the group size and which is the number of groups.

4 groups of bananas

$4 \times \textcircled{3} = 3 + 3 + 3 + 3 = 12$

- **Arrays**: Multiplication can be used to find the total number of items in an *array*—an arrangement of objects into rows and columns.

5 columns

2 rows  2-by-5 array

2 rows of pennies = $2 \times 5 = 10$

- **Area**: Multiplication can be used to find the area of a rectangle

3 units 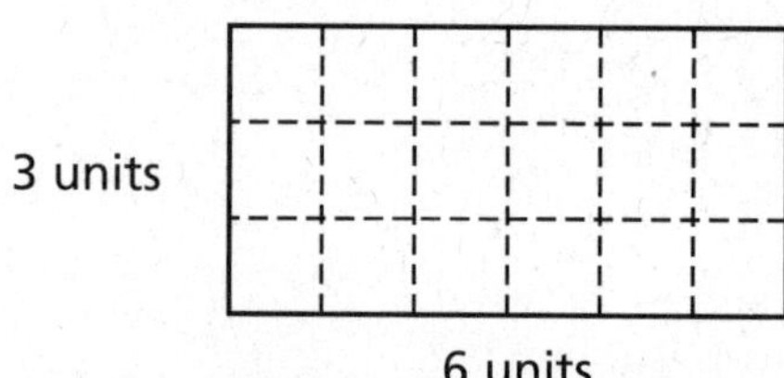

6 units

Area: 3 units × 6 units = 18 square units

Please contact me if you have any questions or comments.

Thank you.

Sincerely,
Your child's teacher

Estimada familia:

En esta unidad y en la que sigue, su niño practicará multiplicaciones y divisiones básicas. *Math Expressions* usa en la clase el estudio, la práctica y la evaluación de las multiplicaciones y divisiones básicas. También su niño debe practicar en casa.

Ayudante de tareas Su niño tendrá tarea de matemáticas casi a diario y necesitará un ayudante para hacer sus tareas. Ese ayudante puede ser cualquier persona: usted, un hermano o hermana mayor, otro familiar, un vecino o un amigo. Por favor decida quién será esta persona y pida a su niño que se lo diga a su maestro mañana. Designe un tiempo específico para la tarea y un lugar para trabajar sin distracciones.

Planes de estudio Todos los días su niño va a completar un plan de estudio, que indica cuáles multiplicaciones y divisiones debe estudiar esa noche. Cuando su niño haya terminado de estudiar (practicar), la persona que lo ayude debe firmar el plan de estudio.

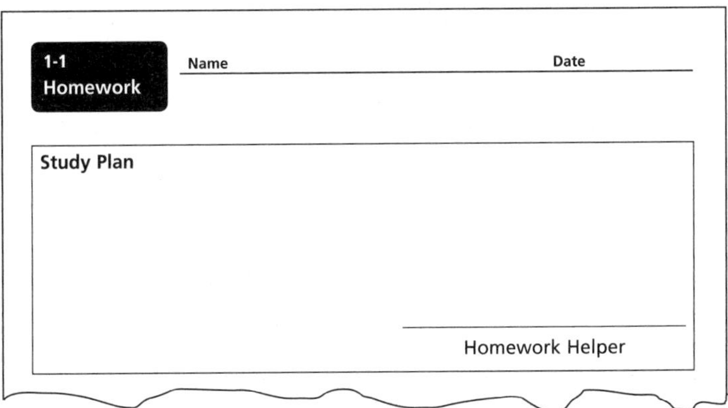

1-1
Homework
Name
Date
Study Plan
Homework Helper

Tablas de práctica Cada vez que se presente un número nuevo, la tarea de los estudiantes incluirá una tabla de práctica. Para practicar, los estudiantes pueden cubrir los productos con un dedo o lápiz.Los niños dicen la multiplicación y deslizan el dedo o lápiz hacia abajo para revelar el producto después de decirlo. También pueden empezar con el último problema de la columna y deslizar el lápiz o el papel hacia arriba. Es importante que su niño practique el conteo y la multiplicación por lo menos 5 minutos cada noche. Su niño debe estudiar cada división en la columna de Desordenados cubriendo el primer factor.

	In Order	Mixed Up
5s	1 × 5 = 5	9 × 5 = 45
	2 × 5 = 10	5 × 5 = 25
	3 × 5 = 15	2 × 5 = 10
	4 × 5 = 20	7 × 5 = 35
	5 × 5 = 25	4 × 5 = 20
	6 × 5 = 30	6 × 5 = 30
	7 × 5 = 35	10 × 5 = 50
	8 × 5 = 40	8 × 5 = 40
	9 × 5 = 45	1 × 5 = 5
	10 × 5 = 50	3 × 5 = 15

Guarde todos los materiales.

Para ayudar a los estudiantes a comprender el concepto de la multiplicación, el programa *Math Expressions* presenta tres maneras de pensar en la multiplicación. Éstas se describen a continuación.

- **Grupos repetidos**: La multiplicación se puede usar para hallar el total con grupos del mismo tamaño que se repiten. Cuando empiezan a trabajar con ecuaciones de grupos repetidos, los estudiantes rodean con un círculo el tamaño del grupo en las ecuaciones, para recordar cuál factor representa el tamaño del grupo y cuál representa el número de grupos.

4 grupos de bananas

$4 \times \textcircled{3} = 3 + 3 + 3 + 3 = 12$

- **Matrices**: Se puede usar la multiplicación para hallar el número total de objetos en una *matriz*, es decir, una disposición de objetos en filas y columnas.

5 columnas

2 filas

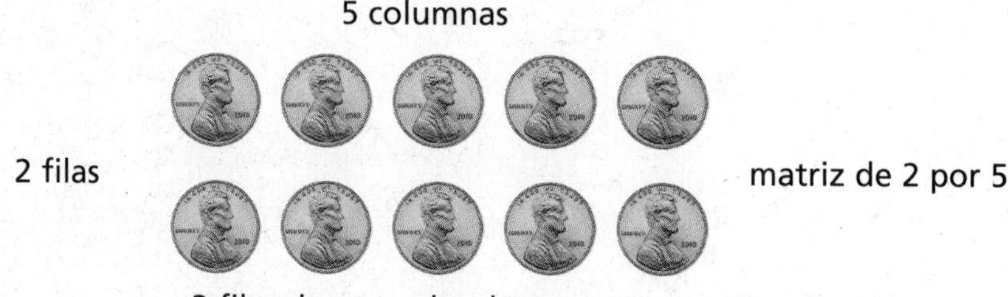

matriz de 2 por 5

2 filas de monedas de un centavo $= 2 \times 5 = 10$

- **Área**: Se puede usar la multiplicación para hallar el área de un rectángulo.

3 unidades

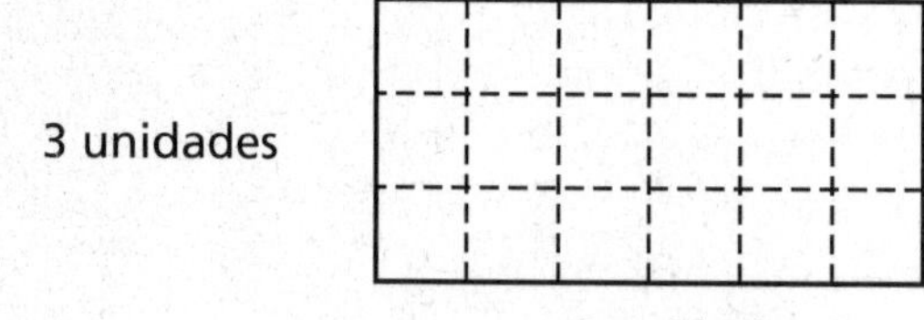

6 unidades

Área: 3 unidades × 6 unidades = 18 unidades cuadradas

Si tiene alguna duda o algún comentario, por favor comuníquese conmigo. Gracias.

Atentamente,
El maestro de su niño

area	**Associative Property of Multiplication**
array	**column**
Associative Property of Addition	**Commutative Property of Addition**

The property that states that changing the way in which factors are grouped does not change the product.

Example:

$(2 \times 3) \times 4 = 2 \times (3 \times 4)$

$6 \times 4 = 2 \times 12$

$24 = 24$

The total number of square units that cover a figure.

Example:

The area of the rectangle is 6 square units.

A part of a table or array that contains items arranged vertically.

An arrangement of objects, pictures, or numbers in columns and rows.

The property that states that changing the order of addends does not change the sum.

Example:

$3 + 7 = 7 + 3$

$10 = 10$

The property that states that changing the way in which addends are grouped does not change the sum.

Example:

$(2 + 3) + 1 = 2 + (3 + 1)$

$5 + 1 = 2 + 4$

$6 = 6$

Commutative Property of Multiplication	**division**
Distributive Property	**divisor**
dividend	**equal groups**

The mathematical operation that separates an amount into smaller equal groups to find the number of groups or the number in each group.

Example:

$12 \div 3 = 4$ is a division number sentence.

The property that states that changing the order of factors does not change the product.

Example:

$5 \times 4 = 4 \times 5$

$20 = 20$

The number that you divide by in division.

Example:

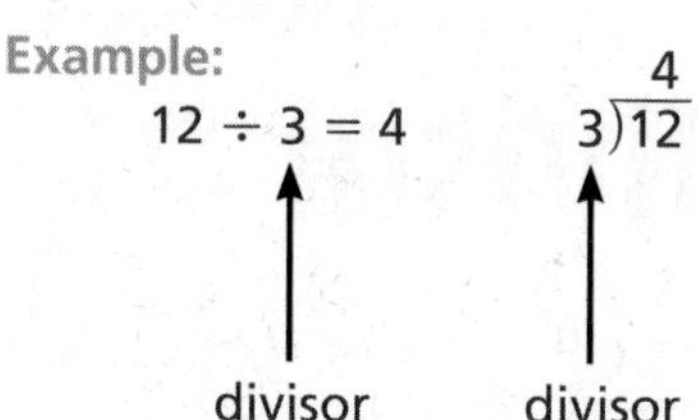

You can multiply a sum by a number, or multiply each addend by the number and add the products; the result is the same.

Example:

$3 \times (2 + 4) = (3 \times 2) + (3 \times 4)$

$3 \times 6 = 6 + 12$

$18 = 18$

Two or more groups with the same number of items in each group.

The number that is divided in division.

Example:

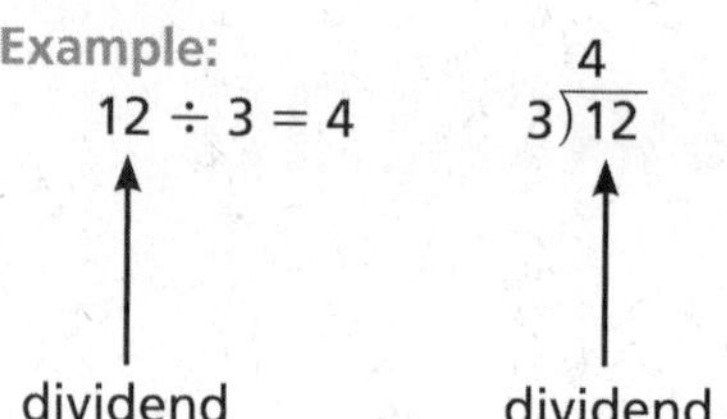

equation

function table

even number

Identity Property of Addition

factor

Identity Property of Multiplication

A table of ordered pairs that shows a function.

For every input number, there is only one possible output number.

Rule: add 2	
Input	**Output**
1	3
2	4
3	5
4	6

A mathematical sentence with an equals sign.

Examples:

$11 + 22 = 33$

$75 - 25 = 50$

If 0 is added to a number, the sum equals that number.

Example:

$3 + 0 = 3$

A whole number that is a multiple of 2. The ones digit in an even number is 0, 2, 4, 6, or 8.

The product of 1 and any number equals that number.

Example:

$10 \times 1 = 10$

Any of the numbers that are multiplied to give a product.

Example:

$4 \times 5 = 20$

factor factor product

(>) is greater than

odd number

(<) is less than

pictograph

multiplication

product

A whole number that is not a multiple of 2. The ones digit in an odd number is 1, 3, 5, 7, or 9.

A symbol used to compare two numbers.

Example:

$6 > 5$

6 *is greater than* 5.

A graph that uses pictures or symbols to represent data.

Favorite Ice Cream Flavors

Peanut Butter Crunch	🍦 (1½ symbols)
Cherry Vanilla	🍦🍦🍦
Chocolate	🍦🍦🍦🍦🍦

Each 🍦 stands for 4 votes.

A symbol used to compare two numbers.

Example:

$5 < 6$

5 *is less than* 6.

The answer when you multiply numbers.

Example:

$4 \times 7 = 28$

factor factor product

A mathematical operation that combines equal groups.

Example:

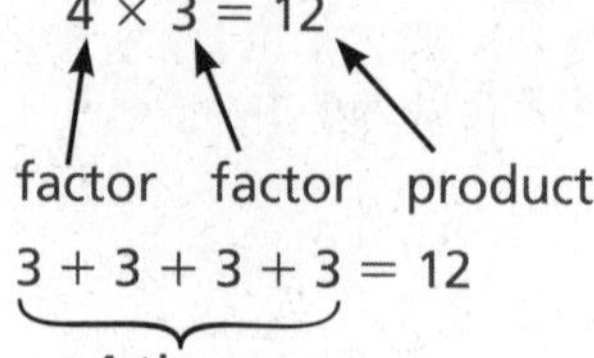

$3 + 3 + 3 + 3 = 12$

4 times

quotient	**variable**
row	**Zero Property of Multiplication**
square unit	

A letter or symbol used to represent an unknown number in an algebraic expression or equation.

Example:

$2 + n$

n is a variable.

The answer when you divide numbers.

Example:

$35 \div 7 = 5$ $\quad 7\overline{)35}$ with 5 above ← quotient

↑ quotient

If 0 is multiplied by a number, the product is 0.

Example:

$3 \times 0 = 0$

A part of a table or array that contains items arranged horizontally.

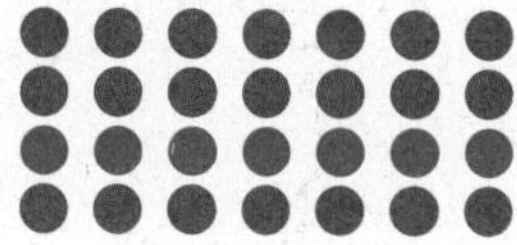

A unit of area equal to the area of a square with one-unit sides.

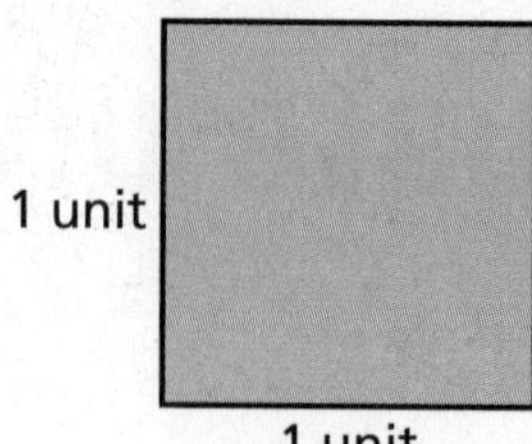

Name ____________________

PATH to FLUENCY

Explore Patterns with 5s

What patterns do you see below?

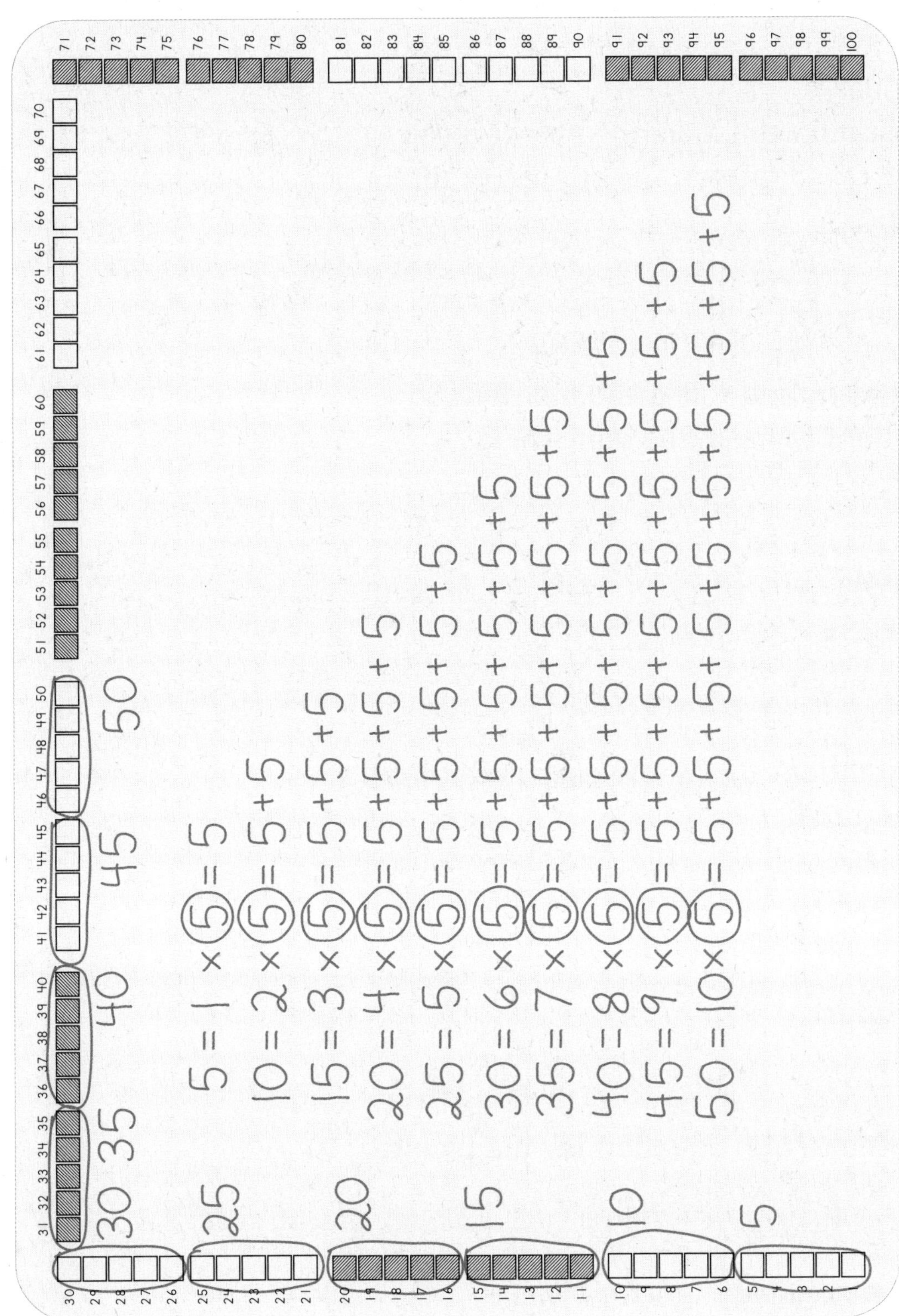

PATH to FLUENCY Practice Multiplications with 5

VOCABULARY
equation
multiplication
factor
product

An **equation** shows that two quantities or expressions are equal.
An equal sign (=) is used to show that the two sides are equal.
In a **multiplication** equation, the numbers you multiply are called **factors**. The answer, or total, is the **product**.

$$3 \times 5 = 15$$

factor factor product

The symbols ×, *, and • all mean *multiply*. So these equations all mean the same thing.

$3 \times 5 = 15$ $3 * 5 = 15$ $3 \bullet 5 = 15$

Write each total.

1. 4 × (5) = 5 + 5 + 5 + 5 = _____
2. 7 • (5) = 5 + 5 + 5 + 5 + 5 + 5 + 5 = _____

Write the 5s additions that show each multiplication. Then write the total.

3. 6 × (5) = ______________________________ = _____
4. 9 * (5) = ______________________________ = _____

Write each product.

5. 8 × 5 = _____
6. 10 × 5 = _____
7. 5 × 5 = _____

Write a 5s multiplication equation for the picture.

8. 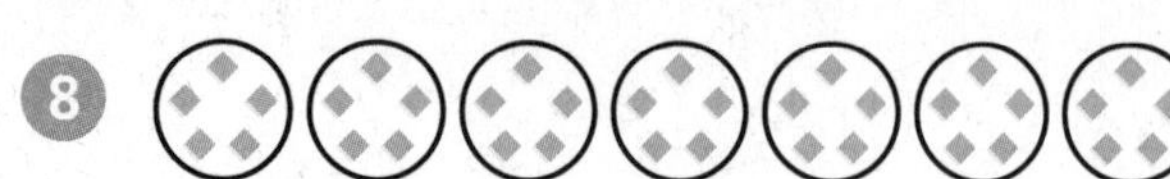 ______________________________

Check Understanding
Describe ways to find 8 × 5.

Name ______________________

PATH to FLUENCY Explore Equal Groups

You can use multiplication to find the total when you have equal groups.

$2 \times \textcircled{5} = 5 + 5 = 10$

PATH to FLUENCY Write Multiplication Equations

Write a multiplication equation to find the total number.

1. How many bananas?

____

2. How many toes?

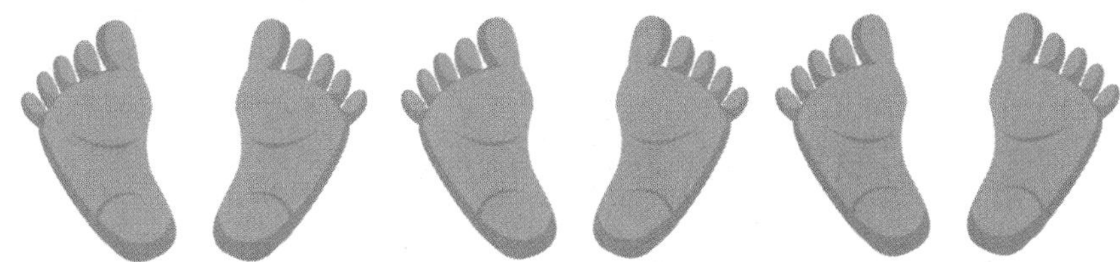

____

3. How many wheels?

____

Make a Math Drawing to Solve Problems

Make a drawing for each problem. Label your drawing with a multiplication equation. Then write the answer to the problem.

Show your work.

4. Sandra bought 4 bags of lemons. There were 6 lemons in each bag. How many lemons did she buy in all?

____

5. Batai baked 2 peach pies. He used 7 peaches per pie. How many peaches did he use in all?

____

6. The Fuzzy Friends pet store has 3 rabbit cages. There are 5 rabbits in each cage. How many rabbits does the store have in all?

____

7. The Paws Plus pet store has 5 rabbit cages. There are 3 rabbits in every cage. How many rabbits does the store have in all?

____

8. There are 7 players on an ultimate frisbee team. The team wants to order 2 game shirts for each player. How many game shirts does the team need to order in all?

____

Name

Explore Equal Shares Drawings

Here is a problem with repeated groups. Read the problem, and think about how you would solve it.

Ms. Thomas bought 4 bags of oranges. Each bag contained 5 oranges. How many oranges did she buy in all?

You could also find the answer to this problem by making an equal shares drawing.

Think:

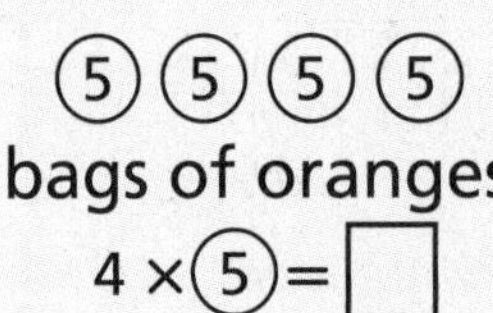

Equal Shares Drawing

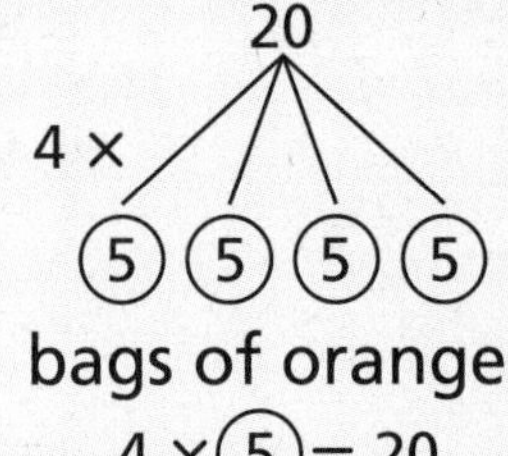

Make an equal shares drawing to solve each problem.

Show your work.

9. Ms. González bought 6 boxes of pencils. There were 5 pencils in each box. How many pencils did she buy in all?

____

10. Mr. Franken made lunch for his 9 nieces and nephews. He put 5 carrot sticks on each of their plates. How many carrot sticks did he use in all?

____

PATH to FLUENCY Practice with Equal Groups

VOCABULARY
function table

Complete each function table.

11

Number of Tricycles	Number of Wheels
1	
2	
3	
4	
5	

12

Number of Rabbits	Number of Ears
1	
2	
3	
4	
5	

13

Number of Cars	Number of Wheels
1	
2	
3	
4	
5	

14

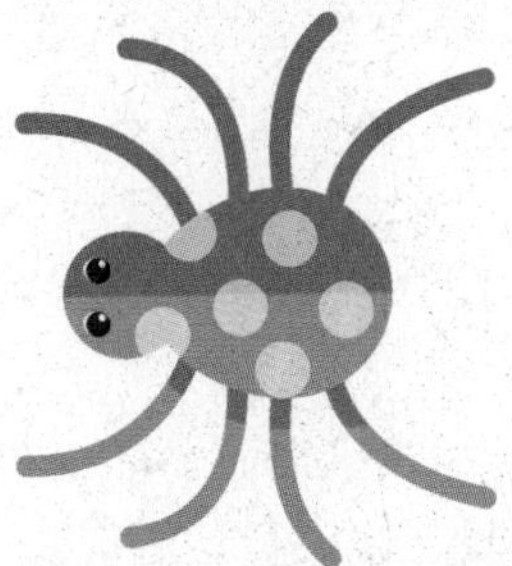

Number of Spiders	Number of Legs
1	
2	
3	
4	
5	

Check Understanding

Draw an equal shares drawing to find the number of markers in 8 packages of markers with 5 markers in each package.

Dear Family:

Over the next few weeks your child will bring home a Practice Chart for each new number to practice multiplications and divisions. Other practice materials will also come home:

- **Home Study Sheets:** A Home Study Sheet includes 3 or 4 practice charts on one page. Your child can use the Home Study Sheets to practice all the count-bys, multiplications, and divisions for a number or to practice just the ones he or she doesn't know for that number. The Homework Helper uses the sheet to test (or retest) your child by giving problems. The Homework Helper should check with your child to see which basic multiplications or divisions he or she is ready to be tested on. The helper should mark any missed problems lightly with a pencil.

  If your child gets all the answers in a column correct, the helper should sign that column on the Home Signature Sheet. When signatures are on all the columns of the Home Signature Sheet, your child should bring the sheet to school.

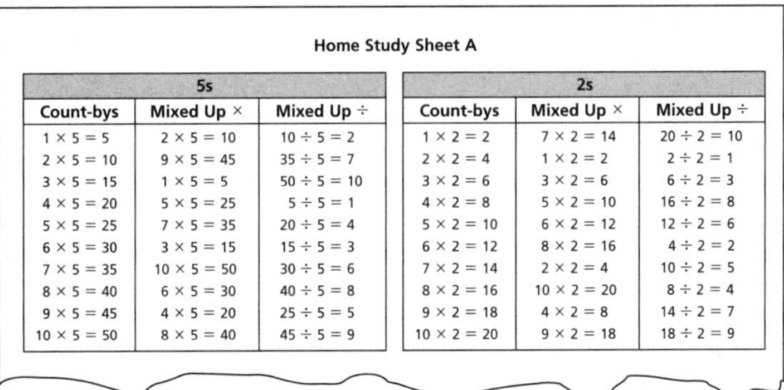

Home Study Sheet A

5s			2s		
Count-bys	Mixed Up ×	Mixed Up ÷	Count-bys	Mixed Up ×	Mixed Up ÷
1 × 5 = 5	2 × 5 = 10	10 ÷ 5 = 2	1 × 2 = 2	7 × 2 = 14	20 ÷ 2 = 10
2 × 5 = 10	9 × 5 = 45	35 ÷ 5 = 7	2 × 2 = 4	1 × 2 = 2	2 ÷ 2 = 1
3 × 5 = 15	1 × 5 = 5	50 ÷ 5 = 10	3 × 2 = 6	3 × 2 = 6	6 ÷ 2 = 3
4 × 5 = 20	5 × 5 = 25	5 ÷ 5 = 1	4 × 2 = 8	5 × 2 = 10	16 ÷ 2 = 8
5 × 5 = 25	7 × 5 = 35	20 ÷ 5 = 4	5 × 2 = 10	6 × 2 = 12	12 ÷ 2 = 6
6 × 5 = 30	3 × 5 = 15	15 ÷ 5 = 3	6 × 2 = 12	8 × 2 = 16	4 ÷ 2 = 2
7 × 5 = 35	10 × 5 = 50	30 ÷ 5 = 6	7 × 2 = 14	2 × 2 = 4	10 ÷ 2 = 5
8 × 5 = 40	6 × 5 = 30	40 ÷ 5 = 8	8 × 2 = 16	10 × 2 = 20	8 ÷ 2 = 4
9 × 5 = 45	4 × 5 = 20	25 ÷ 5 = 5	9 × 2 = 18	4 × 2 = 8	14 ÷ 2 = 7
10 × 5 = 50	8 × 5 = 40	45 ÷ 5 = 9	10 × 2 = 20	9 × 2 = 18	18 ÷ 2 = 9

Children practice by covering the answers with their finger or a pencil and sliding down their finger or pencil to check each answer as soon as they say it.

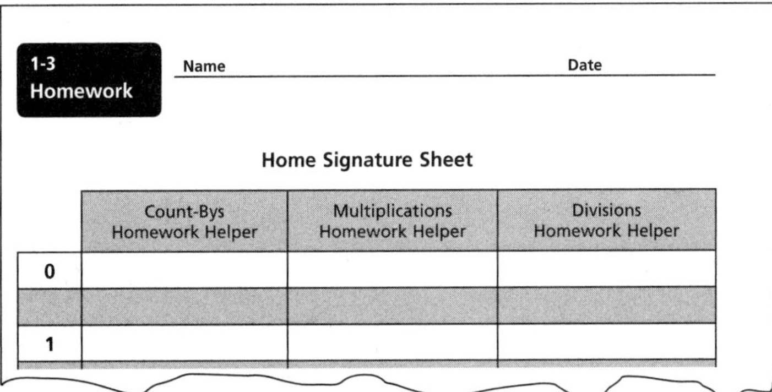

1-3 Homework

Name ______________________ Date ______________

Home Signature Sheet

	Count-Bys Homework Helper	Multiplications Homework Helper	Divisions Homework Helper
0			
1			

Put all practice materials in the folder your child brought home today.

- **Home Check Sheets:** A Home Check Sheet includes columns of 20 multiplications and divisions in mixed order. These sheets can be used to test your child's fluency with basic multiplications and divisions.
- **Strategy Cards:** Your child should use the Strategy Cards to practice multiplication and division by trying to answer the problem on the front. That card is put into one of three piles: *Know Quickly, Know Slowly*, and *Do Not Know*. The *Know Slowly* and *Do Not Know* cards are practiced until they are known quickly.

Sample Multiplication Card

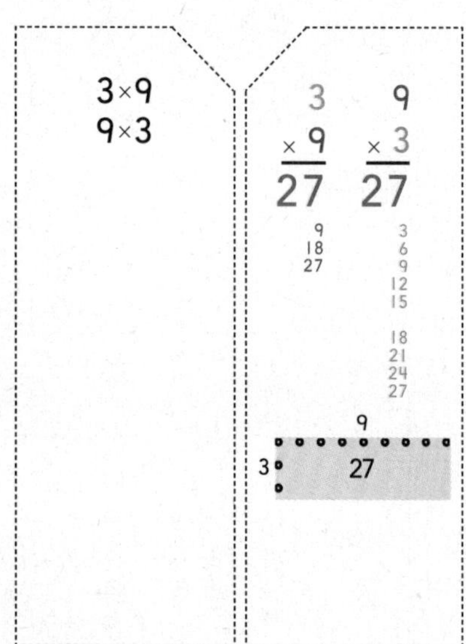

Sample Division Card

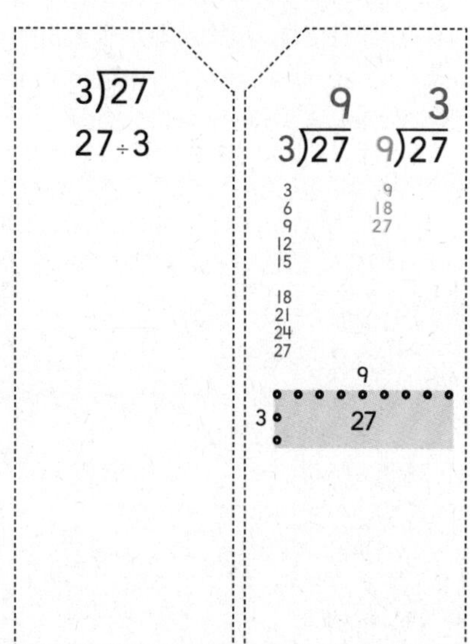

Ask your child to show you these materials and explain how they are used. Your child should practice what they do not know every day.

Please contact me if you have any questions or comments.

Thank you.

Sincerely,
Your child's teacher

Keep all materials in the Home Practice Folder. Keep the folder in a special place.

Estimada familia:

Durante las próximas semanas su niño llevará a casa una tabla de práctica para cada número nuevo para practicar multiplicaciones y divisiones. Otros materiales de práctica también se llevará a casa:

- **Hojas para estudiar en casa:** Una hoja para estudiar en casa incluye 3 ó 4 tablas de práctica en una página. Su niño puede usar las hojas para practicar todos los conteos, multiplicaciones y divisiones de un número, o para practicar sólo las operaciones para ese número que no domine. El ayudante de tareas usa la hoja para hacerle una prueba (o repetir una prueba) con problemas. Esa persona debe hablar con su niño para decidir sobre qué multiplicaciones o divisiones básicas el niño puede hacer la prueba. La persona que ayude debe marcar ligeramente con un lápiz cualquier problema que conteste mal. Si su niño contesta bien todas las operaciones de una columna, la persona que ayude debe firmar esa columna de la hoja de firmas. Cuando todas las columnas de la hoja de firmas estén firmadas, su niño debe llevar la hoja a la escuela.

Home Study Sheet A

5s			2s		
Count-bys	**Mixed Up ×**	**Mixed Up ÷**	**Count-bys**	**Mixed Up ×**	**Mixed Up ÷**
1 × 5 = 5	2 × 5 = 10	10 ÷ 5 = 2	1 × 2 = 2	7 × 2 = 14	20 ÷ 2 = 10
2 × 5 = 10	9 × 5 = 45	35 ÷ 5 = 7	2 × 2 = 4	1 × 2 = 2	2 ÷ 2 = 1
3 × 5 = 15	1 × 5 = 5	50 ÷ 5 = 10	3 × 2 = 6	3 × 2 = 6	6 ÷ 2 = 3
4 × 5 = 20	5 × 5 = 25	5 ÷ 5 = 1	4 × 2 = 8	5 × 2 = 10	16 ÷ 2 = 8
5 × 5 = 25	7 × 5 = 35	20 ÷ 5 = 4	5 × 2 = 10	6 × 2 = 12	12 ÷ 2 = 6
6 × 5 = 30	3 × 5 = 15	15 ÷ 5 = 3	6 × 2 = 12	8 × 2 = 16	4 ÷ 2 = 2
7 × 5 = 35	10 × 5 = 50	30 ÷ 5 = 6	7 × 2 = 14	2 × 2 = 4	10 ÷ 2 = 5
8 × 5 = 40	6 × 5 = 30	40 ÷ 5 = 8	8 × 2 = 16	10 × 2 = 20	8 ÷ 2 = 4
9 × 5 = 45	4 × 5 = 20	25 ÷ 5 = 5	9 × 2 = 18	4 × 2 = 8	14 ÷ 2 = 7
10 × 5 = 50	8 × 5 = 40	45 ÷ 5 = 9	10 × 2 = 20	9 × 2 = 18	18 ÷ 2 = 9

Los niños practican cubriendo las respuestas con su dedo o un lápiz y deslizan su dedo o lápiz hacia abajo para revelar cada respuesta después de decirlo.

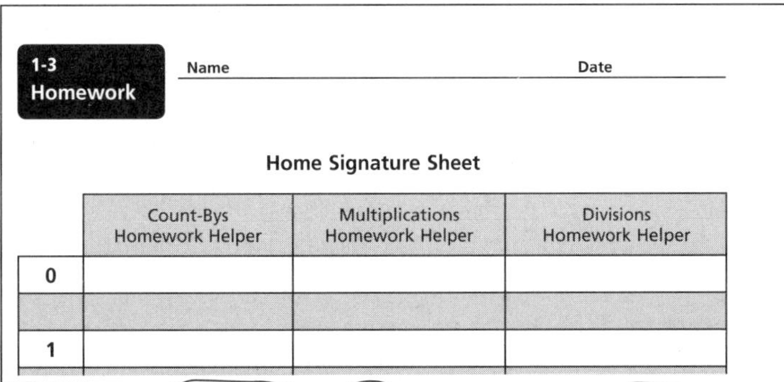

1-3 Homework

Name Date

Home Signature Sheet

	Count-Bys Homework Helper	Multiplications Homework Helper	Divisions Homework Helper
0			
1			

Guarde todos los materiales de práctica en la carpeta que su hijo trajo a casa hoy.

- **Hojas de verificación:** Una hoja de verificación consta de columnas de 20 multiplicaciones y divisiones sin orden fijo. Estas hojas se pueden usar para comprobar el dominio de su niño con las multiplicaciones y divisiones básicas.
- **Tarjetas de estrategias:** Su niño debe usar las Tarjetas de estrategias para practicar la multiplicación y división al responder el problema del frente. Esa tarjeta se pone en una de las tres pilas: *Contesta Rápidamente, Se Demora En Contestar y No Sabe*. Las tarjetas de *Se Demora En Contestar* y *No Sabe* se practican hasta que las contesten rápidamente.

Ejemplo de tarjeta de multiplicación

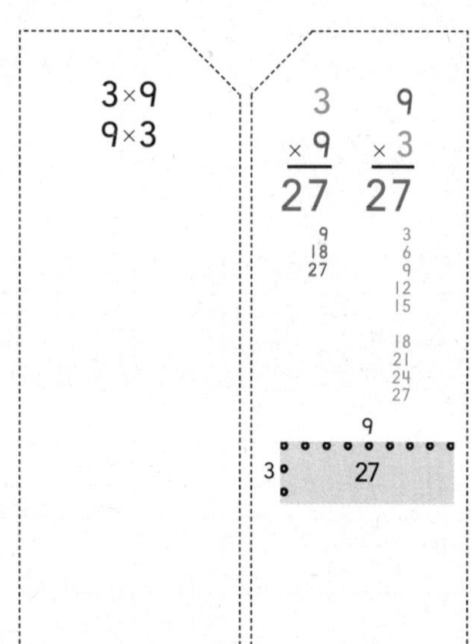

Ejemplo de tarjeta de división

3)27
27÷3
9 3)27
3 9)27
3 6 9 12 15 18 21 24 27
9 18 27
9
3
27

Pida a su niño a que le muestre estos materiales y a que le explique cómo se usan. Su niño debe practicar lo que no sabe todos los días.

Si tiene alguna duda o pregunta, por favor comuníquese conmigo.

Atentamente,
El maestro de su niño

Guarde todos los materiales en la carpeta de práctica en casa.

Name ____________________

Signature Sheet

	Count-Bys Partner	Multiplications Partner	Divisions Partner	Multiplications Check Sheets	Divisions Check Sheets
5s				1:	1:
2s				1:	1:
10s				2:	2:
9s				2:	2:
				3:	3:
3s				4:	4:
4s				4:	4:
1s				5:	5:
0s				5:	5:
				6:	6:
6s				7:	7:
8s				7:	7:
7s				8:	8:
				9:	9:
				10:	10:

Name ____________________

Dash Record Sheet

Dash Number	Accurate	Fast	Really Fast
1			
2			
3			
4			
5			
6			
7			
8			
9			
9A			
9B			
9C			
10			
10A			
10B			
10C			
11			
11A			
11B			
11C			
12			
12A			
12B			
12C			

Dash Number	Accurate	Fast	Really Fast
13			
14			
15			
16			
17			
18			
19			
19A			
19B			
19C			
19D			
20			
20A			
20B			
20C			
20D			
21			
21A			
21B			
21C			
22			
22A			
22B			
22C			

Name

PATH to FLUENCY

Study Sheet A

5s

Count-bys	Mixed Up ×	Mixed Up ÷
1 × 5 = 5	2 × 5 = 10	10 ÷ 5 = 2
2 × 5 = 10	9 × 5 = 45	35 ÷ 5 = 7
3 × 5 = 15	1 × 5 = 5	50 ÷ 5 = 10
4 × 5 = 20	5 × 5 = 25	5 ÷ 5 = 1
5 × 5 = 25	7 × 5 = 35	20 ÷ 5 = 4
6 × 5 = 30	3 × 5 = 15	15 ÷ 5 = 3
7 × 5 = 35	10 × 5 = 50	30 ÷ 5 = 6
8 × 5 = 40	6 × 5 = 30	40 ÷ 5 = 8
9 × 5 = 45	4 × 5 = 20	25 ÷ 5 = 5
10 × 5 = 50	8 × 5 = 40	45 ÷ 5 = 9

2s

Count-bys	Mixed Up ×	Mixed Up ÷
1 × 2 = 2	7 × 2 = 14	20 ÷ 2 = 10
2 × 2 = 4	1 × 2 = 2	2 ÷ 2 = 1
3 × 2 = 6	3 × 2 = 6	6 ÷ 2 = 3
4 × 2 = 8	5 × 2 = 10	16 ÷ 2 = 8
5 × 2 = 10	6 × 2 = 12	12 ÷ 2 = 6
6 × 2 = 12	8 × 2 = 16	4 ÷ 2 = 2
7 × 2 = 14	2 × 2 = 4	10 ÷ 2 = 5
8 × 2 = 16	10 × 2 = 20	8 ÷ 2 = 4
9 × 2 = 18	4 × 2 = 8	14 ÷ 2 = 7
10 × 2 = 20	9 × 2 = 18	18 ÷ 2 = 9

10s

Count-bys	Mixed Up ×	Mixed Up ÷
1 × 10 = 10	1 × 10 = 10	80 ÷ 10 = 8
2 × 10 = 20	5 × 10 = 50	10 ÷ 10 = 1
3 × 10 = 30	2 × 10 = 20	50 ÷ 10 = 5
4 × 10 = 40	8 × 10 = 80	90 ÷ 10 = 9
5 × 10 = 50	7 × 10 = 70	40 ÷ 10 = 4
6 × 10 = 60	3 × 10 = 30	100 ÷ 10 = 10
7 × 10 = 70	4 × 10 = 40	30 ÷ 10 = 3
8 × 10 = 80	6 × 10 = 60	20 ÷ 10 = 2
9 × 10 = 90	10 × 10 = 100	70 ÷ 10 = 7
10 × 10 = 100	9 × 10 = 90	60 ÷ 10 = 6

9s

Count-bys	Mixed Up ×	Mixed Up ÷
1 × 9 = 9	2 × 9 = 18	81 ÷ 9 = 9
2 × 9 = 18	4 × 9 = 36	18 ÷ 9 = 2
3 × 9 = 27	7 × 9 = 63	36 ÷ 9 = 4
4 × 9 = 36	8 × 9 = 72	9 ÷ 9 = 1
5 × 9 = 45	3 × 9 = 27	54 ÷ 9 = 6
6 × 9 = 54	10 × 9 = 90	27 ÷ 9 = 3
7 × 9 = 63	1 × 9 = 9	63 ÷ 9 = 7
8 × 9 = 72	6 × 9 = 54	72 ÷ 9 = 8
9 × 9 = 81	5 × 9 = 45	90 ÷ 9 = 10
10 × 9 = 90	9 × 9 = 81	45 ÷ 9 = 5

Name ______________________

Explore Arrays

VOCABULARY
array column
row

An **array** is an arrangement of objects in **rows** and **columns**. You can use multiplication to find the total number of objects in an array.

2-by-5 array
5 columns

column

2 rows

2 rows of 5 = 2 × 5 = 10

PATH to FLUENCY

Write Multiplication Equations

Write a multiplication equation for each array.

1. How many flowers?

____

2. How many shells?

____

3. How many mugs?

____

4. Math Journal Write a problem that you can solve by using this array. Show how to solve your problem.

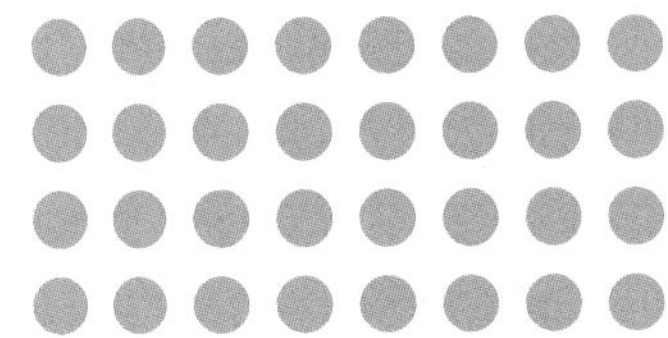

Compare Arrays

VOCABULARY
(>) is greater than
(<) is less than

Without counting the dots in the array, write >, <, or = in the circle.

5 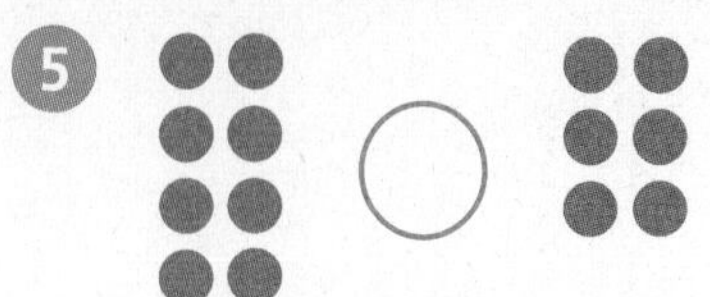

6 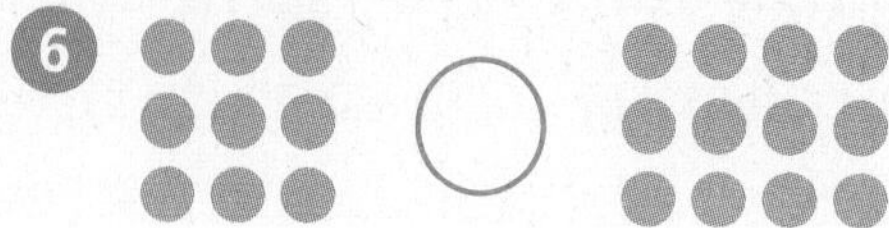

7 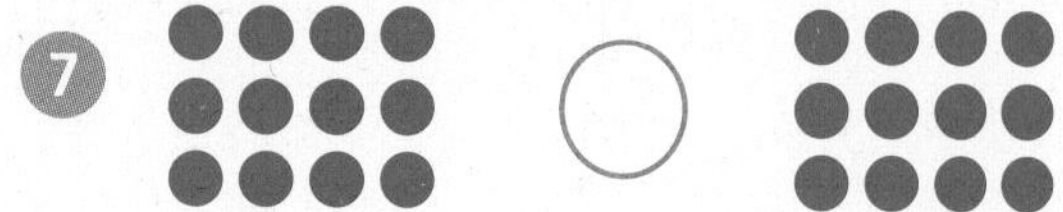

8 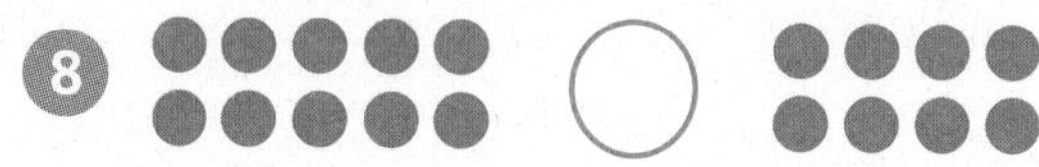

9 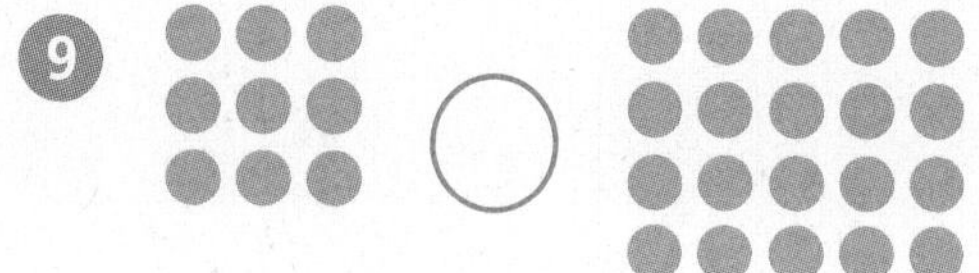

10 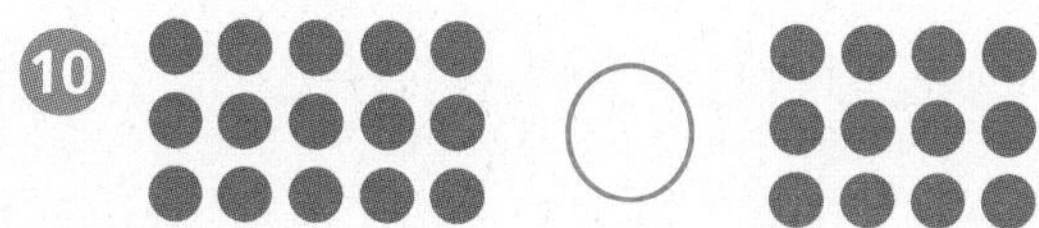

11 

12 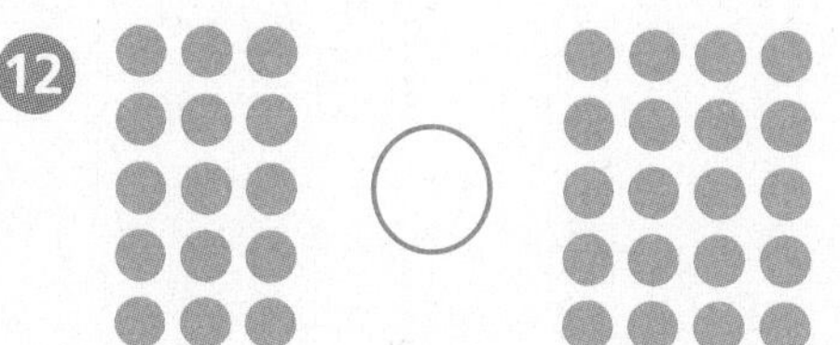

13 **Create Your Own** Draw two dot arrays and compare them using symbols. Then write an equation for each array to show that your comparison is correct.

Name ______________________________

Make a Math Drawing to Solve a Problem

Make a drawing for each problem. Label your drawing with a multiplication equation. Then write the answer to the problem.

Show your work.

14 The clarinet section of the band marched in 6 rows, with 2 clarinet players in each row. How many clarinet players were there in all?

____

15 Mali put some crackers on a tray. She put the crackers in 3 rows, with 5 crackers per row. How many crackers did she put on the tray?

____

16 Ms. Shahin set up some chairs in 7 rows, with 5 chairs in each row. How many chairs did she set up?

____

17 Zak has a box of crayons. The crayons are arranged in 4 rows, with 6 crayons in each row. How many crayons are in the box?

____

Model Commutativity

VOCABULARY
Commutative Property of Multiplication

The **Commutative Property of Multiplication** states that you can switch the order of the factors without changing the product.

Arrays: $4 \times 5 = 5 \times 4$

$4 \times 5 = 20$ $\quad$ $5 \times 4 = 20$

Groups: $4 \times ⑤ = 5 \times ④$

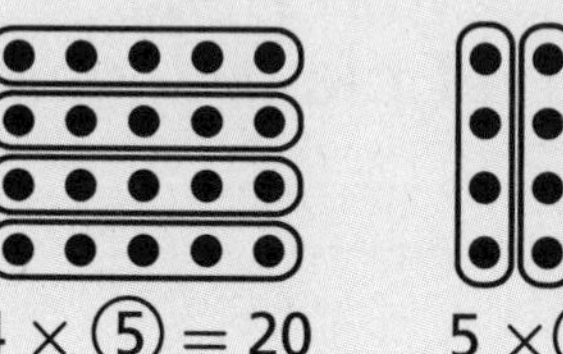

$4 \times ⑤ = 20$ $\quad$ $5 \times ④ = 20$

Solve Problems Using the Commutative Property

Make a math drawing for each problem. Write a multiplication equation and the answer to the problem.

18 Katie put stickers on her folder in 6 rows of 2. How many stickers did she place?

____

19 Marco put stickers on his folder in 2 rows of 6. How many stickers did he place?

____

20 Juan packed glass jars in 3 boxes, with 7 jars per box. How many jars did Juan pack?

____

21 Ty packed glass jars in 7 boxes, with 3 jars per box. How many jars did Ty pack?

____

Check Understanding
Draw arrays to show why 2×5 equals 5×2.

Name ______________________

VOCABULARY
division
dividend
divisor
quotient

Explore Division

Write an equation and solve the problem.

1. Marc bought some bags of limes. There were 5 limes in each bag. He bought 15 limes altogether. How many bags did he buy?

   ____

2. There were 10 photographs on a wall. The photographs were in rows, with 5 photographs in each row. How many rows were there?

   ____

The problems above can be represented by multiplication equations or by **division** equations.

	Multiplication					Division				
Problem 1	□	×	(5)	=	**15**	**15**	÷	(5)	=	□
	number of groups (factor)		group size (factor)		total (product)	total (product)		group size (factor)		number of groups (factor)
Problem 2	□	×	**5**	=	**10**	**10**	÷	**5**	=	□
	number of rows (factor)		number in each row (factor)		total (product)	total (product)		number in each row (factor)		number of rows (factor)

Here are ways to write a division. The following all mean "15 divided by 5 equals 3."

$15 \div 5 = 3$ $15 / 5 = 3$ $\frac{15}{5} = 3$

$5\overline{)15}$ with 3 above: 3 ← quotient; 15 ← dividend; 5 ↑ divisor

The number you divide into is called the **dividend**. The number you divide by is called the **divisor**. The number that is the answer to a division problem is called the **quotient**.

Math Tools: Drawings and Equations

You can use equal shares drawings to help solve division problems. Here is how you might solve Problem 1 on page 23.

Start with the total, 15.

$15 \div \textcircled{5} = \square$

Draw groups of 5, and connect them to the total. Count by 5s as you draw the groups. Stop when you reach 15, the total. Count how many groups you have: 3 groups.

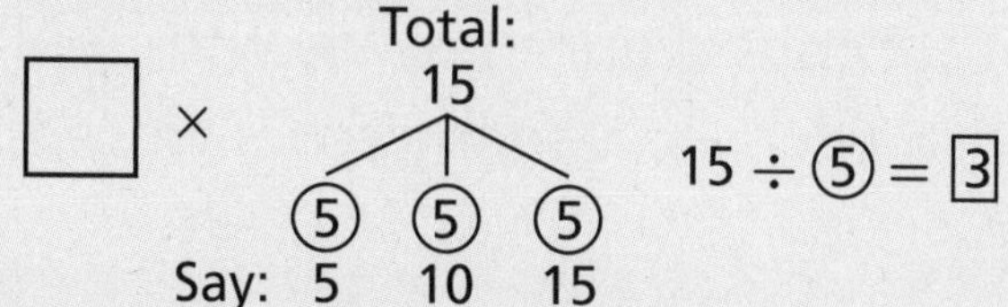

You can use a similar type of drawing to find the number of rows or columns in an array. Here is how you might solve Problem 2 on page 23.

Start with the total, 10.

$10 \div \textcircled{5} = \square$

Draw rows of 5, and connect them to the total. Count by 5s as you draw the rows. Stop when you reach 10, the total. Count how many rows you have: 2 rows.

5 (5)
10 (5)
Total: 10

$10 \div \textcircled{5} = \boxed{2}$

Write an equation and solve the problem.

3 At a bake sale, Luisa bought a lemon square for 35¢. If she paid using only nickels, how many nickels did she use?

____

4 Mr. Su bought a sheet of 20 stamps. There were 5 stamps in each row. How many rows of stamps were there?

____

Name ______________________________

What's the Error?

Dear Math Students,

Today I found the unknown number in this division equation by using a related multiplication. Is my calculation correct?

$40 \div 5 = \square$ $\boxed{9} \times 5 = 40$

If not, please correct my work and tell me what I did wrong. How do you know my answer is wrong?

Your friend,
Puzzled Penguin

5 Write a response to Puzzled Penguin.

____

____

____

____

____

PATH to FLUENCY Relate Division and Multiplication Equations with 5

Find the unknown numbers.

6 $20 \div (5) = \square$ $\square \times (5) = 20$

$20 \div (4) = \square$ $\square \times (4) = 20$

7 $10 \div (5) = \square$ $\square \times (5) = 10$

$10 \div (2) = \square$ $\square \times (2) = 10$

8 $15 \div (5) = \square$ $\square \times (5) = 15$

$15 \div (3) = \square$ $\square \times (3) = 15$

Find the Number in Each Group

Write an equation and solve the problem.

Show your work.

9 Aziz put 15 ice cubes in 5 glasses. He put the same number of ice cubes in each glass. How many ice cubes did he put in each glass?

____

10 Lori's uncle gave her 20 stickers. She put the same number of stickers on each of 5 folders. How many stickers did she put on each folder?

____

11 Todd cut a board that measured 45 inches in length into 5 pieces. Each piece he cut measures the same number of inches. How many inches does each piece measure?

____

12 Ten students gathered into 5 groups to play a math game. The same number of students are in each group. How many students are in each group?

____

Check Understanding

What multiplication equation with an unknown number can you write to find $20 \div 5 = \square$?

____

Solve the equation to find the unknown number. $\square$

Name ______________________________

PATH to FLUENCY

Explore Patterns with 2s

What patterns do you see below?

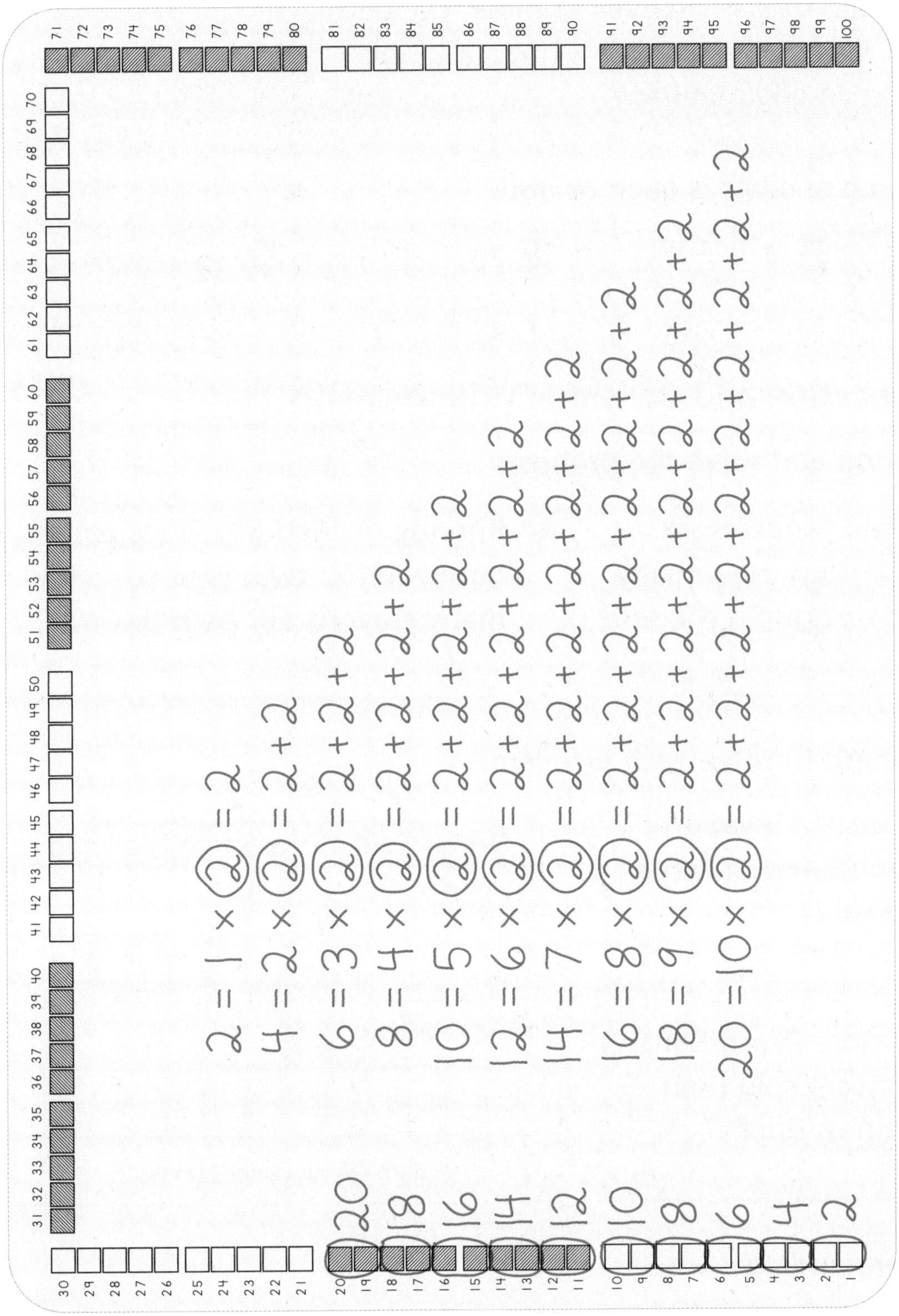

1 2 3 4 5 6 7 8 9 10 11 12 13 14 15 16 17 18 19 20 21 22 23 24 25 26 27 28 29 30 31 32 33 34 35 36 37 38 39 40 41 42 43 44 45 46 47 48 49 50 51 52 53 54 55 56 57 58 59 60 61 62 63 64 65 66 67 68 69 70 71 72 73 74 75 76 77 78 79 80 81 82 83 84 85 86 87 88 89 90 91 92 93 94 95 96 97 98 99 100

2 = 1 × 2 = 2

4 = 2 × 2 = 2 + 2

6 = 3 × 2 = 2 + 2 + 2

8 = 4 × 2 = 2 + 2 + 2 + 2

10 = 5 × 2 = 2 + 2 + 2 + 2 + 2

12 = 6 × 2 = 2 + 2 + 2 + 2 + 2 + 2

14 = 7 × 2 = 2 + 2 + 2 + 2 + 2 + 2 + 2

16 = 8 × 2 = 2 + 2 + 2 + 2 + 2 + 2 + 2 + 2

18 = 9 × 2 = 2 + 2 + 2 + 2 + 2 + 2 + 2 + 2 + 2

20 = 10 × 2 = 2 + 2 + 2 + 2 + 2 + 2 + 2 + 2 + 2 + 2

2 4 6 8 10 12 14 16 18 20

Even and Odd Numbers

VOCABULARY
even number
odd number
pictograph

The 2s count-bys are called *even numbers* because they are multiples of 2. In an **even number,** the ones digit is 0, 2, 4, 6, or 8. If a number is not a multiple of two, it is called an **odd number**.

Tell whether each number is even or odd.

1. 7 ______
2. 4 ______
3. 20 ______
4. 15 ______

Solve Multiplication and Division Problems with 2s

Write an equation and solve the problem.

5. At the art fair, Tamika sold 9 pairs of earrings. How many individual earrings did she sell?

______

6. Rhonda divided 8 crayons equally between her twin brothers. How many crayons did each boy get?

______

Use the pictograph to solve each problem.

7. In all, how many Strawberry Sensation and Citrus Surprise drinks were sold?

______

8. How many more Peach-Banana Blast drinks were sold than Mango Madness drinks?

______

Drinks Sold at the Smoothie Shop	
Strawberry Sensation	
Peach-Banana Blast	
Mango Madness	
Citrus Surprise	
Each stands for 2 drinks.	

Check Understanding

Explain how patterns in the 2s count-bys and multiplications can help you when multiplying.

Name

PATH to FLUENCY

Check Sheet 1: 5s and 2s

5s Multiplications	5s Divisions	2s Multiplications	2s Divisions
2 × 5 = 10	30 / 5 = 6	4 × 2 = 8	8 / 2 = 4
5 • 6 = 30	5 ÷ 5 = 1	2 • 8 = 16	18 ÷ 2 = 9
5 * 9 = 45	15 / 5 = 3	1 * 2 = 2	2 / 2 = 1
4 × 5 = 20	50 ÷ 5 = 10	6 × 2 = 12	16 ÷ 2 = 8
5 • 7 = 35	20 / 5 = 4	2 • 9 = 18	4 / 2 = 2
10 * 5 = 50	10 ÷ 5 = 2	2 * 2 = 4	20 ÷ 2 = 10
1 × 5 = 5	35 / 5 = 7	3 × 2 = 6	10 / 2 = 5
5 • 3 = 15	40 ÷ 5 = 8	2 • 5 = 10	12 ÷ 2 = 6
8 * 5 = 40	25 / 5 = 5	10 * 2 = 20	6 / 2 = 3
5 × 5 = 25	45 / 5 = 9	2 × 7 = 14	14 / 2 = 7
5 • 8 = 40	20 ÷ 5 = 4	2 • 10 = 20	4 ÷ 2 = 2
7 * 5 = 35	15 / 5 = 3	9 * 2 = 18	2 / 2 = 1
5 × 4 = 20	30 ÷ 5 = 6	2 × 6 = 12	8 ÷ 2 = 4
6 • 5 = 30	25 / 5 = 5	8 • 2 = 16	6 / 2 = 3
5 * 1 = 5	10 ÷ 5 = 2	2 * 3 = 6	20 ÷ 2 = 10
5 × 10 = 50	45 / 5 = 9	2 × 2 = 4	14 / 2 = 7
9 • 5 = 45	35 ÷ 5 = 7	1 • 2 = 2	10 ÷ 2 = 5
5 * 2 = 10	50 ÷ 5 = 10	2 * 4 = 8	16 ÷ 2 = 8
3 × 5 = 15	40 / 5 = 8	5 × 2 = 10	12 / 2 = 6
5 • 5 = 25	5 ÷ 5 = 1	7 • 2 = 14	18 ÷ 2 = 9

Name ____________________

PATH to FLUENCY Use the Target

×	0	1	2	3	4	5	6	7	8	9
0	0	0	0	0	0	0	0	0	0	0
1	0	1	2	3	4	5	6	7	8	9
2	0	2	4	6	8	10	12	14	16	18
3	0	3	6	9	12	15	18	21	24	27
4	0	4	8	12	16	20	24	28	32	36
5	0	5	10	15	20	25	30	35	40	45
6	0	6	12	18	24	30	36	42	48	54
7	0	7	14	21	28	35	42	49	56	63
8	0	8	16	24	32	40	48	56	64	72
9	0	9	18	27	36	45	54	63	72	81

1. Discuss how you can use the Target to find the product for 8×5.

2. Discuss how you can use the Target to practice division.

3. Practice using the Target.

4. When using the Target, how are multiplication and division alike? How are they different?

Make Sense of Problems

Write an equation and solve the problem. *Show your work.*

5 Mrs. Cheng bought 8 pairs of mittens. How many individual mittens did she buy?

____

6 Brian divided 10 crayons equally between his two sisters. How many crayons did each girl get?

____

7 Maria has 5 piles of flash cards. There are 9 cards in each pile. How many flash cards does Maria have?

____

8 A parking lot has 5 rows of parking spaces with the same number of spaces in each row. There are 35 parking spaces in the lot. How many spaces are in each row?

____

Write a Word Problem

9 Write a word problem that can be solved using the equation $45 \div 5 = \square$, where 5 is the number of groups.

____

____

____

____

Check Understanding

If you know that $7 \times 2 = 14$, what other multiplications and divisions do you know?

____

Unit 1
Quick Quiz 1

Name ______________________ Date ______________

Write the correct answer.

1. $5 \times 3 = \square$

2. $18 \div 2 = \square$

3. Complete the multiplication sentence.

   $5 \times 6 = 6 \times \square$

4. Andy uses 3 bananas in each of 5 loaves of banana bread he is baking. Write a multiplication expression to represent the total number of bananas Andy uses.

   Show your work.

   ____

5. Solve to find the unknown number in the equation.

   $5 \times \square = 40$

Name ______________________________ Date ______________

Make a drawing. Write an equation. Solve.

1. Imaad has 5 bowls. He wants to serve 4 dumplings in each bowl. How many dumplings does he need in all?

____

2. Marja arranges her toy cars so 7 toy cars are in each row. She makes 3 equal rows of toy cars. How many toy cars does Marja have?

____

3. Noriko pastes stars on the first page of her book. She arranges the stars in 2 rows with 4 stars in each row. On the second page, she pastes 2 stars in a row. There are 4 rows of stars on the second page. How many stars are on each page?

____

Name ____________________

PATH to FLUENCY

Explore Patterns with 10s

What patterns do you see below?

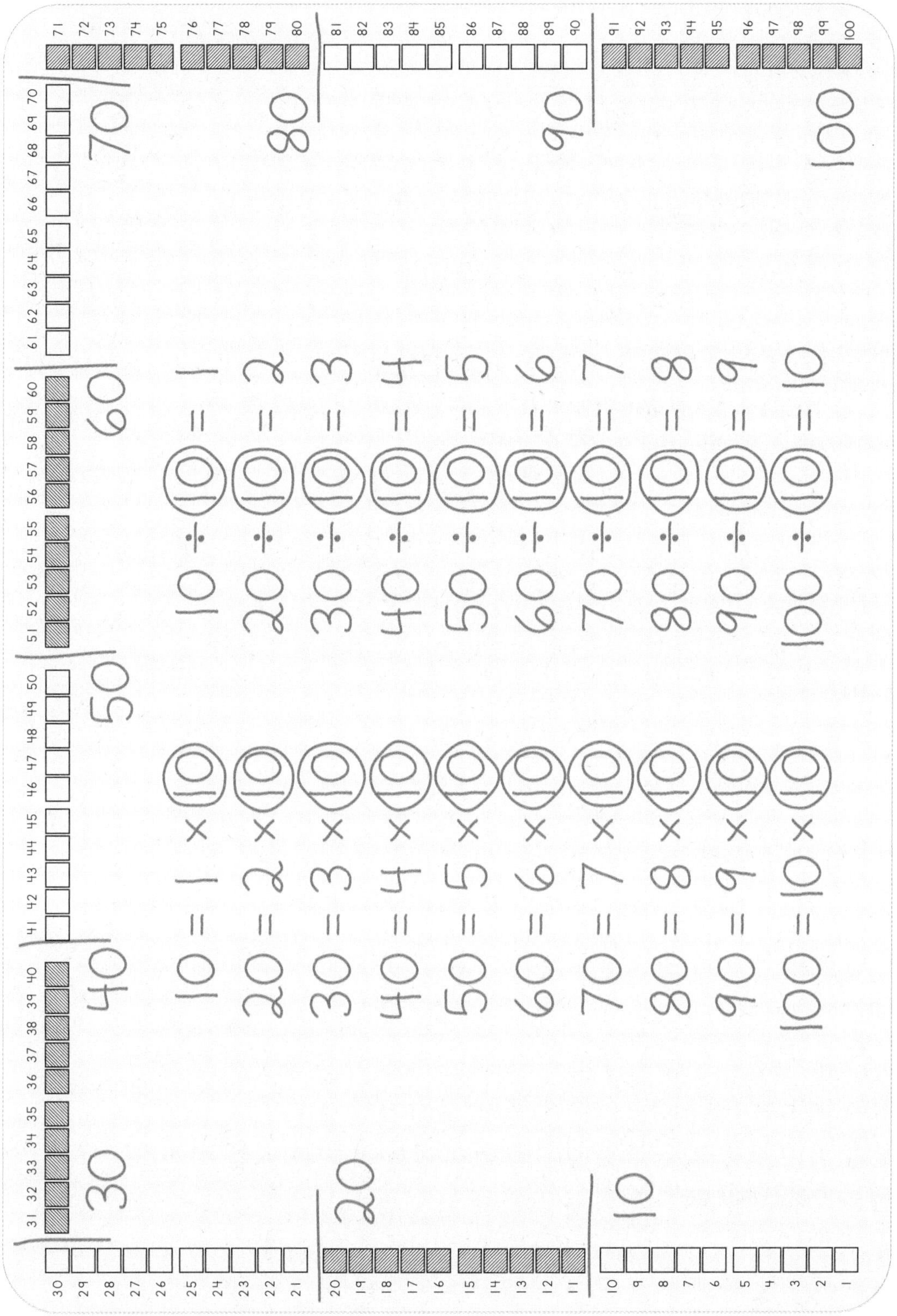

1 2 3 4 5 6 7 8 9 10 | 11 12 13 14 15 16 17 18 19 20 | 21 22 23 24 25 26 27 28 29 30 | 31 32 33 34 35 36 37 38 39 40 | 41 42 43 44 45 46 47 48 49 50 | 51 52 53 54 55 56 57 58 59 60 | 61 62 63 64 65 66 67 68 69 70 | 71 72 73 74 75 76 77 78 79 80 | 81 82 83 84 85 86 87 88 89 90 | 91 92 93 94 95 96 97 98 99 100

10 20 30 40 50 60 70 80 90 100

$10 = 1 \times 10$
$20 = 2 \times 10$
$30 = 3 \times 10$
$40 = 4 \times 10$
$50 = 5 \times 10$
$60 = 6 \times 10$
$70 = 7 \times 10$
$80 = 8 \times 10$
$90 = 9 \times 10$
$100 = 10 \times 10$

$10 \div 10 = 1$
$20 \div 10 = 2$
$30 \div 10 = 3$
$40 \div 10 = 4$
$50 \div 10 = 5$
$60 \div 10 = 6$
$70 \div 10 = 7$
$80 \div 10 = 8$
$90 \div 10 = 9$
$100 \div 10 = 10$

Solve Problems with 10s

Write an equation and solve the problem.

Show your work.

1. Raymundo has 9 dimes. How many cents does he have?

____

2. Yoko has some dimes in her pocket, and no other coins. She has a total of 70¢. How many dimes does she have?

____

3. Jonah picked 40 strawberries. He gave them to 10 of his friends. Each friend got the same number of strawberries. How many strawberries did each friend get?

____

4. There are 10 Space Command trading cards in each pack. Zoe bought 5 packs of cards. How many cards did she buy in all?

____

5. There were 80 students in the auditorium. There were 10 students in each row. How many rows of students were there?

____

6. A roll of ribbon has 60 inches of ribbon. Harper cut all the ribbon into 10 equal length pieces. How many inches long is each piece?

____

Name ______________________

VOCABULARY
variable

Use Variables in Equations

When you write equations you can use a letter to represent an unknown number. This letter is called a **variable**.

Each of these equations has a variable.

$a \times 10 = 60$ $70 = c \times 7$ $w = 80 \div 10$ $9 = 90 \div c$

$2 \times y = 18$ $p = 9 \times 2$ $f = 18 \div 2$ $18 \div n = 2$

Solve each equation.

7 $14 = 7 \times a$

$a =$ ______

8 $90 \div g = 9$

$g =$ ______

9 $10 \div n = 5$

$n =$ ______

10 $8 \times f = 40$

$f =$ ______

Write and Solve Equations with Variables

Write an equation and solve the problem.

11 A box of straws holds 60 straws. There are 10 straws in each row. How many rows are there?

____

12 Ethan used 9 dimes to pay for his book. How much did his book cost?

____

13 There are 10 relay teams with an equal number of people on each team running a race. There are 50 people running the race. How many people are there on each team?

____

14 Amanda has 20 bracelets. She gave the same number of bracelets to 2 of her friends. How many bracelets did she give to each friend?

____

What's the Error?

Dear Math Students,

Today my teacher asked me to write a word problem that can be solved using the division $40 \div 10$. Here is the problem I wrote:

> Kim has 40 apples and puts 4 apples in each bag. How many bags does Kim use?

Is my problem correct? If not, please correct my work and tell me what I did wrong.

Your friend,
Puzzled Penguin

15 **Write an answer to the Puzzled Penguin.**

Write and Solve Problems with 10s

16 Write a word problem that can be solved using the multiplication 10×3. Then write a related division word problem.

Check Understanding

Give an example of a number that is a 10s count-by and explain how you know.

Name ____________________

PATH to FLUENCY

Check Sheet 2: 10s and 9s

10s Multiplications	10s Divisions	9s Multiplications	9s Divisions
9 × 10 = 90	100 / 10 = 10	3 × 9 = 27	27 / 9 = 3
10 • 3 = 30	50 ÷ 10 = 5	9 • 7 = 63	9 ÷ 9 = 1
10 * 6 = 60	70 / 10 = 7	10 * 9 = 90	81 / 9 = 9
1 × 10 = 10	40 ÷ 10 = 4	5 × 9 = 45	45 ÷ 9 = 5
10 • 4 = 40	80 / 10 = 8	9 • 8 = 72	90 / 9 = 10
10 * 7 = 70	60 ÷ 10 = 6	9 * 1 = 9	36 ÷ 9 = 4
8 × 10 = 80	10 / 10 = 1	2 × 9 = 18	18 / 9 = 2
10 • 10 = 100	20 ÷ 10 = 2	9 • 9 = 81	63 ÷ 9 = 7
5 * 10 = 50	90 / 10 = 9	6 * 9 = 54	54 / 9 = 6
10 × 2 = 20	30 / 10 = 3	9 × 4 = 36	72 / 9 = 8
10 • 5 = 50	80 ÷ 10 = 8	9 • 5 = 45	27 ÷ 9 = 3
4 * 10 = 40	70 / 10 = 7	4 * 9 = 36	45 / 9 = 5
10 × 1 = 10	100 ÷ 10 = 10	9 × 1 = 9	63 ÷ 9 = 7
3 • 10 = 30	90 / 10 = 9	3 • 9 = 27	72 / 9 = 8
10 * 8 = 80	60 ÷ 10 = 6	9 * 8 = 72	54 ÷ 9 = 6
7 × 10 = 70	30 / 10 = 3	7 × 9 = 63	18 / 9 = 2
6 • 10 = 60	10 ÷ 10 = 1	6 • 9 = 54	90 ÷ 9 = 10
10 * 9 = 90	40 ÷ 10 = 4	9 * 9 = 81	9 ÷ 9 = 1
10 × 10 = 100	20 / 10 = 2	10 × 9 = 90	36 / 9 = 4
2 • 10 = 20	50 ÷ 10 = 5	2 • 9 = 18	81 ÷ 9 = 9

Name ______________________________

Math Tools: Quick 9s Multiplication

You can use the Quick 9s method to help you multiply by 9. Open your hands and turn them so they are facing you. Imagine that your fingers are numbered like this.

1 2 3 4 5 6 7 8 9 10

To find a number times 9, bend down the finger for that number. For example, to find 4 × 9, bend down your fourth finger.

3 tens 6 ones

fourth finger down
4 × 9 = 36

The fingers to the left of your bent finger are the tens. The fingers to the right are the ones. For this problem, there are 3 tens and 6 ones, so 4 × 9 = 36.

Why does this work? Because 4 × 9 = 4 × (10 − 1) = 40 − 4 = 36

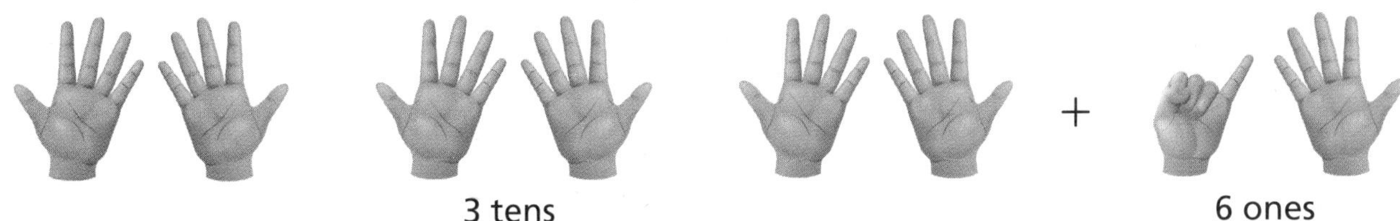

1 Write the multiplication that is shown when the seventh multiplier finger is down.

_____ × _____ = _____

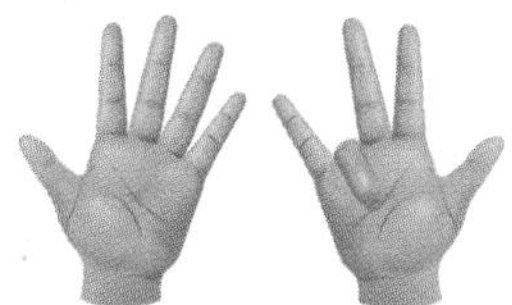

2 Which multiplier finger will be down to show 5 tens and 4 ones?

____

Math Tools: Quick 9s Division

You can also use Quick 9s to help you divide by 9.
For example, to find 72 ÷ 9, show 72 on your fingers.

7 tens 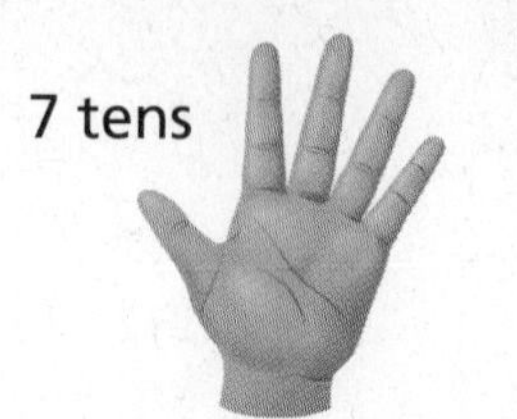 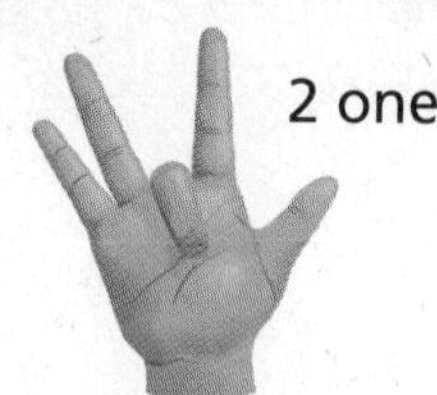 2 ones

Your eighth finger is down, so 72 ÷ 9 = 8.
8 × 9 = 80 − 8 = 72

3 Write the division that is shown when the fifth multiplier finger is down.

_____ ÷ _____ = _____

4 Which multiplier finger will be down to show 81 ÷ 9?

____

5 Which multiplication is shown when the ninth finger is down?

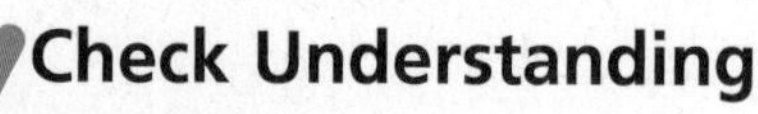

_____ × _____ = _____

Check Understanding

Use the picture below. Draw an X on the finger that you would bend down to find 6 × 9.

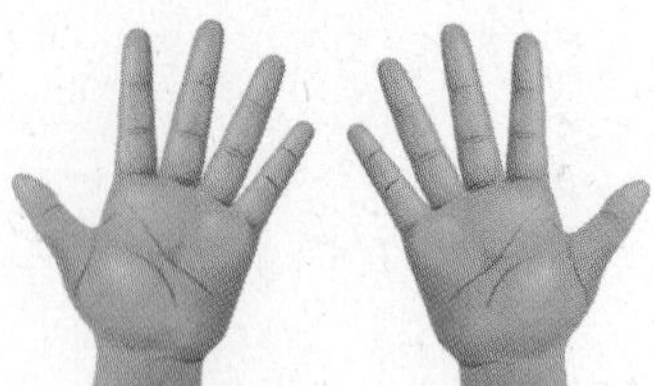

6 × 9 = ☐

Use the picture below. Draw an X on the finger that you would bend down to find 27 ÷ 9.

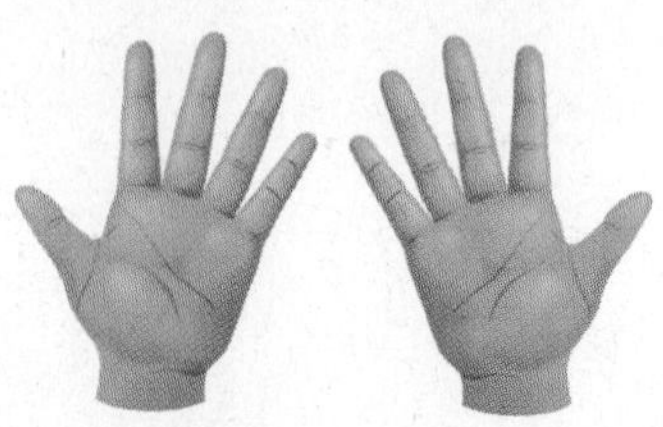

27 ÷ 9 = ☐

Name ______________________________

PATH to FLUENCY Check Sheet 3: 2s, 5s, 9s, and 10s

2s, 5s, 9s, 10s Multiplications	2s, 5s, 9s, 10s Multiplications	2s, 5s, 9s, 10s Divisions	2s, 5s, 9s, 10s Divisions
2 × 10 = 20	5 × 10 = 50	18 / 2 = 9	36 / 9 = 4
10 • 5 = 50	10 • 9 = 90	50 ÷ 5 = 10	70 ÷ 10 = 7
9 * 6 = 54	4 * 10 = 40	72 / 9 = 8	18 / 2 = 9
7 × 10 = 70	2 × 9 = 18	60 ÷ 10 = 6	45 ÷ 5 = 9
2 • 3 = 6	5 • 3 = 15	12 / 2 = 6	45 / 9 = 5
5 * 7 = 35	6 * 9 = 54	30 ÷ 5 = 6	30 ÷ 10 = 3
9 × 10 = 90	10 × 3 = 30	18 / 9 = 2	6 / 2 = 3
6 • 10 = 60	3 • 2 = 6	50 ÷ 10 = 5	50 ÷ 5 = 10
8 * 2 = 16	5 * 8 = 40	14 / 2 = 7	27 / 9 = 3
5 × 6 = 30	9 × 9 = 81	25 / 5 = 5	70 / 10 = 7
9 • 5 = 45	10 • 4 = 40	81 ÷ 9 = 9	20 ÷ 2 = 10
8 * 10 = 80	9 * 2 = 18	20 / 10 = 2	45 / 5 = 9
2 × 1 = 2	5 × 1 = 5	8 ÷ 2 = 4	54 ÷ 9 = 6
3 • 5 = 15	9 • 6 = 54	45 / 5 = 9	80 / 10 = 8
4 * 9 = 36	10 * 1 = 10	63 ÷ 9 = 7	16 ÷ 2 = 8
3 × 10 = 30	7 × 2 = 14	30 / 10 = 3	15 / 5 = 3
2 • 6 = 12	6 • 5 = 30	10 ÷ 2 = 5	90 ÷ 9 = 10
4 * 5 = 20	8 * 9 = 72	40 ÷ 5 = 8	100 ÷ 10 = 10
9 × 7 = 63	10 × 6 = 60	9 / 9 = 1	12 / 2 = 6
1 • 10 = 10	2 • 8 = 16	50 ÷ 10 = 5	35 ÷ 5 = 7

Name ______________________

Make Sense of Problems with 2s, 5s, 9s, and 10s

Write an equation to represent each problem. Then solve the problem.

Show your work.

1. Ian planted tulip bulbs in an array with 5 rows and 10 columns. How many bulbs did he plant?

   ____

2. Erin gave 30 basketball cards to her 5 cousins. Each cousin got the same number of cards. How many cards did each cousin get?

   ____

3. Martina bought 7 cans of racquetballs. There were 2 balls per can. How many racquetballs did she buy in all?

   ____

4. The 27 students in the orchestra stood in rows for their school picture. There were 9 students in every row. How many rows of students were there?

   ____

5. Lindsey needs 40 note cards. The note cards are packaged 10 to a box. How many boxes of cards should Lindsey buy?

   ____

6. There are 25 student desks in the classroom. The desks are arranged in 5 rows with the same number of desks in each row. How many desks are in each row?

   ____

Math Tools: Fast Array Drawings

A fast array drawing shows the number of items in each row and column, but does not show every single item.

Problem 1 on page 45:

Show the number of rows and the number of columns. Make a box in the center to show that you don't know the total.

Here are three ways to find the total.

- Find 5×10.
- Use 10s count-bys to find the total in 5 rows of 10: 10, 20, 30, 40, 50.
- Use 5s count-bys to find the total in 10 columns of 5: 5, 10, 15, 20, 25, 30, 35, 40, 45, 50.

Problem 4 on page 45:

Show the number in each row and the total. Make a box to show that you don't know the number of rows.

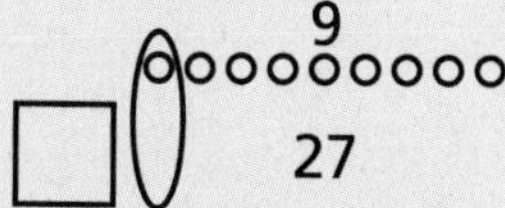

Here are two ways to find the number of rows.

- Find $27 \div 9$ or solve $\square \times 9 = 27$.
- Count by 9s until you reach 27: 9, 18, 27.

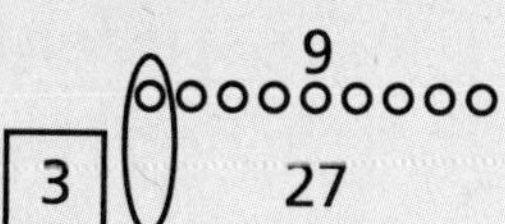

Math Journal Make a fast array drawing to solve each problem.

7. Beth planted trees in 9 rows and 6 columns. How many trees did she plant?

____

8. The 36 boys stood in 4 rows for their team picture. How many boys were in each row?

____

Check Understanding

Which problem has an unknown total?

Circle one: Problem 7 Problem 8

Unit 1
Quick Quiz 2

Name ____________________ **Date** __________

Write the correct answer.

1. $10 \bullet \square = 50$

2. $80 \div 10 = \square$

3. $2 \times \square = 16$

4. $4 \times 9 = \square$

5. $27 \div 9 = \square$

Strategy Check 2

Name ____________________ Date ____________

Complete the pattern below to show 9s multiplication.

1. $1 \times 9 = 10 - 1 = \square$

2. $2 \times 9 = 20 - 2 = \square$

3. $3 \times 9 = 30 - 3 = \square$

4. $4 \times 9 = 40 - \square = \square$

5. $5 \times 9 = \square - \square = \square$

6. $6 \times 9 = \square - \square = \square$

7. $7 \times 9 = \square - \square = \square$

8. $8 \times 9 = \square - \square = \square$

9. $9 \times 9 = \square - \square = \square$

10. $9 \times 10 = \square - \square = \square$

Name ______________________

PATH to FLUENCY

Explore Patterns with 3s

What patterns do you see below?

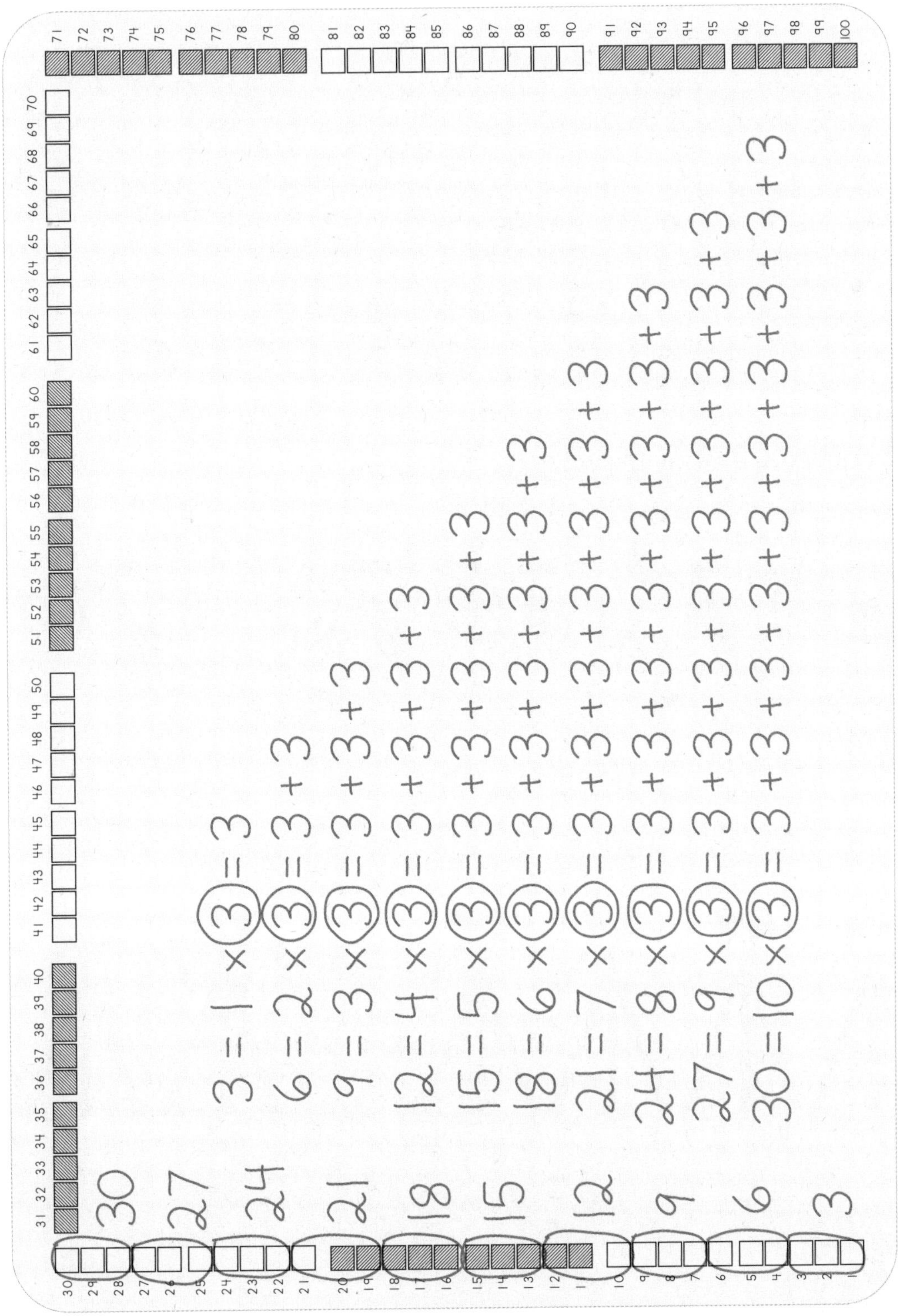

1 2 3 4 5 6 7 8 9 10 11 12 13 14 15 16 17 18 19 20 21 22 23 24 25 26 27 28 29 30

31 32 33 34 35 36 37 38 39 40 41 42 43 44 45 46 47 48 49 50 51 52 53 54 55 56 57 58 59 60 61 62 63 64 65 66 67 68 69 70

71 72 73 74 75 76 77 78 79 80 81 82 83 84 85 86 87 88 89 90 91 92 93 94 95 96 97 98 99 100

3 6 9 12 15 18 21 24 27 30

3 = 1 × 3 = 3
6 = 2 × 3 = 3 + 3
9 = 3 × 3 = 3 + 3 + 3
12 = 4 × 3 = 3 + 3 + 3 + 3
15 = 5 × 3 = 3 + 3 + 3 + 3 + 3
18 = 6 × 3 = 3 + 3 + 3 + 3 + 3 + 3
21 = 7 × 3 = 3 + 3 + 3 + 3 + 3 + 3 + 3
24 = 8 × 3 = 3 + 3 + 3 + 3 + 3 + 3 + 3 + 3
27 = 9 × 3 = 3 + 3 + 3 + 3 + 3 + 3 + 3 + 3 + 3
30 = 10 × 3 = 3 + 3 + 3 + 3 + 3 + 3 + 3 + 3 + 3 + 3

PATH to FLUENCY Use the 5s Shortcut for 3s

Write the 3s count-bys to find the total.

1. How many sides are in 8 triangles?

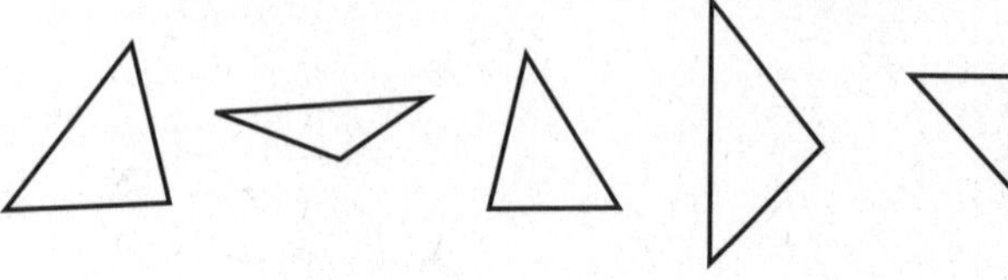
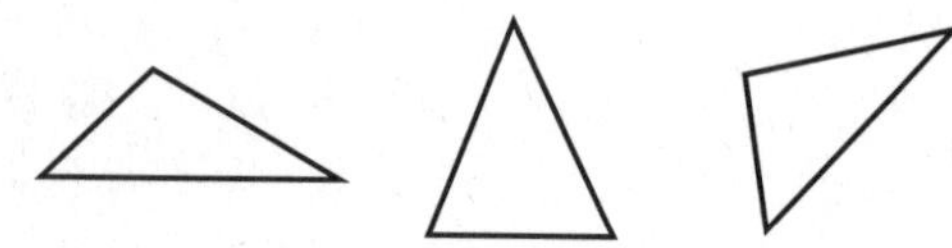

_____ _____ _____ _____ _____ _____ _____ _____

2. How many wheels are on 6 tricycles?

_____ _____ _____ _____ _____ _____

3. How many legs are on 7 tripods?

_____ _____ _____ _____ _____ _____ _____

Name ____________________

PATH to FLUENCY Use the 5s Shortcut for 3s (continued)

Find the total by starting with the fifth count-by and counting by 3s from there.

4 How many sides are in 7 triangles?

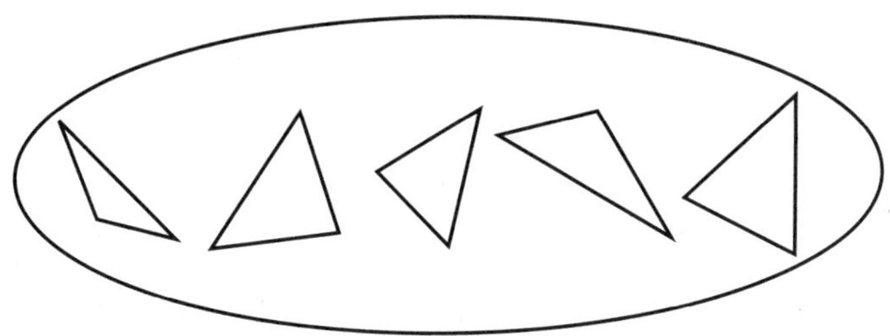
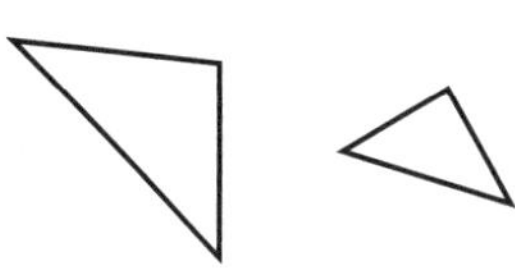

_____ _____ _____

5 How many wheels are on 9 tricycles?

_____ _____ _____ _____ _____

6 How many legs are on 8 tripods?

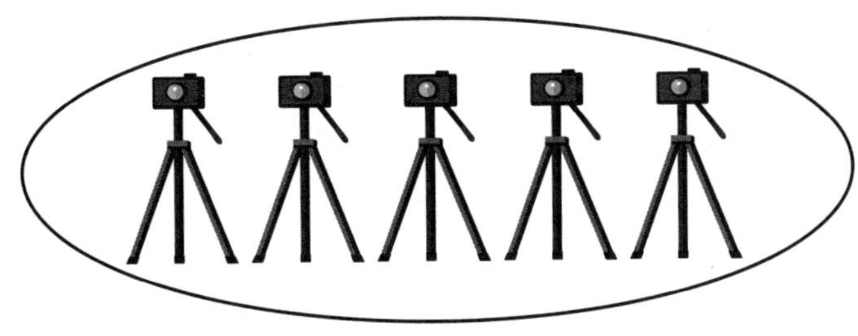

_____ _____ _____ _____

Make Sense of Problems

Write an equation and solve the problem.

Show your work.

7 Spencer arranged his soccer trophies in 3 equal rows. If he has 12 trophies, how many trophies are in each row?

____

8 How many sides do 8 triangles have altogether?

____

9 For Sophie's class picture, the students stood in 3 rows with 5 students in each row. How many students were in the picture?

____

10 Tickets to the school play cost \$3 each. Mr. Cortez spent \$27 on tickets. How many tickets did he buy?

____

11 Hiran wrote 21 vocabulary words. If the words were arranged in rows of 3, how many rows of words did Hiran write?

____

12 Tennis balls come 3 to a can. Coach Pratt bought 6 cans for the tennis team. How many tennis balls did Coach Pratt buy in all?

____

Check Understanding

Draw a picture to show how you can use the 5s Shortcut method to solve Problem 8.

Name ____________________

PATH to FLUENCY

Study Sheet B

3s		
Count-bys	Mixed Up ×	Mixed Up ÷
1 × 3 = 3	5 × 3 = 15	27 ÷ 3 = 9
2 × 3 = 6	1 × 3 = 3	6 ÷ 3 = 2
3 × 3 = 9	8 × 3 = 24	18 ÷ 3 = 6
4 × 3 = 12	10 × 3 = 30	30 ÷ 3 = 10
5 × 3 = 15	3 × 3 = 9	9 ÷ 3 = 3
6 × 3 = 18	7 × 3 = 21	3 ÷ 3 = 1
7 × 3 = 21	9 × 3 = 27	12 ÷ 3 = 4
8 × 3 = 24	2 × 3 = 6	24 ÷ 3 = 8
9 × 3 = 27	4 × 3 = 12	15 ÷ 3 = 5
10 × 3 = 30	6 × 3 = 18	21 ÷ 3 = 7

4s		
Count-bys	Mixed Up ×	Mixed Up ÷
1 × 4 = 4	4 × 4 = 16	12 ÷ 4 = 3
2 × 4 = 8	1 × 4 = 4	36 ÷ 4 = 9
3 × 4 = 12	7 × 4 = 28	24 ÷ 4 = 6
4 × 4 = 16	3 × 4 = 12	4 ÷ 4 = 1
5 × 4 = 20	9 × 4 = 36	20 ÷ 4 = 5
6 × 4 = 24	10 × 4 = 40	28 ÷ 4 = 7
7 × 4 = 28	2 × 4 = 8	8 ÷ 4 = 2
8 × 4 = 32	5 × 4 = 20	40 ÷ 4 = 10
9 × 4 = 36	8 × 4 = 32	32 ÷ 4 = 8
10 × 4 = 40	6 × 4 = 24	16 ÷ 4 = 4

0s	
Count-bys	Mixed Up ×
1 × 0 = 0	3 × 0 = 0
2 × 0 = 0	10 × 0 = 0
3 × 0 = 0	5 × 0 = 0
4 × 0 = 0	8 × 0 = 0
5 × 0 = 0	7 × 0 = 0
6 × 0 = 0	2 × 0 = 0
7 × 0 = 0	9 × 0 = 0
8 × 0 = 0	6 × 0 = 0
9 × 0 = 0	1 × 0 = 0
10 × 0 = 0	4 × 0 = 0

1s		
Count-bys	Mixed Up ×	Mixed Up ÷
1 × 1 = 1	5 × 1 = 5	10 ÷ 1 = 10
2 × 1 = 2	7 × 1 = 7	8 ÷ 1 = 8
3 × 1 = 3	10 × 1 = 10	4 ÷ 1 = 4
4 × 1 = 4	1 × 1 = 1	9 ÷ 1 = 9
5 × 1 = 5	8 × 1 = 8	6 ÷ 1 = 6
6 × 1 = 6	4 × 1 = 4	7 ÷ 1 = 7
7 × 1 = 7	9 × 1 = 9	1 ÷ 1 = 1
8 × 1 = 8	3 × 1 = 3	2 ÷ 1 = 2
9 × 1 = 9	2 × 1 = 2	5 ÷ 1 = 5
10 × 1 = 10	6 × 1 = 6	3 ÷ 1 = 3

2×2

$\begin{array}{r} 2 \\ \times\ 3 \\ \hline \end{array}$ $\begin{array}{r} 3 \\ \times\ 2 \\ \hline \end{array}$

2×4
4×2

$\begin{array}{r} 2 \\ \times\ 5 \\ \hline \end{array}$ $\begin{array}{r} 5 \\ \times\ 2 \\ \hline \end{array}$

2×6
6×2

$\begin{array}{r} 2 \\ \times\ 7 \\ \hline \end{array}$ $\begin{array}{r} 7 \\ \times\ 2 \\ \hline \end{array}$

2×8
8×2

$\begin{array}{r} 2 \\ \times\ 9 \\ \hline \end{array}$ $\begin{array}{r} 9 \\ \times\ 2 \\ \hline \end{array}$

$10 = 2 \times 5$

$10 = 5 \times 2$

5, 10

2, 4, 6, 8, 10

5

2 | 10

$$\begin{array}{r} 2 \\ \times\ 4 \\ \hline 8 \end{array} \qquad \begin{array}{r} 4 \\ \times\ 2 \\ \hline 8 \end{array}$$

2, 4, 6, 8

4, 8

2

4 | 8

$6 = 2 \times 3$

$6 = 3 \times 2$

3, 6

2, 4, 6

3

2 | 6

$$\begin{array}{r} 2 \\ \times\ 2 \\ \hline 4 \end{array}$$

2, 4

2

2 | 4

$18 = 2 \times 9$

$18 = 9 \times 2$

9, 18

2, 4, 6, 8, 10, 12, 14, 16, 18

9

2 | 18

$$\begin{array}{r} 2 \\ \times\ 8 \\ \hline 16 \end{array} \qquad \begin{array}{r} 8 \\ \times\ 2 \\ \hline 16 \end{array}$$

8, 16

2, 4, 6, 8, 10, 12, 14, 16

2

8 | 16

$14 = 2 \times 7$

$14 = 7 \times 2$

7, 14

2, 4, 6, 8, 10, 12, 14

7

2 | 14

$$\begin{array}{r} 2 \\ \times\ 6 \\ \hline 12 \end{array} \qquad \begin{array}{r} 6 \\ \times\ 2 \\ \hline 12 \end{array}$$

6, 12

2, 4, 6, 8, 10, 12

2

6 | 12

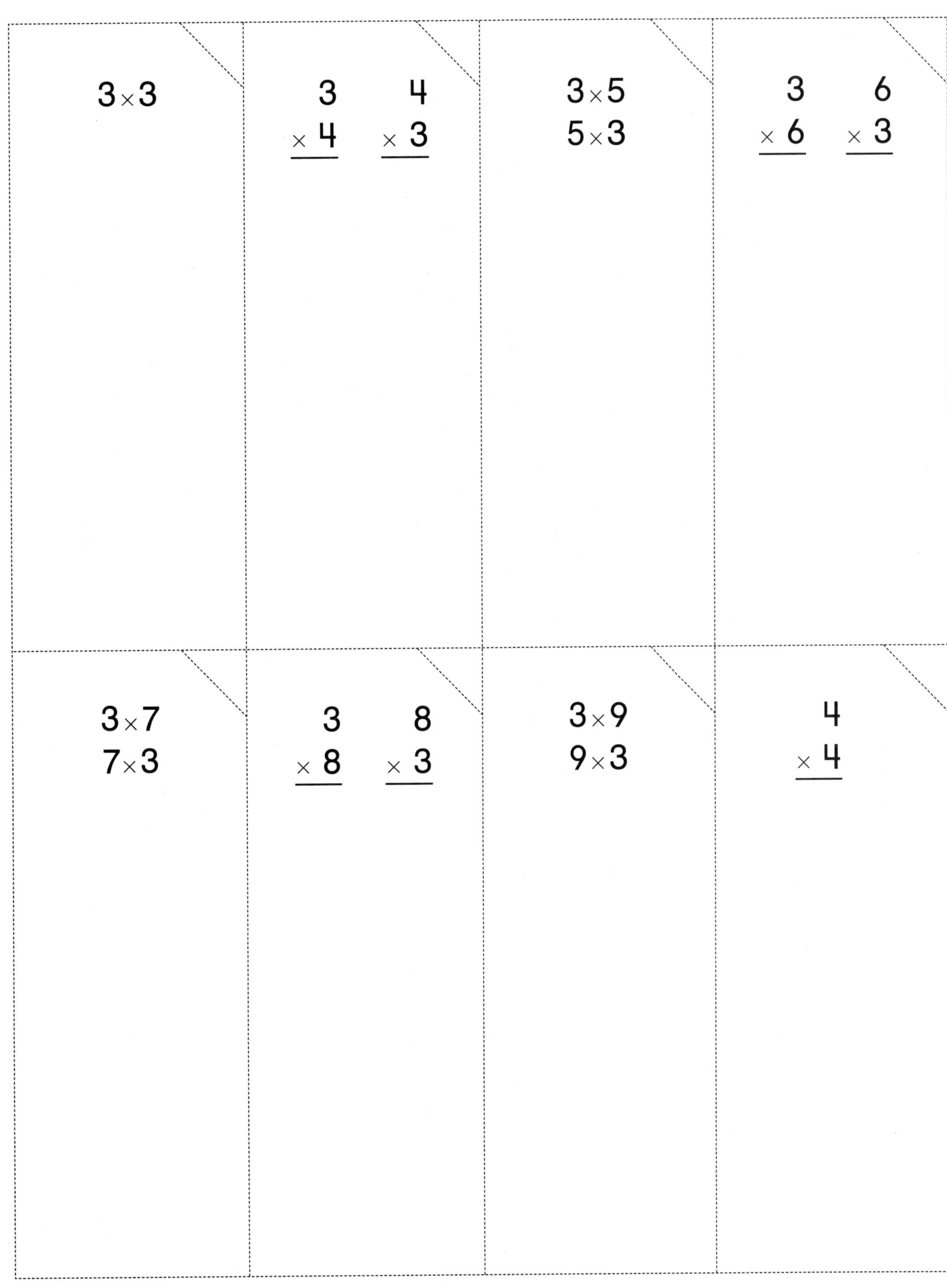
3 × 3
3 × 4
4 × 3
3 × 5
5 × 3
3 × 6
6 × 3
3 × 7
7 × 3
3 × 8
8 × 3
3 × 9
9 × 3
4 × 4

$18 = 3 \times 6$

$18 = 6 \times 3$

6 12 18

3 6 9 12 15 18

6

3 18

$3 \times 5 = 15$

$5 \times 3 = 15$

5 10 15

3 6 9 12 15

3

5 15

$12 = 3 \times 4$

$12 = 4 \times 3$

4 8 12

3 6 9 12

4

3 12

$3 \times 3 = 9$

3 6 9

3

3 9

$16 = 4 \times 4$

4 8 12 16

4

4 16

$3 \times 9 = 27$

$9 \times 3 = 27$

9 18 27

3 6 9 12 15 18 21 24 27

9

3 27

$24 = 3 \times 8$

$24 = 8 \times 3$

8 16 24

3 6 9 12 15 18 21 24

3

8 24

$3 \times 7 = 21$

$7 \times 3 = 21$

7 14 21

3 6 9 12 15 18 21

7

3 21

4 × 5 5 × 4	$\begin{array}{r} 4 \\ \times\ 6 \\ \hline \end{array}$ $\begin{array}{r} 6 \\ \times\ 4 \\ \hline \end{array}$	4 × 7 7 × 4	$\begin{array}{r} 4 \\ \times\ 8 \\ \hline \end{array}$ $\begin{array}{r} 8 \\ \times\ 4 \\ \hline \end{array}$
4 × 9 9 × 4	$\begin{array}{r} 5 \\ \times\ 5 \\ \hline \end{array}$	5 × 6 6 × 5	$\begin{array}{r} 5 \\ \times\ 7 \\ \hline \end{array}$ $\begin{array}{r} 7 \\ \times\ 5 \\ \hline \end{array}$

32 = 4 × 8

32 = 8 × 4

8, 16, 24, 32

4, 8, 12, 16, 20, 24, 28, 32

4 (columns) × 8 (rows): 32

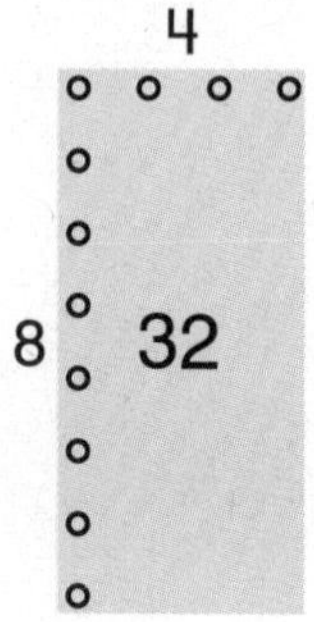

$\begin{array}{r} 4 \\ \times 7 \\ \hline 28 \end{array}$ $\begin{array}{r} 7 \\ \times 4 \\ \hline 28 \end{array}$

7, 14, 21, 28

4, 8, 12, 16, 20, 24, 28

7 (columns) × 4 (rows): 28

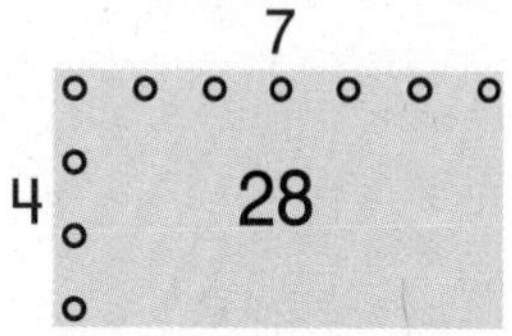

24 = 4 × 6

24 = 6 × 4

6, 12, 18, 24

4, 8, 12, 16, 20, 24

4 (columns) × 6 (rows): 24

$\begin{array}{r} 4 \\ \times 5 \\ \hline 20 \end{array}$ $\begin{array}{r} 5 \\ \times 4 \\ \hline 20 \end{array}$

5, 10, 15, 20

4, 8, 12, 16, 20

5 (columns) × 4 (rows): 20

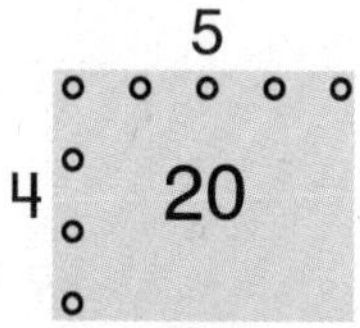

35 = 5 × 7

35 = 7 × 5

7, 14, 21, 28, 35

5, 10, 15, 20, 25, 30, 35

7 (columns) × 5 (rows): 35

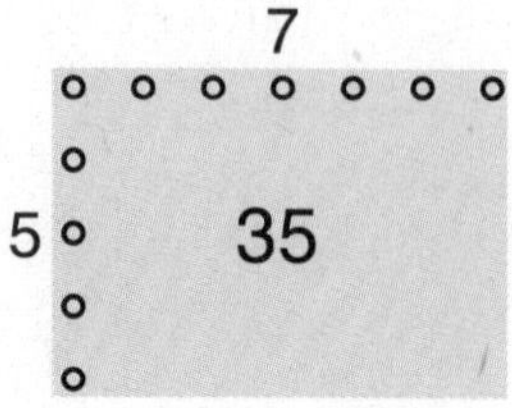

$\begin{array}{r} 5 \\ \times 6 \\ \hline 30 \end{array}$ $\begin{array}{r} 6 \\ \times 5 \\ \hline 30 \end{array}$

6, 12, 18, 24, 30

5, 10, 15, 20, 25, 30

5 (columns) × 6 (rows): 30

25 = 5 × 5

5, 10, 15, 20, 25

5 (columns) × 5 (rows): 25

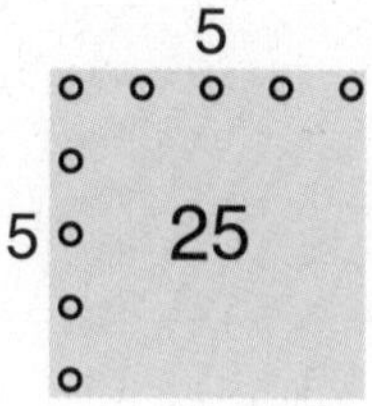

$\begin{array}{r} 4 \\ \times 9 \\ \hline 36 \end{array}$ $\begin{array}{r} 9 \\ \times 4 \\ \hline 36 \end{array}$

9, 18, 27, 36

4, 8, 12, 16, 20, 24, 28, 32, 36

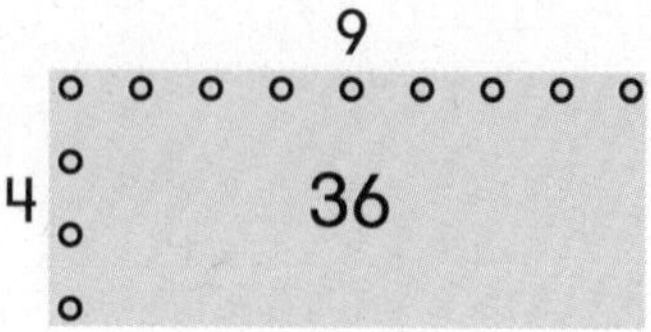

9 (columns) × 4 (rows): 36

5×8
8×5

$\begin{array}{r} 5 \\ \times\ 9 \\ \hline \end{array}$ $\begin{array}{r} 9 \\ \times\ 5 \\ \hline \end{array}$

6×6

$\begin{array}{r} 6 \\ \times\ 7 \\ \hline \end{array}$ $\begin{array}{r} 7 \\ \times\ 6 \\ \hline \end{array}$

6×8
8×6

$\begin{array}{r} 6 \\ \times\ 9 \\ \hline \end{array}$ $\begin{array}{r} 9 \\ \times\ 6 \\ \hline \end{array}$

7×7

$\begin{array}{r} 7 \\ \times\ 8 \\ \hline \end{array}$ $\begin{array}{r} 8 \\ \times\ 7 \\ \hline \end{array}$

42 = 7 × 6

42 = 6 × 7

6 12 18 24 30 36 42

7 14 21 28 35 42

7

6

42

$$\begin{array}{r} 6 \\ \times\ 6 \\ \hline 36 \end{array}$$

6 12 18 24 30 36

6

6

36

45 = 9 × 5

45 = 5 × 9

5 10 15 20 25 30 35 40 45

9 18 27 36 45

9

5

45

$$\begin{array}{r} 8 \\ \times\ 5 \\ \hline 40 \end{array} \qquad \begin{array}{r} 5 \\ \times\ 8 \\ \hline 40 \end{array}$$

5 10 15 20 25 30 35 40

8 16 24 32 40

5

8

40

56 = 7 × 8

56 = 8 × 7

8 16 24 32 40 48 56

7 14 21 28 35 42 49 56

8

7

56

$$\begin{array}{r} 7 \\ \times\ 7 \\ \hline 49 \end{array}$$

7 14 21 28 35 42 49

7

7

49

54 = 9 × 6

54 = 6 × 9

6 12 18 24 30 36 42 48 54

9 18 27 36 45 54

9

6

54

$$\begin{array}{r} 6 \\ \times 8 \\ \hline 48 \end{array} \qquad \begin{array}{r} 8 \\ \times\ 6 \\ \hline 48 \end{array}$$

8 16 24 32 40 48

6 12 18 24 30 36 42 48

8

6

48

7×9 9×7	$\begin{array}{r} 8 \\ \times\ 8 \\ \hline \end{array}$	9×8 8×9	$\begin{array}{r} 9 \\ \times\ 9 \\ \hline \end{array}$

81 = 9 × 9

9
18
27
36
45
54
63
72
81

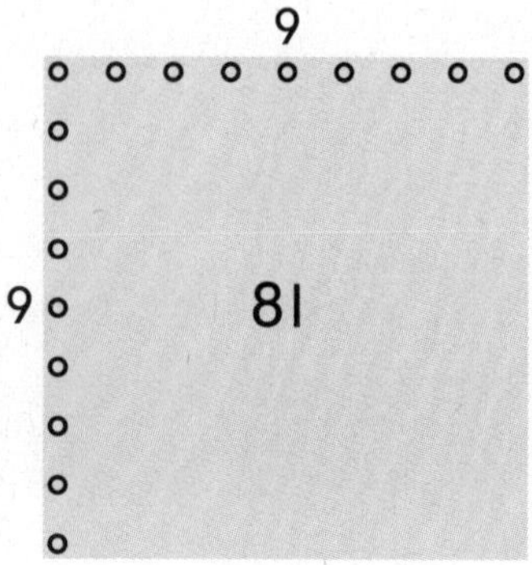

9

9

81

$$\begin{array}{r} 9 \\ \times 8 \\ \hline 72 \end{array} \qquad \begin{array}{r} 8 \\ \times 9 \\ \hline 72 \end{array}$$

8	9
16	18
24	27
32	36
40	45
48	54
56	63
64	72
72	

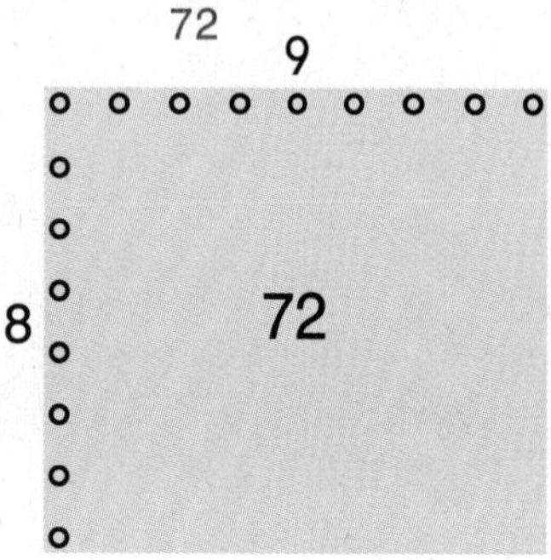

9

8

72

---

64 = 8 × 8

8
16
24
32
40
48
56
64

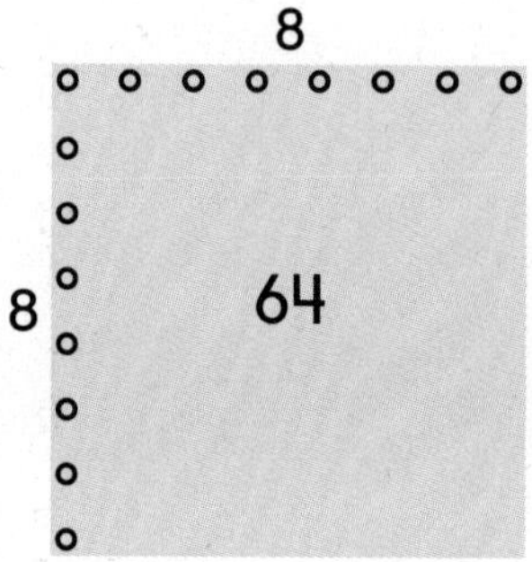

8

8

64

$$\begin{array}{r} 7 \\ \times 9 \\ \hline 63 \end{array} \qquad \begin{array}{r} 9 \\ \times 7 \\ \hline 63 \end{array}$$

9	7
18	14
27	21
36	28
45	35
54	42
63	49
	56
	63

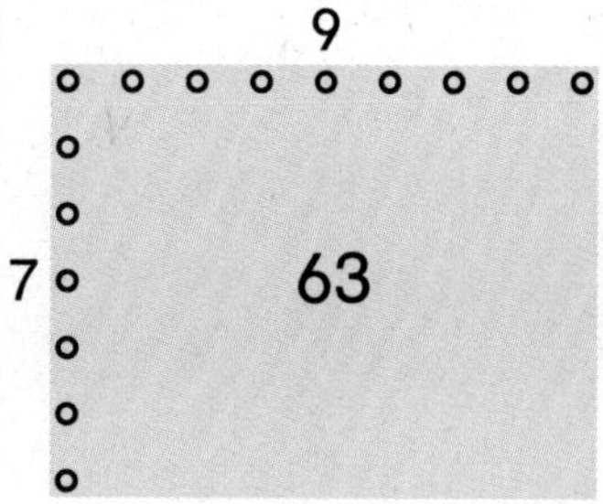

9

7

63

$2\overline{)4}$ $4 \div 2$	$2\overline{)6}$ $6 \div 2$	$2\overline{)8}$ $8 \div 2$	$2\overline{)10}$ $10 \div 2$
$2\overline{)12}$ $12 \div 2$	$2\overline{)14}$ $14 \div 2$	$2\overline{)16}$ $16 \div 2$	$2\overline{)18}$ $18 \div 2$

5	2
2)10	5)10

2
4
6
8
10

5
10

5
2 ○ ○ ○ ○ ○
○ 10

4	2
2)8	4)8

2
4
6
8

4
8

4
2 ○ ○ ○ ○
○ 8

3	2
2)6	3)6

2
4
6

3
6

3
2 ○ ○ ○
○ 6

2

2)4

2
4

2
2 ○ ○
○ 4

9	2
2)18	9)18

2
4
6
8
10

12
14
16
18

9
18

9
2 ○ ○ ○ ○ ○ ○ ○ ○ ○
○ 18

8	2
2)16	8)16

2
4
6
8
10

12
14
16

8
16

8
2 ○ ○ ○ ○ ○ ○ ○ ○
○ 16

7	2
2)14	7)14

2
4
6
8
10

12
14

7
14

7
2 ○ ○ ○ ○ ○ ○ ○
○ 14

6	2
2)12	6)12

2
4
6
8
10

12

6
12

6
2 ○ ○ ○ ○ ○ ○
○ 12

$3\overline{)6}$

$6 \div 3$

$4\overline{)8}$

$8 \div 4$

$5\overline{)10}$

$10 \div 5$

$6\overline{)12}$

$12 \div 6$

$7\overline{)14}$

$14 \div 7$

$8\overline{)16}$

$16 \div 8$

$9\overline{)18}$

$18 \div 9$

$3\overline{)9}$

$9 \div 3$

$\begin{array}{r}2\\6\overline{)12}\end{array}$ $\begin{array}{r}6\\2\overline{)12}\end{array}$

6
12

2
4
6
8
10
12

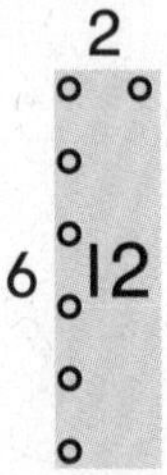

2
6 12

$\begin{array}{r}2\\5\overline{)10}\end{array}$ $\begin{array}{r}5\\2\overline{)10}\end{array}$

5
10

2
4
6
8
10

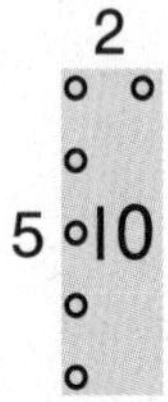

2
5 10

$\begin{array}{r}2\\4\overline{)8}\end{array}$ $\begin{array}{r}4\\2\overline{)8}\end{array}$

4
8

2
4
6
8

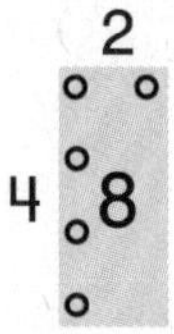

2
4 8

$\begin{array}{r}2\\3\overline{)6}\end{array}$ $\begin{array}{r}3\\2\overline{)6}\end{array}$

3
6

2
4
6

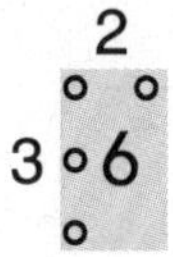

2
3 6

$\begin{array}{r}3\\3\overline{)9}\end{array}$

3
6
9

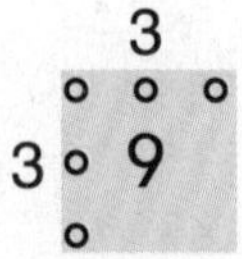

3
3 9

$\begin{array}{r}2\\9\overline{)18}\end{array}$ $\begin{array}{r}9\\2\overline{)18}\end{array}$

9
18

2
4
6
8
10
12
14
16
18

2
9 18

$\begin{array}{r}2\\8\overline{)16}\end{array}$ $\begin{array}{r}8\\2\overline{)16}\end{array}$

8
16

2
4
6
8
10
12
14
16

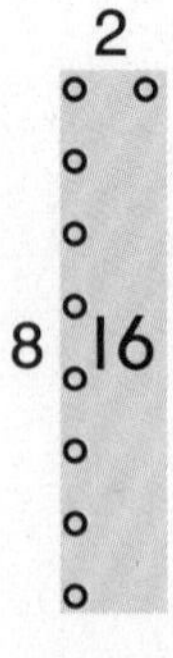

2
8 16

$\begin{array}{r}2\\7\overline{)14}\end{array}$ $\begin{array}{r}7\\2\overline{)14}\end{array}$

7
14

2
4
6
8
10
12
14

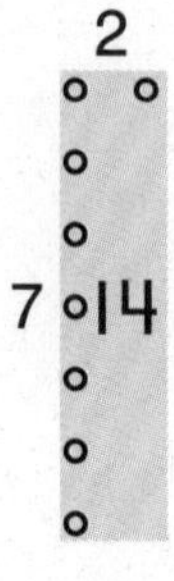

2
7 14

$3\overline{)12}$ $12 \div 3$	$3\overline{)15}$ $15 \div 3$	$3\overline{)18}$ $18 \div 3$	$3\overline{)21}$ $21 \div 3$
$3\overline{)24}$ $24 \div 3$	$3\overline{)27}$ $27 \div 3$	$4\overline{)12}$ $12 \div 4$	$5\overline{)15}$ $15 \div 5$

$3\overline{)21}$ = 7 $\quad$ $7\overline{)21}$ = 3

3, 6, 9, 12, 15, 18, 21 $\quad$ 7, 14, 21

7 × 3 array: 21

$3\overline{)18}$ = 6 $\quad$ $6\overline{)18}$ = 3

3, 6, 9, 12, 15, 18 $\quad$ 6, 12, 18

6 × 3 array: 18

$3\overline{)15}$ = 5 $\quad$ $5\overline{)15}$ = 3

3, 6, 9, 12, 15 $\quad$ 5, 10, 15

5 × 3 array: 15

$3\overline{)12}$ = 4 $\quad$ $4\overline{)12}$ = 3

3, 6, 9, 12 $\quad$ 4, 8, 12

4 × 3 array: 12

$5\overline{)15}$ = 3 $\quad$ $3\overline{)15}$ = 5

5, 10, 15 $\quad$ 3, 6, 9, 12, 15

3 × 5 array: 15

$4\overline{)12}$ = 3 $\quad$ $3\overline{)12}$ = 4

4, 8, 12 $\quad$ 3, 6, 9, 12

3 × 4 array: 12

$3\overline{)27}$ = 9 $\quad$ $9\overline{)27}$ = 3

3, 6, 9, 12, 15, 18, 21, 24, 27 $\quad$ 9, 18, 27

9 × 3 array: 27

$3\overline{)24}$ = 8 $\quad$ $8\overline{)24}$ = 3

3, 6, 9, 12, 15, 18, 21, 24 $\quad$ 8, 16, 24

8 × 3 array: 24

$6\overline{)18}$

$18 \div 6$

$7\overline{)21}$

$21 \div 7$

$8\overline{)24}$

$24 \div 8$

$9\overline{)27}$

$27 \div 9$

$4\overline{)16}$

$16 \div 4$

$4\overline{)20}$

$20 \div 4$

$4\overline{)24}$

$24 \div 4$

$4\overline{)28}$

$28 \div 4$

$$\begin{array}{r}3\\9\overline{)27}\end{array} \quad \begin{array}{r}9\\3\overline{)27}\end{array}$$

9
18
27

3
6
9
12
15

18
21
24
27

3

9 27

$$\begin{array}{r}3\\8\overline{)24}\end{array} \quad \begin{array}{r}8\\3\overline{)24}\end{array}$$

8
16
24

3
6
9
12
15

18
21
24

3

8 24

$$\begin{array}{r}3\\7\overline{)21}\end{array} \quad \begin{array}{r}7\\3\overline{)21}\end{array}$$

7
14
21

3
6
9
12
15

18
21

3

7 21

$$\begin{array}{r}3\\6\overline{)18}\end{array} \quad \begin{array}{r}6\\3\overline{)18}\end{array}$$

6
12
18

3
6
9
12
15

18

3

6 18

$$\begin{array}{r}7\\4\overline{)28}\end{array} \quad \begin{array}{r}4\\7\overline{)28}\end{array}$$

4
8
12
16
20

24
28

7
14
21
28

7

4 28

$$\begin{array}{r}6\\4\overline{)24}\end{array} \quad \begin{array}{r}4\\6\overline{)24}\end{array}$$

4
8
12
16
20

24

6
12
18
24

6

4 24

$$\begin{array}{r}5\\4\overline{)20}\end{array} \quad \begin{array}{r}4\\5\overline{)20}\end{array}$$

4
8
12
16
20

5
10
15
20

5

4 20

$$\begin{array}{r}4\\4\overline{)16}\end{array}$$

4
8
12
16

4

4 16

$4\overline{)32}$

$32 \div 4$

$4\overline{)36}$

$36 \div 4$

$5\overline{)20}$

$20 \div 5$

$6\overline{)24}$

$24 \div 6$

$7\overline{)28}$

$28 \div 7$

$8\overline{)32}$

$32 \div 8$

$9\overline{)36}$

$36 \div 9$

$5\overline{)25}$

$25 \div 5$

4 6
6)24 4)24

6
12
18
24

4
8
12
16
20
24

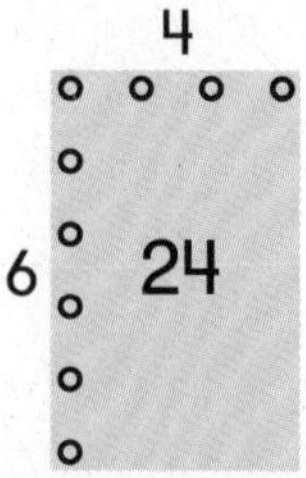

4
6 | 24

4 5
5)20 4)20

5
10
15
20

4
8
12
16
20

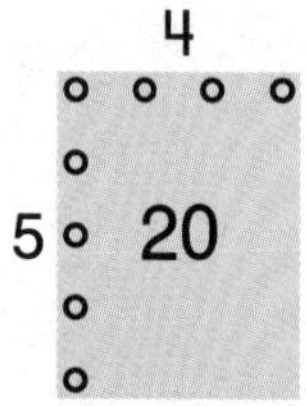

4
5 | 20

9 4
4)36 9)36

4
8
12
16
20
24
28
32
36

9
18
27
36

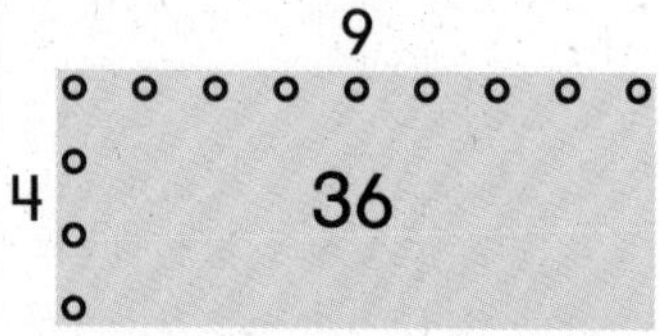

9
4 | 36

8 4
4)32 8)32

4
8
12
16
20
24
28
32

8
16
24
32

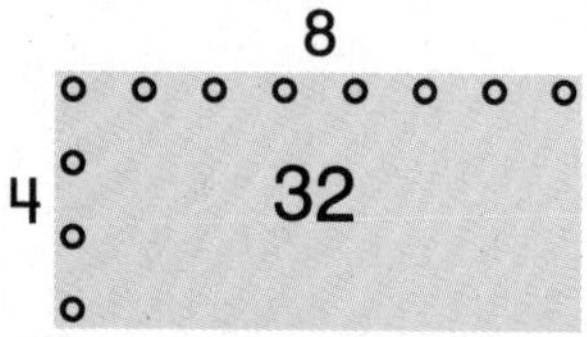

8
4 | 32

5
5)25

5
10
15
20
25

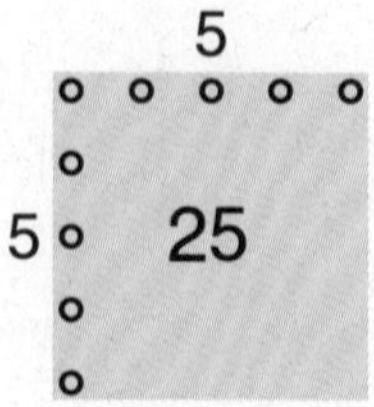

5
5 | 25

4 9
9)36 4)36

9
18
27
36

4
8
12
16
20
24
28
32
36

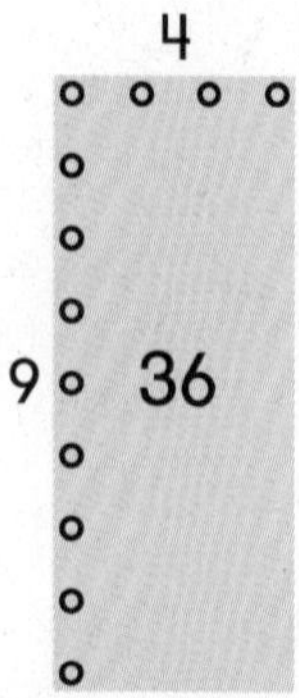

4
9 | 36

4 8
8)32 4)32

8
16
24
32

4
8
12
16
20
24
28
32

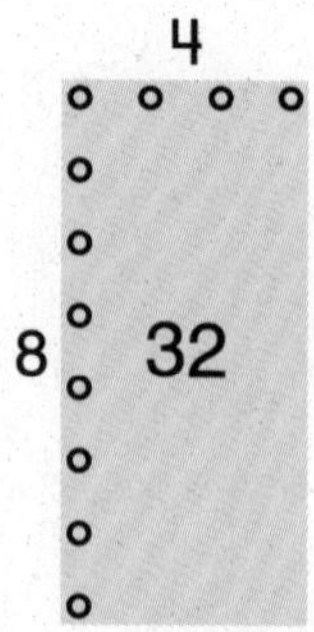

4
8 | 32

4 7
7)28 4)28

7
14
21
28

4
8
12
16
20
24
28

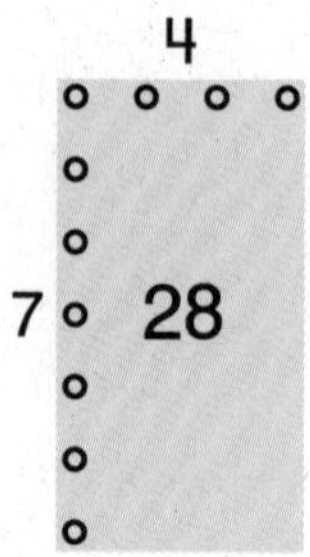

4
7 | 28

$5\overline{)30}$ 30 ÷ 5	$5\overline{)35}$ 35 ÷ 5	$5\overline{)40}$ 40 ÷ 5	$5\overline{)45}$ 45 ÷ 5
$6\overline{)30}$ 30 ÷ 6	$7\overline{)35}$ 35 ÷ 7	$8\overline{)40}$ 40 ÷ 8	$9\overline{)45}$ 45 ÷ 9

$5\overline{)45}$ = 9 | $9\overline{)45}$ = 5

5, 10, 15, 20, 25, 30, 35, 40, 45 | 9, 18, 27, 36, 45

9 × 5 array: 45

$5\overline{)40}$ = 8 | $8\overline{)40}$ = 5

5, 10, 15, 20, 25, 30, 35, 40 | 8, 16, 24, 32, 40

8 × 5 array: 40

$5\overline{)35}$ = 7 | $7\overline{)35}$ = 5

5, 10, 15, 20, 25, 30, 35 | 7, 14, 21, 28, 35

7 × 5 array: 35

$5\overline{)30}$ = 6 | $6\overline{)30}$ = 5

5, 10, 15, 20, 25, 30 | 6, 12, 18, 24, 30

6 × 5 array: 30

$9\overline{)45}$ = 5 | $5\overline{)45}$ = 9

9, 18, 27, 36, 45 | 5, 10, 15, 20, 25, 30, 35, 40, 45

5 × 9 array: 45

$8\overline{)40}$ = 5 | $5\overline{)40}$ = 8

8, 16, 24, 32, 40 | 5, 10, 15, 20, 25, 30, 35, 40

5 × 8 array: 40

$7\overline{)35}$ = 5 | $5\overline{)35}$ = 7

7, 14, 21, 28, 35 | 5, 10, 15, 20, 25, 30, 35

5 × 7 array: 35

$6\overline{)30}$ = 5 | $5\overline{)30}$ = 6

6, 12, 18, 24, 30 | 5, 10, 15, 20, 25, 30

5 × 6 array: 30

$6\overline{)36}$

$36 \div 6$

$6\overline{)42}$

$42 \div 6$

$6\overline{)48}$

$48 \div 6$

$6\overline{)54}$

$54 \div 6$

$7\overline{)42}$

$42 \div 7$

$8\overline{)48}$

$48 \div 8$

$9\overline{)54}$

$54 \div 9$

$7\overline{)49}$

$49 \div 7$

$6\overline{)54}$ = 9 | $9\overline{)54}$ = 6

6, 12, 18, 24, 30, 36, 42, 48, 54 | 9, 18, 27, 36, 45, 54

9 × 6 = 54

$6\overline{)48}$ = 8 | $8\overline{)48}$ = 6

6, 12, 18, 24, 30, 36, 42, 48 | 8, 16, 24, 32, 40, 48

8 × 6 = 48

$6\overline{)42}$ = 7 | $7\overline{)42}$ = 6

6, 12, 18, 24, 30, 36, 42 | 7, 14, 21, 28, 35, 42

7 × 6 = 42

$6\overline{)36}$ = 6

6, 12, 18, 24, 30, 36

6 × 6 = 36

$7\overline{)49}$ = 7

7, 14, 21, 28, 35, 42, 49

7 × 7 = 49

$9\overline{)54}$ = 6 | $6\overline{)54}$ = 9

9, 18, 27, 36, 45, 54 | 6, 12, 18, 24, 30, 36, 42, 48, 54

6 × 9 = 54

$8\overline{)48}$ = 6 | $6\overline{)48}$ = 8

8, 16, 24, 32, 40, 48 | 6, 12, 18, 24, 30, 36, 42, 48

6 × 8 = 48

$7\overline{)42}$ = 6 | $6\overline{)42}$ = 7

7, 14, 21, 28, 35, 42 | 6, 12, 18, 24, 30, 36, 42

6 × 7 = 42

$7\overline{)56}$ 56 ÷ 7	$7\overline{)63}$ 63 ÷ 7	$8\overline{)56}$ 56 ÷ 8	$9\overline{)63}$ 63 ÷ 9
$8\overline{)64}$ 64 ÷ 8	$8\overline{)72}$ 72 ÷ 8	$9\overline{)72}$ 72 ÷ 9	$9\overline{)81}$ 81 ÷ 9

7 9

9)63 7)63

9	7
18	14
27	21
36	28
45	35
54	42
63	49
	56
	63

7

9 63

---

7 8

8)56 7)56

8	7
16	14
24	21
32	28
40	35
48	42
56	49
	56

7

8 56

---

9 7

7)63 9)63

7	9
14	18
21	27
28	36
35	45
42	54
49	63
56	
63	

9

7 63

---

8 7

7)56 8)56

7	8
14	16
21	24
28	32
35	40
42	48
49	56
56	

8

7 56

9

9)81

9
18
27
36
45

54
63
72
81

9

9 81

---

8 9

9)72 8)72

9	8
18	16
27	24
36	32
45	40
54	48
63	56
72	64
	72

8

9 72

---

9 8

8)72 9)72

8	9
16	18
24	27
32	36
40	45
48	54
56	63
64	72
72	

9

8 72

8

8)64

8
16
24
32
40

48
56
64

8

8 64

Name ______________________

VOCABULARY
area
square units

PATH to FLUENCY Find the Area

The **area** of a rectangle is the number of **square units** that fit inside of it.

First, write a multiplication equation to represent the area of each rectangle. Then shade a whole number of rows in each rectangle. Write a multiplication to represent the area of the shaded rectangle and the area of the unshaded rectangle. Then write an addition equation to represent the area of the entire rectangle.

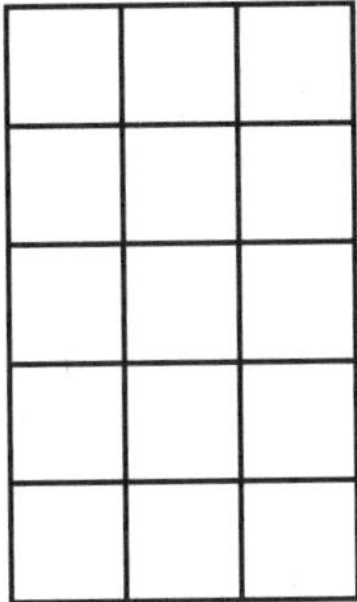

2
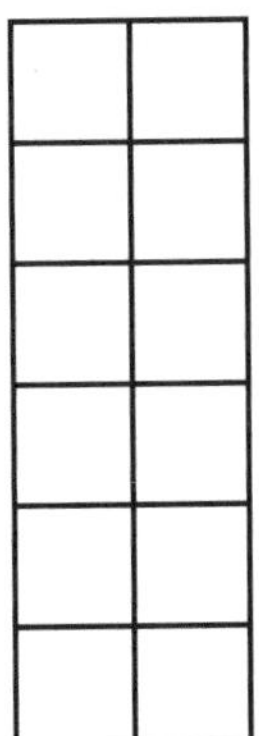

3
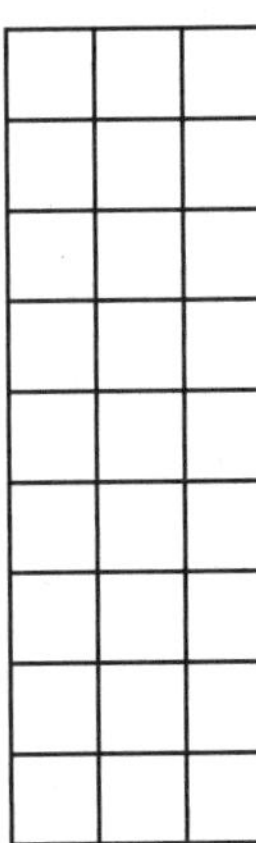

____

____

____

Make a rectangle drawing to represent each problem. Then give the product.

4 $5 \times 3 =$ ______

5 $7 * 2 =$ ______

6 $2 \bullet 9 =$ ______

PATH to FLUENCY Different Ways to Find Area

VOCABULARY
Distributive Property

The large rectangle has been divided into two small rectangles. You can find the area of the large rectangle in two ways:

- Add the areas of the two small rectangles:

  $5 \times 3 =$ 15 square units
  $2 \times 3 =$ 6 square units
  21 square units

  The **Distributive Property** is shown by
  $7 \times 3 = (5 + 2) \times 3 = (5 \times 3) + (2 \times 3)$

- Multiply the number of rows in the large rectangle by the number of square units in each row:

  $7 \times 3 =$ 21 square units

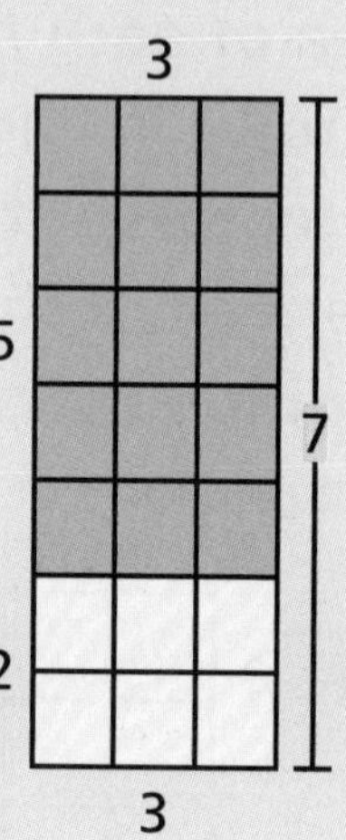

Complete.

7 Find the area of the large rectangle by finding the areas of the two small rectangles and adding them.

____

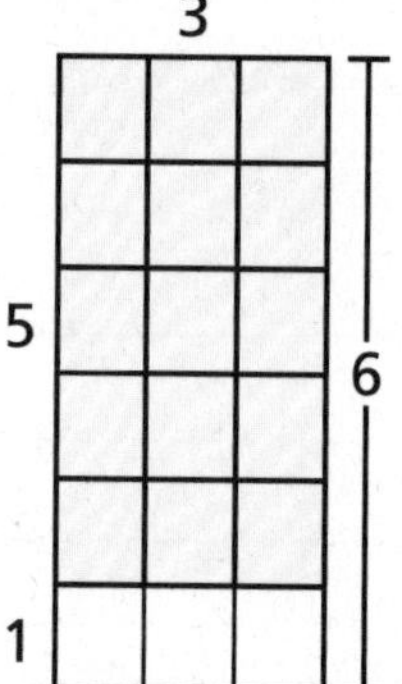

8 Find the area of the large rectangle by multiplying the number of rows by the number of square units in each row.

____

9 $5 \times 4 =$ ______ $2 \times 4 =$ ______ $7 \times 4 =$ ______

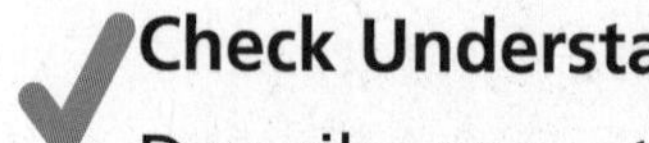

Check Understanding
Describe ways to find the area of this rectangle:

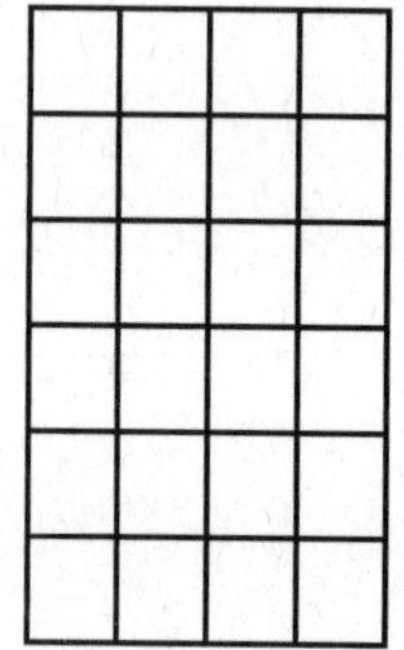

 Name ______________

PATH to FLUENCY

Check Sheet 4: 3s and 4s

3s Multiplications	3s Divisions	4s Multiplications	4s Divisions
8 × 3 = 24	9 / 3 = 3	1 × 4 = 4	40 / 4 = 10
3 • 2 = 6	21 ÷ 3 = 7	4 • 5 = 20	12 ÷ 4 = 3
3 * 5 = 15	27 / 3 = 9	8 * 4 = 32	24 / 4 = 6
10 × 3 = 30	3 ÷ 3 = 1	3 × 4 = 12	8 ÷ 4 = 2
3 • 3 = 9	18 / 3 = 6	4 • 6 = 24	4 / 4 = 1
3 * 6 = 18	12 ÷ 3 = 4	4 * 9 = 36	28 ÷ 4 = 7
7 × 3 = 21	30 / 3 = 10	10 × 4 = 40	32 / 4 = 8
3 • 9 = 27	6 ÷ 3 = 2	4 • 7 = 28	16 ÷ 4 = 4
4 * 3 = 12	24 / 3 = 8	4 * 4 = 16	36 / 4 = 9
3 × 1 = 3	15 / 3 = 5	2 × 4 = 8	20 / 4 = 5
3 • 4 = 12	21 ÷ 3 = 7	4 • 3 = 12	4 ÷ 4 = 1
3 * 3 = 9	3 / 3 = 1	4 * 2 = 8	32 / 4 = 8
3 × 10 = 30	9 ÷ 3 = 3	9 × 4 = 36	8 ÷ 4 = 2
2 • 3 = 6	27 / 3 = 9	1 • 4 = 4	16 / 4 = 4
3 * 7 = 21	30 ÷ 3 = 10	4 * 6 = 24	36 ÷ 4 = 9
6 × 3 = 18	18 / 3 = 6	5 × 4 = 20	12 / 4 = 3
5 • 3 = 15	6 ÷ 3 = 2	4 • 4 = 16	40 ÷ 4 = 10
3 * 8 = 24	15 ÷ 3 = 5	7 * 4 = 28	20 ÷ 4 = 5
9 × 3 = 27	12 / 3 = 4	8 × 4 = 32	24 / 4 = 6
2 • 3 = 6	24 ÷ 3 = 8	10 • 4 = 40	28 ÷ 4 = 7

Name ______________________________

PATH to FLUENCY Explore Patterns with 4s

What patterns do you see below?

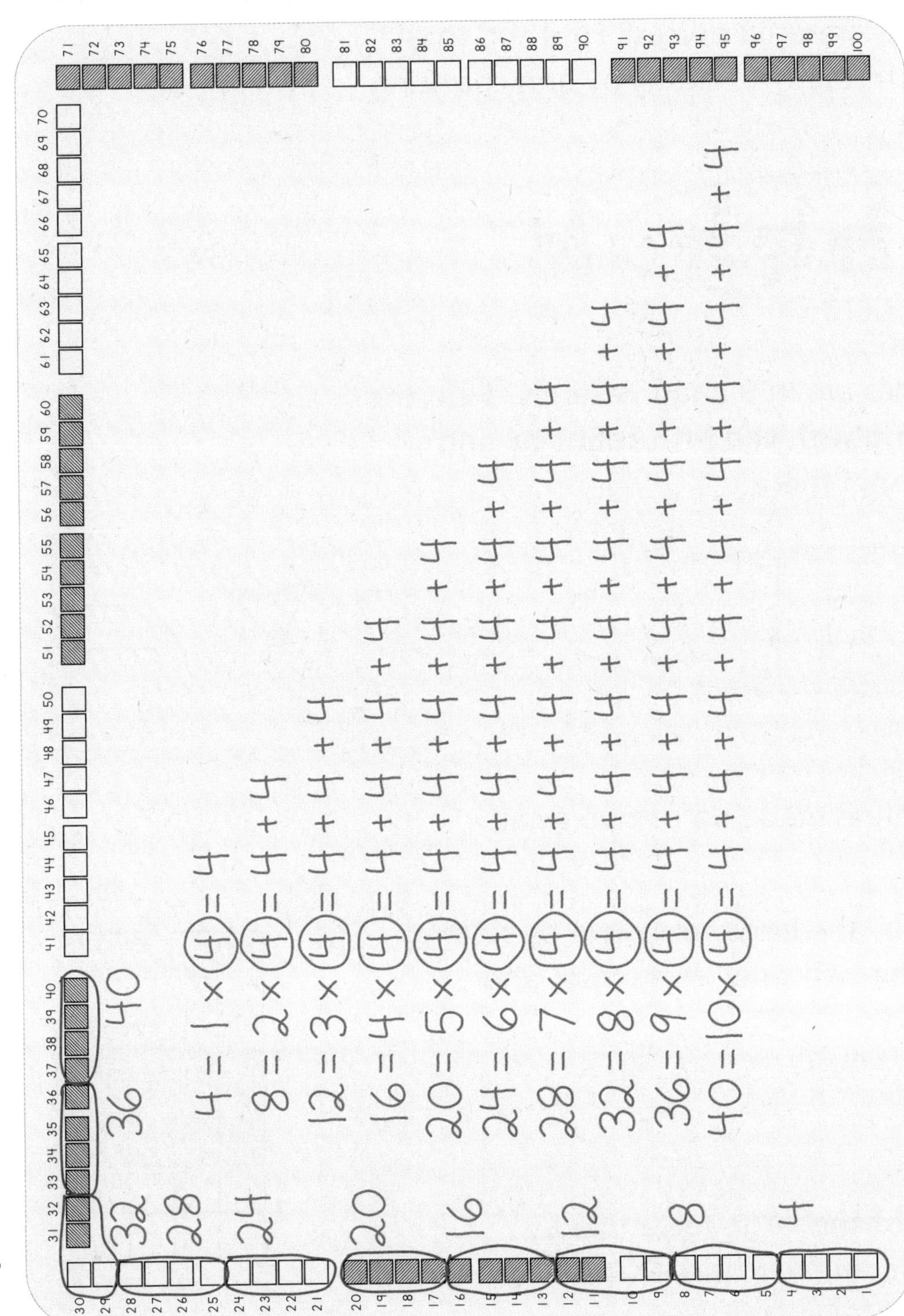

PATH to FLUENCY Use the 5s Shortcut for 4s

Solve each problem.

1. How many legs are on 6 horses? Find the total by starting with the fifth count-by and counting up from there.

_____ _____

2. How many sides are in 8 quadrilaterals? Find the total by starting with the fifth count-by and counting up from there.

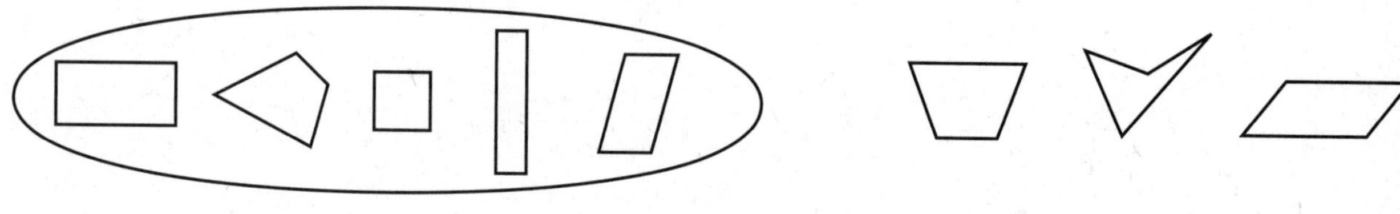

_____ _____ _____ _____

This large rectangle is made up of two small rectangles.

3. Find the area of the large rectangle by finding the areas of the two small rectangles and adding them.

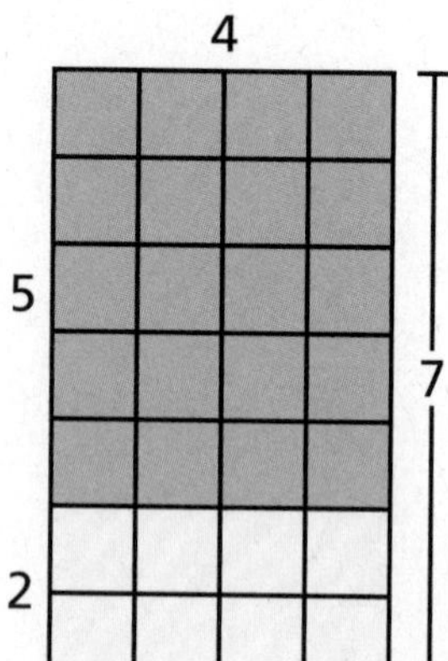

____

____

4. Find the area of the large rectangle by multiplying the number of rows by the number of square units in each row.

____

Name ______________________________

PATH to FLUENCY Use Multiplications You Know

You can combine multiplications to find other multiplications.

This equal shares drawing shows that 7 groups of 4 is the same as 5 groups of 4 plus 2 groups of 4.

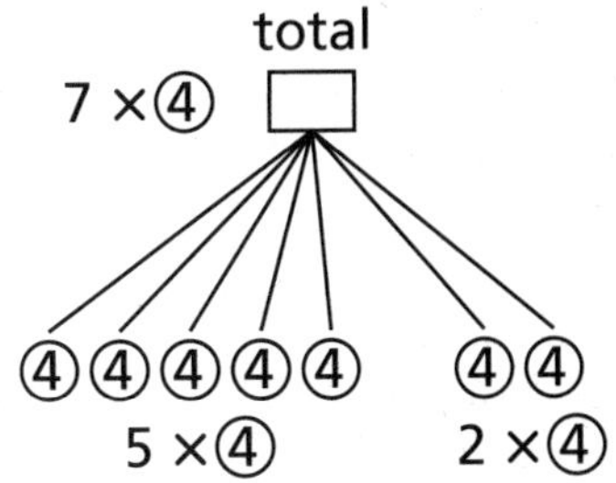

5. Find 5 ×④ and 2 ×④ and add the answers.

____

6. Find 7 ×④. Did you get the same answer as in Exercise 5?

____

7. Find this product: $5 \times 4 =$ ______

8. Find this product: $4 \times 4 =$ ______

9. Use your answers to Exercises 7 and 8 to show that $(5 \times 4) + (4 \times 4) = 9 \times 4 =$ ______

10. Make a drawing to show that your answers to Exercises 7–9 are correct.

What's the Error?

Dear Math Students,

Today I had to find 8 × 4. I didn't know the answer, but I figured it out by combining two multiplications I did know:

$$
\begin{array}{r}
5 \times 2 = 10 \\
3 \times 2 = \ \ 6 \\
\hline
8 \times 4 = 16
\end{array}
$$

Is my answer right? If not, please correct my work and tell me why it is wrong.

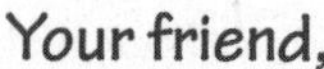

Your friend,
The Puzzled Penguin

11 **Write an answer to the Puzzled Penguin.**

____

____

____

Make Sense of Problems

Write an equation and solve the problem.

12 Galen has 20 pictures to place in his book. If he puts 4 pictures on each page, how many pages will he fill?

____

13 Emery arranged tiles in an array with 4 columns and 7 rows. How many tiles were in the array?

____

Check Understanding
Draw a picture to show how you can use the answers to 5 × 4 and 3 × 4 to find 8 × 4.

 Name ____________________

Make Sense of Problems

Write an equation and solve the problem.

Show your work.

1. The garden shop received a shipment of 12 rose bushes. They arranged the rose bushes in 3 rows with the same number of bushes in each row. How many rose bushes were in each row?

   ____

2. Eric saw 4 stop signs on the way to school. Each stop sign had 8 sides. How many sides were on all 4 stop signs?

   ____

3. Ed needs 14 batteries. If he buys the batteries in packages of 2, how many packages of batteries will he need to buy?

   ____

4. A flag has 5 rows of stars with the same number of stars in each row. There are 35 stars on the flag. How many stars are in each row?

   ____

5. Melia learned in science class that insects have 6 legs. What is the total number of legs on 9 insects?

   ____

6. Stan has 4 model car kits. Each kit comes with 5 tires. How many tires does Stan have altogether?

   ____

Make Sense of Problems (continued)

Write an equation and solve the problem.

Show your work.

7. Maria bought a shoe rack. The shoe rack has 3 rows with places for 6 shoes on each row. How many shoes can be placed on the shoe rack?

____

8. The park has 4 swing sets with the same number of swings on each set. There is a total of 16 swings at the park. How many swings are on each swing set?

____

9. Amanda has 27 seashells in her collection. She displayed the seashells in 3 rows with the same number of seashells in each row. How many seashells are in each row?

____

10. The art room has 4 round tables. There are 6 chairs around each table. Altogether, how many chairs are around the tables?

____

11. Shanna is making bead necklaces for the craft fair. She can make 3 necklaces a day. She plans to make 21 necklaces. How many days will it take her to make the necklaces?

____

✓ Check Understanding

What four equations can you write for this fast array drawing?

____

```
         7
   ○ ○ ○ ○ ○ ○ ○
 3 ○      21
   ○
```


Use the Strategy Cards

Name ___

PATH to FLUENCY

Play *Solve the Stack*

Read the rules for playing *Solve the Stack*. Then play the game with your group.

Rules for *Solve the Stack*

Number of players: 2–4

What you will need: 1 set of Multiplication and Division Strategy Cards

1. Shuffle the cards. Place them exercise side up in the center of the table.
2. Players take turns. On each turn, a player finds the answer to the multiplication or division on the top card and then turns the card over to check the answer.
3. If a player's answer is correct, he or she takes the card. If it is incorrect, the card is placed at the bottom of the stack.
4. Play ends when there are no more cards in the stack. The player with the most cards wins.

PATH to FLUENCY Play *High Card Wins*

Read the rules for playing *High Card Wins*. Then play the game with your partner.

Rules for *High Card Wins*

Number of players: 2

What you will need: 1 set of Multiplication and Division Strategy Cards for 2s, 3s, 4s, 5s, 9s

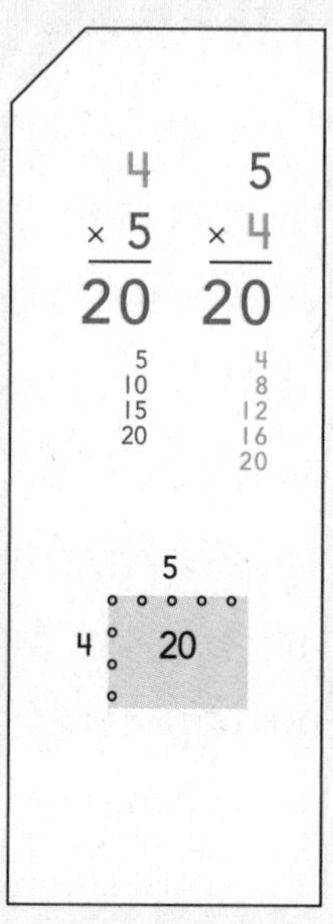

1. Shuffle the cards. Deal all the cards evenly between the two players.
2. Players put their stacks in front of them, exercise side up.
3. Each player takes the top card from his or her stack and puts it exercise side up in the center of the table.
4. Each player says the multiplication or division answer and then turns the card over to check. Then players do one of the following:
   - If one player says the wrong answer, the other player takes both cards and puts them at the bottom of his or her pile.
   - If both players say the wrong answer, both players take back their cards and put them at the bottom of their piles.
   - If both players say the correct answer, the player with the higher product or quotient takes both cards and puts them at the bottom of his or her pile. If the products or quotients are the same, the players set the cards aside and play another round. The winner of the next round takes all the cards.
5. Play continues until one player has all the cards.

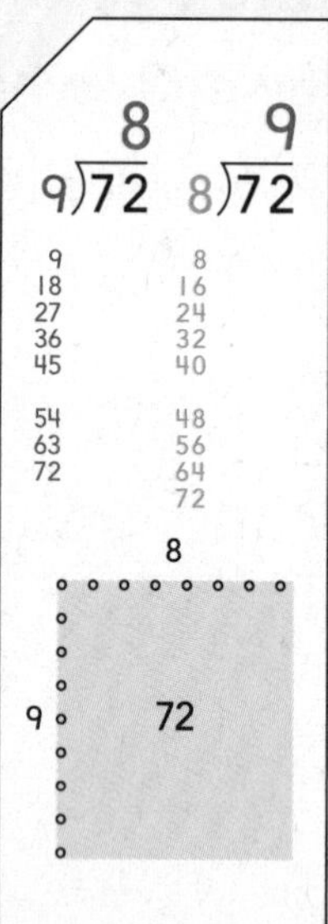

 Name ______________________________

PATH to FLUENCY

Review Strategies

Answer the questions.

1. Emily knows that $4 \times 10 = 40$. How can she use subtraction and multiples of 9 to find 4×9?

____

____

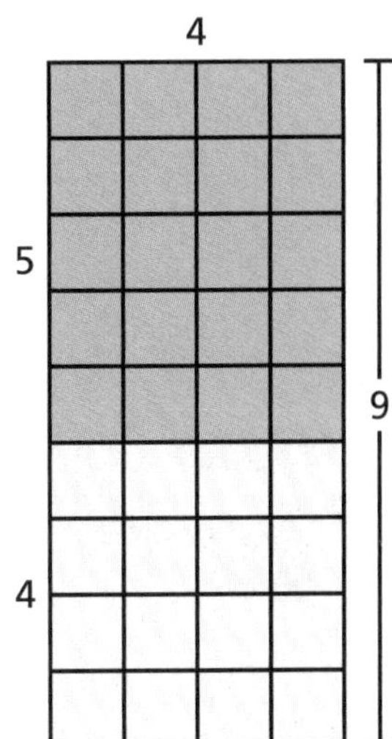

2. Joey knows the multiplications 5×4 and 4×4. How can he use their products to find 9×4?

____

3. Hannah knows that each division has a related multiplication. What related multiplication can she use to find $18 \div 3$?

____

4. Kyle knows that $5 \times 3 = 15$. How can he use the 5s shortcut to find 8×3?

____

____

5. Letitia knows that $5 \times 4 = 20$. How can she use the 5s shortcut to find 9×4?

____

____

6. Jorge knows that $6 \times 9 = 54$. How can he use the Commutative Property or arrays to find 9×6?

____

____

____

Make Sense of Problems

Write an equation and solve the problem.

Show your work.

7 Jordan has 32 peaches. He wants to divide them equally among 4 baskets. How many peaches will he put in each basket?

____

8 A guitar has 6 strings. If Taylor replaces all the strings on 3 guitars, how many strings does he need?

____

9 Kassler puts 5 strawberries in each bowl. Kassler has 40 strawberries. How many bowls will he fill?

____

10 Ruel has a board 36 inches long. He wants to saw it into equal pieces 9 inches long. How many pieces will he get?

____

Write a Word Problem

11 Write a word problem that can be solved using the equation $7 \times 10 = 70$.

____

____

____

Check Understanding

What strategy did you use to solve Problem 10?

____

Unit 1
Quick Quiz 3

Name ______________________ Date ____________

Write an equation and solve the problem.

Show your work.

1. A three-story apartment building has a total of 24 apartments. There are the same number of apartments on each floor. How many apartments are there on one floor?

____

2. Marcus puts shoes on 5 horses at his family's farm. How many horseshoes does Marcus put on the horses altogether?

____

3. The 14 players on the basketball team line up in 2 equal rows to practice passing. How many players are there in each row?

____

4. Marla uses 4 cups of chicken stock for some soup she is cooking. There are 8 ounces in each cup. How many ounces of chicken stock does Marla use?

____

5. Show the area of this rectangle in square units.

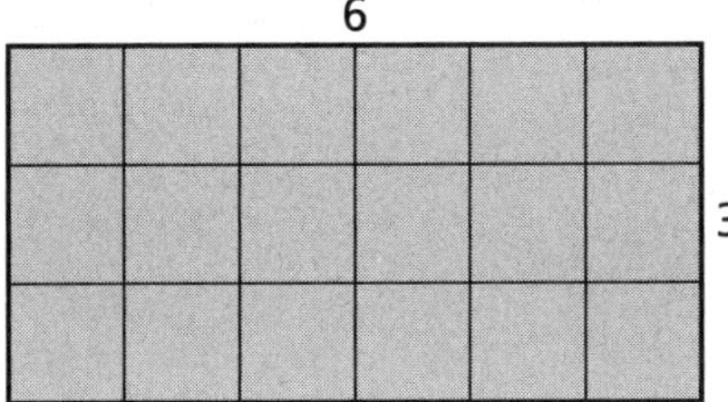

____

Strategy Check 3

Name ______________________ Date ______________

Complete.

1. Rashawn knows the multiplications 6×4 and 2×4. How can he use their products to find 8×4?

____

2. Ruben puts 4 buttons on each puppet. He used 20 buttons for 5 puppets. He needs to put buttons on 3 more puppets. How many buttons does he need for all 8 puppets? Explain.

____

____

3. What multiplication can you use to find $21 \div 3$?

____

4. Find the area of the large rectangle. Explain.

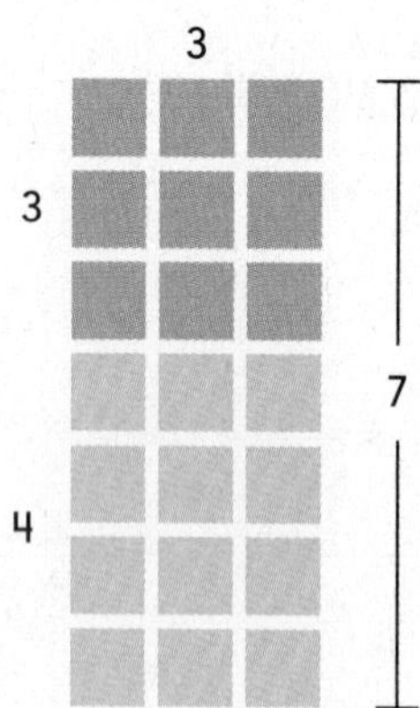

____

____

Name ____________________

Explore Patterns with 1s

What patterns do you see below?

1

$1 = 1 \times 1 = 1$
$2 = 2 \times 1 = 1 + 1$
$3 = 3 \times 1 = 1 + 1 + 1$
$4 = 4 \times 1 = 1 + 1 + 1 + 1$
$5 = 5 \times 1 = 1 + 1 + 1 + 1 + 1$
$6 = 6 \times 1 = 1 + 1 + 1 + 1 + 1 + 1$
$7 = 7 \times 1 = 1 + 1 + 1 + 1 + 1 + 1 + 1$
$8 = 8 \times 1 = 1 + 1 + 1 + 1 + 1 + 1 + 1 + 1$
$9 = 9 \times 1 = 1 + 1 + 1 + 1 + 1 + 1 + 1 + 1 + 1$
$10 = 10 \times 1 = 1 + 1 + 1 + 1 + 1 + 1 + 1 + 1 + 1 + 1$

Explore Patterns with 0s

What patterns do you see below?

2

$1 \times 0 = 0$
$2 \times 0 = 0 + 0$
$3 \times 0 = 0 + 0 + 0$
$4 \times 0 = 0 + 0 + 0 + 0$
$5 \times 0 = 0 + 0 + 0 + 0 + 0$
$6 \times 0 = 0 + 0 + 0 + 0 + 0 + 0$
$7 \times 0 = 0 + 0 + 0 + 0 + 0 + 0 + 0$
$8 \times 0 = 0 + 0 + 0 + 0 + 0 + 0 + 0 + 0$
$9 \times 0 = 0 + 0 + 0 + 0 + 0 + 0 + 0 + 0 + 0$
$10 \times 0 = 0 + 0 + 0 + 0 + 0 + 0 + 0 + 0 + 0 + 0$

PATH to FLUENCY Multiplication Properties and Division Rules

Properties and Rules

Property for 1	Division Rule for 1	Zero Property	Division Rule for 0
$1 \times 6 = 6$	$8 \div 1 = 8$	$6 \times 0 = 0$	$0 \div 6 = 0$
$6 \times 1 = 6$	$8 \div 8 = 1$	$0 \times 6 = 0$	$6 \div 0$ is impossible.

Associative Property of Multiplication

When you group factors in different ways, the product stays the same. The parentheses tell you which numbers to multiply first.

$(3 \times 2) \times 5 = \square$

$6 \times 5 = 30$

$3 \times (2 \times 5) = \square$

$3 \times 10 = 30$

Find each product.

3. $2 \times (6 \times 1) = \square$
4. $(4 \times 2) \times 2 = \square$
5. $7 \times (1 \times 5) = \square$
6. $(9 \times 8) \times 0 = \square$
7. $3 \times (2 \times 3) = \square$
8. $6 \times (0 \times 7) = \square$

Solve each problem.

Show your work.

9. Shawn gave 1 nickel to each of his sisters. If he gave away 3 nickels, how many sisters does Shawn have? ____________

10. Kara has 3 empty boxes. She put 0 toys in each box. How many toys are in the boxes? ____________

11. There are 3 shelves in a bookshelf. Each shelf has 2 piles of books on it. If there are 3 books in each pile, how many books are in the bookshelf?

____

Name ______________________________

PATH to FLUENCY Identify Addition and Multiplication Properties

Addition Properties

A. Commutative Property of Addition The order in which numbers are added does not change their sum.

$$3 + 5 = 5 + 3$$

B. Associative Property of Addition The way in which numbers are grouped does not change their sum.

$$(3 + 2) + 5 = 3 + (2 + 5)$$

C. Identity Property of Addition If 0 is added to a number, the sum equals that number.

$$3 + 0 = 3$$

Multiplication Properties

D. Commutative Property of Multiplication The order in which numbers are multiplied does not change their product.

$$3 \times 5 = 5 \times 3$$

E. Associative Property of Multiplication The way in which numbers are grouped does not change their product.

$$(3 \times 2) \times 5 = 3 \times (2 \times 5)$$

F. Identity Property of Multiplication The product of 1 and any number is that number.

$$3 \times 1 = 3$$

G. Zero Property of Multiplication If 0 is multiplied by a number, the product is 0.

$$3 \times 0 = 0$$

Write the letter of the property that is shown.

12. $1 \times 9 = 9$ ____

13. $5 + (6 + 7) = (5 + 6) + 7$ ____

14. $5 \times 0 = 0$ ____

15. $8 + 0 = 8$ ____

16. $3 \times 9 = 9 \times 3$ ____

17. $(2 \times 1) \times 3 = 2 \times (1 \times 3)$ ____

PATH to FLUENCY

Use Properties to Solve Equations

Use properties and rules to find the unknown numbers.

18 $5 \times 8 = \square \times 5$

19 $4 + 3 = \square + 4$

20 $0 \div 8 = \square$

21 $4 \div 4 = \square$

22 $(3 \times 2) \times 4 = 3 \times (\square \times 4)$

23 $6 \times 2 = 2 \times \square$

24 $5 \times 3 = \square \times 5$

25 $(6 + 2) + 2 = 6 + (\square + 2)$

26 $11 + 0 = \square$

27 $65 \times 1 = \square$

28 $5 \times (2 \times 6) = (5 \times 2) \times \square$

29 $17 \times 0 = \square$

Use Equations to Demonstrate Properties

Write your own equation that shows the property.

30 Commutative Property of Multiplication ______________________

31 Associative Property of Addition ______________________

32 Identity Property of Addition ______________________

33 Identity Property of Multiplication ______________________

34 Associative Property of Multiplication ______________________

35 Zero Property of Multiplication ______________________

36 Commutative Property of Addition ______________________

Check Understanding

Explain what you know about multiplying or dividing a number by 1 and multiplying or dividing a number by 0.

Name ______________________

Identify Types of Problems

Read each problem and decide what type of problem it is. Write the letter from the list below. Then write an equation to solve the problem.

a. Array Multiplication
b. Array Division
c. Equal Groups Multiplication
d. Equal Groups Division with an Unknown Group Size
e. Equal Groups Division with an Unknown Multiplier (number of groups)
f. None of the above

1. Mrs. Ostrega has 3 children. She wants to buy 5 juice boxes for each child. How many juice boxes does she need?

   ____

2. Sophie picked 15 peaches from one tree and 3 peaches from another. How many peaches did she pick in all?

   ____

3. Zamir brought 21 treats to the dog park. He divided the treats equally among the 7 dogs that were there. How many treats did each dog get?

   ____

4. Art said he could make 12 muffins in his muffin pan. The pan has space for 3 muffins in a row. How many rows does the muffin pan have?

   ____

5. Bia is helping with the lights for the school play. Each box of light bulbs has 6 rows, with 3 bulbs in each row. How many light bulbs are in each box?

   ____

6. Tryouts were held to find triplets to act in a commercial for Triple-Crunch Cereal. If 24 children tried out for the commercial, how many sets of triplets tried out?

   ____

Make Sense of Problems

Write an equation and solve the problem.

Show your work.

7. The produce market sells oranges in bags of 6. Santos bought 1 bag. How many oranges did he buy?

____

8. Janine bought a jewelry organizer with 36 pockets. The pockets are arranged in 9 rows with the same number of pockets in each row. How many pockets are in each row?

____

9. A parking lot has 9 rows of parking spaces. Each row has 7 spaces. How many cars can park in the lot?

____

10. The pet store has 3 fish bowls on a shelf. There are 0 fish in each bowl. How many fish are in the bowls?

____

Write a Word Problem

11. Write a word problem that can be solved using $0 \div 5$.

____

____

____

Check Understanding

Which of the problems on this page are array problems? ________

Name ____________________

PATH to FLUENCY

Check Sheet 5: 1s and 0s

1s Multiplications	1s Divisions	0s Multiplications
1 × 4 = 4	10 / 1 = 10	4 × 0 = 0
5 • 1 = 5	5 ÷ 1 = 5	2 • 0 = 0
7 * 1 = 7	7 / 1 = 7	0 * 8 = 0
1 × 8 = 8	9 ÷ 1 = 9	0 × 5 = 0
1 • 6 = 6	3 / 1 = 3	6 • 0 = 0
10 * 1 = 10	10 ÷ 1 = 10	0 * 7 = 0
1 × 9 = 9	2 / 1 = 2	0 × 2 = 0
3 • 1 = 3	8 ÷ 1 = 8	0 • 9 = 0
1 * 2 = 2	6 / 1 = 6	10 * 0 = 0
1 × 1 = 1	9 / 1 = 9	1 × 0 = 0
8 • 1 = 8	1 ÷ 1 = 1	0 • 6 = 0
1 * 7 = 7	5 / 1 = 5	9 * 0 = 0
1 × 5 = 5	3 ÷ 1 = 3	0 × 4 = 0
6 • 1 = 6	4 / 1 = 4	3 • 0 = 0
1 * 1 = 1	2 ÷ 1 = 2	0 * 3 = 0
1 × 10 = 10	8 / 1 = 8	8 × 0 = 0
9 • 1 = 9	4 ÷ 1 = 4	0 • 10 = 0
4 * 1 = 4	7 ÷ 1 = 7	0 * 1 = 0
2 × 1 = 2	1 / 1 = 1	5 × 0 = 0
1 • 3 = 3	6 ÷ 1 = 6	7 • 0 = 0

PATH to FLUENCY Check Sheet 6: Mixed 3s, 4s, 0s, and 1s

3s, 4s, 0s, 1s Multiplications	3s, 4s, 0s, 1s Multiplications	3s, 4s, 1s Divisions	3s, 4s, 1s Divisions
5 × 3 = 15	0 × 5 = 0	18 / 3 = 6	4 / 1 = 4
6 • 4 = 24	10 • 1 = 10	20 ÷ 4 = 5	21 ÷ 3 = 7
9 * 0 = 0	6 * 3 = 18	1 / 1 = 1	16 / 4 = 4
7 × 1 = 7	2 × 4 = 8	21 ÷ 3 = 7	9 ÷ 1 = 9
3 • 3 = 9	5 • 0 = 0	12 / 4 = 3	15 / 3 = 5
4 * 7 = 28	1 * 2 = 2	5 ÷ 1 = 5	8 ÷ 4 = 2
0 × 10 = 0	10 × 3 = 30	15 / 3 = 5	5 / 1 = 5
1 • 6 = 6	5 • 4 = 20	24 ÷ 4 = 6	30 ÷ 3 = 10
3 * 4 = 12	0 * 8 = 0	7 / 1 = 7	12 / 4 = 3
5 × 4 = 20	9 × 1 = 9	12 / 3 = 4	8 / 1 = 8
0 • 5 = 0	10 • 3 = 30	36 ÷ 4 = 9	27 ÷ 3 = 9
9 * 1 = 9	9 * 4 = 36	6 / 1 = 6	40 / 4 = 10
2 × 3 = 6	1 × 0 = 0	12 ÷ 3 = 4	4 ÷ 1 = 4
3 • 4 = 12	1 • 6 = 6	16 / 4 = 4	9 / 3 = 3
0 * 9 = 0	3 * 6 = 18	7 ÷ 1 = 7	16 ÷ 4 = 4
1 × 5 = 5	7 × 4 = 28	9 / 3 = 3	10 / 1 = 10
2 • 3 = 6	6 • 0 = 0	8 ÷ 4 = 2	9 ÷ 3 = 3
4 * 4 = 16	8 * 1 = 8	2 ÷ 1 = 2	20 ÷ 4 = 5
9 × 0 = 0	3 × 9 = 27	6 / 3 = 2	6 / 1 = 6
1 • 1 = 1	1 • 4 = 4	32 ÷ 4 = 8	24 ÷ 3 = 8

Name ______________________________

Write and Solve Equations

Write an equation and solve the problem.

Show your work.

1. The library ordered 1 computer for each of the work stations. If the library ordered 8 computers, how many work stations are in the library?

____

____

2. Ari arranged his baseball cap collection into 9 rows with 2 baseball caps in each row. How many baseball caps are in his collection?

____

____

3. Jess solved 28 multiplication problems. If the problems were arranged in columns with 7 problems in each column, how many columns of problems did Jess solve?

____

____

4. One section on a plane has 9 rows of seats. Five passengers can sit in each row. How many passengers can sit in this section of the plane?

____

____

5. Emily rides her bike 3 miles every day. How many miles does she ride her bike in a week?

____

____

Solve and Discuss

Write an equation and solve the problem.

Show your work.

6 Paige placed 35 books on 5 shelves. She placed the same number of books on each shelf. How many books did she place on each shelf?

____

7 A box of bagels has 24 bagels. There are 4 bagels in each row. How many rows of bagels are in the box?

____

8 Keshawn bought 18 animal stickers for his sisters. He gave 6 stickers to each sister and had none left. How many sisters does Keshawn have?

____

Write a Word Problem

9 Write a word problem that can be solved using $4 \div 1$, where 1 is the group size.

____

____

____

Check Understanding

Write two multiplication equations and two division equations using the numbers 8, 4, and 2 in each.

____

____

Name ____________________

PATH to FLUENCY Play *Multiplication Three-in-a-Row*

Read the rules for playing *Multiplication Three-in-a-Row*. Then play the game with a partner.

Rules for *Multiplication Three-in-a-Row*

Number of players: 2

What You Will Need: A set of Multiplication Strategy Cards, *Three-in-a-Row* Game Grids for each player (see page 83)

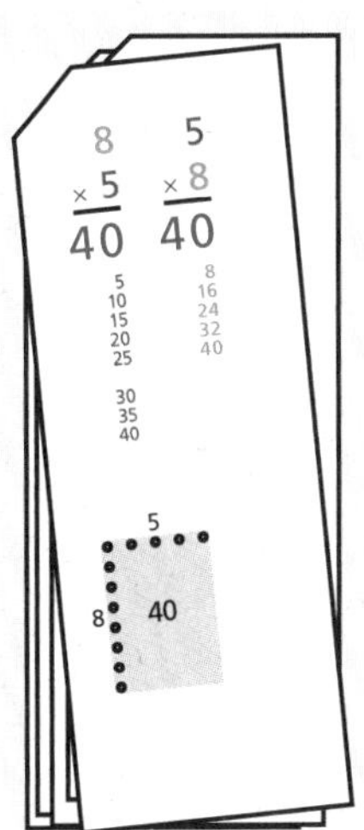

1. Each player looks through the cards and writes any nine of the products in the squares of a Game Grid. A player may write the same product more than once.
2. Shuffle the cards and place them exercise side up in the center of the table.
3. Players take turns. On each turn, a player finds the answer to the multiplication on the top card and then turns the card over to check the answer.
4. If the answer is correct, the player looks to see if the product is on the game grid. If it is, the player puts an X through that grid square. If the answer is wrong, or if the product is not on the grid, the player does not mark anything. The player then puts the card problem side up on the bottom of the stack.
5. The first player to mark three squares in a row (horizontally, vertically, or diagonally) wins.

PATH to FLUENCY Play *Division Race*

Read the rules for playing *Division Race*. Then play the game with a partner.

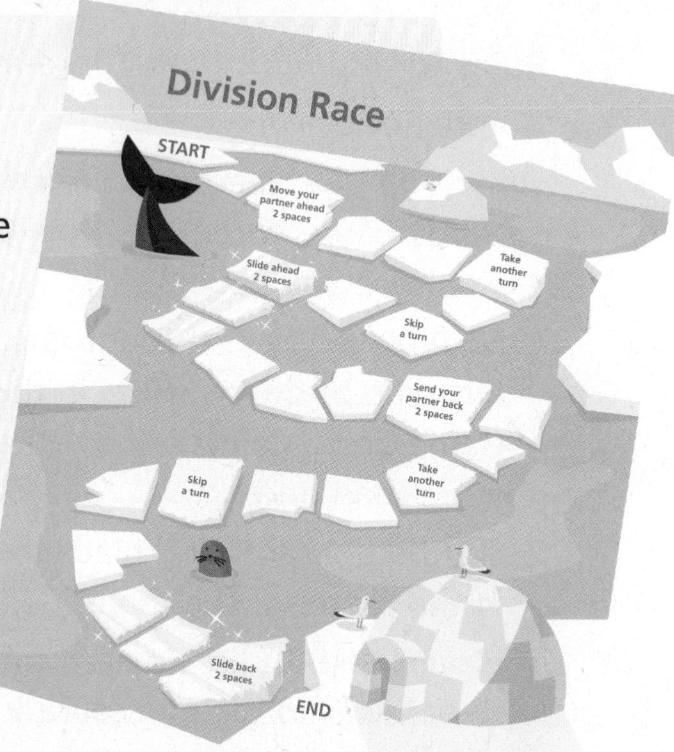

Rules for *Division Race*

Number of players: 2

What You Will Need: a set of Division Strategy Cards, the *Division Race* game board (see page 84), a different game piece for each player

1. Shuffle the cards and then place them exercise side up on the table.
2. Both players put their game pieces on "START."
3. Players take turns. On each turn, a player finds the answer to the division on the top card and then turns the card over to check the answer.
4. If the answer is correct, the player moves *forward* that number of spaces. If a player's answer is wrong, the player moves *back* a number of spaces equal to the correct answer. Players cannot move back beyond the "START" square. The player puts the card on the bottom of the stack.

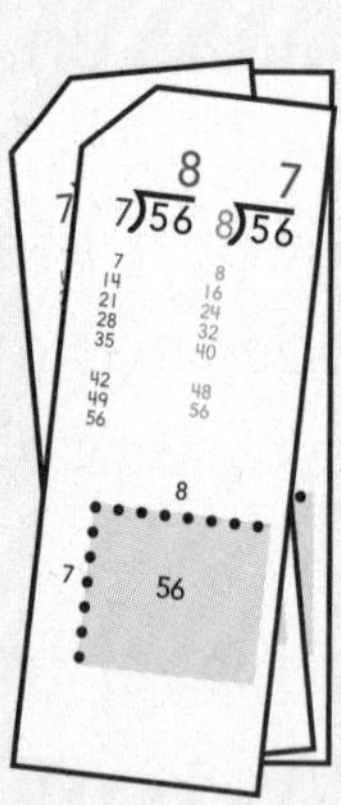

5. If a player lands on a space with special instructions, he or she should follow those instructions.
6. The game ends when everyone lands on or passes the "End" square.

Name ______________________________

Division Race

Name ______________________

PATH to FLUENCY

Dashes 1–4

Complete each Dash. Check your answers on page 89.

Dash 1 **2s and 5s** **Multiplications**	**Dash 2** **2s and 5s** **Divisions**	**Dash 3** **9s and 10s** **Multiplications**	**Dash 4** **9s and 10s** **Divisions**
a. 2 × 6 = ___	a. 18 / 2 = ___	a. 9 × 10 = ___	a. 100 / 10 = ___
b. 9 * 5 = ___	b. 25 ÷ 5 = ___	b. 10 * 3 = ___	b. 9 ÷ 9 = ___
c. 7 • 2 = ___	c. 8 / 2 = ___	c. 1 • 9 = ___	c. 30 / 10 = ___
d. 5 × 8 = ___	d. 45 ÷ 5 = ___	d. 2 × 10 = ___	d. 81 ÷ 9 = ___
e. 2 * 4 = ___	e. 16 / 2 = ___	e. 9 * 9 = ___	e. 70 / 10 = ___
f. 3 • 5 = ___	f. 20 ÷ 5 = ___	f. 10 • 6 = ___	f. 45 ÷ 9 = ___
g. 1 × 2 = ___	g. 4 / 2 = ___	g. 4 × 9 = ___	g. 10 / 10 = ___
h. 5 * 7 = ___	h. 40 ÷ 5 = ___	h. 10 × 10 = ___	h. 54 ÷ 9 = ___
i. 2 • 9 = ___	i. 20 / 2 = ___	i. 9 * 2 = ___	i. 50 / 10 = ___
j. 4 × 5 = ___	j. 35 ÷ 5 = ___	j. 1 • 10 = ___	j. 27 ÷ 9 = ___
k. 5 * 2 = ___	k. 6 / 2 = ___	k. 7 × 9 = ___	k. 20 / 10 = ___
l. 5 • 1 = ___	l. 15 ÷ 5 = ___	l. 10 * 5 = ___	l. 72 ÷ 9 = ___
m. 2 × 2 = ___	m. 14 / 2 = ___	m. 9 • 8 = ___	m. 40 / 10 = ___
n. 10 × 5 = ___	n. 5 ÷ 5 = ___	n. 7 × 10 = ___	n. 18 ÷ 9 = ___
o. 10 * 2 = ___	o. 10 / 2 = ___	o. 3 * 9 = ___	o. 60 / 10 = ___
p. 5 • 6 = ___	p. 10 ÷ 5 = ___	p. 10 • 4 = ___	p. 90 ÷ 9 = ___
q. 2 × 3 = ___	q. 6 / 2 = ___	q. 9 × 5 = ___	q. 90 / 10 = ___
r. 5 * 5 = ___	r. 30 ÷ 5 = ___	r. 8 * 10 = ___	r. 63 ÷ 9 = ___
s. 8 • 2 = ___	s. 2 / 2 = ___	s. 6 • 9 = ___	s. 80 / 10 = ___
t. 6 × 5 = ___	t. 45 ÷ 5 = ___	t. 10 × 9 = ___	t. 36 ÷ 9 = ___

PATH to FLUENCY Dashes 5–8

Complete each Dash. Check your answers on page 89.

Dash 5 3s and 4s Multiplications	Dash 6 3s and 4s Divisions	Dash 7 0s and 1s Multiplications	Dash 8 1s and $n \div n$ Divisions
a. 3 × 9 = ____	a. 12 / 4 = ____	a. 0 × 6 = ____	a. 9 / 9 = ____
b. 4 * 2 = ____	b. 20 ÷ 4 = ____	b. 1 * 4 = ____	b. 8 ÷ 1 = ____
c. 6 • 3 = ____	c. 21 / 3 = ____	c. 4 • 0 = ____	c. 7 / 7 = ____
d. 10 × 4 = ____	d. 16 ÷ 4 = ____	d. 8 × 1 = ____	d. 6 ÷ 1 = ____
e. 3 * 1 = ____	e. 9 / 3 = ____	e. 0 * 2 = ____	e. 1 / 1 = ____
f. 4 • 1 = ____	f. 32 ÷ 4 = ____	f. 1 • 3 = ____	f. 4 ÷ 1 = ____
g. 10 × 3 = ____	g. 24 / 4 = ____	g. 9 × 0 = ____	g. 2 / 2 = ____
h. 5 * 4 = ____	h. 18 ÷ 3 = ____	h. 2 * 1 = ____	h. 2 ÷ 1 = ____
i. 3 • 3 = ____	i. 40 / 4 = ____	i. 0 • 8 = ____	i. 8 / 8 = ____
j. 4 × 4 = ____	j. 12 ÷ 3 = ____	j. 1 × 10 = ____	j. 9 ÷ 1 = ____
k. 8 * 3 = ____	k. 6 / 3 = ____	k. 7 * 0 = ____	k. 3 / 3 = ____
l. 7 • 4 = ____	l. 28 ÷ 4 = ____	l. 1 • 1 = ____	l. 5 ÷ 1 = ____
m. 3 × 2 = ____	m. 24 / 3 = ____	m. 0 × 0 = ____	m. 5 / 5 = ____
n. 4 * 9 = ____	n. 20 ÷ 4 = ____	n. 5 * 1 = ____	n. 10 / 10 = ____
o. 7 • 3 = ____	o. 27 / 3 = ____	o. 1 • 0 = ____	o. 7 ÷ 1 = ____
p. 3 × 4 = ____	p. 15 ÷ 3 = ____	p. 1 × 6 = ____	p. 4 / 4 = ____
q. 3 * 5 = ____	q. 27 / 3 = ____	q. 5 * 0 = ____	q. 10 ÷ 1 = ____
r. 4 • 6 = ____	r. 36 ÷ 4 = ____	r. 0 • 3 = ____	r. 6 / 6 = ____
s. 4 × 3 = ____	s. 8 / 4 = ____	s. 7 × 1 = ____	s. 3 ÷ 1 = ____
t. 8 * 4 = ____	t. 40 ÷ 4 = ____	t. 1 * 9 = ____	t. 1 / 1 = ____

Name ______________________________

PATH to FLUENCY

Dashes 9–12

Complete each Dash. Check your answers on page 90.

Dash 9 2s, 5s, 9s, 10s Multiplications	Dash 10 2s, 5s, 9s, 10s Divisions	Dash 11 3s, 4s, 0s, 1s Multiplications	Dash 12 3s, 4s, 1s Divisions
a. 4 × 5 = ___	a. 8 / 2 = ___	a. 3 × 0 = ___	a. 12 / 4 = ___
b. 10 • 3 = ___	b. 50 ÷ 10 = ___	b. 4 • 6 = ___	b. 5 ÷ 1 = ___
c. 8 * 9 = ___	c. 15 / 5 = ___	c. 9 * 1 = ___	c. 21 / 3 = ___
d. 6 × 2 = ___	d. 63 ÷ 9 = ___	d. 3 × 3 = ___	d. 1 ÷ 1 = ___
e. 5 • 7 = ___	e. 90 / 10 = ___	e. 8 • 4 = ___	e. 16 / 4 = ___
f. 10 * 5 = ___	f. 90 ÷ 9 = ___	f. 0 * 5 = ___	f. 9 ÷ 3 = ___
g. 8 × 2 = ___	g. 35 / 5 = ___	g. 1 × 6 = ___	g. 32 / 4 = ___
h. 6 • 10 = ___	h. 14 ÷ 2 = ___	h. 4 • 3 = ___	h. 8 ÷ 1 = ___
i. 9 * 3 = ___	i. 27 / 9 = ___	i. 7 * 4 = ___	i. 24 / 4 = ___
j. 2 × 9 = ___	j. 45 / 5 = ___	j. 3 × 7 = ___	j. 18 / 3 = ___
k. 5 • 8 = ___	k. 10 ÷ 10 = ___	k. 0 • 1 = ___	k. 10 ÷ 1 = ___
l. 10 * 7 = ___	l. 25 / 5 = ___	l. 10 * 1 = ___	l. 40 / 4 = ___
m. 5 × 5 = ___	m. 54 ÷ 9 = ___	m. 4 × 4 = ___	m. 12 ÷ 3 = ___
n. 1 • 5 = ___	n. 6 / 2 = ___	n. 9 • 3 = ___	n. 6 / 3 = ___
o. 9 * 6 = ___	o. 72 ÷ 9 = ___	o. 8 * 0 = ___	o. 4 ÷ 4 = ___
p. 10 × 10 = ___	p. 40 / 5 = ___	p. 5 × 4 = ___	p. 7 / 1 = ___
q. 4 • 2 = ___	q. 80 ÷ 10 = ___	q. 1 • 6 = ___	q. 28 ÷ 4 = ___
r. 10 * 8 = ___	r. 18 ÷ 2 = ___	r. 3 * 8 = ___	r. 24 ÷ 3 = ___
s. 3 × 9 = ___	s. 36 / 9 = ___	s. 4 × 9 = ___	s. 20 / 4 = ___
t. 9 • 9 = ___	t. 30 ÷ 5 = ___	t. 0 • 4 = ___	t. 27 ÷ 3 = ___

PATH to FLUENCY Dashes 9A–12A

Complete each Dash. Check your answers on page 90.

Dash 9A 2s, 5s, 9s, 10s Multiplications	Dash 10A 2s, 5s, 9s, 10s Divisions	Dash 11A 3s, 4s, 0s, 1s Multiplications	Dash 12A 3s, 4s, 1s Divisions
a. 9 × 9 = ____	a. 30 / 5 = ____	a. 0 × 4 = ____	a. 10 / 1 = ____
b. 4 * 5 = ____	b. 18 ÷ 2 = ____	b. 4 * 9 = ____	b. 40 ÷ 4 = ____
c. 10 • 3 = ____	c. 40 / 5 = ____	c. 3 • 8 = ____	c. 12 / 3 = ____
d. 3 × 9 = ____	d. 6 ÷ 2 = ____	d. 3 × 0 = ____	d. 6 ÷ 3 = ____
e. 10 * 8 = ____	e. 25 / 5 = ____	e. 4 * 6 = ____	e. 4 / 4 = ____
f. 6 • 2 = ____	f. 45 ÷ 5 = ____	f. 9 • 1 = ____	f. 7 ÷ 1 = ____
g. 8 × 9 = ____	g. 14 / 2 = ____	g. 3 × 3 = ____	g. 28 / 4 = ____
h. 4 * 2 = ____	h. 90 ÷ 9 = ____	h. 8 * 4 = ____	h. 24 ÷ 3 = ____
i. 10 • 10 = ____	i. 63 / 9 = ____	i. 0 • 5 = ____	i. 20 / 4 = ____
j. 9 × 6 = ____	j. 50 ÷ 10 = ____	j. 1 × 6 = ____	j. 27 ÷ 3 = ____
k. 5 * 7 = ____	k. 8 / 2 = ____	k. 5 * 4 = ____	k. 12 / 4 = ____
l. 10 • 5 = ____	l. 15 ÷ 5 = ____	l. 8 • 0 = ____	l. 5 ÷ 1 = ____
m. 8 × 2 = ____	m. 90 / 10 = ____	m. 9 × 3 = ____	m. 21 / 3 = ____
n. 6 * 10 = ____	n. 35 ÷ 5 = ____	n. 4 * 4 = ____	n. 1 ÷ 1 = ____
o. 2 * 9 = ____	o. 27 / 9 = ____	o. 10 • 1 = ____	o. 16 / 4 = ____
p. 9 • 6 = ____	p. 10 ÷ 10 = ____	p. 4 × 3 = ____	p. 9 ÷ 3 = ____
q. 1 × 5 = ____	q. 54 / 9 = ____	q. 7 * 4 = ____	q. 32 / 4 = ____
r. 5 * 5 = ____	r. 72 ÷ 9 = ____	r. 3 • 7 = ____	r. 8 ÷ 1 = ____
s. 10 • 7 = ____	s. 80 / 10 = ____	s. 0 × 1 = ____	s. 24 / 4 = ____
t. 5 × 8 = ____	t. 36 ÷ 9 = ____	t. 10 * 1 = ____	t. 18 ÷ 3 = ____

Name

PATH to FLUENCY Answers to Dashes 1–8

Use this sheet to check your answers to the Dashes on pages 85 and 86.

Dash 1 2s and 5s ×	Dash 2 2s and 5s ÷	Dash 3 9s and 10s ×	Dash 4 9s and 10s ÷	Dash 5 3s and 4s ×	Dash 6 3s and 4s ÷	Dash 7 0s and 1s ×	Dash 8 1s and $n \div n$ ÷
a. 12	a. 9	a. 90	a. 10	a. 27	a. 3	a. 0	a. 1
b. 45	b. 5	b. 30	b. 1	b. 8	b. 5	b. 4	b. 8
c. 14	c. 4	c. 9	c. 3	c. 18	c. 7	c. 0	c. 1
d. 40	d. 9	d. 20	d. 9	d. 40	d. 4	d. 8	d. 6
e. 8	e. 8	e. 81	e. 7	e. 3	e. 3	e. 0	e. 1
f. 15	f. 4	f. 60	f. 5	f. 4	f. 8	f. 3	f. 4
g. 2	g. 2	g. 36	g. 1	g. 30	g. 6	g. 0	g. 1
h. 35	h. 8	h. 100	h. 6	h. 20	h. 6	h. 2	h. 2
i. 18	i. 10	i. 18	i. 5	i. 9	i. 10	i. 0	i. 1
j. 20	j. 7	j. 10	j. 3	j. 16	j. 4	j. 10	j. 9
k. 10	k. 3	k. 63	k. 2	k. 24	k. 2	k. 0	k. 1
l. 5	l. 3	l. 50	l. 8	l. 28	l. 7	l. 1	l. 5
m. 4	m. 7	m. 72	m. 4	m. 6	m. 8	m. 0	m. 1
n. 50	n. 1	n. 70	n. 2	n. 36	n. 5	n. 5	n. 1
o. 20	o. 5	o. 27	o. 6	o. 21	o. 9	o. 0	o. 7
p. 30	p. 2	p. 40	p. 10	p. 12	p. 5	p. 6	p. 1
q. 6	q. 3	q. 45	q. 9	q. 15	q. 9	q. 0	q. 10
r. 25	r. 6	r. 80	r. 7	r. 24	r. 9	r. 0	r. 1
s. 16	s. 1	s. 54	s. 8	s. 12	s. 2	s. 7	s. 3
t. 30	t. 9	t. 90	t. 4	t. 32	t. 10	t. 9	t. 1

PATH to FLUENCY Answers to Dashes 9–12, 9A–12A

Use this sheet to check your answers to the Dashes on pages 87 and 88.

Dash 9 ×	Dash 10 ÷	Dash 11 ×	Dash 12 ÷	Dash 9A ×	Dash 10A ÷	Dash 11A ×	Dash 12A ÷
a. 20	a. 4	a. 0	a. 3	a. 81	a. 6	a. 0	a. 10
b. 30	b. 5	b. 24	b. 5	b. 20	b. 9	b. 36	b. 10
c. 72	c. 3	c. 9	c. 7	c. 30	c. 8	c. 24	c. 4
d. 12	d. 7	d. 9	d. 1	d. 27	d. 3	d. 0	d. 2
e. 35	e. 9	e. 32	e. 4	e. 80	e. 5	e. 24	e. 1
f. 50	f. 10	f. 0	f. 3	f. 12	f. 9	f. 9	f. 7
g. 16	g. 7	g. 6	g. 8	g. 72	g. 7	g. 9	g. 7
h. 60	h. 7	h. 12	h. 8	h. 8	h. 10	h. 32	h. 8
i. 27	i. 3	i. 28	i. 6	i. 100	i. 7	i. 0	i. 5
j. 18	j. 9	j. 21	j. 6	j. 54	j. 5	j. 6	j. 9
k. 40	k. 1	k. 0	k. 10	k. 35	k. 4	k. 20	k. 3
l. 70	l. 5	l. 10	l. 10	l. 50	l. 3	l. 0	l. 5
m. 25	m. 6	m. 16	m. 4	m. 16	m. 9	m. 27	m. 7
n. 5	n. 3	n. 27	n. 2	n. 60	n. 7	n. 16	n. 1
o. 54	o. 8	o. 0	o. 1	o. 18	o. 3	o. 10	o. 4
p. 100	p. 8	p. 20	p. 7	p. 54	p. 1	p. 12	p. 3
q. 8	q. 8	q. 6	q. 7	q. 5	q. 6	q. 28	q. 8
r. 80	r. 9	r. 24	r. 8	r. 25	r. 8	r. 21	r. 8
s. 27	s. 4	s. 36	s. 5	s. 70	s. 8	s. 0	s. 6
t. 81	t. 6	t. 0	t. 9	t. 40	t. 4	t. 10	t. 6

Name ______________________________

Solve Word Problems with 2s, 3s, 4s, 5s, and 9s

Write an equation and solve the problem.

Show your work.

1. Toni counted 36 chairs in the restaurant. Each table had 4 chairs. How many tables were there?

____

2. One wall of an art gallery has 5 rows of paintings. Each row has row of 9 paintings. How many paintings are on the wall?

____

3. Josh's muffin pan is an array with 4 rows and 6 columns. How many muffins can Josh make in the pan?

____

4. To get ready for the school spelling bee, Tanya studied 3 hours each night for an entire week. How many hours did she study?

____

5. The 14 trumpet players in the marching band lined up in 2 equal rows. How many trumpet players were in each row?

____

6. The Sunnyside Riding Stable has 9 horses. The owners are going to buy new horseshoes for all the horses. How many horseshoes are needed?

____

Make Sense of Problems

Write an equation and solve the problem.

Show your work.

7 Sadie plans to read 2 books every month for 6 months. How many books will she read during that time?

____

8 A farmer sells pumpkins for $5 each. On Friday the farmer made $35 from the sale of pumpkins. How many pumpkins did the farmer sell on Friday?

____

9 Each student collected 10 leaves for a group science project. If the group collected a total of 80 leaves, how many students are in the group?

____

Write a Word Problem

10 Write and solve a word problem that can be solved using the equation $4 \times 1 = n$.

____

____

Check Understanding

Write a related multiplication or division equation for the equation you wrote for Problem 9.

____

Name ____________________

PATH to FLUENCY Math and Hobbies

A hobby is something you do for fun. Owen's hobby is photography. He took pictures and displayed them on a poster.

Solve.

1. How many photos did Owen display on the poster? Explain the different strategies you can use to find the answer. Write an equation for each.

____

____

____

____

2. What other ways could Owen have arranged the photos in an array on a poster?

____

____

PATH to FLUENCY What is Your Hobby?

Carina asked some third graders, "What is your hobby?" The answers are shown under the photos.

Dancing
Four third graders said dancing.

Photography
Eight more than dancing said photography.

Reading
Six less than photography said reading.

Games
Eight third graders said games.

3 **Use the information above to complete the chart below.**

What is Your Hobby?	
Hobby	Number of Students
Dancing	
Photography	
Games	
Reading	

4 **Use the chart to complete the pictograph below.**

Hobbies	
Dancing	
Photography	
Games	
Reading	

Each ☐ stands for 2 third graders.

5 How many third graders answered Carina's question?

____

Name ______________________ Date ______________

Write an equation and solve the problem.

Show your work.

1. Mrs. Andrews divides 45 milliliters of water equally into 9 test tubes for her science class. How many milliliters of water does she place in each test tube?

____

____

2. The chorus members singing at a school concert stand in 3 rows, with 9 members in each row. How many chorus members are there altogether?

____

3. The 32 students on a field trip are organized into groups of 4 for a tour. How many groups of students are there?

____

Solve.

4. Susan arranges her model cars in 6 rows, with 3 cars in each row. How else can Susan arrange her model cars in equal rows?

____

____

5. Philip bakes 8 muffins and gives each of his friends 1 muffin. He has no muffins left over. To how many of his friends does Philip give a muffin?

____

Fluency Check 1

Name ______________________ Date ______________

Add.

1. $1 + 6 = \square$
2. $3 + 8 = \square$
3. $8 + 5 = \square$
4. $5 + 3 = \square$
5. $2 + 8 = \square$
6. $3 + 9 = \square$
7. $4 + 5 = \square$
8. $6 + 7 = \square$
9. $5 + 9 = \square$
10. $\begin{array}{r} 7 \\ +\,5 \\ \hline \end{array}$
11. $\begin{array}{r} 6 \\ +\,9 \\ \hline \end{array}$
12. $\begin{array}{r} 8 \\ +\,0 \\ \hline \end{array}$
13. $\begin{array}{r} 9 \\ +\,7 \\ \hline \end{array}$
14. $\begin{array}{r} 8 \\ +\,6 \\ \hline \end{array}$
15. $\begin{array}{r} 7 \\ +\,8 \\ \hline \end{array}$

Name ______________________ Date ______________________

1. Write a multiplication equation for the array.

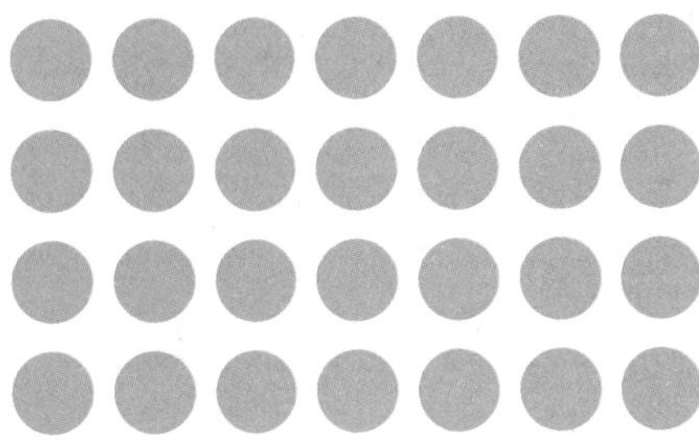

____

2. Write the numbers that complete the pattern.

6	7	8	9	72	81

4	×	9	=	36
5	×	9	=	45
☐	×	9	=	54
7	×	☐	=	63
8	×	9	=	☐

Name ____________________ Date ____________________

3 Read the problem. Choose the type of problem it is. Then write an equation to solve the problem.

Pala is drawing tulips on 9 posters. She draws 4 tulips on each poster. How many tulips does Pala draw on the posters?

The type of problem is

array multiplication
array division
equal groups multiplication

.

Equation: ____________________

____________________ tulips

4 Draw a line to match the equation on the left with the unknown number on the right.

$\frac{45}{5} = \blacksquare$ •	• 0
$9 \times \blacksquare = 0$ •	• 5
$\blacksquare \times 3 = 15$ •	• 8
$\blacksquare \div 3 = 7$ •	• 9
$72 \div \blacksquare = 9$ •	• 14
$7 \times 2 = \blacksquare$ •	• 21

Name ______________________ Date ______________

5 Write the number that completes the multiplication equation.

$6 \times 4 = \square \times 6$

$7 \times 3 = (4 + 3) \times \square$

$5 \times (2 \times 4) = (\square \times \square) \times 4$

6 Sydney wants to find the area of the large rectangle by adding the areas of the two small rectangles.

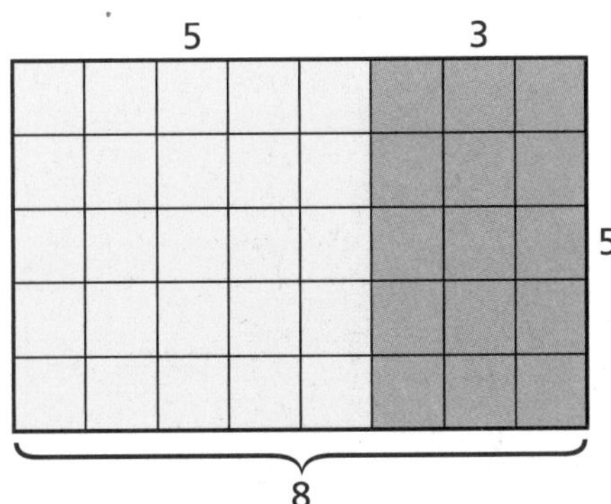

For numbers 6a–6d, choose Yes or No to tell whether or not Sydney could use the expression to find the area of the large rectangle.

6a.	$(8 \times 5) + (5 \times 5)$	○ Yes	○ No
6b.	$25 + 15$	○ Yes	○ No
6c.	$(5 \times 5) + (3 \times 5)$	○ Yes	○ No
6d.	$(5 \times 5) + (5 \times 3)$	○ Yes	○ No

Name Date

7 Look at the rectangle drawing.

Part A

Write a word problem that can be solved using the drawing.

Part B

Solve the problem. Explain how to use the rectangle drawing to check your answer.

Name ______________________ Date ______________________

8 Select the situation which could be represented by the multiplication expression 5×7. Mark all that apply.

Ⓐ total number of stamps on 5 pages with 7 stamps on each page

Ⓑ total number of stamps when there are 5 stamps on one page and 7 stamps on another page

Ⓒ 5 stamps divided evenly onto 7 pages

Ⓓ 5 more stamps than on a page with 7 stamps

Make a drawing for the problem. Then write an equation and solve it.

9 The 28 desks in Mr. Becker's class are arranged in 7 equal rows. How many desks are in each row?

10 Michelle's bookcase has 3 shelves. It holds 9 books on each shelf. How many books will fit in the bookcase?

11 Rami counts 6 birds sitting on each of 5 different wires. How many birds does Rami count?

Name ______________________ Date ______________________

12 Use properties of multiplication to solve.

12a. $9 \times 6 = \square \times 9$

12b. $\square \times 10 = 10$

12c. $\square \times 2 = 0$

12d. $(3 \times \square) \times 5 = 3 \times (4 \times 5)$

13 Chloe buys 10 balloons for her sisters. She gives 5 balloons to each sister and has none left.

Part A

How many sisters does Chloe have? Write an equation and solve the problem.

Equation: ______________

__________ sisters

Part B

Solve the problem in a different way. Tell how the ways are alike and different.

Name ______________________ Date ______________

Make Travel Plans

A group of 40 students is going to a science museum. Some parents have offered to drive the students. The table below shows the vehicles they can use.

Type of Vehicle	Number of Students the Vehicle Can Hold	Number of Vehicles Available
Small Car	2	3
Large Car	3	10
Crossover	4	4
Minivan	5	4
SUV	6	5

1. Plan two different ways the 40 students can ride to the museum. For each plan, be sure all the students have a ride. Describe the plan with words, pictures, equations, or a table. Explain which plan is better and tell why.

2. Plan a way to use the least number of vehicles. Describe the plan with words, pictures, equations, or a table. Explain why the plan uses the least number of vehicles.

Name ______________________ Date ______________

3 If there is another trip, different parents will drive. Will that change the least number of cars that are needed? Explain your answer and show how you know.

4 How would you change your strategy for planning the trip if each vehicle needs to have an adult other than the driver?

Dear Family:

In this unit, students learn multiplications and divisions for 6s, 7s, and 8s, while continuing to practice the rest of the basic multiplications and divisions covered in Unit 1.

Although students practice all the 6s, 7s, and 8s multiplications, they really have only six new multiplications to learn: 6×6, 6×7, 6×8, 7×7, 7×8, and 8×8. The lessons for these multiplications focus on strategies for finding the products using multiplications they know.

This unit also focuses on word problems. Students are presented with a variety of one-step and two-step word problems.

Here is an example of a two-step problem:

> A roller coaster has 7 cars. Each car has 4 seats. If there were 3 empty seats, how many people were on the roller coaster?

Students use the language and context of each problem to determine which operation or operations—multiplication, division, addition, or subtraction—they must use to solve it. Students use a variety of methods to solve two-step word problems.

Please continue to help your child get faster on multiplications and divisions. Use all of the practice materials that your child has brought home. Your support is crucial to your child's learning.

Please contact me if you have any questions or comments.

Thank you.

Sincerely,
Your child's teacher

Estimada familia:

En esta unidad los estudiantes aprenden las multiplicaciones y divisiones con el 6, el 7 y el 8, mientras siguen practicando las demás multiplicaciones y divisiones que se presentaron en la Unidad 1.

Aunque los estudiantes practican todas las multiplicaciones con el 6, el 7 y el 8, en realidad sólo tienen que aprender seis multiplicaciones nuevas: 6×6, 6×7, 6×8, 7×7, 7×8 y 8×8. Las lecciones acerca de estas multiplicaciones se centran en estrategias para hallar los productos usando multiplicaciones que ya se conocen.

Esta unidad también se centra en problemas verbales. A los estudiantes se les presenta una variedad de problemas de uno y de dos pasos.

> Este es un ejemplo de un problema de dos pasos:
> Una montaña rusa tiene 7 carros. Cada carro tiene 7 asientos. Si hay 3 asientos vacíos. Cuántas personas había en la montaña rusa?

Los estudiantes aprovechan el lenguaje y el contexto de cada problema para determinar qué operación u operaciones deben usar para resolverlo: multiplicación, división, suma o resta. Los estudiantes usan una variedad de métodos para resolver problemas de dos pasos.

Por favor continúe ayudando a su niño a practicar las multiplicaciones y las divisiones. Use todos los materiales de práctica que su niño ha llevado a casa. Su apoyo es importante para el aprendizaje de su niño.

Si tiene alguna duda o pregunta, por favor comuníquese conmigo.

Atentamente,
El maestro de su niño

expression

Order of Operations

square number

A combination of numbers, variables, and/or operation signs. An expression does not have an equal sign.

Examples:

$4 + 7$ $a - 3$

A set of rules that state the order in which the operations in an expression should be done.

STEP 1: Perform operations inside parentheses first.
STEP 2: Multiply and divide from left to right.
STEP 3: Add and subtract from left to right.

The product of a whole number and itself.

Example:

$3 \times 3 = 9$

↑

square number

Name ____________________

PATH to FLUENCY

Explore Patterns with 6s

What patterns do you see below?

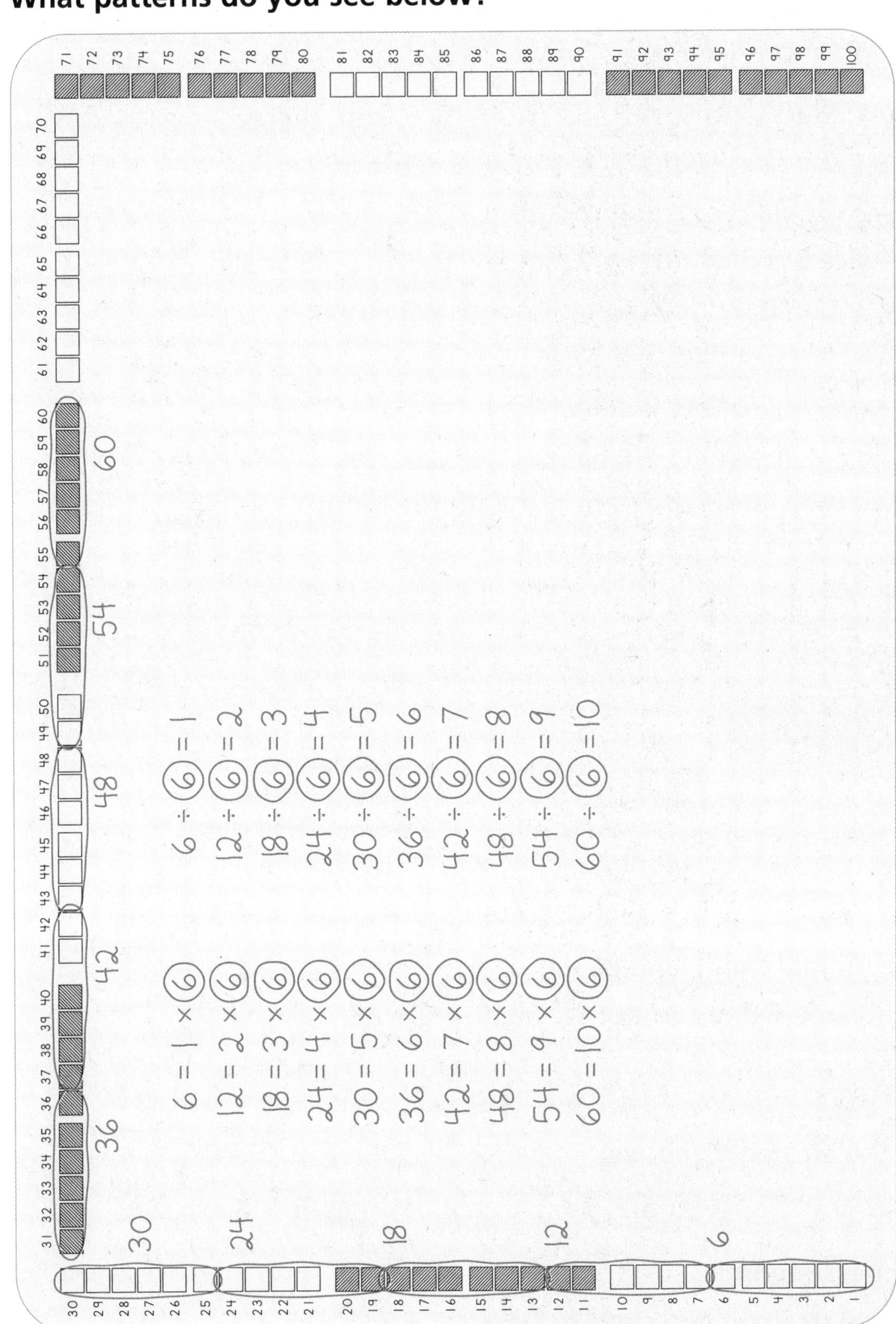

PATH to FLUENCY

Strategies for Multiplying with 6

You can use 6s multiplications that you know to find 6s multiplications that you don't know. Here are some strategies for 6 × 6.

- **Strategy 1:** Start with 5 × 6, and count by 6 from there.
  5 × 6 = 30, the next count-by is 36. So, 6 × 6 = 36.
- **Strategy 2:** Double a 3s multiplication.
  6 × 6 is twice 6 × 3, which is 18. So, 6 × 6 = 18 + 18 = 36.
- **Strategy 3:** Combine two multiplications you know.

4 × 6 = 24	4 sixes are 24.
2 × 6 = 12	2 sixes are 12.
6 × 6 = 36	6 sixes are 36.

Here are two ways to show Strategy 3 with drawings.

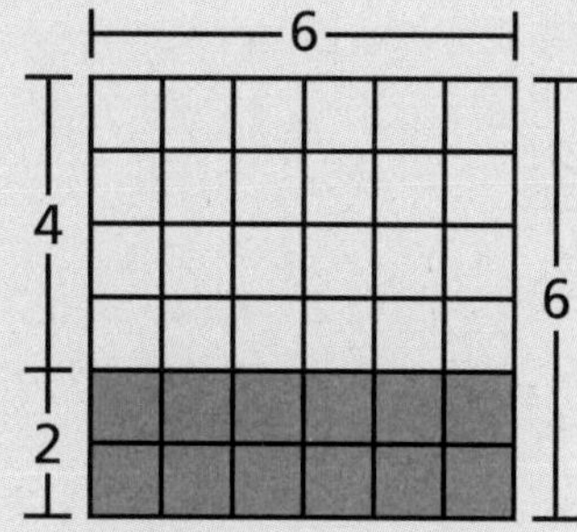

unshaded area: 4 × 6 = 24
shaded area: 2 × 6 = 12
total area: 6 × 6 = 36

6 × ⑥

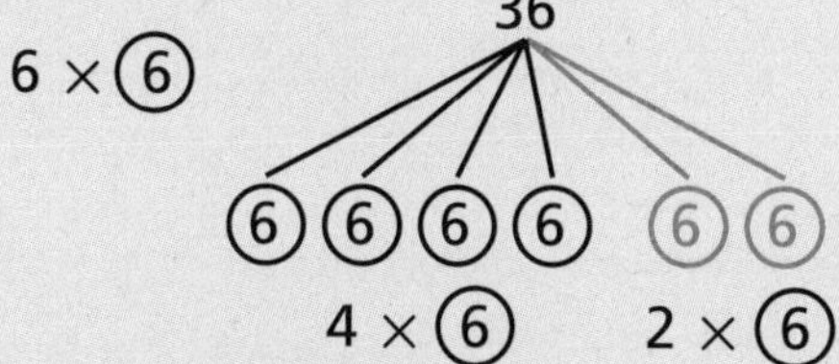

Explanation:
6 groups of 6 is
4 groups of 6 plus
2 groups of 6.

- **Strategy 4:** Add 6 on to the 6s multiplication before or subtract 6 from the multiplication ahead.
  5 × 6 = 30, add 6 more to get 36. So, 6 × 6 = 36.

Apply Strategies for 6s Multiplications

Use any of the strategies above.

1. 7 × 6 = ______
2. 8 × 6 = ______
3. 9 × 6 = ______

Check Understanding

Describe the strategy you used to find 8 × 6.

Name ______________________

PATH to FLUENCY

Study Sheet C

6s		
Count-bys	**Mixed Up ×**	**Mixed Up ÷**
1 × 6 = 6	10 × 6 = 60	54 ÷ 6 = 9
2 × 6 = 12	8 × 6 = 48	30 ÷ 6 = 5
3 × 6 = 18	2 × 6 = 12	12 ÷ 6 = 2
4 × 6 = 24	6 × 6 = 36	60 ÷ 6 = 10
5 × 6 = 30	4 × 6 = 24	48 ÷ 6 = 8
6 × 6 = 36	1 × 6 = 6	36 ÷ 6 = 6
7 × 6 = 42	9 × 6 = 54	6 ÷ 6 = 1
8 × 6 = 48	3 × 6 = 18	42 ÷ 6 = 7
9 × 6 = 54	7 × 6 = 42	18 ÷ 6 = 3
10 × 6 = 60	5 × 6 = 30	24 ÷ 6 = 4

7s		
Count-bys	**Mixed Up ×**	**Mixed Up ÷**
1 × 7 = 7	6 × 7 = 42	70 ÷ 7 = 10
2 × 7 = 14	8 × 7 = 56	14 ÷ 7 = 2
3 × 7 = 21	5 × 7 = 35	28 ÷ 7 = 4
4 × 7 = 28	9 × 7 = 63	56 ÷ 7 = 8
5 × 7 = 35	4 × 7 = 28	42 ÷ 7 = 6
6 × 7 = 42	10 × 7 = 70	63 ÷ 7 = 9
7 × 7 = 49	3 × 7 = 21	21 ÷ 7 = 3
8 × 7 = 56	1 × 7 = 7	49 ÷ 7 = 7
9 × 7 = 63	7 × 7 = 49	7 ÷ 7 = 1
10 × 7 = 70	2 × 7 = 14	35 ÷ 7 = 5

8s		
Count-bys	**Mixed Up ×**	**Mixed Up ÷**
1 × 8 = 8	6 × 8 = 48	16 ÷ 8 = 2
2 × 8 = 16	10 × 8 = 80	40 ÷ 8 = 5
3 × 8 = 24	7 × 8 = 56	72 ÷ 8 = 9
4 × 8 = 32	2 × 8 = 16	32 ÷ 8 = 4
5 × 8 = 40	4 × 8 = 32	8 ÷ 8 = 1
6 × 8 = 48	8 × 8 = 64	80 ÷ 8 = 10
7 × 8 = 56	5 × 8 = 40	64 ÷ 8 = 8
8 × 8 = 64	9 × 8 = 72	24 ÷ 8 = 3
9 × 8 = 72	3 × 8 = 24	56 ÷ 8 = 7
10 × 8 = 80	1 × 8 = 8	48 ÷ 8 = 6

Squares		
Count-bys	**Mixed Up ×**	**Mixed Up ÷**
1 × 1 = 1	3 × 3 = 9	25 ÷ 5 = 5
2 × 2 = 4	9 × 9 = 81	4 ÷ 2 = 2
3 × 3 = 9	4 × 4 = 16	81 ÷ 9 = 9
4 × 4 = 16	6 × 6 = 36	9 ÷ 3 = 3
5 × 5 = 25	2 × 2 = 4	36 ÷ 6 = 6
6 × 6 = 36	7 × 7 = 49	100 ÷ 10 = 10
7 × 7 = 49	10 × 10 = 100	16 ÷ 4 = 4
8 × 8 = 64	1 × 1 = 1	49 ÷ 7 = 7
9 × 9 = 81	5 × 5 = 25	1 ÷ 1 = 1
10 × 10 = 100	8 × 8 = 64	64 ÷ 8 = 8

Name

PATH to FLUENCY

Unknown Number Puzzles

Complete each Unknown Number puzzle.

1

×	5	2	
	30		48
4		8	32
	45		72

2

×		3	
6	30		42
4			28
	40	24	56

3

×	4		8
9		81	
	12		24
	20	45	40

4

×		3	
	60		20
6	36		
	18	9	6

5

×	8		2
7		28	
	16	8	
	32	16	8

6

×	9		
8		56	24
	54	42	18
5			15

7

×	8		7
8		40	
	32	20	28
	24	15	

8

×	3	4	
	27	36	81
7			63
			18

9

×			10
8	48	16	
7	42	14	
	36		60

Tiling and Multiplying to Find Area

Use inch tiles to find the area. Then label the side lengths and find the area using multiplication.

10

Area: ______ ______

11

Area: ______ ______

12

Area: ______ ______

Name ______________________________

Draw Rectangles to Solve Area Word Problems

Draw a rectangle to help solve each problem. Label your answers with the correct units.

Show your work.

13 The mattress has a length of 7 feet and a width of 6 feet. What is the area of the mattress?

____

14 An outdoor stage at Evans Park is shaped like a square with sides 8 feet long. What is the area of the stage?

____

15 Milo's rug has a length of 5 feet and an area of 40 square feet. What is the width of his rug?

____

16 Lana wants to enclose a garden plot. Each side of the garden will be 9 feet. What is the area of the garden?

____

17 A picture has a length of 6 inches and a width of 8 inches. What is the area of the picture?

____

18 A quilt square has sides that are 7 inches long. What is the area of the quilt square?

____

Draw a Picture to Solve a Problem

Draw a picture to help solve each problem.

Show your work.

19 Ana has a ribbon that is 18 inches long. She cut the ribbon into 3 equal pieces. Then she cut each of those pieces in half. How many small pieces of ribbon are there? How long is each piece?

____

____

20 A sign is shaped like a square. Eva draws lines on the sign to make 3 equal rectangles. Each rectangle is 3 inches wide and 9 inches long. What is the area of the square?

____

21 Ty uses 20 feet of fencing to make a rectangular garden. He divides the rectangle into 4 equal squares all in one row. The side of each square is 2 feet long. What is the area of the garden?

____

22 There are 4 cars in a row. Each car is 13 feet long. There are 6 feet between each car. What is the length from the front of the first car to the back of the last car in the row?

____

✓ Check Understanding

Draw a fast area drawing to find the area of a square with sides that are 5 units long.

Name ______________________________

PATH to FLUENCY

Check Sheet 7: 6s and 8s

6s Multiplications	6s Divisions	8s Multiplications	8s Divisions
10 × 6 = 60	24 / 6 = 4	2 × 8 = 16	72 / 8 = 9
6 • 4 = 24	48 ÷ 6 = 8	8 • 10 = 80	16 ÷ 8 = 2
6 * 7 = 42	60 / 6 = 10	3 * 8 = 24	40 / 8 = 5
2 × 6 = 12	12 ÷ 6 = 2	9 × 8 = 72	8 ÷ 8 = 1
6 • 5 = 30	42 / 6 = 7	8 • 4 = 32	80 / 8 = 10
6 * 8 = 48	30 ÷ 6 = 5	8 * 7 = 56	48 ÷ 8 = 6
9 × 6 = 54	6 / 6 = 1	5 × 8 = 40	56 / 8 = 7
6 • 1 = 6	18 ÷ 6 = 3	8 • 6 = 48	24 ÷ 8 = 3
6 * 6 = 36	54 / 6 = 9	1 * 8 = 8	64 / 8 = 8
6 × 3 = 18	36 / 6 = 6	8 × 8 = 64	32 / 8 = 4
6 • 6 = 36	48 ÷ 6 = 8	4 • 8 = 32	80 ÷ 8 = 10
5 * 6 = 30	12 / 6 = 2	6 * 8 = 48	56 / 8 = 7
6 × 2 = 12	24 ÷ 6 = 4	8 × 3 = 24	8 ÷ 8 = 1
4 • 6 = 24	60 / 6 = 10	7 • 8 = 56	24 / 8 = 3
6 * 9 = 54	6 ÷ 6 = 1	8 * 2 = 16	64 ÷ 8 = 8
8 × 6 = 48	42 / 6 = 7	8 × 9 = 72	16 / 8 = 2
7 • 6 = 42	18 ÷ 6 = 3	8 • 1 = 8	72 ÷ 8 = 9
6 * 10 = 60	36 ÷ 6 = 6	8 * 8 = 64	32 ÷ 8 = 4
1 × 6 = 6	30 / 6 = 5	10 × 8 = 80	40 / 8 = 5
4 • 6 = 24	54 ÷ 6 = 9	5 • 8 = 40	48 ÷ 8 = 6

Name ______________________________

PATH to FLUENCY

Explore Patterns with 8s

What patterns do you see below?

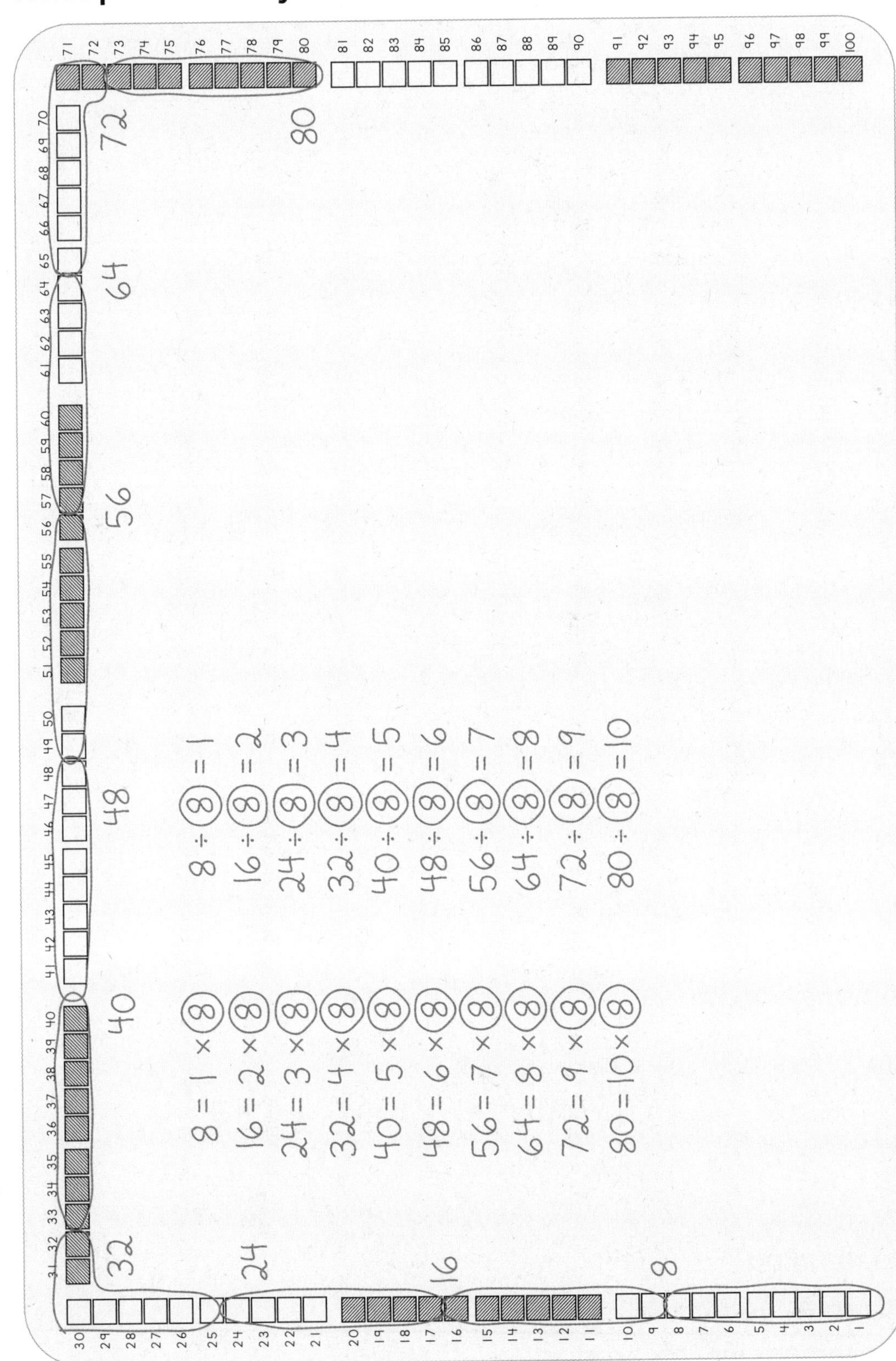

PATH to FLUENCY Fast Array Drawings

Find the unknown number for each fast array drawing.

1. 6, □, 42

2. 8, 6, □

3. □, 8, 64

4. 9, □, 63

5. 6, 4, □

6. □, 5, 20

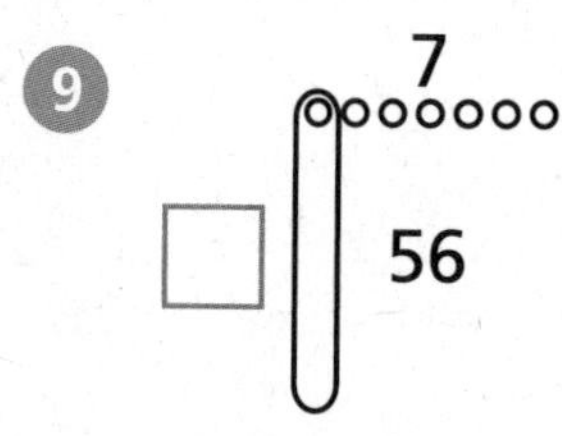

7. □, 9, 45

8. 9, 8, □

9. 7, □, 56

10. 7, 7, □

11. 8, □, 40

12. □, 8, 24

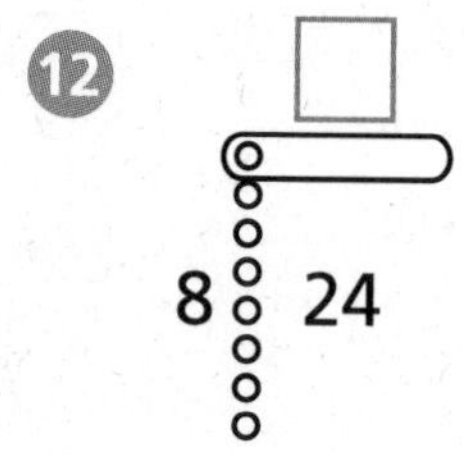

13. 6, 6, □

14. 10, □, 100

15. □, 5, 25

Check Understanding

Describe a strategy you could use to find 9×8 if you do not remember the product.

Name ______________________________

Identify the Type and Choose the Operation

Solve. Then circle what type of problem it is and what operation you use.

1. Students in Mr. Till's class hung their paintings on the wall. They made 6 rows, with 5 paintings in each row. How many paintings did the students hang?

   ____

   Circle one: array   equal groups   area
   Circle one: multiplication   division

2. Write your own problem that is the same type as Problem 1. ______________________________

   ____

   ____

3. There are 8 goldfish in each tank at the pet store. If there are 56 goldfish in all, how many tanks are there?

   ____

   Circle one: array   equal groups   area
   Circle one: multiplication   division

4. Write your own problem that is the same type as Problem 3. ______________________________

   ____

   ____

5. Pierre built a rectangular pen for his rabbits. The pen is 4 feet wide and 6 feet long. What is the area of the pen? ______________________________

   Circle one: array   equal groups   area
   Circle one: multiplication   division

PATH to FLUENCY Identify the Type and Choose the Operation (continued)

6 Write your own problem that is the same type as Problem 5. ____________________

____

____

7 Paulo arranged 72 baseball cards in rows and columns. If there were 9 rows, into how many columns did he arrange the cards? ____________

Circle one: array equal groups area
Circle one: multiplication division

8 Write your own problem that is the same type as Problem 7. ____________________

____

____

9 The store sells bottles of juice in six-packs. Mr. Lee bought 9 six-packs for a picnic. How many bottles did he buy? ____________________

Circle one: array equal groups area
Circle one: multiplication division

10 Write your own problem that is the same type as Problem 9. ____________________

____

____

11 **Math Journal** Write an area multiplication problem. Draw a fast array to solve it.

Name ______________________

What's the Error?

Dear Math Students,

Today my teacher asked me to find the answer to 8×6. Here is what I wrote:

$8 \times 6 = 14$

Is my answer correct? If not, please correct my work and tell me what I did wrong.

Your friend,
Puzzled Penguin

12 Write an answer to the Puzzled Penguin.

____

____

Write and Solve Equations

Write an equation and solve the problem.

13 A large box of crayons holds 60 crayons. There are 10 crayons in each row. How many rows are there?

____

____

14 A sign covers 12 square feet. The sign is 4 feet long. How wide is the sign?

____

____

15 There are 28 students working on a project. There are 7 groups with an equal number of students in each group. How many students are in each group?

____

____

16 Amanda had 15 bracelets. She gave the same number of bracelets to 3 friends. How many bracelets did she give to each friend?

____

____

Write and Solve Equations (continued)

Write an equation and solve the problem.

17. John has 24 baseball cards. He divided them equally among 6 friends. How many cards did each friend get?

____

18. A third grade classroom has 3 tables for 24 students in the class. The same number of students sit at each table. How many students sit at a table?

____

19. Marc bought 18 golf balls. The golf balls were packaged in boxes of 6. How many boxes of golf balls did Marc buy?

____

20. Lara keeps her rock collection in a case that has 10 drawers. Each drawer can hold 6 rocks. How many rocks can the case hold?

____

21. Write a problem that can be solved using the equation $54 \div 6 = n$, where n is the number in each group. Then solve the problem.

____

____

____

Check Understanding

Is Problem 19 an equal groups, array, or area problem?

____

Name ______________________________

PATH to FLUENCY

Explore Patterns with 7s

What patterns do you see below?

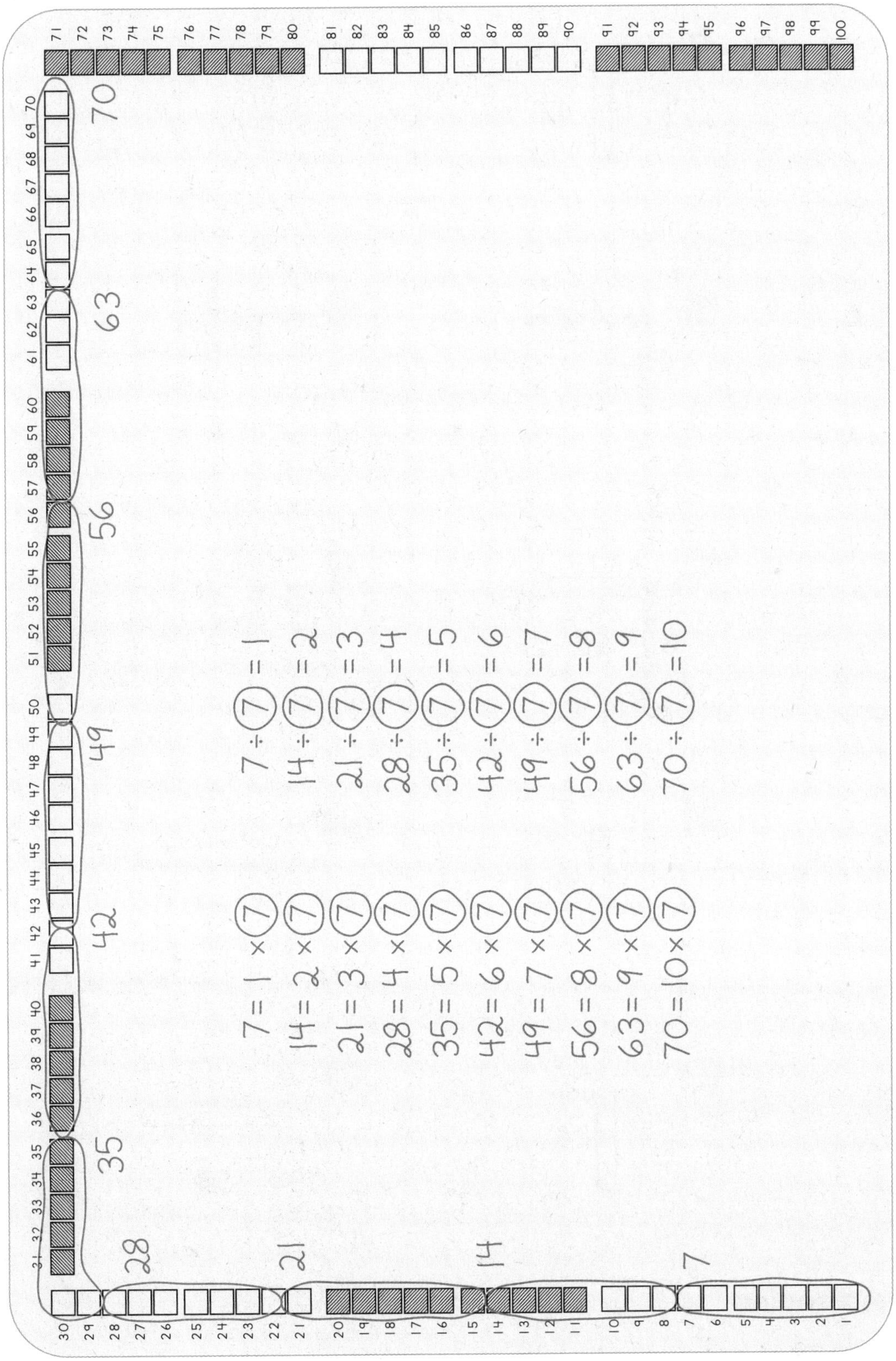

1 2 3 4 5 6 7 8 9 10 11 12 13 14 15 16 17 18 19 20 21 22 23 24 25 26 27 28 29 30 31 32 33 34 35 36 37 38 39 40 41 42 43 44 45 46 47 48 49 50 51 52 53 54 55 56 57 58 59 60 61 62 63 64 65 66 67 68 69 70 71 72 73 74 75 76 77 78 79 80 81 82 83 84 85 86 87 88 89 90 91 92 93 94 95 96 97 98 99 100

7 14 21 28 35 42 49 56 63 70

7 = 1 × 7   7 ÷ 7 = 1
14 = 2 × 7   14 ÷ 7 = 2
21 = 3 × 7   21 ÷ 7 = 3
28 = 4 × 7   28 ÷ 7 = 4
35 = 5 × 7   35 ÷ 7 = 5
42 = 6 × 7   42 ÷ 7 = 6
49 = 7 × 7   49 ÷ 7 = 7
56 = 8 × 7   56 ÷ 7 = 8
63 = 9 × 7   63 ÷ 7 = 9
70 = 10 × 7   70 ÷ 7 = 10

PATH to FLUENCY More Fast Array Drawings

Find the unknown number for each fast array drawing.

1. 7 across, 4 down, □

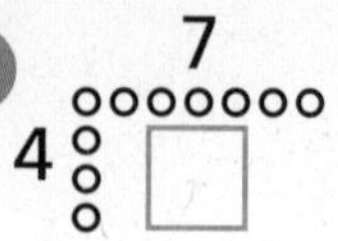

2. 7 across, □ down, 42

3. 5 across, 6 down, □

4. □ across, 3 down, 24

5. 8 across, 6 down, □

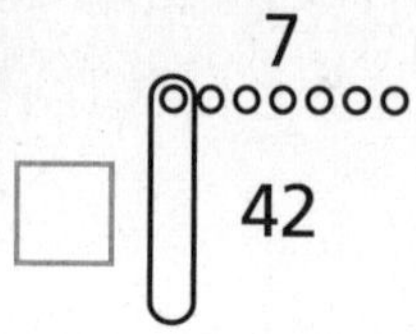

6. 5 across, □ down, 10

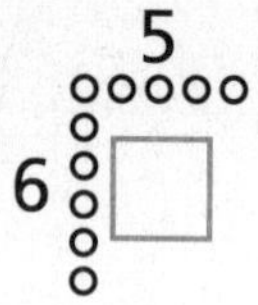

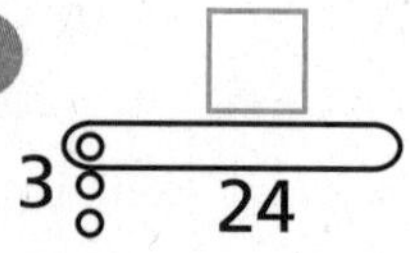

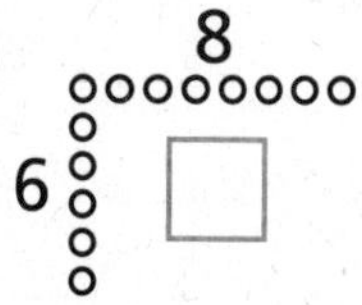

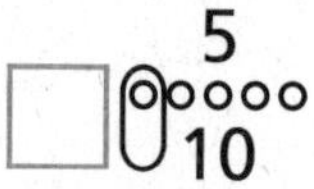

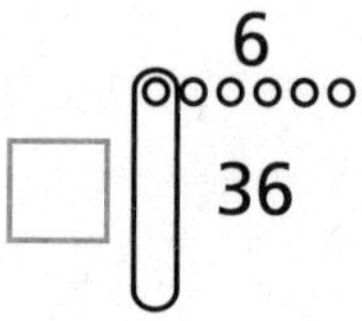

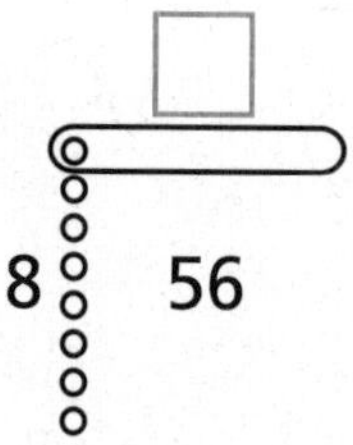

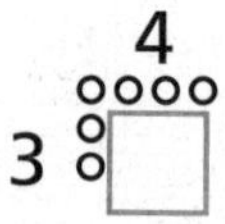

7. 6 across, □ down, 36

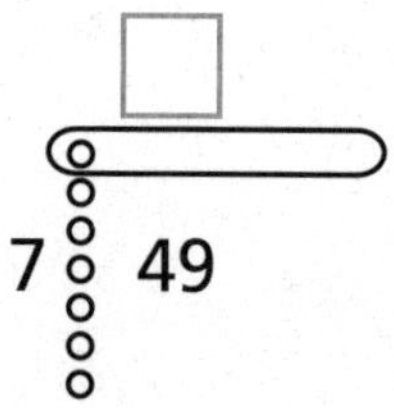

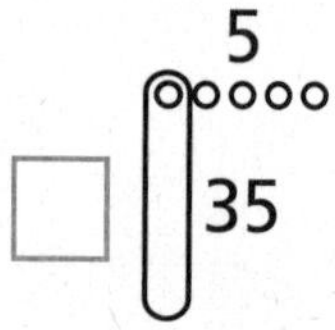

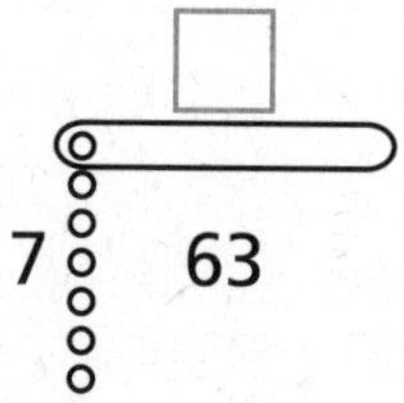

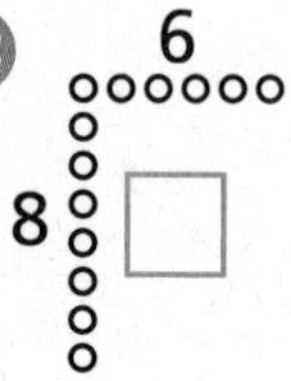

8. □ across, 8 down, 56

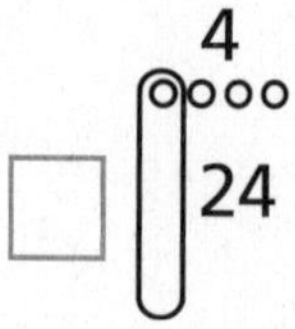

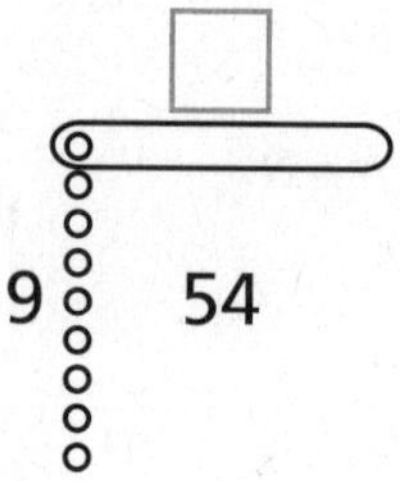

9. 4 across, 3 down, □

10. □ across, 7 down, 49

11. 5 across, □ down, 35

12. □ across, 7 down, 63

13. 6 across, 8 down, □

14. 4 across, □ down, 24

15. □ across, 9 down, 54

Check Understanding

Draw a fast array drawing to find $49 \div 7$.

Name ______________________________

PATH to FLUENCY Check Sheet 8: 7s and Squares

7s Multiplications	7s Divisions	Squares Multiplications	Squares Divisions
4 × 7 = 28	14 / 7 = 2	8 × 8 = 64	81 / 9 = 9
7 • 2 = 14	28 ÷ 7 = 4	10 • 10 = 100	4 ÷ 2 = 2
7 * 8 = 56	70 / 7 = 10	3 * 3 = 9	25 / 5 = 5
7 × 7 = 49	56 ÷ 7 = 8	9 × 9 = 81	1 ÷ 1 = 1
7 • 1 = 7	42 / 7 = 6	4 • 4 = 16	100 / 10 = 10
7 * 10 = 70	63 ÷ 7 = 9	7 * 7 = 49	36 ÷ 6 = 6
3 × 7 = 21	7 / 7 = 1	5 × 5 = 25	49 / 7 = 7
7 • 6 = 42	49 ÷ 7 = 7	6 • 6 = 36	9 ÷ 3 = 3
5 * 7 = 35	21 / 7 = 3	1 * 1 = 1	64 / 8 = 8
7 × 9 = 63	35 / 7 = 5	5 * 5 = 25	16 / 4 = 4
7 • 4 = 28	7 ÷ 7 = 1	1 • 1 = 1	100 ÷ 10 = 10
9 * 7 = 63	63 / 7 = 9	3 • 3 = 9	49 / 7 = 7
2 × 7 = 14	14 ÷ 7 = 2	10 × 10 = 100	1 ÷ 1 = 1
7 • 5 = 35	70 / 7 = 10	4 × 4 = 16	9 / 3 = 3
8 * 7 = 56	21 ÷ 7 = 3	9 * 9 = 81	64 ÷ 8 = 8
7 × 3 = 21	49 / 7 = 7	2 × 2 = 4	4 / 2 = 2
6 • 7 = 42	28 ÷ 7 = 4	6 * 6 = 36	81 ÷ 9 = 9
10 * 7 = 70	56 ÷ 7 = 8	7 × 7 = 49	16 ÷ 4 = 4
1 × 7 = 7	35 / 7 = 5	5 • 5 = 25	25 / 5 = 5
7 • 7 = 49	42 ÷ 7 = 6	8 • 8 = 64	36 ÷ 6 = 6

Name ______________________________

PATH to FLUENCY

Explore Square Numbers

Write an equation to show the area of each large square.

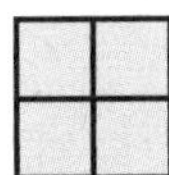
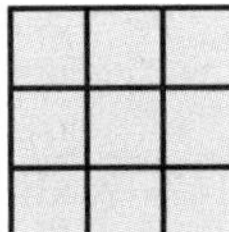
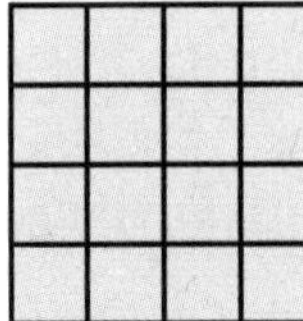

1. $1 \times 1 = 1$
2. 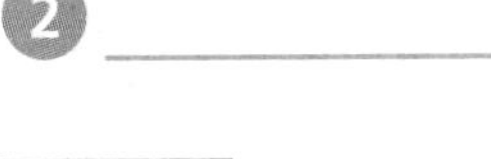 ______________
3.  ______________
4.  ______________

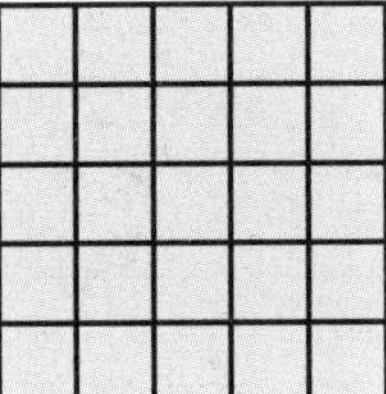
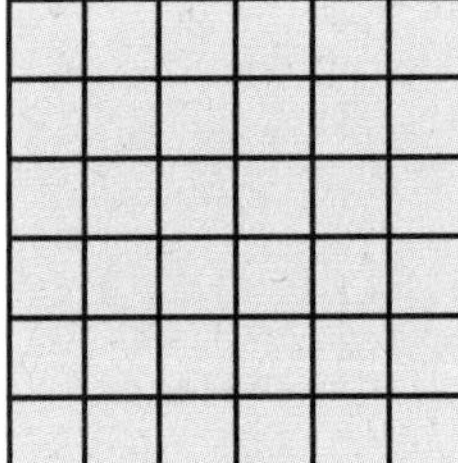

5. ______________________________
6. ______________________________

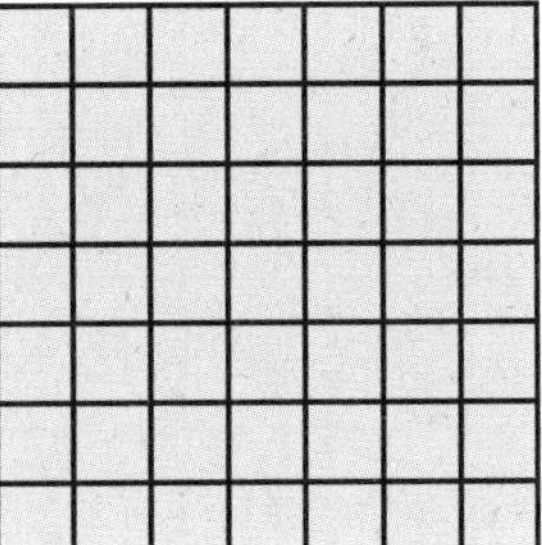

7. ______________________________
8. ______________________________

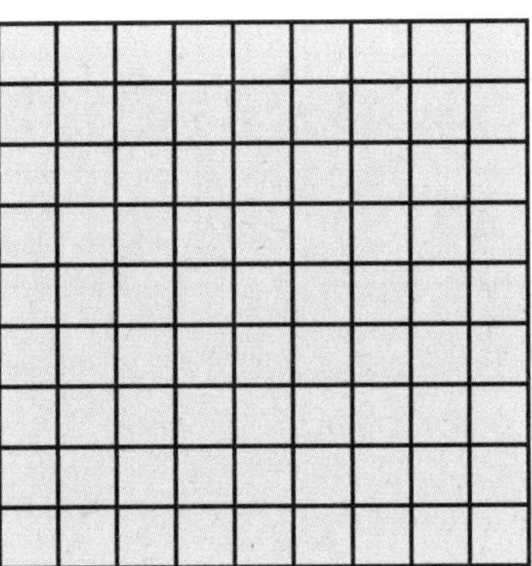
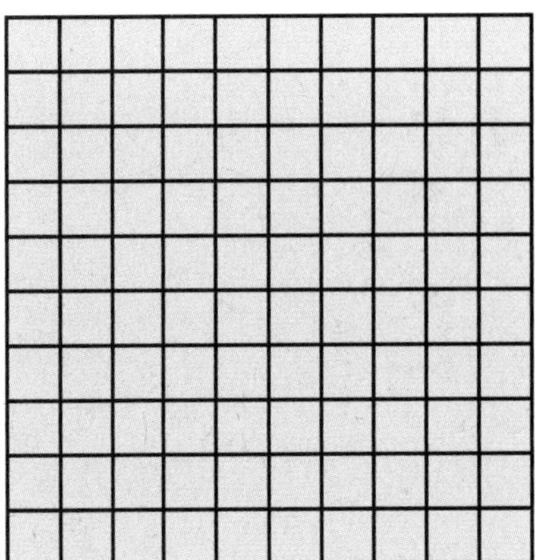

9. ______________________________
10.  ______________________________

Look for Patterns

VOCABULARY
square numbers

11 List the products in Exercises 1–10 in order. Discuss the patterns you see with your class.

___

The numbers you listed in Exercise 11 are called **square numbers** because they are the areas of squares with whole-number lengths of sides. A square number is the product of a whole number and itself. So, if *n* is a whole number, $n \times n$ is a square number.

Patterns on the Multiplication Table

12 In the table on the right, circle the products that are square numbers. Discuss the patterns you see with your class.

X	1	2	3	4	5	6	7	8	9	10
1	1	2	3	4	5	6	7	8	9	10
2	2	4	6	8	10	12	14	16	18	20
3	3	6	9	12	15	18	21	24	27	30
4	4	8	12	16	20	24	28	32	36	40
5	5	10	15	20	25	30	35	40	45	50
6	6	12	18	24	30	36	42	48	54	60
7	7	14	21	28	35	42	49	56	63	70
8	8	16	24	32	40	48	56	64	72	80
9	9	18	27	36	45	54	63	72	81	90
10	10	20	30	40	50	60	70	80	90	100

Check Understanding

Complete the sentence.

The number _____ is a square number because ___________________

___

Name ____________________

PATH to FLUENCY Check Sheet 9: 6s, 7s, and 8s

6s, 7s, and 8s Multiplications	6s, 7s, and 8s Multiplications	6s, 7s, and 8s Divisions	6s, 7s, and 8s Divisions
1 × 6 = 6	0 × 8 = 0	24 / 6 = 4	54 / 6 = 9
6 • 7 = 42	6 • 2 = 12	21 ÷ 7 = 3	24 ÷ 8 = 3
3 * 8 = 24	4 * 7 = 28	16 / 8 = 2	14 / 7 = 2
6 × 2 = 12	8 × 3 = 24	24 ÷ 8 = 3	32 ÷ 8 = 4
7 • 5 = 35	5 • 6 = 30	14 / 7 = 2	18 / 6 = 3
8 * 4 = 32	7 * 2 = 14	30 ÷ 6 = 5	56 ÷ 7 = 8
6 × 6 = 36	3 × 8 = 24	35 / 7 = 5	40 / 8 = 5
8 • 7 = 56	6 • 4 = 24	24 ÷ 8 = 3	35 ÷ 7 = 5
9 * 8 = 72	0 * 7 = 0	18 / 6 = 3	12 / 6 = 2
6 × 10 = 60	8 × 1 = 8	12 / 6 = 2	21 / 7 = 3
7 • 1 = 7	8 • 6 = 48	42 ÷ 7 = 6	16 ÷ 8 = 2
8 * 3 = 24	7 * 9 = 63	56 / 8 = 7	42 / 6 = 7
5 × 6 = 30	10 × 8 = 80	49 ÷ 7 = 7	80 ÷ 8 = 10
4 • 7 = 28	6 • 10 = 60	16 / 8 = 2	36 / 6 = 6
2 * 8 = 16	3 * 7 = 21	60 ÷ 6 = 10	7 ÷ 7 = 1
7 × 7 = 49	8 × 4 = 32	54 / 6 = 9	64 / 8 = 8
7 • 6 = 42	6 • 5 = 30	8 ÷ 8 = 1	24 ÷ 6 = 4
8 * 8 = 64	7 * 4 = 28	28 ÷ 7 = 4	21 ÷ 7 = 3
9 × 6 = 54	8 × 8 = 64	72 / 8 = 9	49 / 7 = 7
10 • 7 = 70	6 • 9 = 54	56 ÷ 7 = 8	24 ÷ 8 = 3

PATH to FLUENCY Check Sheet 10: 0s–10s

0s–10s Multiplications	0s–10s Multiplications	0s–10s Divisions	0s–10s Divisions
9 × 0 = 0	9 × 4 = 36	9 / 1 = 9	90 / 10 = 9
1 • 1 = 1	5 • 9 = 45	12 ÷ 3 = 4	64 ÷ 8 = 8
2 * 3 = 6	6 * 10 = 60	14 / 2 = 7	15 / 5 = 3
1 × 3 = 3	7 × 3 = 21	20 ÷ 4 = 5	12 ÷ 6 = 2
5 • 4 = 20	5 • 3 = 15	10 / 5 = 2	14 / 7 = 2
7 * 5 = 35	4 * 1 = 4	48 ÷ 8 = 6	45 ÷ 9 = 5
6 × 9 = 54	7 × 5 = 35	35 / 7 = 5	8 / 1 = 8
4 • 7 = 28	6 • 3 = 18	60 ÷ 6 = 10	30 ÷ 3 = 10
1 * 8 = 8	8 * 7 = 56	81 / 9 = 9	16 / 4 = 4
9 × 8 = 72	5 × 8 = 40	20 / 10 = 2	8 / 2 = 4
2 • 10 = 20	9 • 9 = 81	16 ÷ 2 = 8	80 ÷ 10 = 8
0 * 7 = 0	9 * 10 = 90	30 / 5 = 6	36 / 4 = 9
4 × 1 = 4	0 × 0 = 0	49 ÷ 7 = 7	25 ÷ 5 = 5
2 • 4 = 8	1 • 0 = 0	60 / 6 = 10	42 / 7 = 6
10 * 3 = 30	1 * 6 = 6	30 ÷ 3 = 10	36 ÷ 6 = 6
8 × 4 = 32	7 × 2 = 14	8 / 1 = 8	90 / 9 = 10
5 • 8 = 40	6 • 3 = 18	16 ÷ 4 = 4	24 ÷ 8 = 3
4 * 6 = 24	4 * 5 = 20	16 ÷ 8 = 2	6 ÷ 2 = 3
7 × 6 = 42	6 × 6 = 36	40 / 10 = 4	9 / 3 = 3
1 • 8 = 8	10 • 7 = 70	36 ÷ 9 = 4	1 ÷ 1 = 1

Name ____________________

PATH to FLUENCY

Play Quotient Match and Division Blockout

Read the rules for playing a game.
Then play the game.

Rules for Quotient Match

Number of players: 2 or 3

What each player will need: Division Strategy Cards for 6s, 7s, and 8s

1. Shuffle the cards. Put the division cards, sides without answers, face up on the table in 6 rows of 4.
2. Players take turns. On each turn, a player chooses three cards that he or she thinks have the same quotient and turns them over.
3. If all three cards do have the same quotient the player takes them. If the cards do not have the same quotient, the player turns them back over so the without answers side is up.
4. Play continues until no cards remain.

Rules for Division Blockout

Number of players: 3

What each player will need: *Blockout* Game Board (TRB M70), Division Strategy Cards for 6s, 7s, and 8s

1. Players do not write anything on the game board. The first row is for 6s, the second row for 7s, and the third row for 8s, as indicated in the gray column on the left.
2. Each player shuffles his or her Division Strategy Cards for 6s, 7s, 8s, making sure the division sides without answers are face up.
3. Repeat Steps 2, 3, and 4 above. This time players will place the Strategy Cards in the appropriate row to indicate whether the unknown factor is 6, 7, or 8.

PATH to FLUENCY Play Multiplication Blockout

Read the rules for playing *Multiplication Blockout*. Then play the game.

Rules for *Multiplication Block Out*

Number of players: 3

What each player will need: *Blockout* Game Board (TRB M70), Multiplication Strategy Cards for 6s, 7s, and 8s

1. Players choose any 5 factors from 2–9 and write them in any order in the gray spaces at the top of the game board. The players then write the products in the large white spaces. The result will be a scrambled multiplication table.
2. Once the table is complete, players cut off the gray row and gray column that show the factors so that only the products are showing. This will be the game board.
3. Each player shuffles his or her Multiplication Strategy Cards for 6s, 7s, and 8s, making sure the multiplication sides without answers are facing up.
4. One player says, "Go!" and everyone quickly places their Strategy Cards on the game board spaces showing the corresponding products. When a player's game board is completely filled, he or she calls out, "Blockout!"
5. Everyone stops and checks the player's work. If all the cards are placed correctly, that player is the winner. If the player has made a mistake, he or she sits out and waits for the next player to call out, "Blockout!"

Name ______________________________

PATH to FLUENCY

Solve Word Problems with 6s, 7s, 8s

Write an equation and solve the problem.

1. Terri's class has 32 students. The students worked on an art project in groups of 4 students. How many groups were there?

   ____

2. Kyle saw 9 ladybugs while he was camping. Each one had 6 legs. How many legs did the 9 ladybugs have in all?

   ____

3. Adam walks 3 miles a day. How many miles does he walk in a week?

   ____

4. Nancy's dog Rover eats 6 cups of food a day. In 8 days, how many cups of food does Rover eat?

   ____

5. The school library has 72 books on the topic of weather. If Tanya arranged the books in 8 equal-sized stacks, how many books were in each stack?

   ____

6. The 42 trumpet players in the marching band lined up in 6 equal rows. How many trumpet players were in each row?

   ____

Solve Word Problems with 6s, 7s, and 8s (continued)

Write an equation and solve the problem.

7 Susan is having a party. She has 18 cups. She puts them in 6 equal stacks. How many cups are in each stack?

____

8 Regina made an array with 7 rows of 9 blocks. How many blocks are in the array?

____

9 Mr. Rodriguez plans to invite 40 students to a picnic. The invitations come in packs of 8. How many packs of invitations does Mr. Rodriguez need to buy?

____

10 A classroom has 7 rows of 4 desks. How many desks are there in the classroom?

____

11 Write a word problem for $48 \div 6$ where 6 is the size of the group.

____

____

12 Write a word problem for 7×9 where 9 is the number of items in one group.

____

____

Check Understanding

Explain how you know when a word problem can be solved by using division.

Name ______________________________

PATH to FLUENCY

Complete a Multiplication Table

1. Look at the factors to complete the Multiplication Table. Leave blanks for the products you do not know.

×	1	2	3	4	5	6	7	8	9	10
1										
2										
3										
4										
5										
6										
7										
8										
9										
10										

2. Write the multiplications you need to practice.

____

____

____

____

____

____

PATH to FLUENCY Scrambled Multiplication Tables

Complete each table.

A

×										
	6	30	54	60	42	24	18	12	48	36
	2	10	18	20	14	8	6	4	16	12
	10	50	90	100	70	40	30	20	80	60
	8	40	72	80	56	32	24	16	64	48
	5	25	45	50	35	20	15	10	40	30
	1	5	9	10	7	4	3	2	8	6
	9	45	81	90	63	36	27	18	72	54
	4	20	36	40	28	16	12	8	32	24
	7	35	63	70	49	28	21	14	56	42
	3	15	27	30	21	12	9	6	24	18

B

×										
	27	6	24	21	18	15	12	9	3	
	36	8	32	28	24		16	12	4	40
	9	2	8	7	6	5	4	3	1	10
	18	4	16	14		10	8	6	2	20
		14	56	49	42		28	21	7	
	72		64	56	48	40	32	24	8	80
	45	10	40		30	25	20	15	5	
	54	12	48	42	36	30	24	18	6	60
	90		80	70	60		40	30	10	100
	81	18	72		54	45	36	27	9	

C

×										
	100		20		70	50		90		10
	50	15		20	35		30		40	5
	10	3		4	7		6	9		1
		9		12	21	15		27	24	
		6	4	8			12	18	16	2
		12	8	16	28	20		36	32	
	90	27	18	36	63	45	54		72	
		18	12	24		30	36	54	48	6
		21		28	49		42		56	7
		24		32	56	40		72	64	8

D

×										
	48		42	12	36		18	6		30
	56	28		14		70	21		63	35
			70		60			10		50
		20	35		30		15	5	45	
	32			8		40			36	
	8	4		2			3	1		5
		8	14		12		6		18	10
	64		56		48	80	24	8		40
	72	36		18			27		81	
	24		21		18	30		3	27	

Check Understanding

Complete the sentences.

The numbers in the blue boxes are ______________________.

The numbers in the white boxes are ______________________.

Name ______

PATH to FLUENCY

Dashes 13–16

Complete each Dash. Check your answers on page 141.

Dash 13 6s and 8s Multiplications	Dash 14 6s and 8s Divisions	Dash 15 7s and 8s Multiplications	Dash 16 7s and 8s Divisions
a. 6 × 9 = ___	a. 72 / 8 = ___	a. 7 × 3 = ___	a. 63 / 7 = ___
b. 8 * 2 = ___	b. 12 ÷ 6 = ___	b. 8 * 5 = ___	b. 80 ÷ 8 = ___
c. 4 • 6 = ___	c. 16 / 8 = ___	c. 2 • 7 = ___	c. 14 / 7 = ___
d. 7 × 8 = ___	d. 24 ÷ 6 = ___	d. 1 × 8 = ___	d. 16 ÷ 8 = ___
e. 6 * 1 = ___	e. 8 / 8 = ___	e. 7 * 9 = ___	e. 7 / 7 = ___
f. 8 • 9 = ___	f. 6 ÷ 6 = ___	f. 8 • 4 = ___	f. 48 ÷ 8 = ___
g. 3 × 6 = ___	g. 40 / 8 = ___	g. 4 × 7 = ___	g. 35 / 7 = ___
h. 4 * 8 = ___	h. 42 ÷ 6 = ___	h. 7 * 8 = ___	h. 32 ÷ 8 = ___
i. 6 • 8 = ___	i. 24 / 8 = ___	i. 7 • 1 = ___	i. 21 / 7 = ___
j. 8 × 1 = ___	j. 18 ÷ 6 = ___	j. 8 × 2 = ___	j. 8 ÷ 8 = ___
k. 2 * 6 = ___	k. 48 / 8 = ___	k. 5 * 7 = ___	k. 28 / 7 = ___
l. 3 • 8 = ___	l. 48 ÷ 6 = ___	l. 9 • 8 = ___	l. 40 ÷ 8 = ___
m. 6 × 5 = ___	m. 64 / 8 = ___	m. 7 × 6 = ___	m. 49 / 7 = ___
n. 8 * 8 = ___	n. 42 ÷ 6 = ___	n. 8 * 3 = ___	n. 72 ÷ 8 = ___
o. 6 • 6 = ___	o. 56 / 8 = ___	o. 7 • 7 = ___	o. 42 / 7 = ___
p. 5 × 8 = ___	p. 30 ÷ 6 = ___	p. 8 × 8 = ___	p. 24 ÷ 8 = ___
q. 6 * 7 = ___	q. 32 / 8 = ___	q. 7 * 0 = ___	q. 56 / 7 = ___
r. 8 × 0 = ___	r. 54 ÷ 6 = ___	r. 6 • 8 = ___	r. 64 ÷ 8 = ___
s. 0 * 6 = ___	s. 80 / 8 = ___	s. 8 × 0 = ___	s. 70 / 7 = ___
t. 6 • 10 = ___	t. 60 ÷ 6 = ___	t. 7 * 10 = ___	t. 56 ÷ 8 = ___

PATH to FLUENCY

Dashes 17–20

Complete each Dash. Check your answers on page 141.

Dash 17 6s and 7s Multiplications	Dash 18 6s and 7s Divisions	Dash 19 6s, 7s, 8s Multiplications	Dash 20 6s, 7s, 8s Divisions
a. 6 × 6 = ___	a. 70 / 7 = ___	a. 7 × 7 = ___	a. 21 / 7 = ___
b. 7 * 7 = ___	b. 60 ÷ 6 = ___	b. 6 • 3 = ___	b. 16 ÷ 8 = ___
c. 3 • 6 = ___	c. 28 / 7 = ___	c. 8 * 6 = ___	c. 54 / 6 = ___
d. 8 × 7 = ___	d. 30 ÷ 6 = ___	d. 6 × 6 = ___	d. 48 ÷ 8 = ___
e. 6 * 1 = ___	e. 42 / 7 = ___	e. 7 • 6 = ___	e. 64 / 8 = ___
f. 7 • 2 = ___	f. 24 ÷ 6 = ___	f. 4 * 7 = ___	f. 42 ÷ 6 = ___
g. 9 × 6 = ___	g. 35 / 7 = ___	g. 9 × 7 = ___	g. 56 / 7 = ___
h. 9 * 7 = ___	h. 12 ÷ 6 = ___	h. 6 • 9 = ___	h. 72 ÷ 8 = ___
i. 6 • 8 = ___	i. 7 / 7 = ___	i. 6 * 4 = ___	i. 18 / 6 = ___
j. 7 × 3 = ___	j. 36 ÷ 6 = ___	j. 8 × 8 = ___	j. 28 / 7 = ___
k. 7 * 6 = ___	k. 21 / 7 = ___	k. 7 • 3 = ___	k. 56 ÷ 8 = ___
l. 1 • 7 = ___	l. 48 ÷ 6 = ___	l. 8 * 7 = ___	l. 30 / 6 = ___
m. 6 × 2 = ___	m. 63 / 7 = ___	m. 6 × 7 = ___	m. 63 ÷ 7 = ___
n. 7 * 5 = ___	n. 6 ÷ 6 = ___	n. 3 • 6 = ___	n. 32 / 8 = ___
o. 4 • 6 = ___	o. 56 / 7 = ___	o. 2 * 7 = ___	o. 48 ÷ 6 = ___
p. 6 × 7 = ___	p. 18 ÷ 6 = ___	p. 9 × 8 = ___	p. 49 / 7 = ___
q. 6 * 5 = ___	q. 49 / 7 = ___	q. 5 • 6 = ___	q. 36 ÷ 6 = ___
r. 7 • 4 = ___	r. 42 ÷ 6 = ___	r. 7 * 8 = ___	r. 24 ÷ 8 = ___
s. 6 × 10 = ___	s. 14 / 7 = ___	s. 3 × 7 = ___	s. 42 / 7 = ___
t. 7 × 10 = ___	t. 54 ÷ 6 = ___	t. 9 • 6 = ___	t. 24 ÷ 6 = ___

Name ____________________

PATH to FLUENCY

Dashes 9B–12B

Complete each multiplication and division Dash.
Check your answers on page 142.

Dash 9B 2s, 5s, 9s, 10s Multiplications	Dash 10B 2s, 5s, 9s, 10s Divisions	Dash 11B 0s, 1s, 3s, 4s Multiplications	Dash 12B 1s, 3s, 4s Divisions
a. 6 × 2 = ___	a. 18 / 2 = ___	a. 7 × 1 = ___	a. 2 / 1 = ___
b. 9 • 4 = ___	b. 25 ÷ 5 = ___	b. 0 • 6 = ___	b. 28 ÷ 4 = ___
c. 8 * 5 = ___	c. 70 / 10 = ___	c. 4 * 4 = ___	c. 3 / 3 = ___
d. 1 × 10 = ___	d. 54 ÷ 9 = ___	d. 7 × 3 = ___	d. 1 ÷ 1 = ___
e. 2 • 7 = ___	e. 50 / 5 = ___	e. 3 • 1 = ___	e. 40 / 4 = ___
f. 9 * 9 = ___	f. 81 ÷ 9 = ___	f. 4 * 7 = ___	f. 21 ÷ 3 = ___
g. 5 × 6 = ___	g. 8 / 2 = ___	g. 9 × 0 = ___	g. 5 / 1 = ___
h. 10 • 4 = ___	h. 90 ÷ 10 = ___	h. 1 • 1 = ___	h. 16 ÷ 4 = ___
i. 7 * 5 = ___	i. 35 / 5 = ___	i. 3 * 4 = ___	i. 15 / 3 = ___
j. 8 × 2 = ___	j. 27 / 9 = ___	j. 4 × 9 = ___	j. 6 / 1 = ___
k. 10 • 10 = ___	k. 2 ÷ 2 = ___	k. 8 • 1 = ___	k. 12 ÷ 4 = ___
l. 5 * 3 = ___	l. 36 / 9 = ___	l. 3 * 3 = ___	l. 27 / 3 = ___
m. 9 × 7 = ___	m. 45 ÷ 5 = ___	m. 0 × 4 = ___	m. 9 ÷ 1 = ___
n. 9 • 2 = ___	n. 14 / 2 = ___	n. 10 • 3 = ___	n. 8 / 4 = ___
o. 5 * 5 = ___	o. 20 ÷ 10 = ___	o. 6 * 4 = ___	o. 12 ÷ 3 = ___
p. 6 × 9 = ___	p. 9 / 9 = ___	p. 1 × 4 = ___	p. 3 / 1 = ___
q. 5 • 2 = ___	q. 20 ÷ 5 = ___	q. 3 • 6 = ___	q. 36 ÷ 4 = ___
r. 9 * 5 = ___	r. 45 ÷ 9 = ___	r. 4 * 8 = ___	r. 6 ÷ 3 = ___
s. 8 × 10 = ___	s. 5 / 5 = ___	s. 7 × 0 = ___	s. 4 / 1 = ___
t. 5 • 10 = ___	t. 4 ÷ 2 = ___	t. 5 • 3 = ___	t. 4 ÷ 4 = ___

PATH to FLUENCY Dashes 9C–12C

Complete each Dash. Check your answers on page 142.

Dash 9C 2s, 5 ,9s, 10s Multiplications	Dash 10C 2s, 5, 9s, 10s Divisions	Dash 11C 0s, 1s ,3s, 4s Multiplications	Dash 12C 1s, 3s, 4s Divisions
a. 5 × 8 = ____	a. 36 ÷ 9 = ____	a. 0 × 7 = ____	a. 4 / 1 = ____
b. 9 * 9 = ____	b. 30 / 5 = ____	b. 1 * 4 = ____	b. 15 ÷ 3 = ____
c. 10 • 7 = ____	c. 18 ÷ 2 = ____	c. 3 • 6 = ____	c. 24 / 4 = ____
d. 4 × 5 = ____	d. 80 / 10 = ____	d. 4 × 9 = ____	d. 9 ÷ 1 = ____
e. 5 * 5 = ____	e. 40 ÷ 5 = ____	e. 8 * 0 = ____	e. 21 / 3 = ____
f. 10 • 3 = ____	f. 72 / 9 = ____	f. 7 * 1 = ____	f. 12 ÷ 4 = ____
g. 1 × 5 = ____	g. 6 ÷ 2 = ____	g. 4 • 3 = ____	g. 5 / 1 = ____
h. 3 * 9 = ____	h. 54 / 9 = ____	h. 4 × 4 = ____	h. 3 ÷ 3 = ____
i. 9 • 6 = ____	i. 25 ÷ 5 = ____	i. 0 * 5 = ____	i. 32 / 4 = ____
j. 10 × 8 = ____	j. 10 / 10 = ____	j. 1 • 6 = ____	j. 2 ÷ 1 = ____
k. 2 * 9 = ____	k. 45 ÷ 5 = ____	k. 3 × 2 = ____	k. 18 / 3 = ____
l. 6 • 2 = ____	l. 27 / 9 = ____	l. 4 * 7 = ____	l. 36 ÷ 4 = ____
m. 6 × 10 = ____	m. 14 ÷ 2 = ____	m. 1 • 0 = ____	m. 7 / 1 = ____
n. 8 * 9 = ____	n. 35 / 5 = ____	n. 2 × 1 = ____	n. 24 ÷ 3 = ____
o. 8 • 2 = ____	o. 90 ÷ 9 = ____	o. 9 * 3 = ____	o. 4 / 4 = ____
p. 4 × 2 = ____	p. 90 / 10 = ____	p. 2 • 4 = ____	p. 6 ÷ 1 = ____
q. 10 * 5 = ____	q. 63 ÷ 9 = ____	q. 0 × 3 = ____	q. 12 / 3 = ____
r. 10 • 10 = ____	r. 15 / 5 = ____	r. 1 * 1 = ____	r. 20 ÷ 4 = ____
s. 9 × 6 = ____	s. 50 ÷ 10 = ____	s. 3 • 9 = ____	s. 8 / 1 = ____
t. 5 * 7 = ____	t. 8 / 2 = ____	t. 4 × 5 = ____	t. 27 ÷ 3 = ____

Name ____________________

PATH to FLUENCY

Answers to Dashes 13–20

Use this sheet to check your answers to the Dashes on pages 137 and 138.

Dash 13 ×	Dash 14 ÷	Dash 15 ×	Dash 16 ÷	Dash 17 ×	Dash 18 ÷	Dash 19 ×	Dash 20 ÷
a. 54	a. 9	a. 21	a. 9	a. 36	a. 10	a. 49	a. 3
b. 16	b. 2	b. 40	b. 10	b. 49	b. 10	b. 18	b. 2
c. 24	c. 2	c. 14	c. 2	c. 18	c. 4	c. 48	c. 9
d. 56	d. 4	d. 8	d. 2	d. 56	d. 5	d. 36	d. 6
e. 6	e. 1	e. 63	e. 1	e. 6	e. 6	e. 42	e. 8
f. 72	f. 1	f. 32	f. 6	f. 14	f. 4	f. 28	f. 7
g. 18	g. 5	g. 28	g. 5	g. 54	g. 5	g. 63	g. 8
h. 32	h. 7	h. 56	h. 4	h. 63	h. 2	h. 54	h. 9
i. 48	i. 3	i. 7	i. 3	i. 48	i. 1	i. 24	i. 3
j. 8	j. 3	j. 16	j. 1	j. 21	j. 6	j. 64	j. 4
k. 12	k. 6	k. 35	k. 4	k. 42	k. 3	k. 21	k. 7
l. 24	l. 8	l. 72	l. 5	l. 7	l. 8	l. 56	l. 5
m. 30	m. 8	m. 42	m. 7	m. 12	m. 9	m. 42	m. 9
n. 64	n. 7	n. 24	n. 9	n. 35	n. 1	n. 18	n. 4
o. 36	o. 7	o. 49	o. 6	o. 24	o. 8	o. 14	o. 8
p. 40	p. 5	p. 64	p. 3	p. 42	p. 3	p. 72	p. 7
q. 42	q. 4	q. 0	q. 8	q. 30	q. 7	q. 30	q. 6
r. 0	r. 9	r. 48	r. 8	r. 28	r. 7	r. 56	r. 3
s. 0	s. 10	s. 0	s. 10	s. 60	s. 2	s. 21	s. 6
t. 60	t. 10	t. 70	t. 7	t. 70	t. 9	t. 54	t. 4

PATH to FLUENCY Answers to Dashes 9B–12B, 9C–12C

Use this sheet to check your answers to the Dashes on pages 139 and 140.

Dash 9B ×	Dash 10B ÷	Dash 11B ×	Dash 12B ÷	Dash 9C ×	Dash 10C ÷	Dash 11C ×	Dash 12C ÷
a. 12	a. 9	a. 7	a. 2	a. 40	a. 4	a. 0	a. 4
b. 36	b. 5	b. 0	b. 7	b. 81	b. 6	b. 4	b. 5
c. 40	c. 7	c. 16	c. 1	c. 70	c. 9	c. 18	c. 6
d. 10	d. 6	d. 21	d. 1	d. 20	d. 8	d. 36	d. 9
e. 14	e. 10	e. 3	e. 10	e. 25	e. 8	e. 0	e. 7
f. 81	f. 9	f. 28	f. 7	f. 30	f. 8	f. 7	f. 3
g. 30	g. 4	g. 0	g. 5	g. 5	g. 3	g. 12	g. 5
h. 40	h. 9	h. 1	h. 4	h. 27	h. 6	h. 16	h. 1
i. 35	i. 7	i. 12	i. 5	i. 54	i. 5	i. 0	i. 8
j. 16	j. 3	j. 36	j. 6	j. 80	j. 1	j. 6	j. 2
k. 100	k. 1	k. 8	k. 3	k. 18	k. 9	k. 6	k. 6
l. 15	l. 4	l. 9	l. 9	l. 12	l. 3	l. 28	l. 9
m. 63	m. 9	m. 0	m. 9	m. 60	m. 7	m. 0	m. 7
n. 18	n. 7	n. 30	n. 2	n. 72	n. 7	n. 2	n. 8
o. 25	o. 2	o. 24	o. 4	o. 16	o. 10	o. 27	o. 1
p. 54	p. 1	p. 4	p. 3	p. 8	p. 9	p. 8	p. 6
q. 10	q. 4	q. 18	q. 9	q. 50	q. 7	q. 0	q. 4
r. 45	r. 5	r. 32	r. 2	r. 100	r. 3	r. 1	r. 5
s. 80	s. 1	s. 0	s. 4	s. 54	s. 5	s. 27	s. 8
t. 50	t. 2	t. 15	t. 1	t. 35	t. 4	t. 20	t. 9

Unit 2
Quick Quiz 1

Name ____________________ Date ____________

Write an equation and solve the problem.

Show your work.

1. The area of the rectangle shown is 42 square inches. What is the value of n?

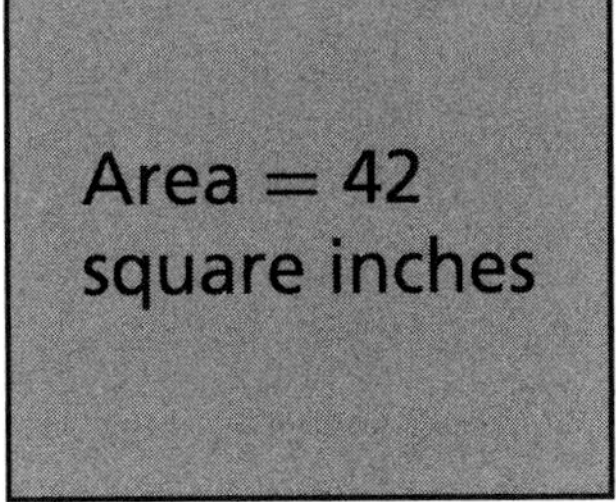

____

2. There are 81 bottles of apple juice to be equally shared among 9 people. How many bottles will each of those 9 people receive?

____

Solve.

3. $7 \times \square = 56$

$\square =$ ____

4. $9 \times 9 = \square$

$\square =$ ____

5. Jaewon arranges his stamps in 6 equal rows. If he has 48 stamps, how many stamps will be in each row?

____

Strategy Check 4

Name ______________________ Date ______________

Write an equation and solve the problem.

Show your work.

1. There are 7 rows of 9 mango trees in an orchard. How many mango trees are there in all?

   ____

2. A carrot seed needs about 8 weeks to become a carrot. How many days is that?

   ____

3. It takes a little more than 63 days for pea seeds to become peas that you can eat. How many weeks are 63 days?

   ____

4. During harvest season each 24-hour day is split into 3 equal shifts. How long is each shift?

   ____

5. Hal packs 6 boxes of oranges. Each box weighs 6 pounds. How much do the boxes weigh in all?

   ____

Name ____________________

PATH to FLUENCY Choose the Operation

Write an equation and solve the problem.

1. Ernie helped his mother work in the yard for 3 days. He earned $6 each day. How much did he earn in all?

   ____

2. Ernie helped his mother work in the yard for 3 days. He earned $6 the first day, $5 the second day, and $7 the third day. How much did he earn in all?

   ____

3. Troy had $18. He gave $6 to each of his brothers and had no money left. How many brothers does Troy have?

   ____

4. Troy gave $18 to his brothers. He gave $4 to Raj, $7 to Darnell, and the rest to Jai. How much money did Jai get?

   ____

5. Jinja has 4 cousins. Grant has 7 more cousins than Jinja. How many cousins does Grant have?

   ____

6. Jinja has 4 cousins. Grant has 7 times as many cousins as Jinja. How many cousins does Grant have?

   ____

7. Camille has 15 fewer books than Jane has. Camille has 12 books. How many does Jane have?

   ____

8. Camille has 4 more books than Jane has. Camille has 15 books. How many books does Jane have?

   ____

Write an Equation

Write an equation and solve the problem.

Show your work.

9. Luke had a $5 bill. He spent $3 on a sandwich. How much change did he get?

____

10. Ramona is putting tiles on the kitchen floor. She will lay 8 rows of tiles, with 7 tiles in each row. How many tiles will Ramona use?

____

11. Josh earned a perfect score on 6 tests last year. Jenna earned a perfect score on 6 times as many tests. How many perfect scores did Jenna earn?

____

12. Sophie bought a stuffed animal for $3 and a board game for $7. How much money did Sophie spend?

____

13. Mr. Duarte buys 15 dog treats. He gives each of his 3 dogs the same number of treats. How many treats does each dog get?

____

14. Ahmed spent $9 on a book. Zal paid $6 more for the same book at a different store. How much did Zal spend on the book?

____

Name ______________________________

Write the Question

Write a question for the given information and solve.

15 Anna read 383 pages this month. Chris read 416 pages.

Question: ______________________________

Solution: ______________________________

16 Marisol had 128 beads in her jewelry box. She gave away 56 of them.

Question: ______________________________

Solution: ______________________________

17 Louis put 72 marbles in 8 bags. He put the same number of marbles in each bag.

Question: ______________________________

Solution: ______________________________

18 Geoff planted seeds in 4 pots. He planted 6 seeds in each pot.

Question: ______________________________

Solution: ______________________________

19 Marly put 10 books on each of 5 shelves in the library.

Question: ______________________________

Solution: ______________________________

Write the Problem

Write a problem that can be solved using the given equation. Then solve.

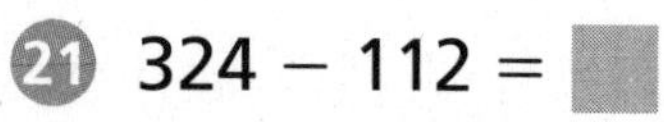

20 $9 \times 6 = \blacksquare$ **Solution:** ______

______

______

______

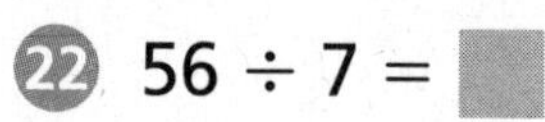

21 $324 - 112 = \blacksquare$ **Solution:** ______

______

______

______

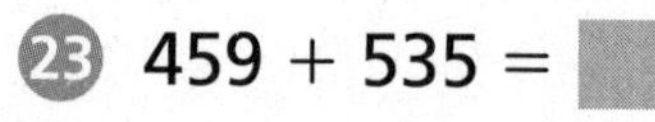

22 $56 \div 7 = \blacksquare$ **Solution:** ______

______

______

______

23 $459 + 535 = \blacksquare$ **Solution:** ______

______

______

______

Check Understanding

Describe how you would begin to write a word problem for $42 \div 6 = n$.

 Name ______

VOCABULARY
expression
Order of Operations

Use Order of Operations

This **expression** involves subtraction and multiplication:

$$10 - 3 \times 2$$

1 What do you get if you subtract first and then multiply? ______

2 What do you get if you multiply first and then subtract? ______

To make sure everyone has the same answer, people follow the **Order of Operations** rules. Using the Order of Operations, multiplication and division is done *before* addition and subtraction. The answer you found in question 2 is correct.

In the Order of Operations rules, using parentheses means "Do this first." For example, if you want people to subtract first in the exercise above, write it like this:

$$(10 - 3) \times 2$$

Find the answer.

3 $5 + 4 \times 2 =$ ______

4 $(9 - 3) \times 6 =$ ______

5 $8 \div 2 + 2 =$ ______

6 $6 \times (8 - 1) =$ ______

Rewrite each statement, using symbols and numbers instead of words.

7 Add 4 and 3, and multiply the total by 8. ______

8 Multiply 3 by 8, and add 4 to the total. ______

What's the Error?

Dear Math Students,

Today I found the answer to $6 + 3 \times 2$.
Here is how I found the answer.

$6 + 3 \times 2$

$9 \times 2 = 18$

Is my answer correct? If not, please correct my work and tell me what I did wrong.

Your friend,
Puzzled Penguin

9 Write an answer to the Puzzled Penguin.

____

____

____

Find the answer.

10 $4 + 3 \times 5 =$ _______

11 $10 \div 2 + 3 =$ _______

12 $12 - 9 \div 3 =$ _______

13 $3 \times 5 - 2 =$ _______

14 $(4 + 3) \times 5 =$ _______

15 $10 \div (2 + 3) =$ _______

16 $(12 - 9) \div 3 =$ _______

17 $3 \times (5 - 2) =$ _______

Name ______________________________

Write First-Step Questions

Write the first-step question and answer.
Then solve the problem.

Show your work.

18 A roller coaster has 7 cars. Each car has 4 seats. If there were 3 empty seats, how many people were on the roller coaster?

____

____

19 Each week, Marta earns $10 babysitting. She always spends $3 and saves the rest. How much does she save in 8 weeks?

____

____

20 Abu bought 6 packs of stickers. Each pack had 8 stickers. Then Abu's friend gave him 10 more stickers. How many stickers does Abu have now?

____

____

21 Zoe made some snacks. She put 4 apple slices and 2 melon slices on each plate. She prepared 5 plates. How many slices of fruit did Zoe use in all?

____

____

22 Kyle ordered 8 pizzas for his party. Each pizza was cut into 8 slices. 48 of the slices were plain cheese, and the rest had mushrooms. How many slices of pizza had mushrooms?

____

____

Write First-Step Questions (continued)

Write the first-step question and answer. Then solve the problem.

Show your work.

23 Kagami baked 86 blueberry muffins. Her sisters ate 5 of them. Kagami divided the remaining muffins equally among 9 plates. How many muffins did she put on each plate?

____

____

24 Lucia had 42 plums. Jorge had 12 more plums than Lucia. Jorge divided his plums equally among 6 people. How many plums did each person get?

____

____

25 On his way to school, Kevin counted 5 mountain bikes and 3 road bikes. How many wheels were on the bikes altogether?

____

____

26 Juana has 21 shirts. Leslie had 7 fewer shirts than Juana, but then she bought 4 more. How many shirts does Leslie have now?

____

____

✓ Check Understanding

Describe the difference between solving $6 + 4 \times 2 = n$ and $(6 + 4) \times 2 = n$.

 Name ______________________

Make Sense of Two-Step Word Problems

Write an equation and solve the problem.

Show your work.

1. Nine hens laid 6 eggs each. Five of the eggs broke. How many eggs are left?

   ____

2. There are 8 houses on Jeremiah's street. Each house has 1 willow tree, 6 apple trees, and 2 olive trees. How many trees are on Jeremiah's street in all?

   ____

3. Tim has 9 marbles. Ryan has 3 fewer marbles than Tim. Leslie has 5 more marbles than Ryan. How many marbles does Leslie have?

   ____

4. Mr. Helms has 2 stables with 4 horses in each stable. Ms. Martinez has 4 more horses than Mr. Helms. How many horses does Ms. Martinez have?

   ____

5. Angela had $4. She bought 2 small pumpkins for $1 each. How much money does Angela have now?

   ____

6. Ahmad had $40. He bought an action figure for $5 and a backpack for $14. How much money does Ahmad have left?

   ____

More Make Sense of Two-Step Problems

Write an equation and solve the problem.

Show your work.

7. In the locker room, there are 8 rows of 9 lockers. All of the lockers were full in the morning, but by afternoon 6 lockers had emptied out. How many lockers were still full in the afternoon?

____

8. Anita sent 3 cards to friends and 2 cards to cousins each month for 3 months. How many cards is that?

____

9. The library has 6 books about the desert and 8 books about the rainforest. The books were divided into groups of 2. How many groups of books are there?

____

10. Each pack of pencils contains 8 pencils. Sahil bought 3 packs and divided them equally among 6 people. How many pencils did each person get?

____

11. Kaya has 20 photos of dogs and 30 photos of cats. She displayed an equal number of them on 10 posters for an animal shelter fundraiser. How many photos were on each poster?

____

Check Understanding

Draw a picture that represents Problem 10 and the solution.

 Name ______

Multiply with Multiples of 10

When a number of ones is multiplied by 10, the ones become tens.

1 ten × 5 ones = 5 tens

$10 \times 5 =$ ____

To multiply with multiples of 10, use place value and properties.

$2 \times 3 = (2 \times 1) \times (3 \times 1) = (2 \times 3) \times (1 \times 1) = 6 \times 1 = 6$

$2 \times 30 = (2 \times 1) \times (3 \times 10) = (2 \times 3) \times (1 \times 10) = 6 \times 10 = 60$

Use a shortcut.

Find the basic multiplication product. Then multiply by 10.

2×30

$6 \times 10 = 60$

Multiply.

1. 6×40

   ☐ $\times 10 =$ ____

2. 4×50

   ☐ $\times 10 =$ ____

3. 70×8

   ☐ $\times 10 =$ ____

4. 90×3

   ☐ $\times 10 =$ ____

Multiply Using Mental Math

Use a basic multiplication and mental math to complete.

5. $3 \times 4 =$ ______
   $3 \times 40 =$ ______
6. $1 \times 2 =$ ______
   $10 \times 2 =$ ______
7. $9 \times 8 =$ ______
   $9 \times 80 =$ ______
8. $2 \times 9 =$ ______
   $2 \times 90 =$ ______
9. $5 \times 5 =$ ______
   $5 \times 50 =$ ______
10. $3 \times 5 =$ ______
    $3 \times 50 =$ ______
11. $1 \times 1 =$ ______
    $10 \times 1 =$ ______
12. $2 \times 3 =$ ______
    $20 \times 3 =$ ______
13. $5 \times 6 =$ ______
    $5 \times 60 =$ ______
14. $2 \times 4 =$ ______
    $2 \times 40 =$ ______
15. $6 \times 3 =$ ______
    $6 \times 30 =$ ______
16. $9 \times 2 =$ ______
    $9 \times 20 =$ ______
17. $2 \times 30 =$ ______
18. $5 \times 40 =$ ______
19. $9 \times 60 =$ ______
20. $3 \times 80 =$ ______
21. $2 \times 70 =$ ______
22. $5 \times 90 =$ ______
23. $9 \times 50 =$ ______
24. $5 \times 20 =$ ______
25. $3 \times 30 =$ ______
26. $5 \times 80 =$ ______
27. $9 \times 90 =$ ______
28. $5 \times 60 =$ ______
29. $70 \times 5 =$ ______
30. $8 \times 50 =$ ______
31. $60 \times 4 =$ ______

Check Understanding

Describe how you can use a multiplication strategy to find 7×40.

Name ______________________________

PATH to FLUENCY Dashes 21–22, 19A–20A

Complete each Dash. Check your answers on page 161.

Dash 21 **2s, 3s, 4s, 5s, 9s** **Multiplications**	**Dash 22** **2s, 3s, 4s, 5s, 9s** **Divisions**	**Dash 19A** **6s, 7s, 8s** **Multiplications**	**Dash 20A** **6s, 7s, 8s** **Divisions**
a. 6 × 3 = ___	a. 16 / 4 = ___	a. 9 × 6 = ___	a. 24 ÷ 6 = ___
b. 4 • 7 = ___	b. 54 ÷ 9 = ___	b. 7 * 7 = ___	b. 21 / 7 = ___
c. 8 * 2 = ___	c. 4 / 2 = ___	c. 3 • 7 = ___	c. 42 ÷ 7 = ___
d. 5 × 3 = ___	d. 28 ÷ 4 = ___	d. 6 × 3 = ___	d. 16 / 8 = ___
e. 4 • 4 = ___	e. 25 / 5 = ___	e. 7 * 8 = ___	e. 24 ÷ 8 = ___
f. 3 • 9 = ___	f. 21 ÷ 3 = ___	f. 8 • 6 = ___	f. 54 / 6 = ___
g. 9 × 9 = ___	g. 40 / 4 = ___	g. 5 × 6 = ___	g. 36 ÷ 6 = ___
h. 8 • 9 = ___	h. 81 ÷ 9 = ___	h. 6 * 6 = ___	h. 48 / 8 = ___
i. 6 * 4 = ___	i. 35 / 5 = ___	i. 9 • 8 = ___	i. 49 ÷ 7 = ___
j. 3 × 3 = ___	j. 12 / 3 = ___	j. 7 × 6 = ___	j. 64 / 8 = ___
k. 2 • 7 = ___	k. 2 ÷ 2 = ___	k. 2 * 7 = ___	k. 48 ÷ 6 = ___
l. 8 • 5 = ___	l. 63 / 9 = ___	l. 4 • 7 = ___	l. 42 / 6 = ___
m. 4 × 9 = ___	m. 36 ÷ 4 = ___	m. 3 × 6 = ___	m. 32 ÷ 8 = ___
n. 9 • 5 = ___	n. 18 / 2 = ___	n. 9 * 7 = ___	n. 56 / 7 = ___
o. 7 * 3 = ___	o. 9 ÷ 3 = ___	o. 6 • 7 = ___	o. 63 ÷ 7 = ___
p. 2 × 2 = ___	p. 36 / 9 = ___	p. 6 × 9 = ___	p. 72 / 8 = ___
q. 8 • 4 = ___	q. 40 ÷ 5 = ___	q. 8 * 7 = ___	q. 30 ÷ 6 = ___
r. 5 * 1 = ___	r. 12 ÷ 4 = ___	r. 6 • 4 = ___	r. 18 / 6 = ___
s. 5 × 5 = ___	s. 9 / 9 = ___	s. 7 × 3 = ___	s. 56 ÷ 8 = ___
t. 6 • 9 = ___	t. 14 ÷ 2 = ___	t. 8 * 8 = ___	t. 28 / 7 = ___

PATH to FLUENCY Dashes 21A–22A, 19B–20B

Complete each Dash. Check your answers on page 161.

Dash 21A
2s, 3s, 4s, 5s, 9s
Multiplications

a. 6 × 9 = ____
b. 6 * 3 = ____
c. 4 • 7 = ____
d. 5 × 5 = ____
e. 8 * 2 = ____
f. 5 • 1 = ____
g. 5 × 3 = ____
h. 8 * 4 = ____
i. 4 • 4 = ____
j. 2 × 2 = ____
k. 3 * 9 = ____
l. 7 • 3 = ____
m. 9 × 9 = ____
n. 9 * 5 = ____
o. 8 • 9 = ____
p. 4 × 9 = ____
q. 6 * 4 = ____
r. 8 • 5 = ____
s. 2 × 7 = ____
t. 3 * 3 = ____

Dash 22A
2s, 3s, 4s, 5s, 9s
Divisions

a. 14 ÷ 2 = ____
b. 16 / 4 = ____
c. 9 ÷ 9 = ____
d. 54 / 9 = ____
e. 12 ÷ 4 = ____
f. 4 / 2 = ____
g. 40 ÷ 5 = ____
h. 28 / 4 = ____
i. 36 ÷ 9 = ____
j. 25 / 5 = ____
k. 9 ÷ 3 = ____
l. 21 / 3 = ____
m. 18 ÷ 2 = ____
n. 40 / 4 = ____
o. 36 ÷ 4 = ____
p. 81 / 9 = ____
q. 63 ÷ 9 = ____
r. 35 / 5 = ____
s. 12 ÷ 3 = ____
t. 2 / 2 = ____

Dash 19B
6s, 7s, 8s
Multiplications

a. 6 × 2 = ____
b. 7 * 7 = ____
c. 8 • 5 = ____
d. 4 × 6 = ____
e. 3 * 7 = ____
f. 1 • 8 = ____
g. 6 × 9 = ____
h. 7 * 5 = ____
i. 8 • 3 = ____
j. 4 × 6 = ____
k. 9 * 7 = ____
l. 8 • 8 = ____
m. 6 × 1 = ____
n. 7 * 4 = ____
o. 8 • 6 = ____
p. 7 × 6 = ____
q. 2 * 7 = ____
r. 9 • 8 = ____
s. 6 × 5 = ____
t. 7 * 6 = ____

Dash 20B
6s, 7s, 8s
Divisions

a. 36 ÷ 6 = ____
b. 63 / 7 = ____
c. 24 ÷ 8 = ____
d. 18 / 6 = ____
e. 28 ÷ 7 = ____
f. 48 / 8 = ____
g. 54 ÷ 6 = ____
h. 42 / 7 = ____
i. 72 ÷ 8 = ____
j. 6 / 6 = ____
k. 14 ÷ 7 = ____
l. 56 / 8 = ____
m. 12 ÷ 6 = ____
n. 7 / 7 = ____
o. 16 ÷ 8 = ____
p. 30 / 6 = ____
q. 56 ÷ 7 = ____
r. 8 / 8 = ____
s. 48 ÷ 6 = ____
t. 21 / 7 = ____

Name ______________________________

PATH to FLUENCY

Dashes 21B–22B, 19C–20C

Complete each Dash. Check your answers on page 162.

Dash 21B 2s, 3s, 4s, 5s, 9s Multiplications	Dash 22B 2s, 3s, 4s, 5s, 9s Divisions	Dash 19C 6s, 7s, 8s Multiplications	Dash 20C 6s, 7s, 8s Divisions
a. 2 × 3 = ___	a. 8 ÷ 2 = ___	a. 6 × 8 = ___	a. 54 ÷ 6 = ___
b. 3 * 8 = ___	b. 18 / 3 = ___	b. 7 * 3 = ___	b. 49 / 7 = ___
c. 4 • 4 = ___	c. 12 ÷ 4 = ___	c. 8 • 6 = ___	c. 24 ÷ 8 = ___
d. 5 × 6 = ___	d. 25 / 5 = ___	d. 2 × 6 = ___	d. 6 / 6 = ___
e. 9 * 8 = ___	e. 63 ÷ 9 = ___	e. 8 * 7 = ___	e. 35 ÷ 7 = ___
f. 9 • 2 = ___	f. 16 / 2 = ___	f. 9 • 8 = ___	f. 72 / 8 = ___
g. 3 × 3 = ___	g. 3 ÷ 3 = ___	g. 6 × 4 = ___	g. 18 ÷ 6 = ___
h. 4 * 2 = ___	h. 28 / 4 = ___	h. 7 * 1 = ___	h. 28 / 7 = ___
i. 9 • 5 = ___	i. 45 ÷ 5 = ___	i. 8 • 3 = ___	i. 8 ÷ 8 = ___
j. 9 × 4 = ___	j. 27 / 9 = ___	j. 5 × 6 = ___	j. 30 / 6 = ___
k. 2 * 7 = ___	k. 12 ÷ 2 = ___	k. 9 * 7 = ___	k. 21 ÷ 7 = ___
l. 3 • 5 = ___	l. 12 / 3 = ___	l. 4 • 8 = ___	l. 40 / 8 = ___
m. 4 × 8 = ___	m. 20 ÷ 4 = ___	m. 6 × 6 = ___	m. 42 ÷ 6 = ___
n. 5 * 3 = ___	n. 40 / 5 = ___	n. 7 * 5 = ___	n. 63 / 7 = ___
o. 9 • 6 = ___	o. 54 ÷ 9 = ___	o. 8 • 8 = ___	o. 32 ÷ 8 = ___
p. 2 × 8 = ___	p. 2 / 2 = ___	p. 1 × 6 = ___	p. 36 / 6 = ___
q. 3 * 7 = ___	q. 9 ÷ 3 = ___	q. 2 * 7 = ___	q. 14 ÷ 7 = ___
r. 4 • 1 = ___	r. 36 / 4 = ___	r. 5 • 8 = ___	r. 56 / 8 = ___
s. 5 × 8 = ___	s. 15 ÷ 5 = ___	s. 6 × 9 = ___	s. 24 ÷ 6 = ___
t. 9 * 9 = ___	t. 9 / 9 = ___	t. 7 * 7 = ___	t. 42 / 7 = ___

PATH to FLUENCY Dashes 21C–22C, 19D–20D

Complete each Dash. Check your answers on page 162.

Dash 21C 2s, 3s, 4s, 5s, 9s Multiplications	Dash 22C 2s, 3s, 4s, 5s, 9s Divisions	Dash 19D 6s, 7s, 8s Multiplications	Dash 20D 6s, 7s, 8s Divisions
a. 2 × 9 = ____	a. 8 ÷ 2 = ____	a. 6 × 9 = ____	a. 18 / 6 = ____
b. 3 * 7 = ____	b. 6 / 3 = ____	b. 7 * 6 = ____	b. 42 ÷ 7 = ____
c. 4 • 5 = ____	c. 4 ÷ 4 = ____	c. 8 • 2 = ____	c. 32 / 8 = ____
d. 5 × 3 = ____	d. 20 / 5 = ____	d. 3 × 6 = ____	d. 54 ÷ 6 = ____
e. 9 * 1 = ____	e. 63 ÷ 9 = ____	e. 4 * 7 = ____	e. 49 / 7 = ____
f. 1 • 2 = ____	f. 16 / 2 = ____	f. 9 • 8 = ____	f. 8 / 8 = ____
g. 4 × 3 = ____	g. 15 ÷ 3 = ____	g. 6 × 6 = ____	g. 30 ÷ 6 = ____
h. 4 * 1 = ____	h. 32 / 4 = ____	h. 7 * 2 = ____	h. 35 / 7 = ____
i. 7 • 5 = ____	i. 30 ÷ 5 = ____	i. 8 • 1 = ____	i. 48 ÷ 8 = ____
j. 9 × 9 = ____	j. 45 / 9 = ____	j. 2 × 6 = ____	j. 24 / 6 = ____
k. 2 * 3 = ____	k. 2 ÷ 2 = ____	k. 8 * 7 = ____	k. 14 ÷ 7 = ____
l. 3 • 8 = ____	l. 21 / 3 = ____	l. 3 • 8 = ____	l. 56 / 8 = ____
m. 4 × 4 = ____	m. 12 ÷ 4 = ____	m. 6 × 4 = ____	m. 6 ÷ 6 = ____
n. 5 * 2 = ____	n. 10 / 5 = ____	n. 7 * 5 = ____	n. 21 / 7 = ____
o. 9 • 6 = ____	o. 9 ÷ 9 = ____	o. 8 • 8 = ____	o. 40 ÷ 8 = ____
p. 6 × 2 = ____	p. 12 / 2 = ____	p. 1 × 6 = ____	p. 48 / 6 = ____
q. 9 * 3 = ____	q. 27 ÷ 3 = ____	q. 3 * 7 = ____	q. 56 ÷ 7 = ____
r. 6 • 4 = ____	r. 20 / 4 = ____	r. 4 • 8 = ____	r. 64 / 8 = ____
s. 5 × 5 = ____	s. 40 ÷ 8 = ____	s. 6 × 7 = ____	s. 36 ÷ 6 = ____
t. 3 * 9 = ____	t. 81 / 9 = ____	t. 7 * 7 = ____	t. 7 / 7 = ____

Name ______________________________

Answers to Dashes 21–22, 19A–22A, 19B–20B

Use this sheet to check your answers to the Dashes on pages 157 and 158.

	Dash 21 ×	Dash 22 ÷	Dash 19A ×	Dash 20A ÷	Dash 21A ×	Dash 22A ÷	Dash 19B ×	Dash 20B ÷
a.	18	4	54	4	54	7	12	6
b.	28	6	49	3	18	4	49	9
c.	16	2	21	6	28	1	40	3
d.	15	7	18	2	25	6	24	3
e.	16	5	56	3	16	3	21	4
f.	27	7	48	9	5	2	8	6
g.	81	10	30	6	15	8	54	9
h.	72	9	36	6	32	7	35	6
i.	24	7	72	7	16	4	24	9
j.	9	4	42	8	4	5	24	1
k.	14	1	14	8	27	3	63	2
l.	40	7	28	7	21	7	64	7
m.	36	9	18	4	81	9	6	2
n.	45	9	63	8	45	10	28	1
o.	21	3	42	9	72	9	48	2
p.	4	4	54	9	36	9	42	5
q.	32	8	56	5	24	7	14	8
r.	5	3	24	3	40	7	72	1
s.	25	1	21	7	14	4	30	8
t.	54	7	64	4	9	1	42	3

Answers to Dashes 21B–22B, 19C–22C, 19D–20D

Use this sheet to check your answers to the Dashes on pages 159 and 160.

Dash 21B ×	Dash 22B ÷	Dash 19C ×	Dash 20C ÷	Dash 21C ×	Dash 22C ÷	Dash 19D ×	Dash 20D ÷
a. 6	a. 4	a. 48	a. 9	a. 18	a. 4	a. 54	a. 3
b. 24	b. 6	b. 21	b. 7	b. 21	b. 2	b. 42	b. 6
c. 16	c. 3	c. 48	c. 3	c. 20	c. 1	c. 16	c. 4
d. 30	d. 5	d. 12	d. 1	d. 15	d. 4	d. 18	d. 9
e. 72	e. 7	e. 56	e. 5	e. 9	e. 7	e. 28	e. 7
f. 18	f. 8	f. 72	f. 9	f. 2	f. 8	f. 72	f. 1
g. 9	g. 1	g. 24	g. 3	g. 12	g. 5	g. 36	g. 5
h. 8	h. 7	h. 7	h. 4	h. 4	h. 8	h. 14	h. 5
i. 45	i. 9	i. 24	i. 1	i. 35	i. 6	i. 8	i. 6
j. 36	j. 3	j. 30	j. 5	j. 81	j. 5	j. 12	j. 4
k. 14	k. 6	k. 63	k. 3	k. 6	k. 1	k. 56	k. 2
l. 15	l. 4	l. 32	l. 5	l. 24	l. 7	l. 24	l. 7
m. 32	m. 5	m. 36	m. 7	m. 16	m. 3	m. 24	m. 1
n. 15	n. 8	n. 35	n. 9	n. 10	n. 2	n. 35	n. 3
o. 54	o. 6	o. 64	o. 4	o. 54	o. 1	o. 64	o. 5
p. 16	p. 1	p. 6	p. 6	p. 12	p. 6	p. 6	p. 8
q. 21	q. 3	q. 14	q. 2	q. 27	q. 9	q. 21	q. 8
r. 4	r. 9	r. 40	r. 7	r. 24	r. 5	r. 32	r. 8
s. 40	s. 3	s. 54	s. 4	s. 25	s. 5	s. 42	s. 6
t. 81	t. 1	t. 49	t. 6	t. 27	t. 9	t. 49	t. 1

Name ______________________

Solve Two-Step Word Problems

Write an equation and solve the problem.

Show your work.

1. Raul spent 10 minutes doing homework for each of 5 subjects and 15 minutes for another subject. How many minutes did Raul spend on his homework?

   ____

2. At Sonya's cello recital, there were 8 rows of chairs, with 6 chairs in each row. There was a person in each chair, and there were 17 more people standing. How many people were in the audience altogether?

   ____

3. Jana played a game with a deck of cards. She placed the cards on the floor in 3 rows of 10. If the deck has 52 cards, how many cards did Jana leave out?

   ____

4. Mukesh was making 7 salads. He opened a can of olives and put 6 olives on each salad. Then he ate the rest of the olives in the can. If there were 51 olives to start with, how many olives did Mukesh eat?

   ____

5. Peter wallpapered a wall that was 8 feet wide and 9 feet high. He had 28 square feet of wallpaper left over. How many square feet of wallpaper did he start with?

   ____

PATH to FLUENCY What's My Rule?

A function table is a table of ordered pairs. For every input number, there is only one output number. The rule describes what to do to the input number to get the output number.

Write the rule and then complete the function table.

6 **Rule:** ______

Input	Output
7	42
8	___
___	54
6	36
4	24
5	___

7 **Rule:** ______

Input	Output
81	9
45	5
72	___
___	7
27	___
54	6

8 **Rule:** ______

Input	Output
21	7
27	9
___	6
15	___
___	8
9	3

9 **Rule:** ______

Input	Output
5	25
___	40
9	___
3	15
7	35
___	20

Check Understanding

Explain how you chose the rule for the table in Exercise 9.

Name ____________________

PATH to FLUENCY

Play *Division Three-in-a-Row*

Rules for *Division Three-in-a-Row*

Number of players: 2
What You Will Need: Product Cards, one *Three-in-a-Row* Game Grid for each player

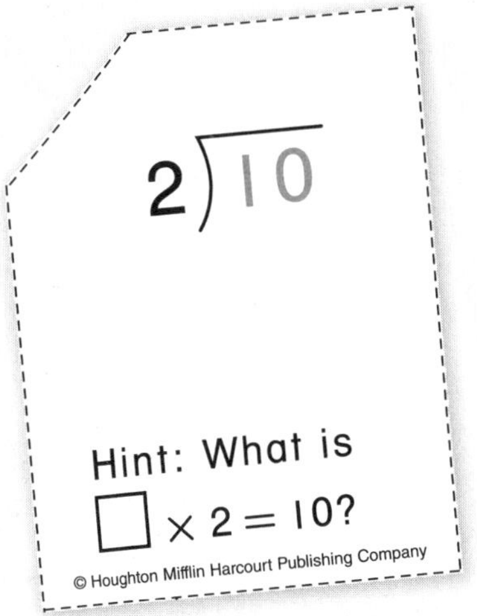

1. Players write a number in each of the squares on their game grids. They may use only numbers from 1 to 9, but they may use the same number more than once.

2. Shuffle the cards. Place them division side up in a stack in the center of the table.

3. Players take turns. On each turn, a player completes the division on the top card and then partners check the answer.

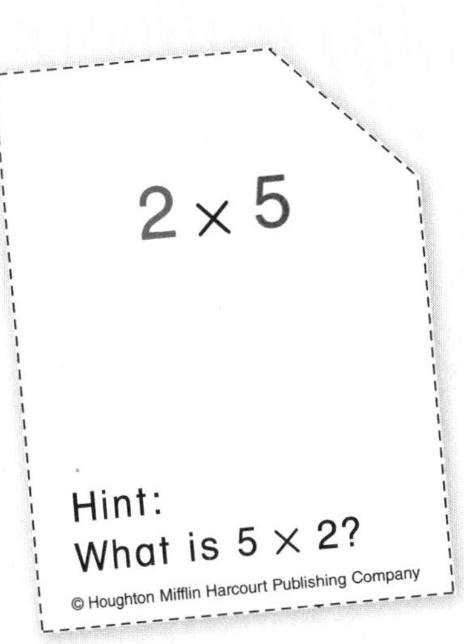

4. For a correct answer, if the quotient is on the game grid, the player puts an X through that grid square. If the answer is wrong, or if the quotient is not on the grid, the player doesn't mark anything. The player puts the card division side up on the bottom of the stack.

5. The first player to mark three squares in a row (horizontally, vertically, or diagonally) wins.

2×2 	$2 \bullet 3$ Hint: What is $3 \cdot 2$? 	$2 * 4$ Hint: What is $4 * 2$? 	2×5 Hint: What is 5×2?
2×6 Hint: What is 6×2? 	$2 \bullet 7$ Hint: What is $7 \cdot 2$? 	$2 * 8$ Hint: What is $8 * 2$? 	2×9 Hint: What is 9×2?
5×2 Hint: What is 2×5? 	$5 \bullet 3$ Hint: What is $3 \cdot 5$? 	$5 * 4$ Hint: What is $4 * 5$? 	5×5
5×6 Hint: What is 6×5? 	$5 \bullet 7$ Hint: What is $7 \cdot 5$? 	$5 * 8$ Hint: What is $8 * 5$? 	5×9 Hint: What is 9×5?

$2\overline{)10}$

Hint: What is

☐ × 2 = 10?

$2\overline{)8}$

Hint: What is

☐ × 2 = 8?

$2\overline{)6}$

Hint: What is

☐ × 2 = 6?

$2\overline{)4}$

Hint: What is

☐ × 2 = 4?

$2\overline{)18}$

Hint: What is

☐ × 2 = 18?

$2\overline{)16}$

Hint: What is

☐ × 2 = 16?

$2\overline{)14}$

Hint: What is

☐ × 2 = 14?

$2\overline{)12}$

Hint: What is

☐ × 2 = 12?

$5\overline{)25}$

Hint: What is

☐ × 5 = 25?

$5\overline{)20}$

Hint: What is

☐ × 5 = 20?

$5\overline{)15}$

Hint: What is

☐ × 5 = 15?

$5\overline{)10}$

Hint: What is

☐ × 5 = 10?

$5\overline{)45}$

Hint: What is

☐ × 5 = 45?

$5\overline{)40}$

Hint: What is

☐ × 5 = 40?

$5\overline{)35}$

Hint: What is

☐ × 5 = 35?

$5\overline{)30}$

Hint: What is

☐ × 5 = 30?

9×2 Hint: What is 2×9? 	$9 \bullet 3$ Hint: What is $3 \cdot 9$? 	$9 * 4$ Hint: What is $4 * 9$? 	9×5 Hint: What is 5×9?
9×6 Hint: What is 6×9? 	$9 \bullet 7$ Hint: What is $7 \cdot 9$? 	$9 * 8$ Hint: What is $8 * 9$? 	9×9
$\times$	$\bullet$	$*$	$\times$
$\times$	$\bullet$	$*$	$\times$

You can write any numbers on the last 8 cards. Use them to practice difficult problems or if you lose a card.

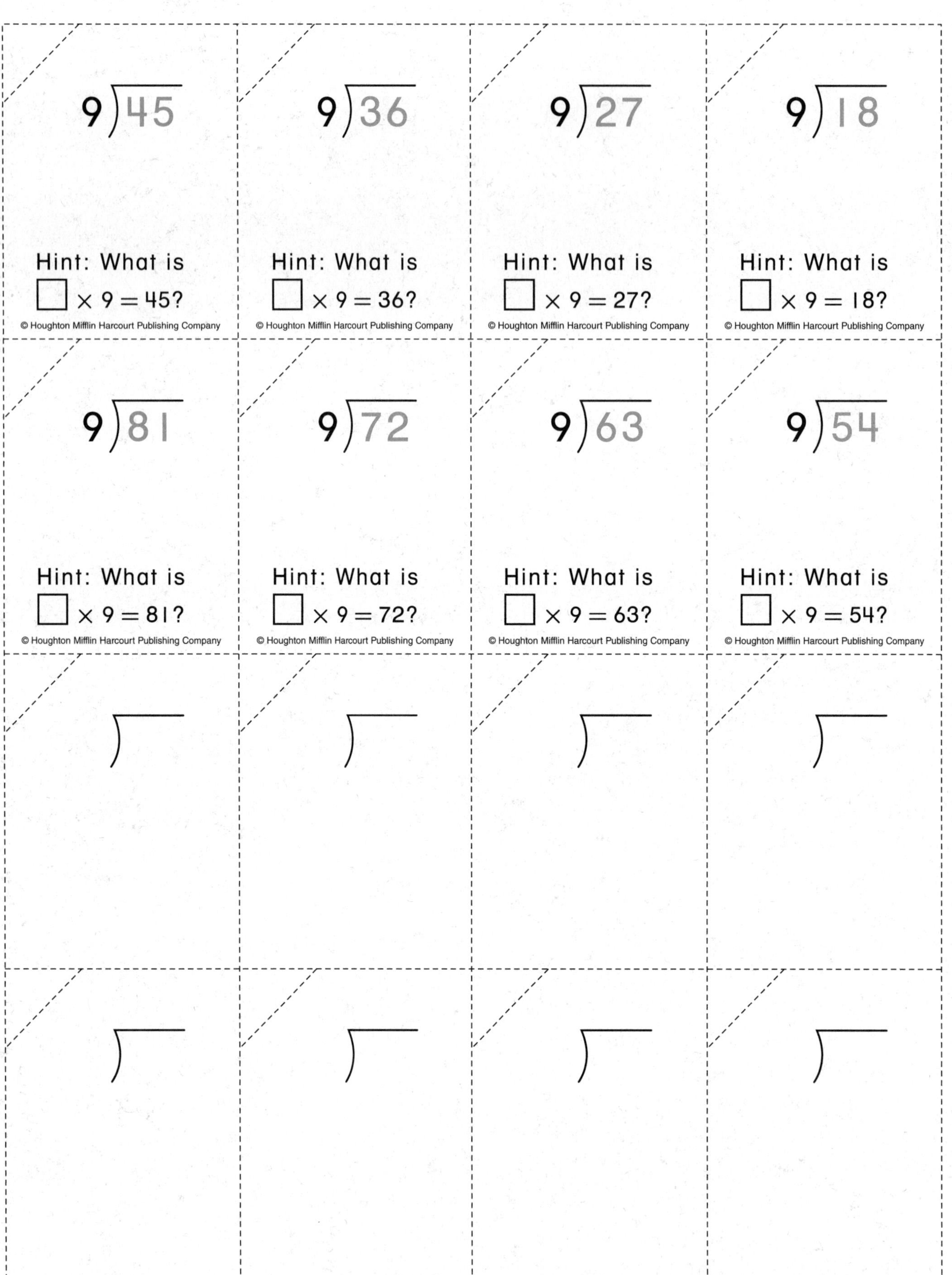

You can write any numbers on the last 8 cards. Use them to practice difficult problems or if you lose a card.

3×2 Hint: What is 2×3? 	$3 \bullet 3$ 	$3 * 4$ Hint: What is $4 * 3$? 	3×5 Hint: What is 5×3?
3×6 Hint: What is 6×3? 	$3 \bullet 7$ Hint: What is $7 \cdot 3$? 	$3 * 8$ Hint: What is $8 * 3$? 	3×9 Hint: What is 9×3?
4×2 Hint: What is 2×4? 	$4 \bullet 3$ Hint: What is $3 \cdot 4$? 	$4 * 4$ 	4×5 Hint: What is 5×4?
4×6 Hint: What is 6×4? 	$4 \bullet 7$ Hint: What is $7 \cdot 4$? 	$4 * 8$ Hint: What is $8 * 4$? 	4×9 Hint: What is 9×4?

$3\overline{)15}$

Hint: What is
☐ × 3 = 15?

$3\overline{)12}$

Hint: What is
☐ × 3 = 12?

$3\overline{)9}$

Hint: What is
☐ × 3 = 9?

$3\overline{)6}$

Hint: What is
☐ × 3 = 6?

$3\overline{)27}$

Hint: What is
☐ × 3 = 27?

$3\overline{)24}$

Hint: What is
☐ × 3 = 24?

$3\overline{)21}$

Hint: What is
☐ × 3 = 21?

$3\overline{)18}$

Hint: What is
☐ × 3 = 18?

$4\overline{)20}$

Hint: What is
☐ × 4 = 20?

$4\overline{)16}$

Hint: What is
☐ × 4 = 16?

$4\overline{)12}$

Hint: What is
☐ × 4 = 12?

$4\overline{)8}$

Hint: What is
☐ × 4 = 8?

$4\overline{)36}$

Hint: What is
☐ × 4 = 36?

$4\overline{)32}$

Hint: What is
☐ × 4 = 32?

$4\overline{)28}$

Hint: What is
☐ × 4 = 28?

$4\overline{)24}$

Hint: What is
☐ × 4 = 24?

6×2 Hint: What is 2×6? © Houghton Mifflin Harcourt Publishing Company	$6 \bullet 3$ Hint: What is $3 \cdot 6$? © Houghton Mifflin Harcourt Publishing Company	$6 * 4$ Hint: What is $4 * 6$? © Houghton Mifflin Harcourt Publishing Company	6×5 Hint: What is 5×6? © Houghton Mifflin Harcourt Publishing Company
6×6 © Houghton Mifflin Harcourt Publishing Company	$6 \bullet 7$ Hint: What is $7 \cdot 6$? © Houghton Mifflin Harcourt Publishing Company	$6 * 8$ Hint: What is $8 * 6$? © Houghton Mifflin Harcourt Publishing Company	6×9 Hint: What is 9×6? © Houghton Mifflin Harcourt Publishing Company
7×2 Hint: What is 2×7? © Houghton Mifflin Harcourt Publishing Company	$7 \bullet 3$ Hint: What is $3 \cdot 7$? © Houghton Mifflin Harcourt Publishing Company	$7 * 4$ Hint: What is $4 * 7$? © Houghton Mifflin Harcourt Publishing Company	7×5 Hint: What is 5×7? © Houghton Mifflin Harcourt Publishing Company
7×6 Hint: What is 6×7? © Houghton Mifflin Harcourt Publishing Company	$7 \bullet 7$ © Houghton Mifflin Harcourt Publishing Company	$7 * 8$ Hint: What is $8 * 7$? © Houghton Mifflin Harcourt Publishing Company	7×9 Hint: What is 9×7? © Houghton Mifflin Harcourt Publishing Company

$6\overline{)30}$

Hint: What is

☐ × 6 = 30?

$6\overline{)24}$

Hint: What is

☐ × 6 = 24?

$6\overline{)18}$

Hint: What is

☐ × 6 = 18?

$6\overline{)12}$

Hint: What is

☐ × 6 = 12?

$6\overline{)54}$

Hint: What is

☐ × 6 = 54?

$6\overline{)48}$

Hint: What is

☐ × 6 = 48?

$6\overline{)42}$

Hint: What is

☐ × 6 = 42?

$6\overline{)36}$

Hint: What is

☐ × 6 = 36?

$7\overline{)35}$

Hint: What is

☐ × 7 = 35?

$7\overline{)28}$

Hint: What is

☐ × 7 = 28?

$7\overline{)21}$

Hint: What is

☐ × 7 = 21?

$7\overline{)14}$

Hint: What is

☐ × 7 = 14?

$7\overline{)63}$

Hint: What is

☐ × 7 = 63?

$7\overline{)56}$

Hint: What is

☐ × 7 = 56?

$7\overline{)49}$

Hint: What is

☐ × 7 = 49?

$7\overline{)42}$

Hint: What is

☐ × 7 = 42?

8×2 Hint: What is 2×8? 	$8 \bullet 3$ Hint: What is $3 \cdot 8$? 	$8 * 4$ Hint: What is $4 * 8$? 	8×5 Hint: What is 5×8?
8×6 Hint: What is 6×8? 	$8 \bullet 7$ Hint: What is $7 \cdot 8$? 	$8 * 8$ 	8×9 Hint: What is 9×8?
$\times$	$\bullet$	$*$	$\times$
$\times$	$\bullet$	$*$	$\times$

You can write any numbers on the last 8 cards. Use them to practice difficult problems or if you lose a card.

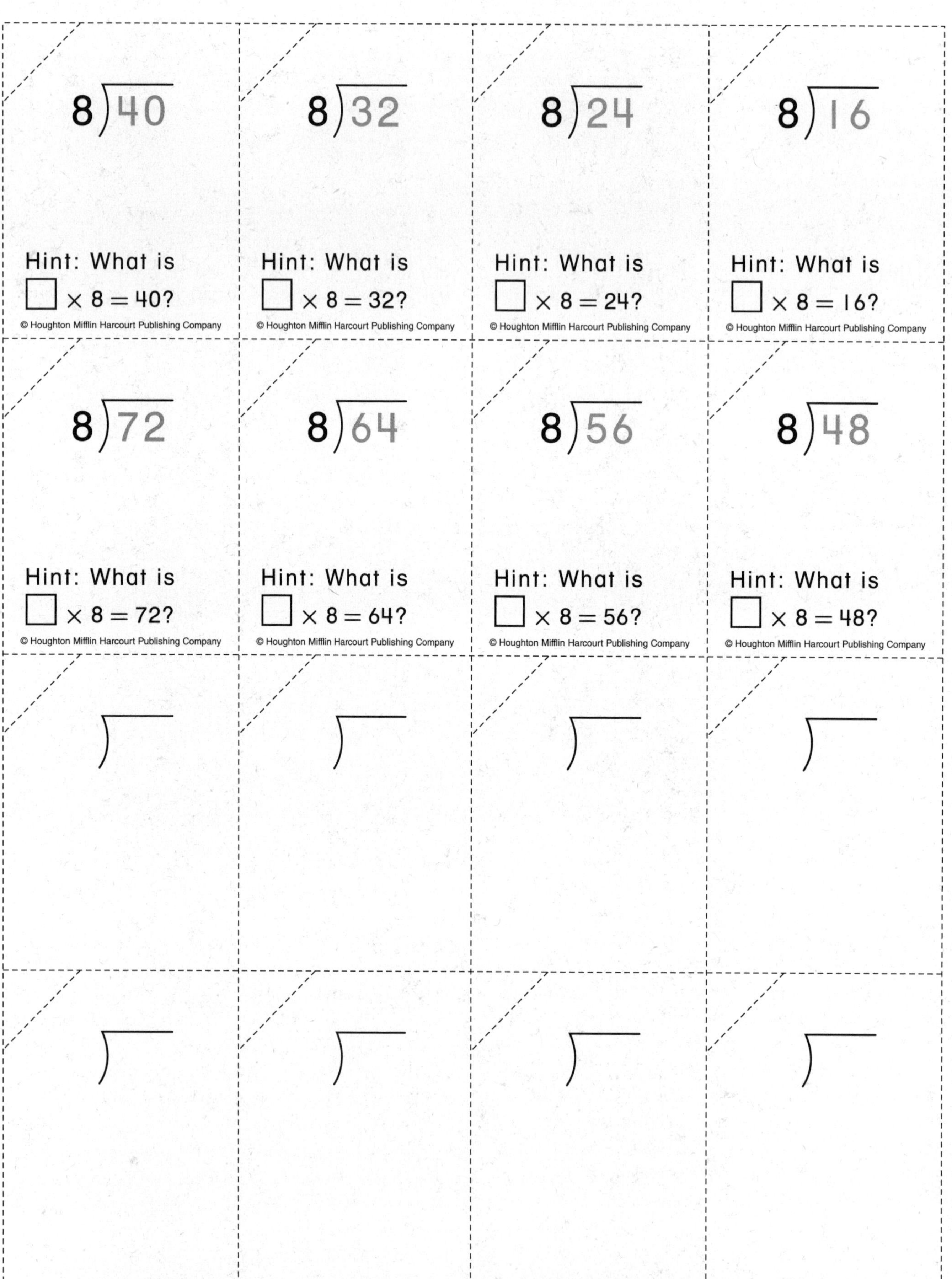

You can write any numbers on the last 8 cards. Use them to practice difficult problems or if you lose a card.

Name ______________________

PATH to FLUENCY Diagnostic Checkup for Basic Multiplication

1. 7 × 5 = ___
2. 2 × 3 = ___
3. 9 × 9 = ___
4. 9 × 6 = ___
5. 6 × 2 = ___
6. 3 × 0 = ___
7. 3 × 4 = ___
8. 6 × 8 = ___
9. 5 × 9 = ___
10. 3 × 3 = ___
11. 2 × 9 = ___
12. 5 × 7 = ___
13. 6 × 10 = ___
14. 4 × 1 = ___
15. 6 × 4 = ___
16. 4 × 8 = ___
17. 5 × 2 = ___
18. 1 × 3 = ___
19. 3 × 9 = ___
20. 7 × 6 = ___
21. 7 × 2 = ___
22. 9 × 0 = ___
23. 8 × 9 = ___
24. 8 × 7 = ___
25. 8 × 10 = ___
26. 6 × 3 = ___
27. 4 × 4 = ___
28. 3 × 8 = ___
29. 5 × 5 = ___
30. 6 × 0 = ___
31. 7 × 9 = ___
32. 6 × 6 = ___
33. 9 × 2 = ___
34. 8 × 3 = ___
35. 5 × 4 = ___
36. 7 × 7 = ___
37. 5 × 10 = ___
38. 5 × 1 = ___
39. 10 × 9 = ___
40. 5 × 6 = ___
41. 6 × 5 = ___
42. 9 × 3 = ___
43. 4 × 2 = ___
44. 7 × 8 = ___
45. 8 × 2 = ___
46. 5 × 0 = ___
47. 4 × 9 = ___
48. 6 × 7 = ___
49. 9 × 5 = ___
50. 6 × 1 = ___
51. 7 × 4 = ___
52. 9 × 8 = ___
53. 4 × 10 = ___
54. 5 × 3 = ___
55. 6 × 9 = ___
56. 8 × 6 = ___
57. 8 × 5 = ___
58. 8 × 0 = ___
59. 8 × 4 = ___
60. 4 × 7 = ___
61. 3 × 5 = ___
62. 7 × 3 = ___
63. 5 × 9 = ___
64. 3 × 6 = ___
65. 7 × 10 = ___
66. 8 × 1 = ___
67. 0 × 4 = ___
68. 9 × 7 = ___
69. 4 × 5 = ___
70. 4 × 3 = ___
71. 1 × 9 = ___
72. 8 × 8 = ___

Name ____________________

PATH to FLUENCY Diagnostic Checkup for Basic Division

1. $12 \div 2 =$ ___	2. $8 \div 1 =$ ___	3. $36 \div 9 =$ ___	4. $35 \div 7 =$ ___
5. $20 \div 5 =$ ___	6. $24 \div 3 =$ ___	7. $12 \div 4 =$ ___	8. $6 \div 6 =$ ___
9. $6 \div 2 =$ ___	10. $3 \div 3 =$ ___	11. $18 \div 9 =$ ___	12. $63 \div 7 =$ ___
13. $20 \div 10 =$ ___	14. $0 \div 1 =$ ___	15. $40 \div 4 =$ ___	16. $48 \div 8 =$ ___
17. $18 \div 2 =$ ___	18. $6 \div 3 =$ ___	19. $8 \div 4 =$ ___	20. $36 \div 6 =$ ___
21. $8 \div 2 =$ ___	22. $9 \div 1 =$ ___	23. $9 \div 9 =$ ___	24. $56 \div 7 =$ ___
25. $40 \div 5 =$ ___	26. $9 \div 3 =$ ___	27. $36 \div 4 =$ ___	28. $56 \div 8 =$ ___
29. $80 \div 10 =$ ___	30. $7 \div 1 =$ ___	31. $45 \div 9 =$ ___	32. $48 \div 6 =$ ___
33. $5 \div 5 =$ ___	34. $30 \div 3 =$ ___	35. $16 \div 4 =$ ___	36. $72 \div 8 =$ ___
37. $10 \div 2 =$ ___	38. $1 \div 1 =$ ___	39. $54 \div 9 =$ ___	40. $21 \div 7 =$ ___
41. $25 \div 5 =$ ___	42. $15 \div 3 =$ ___	43. $32 \div 4 =$ ___	44. $24 \div 8 =$ ___
45. $90 \div 10 =$ ___	46. $18 \div 3 =$ ___	47. $63 \div 9 =$ ___	48. $54 \div 6 =$ ___
49. $45 \div 5 =$ ___	50. $6 \div 1 =$ ___	51. $20 \div 4 =$ ___	52. $49 \div 7 =$ ___
53. $15 \div 5 =$ ___	54. $0 \div 3 =$ ___	55. $28 \div 4 =$ ___	56. $30 \div 6 =$ ___
57. $16 \div 2 =$ ___	58. $21 \div 3 =$ ___	59. $81 \div 9 =$ ___	60. $64 \div 8 =$ ___
61. $30 \div 5 =$ ___	62. $12 \div 3 =$ ___	63. $27 \div 9 =$ ___	64. $42 \div 7 =$ ___
65. $40 \div 10 =$ ___	66. $10 \div 1 =$ ___	67. $24 \div 4 =$ ___	68. $18 \div 6 =$ ___
69. $35 \div 5 =$ ___	70. $27 \div 3 =$ ___	71. $72 \div 9 =$ ___	72. $42 \div 6 =$ ___

Name ______

PATH to FLUENCY Patterns With 10s, 5s, and 9s

These multiplication tables help us see some patterns that make recalling basic multiplications easier.

1. What pattern do you see in the 10s count-bys?

______

2. Look at the 5s and the 10s together. What patterns do you see?

______

3. Look at the 9s count-bys. How does each 9s count-by relate to the 10s count-by in the next row?

______

How could this pattern help you remember the 9s count-bys?

______

______

4. Look at the digits in each 9s product. What is the sum of the digits in each 9s product?

______

How could you use this knowledge to check your answers when you multiply by 9?

______

5s and 10s

×	1	2	3	4	5	6	7	8	9	10
1	1	2	3	4	5	6	7	8	9	10
2	2	4	6	8	10	12	14	16	18	20
3	3	6	9	12	15	18	21	24	27	30
4	4	8	12	16	20	24	28	32	36	40
5	5	10	15	20	25	30	35	40	45	50
6	6	12	18	24	30	36	42	48	54	60
7	7	14	21	28	35	42	49	56	63	70
8	8	16	24	32	40	48	56	64	72	80
9	9	18	27	36	45	54	63	72	81	90
10	10	20	30	40	50	60	70	80	90	100

9s

×	1	2	3	4	5	6	7	8	9	10
1	1	2	3	4	5	6	7	8	9	10
2	2	4	6	8	10	12	14	16	18	20
3	3	6	9	12	15	18	21	24	27	30
4	4	8	12	16	20	24	28	32	36	40
5	5	10	15	20	25	30	35	40	45	50
6	6	12	18	24	30	36	42	48	54	60
7	7	14	21	28	35	42	49	56	63	70
8	8	16	24	32	40	48	56	64	72	80
9	9	18	27	36	45	54	63	72	81	90
10	10	20	30	40	50	60	70	80	90	100

PATH to FLUENCY Patterns With Other Numbers

On these grids, find patterns with 2s, 4s, 6s, and 8s.

5 Look at the ones digits in all the 2s, 4s, 6s, and 8s count-bys. What pattern do you see?

____

6 Are the 2s, 4s, 6s, and 8s products even numbers or odd numbers?

____

2s, 4s, 6s, 8s

×	1	2	3	4	5	6	7	8	9
1	1	2	3	4	5	6	7	8	9
2	2	4	6	8	10	12	14	16	18
3	3	6	9	12	15	18	21	24	27
4	4	8	12	16	20	24	28	32	36
5	5	10	15	20	25	30	35	40	45
6	6	12	18	24	30	36	42	48	54
7	7	14	21	28	35	42	49	56	63
8	8	16	24	32	40	48	56	64	72
9	9	18	27	36	45	54	63	72	81
10	10	20	30	40	50	60	70	80	90

On the multiplication table labeled Doubles, look for rows that have products that are double the products in other rows.

7 Name the factors that have products that are double the products of another factor.

____

____

____

____

Doubles

×	1	2	3	4	5	6	7	8	9
1	1	2	3	4	5	6	7	8	9
2	2	4	6	8	10	12	14	16	18
3	3	6	9	12	15	18	21	24	27
4	4	8	12	16	20	24	28	32	36
5	5	10	15	20	25	30	35	40	45
6	6	12	18	24	30	36	42	48	54
7	7	14	21	28	35	42	49	56	63
8	8	16	24	32	40	48	56	64	72
9	9	18	27	36	45	54	63	72	81
10	10	20	30	40	50	60	70	80	90

8 How can you find 6×8 if you know 3×8?

____

Rewrite each list so that the count-by list is correct.

9 4, 8, 12, 18, 20, 24, 28 _______________

10 18, 28, 36, 45, 54, 63, 70 _______________

Check Understanding

Cross out the number that does not belong in this count-by list: 16, 24, 28, 32, 40, 48, 56, 64, 72.

Name ______________________

Math and Recipes

The animal keepers at zoos feed and care for the animals. The animal keepers consult a zoo nutritionist to decide what and how much to feed the animals. In the zoo kitchens there are recipes posted for each type of animal such as the one shown below.

Gorilla's Zoo Stew

32 carrots	8 yams
32 oranges	8 eggs
24 apples	16 bananas
64 ounces Monkey's Chow	72 grapes
48 ounces primate-diet food	56 stalks of celery
8 heads lettuce, any variety	bales of hydroponic grass to taste

Toss all ingredients lightly. Divide among 8 trays.

The recipe makes 8 gorilla servings.

Write an equation and solve the problem.

1. How much of each ingredient is in 1 gorilla serving?

____

____

____

____

2. How much of each ingredient in the Gorilla's Zoo Stew recipe is needed to serve 6 gorillas?

____

____

____

____

Favorite Zoo Animals

The students in third grade took a field trip to a zoo. The students were asked to name their favorite zoo animal. The pictograph below shows the animals the students chose.

Favorite Zoo Animal	
Bear	☺ ☺ ☺ ☺ ☺ ☺ ☺
Elephant	☺ ☺ ☺ ☺ ☺ ☺ ☺ ☺
Giraffe	☺ ☺ ☺ ☺
Gorilla	☺ ☺ ☺ ☺ ☺ ☺
Lion	☺ ☺

Each ☺ stands for 7 students.

3 Use the information in the pictograph to complete the chart to show the number of students that chose each zoo animal.

Favorite Zoo Animal	
Zoo Animal	**Number of Students**
Bear	
Elephant	
Giraffe	
Gorilla	
Lion	

Solve.

4 If 63 students chose a zebra as their favorite zoo animal, how many symbols would you use to show that on the pictograph?

____

Unit 2
Quick Quiz 2

Name ______________________ Date ______________

Solve.

1. $6 + 8 \div 4 = \square$

   $\square = $ ______

2. $3 \times 40 = \square$

   $\square = $ ______

Write an equation and solve the problem.

Show your work.

3. The pet shop had 8 cages of mice, with 4 mice in each cage. 5 mice escaped. How many mice were left in cages?

   ____

4. Ingrid baked 47 cookies, but 5 were burned and thrown away. The rest were shared equally among 6 people. How many cookies did each person get?

   ____

5. Maria had \$4. Then she earned \$7 each day for 8 days. How much money does she have now?

   ____

Fluency Check 2 Name Date

PATH to FLUENCY

Subtract.

1. $8 - 6 = \square$
2. $6 - 4 = \square$
3. $5 - 5 = \square$
4. $11 - 6 = \square$
5. $12 - 8 = \square$
6. $10 - 1 = \square$
7. $13 - 8 = \square$
8. $14 - 7 = \square$
9. $15 - 9 = \square$
10. $\begin{array}{r} 17 \\ -\ 8 \\ \hline \end{array}$
11. $\begin{array}{r} 12 \\ -\ 6 \\ \hline \end{array}$
12. $\begin{array}{r} 15 \\ -\ 7 \\ \hline \end{array}$
13. $\begin{array}{r} 19 \\ -\ 9 \\ \hline \end{array}$
14. $\begin{array}{r} 14 \\ -\ 9 \\ \hline \end{array}$
15. $\begin{array}{r} 16 \\ -\ 8 \\ \hline \end{array}$

Name ____________________ Date ____________

Solve.

1. Write the numbers that complete the unknown number puzzle.

3 5 8 10 12 24 54

×	9		2
6		18	
	45	15	◯
	72	24	16

Explain how you found the number in the circle.

2. There are 56 books on a library cart. Each student helper puts 7 books on a shelf. How many student helpers are there?

For numbers 2a–2d, choose Yes or No to tell whether the equation could be used to solve the problem.

2a. $56 \times 7 = \square$ ○ Yes ○ No

2b. $56 \div 7 = \square$ ○ Yes ○ No

2c. $7 \times \square = 56$ ○ Yes ○ No

2d. $7 \div \square = 56$ ○ Yes ○ No

Name ______________________ Date ______________

3 Raul makes a sign for the school fair. It has a length of 9 inches and a width of 8 inches. What is the area of the sign?

Draw a rectangle to help solve the problem. Label your drawing.

Write an equation to solve the problem.

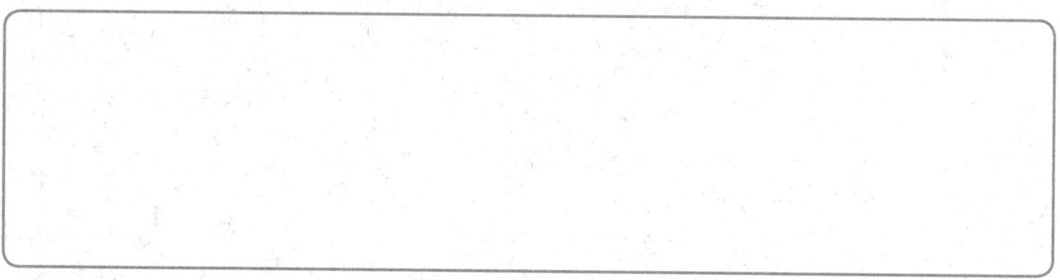

Area of the sign: __________ square inches

4 For numbers 4a–4c, select True or False for each statement.

4a. The first step to solve $3 + 2 \times 4$ is $3 + 2$. ○ True ○ False

4b. The first step to solve $5 \times 4 \div 2$ is 5×4. ○ True ○ False

4c. The first step to solve $(9 - 6) \div 3$ is $9 - 6$. ○ True ○ False

5 Write a problem that can be solved using the given equation. Then solve.

$7 \times 6 = \blacksquare$

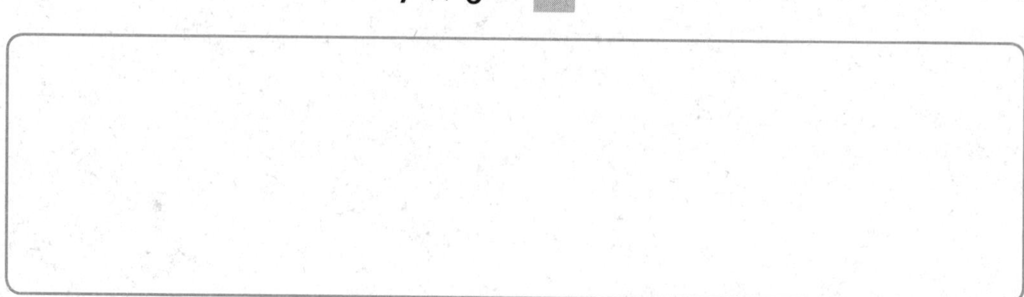

Solution: ______________ tickets

Name ______________________ Date ______________________

6 Select the equation below where the unknown number is 8. Select all that apply.

Ⓐ $7 \times \square = 63$

Ⓑ $4 \times \square = 32$

Ⓒ $36 \div 4 = \square$

Ⓓ $\square \times 9 = 72$

Ⓔ $24 \div \square = 3$

Ⓕ $18 \div 2 = \square$

7 For numbers 7a–7d, choose Yes or No to tell whether the product is correct.

7a. $3 \times 30 = 900$ ○ Yes ○ No

7b. $5 \times 40 = 200$ ○ Yes ○ No

7c. $2 \times 40 = 800$ ○ Yes ○ No

7d. $9 \times 60 = 540$ ○ Yes ○ No

8 Carrie finds 7 seashells at the beach. Her brother finds 8 seashells. They divide the seashells equally among 3 people. How many seashells did each person get? Write an equation to solve the problem.

Equation: ______________________

__________ seashells

Name ______________________ Date ______________

9 A toy store sells 7 different model cars. Each model car comes in 5 different colors. How many different model cars are there?

Part A

Solve the problem.

_______ different model cars

Part B

Choose the type of problem and the operation you use to solve.

The type is [array | equal groups | area]. The operation is [multiplication | division].

Write another problem that is the same type.

10 Write a question for the given information. Then write an equation and solve.

A museum has 297 visitors on Friday. It has 468 visitors on Saturday.

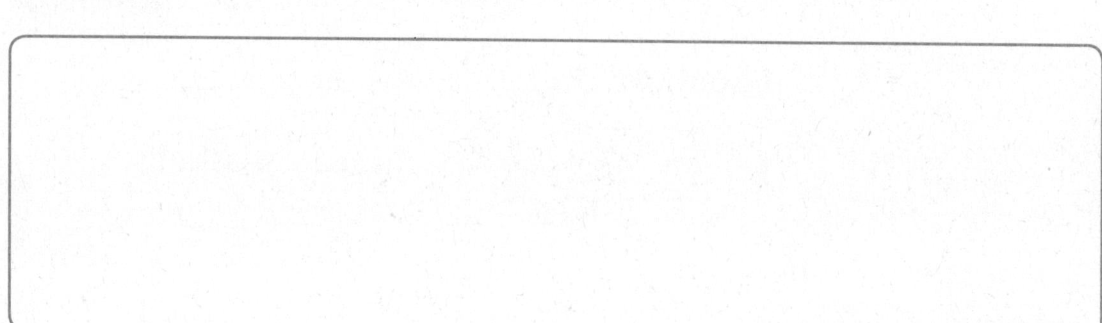

Solution: ______________________ visitors

Name ______________________ Date ______________

11 How can you use a pattern to find 6×9 if you know 3×9? Complete the given part of the multiplication table to help you explain.

×	1	2	3	4	5	6	7	8	9
3									
6									

12 Select the equations that show square numbers. Select all that apply.

Ⓐ $2 \times 5 = 10$

Ⓑ $4 \times 4 = 16$

Ⓒ $8 \times 8 = 64$

Ⓓ $6 \times 6 = 36$

Ⓔ $8 \times 4 = 32$

Ⓕ $5 \times 5 = 25$

Draw a picture for one of the equations you chose. Explain why it is a square number.

Name ____________________ Date ____________________

13 Read the problem. Write the first step question and answer. Then write an equation to solve the problem.

A school buys games for 6 classrooms. The school buys 3 board games, 4 puzzle games, and 1 video game for each classroom. How many games does the school buy?

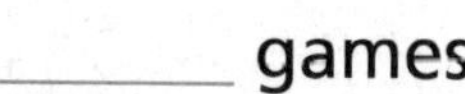 games

14 Draw a line to match each expression on the left with an expression on the right that has the same value.

$2 \times 4 \times 4$ •	• 5×6
7×7 •	• $7 \times 5 + 7 \times 2$
$2 + 2 \times 4$ •	• $2 + 2$
$5 \times 3 \times 2$ •	• 8×4
$8 \div 4 + 2$ •	• $2 + 8$

15 Choose the equations that make the statements true.

You know that [$3 \times 9 = 27$ / $3 \times 5 = 15$ / $8 \times 6 = 48$ / $4 \times 7 = 28$]. So, you know that [$24 \div 3 = 8$ / $18 \div 9 = 2$ / $36 \div 6 = 6$ / $48 \div 8 = 6$].

Name ________________________________ Date ____________

Play a Target Game

The object of this target game is to score 100 points, or as close to 100 points as possible without going over.

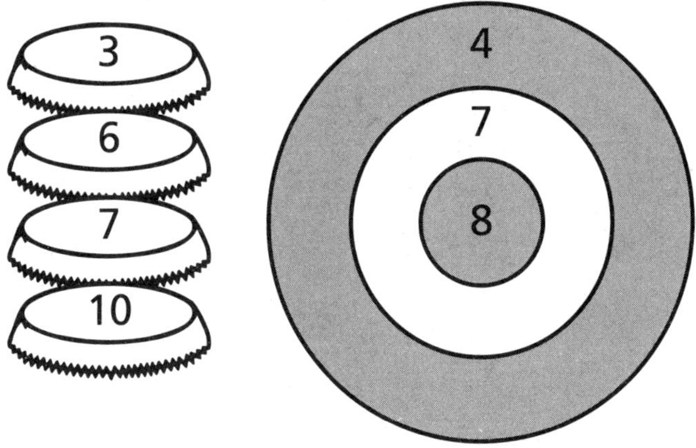

- You may drop two, three, or four bottle caps onto the target. To calculate the points for each drop, multiply the points on the cap by the points on the ring. For example, if the 3 cap lands on the 4 ring, the score would be $3 \times 4 = 12$.
- To find your final score, add the points for all your drops.

  Example: If the 3 bottle cap lands on the 4 ring, and the 7 bottle cap lands on the 8 ring, you could calculate your score using this equation.

  $(3 \times 4) + (7 \times 8) =$

  $12 \quad + \quad 56 \quad = 68$

- Repeat the process by tossing other caps. Keep track of your scores and your equations for finding your scores.

Name ______________________ Date ____________

1. What is the best possible score you can get with 2 bottle caps? Show your work.

2. How do you know that you found the best possible score with 2 caps? What strategy did you use?

3. What are two different scores you could get with the same 3 caps? Show your work.

4. Can you score exactly 100 points with 3 caps? Show your work. Show your work.

5. Michael says that he can score exactly 100 points with 4 bottle caps. Is that true? Show your work.

Dear Family:

Your child is currently participating in math activities that help him or her to understand place value, rounding, and addition, subtraction, and multiplication of greater numbers.

- **Place Value Drawings:** Students learn to represent numbers with drawings that show how many hundreds, tens, and ones are in the numbers. Hundreds are represented by boxes. Tens are represented by vertical line segments, called ten sticks. Ones are represented by small circles. The drawings are also used to help students understand regrouping in addition and subtraction. Here is a place value drawing for the number 178.

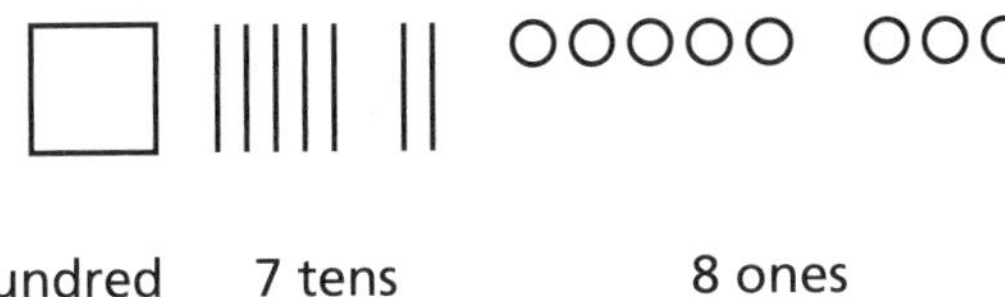

1 hundred 7 tens 8 ones

The 7 ten sticks and 8 circles are grouped in 5s so students can see the quantities easily and avoid errors.

- **Secret Code Cards:** Secret Code Cards are a set of cards for hundreds, tens, and ones. Students learn about place value by assembling the cards to show two- and three-digit numbers. Here is how the number 148 would be assembled.

Hundreds card Tens card Ones card Assembled cards

Estimate Sums and Differences Students learn to estimate sums and differences by rounding numbers. They also use estimates to check that their actual answers are reasonable.

	Rounded to the nearest hundred	Rounded to the nearest ten
493	500	490
129	100	130
+ 369	+ 400	+ 370
991	Estimate: 1,000	Estimate: 990

Addition Methods: Students may use the common U.S. method, referred to as the New Groups Above Method, as well as two alternative methods. In the New Groups Below Method, students add from right to left and write the new ten and new hundred on the line. In the Show All Totals Method, students add in either direction, write partial sums and then add the partial sums to get the total. Students also use proof drawings to demonstrate grouping 10 ones to make a new ten and grouping 10 tens to make a new hundred.

The New Groups Below Method shows the teen number 13 better than the New Groups Above Method, where the 1 and 3 are separated. Also, addition is easier in New Groups Below, where you add the two numbers you see and just add 1.

New Groups Above:

```
  1 ← the new ten
  46
+ 37
  83
```

New Groups Below:

```
  46
+ 37   ← the new ten
  1
  83
  ←
```

Add right to left.

Show All Totals:

```
  46
+ 37
  70
  13   ← the new ten
  83
  →
```

Add left to right.

Proof Drawing:

8 tens 3 ones

the new ten

Subtraction Methods: Students may use the common U.S. method in which the subtraction is done right to left, with the ungrouping done before each column is subtracted. They also learn an alternative method in which all the ungrouping is done *before* the subtracting. If they do all the ungrouping first, students can subtract either from left to right or from right to left.

The Ungroup First Method helps students avoid the common error of subtracting a smaller top number from a larger bottom number.

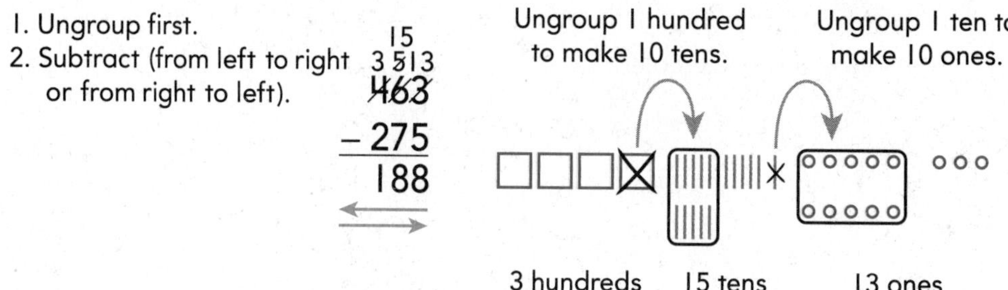

Please contact me if you have any questions or comments.

Thank you.

Sincerely,
Your child's teacher

Estimada familia:

Su niño está participando en actividades matemáticas que le servirán para comprender el valor posicional, el redondeo y la suma, resta y multiplicación de números mayores.

- **Dibujos de valor posicional:** Los estudiantes aprenden a representar números por medio de dibujos que muestran cuántas centenas, decenas y unidades contienen. Las centenas están representadas con casillas, las decenas con segmentos verticales, llamados palitos de decenas, y las unidades con círculos pequeños. Los dibujos también se usan para ayudar a los estudiantes a comprender cómo se reagrupa en la suma y en la resta. Este es un dibujo de valor posicional para el número 178.

1 centena 7 decenas 8 unidades

Los palitos de decenas y los círculos se agrupan en grupos de 5 para que las cantidades se puedan ver más fácilmente y se eviten errores.

- **Tarjetas de código secreto:** Las tarjetas de código secreto son un conjunto de tarjetas con centenas, decenas y unidades. Los estudiantes aprenden acerca del valor posicional organizando las tarjetas de manera que muestren números de dos y de tres dígitos. Así se puede formar el número 148:

Tarjeta de centenas — Tarjeta de decenas — Tarjeta de unidades — Tarjetas organizadas

Estimar sumas y diferencias: Los estudiantes aprenden a estimar sumas y diferencias redondeando números. También usan las estimaciones para comprobar que sus respuestas son razonables.

	Redondear a la centena más próxima	Redondear a la decena más próxima
493	500	490
129	100	130
+ 369	+ 400	+ 370
991	Estimación: 1,000	Estimación: 990

Métodos de suma: Los estudiantes pueden usar el método común de EE. UU., conocido como Grupos nuevos arriba, y otros dos métodos alternativos. En el método de Grupos nuevos abajo, los estudiantes suman de derecha a izquierda y escriben la nueva decena y la nueva centena en el renglón. En el método de Mostrar todos los totales, los estudiantes suman en cualquier dirección, escriben sumas parciales y luego las suman para obtener el total. Los estudiantes también usan dibujos de comprobación para demostrar cómo se agrupan 10 unidades para formar una nueva decena, y 10 decenas para formar una nueva centena.

El método de Grupos nuevos abajo muestra el número 13 mejor que el método de Grupos nuevos arriba, en el que se separan los números 1 y 3. Además, es más fácil sumar con Grupos nuevos abajo, donde se suman los dos números que se ven y simplemente se añade 1.

Grupos nuevos arriba:

```
  1 ← la decena nueva
  46
+ 37
  83
```

Grupos nuevos abajo:

```
  46
+ 37
  1   ← la decena nueva
  83
  ←
```

Sumar de derecha a izquierda.

Mostrar todos los totales:

```
  46
+ 37
  70
  13
  83
  →
```

Sumar de izquierda a derecha.

Dibujo de comprobación:

la decena nueva

8 decenas 3 unidades

Métodos de resta: Los estudiantes pueden usar el método común de EE. UU., en el cual la resta se hace de derecha a izquierda, desagrupando antes de restar cada columna. También aprenden un método alternativo en el que desagrupan todo *antes* de restar. Si los estudiantes desagrupan todo primero, pueden restar de izquierda a derecha o de derecha a izquierda.

El método de Desagrupar primero ayuda a los estudiantes a evitar el error común de restar un número pequeño de arriba, de un número más grande de abajo.

1. Desagrupar primero.
2. Restar (de izquierda a derecha o de derecha a izquierda).

```
   15
  3 5 13
  4̸ 6̸ 3̸
- 2 7 5
  1 8 8
  ←→
```

Desagrupar 1 centena para formar 10 decenas.

Desagrupar 1 decena para formar 10 unidades.

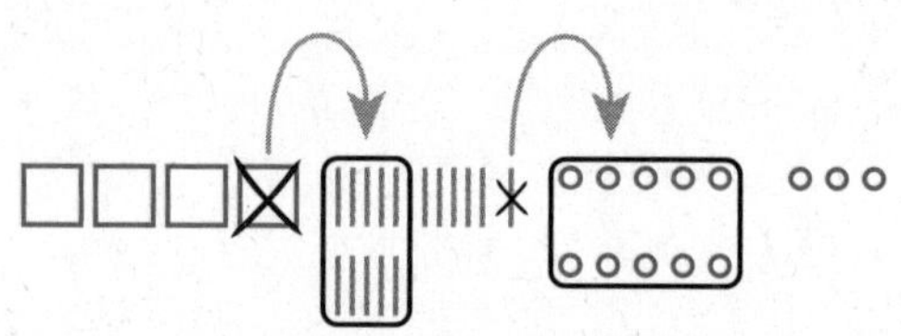

3 centenas 15 decenas 13 unidades

Si tiene alguna pregunta o algún comentario, por favor comuníquese conmigo. Gracias.

Atentamente,
El maestro de su niño

compatible numbers

expanded form

equal (=)

greatest

estimate

hundreds

A number written to show the value of each of its digits.

Examples:

347 = 300 + 40 + 7

347 = 3 hundreds + 4 tens + 7 ones

Numbers that are easy to compute mentally. Compatible numbers can be used to check if answers are reasonable.

Example:

692 + 234

Some compatible numbers for the addends are 700 and 200 or 700 and 234.

56 29 64

64 is the greatest number.

A symbol used to compare two amounts or values. It shows that what is on the left of the sign is equal to or the same value as what is on the right of the sign.

Example:

3,756 = 3,756

3,756 *is equal* to 3,756.

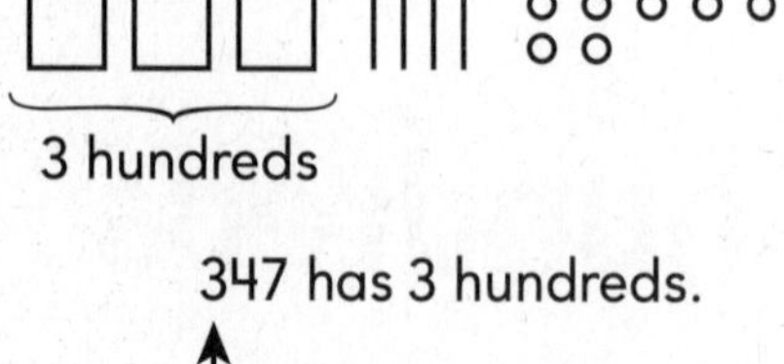

A reasonable guess about how many or about how much.

hundred thousands	**ones**
input-output table	**place value**
least	**round**

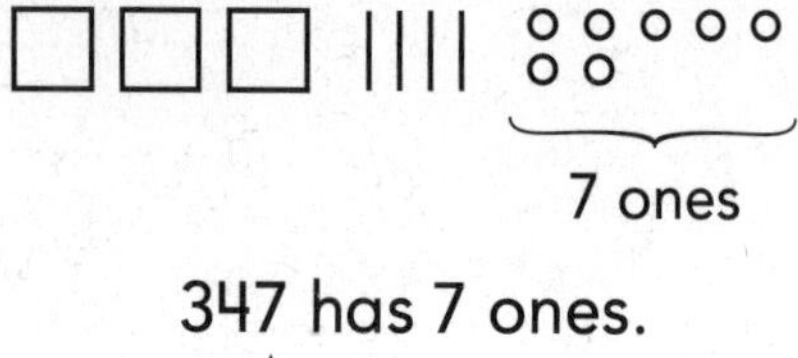

347 has 7 ones.

↑

ones

Hundred Thousands	Ten Thousands	Thousands	Hundreds	Tens	Ones
5	4	6	7	8	2

There are 5 hundred thousands in 546,782.

The value assigned to the place that a digit occupies in a number.

9	6	2
↑	↑	↑
hundreds	tens	ones

A table that displays ordered pairs of numbers that follow a specific rule.

Example:

Rule: Add 4	
Input	**Output**
3	7
5	9
9	13
11	15
15	19

To find about how many or how much by expressing a number to the nearest ten, hundred, thousand, and so on.

72 41 89
41 is the least number.

standard form	**thousands**
tens	**unit square**
ten thousands	

Hundred Thousands	Ten Thousands	Thousands	Hundreds	Tens	Ones
5	4	6	7	8	2

There are 6 thousands in 546,782.

The name of a number written using digits.

Example:
1,829

A square whose area is 1 square unit.

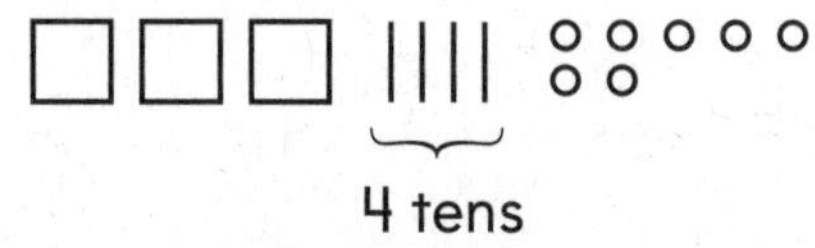

347 has 4 tens.

tens

Hundred Thousands	Ten Thousands	Thousands	Hundreds	Tens	Ones
5	4	6	7	8	2

There are 4 ten thousands in 546,782.

Name ______________________

VOCABULARY
place value

Practice Place Value Drawings to 999

Write the number for each dot drawing.

1 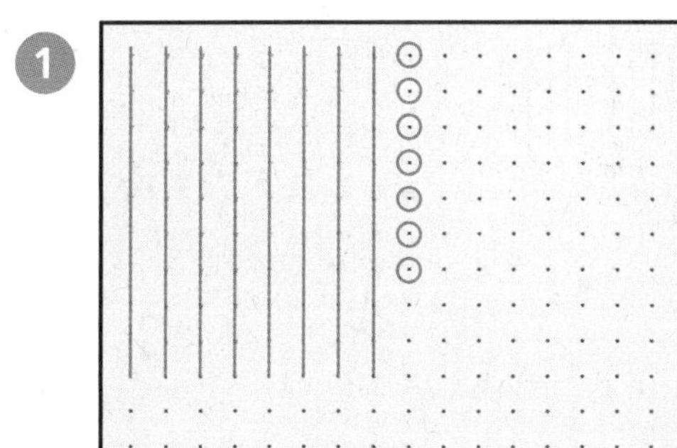

____

2 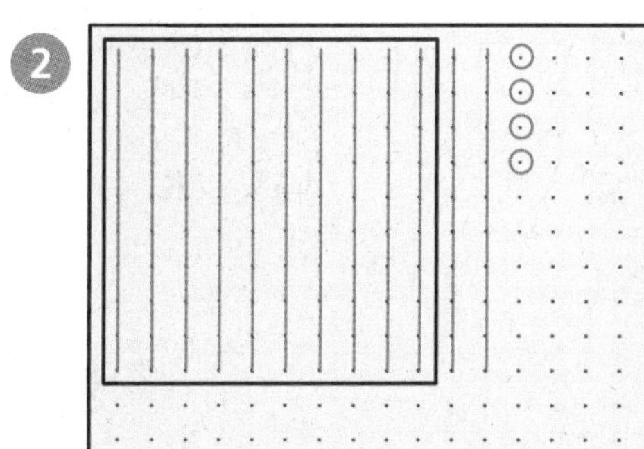

____

Write the number for each place value drawing.

3 □ □ ||||| || ○○○○○ ○○

____

4 □ □ □ ||||| | ○

____

5 □ □ □ □ □ □ || ○○○

____

6 □ □ □ □ |||| ○○○○○ ○○○○

____

Make a place value drawing for each number.

7 86

8 587

Practice with the Thousand Model

Write the number for each place value drawing.

9 ______

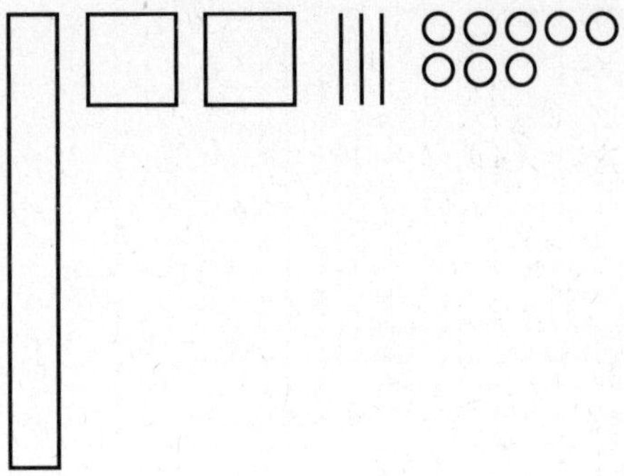

10 ______

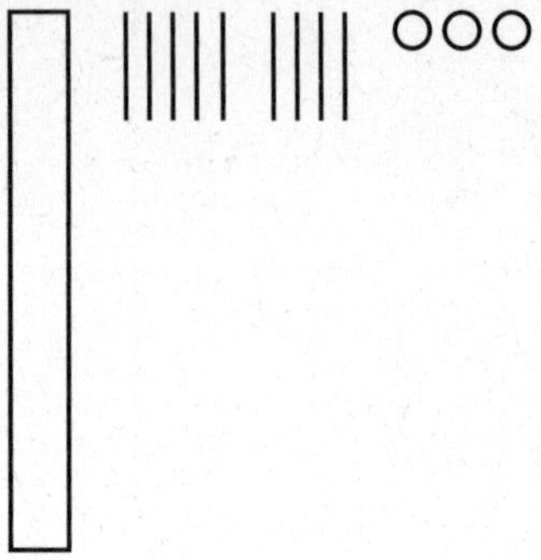

Make a place value drawing for each number.

11 2,368

12 5,017

Write Numbers for Word Names

Write the number for the words.

13 eighty-two ______

14 ninety-nine ______

15 four hundred sixty-seven ______

16 nine hundred six ______

17 one thousand, fifteen ______

18 eight thousand, one hundred twenty ______

Check Understanding

Use place value drawings to show how the numbers 251 and 521 are different.

1	2	10	20
1	2	1 0	2 0

3	4	30	40
3	4	3 0	4 0

5	6	50	60
5	6	5 0	6 0

7	8	70	80
7	8	7 0	8 0

9	90	100
9	9 0	1 0 0

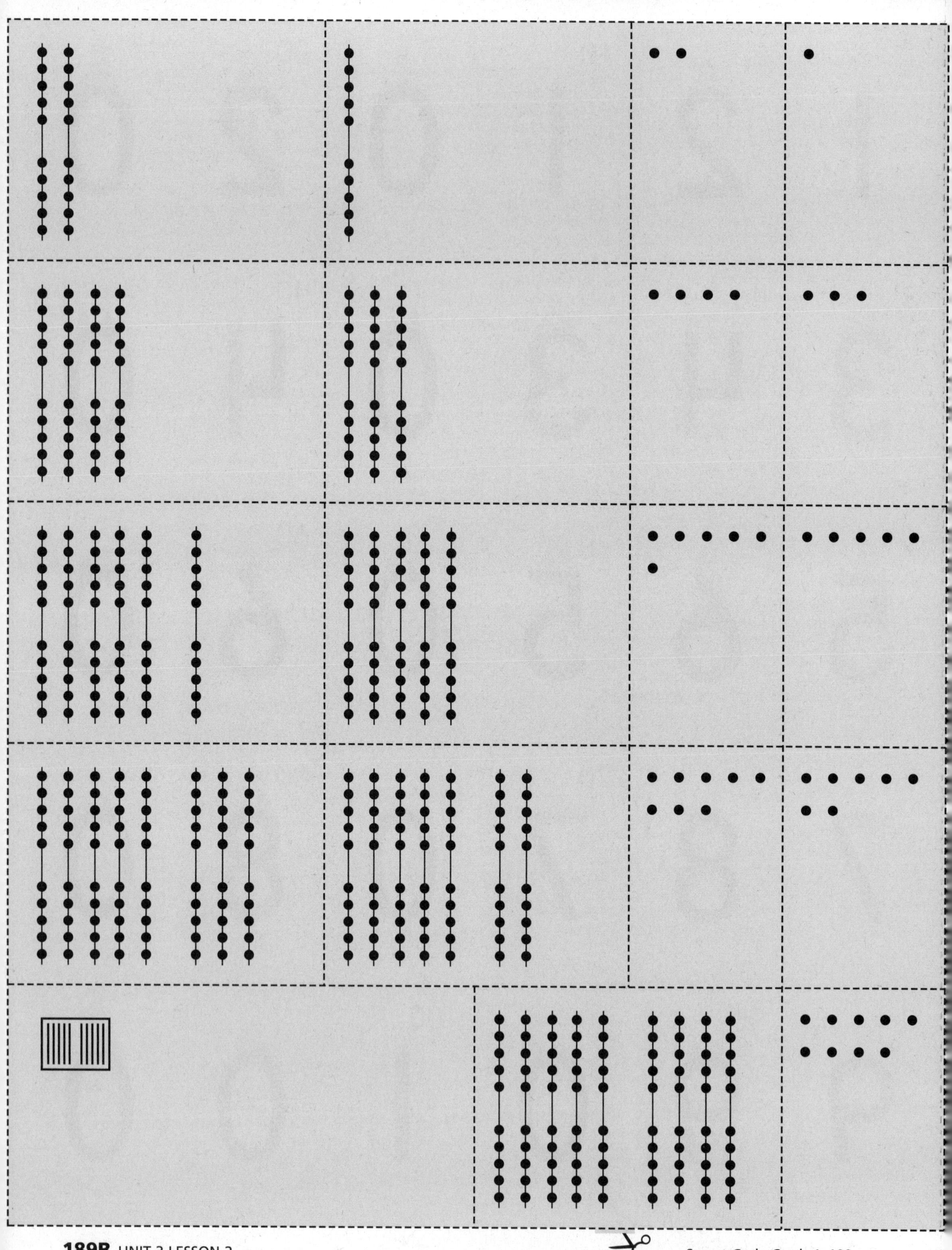

Secret Code Cards 1–100

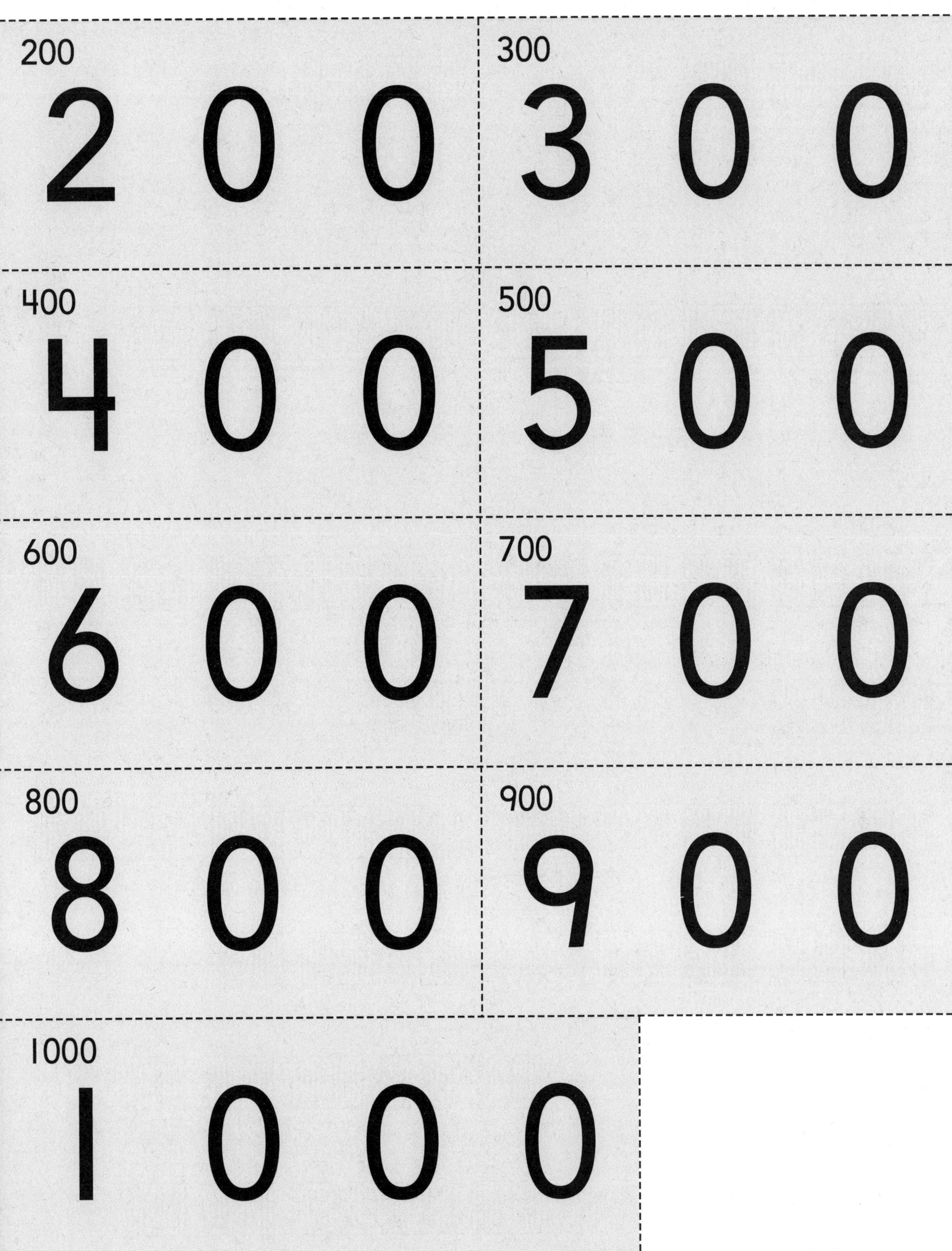
200
2 0 0
300
3 0 0
400
4 0 0
500
5 0 0
600
6 0 0
700
7 0 0
800
8 0 0
900
9 0 0
1000
1 0 0 0

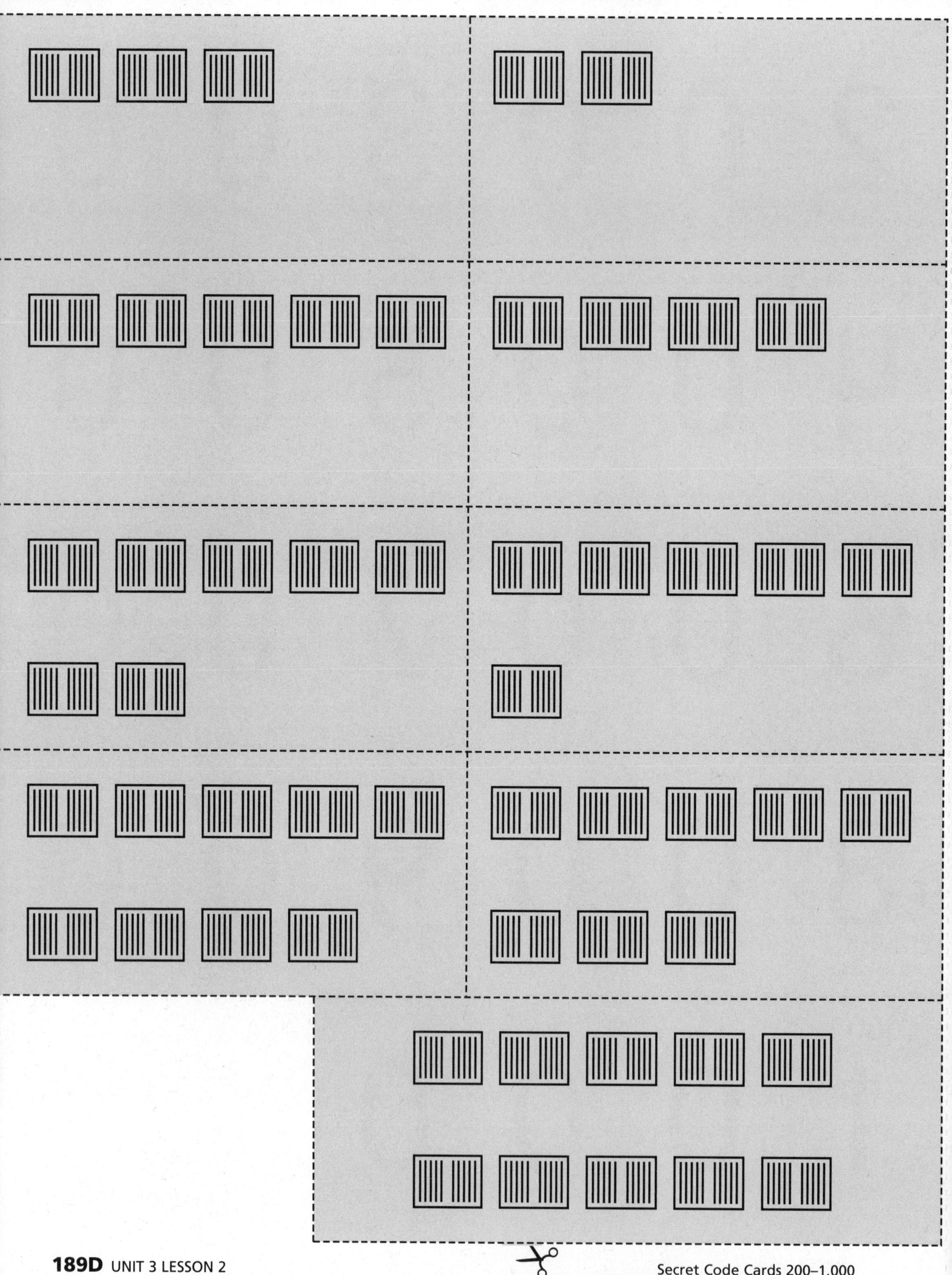

Name ____________________

Build and Discuss Other Numbers

VOCABULARY
hundreds
tens
ones
thousands
expanded form

Write the number.

1. 700 + 20 + 9 = ______

2. 1,000 + 600 + 80 + 4 = ______

3. 400 + 5 = ______

4. 3 **hundreds** + 4 **tens** + 7 **ones** = ______

5. 8 hundreds + 1 ten = ______

6. 1 **thousand** + 9 hundreds + 1 ten + 8 ones = ______

Write the number in expanded form in two ways.

7. 585

______

______

8. 1,367

______

______

9. 213

______

______

What's the Error?

Dear Math Students,

I was asked to build the number 238 with Secret Code Cards. I made the number with these cards.

200 | 3 | 8

238

My teacher says that what I showed is not correct. Can you help me?

Your friend,
Puzzled Penguin

10 Write an answer to Puzzled Penguin.

____

____

____

____

Check Understanding

Use the number 456 to complete the sentences. Build the number with Secret Code Cards to check your answer.

The value of the digit 4 is ________.

The value of the digit 5 is ________.

The value of the digit 6 is ________.

 Name ______________________

VOCABULARY
standard form

Read and Write Numbers

Write the number for the words.

1. two hundred twelve ________
2. two thousand, eight ________
3. nine hundred ninety-one ________
4. six thousand, fifty-one ________
5. four hundred sixteen ________
6. six hundred nine ________
7. nine hundred eighty-seven ________
8. five thousand, thirty ________
9. four thousand, seventeen ________
10. eight thousand, six hundred ________

Write the word name for each number.

11. 783 ____________________
12. 907 ____________________
13. 3,001 ____________________
14. 8,043 ____________________

Write each number in expanded form.

15. 314 ____________________
16. 2,148 ____________________
17. 7,089 ____________________
18. 8,305 ____________________

Write each number in standard form.

19. 5 thousands + 8 tens + 7 ones ________
20. 6 thousands + 4 hundreds + 5 ones ________

Solve and Discuss

Use a place value drawing to help you solve each problem. Label your answers.

Show your work.

21 Scott baked a batch of rolls. He gave a bag of 10 rolls to each of 7 friends. He kept 1 roll for himself. How many rolls did he bake in all?

____

22 Sixty-two bags of hot dog buns were delivered to the school cafeteria. Each bag had 10 buns. How many buns were delivered?

____

Mario and Rosa baked 89 corn muffins. They put the muffins in boxes of 10.

23 How many boxes did they fill?

____

24 How many muffins were left over?

____

Zoe's scout troop collected 743 cans of food to donate to a shelter. They put the cans in boxes of 10.

25 How many boxes did they fill?

____

26 How many cans were left over?

____

Check Understanding

Write the number 4,250 in expanded form in two different ways.

4,250 = __________ hundreds + __________ tens or

__________ thousands + __________ hundreds + __________ ones

Name ______________________

Scrambled Place Value Names

Unscramble the place values and write the number.

1. 8 ones + 6 hundreds + 4 tens

   ____

2. 9 hundreds + 7 tens + 1 one

   ____

3. 5 ones + 0 tens + 7 hundreds

   ____

4. 5 tens + 4 ones + 3 hundreds

   ____

5. 2 tens + 2 hundreds + 2 ones

   ____

6. 8 hundreds + 3 ones + 6 tens

   ____

Unscramble the place values and write the number. Then, make a place value drawing for the number.

7. 6 hundreds + 9 ones + 3 tens

   ____

8. 9 ones + 3 tens + 8 hundreds

   ____

9. 8 ones + 3 hundreds + 4 tens

   ____

10. 2 hundreds + 9 tens + 1 one

    ____

Solve and Discuss

Solve each problem. Label your answer.

11 The bookstore received 35 boxes of books. Each box held 10 books. How many books did the store receive?

____

Maya's family picked 376 apples and put them in baskets. Each basket held 10 apples.

12 How many baskets did they fill?

____

13 How many apples were left over?

____

Aidee had 672 digital photos. She put them in folders of 100 each.

14 How many folders did Aidee fill?

____

15 How many photos were left over?

____

Joe had 543 pennies in his coin bank. He grouped the pennies into piles of 100.

16 How many piles of 100 did Joe make?

____

17 How many extra pennies did he have?

____

Check Understanding

Make a place value drawing to represent the 543 pennies in Joe's coin bank.

Name ____________________

VOCABULARY
estimate
round

Estimate

Solve the problem.

1 Tasha read three books over the summer. Here is the number of pages in each book:

Watership Down	494 pages
Sounder	128 pages
The Secret Garden	368 pages

About how many pages did Tasha read? Explain how you made your **estimate.**

____

____

Practice Rounding

Round each number to the nearest hundred. Use drawings or Secret Code Cards, if they help you.

2 128 ________ 3 271 ________ 4 376 ________

5 649 ________ 6 415 ________ 7 550 ________

8 62 ________ 9 1,481 ________ 10 2,615 ________

11 **Explain Your Thinking** When you round a number to the nearest hundred, how do you know whether to round up or round down?

____

____

____

____

____

Solve Problems by Estimating

Solve by rounding to the nearest hundred.

Show your work.

12 On Saturday, the stadium snack bar sold 286 small drinks, 341 medium drinks, and 277 large drinks. About how many drinks were sold?

____

13 Last week, Mrs. Larson drove 191 miles on Monday, 225 miles on Wednesday, and 107 miles on Friday. About how many miles did she drive altogether?

____

14 Of the 832 people at the hockey game, 292 sat on the visiting team side. The rest sat on the home team side. About how many people sat on the home team side?

____

Reasonable Answers

Use rounding to decide if the answer is reasonable. Write your estimate. Then write *yes* or *no* for the reasonableness of the answer.

15 $604 - 180 = 586$

____

16 $377 + 191 = 568$

____

17 $268 - 57 = 107$

____

18 $41 + 395 = 300$

____

Check Understanding

Explain how to round a number with a 7 in the tens place to the nearest hundred.

Name 

Round 2-Digit Numbers to the Nearest Ten

Round each number to the nearest ten.

1. 63 ______
2. 34 ______
3. 78 ______
4. 25 ______
5. 57 ______
6. 89 ______
7. 42 ______
8. 92 ______

Round 3-Digit Numbers to the Nearest Ten

Round each number to the nearest ten.

9. 162 ______
10. 741 ______
11. 309 ______
12. 255 ______
13. 118 ______
14. 197 ______
15. 503 ______
16. 246 ______
17. **Explain Your Thinking** When you round a number to the nearest ten, how do you know whether to round up or round down?

______

______

______

______

Estimate the Answer

Solve each problem.

18 The chart at the right shows how many smoothies were sold at the Juice Hut yesterday. By rounding each number to the nearest ten, estimate how many smoothies were sold in all.

Smoothies Sold at Juice Hut

13 raspberry-peach smoothies

38 strawberry-banana smoothies

44 guava-mango smoothies

61 peach-blueberry smoothies

____

19 A store has 52 necklaces, 75 bracelets, 36 rings, and 23 earrings. Round each number to the nearest ten to find *about* how many pieces of jewelry the store has.

____

20 Roz rented a movie that is 123 minutes long. She watched 48 minutes of it. Round each number to the nearest ten to estimate how many more minutes she has to watch.

____

Use the table at the right to solve Problems 21–23.

21 Estimate the total number of books the school received by rounding each number to the nearest hundred.

____

Jefferson Elementary School Books Received	
Math	436
Reading	352

22 Estimate the total number of books the school received by rounding each number to the nearest ten.

____

23 Find the total number of math and reading books. Which of your estimates is closer to the actual total?

____

____

Name ____________________

Reasonable Answers

Use rounding to decide if the answer is reasonable. Write your estimate. Write *yes* or *no* for the reasonableness of the answer.

24. 93 − 29 = 64

____

25. 113 + 57 = 140

____

26. 83 + 19 = 102

____

27. 336 + 258 = 594

____

28. 468 − 158 = 280

____

29. 437 + 149 = 536

____

30. 725 − 285 = 590

____

31. 249 + 573 = 822

____

32. 542 − 167 = 475

____

What's the Error?

Dear Math Students,

Today my teacher asked me to estimate the answer to this problem:

Ms. Smith's class brought in 384 cans for the food drive. Mr. Alvarez's class brought in 524 cans. About how many cans did the two classes bring in?

$$\begin{array}{r} 384 \\ +\,524 \\ \hline \end{array} \;\rightarrow\; \begin{array}{r} 300 \\ +\,500 \\ \hline 800 \end{array}$$

About 800 cans were brought in.

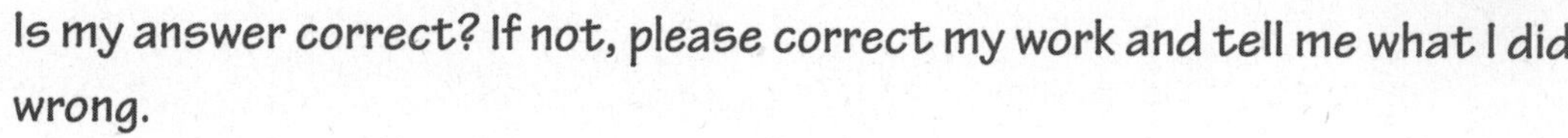

Is my answer correct? If not, please correct my work and tell me what I did wrong.

Your friend,
Puzzled Penguin

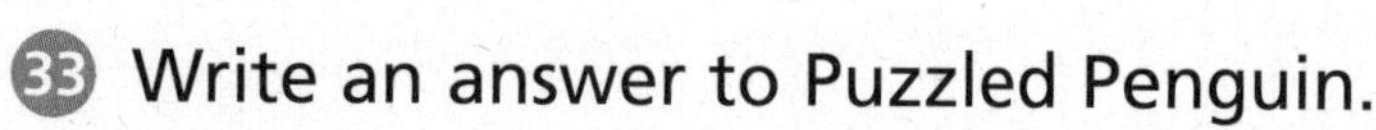

33 Write an answer to Puzzled Penguin.

____

____

Estimate the Number of Objects

Jar D has 100 Beans. Estimate how many beans are in the other jars.

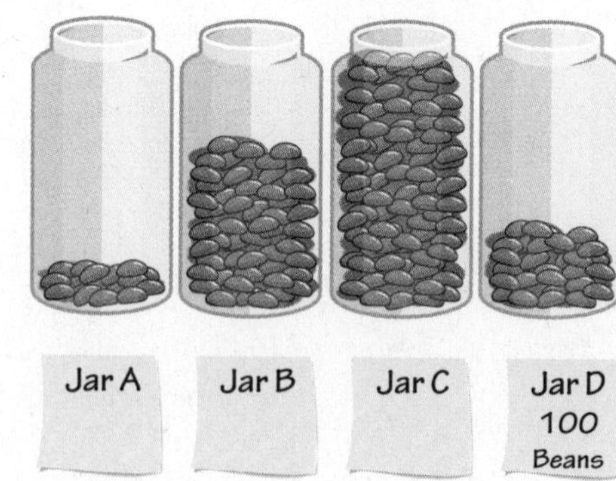

34 Jar A ______________

35 Jar B ______________

36 Jar C ______________

✓ Check Understanding

Round each number to the nearest ten.

83 ________ 98 ________ 245 ________ 362 ________

Name ____________________ Date ____________

Write the correct answer.

1. Round to the nearest hundred.

   678

   ____

2. Round to the nearest ten.

   524

   ____

3. Write the number shown by the place value drawing.

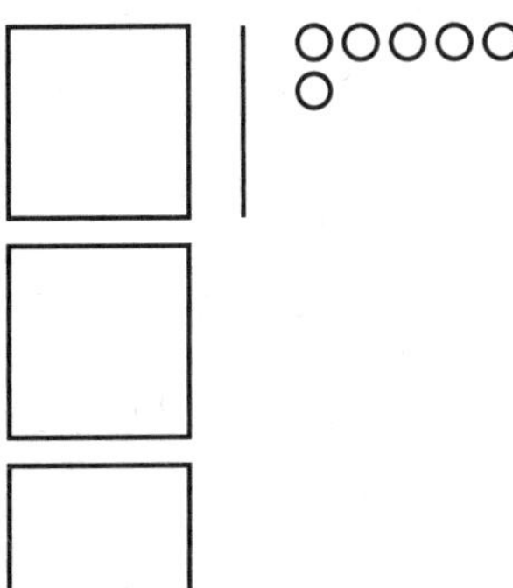

   ____

4. Round to the nearest ten.

   567

   ____

5. Gerard has 365 baseball cards. He puts as many of them as he can into piles of 100. How many piles of 100 does he make?

   ____

Fluency Check 3

Name ______________________ Date ______________

PATH to FLUENCY

Multiply.

1. $1 \times 3 = \square$
2. $3 \times 2 = \square$
3. $4 \times 3 = \square$
4. $4 \times 1 = \square$
5. $2 \times 5 = \square$
6. $6 \times 1 = \square$
7. $6 \times 6 = \square$
8. $8 \times 4 = \square$
9. $5 \times 7 = \square$
10. $9 \times 3 = \square$
11. $8 \times 8 = \square$
12. $6 \times 9 = \square$
13. $7 \times 10 = \square$
14. $10 \times 10 = \square$
15. $8 \times 9 = \square$

Name ______________________________

Solve and Discuss

Solve each problem. Label your answer. Use your MathBoard or a separate sheet of paper.

1. Elena made necklaces for her friends. She used 586 green beads and 349 red beads. How many beads did Elena use in all? ______________

2. Fabrice has a collection of 485 basketball cards and 217 baseball cards. How many sports cards does Fabrice have in all? ______________

PATH to FLUENCY Introduce Addition Methods

Tonya and Mark collect seashells. Tonya has 249 shells and Mark has 386 shells. How many shells do they have in all?

Here are three ways to find the answer:

Show All Totals Method	New Groups Below Method	New Groups Above Method
$\begin{array}{r} 249 \\ +\ 386 \\ \hline 500 \\ 120 \\ +\ \ 15 \\ \hline 635 \end{array}$	$\begin{array}{r} 249 \\ +\ 386 \\ \hline {}^{1\,1}\ \ \\ 635 \end{array}$	$\begin{array}{r} {}^{1\,1}\ \ \\ 249 \\ +\ 386 \\ \hline 635 \end{array}$

Proof Drawing:

6 hundreds
(5 hundreds
+ I new hundred)

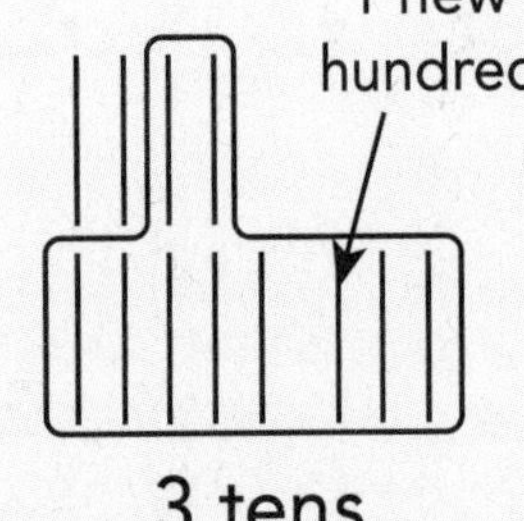

3 tens
(2 tens + I new ten)

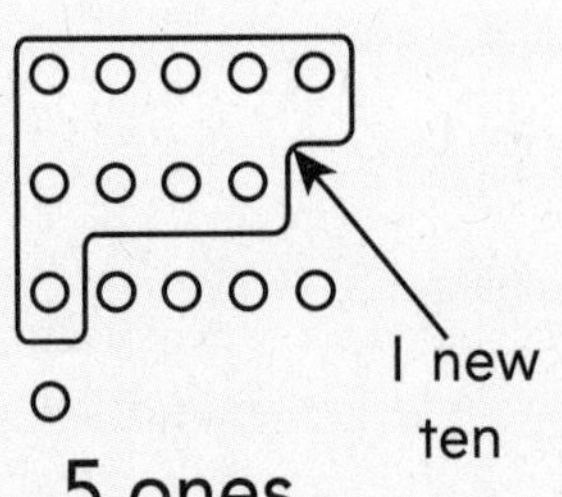

5 ones

PATH to FLUENCY Practice Addition Methods

Solve each problem. Make proof drawings to show that your answers are correct.

3 Ryan has two stamp albums. One album has 554 stamps, and the other has 428 stamps. How many stamps does Ryan have in all?

____

4 Ali has 128 photos of her pets and 255 photos of her family. How many photos does Ali have altogether?

____

5 One week Ashley read 269 pages. The next week she read 236 pages. What is the total number of pages she read in the two weeks?

____

6 The online store has 445 comedy movies and 515 drama movies. How many comedy and drama movies does the store have altogether?

____

Check Understanding

Tell which addition method you prefer and why.

Name ______________________________

Solve and Discuss

Solve each problem using a numerical method and a proof drawing.

1. There are 359 cars and 245 trucks in the parking garage. How many vehicles are in the garage?

   ____

2. The Creepy Crawler exhibit at the science museum has 693 spiders and 292 centipedes. How many spiders and centipedes are there in all?

   ____

3. On Saturday, 590 people went to the art museum. On Sunday, 355 went to the museum. How many people went to the museum altogether?

   ____

4. There were 120 people on the ferry yesterday. Today the ferry had 767 people. How many people in all were on the ferry during the past two days?

   ____

What's the Error?

Dear Math Students,

Today I found the answer to 168 + 78, but I don't know if I added correctly. Please look at my work. Is my answer right? If not, please correct my work and tell what I did wrong.

$$\begin{array}{r} 168 \\ +\ 78 \\ \hline 948 \end{array}$$

Your friend,
Puzzled Penguin

5 Write an answer to Puzzled Penguin.

____

____

PATH to FLUENCY **Line Up the Places to Add**

Write each addition vertically. Line up the places correctly. Then add and make a proof drawing.

6 179 + 38 = ______

7 650 + 345 = ______

8 407 + 577 = ______

Check Understanding

Explain why it is important to line up place values before adding.

Name ______________________________

Decide When to Group

**Decide which new groups you will make.
Then add to see if you were correct.**

1. $\begin{array}{r} 123 \\ +\ 247 \\ \hline \end{array}$

2. $\begin{array}{r} 358 \\ +\ 434 \\ \hline \end{array}$

3. $\begin{array}{r} 732 \\ +\ 189 \\ \hline \end{array}$

4. $\begin{array}{r} 416 \\ +\ 396 \\ \hline \end{array}$

Add.

5. $\begin{array}{r} 647 \\ +\ 178 \\ \hline \end{array}$

6. $\begin{array}{r} 132 \\ +\ 763 \\ \hline \end{array}$

7. $\begin{array}{r} 554 \\ +\ 257 \\ \hline \end{array}$

8. $\begin{array}{r} 168 \\ +\ 692 \\ \hline \end{array}$

9. $\begin{array}{r} 384 \\ +\ 586 \\ \hline \end{array}$

10. $\begin{array}{r} 631 \\ +\ 189 \\ \hline \end{array}$

11. $\begin{array}{r} 464 \\ +\ 446 \\ \hline \end{array}$

12. $\begin{array}{r} 313 \\ +\ 649 \\ \hline \end{array}$

13. 576 + 265 = ____________

14. 568 + 219 = ____________

15. 389 + 511 = ____________

16. 137 + 284 = ____________

Write an equation and solve the problem.

17. The first animated film at the movie theatre lasted 129 minutes. The second film lasted 104 minutes. How many minutes in all did the two movies last?

____

Solve and Discuss

Write an equation and solve the problem.

Show your work.

18 Jacob has 347 basketball cards in his collection. He has 256 baseball cards. How many cards does he have altogether?

____

19 Jasmine's family drove for two days to visit her grandparents. They drove 418 miles on the first day and 486 miles on the second day. How many miles did they drive in all?

____

20 The florist ordered 398 roses and 562 tulips. How many flowers did the florist order in all?

____

21 The suitcase that Emilio packed weighed 80 pounds. His wife packed three suitcases. Each of her suitcases weighed 30 pounds. How many pounds in all did their suitcases weigh?

____

22 Write and solve an addition word problem where 287 and 614 are addends.

____

____

____

Check Understanding

Explain how you know when you need to group when adding two 3-digit numbers.

Name ____________________

Add Three-Digit Numbers

School Carnival Rides	
Rides	**Tickets Sold**
Twister	298
Monster Mix	229
Crazy Coaster	193
Mega Wheel	295
Bumper Cars	301

Write an equation and solve the problem. *Show your work.*

1. How many people went on the two most popular rides?

____

2. The total tickets sold for which two rides was 494?

____

3. Tickets for the Monster Mix and Crazy Coaster sold for $2. How much money did the school earn on the ticket sales for these two rides?

____

4. About how many tickets were sold for Twister, Monster Mix, and Mega Wheel altogether?

____

5. The total tickets sold for which three rides equals about 900?

____

Use Addition to Solve Problems

Student Collections	
Type of Collection	**Number of Objects**
rocks	403
stamps	371
shells	198
buttons	562
miniature cars	245

Write an equation and solve the problem. *Show your work.*

6 How many objects are in the two smallest collections?

____

7 The total number of objects in two collections is 760. What are the collections?

____

8 Are the combined collections of shells and buttons greater than or less than the combined collections of rocks and stamps?

____

9 Is the estimated sum of stamps, shells, and miniature cars closer to 700 or to 800?

____

10 Yuji has a number of sports cards that is 154 greater than the number of rocks. How many cards does Yuji have?

____

Check Understanding

Suppose your classmate got a sum of 343 for Problem 6. Describe the error. _______________

Unit 3
Quick Quiz 2

Name ______________________________ Date ______________

Write the correct answer.

Show your work.

1. The bookstore sold 273 books in the morning and 385 books in the afternoon before it closed. How many books did it sell that day?

____

2. What new groups will need to be made to add 345 and 276?

____

____

3. Holly's farm has 143 goats and 287 sheep. How many animals does the farm have in all? Write an equation and solve the problem.

____

Add.

4. 227 + 98 = ________

5. 47 + 26 = ________

Fluency Check 4

Name Date

PATH to FLUENCY

Divide.

1. 3 ÷ 3 = ☐
2. 8 ÷ 2 = ☐
3. 9 ÷ 3 = ☐
4. 16 ÷ 2 = ☐
5. 25 ÷ 5 = ☐
6. 28 ÷ 4 = ☐
7. 32 ÷ 8 = ☐
8. 40 ÷ 4 = ☐
9. 48 ÷ 6 = ☐
10. 56 ÷ 7 = ☐
11. 63 ÷ 9 = ☐
12. 54 ÷ 6 = ☐
13. 64 ÷ 8 = ☐
14. 72 ÷ 8 = ☐
15. 90 ÷ 9 = ☐

 Name ______________________

PATH to FLUENCY

Discuss Subtraction Methods

Solve this word problem.

Mr. Kim had 134 kites in his hobby store. He sold 58 of them. How many kites does he have now?

1. Write a subtraction that you could do to answer this question.

____

2. Make a place value drawing for 134. Take away 58. How many are left?

3. Write a numerical solution method for what you did in the drawing.

4. Describe how you ungrouped to subtract.

____

____

____

____

____

What's the Error?

Dear Math Students,

Today I found the answer to 134 − 58, but I don't know if I did it correctly. Please look at my work. Is my answer right? If not, please correct my work and tell what I did wrong.

$$\begin{array}{r} 134 \\ -\ 58 \\ \hline 124 \end{array}$$

Your friend,
Puzzled Penguin

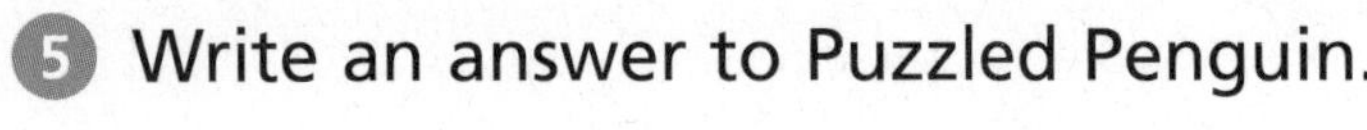

5 Write an answer to Puzzled Penguin.

____

____

PATH to FLUENCY Subtraction Detective

To avoid making subtraction mistakes, look at the top number closely. Do all the ungrouping *before* you subtract. The magnifying glass around the top number helps you remember to be a "subtraction detective."

Subtract. Show your ungroupings numerically and with proof drawings.

6 

$$\begin{array}{r} 371 \\ -\ 86 \\ \hline \end{array}$$

7 

$$\begin{array}{r} 163 \\ -\ 47 \\ \hline \end{array}$$

8 

$$\begin{array}{r} 459 \\ -175 \\ \hline \end{array}$$

Check Understanding

Complete. Always subtract the ______________ number from the ______________ number.

 Name ____________________

PATH to FLUENCY Ungroup to Subtract

Solve each problem. Show your work numerically and with proof drawings.

1. Lakesha bought a box of 500 paper clips. So far, she has used 138 of them. How many are left?

   ____

2. A movie theater has 400 seats. At the noon show, 329 seats were filled. How many seats were empty?

   ____

3. At the start of the school year, Ms. Endo had a new box of 300 crayons for her class. Now 79 crayons are broken. How many unbroken crayons are there?

   ____

PATH to FLUENCY Subtract Across Zeros

Solve each problem. Show your work numerically and with proof drawings.

4. The students at Freedom Elementary School have a goal of reading 900 books. They have read 342 books. How many books do the students have left to read?

____

5. There are 500 fiction books in the Lee School Library. There are 179 fewer non-fiction books than fiction books. How many books are non-fiction?

____

6. The students at Olympia Elementary School collected 1,000 bottles for recycling. The students at Sterling Elementary collected 768 bottles. How many more bottles did the students at Olympia collect?

____

Name ____________________

PATH to FLUENCY Practice Subtracting Across Zeros

Subtract. Make proof drawings for Exercises 7–10.

7.
$$\begin{array}{r} 800 \\ -\ 391 \\ \hline \end{array}$$

8.
$$\begin{array}{r} 500 \\ -\ 333 \\ \hline \end{array}$$

9.
$$\begin{array}{r} 400 \\ -\ 217 \\ \hline \end{array}$$

10.
$$\begin{array}{r} 900 \\ -\ 818 \\ \hline \end{array}$$

11.
$$\begin{array}{r} 600 \\ -\ 575 \\ \hline \end{array}$$

12.
$$\begin{array}{r} 700 \\ -\ 248 \\ \hline \end{array}$$

13.
$$\begin{array}{r} 200 \\ -\ 109 \\ \hline \end{array}$$

14.
$$\begin{array}{r} 800 \\ -\ 519 \\ \hline \end{array}$$

15. **Math Journal** Write a word problem that is solved by subtracting a 2-digit number from a 3-digit number that has a zero in both the ones and tens places. Then solve the problem.

PATH to FLUENCY

Practice Deciding When to Ungroup

Subtract. Make proof drawings if you need to on MathBoards or on a separate sheet of paper.

16. 912 − 265

17. 323 − 147

18. 280 − 136

19. 489 − 263

20. $\begin{array}{r} 754 \\ -\ 389 \\ \hline \end{array}$

21. $\begin{array}{r} 912 \\ -\ 437 \\ \hline \end{array}$

22. $\begin{array}{r} 341 \\ -\ 178 \\ \hline \end{array}$

23. $\begin{array}{r} 603 \\ -\ 464 \\ \hline \end{array}$

Check Understanding

Subtract. 300 – 156. Make a proof drawing to show that your answer is correct.

Name ______________________________

PATH to FLUENCY Ungroup from Left or Right

Tony and Maria each solved this problem:

On Tuesday morning, a bookstore had 463 copies of a new bestseller. By the end of the day, 275 copies were sold. How many copies were left?

Tony

Tony started ungrouping from the left.

1. He has enough hundreds.
2. He does not have enough tens. He ungroups 1 hundred to make 10 more tens.

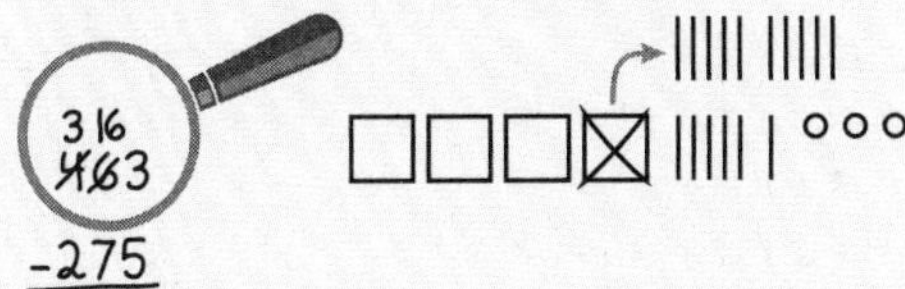

3. He does not have enough ones. He ungroups 1 ten to make 10 more ones.

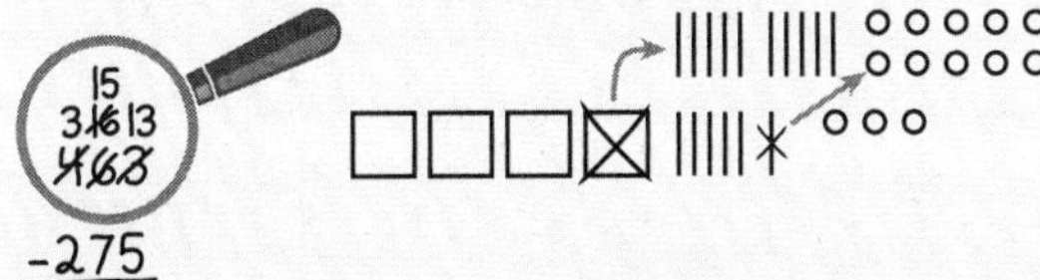

4. Complete the subtraction.

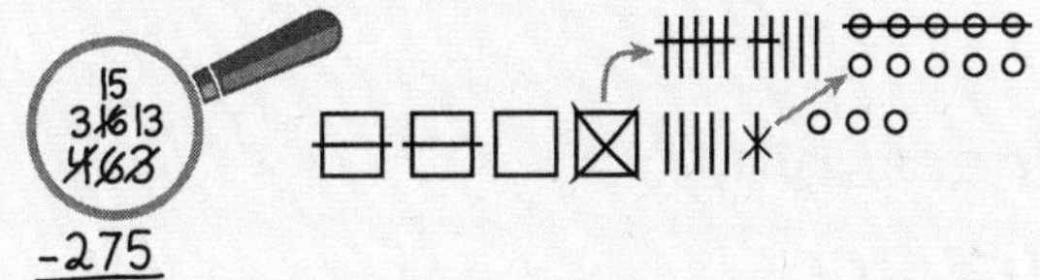

Maria

Maria started ungrouping from the right.

1. She does not have enough ones. She ungroups 1 ten to make 10 more ones.

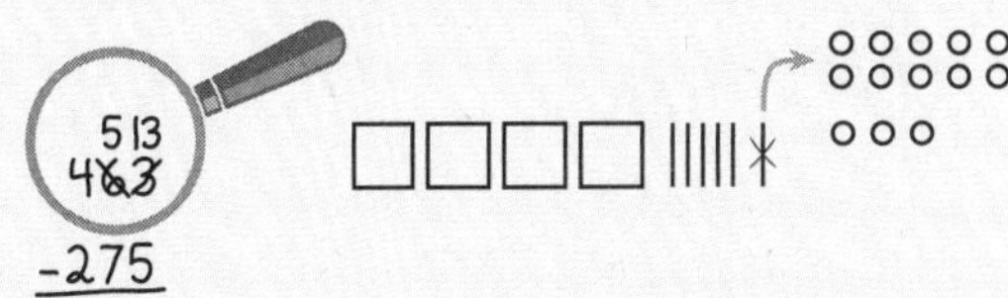

2. She does not have enough tens. She ungroups 1 hundred to get 10 more tens.

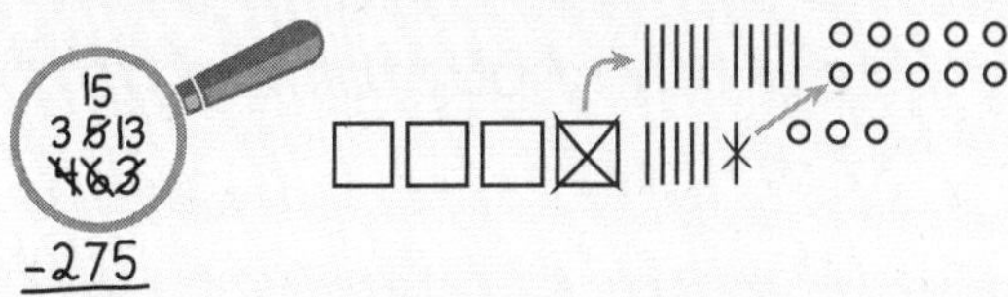

3. She has enough hundreds.
4. Complete the subtraction.

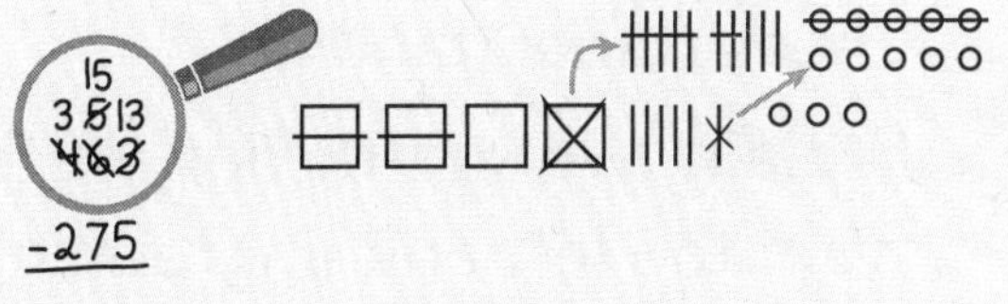

PATH to FLUENCY Choose a Method to Subtract

Subtract.

1. $\begin{array}{r} 686 \\ -\ 387 \\ \hline \end{array}$

2. $\begin{array}{r} 340 \\ -\ 167 \\ \hline \end{array}$

3. $\begin{array}{r} 765 \\ -\ 498 \\ \hline \end{array}$

4. $\begin{array}{r} 841 \\ -\ 253 \\ \hline \end{array}$

5. $\begin{array}{r} 912 \\ -\ 575 \\ \hline \end{array}$

6. $\begin{array}{r} 853 \\ -\ 194 \\ \hline \end{array}$

7. $\begin{array}{r} 705 \\ -\ 429 \\ \hline \end{array}$

8. $\begin{array}{r} 998 \\ -\ 299 \\ \hline \end{array}$

9. $\begin{array}{r} 513 \\ -\ 156 \\ \hline \end{array}$

10. 627 − 348

11. 544 − 169

12. 810 − 261

Solve.

13. Rory is putting 302 digital photos in an album. Of these, 194 are from her trip to Florida. How many photos are not from Rory's trip?

14. There were 645 bike riders in a race. Toby finished eighty-seventh. How many riders finished after Toby?

Check Understanding

Explain two subtraction methods—ungrouping from the left and ungrouping from the right.

 Name ______________________

PATH to FLUENCY Relate Addition and Subtraction

Solve each problem. Make a proof drawing if you need to.

1. There were 138 students in the gym for the assembly. Then 86 more students came in. How many students were in the gym altogether?

____

2. There were 224 students in the gym for the assembly. Then 86 students left. How many students were still in the gym?

____

3. Look at your addition, subtraction, and proof drawings from Problems 1 and 2. How are addition and subtraction related?

____

____

____

Solve and Discuss

Solve. Label your answers.

4 Marly had 275 baseball cards. Her brother gave her a collection of 448 baseball cards. How many baseball cards does Marly have now?

5 Write a subtraction word problem related to the addition word problem in Problem 4. Then find the answer without doing any calculations.

6 Bill drove 375 miles on the first day of his cross-country trip. The next day he drove an additional 528 miles. How many miles did Bill drive on the first two days of his trip?

7 Write a subtraction problem related to the addition word problem in Problem 6. Then find the answer without doing any calculations.

Check Understanding

Draw a Math Mountain to show the relationship between the numbers in Problems 6 and 7.

Name ______________________________

Subtract and Check

Show your work.

Solve each problem.

1. Ken collects photographs as a hobby. He has 375 photographs in his collection at home. If Ken brought 225 of his photographs to share with his classmates, how many photographs did he leave at home?

____

2. Of the 212 third- and fourth-grade students, 165 attended the school festival. How many students did not attend the festival?

____

3. Becky has 653 marbles in her collection. Riley has 438 marbles in her collection. How many more marbles does Becky have than Riley?

____

4. Andrea and John need 750 tickets to get a board game. They have 559 tickets. How many more tickets do they need?

____

PATH to FLUENCY Practice Deciding When to Ungroup

Answer each question.

Adair subtracted 595 from 834.

5. Did she have to ungroup to make more tens? Explain.

6. Did she have to ungroup to make more ones? Explain.

Beatrice subtracted 441 from 950.

7. Did she have to ungroup to make more tens? Explain.

8. Did she have to ungroup to make more ones? Explain.

Wan subtracted 236 from 546.

9. Did he have to ungroup to make more tens? Explain.

10. Did he have to ungroup to make more ones? Explain.

Check Understanding

Explain how to decide when to ungroup in a subtraction problem.

 Name ____________________

PATH to FLUENCY Practice Addition and Subtraction

Add or subtract.

1. $\begin{array}{r} 112 \\ +\ 459 \\ \hline \end{array}$

2. $\begin{array}{r} 572 \\ -\ 357 \\ \hline \end{array}$

3. $\begin{array}{r} 253 \\ +\ 328 \\ \hline \end{array}$

4. $\begin{array}{r} 710 \\ -\ 464 \\ \hline \end{array}$

5. $\begin{array}{r} 461 \\ -\ 182 \\ \hline \end{array}$

6. $\begin{array}{r} 540 \\ +\ 175 \\ \hline \end{array}$

7. $\begin{array}{r} 921 \\ -\ 653 \\ \hline \end{array}$

8. $\begin{array}{r} 398 \\ -\ 99 \\ \hline \end{array}$

9. $\begin{array}{r} 712 \\ +\ 189 \\ \hline \end{array}$

10. $\begin{array}{r} 600 \\ -\ 223 \\ \hline \end{array}$

11. $\begin{array}{r} 809 \\ -\ 576 \\ \hline \end{array}$

12. $\begin{array}{r} 634 \\ +\ 287 \\ \hline \end{array}$

Solve.

13. The height of Angeline Falls in Washington is 450 feet. Snoqualmie Falls in Washington is 182 feet lower than Angeline Falls. What is the height of Snoqualmie Falls?

____

14. Jill scored 534 points at the arcade on Friday night. She scored 396 points on Saturday night. How many points did she score altogether?

____

Solve Real World Problems

The students at Liberty Elementary collected pennies for a fundraiser.

Pennies Collected					
Grade	1	2	3	4	5
Number of Pennies	225	436	517	609	342

Write an equation and solve the problem.

Show your work.

15 How many pennies did Grades 2 and 5 collect?

____

16 How many more pennies did Grades 1 and 3 together collect than Grade 4?

____

17 Is the total number of pennies collected by Grades 1 and 4 greater than or less than the total number collected by Grades 3 and 5?

____

18 The total number of pennies collected by which three grades equals about 900?

____

19 The Kindergarten students collected 198 fewer pennies than the Grade 3 students. How many pennies did the Kindergarteners collect?

____

Check Understanding

Describe a real world situation in which you would need to add or subtract.

Name ______________________

Solve Multistep Word Problems

Solve each problem. Label your answers. *Show your work.*

1. Isabel bought 36 pieces of fruit for her soccer team. There are 16 apples, 12 bananas, and the rest are pears. How many pieces of fruit are pears?

   ____

2. Toby has a collection of sports cards. He had 13 baseball cards, 16 basketball cards, and 14 football cards. Toby sold 15 cards and he bought 17 hockey cards. What is the total number of cards in Toby's collection now?

   ____

3. There are 15 more boys than girls in the school band. There are 27 girls. How many students are in the school band?

   ____

4. Finn delivered 13 pizzas. Then he delivered 8 more pizzas. Altogether, he delivered 6 fewer pizzas than Liz. How many pizzas did Liz deliver?

   ____

5. Majeed built 7 car models and 14 airplane models. Jasmine built 9 more car models than Majeed and 6 fewer airplane models. How many models did Jasmine build in all?

   ____

Reasonable Answers

VOCABULARY
compatible numbers

Use compatible numbers to decide if the solution is reasonable. Write *yes* or *no*. Then add or subtract to see if you were correct.

6. Nathan counted 28 large dogs and 37 small dogs at the dog park. He said he saw 55 dogs in all.

____

7. There are 122 fish in a tank. There are 67 spotted fish and the rest are striped, so there are 55 striped fish in the tank.

____

Make an estimate for each problem. Then write whether or not Jana's answer is reasonable and solve the problem.

8. There were 432 people at the basketball game. 257 people sat on the home team side. How many people sat on the visiting team side?

   Jana's answer: 689 people

   Estimate: 432 − 257 → _____ − _____ = _____

   Jana's answer is ______________________________.

   My answer: ______________________________

9. The Pecos River is 234 miles longer the Yellowstone River. The Yellowstone River is 692 miles long. How long is the Pecos River?

   Jana's answer: 462 miles

   Estimate: 692 + 234 → _____ + _____ = _____

   Jana's answer is ______________________________.

   My answer: ______________________________

Name ________________________________

Solve Word Problems with Greater Numbers

Solve each problem. Then use compatible numbers to check your answer.

Show your work.

10 Jenna has $250 in a bank account. After her birthday she adds $135 to the account. Then the next week, she takes out $40 to buy a game for her computer. How much money is in the account now?

____

11 Alex and his father each have a collection of sports cards. Alex's father has 900 cards and Alex has 350 fewer cards than his father. After Alex's friend gives Alex 72 more cards, how many does Alex have?

____

12 A truck has 2,600 cans of tomatoes to deliver to stores. The first store takes 450 cans. How many cans of tomatoes are left on the truck?

____

13 There are 1,250 people living in Union. There are 2,100 more people living in Grantville than in Union. What is the population of Grantville?

____

14 Valley View Farm grew 2,549 pounds of potatoes during the summer. The Valley View Farm store sold 1,083 pound of potatoes. How many pounds of potatoes were left?

____

Solve Word Problems with Greater Numbers (continued)

Solve each problem. Then use compatible numbers to check your answer for reasonableness.

Show your work.

15 The PTA has $3,029 in its account to pay for school field trips. A field trip costs $576. If the PTA pays for the field trip, how much will be left in the account? Is your answer reasonable? Explain.

____

____

16 The Scott family is taking a trip to Washington, D.C. which is 1,395 miles from their home. So far they have driven 612 miles. How many more miles do they need to drive? Is your answer reasonable? Explain.

____

____

____

17 Last week 5,089 books were checked out from the city library. There were 4,962 books returned last week. How many more books were checked out than returned? Is your answer reasonable? Explain.

____

____

____

Check Understanding

Describe how you decide whether an answer is reasonable or not.

Name ______________________________

Math and Maps

The Pony Express was a mail service from St. Joseph, Missouri, to Sacramento, California. The Pony Express service carried mail by horseback riders in relays.

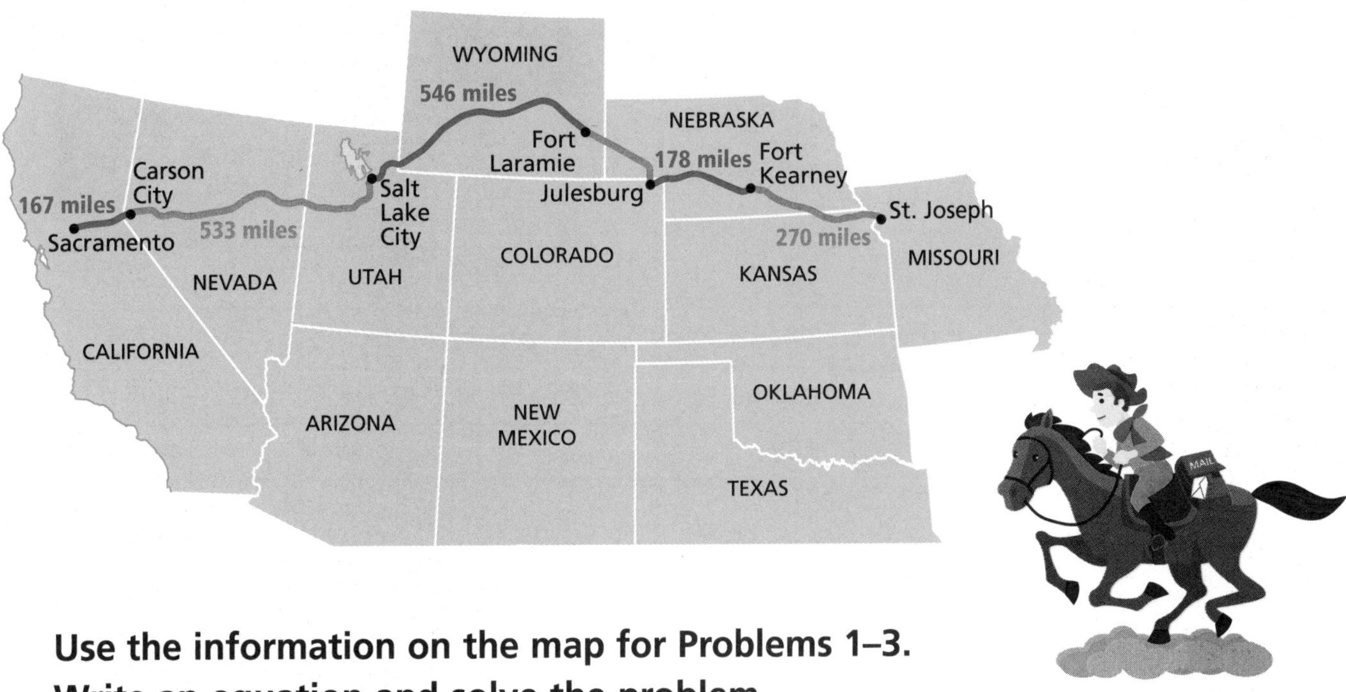

Use the information on the map for Problems 1–3. Write an equation and solve the problem.

1. How many miles did the Pony Express riders travel on a trip from Sacramento to Salt Lake City?

____

2. The total distance from St. Joseph to Fort Laramie is 616 miles. How many miles is it from Julesburg to Fort Laramie?

____

3. Write and solve a problem that can be answered using the map.

____

____

Use a Table

It took the Pony Express 10 days to deliver letters between Sacramento and St. Joseph. Today we send text messages that are delivered within a few seconds. The chart below shows the number of messages sent in a month by different students.

Number of Messages Sent last Month					
Name	Robbie	Samantha	Ellen	Bryce	Callie
Number	528	462	942	388	489

Use the information in the table for Problems 4–6. Write an equation and solve the problem.

4. How many more messages did Robbie send than Callie?

____

5. How many more messages did Ellen send than Bryce and Samantha combined?

____

6. Tamara said that Robbie and Bryce together sent 806 messages. Is that number reasonable? Explain. Then find the actual number to see if you are correct.

____

____

____

Unit 3
Quick Quiz 3

Name ______________________ Date __________

Subtract.

1 765 − 56 = ________

2 72 − 35 = ________

Solve.

3 524 people watch the town parade. 178 of them are children. How many people watching the parade are adults?

____

4 Roberto has a collection of 243 CDs. He scratched 152 of them. How many of his CDs are not scratched?

____

5 Amaya has 476 pennies. Then she finds 359 more pennies. How many pennies does she have now?

____

Fluency Check 5

Name ______________________ Date ________

PATH to FLUENCY

Multiply or divide.

1. $1 \div 1 = \square$
2. $3 \times 5 = \square$
3. $6 \div 2 = \square$
4. $4 \times 3 = \square$
5. $9 \div 3 = \square$
6. $8 \times 2 = \square$
7. $12 \div 3 = \square$
8. $7 \times 6 = \square$
9. $8 \div 1 = \square$
10. $7 \times 3 = \square$
11. $20 \div 4 = \square$
12. $5 \times 7 = \square$
13. $36 \div 9 = \square$
14. $9 \times 2 = \square$
15. $54 \div 9 = \square$

Name ______________________________

VOCABULARY
hundred thousands
ten thousands

Identify Place Value Through Hundred Thousands

Write each number in the place-value chart.

1. 12,072
2. 6,908
3. 90,542
4. 175,163

	Hundred Thousands	Ten Thousands	Thousands	Hundreds	Tens	Ones
1.						
2.						
3.						
4.						

Write the value of the underlined digit.

5. 13,456 ____________
6. 190,765 ____________
7. 88,763 ____________
8. 4,567 ____________
9. 25,783 ____________
10. 95,426 ____________

Write Numbers Different Ways

Write each number in standard form.

11. sixty thousand, one hundred eight ____________
12. one hundred sixty-six thousand, eighty ____________

Write each number in word form.

13. 17,893 ______________________________
14. 175,635 ______________________________

Write each number in expanded form.

15. 23,059 ______________________________
16. 103,814 ______________________________

More and Less

Write the number that is 10,000 more and the number that is 10,000 less.

17 87,630 10,000 more ________ 10,000 less ________

18 19,455 10,000 more ________ 10,000 less ________

Write the number that is 1,000 more and the number that is 1,000 less.

19 5,176 1,000 more ________ 1,000 less ________

20 26,709 1,000 more ________ 1,000 less ________

Write the number that is 100 more and the number that is 100 less.

21 2,547 100 more ________ 100 less ________

22 30,169 100 more ________ 100 less ________

What's the Error?

Dear Math Students,

Today my teacher asked me to find the number that is 1,000 more than 15,319, but I don't know if my answer is correct. I wrote:

1,000 more than 15,319 is 25,319.

Your friend,
Puzzled Penguin

23 Write an answer to Puzzled Penguin.

____

____

____

____

Name ______________________________

Compare and Order Numbers Through Hundred Thousands

VOCABULARY
greatest
least

Discuss the problem below.

Jim has 24 trading cards and Hattie has 42 trading cards. Who has more trading cards? How do you know?

Write greater than (>), less than (<), or equal (=) to make each statement true.

24 3,989 ◯ 3,899

25 2,385 ◯ 2,385

26 3,235 ◯ 2,350

27 4,008 ◯ 4,108

28 2,563 ◯ 2,563

29 8,567 ◯ 9,765

30 23,836 ◯ 7,859

31 5,206 ◯ 52,026

32 89,748 ◯ 98,478

33 12,904 ◯ 12,904

34 14,538 ◯ 41,830

35 61,564 ◯ 60,569

Write each group of numbers in order from greatest to least.

36 8,456 4,567 4,675

____

37 3,465 3,654 3,546

____

38 8,091 10,981 9,081

____

39 13,230 11,710 5,608

____

40 30,714 32,740 30,174

____

41 89,518 85,981 89,815

____

42 Fremont has a population of 26,397. Hastings has a population of 24,907. Which city has the greater population?

____

43 Bella, Jason, and Nico each took a car trip over the summer. Bella traveled 3,208 miles. Jason traveled 4,796 miles. Nico traveled 958 miles. Who traveled the greatest distance?

____

Rounding with Greater Numbers

Round each number to the nearest ten thousand.

44 87,630 ____________ 45 46,433 ____________

46 34,641 ____________ 47 27,309 ____________

Round each number to the nearest thousand.

48 1,380 ____________ 49 5,998 ____________

50 41,632 ____________ 51 65,594 ____________

Round to the place of the underlined digit.

52 $\underline{1}$4,594 ____________ 53 2$\underline{4}$,596 ____________

54 23,$\underline{3}$07 ____________ 55 4,$\underline{1}$36 ____________

Estimate with Greater Numbers

Round each number to the greatest place to estimate each sum or difference.

56 $\begin{array}{r} 2{,}491 \\ +\ 1{,}309 \\ \hline \end{array}$

57 $\begin{array}{r} 7{,}463 \\ -\ 3{,}270 \\ \hline \end{array}$

58 $\begin{array}{r} 65{,}594 \\ -\ 12{,}407 \\ \hline \end{array}$

59 $\begin{array}{r} 20{,}365 \\ +\ 18{,}679 \\ \hline \end{array}$

Check Understanding

How is rounding 46,037 to the nearest ten thousand like rounding 482 to the nearest hundred?

 Name ______________________

VOCABULARY
unit square

Model a Product of Ones and Tens

The number of **unit squares** in an array of connected unit squares is the area of the rectangle formed by the squares. We sometimes just show the measurement of length and width.

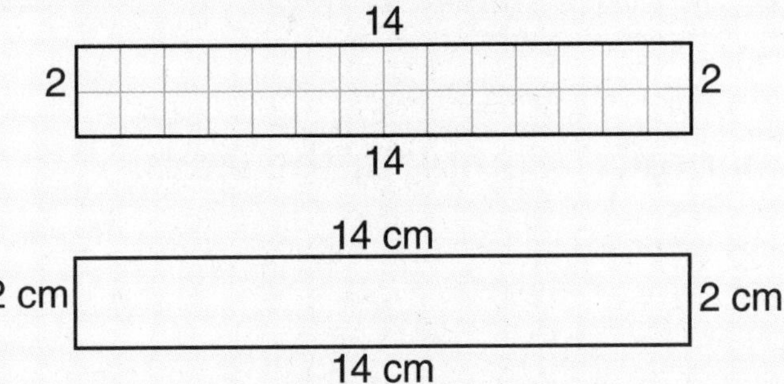

You can draw a rectangle for any multiplication. In the real world, we use multiplication for finding both sizes of arrays and areas of figures.

A 2 × 14 rectangle has 28 unit squares inside, so 2 × 14 = 28.

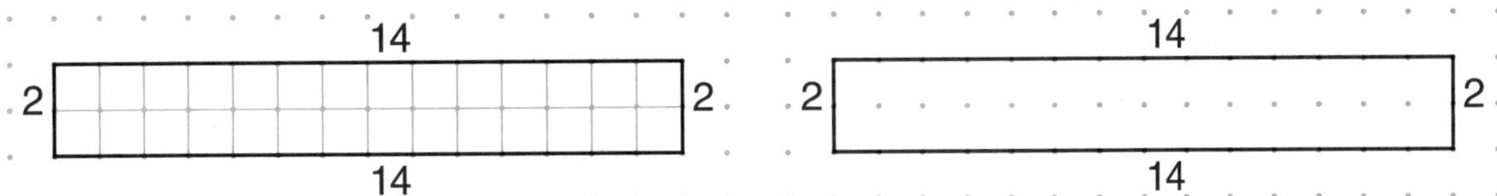

1. On your MathBoard, draw a 14 × 2 rectangle. How is the 14 × 2 rectangle similar to the 2 × 14 rectangle? How is it different?

____

____

____

____

2. How do the areas of the 2 × 14 and 14 × 2 rectangles compare?

____

Factor the Tens to Multiply Ones and Tens

This 3 × 40 rectangle contains 12 groups of 10 square units, so its area is 120 square units.

	40 = 10	+	10	+	10	+	10	
1	1 × 10 = 10		1 × 10 = 10		1 × 10 = 10		1 × 10 = 10	1
1	1 × 10 = 10		1 × 10 = 10		1 × 10 = 10		1 × 10 = 10	1
1	1 × 10 = 10		1 × 10 = 10		1 × 10 = 10		1 × 10 = 10	1
	10	+	10	+	10	+	10	

3 How can we show this numerically? Complete the steps.

$3 \times 40 = (3 \times 1) \times (\_\_\_\_ \times 10)$

$= (\_\_\_\_ \times \_\_\_\_) \times (1 \times 10)$

$= \_\_\_\_ \times 10 = 120$

4 On your MathBoard, draw a 40 × 3 rectangle and find its area.

____

5 How is the 40 × 3 rectangle similar to the 3 × 40 rectangle? How is it different?

____

____

____

____

6 Write out the steps for finding 4 × 30 by factoring the tens. Use your MathBoard if you need to.

____

____

____

Name ______________________

Explore the Area Model

Copy this rectangle on your MathBoard.

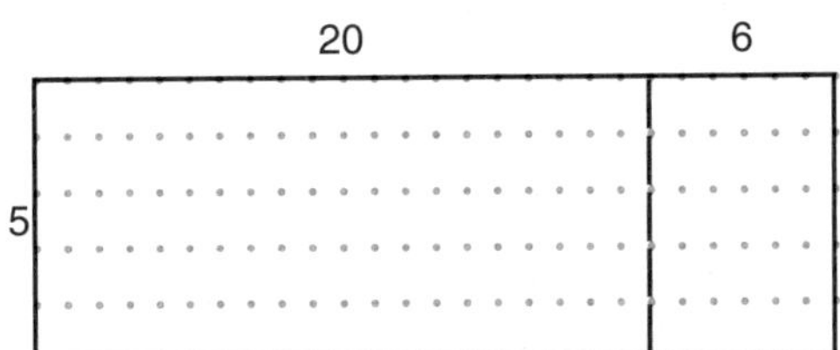

7 How many square units of area are there in the tens part of the drawing? ______________

8 What multiplication equation gives the area of the tens part of the drawing? ______________ Write this equation in its rectangle.

9 How many square units of area are there in the ones part of the drawing? ______________

10 What multiplication equation gives the area of the ones part? ______________ Write this equation in its rectangle.

11 What is the total of the two areas? ______________

12 How do you know that 130 is the correct product of 5×26?

____

____

13 **Read Problems A and B.**

A. Brad's photo album has 26 pages. Each page has 5 photos. How many photos are in Brad's album?

B. Nick took 5 photos. Haley took 26 photos. How many more photos did Haley take than Nick?

Which problem could you solve using the multiplication you just did? Explain why.

____

____

Use Rectangles to Multiply

Draw a rectangle for each problem on your MathBoard. Find the tens product, the ones product, and the total.

14 8 × 38 ________ ________ ________

15 3 × 29 ________ ________ ________

16 4 × 28 ________ ________ ________

17 7 × 34 ________ ________ ________

18 2 × 38 ________ ________ ________

19 3 × 28 ________ ________ ________

20 5 × 30 ________ ________ ________

21 5 × 28 ________ ________ ________

Solve each problem.

22 Lucille put 9 rows of tile on her mudroom floor. Each row has 16 tiles. How many tiles are on Lucille's mudroom floor?

Show your work.

____

23 A pizzeria can make pizzas on thin crusts, thick crusts, or flatbreads. The pizzeria has a total of 57 different ways to top the pizzas. How many different combinations of crusts and pizza toppings can the pizzeria make?

____

24 Complete this word problem. Then solve it.

________ has ____ boxes of ________.

There are ____ ________ in each box.

How many ________ does ________

have altogether? ________________

Name ______________________________

Make a Rectangle Drawing to Solve a Problem

Draw an area model for each problem.
Label your drawing with a multiplication equation.
Then write the answer to the problem.

Show your work.

25 A craft store has an artist kit with 8 rows of color pencils. Each row has 34 pencils. How many pencils are there in all?

____

26 Mali put some cheese on a tray. She put the cheese in 7 rows, with 18 slices per row. How many slices did she put on the tray?

____

27 Arch created a new walkway. He set 56 rows of pavers. In each row, Arch set 9 pavers. How many pavers did he set in the walkway?

____

28 Mr. Chung set up some extra chairs in the back of the auditorium. He was able to set 47 chairs in each row. He set 4 rows of chairs. How many chairs did he set up?

____

What's the Error?

Dear Math Students,

Today I found the answer to 4 × 29.
Here is how I found the answer.

	2	9
4	4 × 2 = 8	4 × 9 = 36

4 × 29 = 44

Is my answer correct? If not, please correct my work and tell me what I did wrong.

Your friend,
Puzzled Penguin

29 Write an answer to the Puzzled Penguin.

____

____

____

Practice 2-Digit by 1-Digit Multiplication

Use an area model to find the answer.

30 96 × 2 = ________

31 50 × 3 = ________

32 78 × 5 = ________

33 3 × 52 = ________

Check Understanding

Explain how the rectangle you draw to solve Problem 33 is similar to the rectangle you can draw to solve 52 × 3.

 Name ________________

Multiply 1-Digit Numbers by Hundreds

You can use an area model to multiply a 1-digit number by a 3-digit number.

$3 \times 249 = \square$

249 =	200	40	9
3	$3 \times 200 = 600$	$3 \times 40 = 120$	$3 \times 9 = 27$

1. What two operations are used to find the product of 3×249 using the area model?

   ________________ ________________

2. What multiplication equation gives the area of the hundreds part of the model? ________________

3. What multiplication equation gives the area of the tens part of the model? ________________

4. What multiplication equation gives the area of the ones part of the model? ________________

5. What is the total of the three areas? ________________

PATH to FLUENCY Use an Area Model to Solve

For each acre of land that a farmer cuts, he gets 127 bales of hay. The farmer cuts his land 4 times every year. What is the total number of bales of hay the farmer will get from each acre this year?

6 Draw rectangles to represent the problem.

7 Explain how to use the area model to solve the problem above.

____

____

____

8 Use your rectangle drawing and the steps you described to find the answer to the problem.

____

Write the equation.

9 If the farmer has 9 acres of land, how many bales of hay will the farmer cut each year? Complete the area model to find the answer.

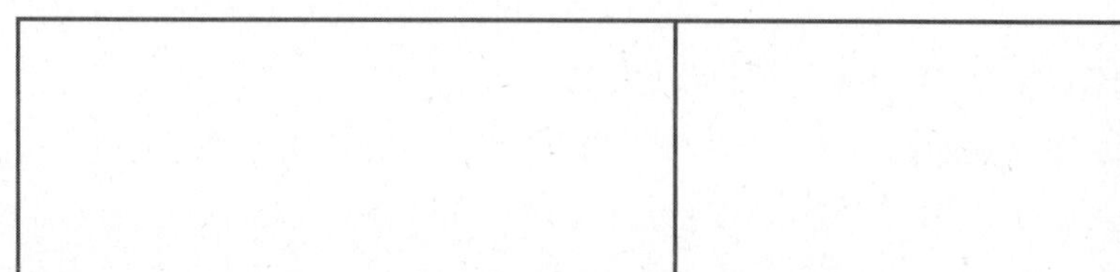

Equation: ______________

Name

PATH to FLUENCY Draw a Model to Solve a Problem

Draw a model for each problem. Label your drawing with a multiplication equation. Then write the answer to the problem.

Show your work.

10 The length of a soccer field is 130 yards. Lou runs the length of the field 7 times during practice. How many yards does Lou run in all?

____

11 A large airplane travels about 567 miles in an hour. How many miles does the airplane travel in 4 hours?

____

12 A store receives a shipment of 9 boxes of oranges. Each box has 126 oranges. How many oranges does the store receive in the shipment?

____

13 A school theater program has 248 tickets available for each show. The theater sells all of the tickets for 5 shows. How many tickets does the theater program sell?

____

PATH to FLUENCY Use Rectangles to Multiply

Draw an area model for each problem on your MathBoard. Find the hundreds product, the tens product, the ones product, and the total.

14 8 × 387

______
______
______
______

15 3 × 299

______
______
______
______

16 4 × 528

______
______
______
______

17 5 × 467

______
______
______
______

18 2 × 838

______
______
______
______

19 6 × 506

______
______
______
______

Solve.

20 During the grand opening, an ice cream shop is giving away 5 free ice creams to the first 275 people through the door. What is the total number of ice creams that the shop is giving away?

______

Check Understanding

Complete. An area model for 2 × 413 shows the hundreds part is ______, the tens part is ______, and the ones part is ______, for a total area of ______.

Name ______________________________

VOCABULARY
rule
input-output table

PATH to FLUENCY

Complete Input-Output Tables

Use the rule to complete each input-output table.

1 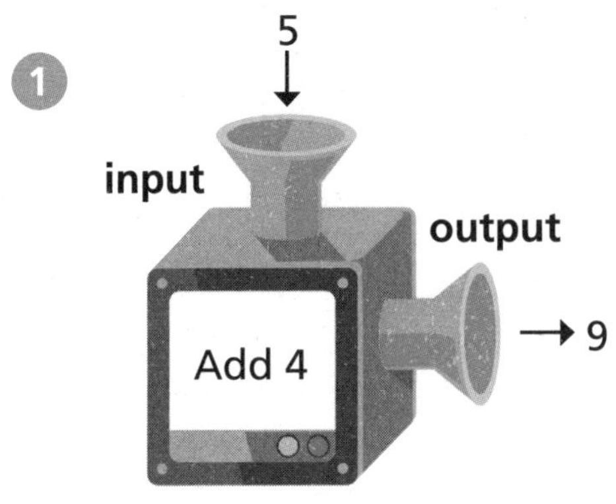

Rule: Add 4	
Input	Output
5	9
6	
8	
10	
13	

2 3 → input → Multiply by 3 → output → 9

Rule: Multiply by 3	
Input	Output
3	9
4	
5	
7	
9	

3

Rule: Add 8	
Input	Output
7	15
10	
24	
31	
50	

4

Rule: Subtract 10	
Input	Output
21	11
42	
59	
77	
95	

5

Rule: Multiply by 4	
Input	Output
3	12
4	
6	
8	
10	

6

Rule: Subtract 15	
Input	Output
16	1
31	
35	
49	
70	

PATH to FLUENCY Find the Rule

Find the rule for each input-output table. Then complete the table.

Rule:	
Number of Bicycles	Number of Wheels
Input	Output
1	2
2	
3	
4	
5	

8

Rule:	
Input	Output
15	16
21	22
32	33
45	
49	

9

Rule:	
Input	Output
16	10
20	14
46	40
59	
84	

10

Rule:	
Input	Output
2	10
3	15
4	20
7	
10	

11 Blair is selling tickets to the school play. He records the number of tickets he sells to each family and the amount of money he collects. Complete the table. Then use the table to find the cost of each ticket.

Tickets Sold	2	3	5	7		10
Amount Collected		$21	$35	$49	$63	

Answer: ______________________________

Check Understanding

Create an input-output table that uses the rule add 10.

Rule	Add 10				
Input					
Output					

Name ____________________ Date ____________

1. Write the number that is 10,000 more than 89,086.

____

2. Round to the nearest thousand to estimate the difference.

$$\begin{array}{r} 36,969 \\ -\ \ 3,489 \\ \hline \end{array}$$

For questions 3 and 4, draw a model to solve.

3. An orchard has 8 rows of apple trees. There are 24 apple trees in each row. How many apple trees does the orchard have in all?

____

4. Yolanda's book of puzzles has 365 pages. Each page has 3 puzzles. How many puzzles are in the book?

____

5. Use the rule to complete the table.

Rule: Add 10	
Input	**Output**
3	13
13	
43	
63	
93	

Fluency Check 6

Name ____________________ Date ____________

PATH to FLUENCY

Multiply or divide.

1. $7 \div 1 = \square$
2. $8 \times 5 = \square$
3. $6 \div 3 = \square$
4. $9 \times 3 = \square$
5. $3 \div 3 = \square$
6. $8 \times 7 = \square$
7. $15 \div 3 = \square$
8. $9 \times 6 = \square$
9. $36 \div 6 = \square$
10. $4 \times 3 = \square$
11. $28 \div 4 = \square$
12. $5 \times 9 = \square$
13. $72 \div 9 = \square$
14. $6 \times 2 = \square$
15. $63 \div 9 = \square$

Name ______________________ Date ______________

1. Select the way that shows three hundred fifty-seven. Mark all that apply.

Ⓐ 357

Ⓑ 3 hundreds + 57 tens

Ⓒ 3 hundreds + 5 tens + 7 ones

Ⓓ 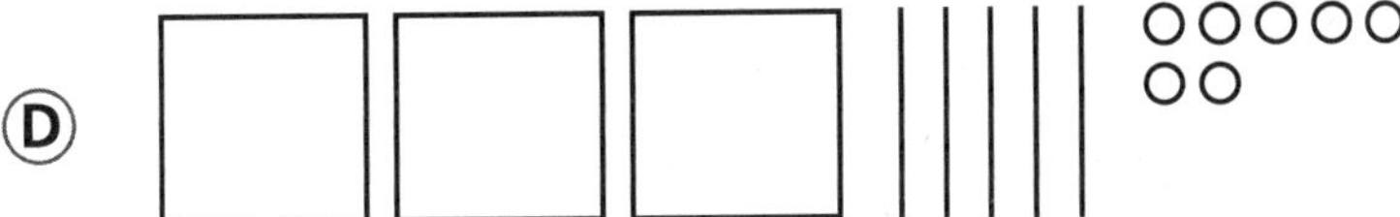

Ⓔ 300 + 5 + 7

2. Make a place value drawing for the number.

691

3. The museum sells 15,564 posters. It sells 18,836 calendars. Round each number to the nearest thousand to estimate how many more calendars the museum sells than posters.

about ________ more calendars

Name Date

4 Write the number in the box that shows how it should be rounded to the nearest hundred.

479 440 655 405 643

400	500	600	700

5 Use the rule to complete the table.

Rule: Multiply by 6	
Input	Output
2	12
3	
6	
7	
8	

6 Use the model to multiply 426 by 7.

426 = ☐ ☐ ☐

☐

$7 \times 426 =$ ☐

Name ______________________ Date ______________

7 Subtract.

700 − 255 =

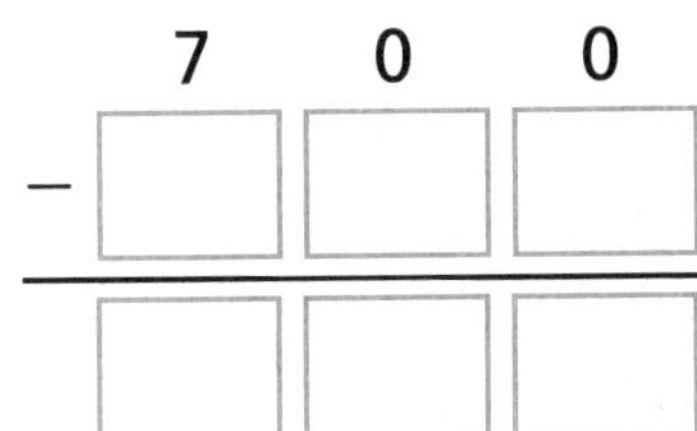

8 Select the number that has the digit 5 in the thousands place. Select all that apply.

Ⓐ 64,500 Ⓒ 25,700

Ⓑ 59,700 Ⓓ 16,705

For numbers 9 and 10, add or subtract. Make a proof drawing to show that your answer is correct.

9
```
  497
+ 326
```

10
```
  690
− 493
```

Name ______________________ Date ______________

For numbers 11 and 12, add or subtract.

Show your work.

11. $\begin{array}{r} 437 \\ +\ 273 \\ \hline \end{array}$

Which method did you use to add?

I used the [New Groups Above / New Groups Below / Show All Totals] Method.

12. $\begin{array}{r} 617 \\ -\ 549 \\ \hline \end{array}$

Did you ungroup to subtract? Explain why or why not.

13. Andre buys 860 bricks. He buys 575 red bricks and 147 tan bricks. The rest of the bricks are gray. Write and solve an equation to find how many gray bricks Andre buys.

Equation: ______________

______ gray bricks

14. A company sells 6,409 cases of fruit. It sells 3,620 cases of oranges and the rest are cases of grapefruit. How many cases of grapefruit does the company sell?

______ cases

Name ______________________ Date ______________

15 Pia collects 245 acorns in a jar. For numbers 15a–15d, select True or False for each statement.

15a. Pia collects 193 more acorns. She now has 338 acorns. ○ True ○ False

15b. Pia gives 160 acorns to Ana. She now has 85 acorns. ○ True ○ False

15c. Pia collects 286 more acorns. She uses 143 to decorate a tray. She now has 388 acorns. ○ True ○ False

15d. Pia gives her two sisters 85 acorns each. She now has 160 acorns. ○ True ○ False

16 Li earns 321 points in the first round of a math contest. He earns another 278 points in the second round and 315 points in the third round. Li says he has 804 points.

Is Li's answer reasonable? Explain.

Find the actual answer to check if you are correct.

Name _________________________ Date _____________

17 Darian sells 293 bags of popcorn and 321 bags of peanuts.

Part A

How many bags of popcorn and peanuts does Darian sell?

_______ bags

Part B

Write a subtraction word problem related to how many bags of popcorn and peanuts Darian sells. Then find the answer without doing any calculations.

18 Sanaz makes 28 puppets for the craft fair. She needs 2 buttons on each puppet. How many buttons does Sanaz need in all?

_______ buttons

Name ______________________ Date ______________

Raise Money

The students at Kevin's school are collecting pennies for a service project. They plan to use the money to buy flowers to plant at a local park. They need 1,000 pennies to buy each flat of flowers.

1. Kevin has collected 873 pennies. Round 873 to the nearest 100. Is the rounded number less than 1,000? Explain.

2. What would you have to add to 873 to get 1,000? How do you know your answer is reasonable?

3. Write an addition word problem related to Problem 2. Explain how the problems are related.

Name ____________________ Date ____________

4 June, Ella, and Joshua also are collecting pennies for the service project. June collected 324 pennies, Ella collected 442 pennies, and Joshua collected 248 pennies.

Part A

Estimate to decide whether these three students collected enough pennies to buy a flat of flowers.

Part B

Find the actual answer to check if you are correct. Explain your strategy.

Part C

How many more pennies do the students need to collect to buy a second flat of flowers? Show your work.

Part D

Write an addition word problem related to Part C. Explain how the problems are related.

Fractions in Measurement

Halves	Quarters
Length	
0 1 2 3	0 1 2 3
Money	
50¢ 50¢ Half-Dollar Half-Dollar	25¢ 25¢ 25¢ 25¢ 4 Quarters
Time	
12 30 30 6 30 minutes + 30 minutes = 60 minutes = 1 hour	 15 minutes + 15 minutes + 15 minutes + 15 minutes = 60 minutes = 1 hour
Liquid Capacity	
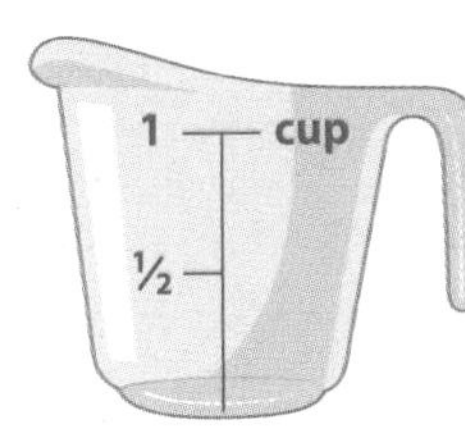	

Measures and Units of Time

Table of Measures

Metric	Customary
Length/Area	
1 meter (m) = 10 decimeters (dm) 1 meter (m) = 100 centimeters (cm) 1 decimeter (dm) = 10 centimeters (cm) 1 square centimeter = 1 cm^2 A metric unit for measuring area. It is the area of a square that is one centimeter on each side.	1 foot (ft) = 12 inches (in.) 1 yard (yd) = 3 feet (ft) 1 mile (mi) = 5,280 feet (ft) 1 square inch = 1 in^2 A customary unit for measuring area. It is the area of a square that is one inch on each side.
Liquid Volume	
1 liter (L) = 1,000 milliliters (mL)	1 tablespoon (tbsp) = $\frac{1}{2}$ fluid ounce (fl oz) 1 cup (c) = 8 fluid ounces (fl oz) 1 pint (pt) = 2 cups (c) 1 quart (qt) = 2 pints (pt) 1 gallon (gal) = 4 quarts (qt)

Table of Units of Time

Time	
1 minute (min) = 60 seconds (sec) 1 hour (hr) = 60 minutes 1 day = 24 hours 1 week (wk) = 7 days 1 month, about 30 days 1 year (yr) = 12 months (mo) or about 52 weeks	1 year = 365 days 1 leap year = 366 days

Properties of Operations

Associative Property of Addition	
$(a + b) + c = a + (b + c)$	$(2 + 5) + 3 = 2 + (5 + 3)$
Commutative Property of Addition	
$a + b = b + a$	$4 + 6 = 6 + 4$
Identity Property of Addition	
$a + 0 = 0 + a = a$	$3 + 0 = 0 + 3 = 3$
Associative Property of Multiplication	
$(a \cdot b) \cdot c = a \cdot (b \cdot c)$	$(3 \cdot 5) \cdot 7 = 3 \cdot (5 \cdot 7)$
Commutative Property of Multiplication	
$a \cdot b = b \cdot a$	$6 \cdot 3 = 3 \cdot 6$
Identity Property of Multiplication	
$a \cdot 1 = 1 \cdot a = a$	$8 \cdot 1 = 1 \cdot 8 = 8$
Zero Property of Multiplication	
$a \cdot 0 = 0 \cdot a = 0$	$5 \cdot 0 = 0 \cdot 5 = 0$
Distributive Property of Multiplication over Addition	
$a \cdot (b + c) = (a \cdot b) + (a \cdot c)$	$2 \cdot (4 + 3) = (2 \cdot 4) + (2 \cdot 3)$

Addition and Subtraction Problem Types

	Result Unknown	Change Unknown	Start Unknown
Add to	Aisha had 274 stamps in her collection. Then her grandfather gave her 65 stamps. How many stamps does she have now? *Situation and solution equation:*[1] $274 + 65 = s$	Aisha had 274 stamps in her collection. Then her grandfather gave her some stamps. Now she has 339 stamps. How many stamps did her grandfather give her? *Situation equation:* $274 + s = 339$ *Solution equation:* $s = 339 - 274$	Aisha had some stamps in her collection. Then her grandfather gave her 65 stamps. Now she has 339 stamps. How many stamps did she have to start? *Situation equation* $s + 65 = 339$ *Solution equation:* $s = 339 - 65$
Take from	A store had 750 bottles of water at the start of the day. During the day, the store sold 490 bottles. How many bottles did they have at the end of the day? *Situation and solution equation:* $750 - 490 = b$	A store had 750 bottles of water at the start of the day. The store had 260 bottles left at the end of the day. How many bottles did the store sell? *Situation equation:* $750 - b = 260$ *Solution equation:* $b = 750 - 260$	A store had a number of bottles of water at the start of the day. The store sold 490 bottles of water. At the end of the day 260 bottles were left. How many bottles did the store have to start with? *Situation equation:* $b - 490 = 260$ *Solution equation:* $b = 260 + 490$

[1]A situation equation represents the structure (action) in the problem situation. A solution equation shows the operation used to find the answer.

Addition and Subtraction Problem Types (continued)

<table>
<tr><th></th><th>Total Unknown</th><th>Addend Unknown</th><th>Other Addends Unknown</th></tr>
<tr><td rowspan="2">Put Together/ Take Apart</td>
<td>A clothing store has 375 shirts with short sleeves and 148 shirts with long sleeves. How many shirts does the store have in all?

Math drawing:[1]

Situation and solution equation:
375 + 148 = s</td>
<td>Of the 523 shirts in a clothing store, 375 have short sleeves. The rest have long sleeves. How many shirts have long sleeves?

Math drawing:

Situation equation:
523 = 375 + s

Solution equation:
s = 523 − 375</td>
<td>A clothing store has 523 shirts. Some have short sleeves and 148 have long sleeves. How many of the shirts have short sleeves?

Math drawing:

Situation equation
523 = s + 148

Solution equation:
s = 523 − 148</td></tr>
<tr><td colspan="2">Both Addends Unknown is a productive extension of this basic situation, especially for small numbers less than or equal to 10. Such take apart situations can be used to show all the decompositions of a given number. The associated equations, which have the total on the left of the equal sign, help students understand that the = sign does not always mean makes or results in but always does mean is the same number as.</td>
<td>Both Addends Unknown

A clothing store has 523 shirts. Some have short sleeves and some have long sleeves. Write a situation equation for how many shirts with long sleeves and how many shirts with short sleeves the store could have.

Math Drawing:
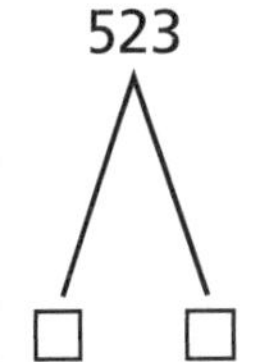

Situation Equation:
523 = □ + □</td></tr>
</table>

[1]These math drawings are called math mountains in Grades 1–3 and break apart drawings in Grades 4 and 5.

Addition and Subtraction Problem Types (continued)

	Difference Unknown	Greater Unknown	Smaller Unknown
Compare	At a zoo, the female black bear weighs 175 pounds. The male black bear weighs 260 pounds. How much more does the male black bear weigh than the female black bear? At a zoo, the female black bear weighs 175 pounds. The male black bear weighs 260 pounds. How much less does the female black bear weigh than the male black bear? *Math drawing:* 260 175 | d *Situation equation:* $175 + d = 260$, or $d = 260 - 175$ *Solution equation:* $d = 260 - 175$	**Leading Language** At a zoo, the female black bear weighs 175 pounds. The male black bear weighs 85 pounds more than the female black bear. How much does the male black bear weigh? **Misleading Language** At a zoo, the female black bear weighs 175 pounds. The female black bear weighs 85 pounds less than the male black bear. How much does the male black bear weigh? *Math drawing:* m 175 | 85 *Situation and solution equation:* $175 + 85 = m$	**Leading Language** At a zoo, the male black bear weighs 260 pounds. The female black bear weighs 85 pounds less than the male black bear. How much does the female black bear weigh? **Misleading Language** At a zoo, the male black bear weighs 260 pounds. The male black bear weighs 85 pounds more than the female black bear. How much does the female black bear weigh? *Math drawing:* 260 f | 85 *Situation equation* $f + 85 = 260$, or $f = 260 - 85$ *Solution equation:* $f = 260 - 85$

A comparison sentence can always be said in two ways. One way uses *more*, and the other uses *fewer* or *less*. Misleading language suggests the wrong operation. For example, it says *the female black bear weighs 85 pounds less than the male*, but you have to add 85 pounds to the female's weight to get the male's weight.

Multiplication and Division Problem Types

	Product Unknown	Group Size Unknown	Number of Groups Unknown
Equal Groups	A teacher bought 5 boxes of markers. There are 8 markers in each box. How many markers did the teacher buy? *Math drawing:* 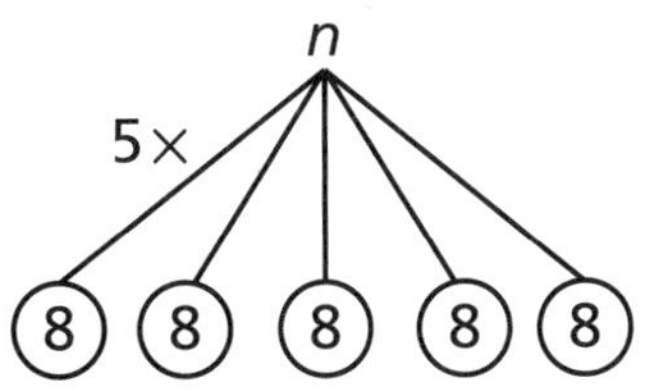 n; 5×; 8 8 8 8 8 *Situation and solution equation:* $n = 5 \cdot 8$	A teacher bought 5 boxes of markers. She bought 40 markers in all. How many markers are in each box? *Math drawing:* 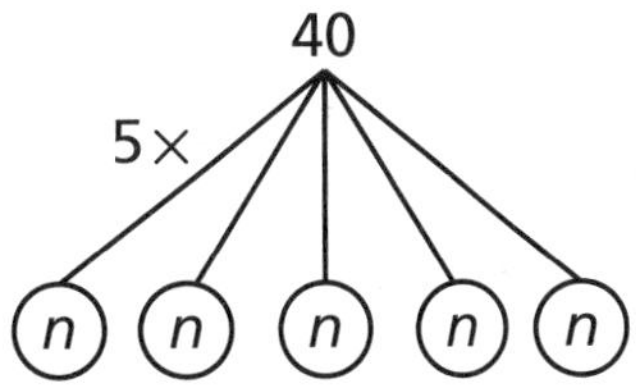 40; 5×; n n n n n *Situation equation:* $5 \cdot n = 40$ *Solution equation:* $n = 40 \div 5$	A teacher bought boxes of 8 markers. She bought 40 markers in all. How many boxes of markers did she buy? *Math drawing:* 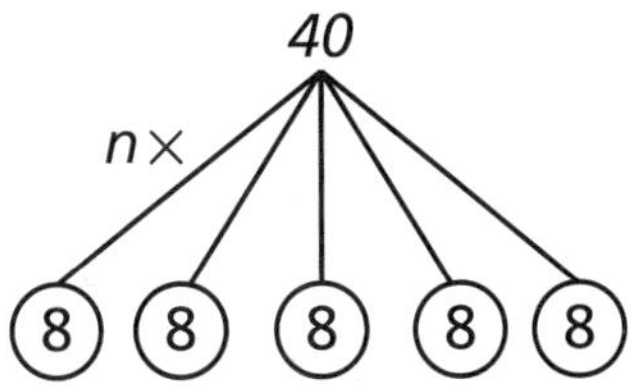 40; n×; 8 8 8 8 8 *Situation equation* $n \cdot 8 = 40$ *Solution equation:* $n = 40 \div 8$

Multiplication and Division Problem Types (continued)

	Product Unknown	Factor Unknown	Factor Unknown
Arrays	For the yearbook photo, the drama club stood in 3 rows of 7 students. How many students were in the photo in all? *Math drawing:* 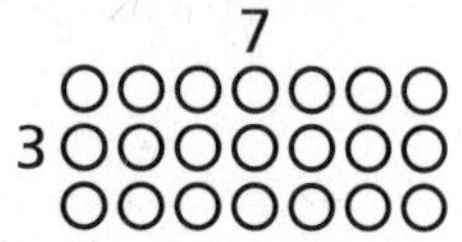 7 3 OOOOOOO OOOOOOO OOOOOOO *Situation and solution equation:* $n = 3 \cdot 7$	For the yearbook photo, the 21 students in drama club stood in 3 equal rows. How many students were in each row? *Math drawing:* 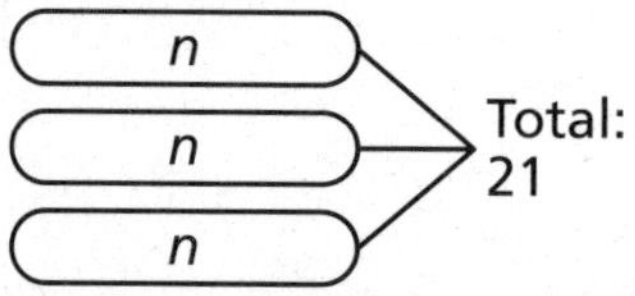 n, n, n — Total: 21 *Situation equation:* $3 \cdot n = 21$ *Solution equation:* $n = 21 \div 3$	For the yearbook photo, the 21 students in drama club stood in rows of 7 students. How many rows were there? *Math drawing:* 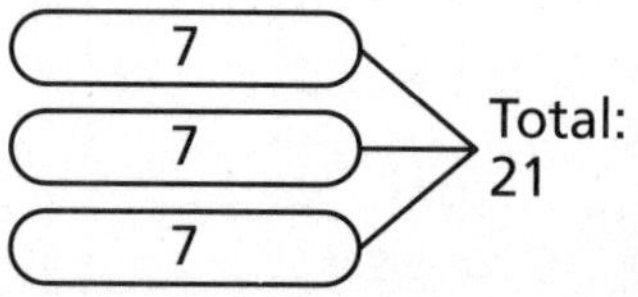 7, 7, 7 — Total: 21 *Situation equation* $n \cdot 7 = 21$ *Solution equation:* $n = 21 \div 7$
Area	The floor of the kitchen is 2 meters by 5 meters. What is the area of the floor? *Math drawing:* 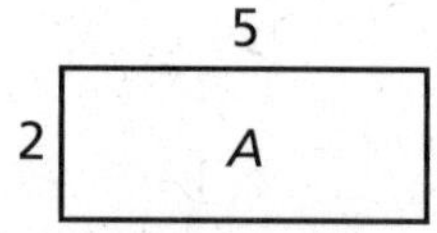 5 2 [A] *Situation and solution equation:* $A = 5 \cdot 2$	The floor of the kitchen is 5 meters long. The area of the floor is 10 square meters. What is the width of the floor? *Math drawing:* 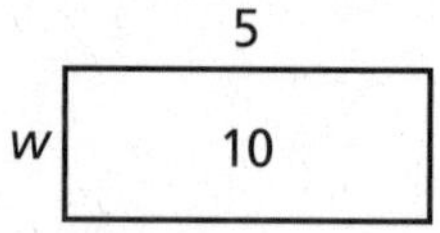 5 w [10] *Situation equation:* $5 \cdot w = 10$ *Solution equation:* $w = 10 \div 5$	The floor of the kitchen is 2 meters wide. The area of the floor is 10 square meters. What is the length of the floor? *Math drawing:* 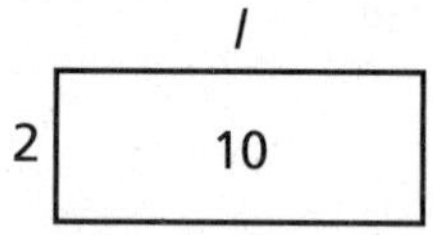 l 2 [10] *Situation equation* $l \cdot 2 = 10$ *Solution equation:* $l = 10 \div 2$

MathWord **Power**

Word Review

Work with a partner. Choose a word from a current unit or a review word from a previous unit. Use the word to complete one of the activities listed on the right. Then ask your partner if they have any edits to your work or questions about what you described. Repeat, having your partner choose a word.

Activities

- Give the meaning in words or gestures.
- Use the word in a sentence.
- Give another word that is related to the word in some way and explain the relationship.

Crossword Puzzle

Create a crossword puzzle similar to the example below. Use vocabulary words from the unit. You can add other related words, too. Challenge your partner to solve the puzzle.

<table>
<tr><td></td><td></td><td></td><td></td><td>1 s</td><td>u</td><td>m</td><td></td></tr>
<tr><td></td><td>2 a</td><td></td><td></td><td>u</td><td></td><td></td><td></td></tr>
<tr><td></td><td>d</td><td></td><td></td><td>b</td><td></td><td></td><td></td></tr>
<tr><td>3 a</td><td>d</td><td>d</td><td>i</td><td>t</td><td>i</td><td>o</td><td>4 n</td></tr>
<tr><td></td><td>e</td><td></td><td></td><td>r</td><td></td><td></td><td>u</td></tr>
<tr><td></td><td>n</td><td></td><td></td><td>a</td><td></td><td></td><td>m</td></tr>
<tr><td>5 a</td><td>d</td><td>d</td><td></td><td>c</td><td></td><td></td><td>b</td></tr>
<tr><td></td><td></td><td></td><td></td><td>t</td><td></td><td></td><td>e</td></tr>
<tr><td></td><td></td><td></td><td></td><td>i</td><td></td><td></td><td>r</td></tr>
<tr><td>6 r</td><td>e</td><td>g</td><td>r</td><td>o</td><td>u</td><td>p</td><td></td></tr>
<tr><td></td><td></td><td></td><td></td><td>n</td><td></td><td></td><td></td></tr>
</table>

Across

1. The answer to an addition problem
3. __________ and subtraction are operations that undo each other.
5. To put amounts together
6. When you trade 10 ones for 1 ten, you __________.

Down

1. The operation that you can use to find out how much more one number is than another
2. In 24 + 65 = 89, 24 is an _____.
4. A combination of the digits 0, 1, 2, 3, 4, 5, 6, 7, 8, and 9

Word Wall

With your teacher's permission, start a word wall in your classroom. As you work through each lesson, put the math vocabulary words on index cards and place them on the word wall. You can work with a partner or a small group choosing a word and giving the definition.

Word Web 

Make a word web for a word or words you do not understand in a unit. Fill in the web with words or phrases that are related to the vocabulary word.

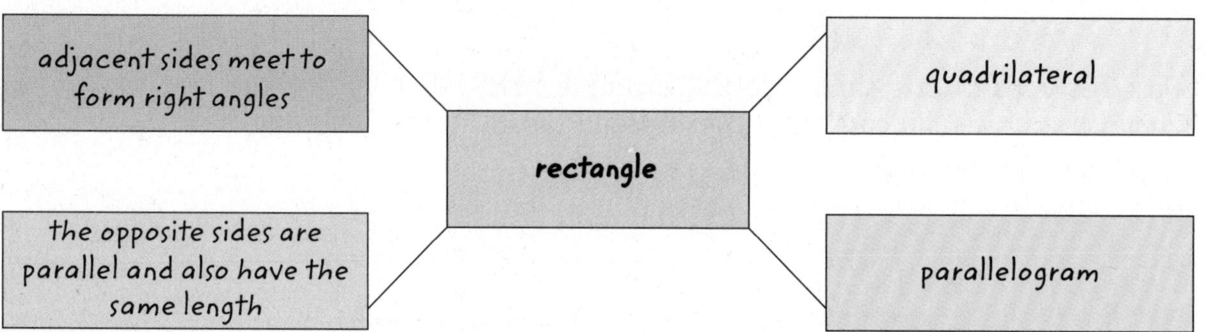

Alphabet Challenge 

Take an alphabet challenge. Choose three letters from the alphabet. Think of three vocabulary words for each letter. Then write the definition or draw an example for each word.

A	D	L
addition	data	liter
array	denominator	line segment
area	divide	line plot

Concentration 

Write the vocabulary words and related words from a unit on index cards. Write the definitions on a different set of index cards. Choose 3 to 6 pairs of vocabulary words and definitions. Mix up the set of pairs. Then place the cards facedown on a table. Take turns turning over two cards. If one card is a word and one card is a definition that matches the word, take the pair. Continue until each word has been matched with its definition.

Math Journal 

As you learn new words, write them in your Math Journal. Write the definition of the word and include a sketch or an example. As you learn new information about the word, add notes to your definition.

polygon: a closed plane figure with sides made of straight line segments.

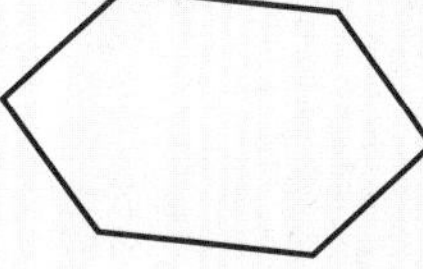

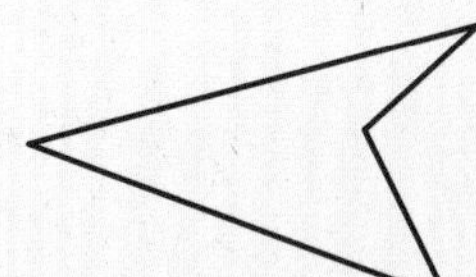

In concave polygons, there exists a line segment with endpoints inside the polygon and a point on the line segment that is outside the polygon.

What's the Word? 

Work together to make a poster or bulletin board display of the words in a unit. Write definitions on a set of index cards. Mix up the cards. Work with a partner, choosing a definition from the index cards. Have your partner point to the word on the poster and name the matching math vocabulary word. Switch roles and try the activity again.

the bottom number in a fraction that shows the total number of equal parts in the whole

fraction
unit fraction
denominator
numerator
equivalent
equivalent fractions
equivalence chain
thirds
fourths
eighths
halves
sixths

A

addend
One of two or more numbers to be added together to find a sum.

Example:

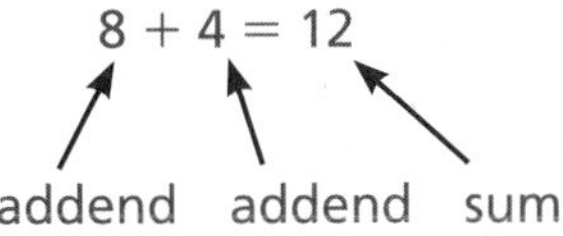

addition
A mathematical operation that combines two or more numbers.

Example:

23 + 52 = 75

addend addend sum

adjacent sides
Two sides of a figure that meet at a point.

Example:

Sides *a* and *b* are adjacent.

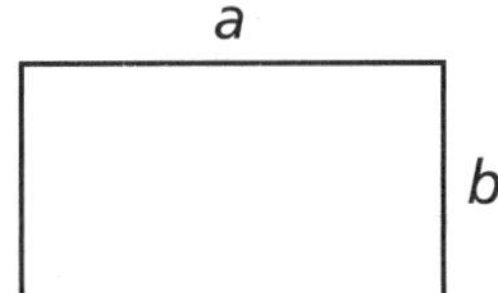

A.M.
The time period between midnight and noon.

analog clock
A clock with a face and hands.

angle
A figure formed by two rays or two line segments that meet at an endpoint.

area
The total number of square units that cover a figure.

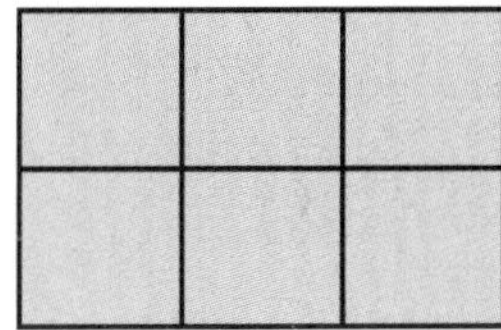

Example:

The area of the rectangle is 6 square units.

array
An arrangement of objects, pictures, or numbers in columns and rows.

Associative Property of Addition (Grouping Property of Addition)
The property that states that changing the way in which addends are grouped does not change the sum.

Example:

(2 + 3) + 1 = 2 + (3 + 1)

5 + 1 = 2 + 4

6 = 6

Associative Property of Multiplication (Grouping Property of Multiplication)

The property that states that changing the way in which factors are grouped does not change the product.

Example:

$(2 \times 3) \times 4 = 2 \times (3 \times 4)$

$6 \times 4 = 2 \times 12$

$24 = 24$

axis (plural: axes)

A reference line for a graph. A graph has two axes; one is horizontal and the other is vertical.

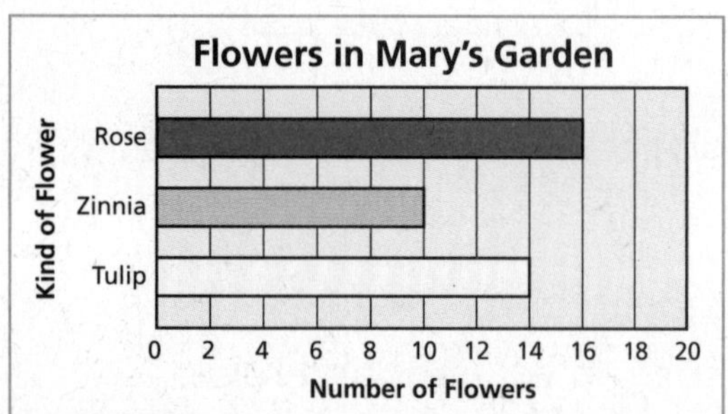

B

bar graph

A graph that uses bars to show data. The bars may be horizontal, as in the graph above, or vertical, as in the graph below.

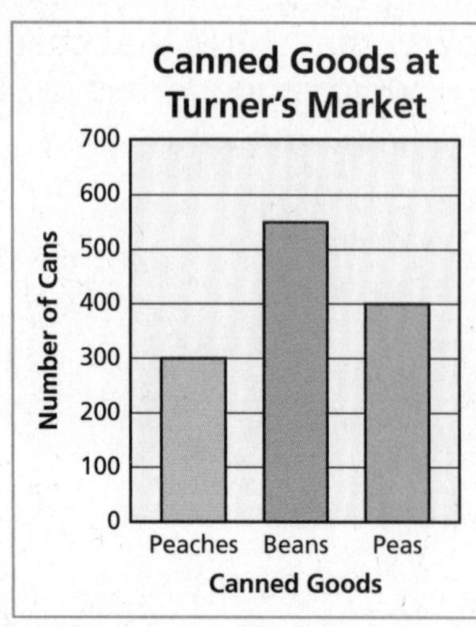

C

capacity

The amount a container can hold.

Celsius (°C)

A scale used to measure temperature.

Examples:

Water freezes at 0°C.

Water boils at 100°C.

centimeter (cm)

A metric unit used to measure length.

100 centimeters = 1 meter

column

A part of a table or array that contains items arranged vertically.

● ● ● ●
● ● ● ●
● ● ● ●
● ● ● ●

Commutative Property of Addition (Order Property of Addition)

The property that states that changing the order of addends does not change the sum.

Example:

$3 + 7 = 7 + 3$

$10 = 10$

Commutative Property of Multiplication (Order Property of Multiplication)

The property that states that changing the order of factors does not change the product.

Example:

$5 \times 4 = 4 \times 5$

$20 = 20$

comparison bars*

Bars that represent the greater amount, lesser amount, and difference in a comparison problem.

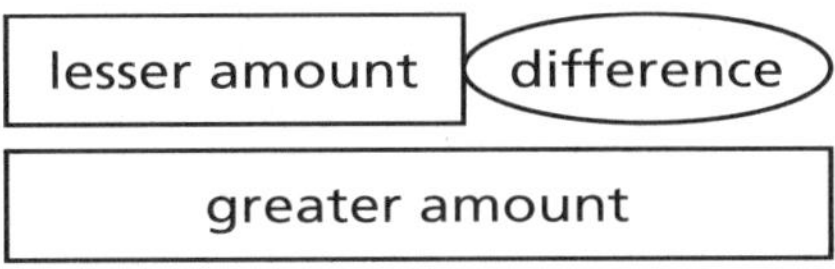

compatible numbers

Numbers that are easy to compute mentally. Compatible numbers can be used to check if answers are reasonable.

Example:

692 + 234

Some compatible numbers for the addends are 700 and 200 or 700 and 234.

concave

A polygon for which you can connect two points inside the polygon with a segment that passes outside the polygon.

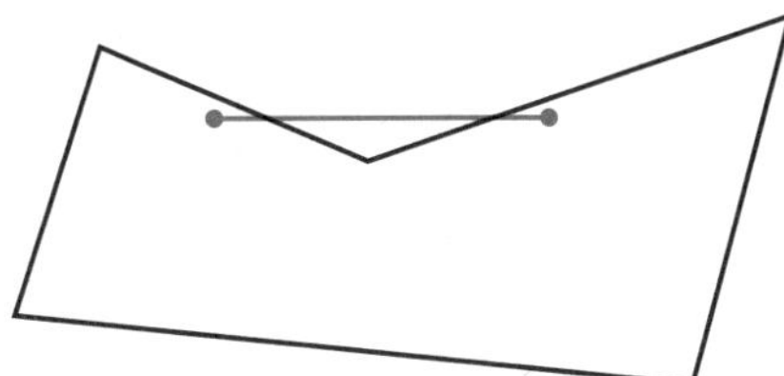

convex

A polygon is convex if all of its diagonals are inside it.

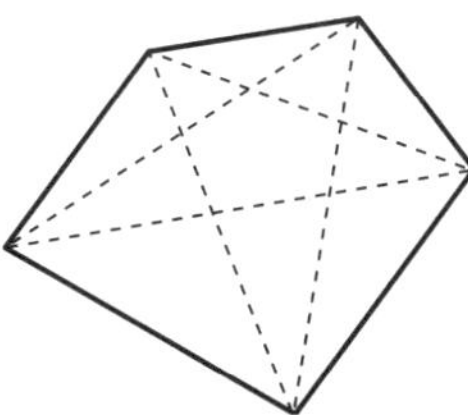

cup (c)

A U.S. customary unit of measure used to measure capacity.

1 cup = 8 fluid ounces

2 cups = 1 pint

4 cups = 1 quart

16 cups = 1 gallon

D

data

A collection of information about people or things.

decagon

A polygon with 10 sides.

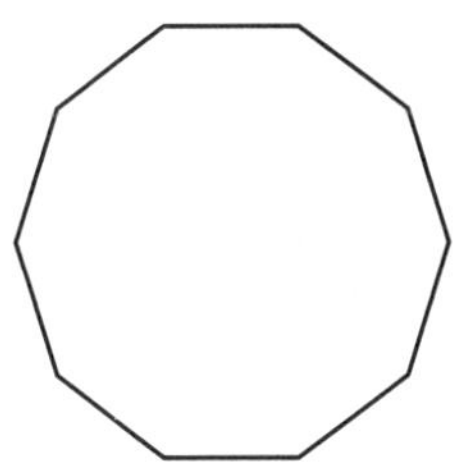

decimeter (dm)

A metric unit used to measure length.

1 decimeter = 10 centimeters

decompose

To separate or break apart (a geometric figure or a number) into smaller parts.

denominator

The bottom number in a fraction that shows the total number of equal parts in the whole.

Example:

$\frac{1}{3}$ ← denominator

diagonal

A line segment that connects two corners of a figure and is not a side of the figure.

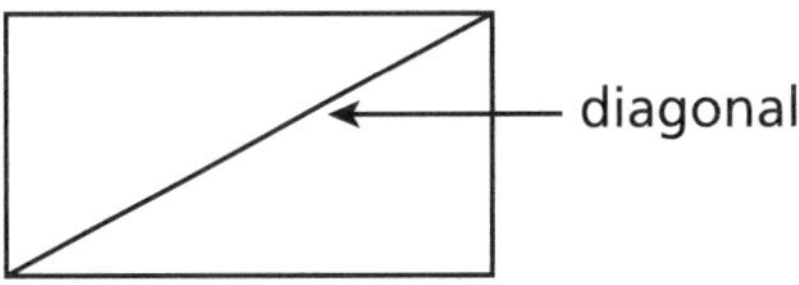

difference

The result of subtraction or of comparing.

*A classroom research-based term developed for *Math Expressions*

digit
Any of the symbols 0, 1, 2, 3, 4, 5, 6, 7, 8, 9.

digital clock
A clock that displays the hour and minutes with numbers.

Distributive Property
You can multiply a sum by a number, or multiply each addend by the number and add the products; the result is the same.

Example:
$3 \times (2 + 4) = (3 \times 2) + (3 \times 4)$

$3 \times 6 = 6 + 12$

$18 = 18$

dividend
The number that is divided in division.

Examples:

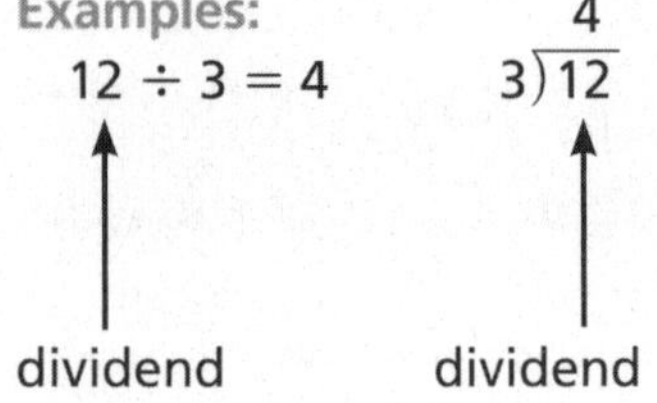

division
The mathematical operation that separates an amount into smaller equal groups to find the number of groups or the number in each group.

Example:
12 ÷ 3 = 4 is a division number sentence.

divisor
The number that you divide by in division.

Example: 12 ÷ 3 = 4 3)12 (quotient 4)

divisor divisor

E

elapsed time
The time that passes between the beginning and the end of an activity.

endpoint
The point at either end of a line segment or the beginning point of a ray.

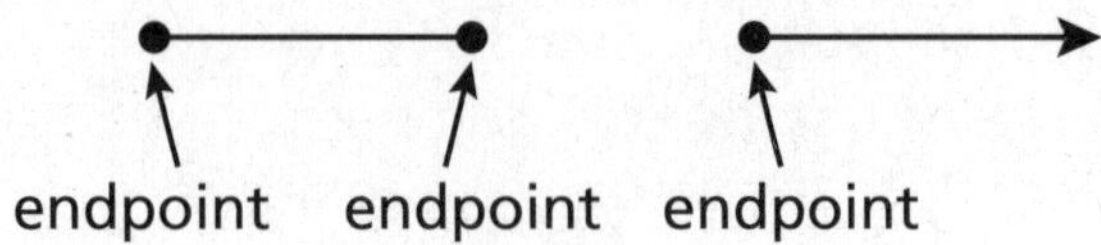

endpoint endpoint endpoint

equal (=)
A symbol used to compare two amounts or values. It shows that what is on the left of the sign is equal to or the same value as what is on the right of the sign.

Example:
3,756 = 3,756

3,756 *is equal to* 3,756.

equal groups
Two or more groups with the same number of items in each group.

equation
A mathematical sentence with an equals sign.

Examples:
11 + 22 = 33

75 − 25 = 50

equivalent
Equal, or naming the same amount.

equivalent fractions
Fractions that name the same amount.

Example:

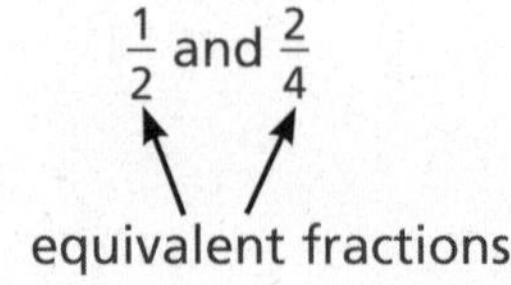

equivalent fractions

estimate
A reasonable guess about how many or about how much.

even number
A whole number that is a multiple of 2. The ones digit in an even number is 0, 2, 4, 6, or 8.

expanded form
A number written to show the value of each of its digits.

Examples:
347 = 300 + 40 + 7
347 = 3 hundreds + 4 tens + 7 ones

expression
A combination of numbers, variables, and/or operation signs. An expression does not have an equal sign.

Examples:
$4 + 7$ $a - 3$

F

factor
Any of the numbers that are multiplied to give a product.

Example:
$4 \times 5 = 20$

factor factor product

Fahrenheit (°F)
A scale used to measure temperature.

Examples:
Water freezes at 32°F.
Water boils at 212°F.

fluid ounce (fl oz)
A unit of liquid volume in the U.S. customary system that equals $\frac{1}{8}$ cup or 2 tablespoons.

foot (ft)
A U.S. customary unit used to measure length.

1 foot = 12 inches

fraction
A number that names part of a whole or part of a set.

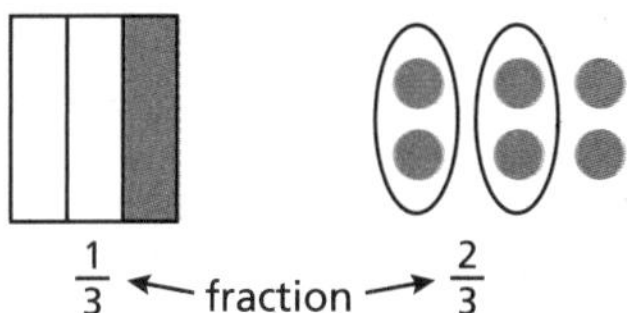
$\frac{1}{3}$ ← fraction → $\frac{2}{3}$

frequency table
A table that shows how many times each event, item, or category occurs.

Frequency Table	
Age	Number of Players
7	1
8	3
9	5
10	4
11	2

function table
A table of ordered pairs that shows a function.

For every input number, there is only one possible output number.

Rule: Add 2	
Input	Output
1	3
2	4
3	5
4	6

G

gallon (gal)
A U.S. customary unit used to measure capacity.

1 gallon = 4 quarts = 8 pints = 16 cups

gram (g)
A metric unit of mass. One paper clip has a mass of about 1 gram.

1,000 grams = 1 kilogram

greatest
56 29 64

64 is the greatest number.

group
To combine numbers to form new tens, hundreds, thousands, and so on.

H

height
A vertical distance, or how tall something is.

hexagon
A polygon with six sides.

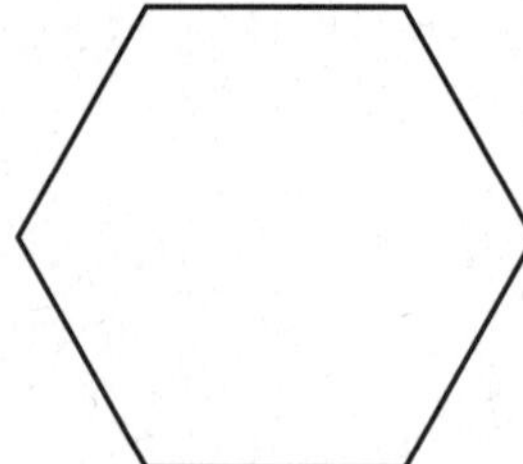

horizontal
Extending in two directions, left and right.

horizontal bar graph
A bar graph with horizontal bars.

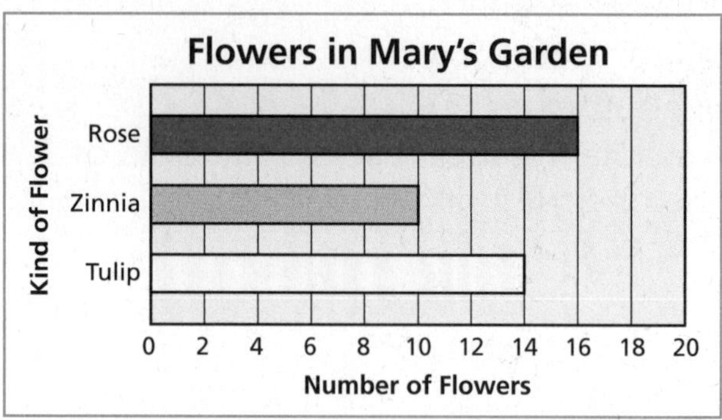

hundred thousands

Hundred Thousands	Ten Thousands	Thousands	Hundreds	Tens	Ones
5	4	6	7	8	2

There are 5 hundred thousands in 546,782.

hundreds

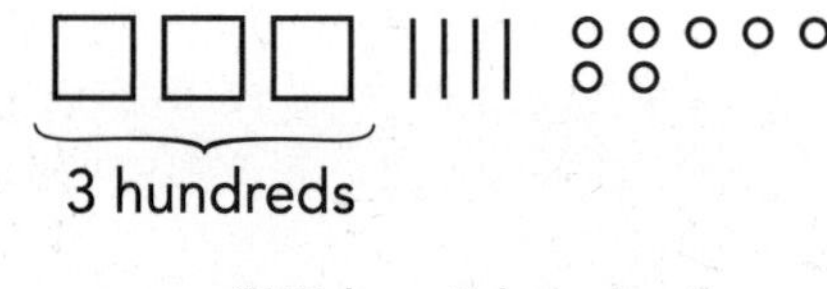

3 hundreds

347 has 3 hundreds.

hundreds

I

Identity Property of Addition
If 0 is added to a number, the sum equals that number.

Example:
$3 + 0 = 3$

Identity Property of Multiplication
The product of 1 and any number equals that number.

Example:
$10 \times 1 = 10$

improper fraction
A fraction in which the numerator is equal to or is greater than the denominator. Improper fractions are equal to or greater than 1.

$\frac{5}{5}$ and $\frac{8}{3}$ are improper fractions.

inch (in.)
A U.S. customary unit used to measure length.

12 inches = 1 foot

input-output table
A table that displays ordered pairs of numbers that follow a specific rule.

Rule: Add 4	
Input	**Output**
3	7
5	9
9	13
11	15
15	19

is greater than (>)
A symbol used to compare two numbers.

Example:

$6 > 5$

6 *is greater than* 5.

is less than (<)
A symbol used to compare two numbers.

Example:

$5 < 6$

5 *is less than* 6.

K

key
A part of a map, graph, or chart that explains what symbols mean.

kilogram (kg)
A metric unit of mass.

1 kilogram = 1,000 grams

kilometer (km)
A metric unit of length.

1 kilometer = 1,000 meters

L

least
72 41 89

41 is the least number.

line
A straight path that goes on forever in opposite directions.

line plot
A diagram that shows frequency of data on a number line. Also called a *dot plot*.

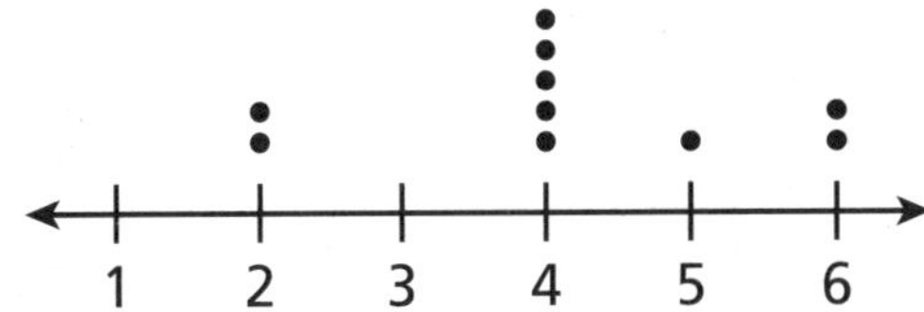

line segment
A part of a line. A line segment has two endpoints.

liquid volume
A measure of how much a container can hold. Also called *capacity*.

liter (L)
A metric unit used to measure capacity.

1 liter = 1,000 milliliters

M

mass
The amount of matter in an object.

mental math
A way to solve problems without using pencil and paper or a calculator.

meter (m)
A metric unit used to measure length.
1 meter = 100 centimeters

method
A procedure, or way, of doing something.

mile (mi)
A U.S. customary unit of length.
1 mile = 5,280 feet

milliliter (mL)
A metric unit used to measure capacity.
1,000 milliliters = 1 liter

mixed number
A whole number and a fraction.
$1\frac{3}{4}$ is a mixed number.

multiple
A number that is the product of the given number and any whole number.

multiplication
A mathematical operation that combines equal groups.

Example:

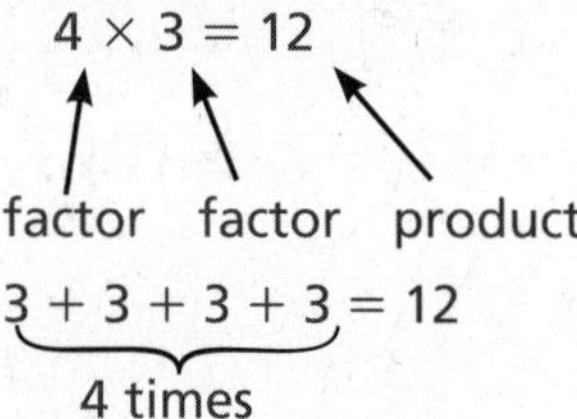

N

number line
A line on which numbers are assigned to lengths.

numerator
The top number in a fraction that shows the number of equal parts counted.

Example:

$\frac{1}{3}$ ← numerator

O

octagon
A polygon with eight sides.

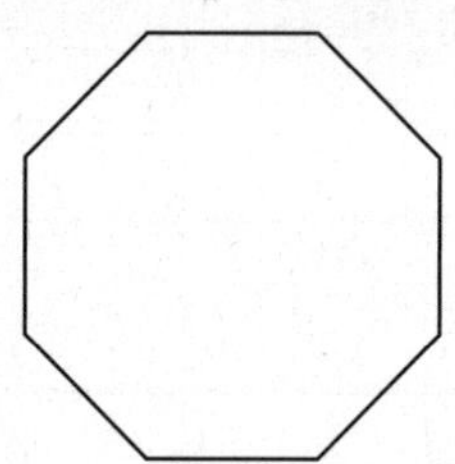

odd number
A whole number that is not a multiple of 2. The ones digit in an odd number is 1, 3, 5, 7, or 9.

ones

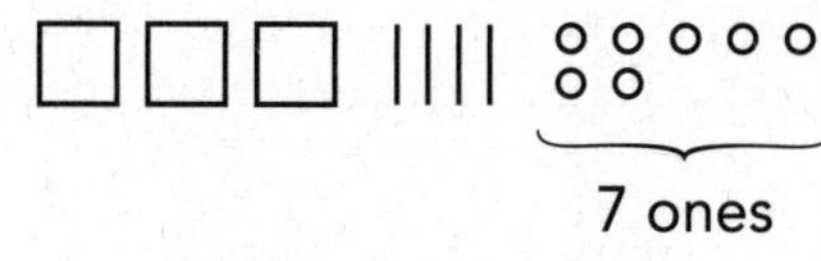

347 has 7 ones.

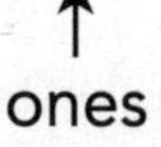

opposite sides

Sides of a polygon that are across from each other; they do not meet at a point.

Example:

Sides *a* and *c* are opposite.

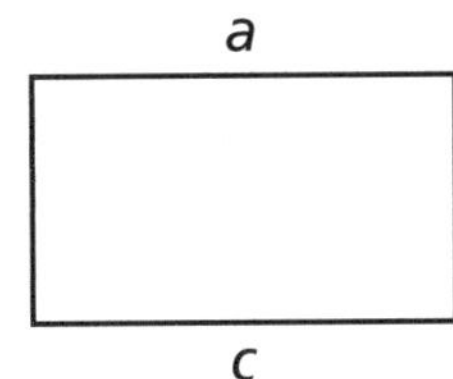

Order of Operations

A set of rules that state the order in which the operations in an expression should be done.

STEP 1: Perform operations inside parentheses first.

STEP 2: Multiply and divide from left to right.

STEP 3: Add and subtract from left to right.

ounce (oz)

A U.S. customary unit used to measure weight.

16 ounces = 1 pound

P

parallel

Two lines are parallel if they never cross or meet. They are the same distance apart.

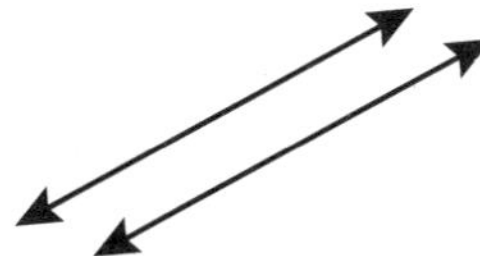

parallelogram

A quadrilateral with both pairs of opposite sides parallel.

pentagon

A polygon with five sides.

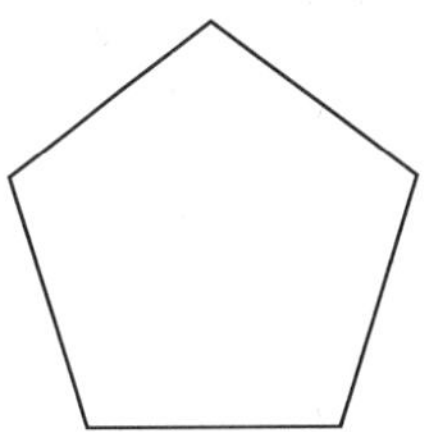

perimeter

The distance around a figure.

Example:

Perimeter = 3 cm + 5 cm + 3 cm + 5 cm = 16 cm

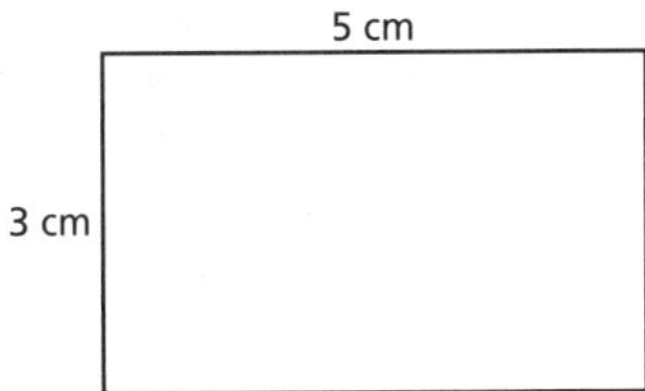

perpendicular

Two lines are perpendicular if they cross or meet to form square corners.

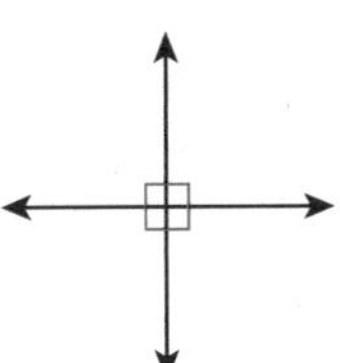

pictograph

A graph that uses pictures or symbols to represent data.

pint (pt)

A U.S. customary unit used to measure capacity.

1 pint = 2 cups

place value

The value assigned to the place that a digit occupies in a number.

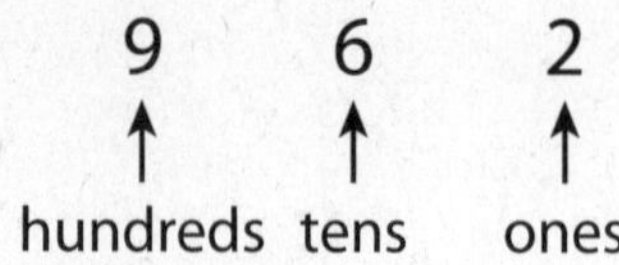

place value drawing

A drawing that represents a number. Hundreds are represented by boxes, tens by vertical lines, and ones by small circles.

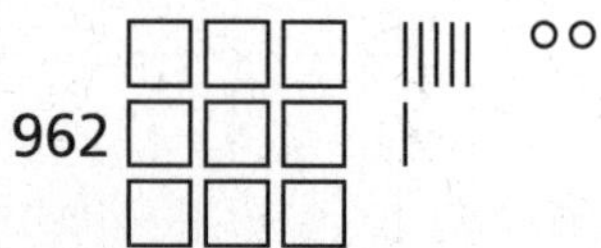

P.M.

The time period between noon and midnight.

polygon

A closed plane figure with sides made up of straight line segments.

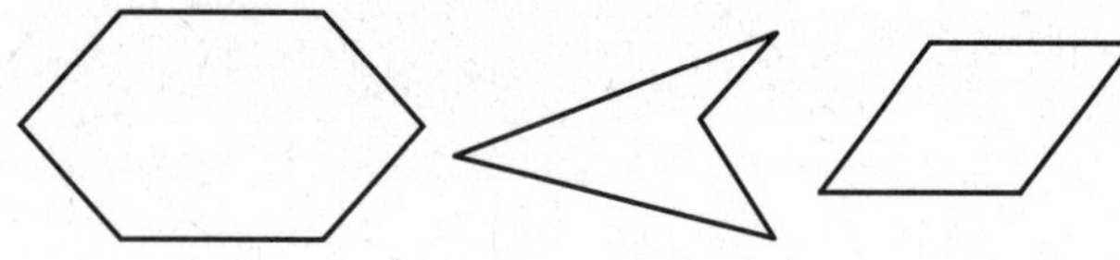

pound (lb)

A U.S. customary unit used to measure weight.

1 pound = 16 ounces

product

The answer when you multiply numbers.

Example:

$4 \times 7 = 28$

factor factor product

proof drawing*

A drawing used to show that an answer is correct.

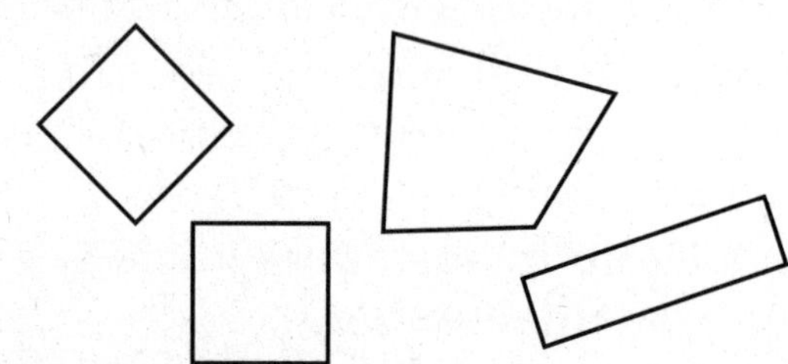

Q

quadrilateral

A polygon with four sides.

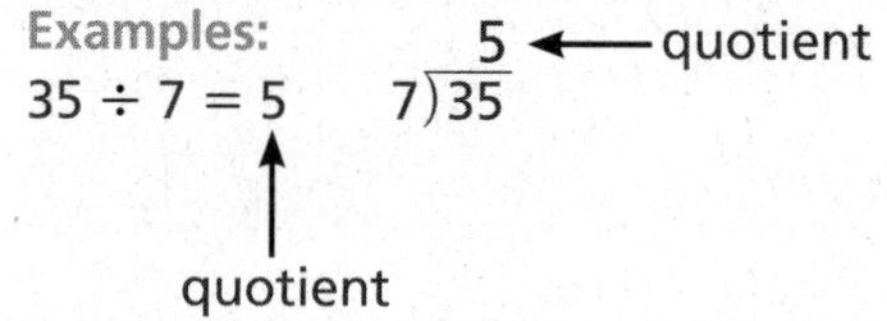

quart (qt)

A U.S. customary unit used to measure capacity.

1 quart = 4 cups

quotient

The answer when you divide numbers.

Examples:

$35 \div 7 = 5$ (quotient: 5)

$7\overline{)35}$ with 5 ← quotient

R

ray

A part of a line that has one endpoint and goes on forever in one direction.

*A classroom research-based term developed for *Math Expressions*

rectangle
A parallelogram that has four right angles.

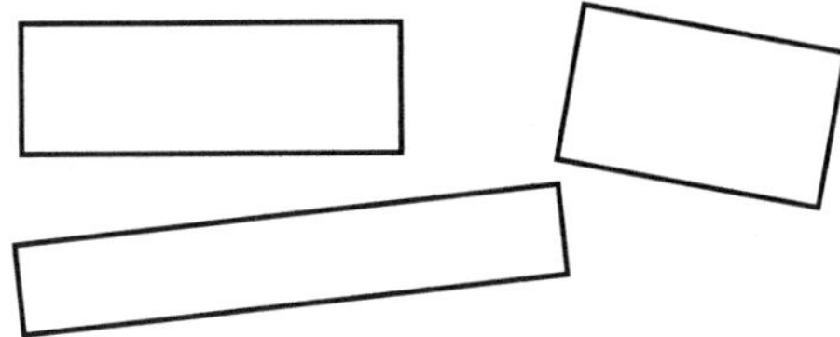

rhombus
A parallelogram with equal sides.

right angle
An angle that measures 90°.

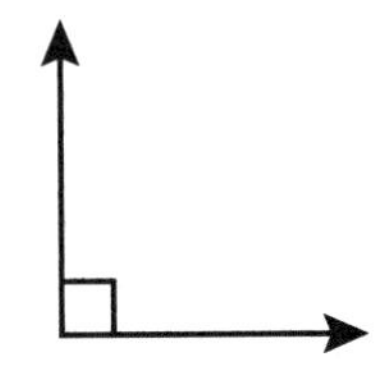

round
To find about how many or how much by expressing a number to the nearest ten, hundred, thousand, and so on.

row
A part of a table or array that contains items arranged horizontally.

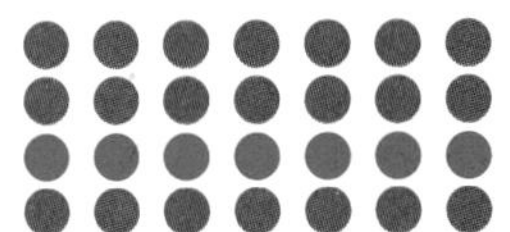

rule
For an input-output table, a *rule* is applied to the input to find the output.

Rule: Add 4	
Input	**Output**
3	7
5	9
9	13
11	15
15	19

S

scale
An arrangement of numbers in order with equal intervals.

side (of a figure)
One of the line segments that make up a polygon.

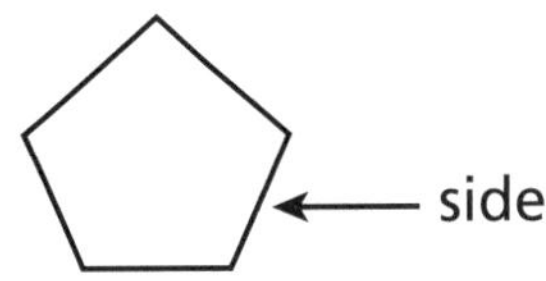

simplify
To write an equivalent fraction with a smaller numerator and denominator.

situation equation*
An equation that shows the action or the relationship in a problem.

Example:
$35 + n = 40$

solution equation*
An equation that shows the operation to perform in order to solve the problem.

Example:
$n = 40 - 35$

square
A rectangle with four sides of the same length.

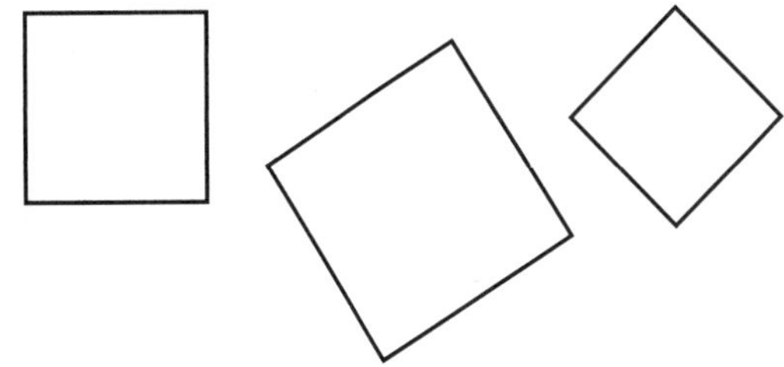

*A classroom research-based term developed for *Math Expressions*

square number
The product of a whole number and itself.

Example:
4 × 4 = 16

↑

square number

square unit
A unit of area equal to the area of a square with one-unit sides.

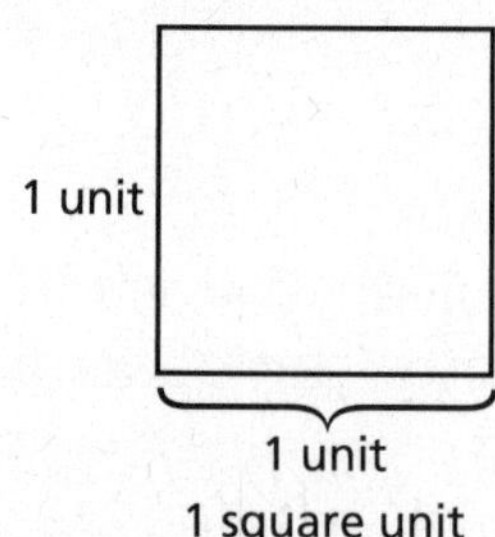

standard form
The name of a number written using digits.

Example:
1,829

subtract
To find the difference of two numbers.

Example:
18 − 11 = 7

subtraction
A mathematical operation on two numbers that gives the difference.

Example:
43 − 40 = 3

sum
The answer when adding two or more addends.

Example:
37 + 52 = 89

addend addend sum

T

table
An easy-to-read arrangement of data, usually in rows and columns.

Favorite Team Sport	
Sport	**Number of Students**
Baseball	35
Soccer	60
Basketball	40

tally chart
A chart used to record and organize data with tally marks.

Tally Chart	
Age	**Tally**
7	I
8	III
9	𝍸

tally marks
Short line segments drawn in groups of 5. Each mark, including the slanted mark, stands for 1 unit.

𝍸 𝍸 ||| means 13
5 5 3

temperature
The measure of how hot or cold something is.

ten thousands

Hundred Thousands	Ten Thousands	Thousands	Hundreds	Tens	Ones
5	4	6	7	8	2

There are 4 ten thousands in 546,782.

tens

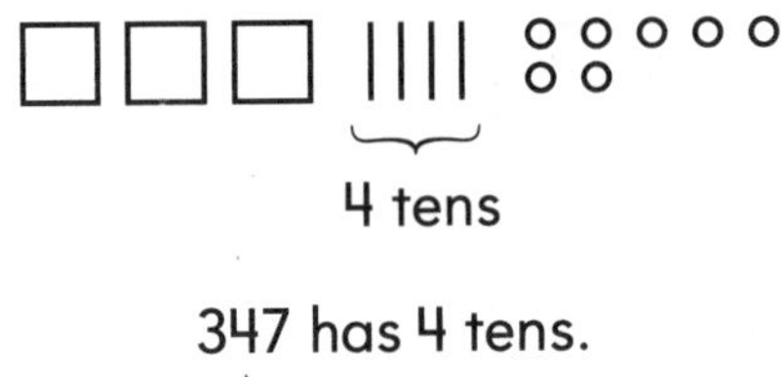

thermometer

A tool that is used to measure temperature.

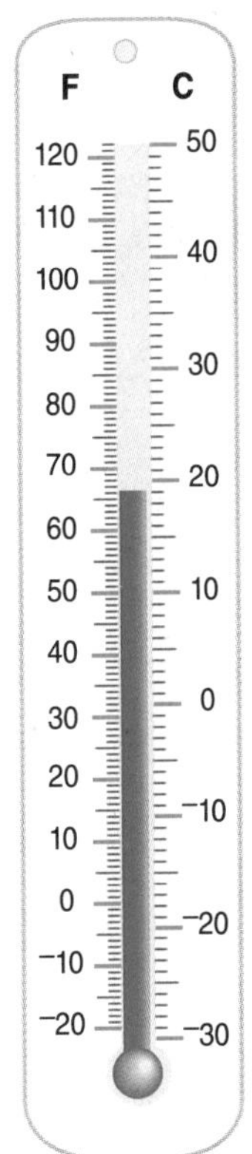

thousands

Hundred Thousands	Ten Thousands	Thousands	Hundreds	Tens	Ones
5	4	6	7	8	2

There are 6 thousands in 546,782.

total

The answer when adding two or more addends. The sum of two or more numbers.

Example:

672 + 228 = 900

addend addend total, or sum

trapezoid

A quadrilateral with exactly one pair of parallel sides.

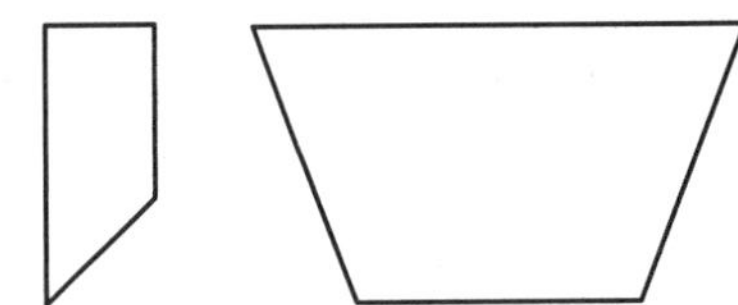

triangle

A polygon with three sides.

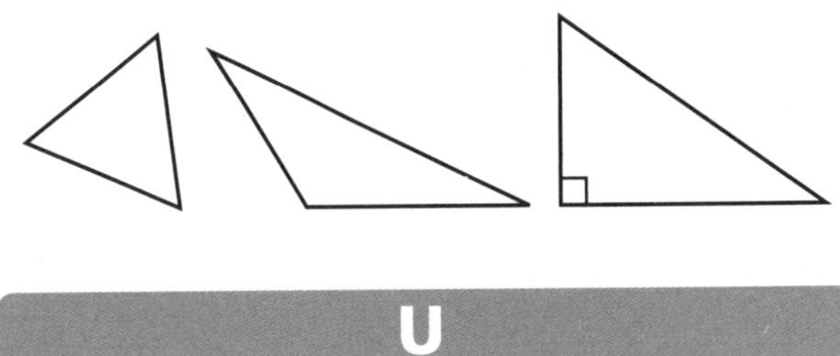

U

ungroup*

To open up 1 in a given place to make 10 of the next smaller place value in order to subtract.

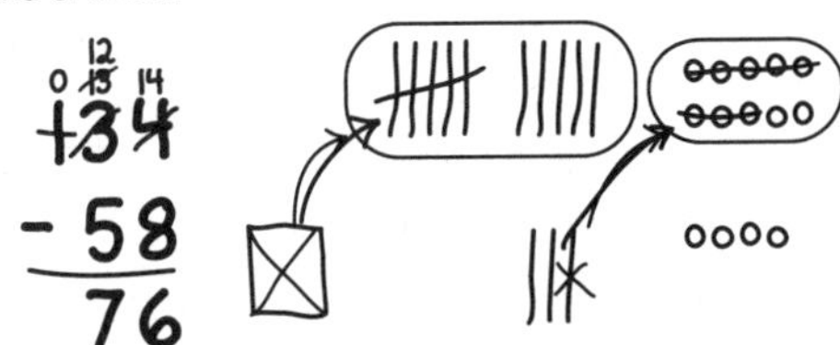

unit fraction

A fraction whose numerator is 1. It shows one equal part of a whole.

Example:

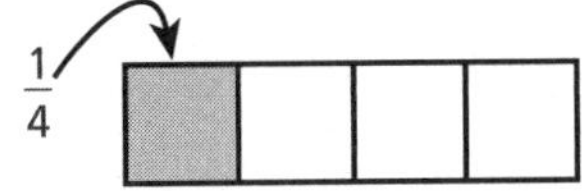

*A classroom research-based term developed for *Math Expressions*

unit square
A square whose area is 1 square unit.

V

variable
A letter or symbol used to represent an unknown number in an algebraic expression or equation.

Example:
$2 + n$
n is a variable.

Venn diagram
A diagram that uses circles to show the relationship among sets of objects.

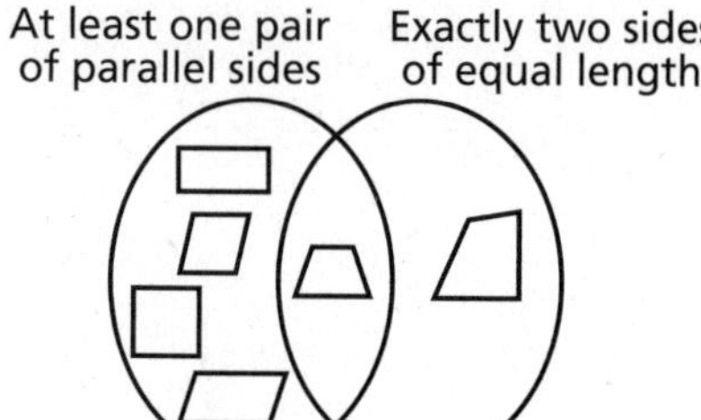

vertex
A point where sides, rays, or edges meet.

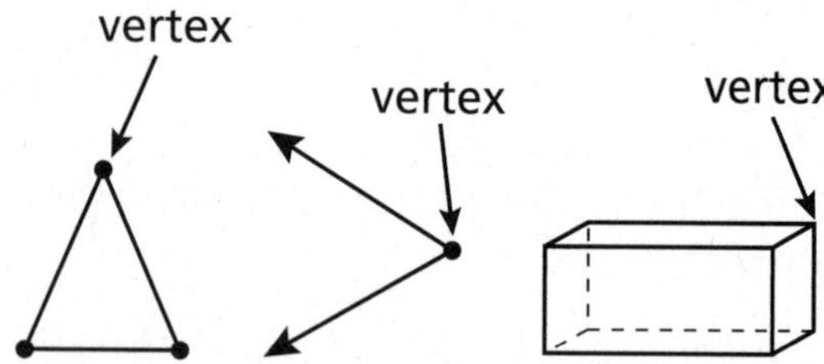

vertical
Extending in two directions, up and down.

vertical bar graph
A bar graph with vertical bars.

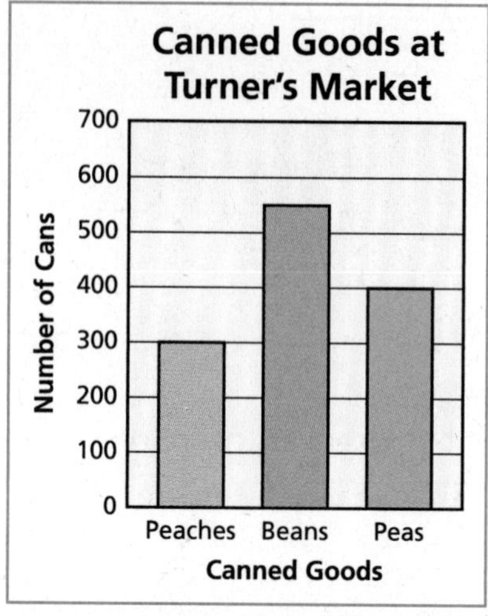

W

weight
The measure of how heavy something is.

word form
A name of a number written using words instead of digits.

Example:
Nine hundred eighty-four

Y

yard (yd)
A U.S. customary unit used to measure length.
1 yard = 3 feet = 36 inches

Z

Zero Property of Multiplication
If 0 is multiplied by a number, the product is 0.

Example:
$3 \times 0 = 0$

3.ARO Algebraic Reasoning and Operations

3.ARO.1	Given an expression such as 3 × 8, describe the product as the total number of objects in 3 groups of 8 objects.	Unit 1 Lessons 1, 2, 3, 4, 5, 6, 7, 8, 9, 10, 12, 13, 14, 16, 18, 19; Unit 2 Lessons 2, 4, 7, 9, 10, 11, 13, 15
3.ARO.2	Given an expression such as 35 ÷ 7, describe the quotient as the *number of objects in a group* when 35 objects are separated into equal shares, or the *number of equal shares* when 35 objects are separated into equal groups of 7 objects.	Unit 1 Lessons 4, 5, 6, 7, 9, 10, 12, 13, 14, 16, 17, 18, 19; Unit 2 Lessons 2, 4, 7, 9, 10, 11, 13, 15
3.ARO.3	Solve multiplication and division word problems through 100 involving arrays, equal groups, and measurements (example: area model); represent the problem using for example, pictures and equations that have symbols for the unknown quantity.	Unit 1 Lessons 2, 3, 4, 5, 6, 7, 9, 10, 12, 13, 14, 16, 17, 18, 19; Unit 2 Lessons 2, 4, 7, 9, 10, 11, 13, 15; Unit 3 Lessons 20, 21; Unit 4 Lesson 15; Unit 5 Lesson 5; Unit 6 Lessons 2, 3, 8, 9, 10, 11; Unit 7 Lessons 1, 2, 3, 4
3.ARO.4	Given a multiplication or division equation involving 3 whole numbers, find the unknown quantity that makes the equation true.	Unit 1 Lessons 1, 4, 5, 6, 7, 8, 9, 10, 12, 13, 14, 16, 17, 18, 19; Unit 2 Lessons 1, 2, 3, 4, 5, 6, 7, 8, 9, 10, 11, 13, 14, 15; Unit 5 Lesson 2; Unit 6 Lessons 2, 3
3.ARO.5	Use properties of operations as strategies for multiplying and dividing.	Unit 1 Lessons 3, 6, 11, 12, 14, 15, 19; Unit 2 Lessons 1, 8, 12, 15; Unit 5 Lesson 2
3.ARO.6	Use multiplication knowledge to recognize that division can be thought of as an unknown factor problem.	Unit 1 Lessons 4, 5, 6, 7, 8, 9, 10, 11, 12, 13, 14, 15, 16, 17, 18; Unit 2 Lessons 1, 2, 3, 4, 5, 6, 7, 8, 9, 10, 11, 12, 13, 14; Unit 5 Lesson 2
3.ARO.7	Demonstrate fluency in multiplying and dividing through 100 by using strategies like the properties of operations or the relationship between multiplication and division (example: if you know 4 × 7 = 28 then you know 28 ÷ 4 = 7). Know the products of two 1-digit numbers from memory by the end of Grade 3.	Unit 1 Lessons 1, 2, 3, 4, 5, 6, 7, 8, 9, 10, 11, 12, 13, 14, 15, 16, 17, 18, 19; Unit 2 Lessons 1, 2, 3, 4, 5, 6, 7, 8, 9, 10, 11, 12, 13, 14, 15

3.ARO.8	Use the four operations to solve two-step word problems; represent the problems with equations using a letter for an unknown quantity. Determine if an answer is reasonable by estimating (example: round to estimate the answer) and using mental math.	Unit 2 Lessons 9, 10, 11, 13; Unit 3 Lessons 17, 19; Unit 6 Lessons 7, 8, 9, 10, 11
3.ARO.9	Find arithmetic patterns (example: find patterns in addition and multiplication tables). Use properties of operations to explain the patterns.	Unit 1 Lessons 1, 5, 6, 7, 8, 10, 12, 15, 19; Unit 2 Lessons 1, 3, 5, 6, 8, 14, 15; Unit 3 Lesson 17
3.ARO.10	Create, describe, and apply single-operation input-output rules involving addition, subtraction and multiplication to solve problems in various contexts.	Unit 3 Lesson 22

3.PVO Place Value and Operations		
3.PVO.1	Understand how to use place value when rounding whole numbers to the nearest 10, 100, 1,000, and 10,000.	Unit 3 Lessons 1, 2, 3, 4, 5, 6, 10, 18, 19; Unit 6 Lessons 4, 8
3.PVO.2	Use strategies and algorithms reflecting properties of operations, place value, and/or the fact that addition and subtraction are related, to fluently add and subtract through 1,000.	Unit 3 Lessons 2, 3, 4, 5, 6, 7, 8, 9, 10, 11, 12, 13, 14, 15, 16, 18; Unit 4 Lessons 12, 13; Unit 6 Lessons 1, 2, 3, 4, 5, 6, 8, 9, 10, 11; Unit 7 Lessons 1, 2, 3
3.PVO.3	Use place value and properties of operations to multiply a 1-digit number and a multiple of 10 through 90 (example: 6×40 and 9×70).	Unit 2 Lesson 12; Unit 3 Lessons 20, 21
3.PVO.4	Read, write and demonstrate multiple equivalent representations for numbers up to 100,000 using objects, visual representations, including standard form, word form, expanded form, and expanded notation.	Unit 3 Lesson 19
3.PVO.5	Compare whole numbers through the hundred thousands and represent the comparisons using the symbols $>$, $<$, or $=$.	Unit 3 Lesson 19
3.PVO.6	Find 10,000 more or 10,000 less than a given five-digit number. Find 1,000 more or 1,000 less than a given four- or five-digit. Find 100 more or 100 less than a given four- or five-digit number.	Unit 3 Lesson 19
3.PVO.7	Use strategies and algorithms based on knowledge of place value, equality and properties of addition and multiplication to multiply a two- or three-digit number by a one-digit number.	Unit 3 Lessons 20, 21

3.FO Fractions and Operations		
3.FO.1	Understand that a unit fraction, $\frac{1}{b}$, represents one part of a whole that has been separated into *b* equal parts (example: $\frac{1}{3}$ is one of 3 equal parts) and the fraction $\frac{a}{b}$ is formed by $\frac{1}{b}$-size parts (example: $\frac{2}{3}$ can be thought of as putting together two $\frac{1}{3}$ parts). Find parts of a set using visual representations.	Unit 4 Lessons 1, 2, 4, 5; Unit 5 Lessons 9, 10
3.FO.2	Recognize that fractions can be indicated on a number line. Use a number line to represent fractions.	Unit 4 Lessons 2, 3, 4
3.FO.2.a	Use a number line to show a unit fraction $\frac{1}{b}$. Know that the interval from 0 to 1 represents the whole; to show $\frac{1}{b}$ the whole must be separated into b equal parts. Understand that from 0 to the first endpoint of the partitioned whole is where the fraction $\frac{1}{b}$ is located.	Unit 4 Lessons 2, 3; Unit 5 Lesson 8
3.FO.2.b	Draw a number line to locate fractions; starting at 0 and ending at 1, separate the whole into *a* equal-size parts, $\frac{1}{b}$. Understand that the length of the interval created is $\frac{a}{b}$, and the endpoint of the interval locates $\frac{a}{b}$.	Unit 4 Lessons 2, 3, 4; Unit 5 Lesson 8
3.FO.3	Understand special cases of equivalent fractions and explain why such fractions are equivalent. Reason about size to compare and order fractions.	Unit 4 Lessons 2, 3, 4, 5; Unit 5 Lessons 7, 9, 10
3.FO.3.a	Given two fractions, understand that they are equivalent if their size is the same, or if they are located at the same point on the number line.	Unit 4 Lesson 3; Unit 5 Lessons 8, 9
3.FO.3.b	Recognize and find equivalent fractions less than 1 (example: $\frac{1}{3} = \frac{3}{6}$ and $\frac{1}{4} = \frac{2}{8}$). Use methods such as, making models, to explain why the fractions are equivalent.	Unit 5 Lessons 7, 8, 9, 10
3.FO.3.c	Write a whole number as a fraction; identify fractions equivalent to whole numbers.	Unit 4 Lessons 2, 3; Unit 5 Lessons 8, 9
3.FO.3.d	Use reasoning about size to compare and order fractions with the same numerator but different denominators, or with the same denominator. Understand that to make an accurate comparison, the two fractions must refer to the same whole. Record the comparison with symbols >, <, or =, and justify the results (example: use a picture or other model).	Unit 4 Lessons 4, 5; Unit 5 Lessons 9, 10
3.FO.4	Explain and demonstrate how fractions $\frac{1}{4}, \frac{1}{2}, \frac{3}{4}$ and a whole relate to time, measurement, and money, and demonstrate using visual representation.	Unit 4 Lesson 11; Unit 5 Lesson 9

3.MDA Measurement and Data Analysis		
3.MDA.1	Know how to tell and write time to the nearest minute and measure time in minutes. Use a number line, or other methods, to solve word problems that involve adding and subtracting time in minutes. Know relationships among units of time.	Unit 4 Lessons 7, 8, 9, 10, 11
3.MDA.2	Use the standard units, liter (L), grams (g), and kilograms (kg) to measure and estimate liquid volume and mass. Solve one-step problems about mass or volume given in the same units and that involve the four operations. Represent the problem by using a diagram (example: a number line) or other methods.	Unit 7 Lessons 1, 2, 3, 4
3.MDA.2.a	Solve problems and make change involving money using a combination of coins and bills.	Unit 5 Lessons 11, 12
3.MDA.2.b	Solve problems involving estimating of temperature and use an analog thermometer to determine temperature to the nearest degree in Fahrenheit and Celsius.	Unit 4 Lesson 14; Unit 5 Lessons 11, 12
3.MDA.3	Given a collection of data in several categories, make a picture graph and bar graph with labeled scales. Use information from bar graphs to solve one- and two-step problems to answer *how many more* and *how many less* questions. Collect data through observations, surveys, and experiments.	Unit 4 Lessons 12, 13, 14, 15
3.MDA.4	Create a group of data by estimating and measuring lengths with customary units (inch, half-inch, quarter-inch) or the metric unit, centimeter. Use a line plot to display the data, labeling the horizontal scale with the correct units (example: whole inches, half-inches, or quarter-inches).	Unit 4 Lessons 6, 14, 15, 16
3.MDA.5	Know that area is an attribute of two-dimensional (plane) figures; understand concepts of area measurement.	Unit 1 Lesson 11; Unit 2 Lesson 2; Unit 4 Lesson 6; Unit 5 Lessons 1, 3, 5, 6
3.MDA.5.a	Recognize that a *unit square* has a side length of *1 unit* and an area of *1 square unit* and can be used to measure area of plane figures.	Unit 1 Lesson 11; Unit 2 Lesson 2; Unit 5 Lessons 1, 3
3.MDA.5.b	Understand that if a plane figure can be covered by n unit squares without having gaps or overlaps, then the figure has an area of n square units.	Unit 1 Lesson 11; Unit 2 Lesson 2; Unit 5 Lessons 1, 3, 6
3.MDA.6	Count unit squares to find the area of a figure; use standard units (square inch, square foot, square centimeter, square meter) and non-standard units (example: tiles) to measure area.	Unit 1 Lesson 11; Unit 5 Lessons 1, 2, 4, 6

3.MDA.7	Understand the relationship between area and the operations of multiplication and addition.	Unit 1 Lessons 11, 12; Unit 2 Lesson 1; Unit 3 Lessons 20, 21; Unit 5 Lessons 1, 2, 3; Unit Lesson 9
3.MDA.7.a	Use tiling to find the area of rectangles with given side lengths; show that the resulting area can also be found by multiplying the two side lengths.	Unit 1 Lesson 11; Unit 2 Lesson 2; Unit 5 Lessons 1, 2
3.MDA.7.b	Solve real-world and other mathematical problems that involve finding the area of rectangles by multiplying the side lengths (given in whole-numbers); use reasoning to illustrate the products as rectangular areas.	Unit 1 Lessons 11,12; Unit 2 Lessons 2, 6; Unit 5 Lessons 1, 2, 3, 4, 5; Unit 7 Lesson 9
3.MDA.7.c	Use reasoning and area models to represent the Distributive Property: given a rectangle that has side lengths a and $b + c$ use tiles to illustrate understanding that the area is the sum of $a \times b$ and $a \times c$.	Unit 1 Lessons 11, 12, 14; Unit 2 Lesson 1; Unit 5 Lesson 2
3.MDA.7.d	Recognize that addition can be used to find area. Partition rectilinear figures (example: composite rectangular figures) into rectangles having no overlaps, then find the area of the original figure by adding the areas of the parts; use this approach to solve real-world problems.	Unit 1 Lessons 11, 12; Unit 5 Lessons 2, 4, 5, 6
3.MDA.8	Solve problems (real world and other mathematical contexts) that involve perimeters of polygons in the following situations: given side lengths, find perimeter; given perimeter and a side length, find the unknown length; find rectangles with the same perimeter and different areas or same area and different perimeters.	Unit 5 Lessons 1, 2, 3, 5; Unit 7 Lesson 9
3.MDA.9	Measure distances around objects.	Unit 4 Lesson 14

3.GSR Geometry and Spatial Reasoning

3.GSR.1	Recognize that geometric figures belonging to different categories may have attributes in common and these shared attributes can form a larger category (example: although squares, rectangles, and rhombuses belong to different categories they share the attributes four sides, four angles, and four vertices and belong to the larger category, quadrilaterals.) Know that squares, rectangles, and rhombuses are quadrilaterals; sketch quadrilaterals that are not in those categories.	Unit 7 Lessons 5, 6, 7, 8, 9
3.GSR.2	Separate geometric figures into parts with equal areas. Represent the area of a part as a unit fraction of the whole.	Unit 4 Lessons 1, 2, 4, 5; Unit 5 Lesson 10; Unit 7 Lesson 5
3.GSR.3	Identify parallel and perpendicular lines in various contexts, and use them to describe and create geometric figures such as right triangles, rectangles, parallelograms and trapezoids.	Unit 7 Lessons 5, 6, 7, 8

Mathematical Processes and Practices

MPP1	
Problem Solving	Unit 1 Lessons 3, 4, 5, 6, 7, 9, 10, 12, 13, 14, 16, 18, 19 Unit 2 Lessons 1, 2, 4, 7, 9, 10, 13, 15 Unit 3 Lessons 3, 4, 5, 6, 7, 8, 9, 10, 11, 12, 14, 15, 16, 17, 18, 20, 21 Unit 4 Lessons 9, 10, 11, 12, 13, 14, 15, 16 Unit 5 Lessons 2, 5, 9, 10, 11 Unit 6 Lessons 1, 2, 3, 4, 5, 6, 7, 8, 9, 10, 11 Unit 7 Lessons 1, 2, 3, 4, 5, 9
MPP2	
Abstract and Quantitative Reasoning	Unit 1 Lessons 1, 3, 5, 7, 8, 10, 11, 12, 19 Unit 2 Lessons 1, 2, 3, 5, 6, 8, 13, 15 Unit 3 Lessons 1, 2, 5, 6, 8, 9, 11, 12, 13, 14, 15, 16, 17, 18, 19, 20, 22 Unit 4 Lessons 1, 2, 3, 4, 5, 6, 9, 11, 12, 16 Unit 5 Lessons 1, 2, 3, 4, 5, 7, 8, 9, 10 Unit 6 Lessons 1, 2, 3, 4, 8, 11 Unit 7 Lessons 1, 2, 3, 5, 9
MPP3	
Use and Evaluate Logical Reasoning	Unit 1 Lessons 1, 2, 3, 4, 5, 6, 7, 8, 9, 10, 11, 12, 13, 14, 15, 16, 18, 19 Unit 2 Lessons 1, 2, 3, 4, 5, 6, 8, 9, 10, 11, 12, 13, 14, 15 Unit 3 Lessons 1, 2, 3, 4, 5, 6, 7, 8, 9, 10, 11, 12, 13, 14, 15, 16, 17, 18, 20, 21, 22 Unit 4 Lessons 1, 2, 3, 4, 5, 6, 7, 8, 9, 10, 11, 12, 13, 14, 15, 16 Unit 5 Lessons 1, 2, 3, 4, 5, 7, 8, 9, 10, 11, 12 Unit 6 Lessons 1, 2, 3, 4, 5, 6, 7, 8, 9, 10, 11 Unit 7 Lessons 1, 2, 3, 4, 5, 6, 8, 9
MPP4	
Mathematical Modeling	Unit 1 Lessons 1, 2, 3, 4, 5, 6, 7, 9, 10, 12, 13, 14, 15, 16, 17, 18, 19 Unit 2 Lessons 2, 4, 7, 9, 11, 13, 15 Unit 3 Lessons 3, 4, 8, 9, 10, 11, 12, 14, 16, 17, 18, 20, 21, 22 Unit 4 Lessons 9, 10, 11, 12, 13, 14, 16 Unit 5 Lessons 2, 5, 9, 10, 11 Unit 6 Lessons 1, 2, 3, 4, 8, 9, 10, 11 Unit 7 Lessons 1, 2, 3, 4, 5, 9

MPP5	
Use Mathematical Tools	Unit 1 Lessons 1, 2, 3, 4, 5, 6, 7, 8, 9, 10, 11, 12, 13, 14, 15, 16, 17, 18 Unit 2 Lessons 1, 2, 3, 4, 5, 6, 7, 8, 9, 10, 11, 12, 13, 14, 15 Unit 3 Lessons 1, 2, 3, 4, 5, 6, 7, 8, 13, 17, 18, 19, 20, 21 Unit 4 Lessons 1, 2, 3, 5, 6, 7, 8, 9, 10, 11, 14, 16 Unit 5 Lessons 1, 2, 6, 7, 8, 11, 12 Unit 6 Lessons 4, 11 Unit 7 Lessons 2, 3, 5, 7, 8, 9
MPP6	
Use Precise Mathematical Language	Unit 1 Lessons 1, 2, 3, 4, 5, 6, 7, 8, 9, 10, 11, 12, 13, 14, 15, 16, 18, 19 Unit 2 Lessons 1, 2, 3, 4, 5, 6, 7, 8, 9, 10, 11, 12, 13, 14, 15 Unit 3 Lessons 1, 2, 3, 4, 5, 6, 7, 8, 9, 10, 11, 12, 13, 14, 15, 16, 17, 18, 19, 20, 21, 22 Unit 4 Lessons 1, 2, 3, 4, 5, 6, 7, 8, 9, 10, 11, 12, 13, 14, 15, 16 Unit 5 Lessons 1, 2, 3, 4, 5, 7, 8, 9, 11 Unit 6 Lessons 1, 2, 3, 4, 5, 6, 7, 8, 9, 10, 11 Unit 7 Lessons 1, 2, 3, 4, 5, 6, 7, 8, 9
MPP7	
See Structure	Unit 1 Lessons 1, 2, 4, 5, 6, 7, 8, 10, 11, 12, 13, 15, 17, 18, 19 Unit 2 Lessons 1, 3, 5, 6, 14, 15 Unit 3 Lessons 1, 2, 3, 4, 11, 14, 16, 17, 18, 19, 21, 22 Unit 4 Lessons 1, 2, 3, 13, 16 Unit 5 Lessons 1, 4, 6, 7, 10 Unit 6 Lessons 1, 2, 3, 5, 8, 11 Unit 7 Lessons 1, 5, 6, 7, 8, 9
MPP8	
Generalize	Unit 1 Lessons 1, 3, 5, 7, 8, 10, 11, 13, 15, 19 Unit 2 Lessons 1, 3, 5, 6, 10, 12, 14, 15 Unit 3 Lessons 5, 6, 14, 17, 18, 19, 20 Unit 4 Lessons 1, 2, 3, 4, 5, 6, 15, 16 Unit 5 Lessons 3, 6, 7, 8, 9, 10, 11 Unit 6 Lessons 1, 2, 4, 11 Unit 7 Lessons 3, 5, 8, 9

A

B

C

F

G

H

I

K

L

M

N

Q

R

Multiplication Table and Scrambled Tables (Volume 1)

A

×	1	2	3	4	5	6	7	8	9	10
1	1	2	3	4	5	6	7	8	9	10
2	2	4	6	8	10	12	14	16	18	20
3	3	6	9	12	15	18	21	24	27	30
4	4	8	12	16	20	24	28	32	36	40
5	5	10	15	20	25	30	35	40	45	50
6	6	12	18	24	30	36	42	48	54	60
7	7	14	21	28	35	42	49	56	63	70
8	8	16	24	32	40	48	56	64	72	80
9	9	18	27	36	45	54	63	72	81	90
10	10	20	30	40	50	60	70	80	90	100

B

×	2	4	3	1	5	10	6	8	7	9
5	10	20	15	5	25	50	30	40	35	45
3	6	12	9	3	15	30	18	24	21	27
1	2	4	3	1	5	10	6	8	7	9
4	8	16	12	4	20	40	24	32	28	36
2	4	8	6	2	10	20	12	16	14	18
7	14	28	21	7	35	70	42	56	49	63
9	18	36	27	9	45	90	54	72	63	81
10	20	40	30	10	50	100	60	80	70	90
8	16	32	24	8	40	80	48	64	56	72
6	12	24	18	6	30	60	36	48	42	54

C

×	8	6	4	9	7	9	6	7	4	8
5	40	30	20	45	35	45	30	35	20	40
3	24	18	12	27	21	27	18	21	12	24
2	16	12	8	18	14	18	12	14	8	16
3	24	18	12	27	21	27	18	21	12	24
5	40	30	20	45	35	45	30	35	20	40
9	72	54	36	81	63	81	54	63	36	72
4	32	24	16	36	28	36	24	28	16	32
7	56	42	28	63	49	63	42	49	28	56
6	48	36	24	54	42	54	36	42	24	48
8	64	48	32	72	56	72	48	56	32	64

D

×	6	7	8	7	8	6	7	8	6	8
2	12	14	16	14	16	12	14	16	12	16
3	18	21	24	21	24	18	21	24	18	24
4	24	28	32	28	32	24	28	32	24	32
5	30	35	40	35	40	30	35	40	30	40
7	42	49	56	49	56	42	49	56	42	56
8	48	56	64	56	64	48	56	64	48	64
6	36	42	48	42	48	36	42	48	36	48
9	54	63	72	63	72	54	63	72	54	72
8	48	56	64	56	64	48	56	64	48	64
6	36	42	48	42	48	36	42	48	36	48

Illustrator: Josh Brill

Did you ever try to use shapes to draw animals like the moose on the cover?

Over the last 10 years Josh has been using geometric shapes to design his animals. His aim is to keep the animal drawings simple and use color to make them appealing.

Add some color to the moose Josh drew. Then try drawing a cat or dog or some other animal using the shapes below.

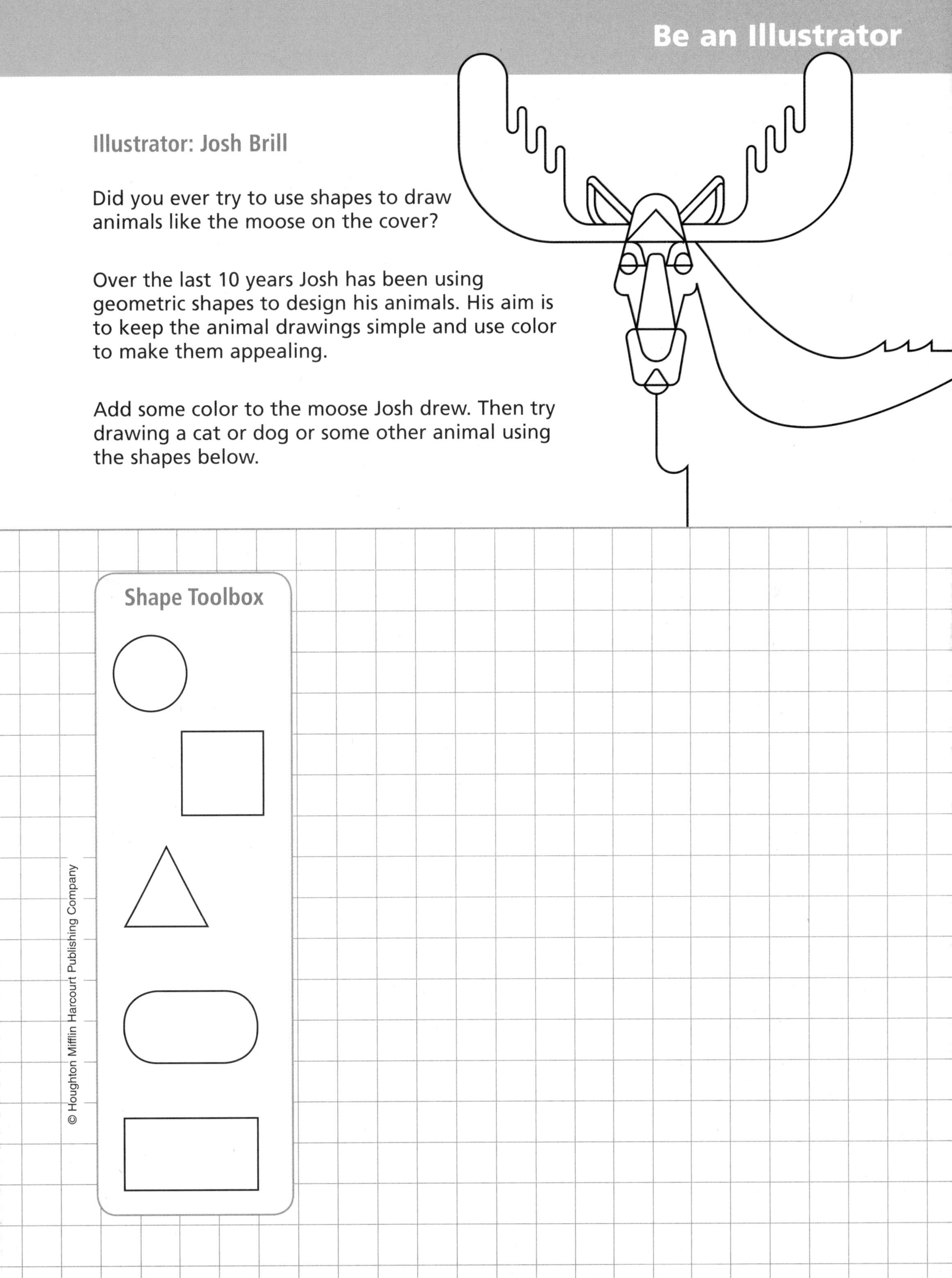

Shape Toolbox

math expressions

Dr. Karen C. Fuson

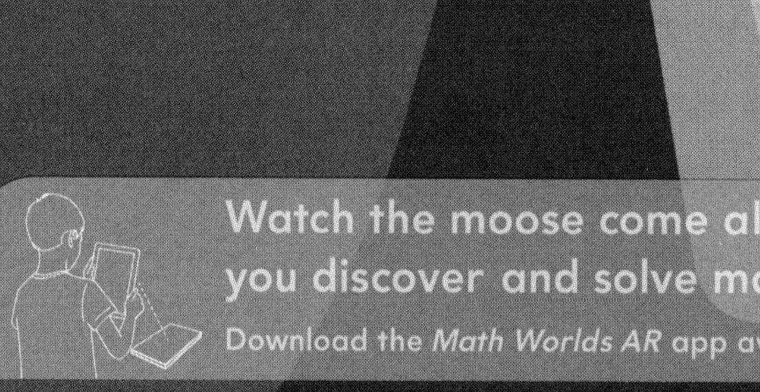

Grade 3

Volume 2

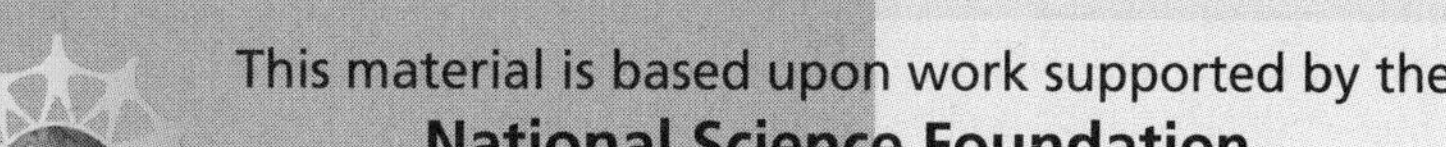

This material is based upon work supported by the
National Science Foundation
under Grant Numbers
ESI-9816320, REC-9806020, and RED-935373.

Any opinions, findings, and conclusions, or recommendations expressed in this material are those of the author and do not necessarily reflect the views of the National Science Foundation.

Cover Illustration: ©Josh Brill

Printed in the U.S.A.

ISBN 978-1-328-74388-6

7 8 9 10 0928 26 25 24 23 22 21 20

4500817361 C D E F G

Unit 4 | Fractions, Time, and Data

BIG IDEA 1 - Fraction Concepts

BIG IDEA 2 - Time

BIG IDEA 3 - Pictographs, Bar Graphs, and Line Plots

Unit 5 Measurement and Fractions

BIG IDEA 1 - Area and Perimeter

BIG IDEA 2 - Equivalent Fractions

BIG IDEA 3 - Money and Temperature

Unit 6

Write Equations to Solve Word Problems

BIG IDEA 1 - Types of Word Problems

BIG IDEA 2 - Solve Two-Step Word Problems

Unit 7 Measurement and Polygons

BIG IDEA 1 - Capacity, Weight, and Mass

BIG IDEA 2 - Analyzing Triangles and Quadrilaterals

Student Resources

Dear Family:

In this unit, your child will be introduced to fractions. Students will build fractions from unit fractions and explore fractions as parts of a whole.

Unit Fraction

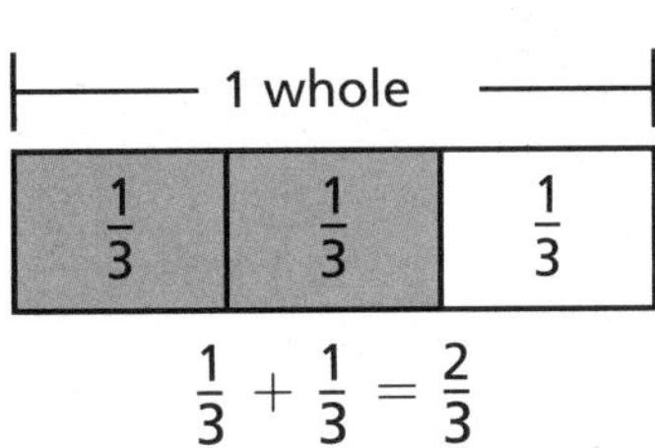

$\frac{1}{3} + \frac{1}{3} = \frac{2}{3}$

Fraction of a Whole

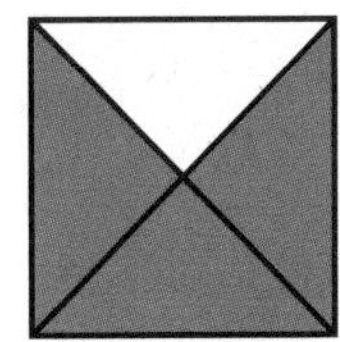

$\frac{3}{4}$ ← numerator ← denominator

Students will compare and order fractions with either the same denominator or the same numerator.

1 whole					
$\frac{1}{2}$			$\frac{1}{2}$		
$\frac{1}{6}$	$\frac{1}{6}$	$\frac{1}{6}$	$\frac{1}{6}$	$\frac{1}{6}$	$\frac{1}{6}$

$\frac{2}{6} < \frac{3}{6}$

$\frac{1}{2} > \frac{1}{6}$

Students will also generate measurement data with halves and fourths and relate the fractions to length, time, and money. They graph their data in a line plot.

You can help your child become familiar with units of length, time, and money by working with these concepts together. For example, you might estimate and measure the length of something in inches or the amount of time something takes in seconds.

Please contact me if you have any questions or comments.

Sincerely,
Your child's teacher

Estimada familia:

En esta unidad, se le presentarán por primera vez las fracciones a su niño. Los estudiantes formarán fracciones con fracciones unitarias y explorarán las fracciones como partes de un entero.

Fracción unitaria

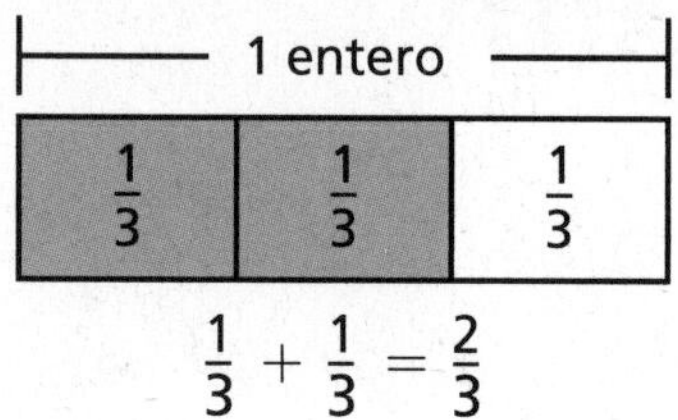

Fracción de un entero

$\frac{3}{4}$ 3 ← numerador
4 ← denominador

Los estudiantes compararán y ordenarán fracciones del mismo denominador o del mismo numerador.

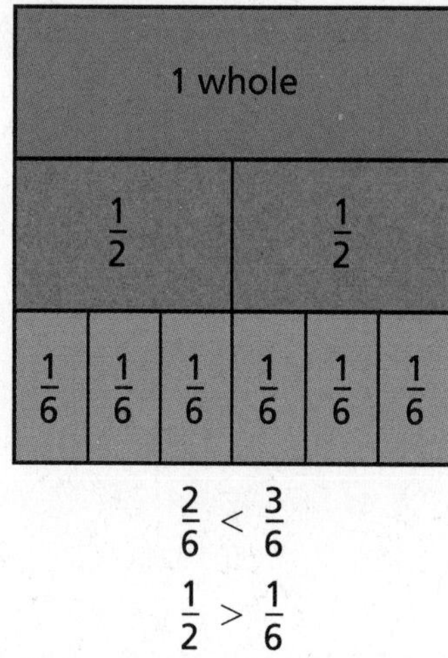

Los estudiantes también generarán datos de medición con mitades y cuartos y relacionarán las fracciones a longitud, tiempo y dinero. Graficarán sus datos en un diagrama de puntos.

Puede ayudar a su niño a familiarizarse con las unidades de longitud, tiempo y dinero trabajando con estos conceptos en conjunto. Por ejemplo, es posible estimar y medir la longitud de algo en pulgadas o el tiempo que toma algo en segundos..

Si tiene alguna duda o algún comentario, por favor comuníquese conmigo.

Atentamente,
El maestro de su niño

denominator	**frequency table**
elapsed time	**horizontal bar graph**
fraction	**inch (in.)**

A table that shows how many times each event, item, or category occurs.

Frequency Table	
Age	**Tally**
7	1
8	3
9	5
10	4
11	2

The bottom number in a fraction that shows the total number of equal parts in the whole.

Example:

$\frac{1}{3}$ ← denominator

A bar graph with horizontal bars.

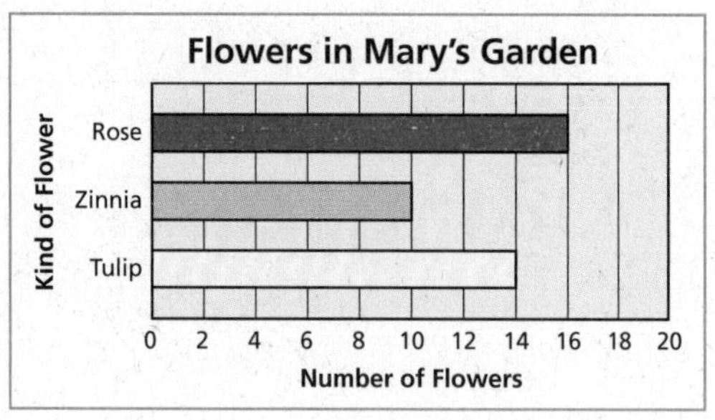

The time that passes between the beginning and the end of an activity.

A customary unit used to measure length.

12 inches = 1 foot

A number that names part of a whole or part of a set.

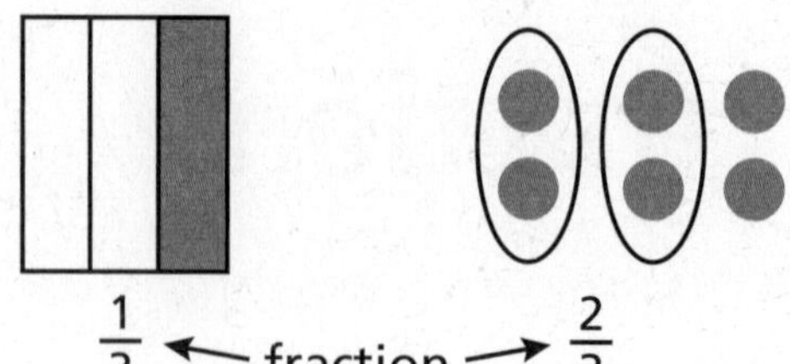

$\frac{1}{3}$ ← fraction → $\frac{2}{3}$

key	**mixed number**
line plot	**numerator**
line segment	**tally chart**

A whole number and a fraction.

$1\frac{3}{4}$ is a mixed number.

A part of a map, graph, or chart that explains what symbols mean.

The top number in a fraction that shows the number of equal parts counted.

Example:

$\frac{1}{3}$ ← numerator

A diagram that shows frequency of data on a number line. Also called a *dot plot*.

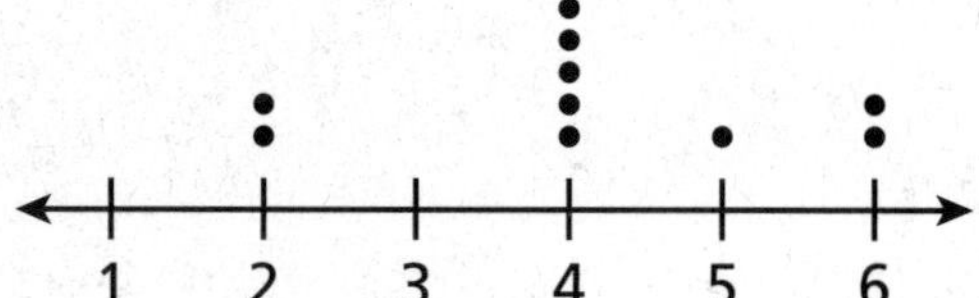

A chart used to record and organize data with tally marks.

Tally Chart	
Age	**Tally**
7	I
8	III
9	~~IIII~~
10	IIII
11	II

A part of a line. A line segment has two endpoints.

unit fraction

vertical bar graph

A fraction whose numerator is 1. It shows one equal part of a whole.

Example:

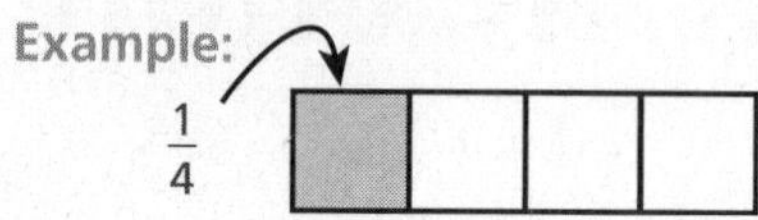

A bar graph with vertical bars.

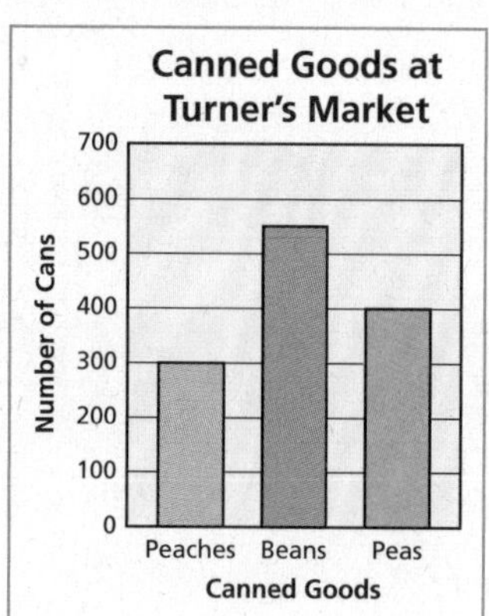

Name ____________________

Fraction Rectangles

Cut out the bottom rectangle first.
Then cut on the dotted lines to make 4 rectangles.
Wait to cut out the top rectangle.

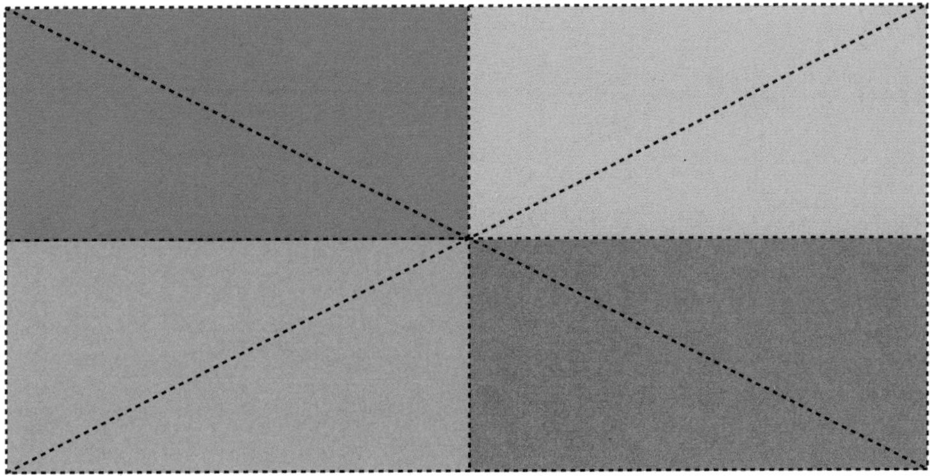

Name ______________________________

Explore Unit Fractions

Use your rectangles from page 263A to make the whole shape. Count the equal parts. What unit fraction of the whole shape is one of the rectangles?

1.

Number of equal parts ______ Unit fraction ______

2.

Number of equal parts ______ Unit fraction ______

3.

Number of equal parts ______ Unit fraction ______

Explore Unit Fractions (continued)

Use your triangles from page 263A to make a whole shape like the model shown. Count the equal parts in the whole. What unit fraction of the whole shape is the blue triangle?

4 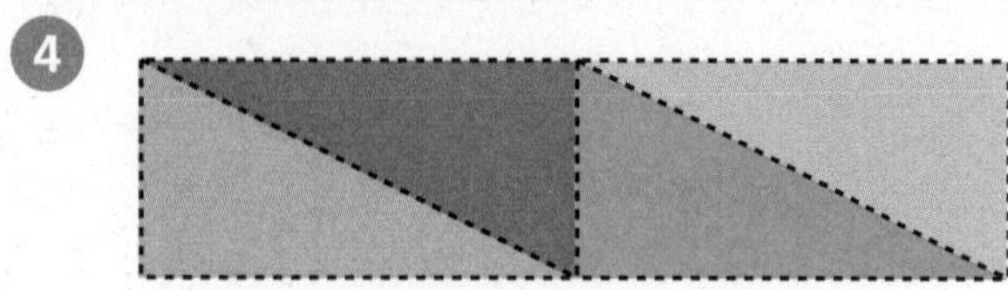

There are ______ equal parts in the whole shape.

The blue triangle is ______ of the whole shape.

5 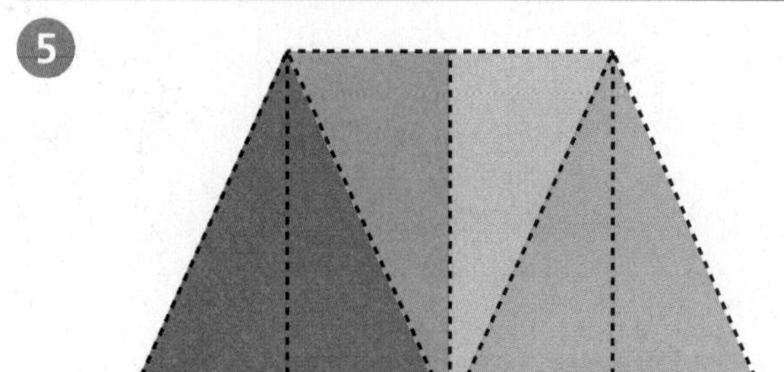

There are ______ equal parts in the whole shape.

The blue triangle is ______ of the whole shape.

6 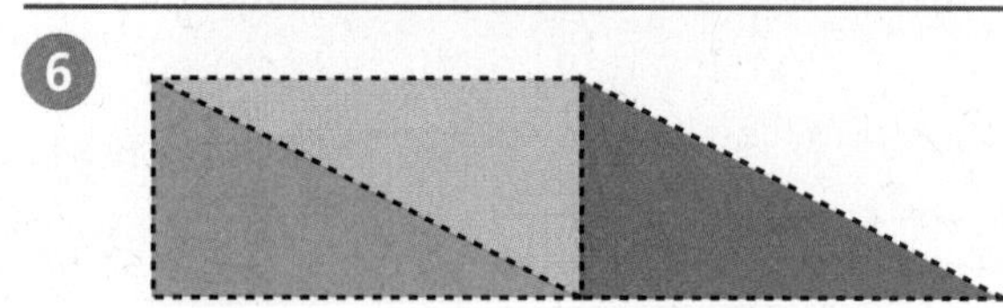

There are ______ equal parts in the whole shape.

The blue triangle is ______ of the whole shape.

7 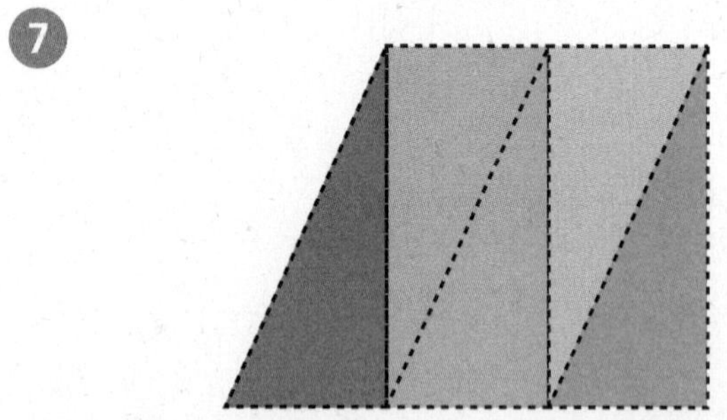

There are ______ equal parts in the whole shape.

The blue triangle is ______ of the whole shape.

8 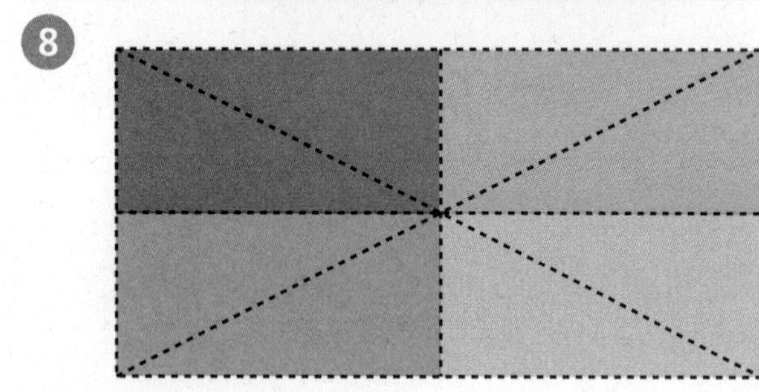

There are ______ equal parts in the whole shape.

One blue triangle is ______ of the whole shape.

Name ____________________

Unit Fractions and Fraction Bars

VOCABULARY
fraction
denominator
numerator
unit fraction

You can represent a **fraction** with a fraction bar. The **denominator** tells how many equal parts the whole is divided into. The **numerator** tells how many equal parts you are talking about.

1 whole

$\frac{1}{3}$ 1 ← numerator, 3 ← denominator

Shade 1 part.

A **unit fraction** has a numerator of 1. Shade the rest of the fraction bars at the right below to represent unit fractions. What patterns do you see?

1 whole	→	Shade 1 whole.	1	one
Divide the whole into 2 equal parts.	→	Shade 1 part.	$\frac{1}{2}$	one half
Divide the whole into 3 equal parts.	→	Shade 1 part.	$\frac{1}{3}$	one third
Divide the whole into 4 equal parts.	→	Shade 1 part.	$\frac{1}{4}$	one fourth
Divide the whole into 5 equal parts.	→	Shade 1 part.	$\frac{1}{5}$	one fifth
Divide the whole into 6 equal parts.	→	Shade 1 part.	$\frac{1}{6}$	one sixth
Divide the whole into 7 equal parts.	→	Shade 1 part.	$\frac{1}{7}$	one seventh
Divide the whole into 8 equal parts.	→	Shade 1 part.	$\frac{1}{8}$	one eighth

Build Fractions from Unit Fractions

Write the unit fractions for each whole. Next, shade the correct number of parts. Then show each shaded fraction as a sum of unit fractions.

9 → 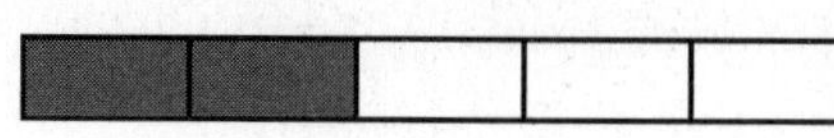 Shade 2 parts.

Divide the whole into 5 equal parts.

$\frac{1}{5} + \frac{1}{5} + \frac{1}{5} + \frac{1}{5} + \frac{1}{5}$ $\qquad$ $\frac{1}{5} + \frac{1}{5} = \frac{2}{5}$

10 → Shade 2 parts.

Divide the whole into 3 equal parts.

11 → 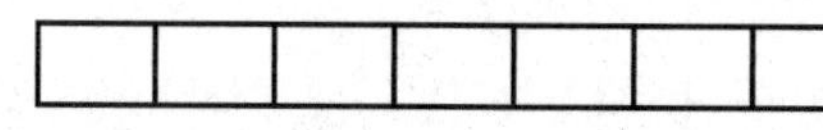 Shade 5 parts.

Divide the whole into 7 equal parts.

12 → Shade 7 parts.

Divide the whole into 8 equal parts.

  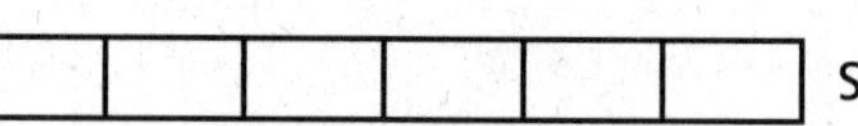 Shade 3 parts.

Divide the whole into 6 equal parts.

Check Understanding

A fraction bar is divided into 8 equal parts.
What unit fraction represents each part? ____.
Write an equation that shows 5 parts shaded.

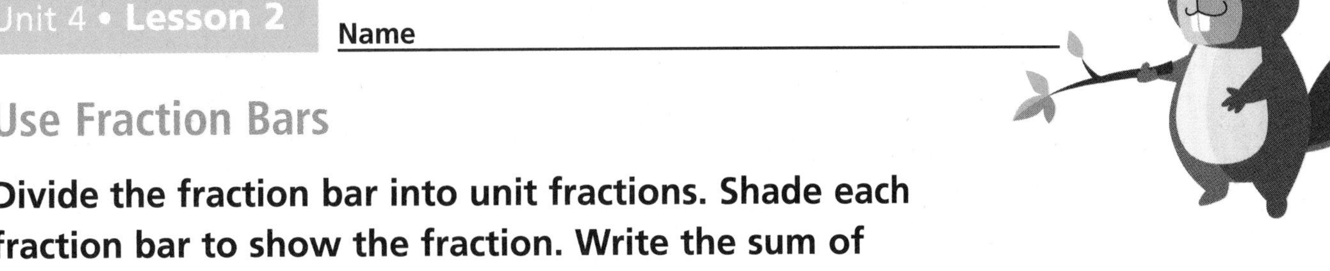

Use Fraction Bars

Divide the fraction bar into unit fractions. Shade each fraction bar to show the fraction. Write the sum of the unit fractions under the shaded parts.

1. $\frac{1}{6}$ — 1 whole

2. $\frac{2}{3}$ — 1 whole

3. $\frac{7}{8}$ — 1 whole

4. $\frac{2}{4}$ — 1 whole

5. $\frac{5}{6}$ — 1 whole

6. $\frac{3}{8}$ — 1 whole

Use Number Lines

First, divide each number line into the correct unit fractions. Then label each point. Show the target fraction by looping the unit fractions that make it.

7 $\frac{1}{6}$

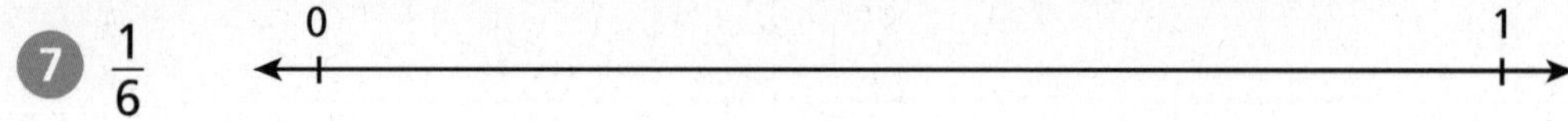

8 $\frac{2}{3}$

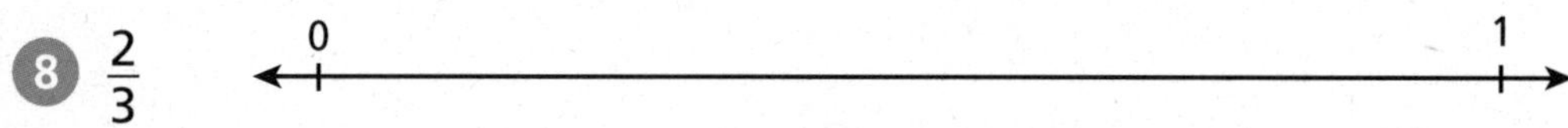

9 $\frac{7}{8}$

0 1

10 $\frac{2}{4}$

0 1

11 $\frac{5}{6}$

0 1

12 $\frac{3}{8}$

0 1

Check Understanding

Explain how Exercise 6 and Exercise 12 can both be used to show $\frac{3}{8}$.

Name ____________________

Locate Fractions Less Than 1

Divide each number line into the correct unit fractions. Then label each point. Show the target fraction by looping the unit fractions that make it.

1. $\frac{1}{4}$

0 1

2. $\frac{1}{8}$

0 1

3. $\frac{3}{4}$

0 1

4. $\frac{5}{6}$

0 1

5. $\frac{2}{3}$

Plot the target fractions $\frac{2}{3}$ and $\frac{5}{6}$ on the number line below.

6.

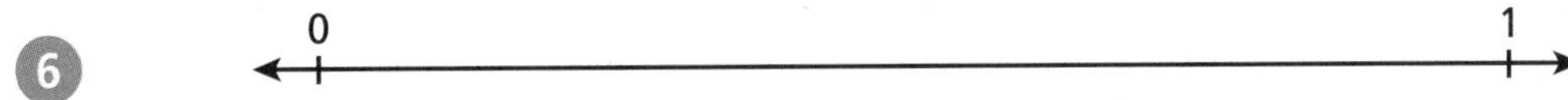

Locate Fractions Greater Than 1

VOCABULARY
mixed number

Divide each number line into the correct unit fractions. Then label each point. Show the target fraction by looping the unit fractions that make it.

7 $\frac{5}{4}$

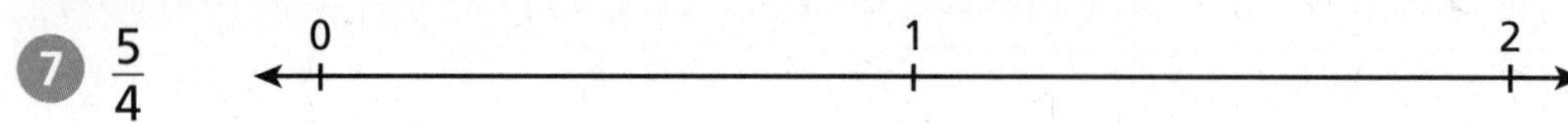

8 $\frac{8}{3}$

0 1 2 3

9 $\frac{5}{1}$

0 1 2 3 4 5 6 7 8 9 10

10 $\frac{6}{2}$

0 1 2 3 4 5

Introduce Mixed Numbers

A fraction greater than 1 that cannot be named as a whole number can be named as a mixed number. **Mixed numbers** have a whole-number part and a fraction part.

Examples of mixed numbers:

$1\frac{1}{2}$

$3\frac{2}{3}$

$4\frac{2}{4}$

Complete.

11 $\frac{5}{4} = \frac{4}{4} + \frac{1}{4}$
$= 1 + \frac{1}{4}$
$= \square$

$\frac{8}{3} = \frac{3}{3} + \frac{3}{3} + \frac{\square}{3}$
$= 1 + 1 + \square$
$= \square$

$\frac{8}{6} = \frac{\square}{6} + \frac{\square}{6}$
$= 1 + \square$
$= \square$

Name ______________________________

Find 1

Divide each number line into the correct unit fractions. Label each point. Then locate 1 on the number line.

12 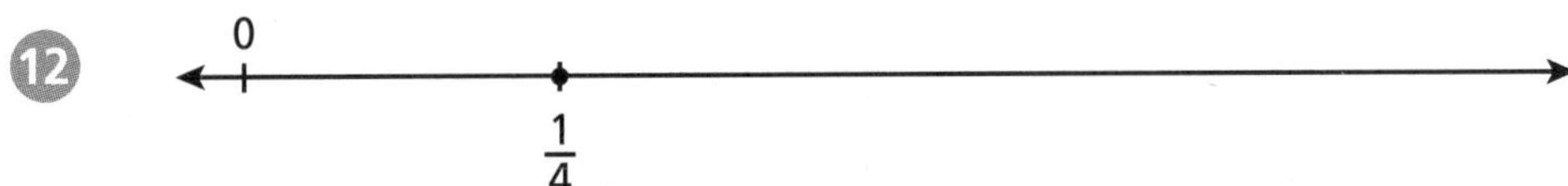

13 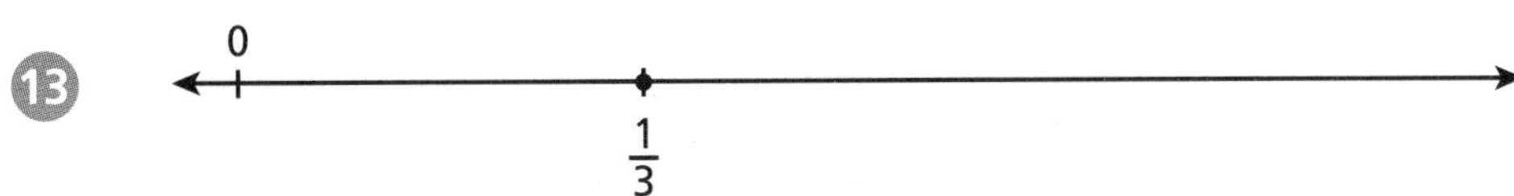

14 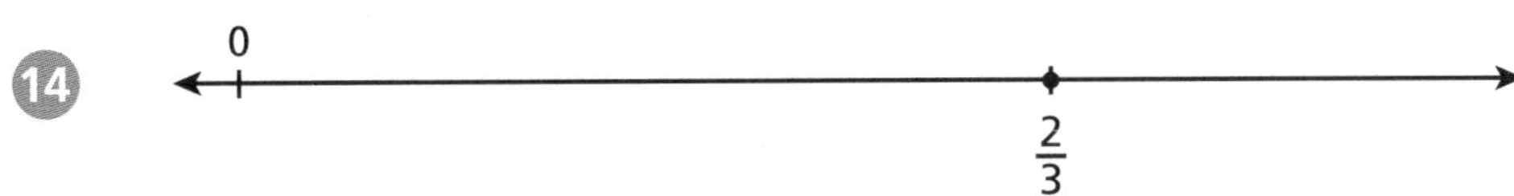

15 

16 0 $\frac{11}{4}$

17 Explain how you located 1 for Exercise 15.

____

____

____

Find Fractions

Divide each number line into the correct unit fractions. Then label each point. Use loops to show the target fraction.

18. $\frac{3}{4}$

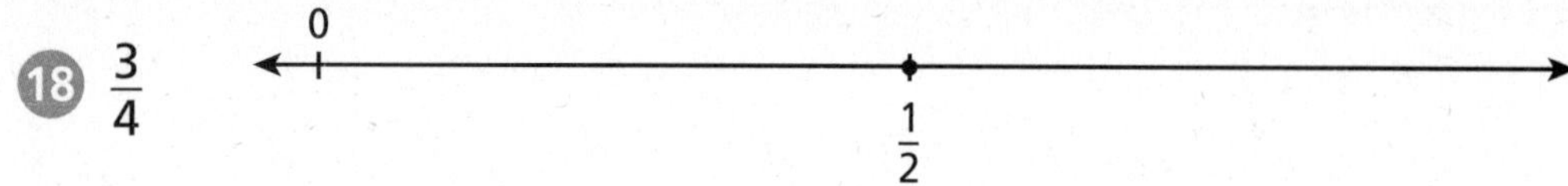

19. $\frac{5}{6}$

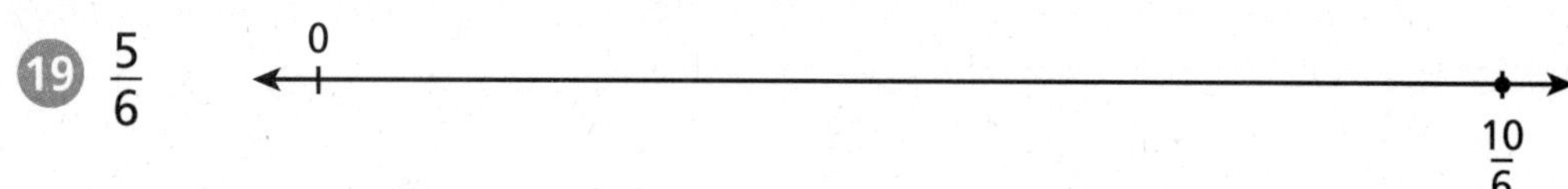

20. $\frac{3}{8}$

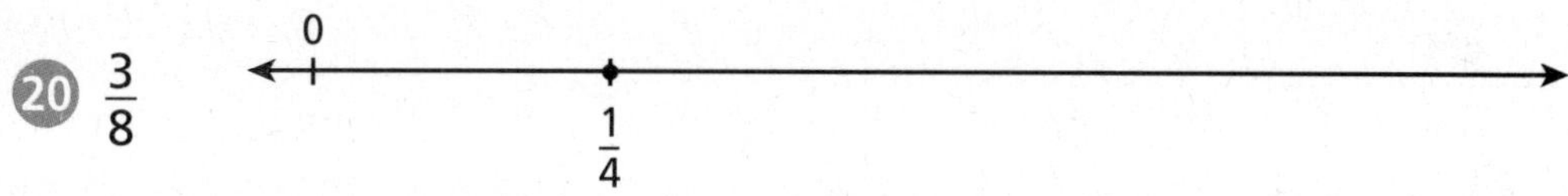

21. $\frac{5}{3}$

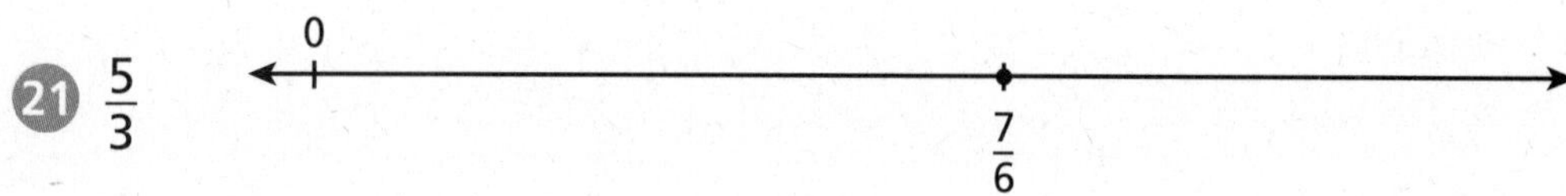

22. $\frac{1}{6}$

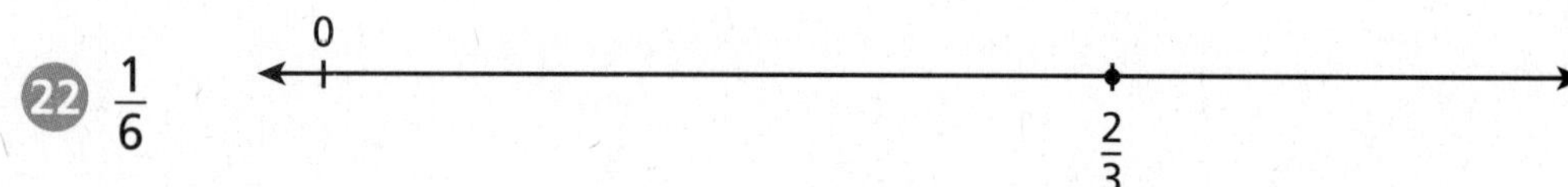

23. $\frac{10}{8}$

0

$\frac{4}{2}$

Check Understanding

Complete the sentence. The two fractions used to find 1 on the number line in Problem 23 are ________ and ________.

Name ______________________________

Compare Unit Fractions with Fraction Bars

The fraction bars are made up of unit fractions. Look for patterns.

1. Describe two patterns that you see in the fraction bars.

____

____

____

____

Compare. Use <, >, or =.

2. $\frac{1}{3} \bigcirc \frac{1}{7}$

3. $\frac{1}{3} \bigcirc \frac{1}{2}$

4. $\frac{1}{6} \bigcirc \frac{1}{7}$

Compare and Order Unit Fractions with Number Lines

The number line shows unit fractions.
Look for patterns in the number line.

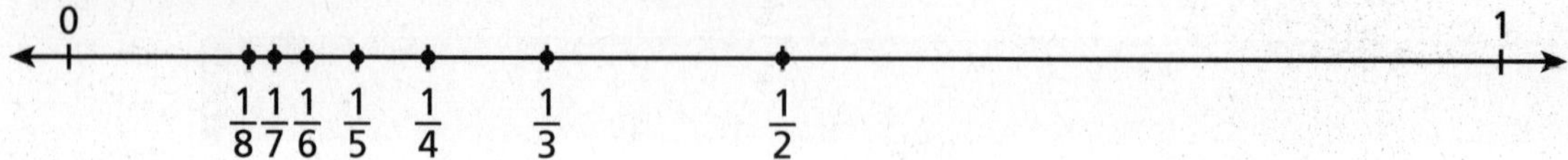

5 Describe a pattern that you see in the number line.

____

____

Compare. Use the fraction bars or the number line, if needed.

6 $\frac{1}{3}$ ○ $\frac{1}{8}$

7 $\frac{1}{4}$ ○ $\frac{1}{2}$

8 $\frac{1}{5}$ ○ $\frac{1}{8}$

Order the fractions from least to greatest. Use the fraction bars or the number line, if needed.

9 $\frac{1}{3}$ $\frac{1}{2}$ $\frac{1}{5}$

____, ____, ____

10 $\frac{1}{8}$ $\frac{1}{5}$ $\frac{1}{6}$

____, ____, ____

11 $\frac{1}{4}$ $\frac{1}{6}$ $\frac{1}{7}$

____, ____, ____

Solve. Use the fraction bars or the number line.

12 Between which two unit fractions is $\frac{1}{5}$ on a number line? ____________

13 Think about making a fraction bar for tenths.

a. How many unit fractions would be in the fraction bar? ____________

b. How do you write the unit fraction? ____________

Check Understanding

Draw a picture to show how you can compare $\frac{1}{6}$ and $\frac{1}{8}$.

Name ___________________________________

Fraction Circles

Each circle is the same size and represents the same whole. So, you can use these circles to compare fractions. Label each unit fraction.Then cut out the fraction circles on the dashed lines.

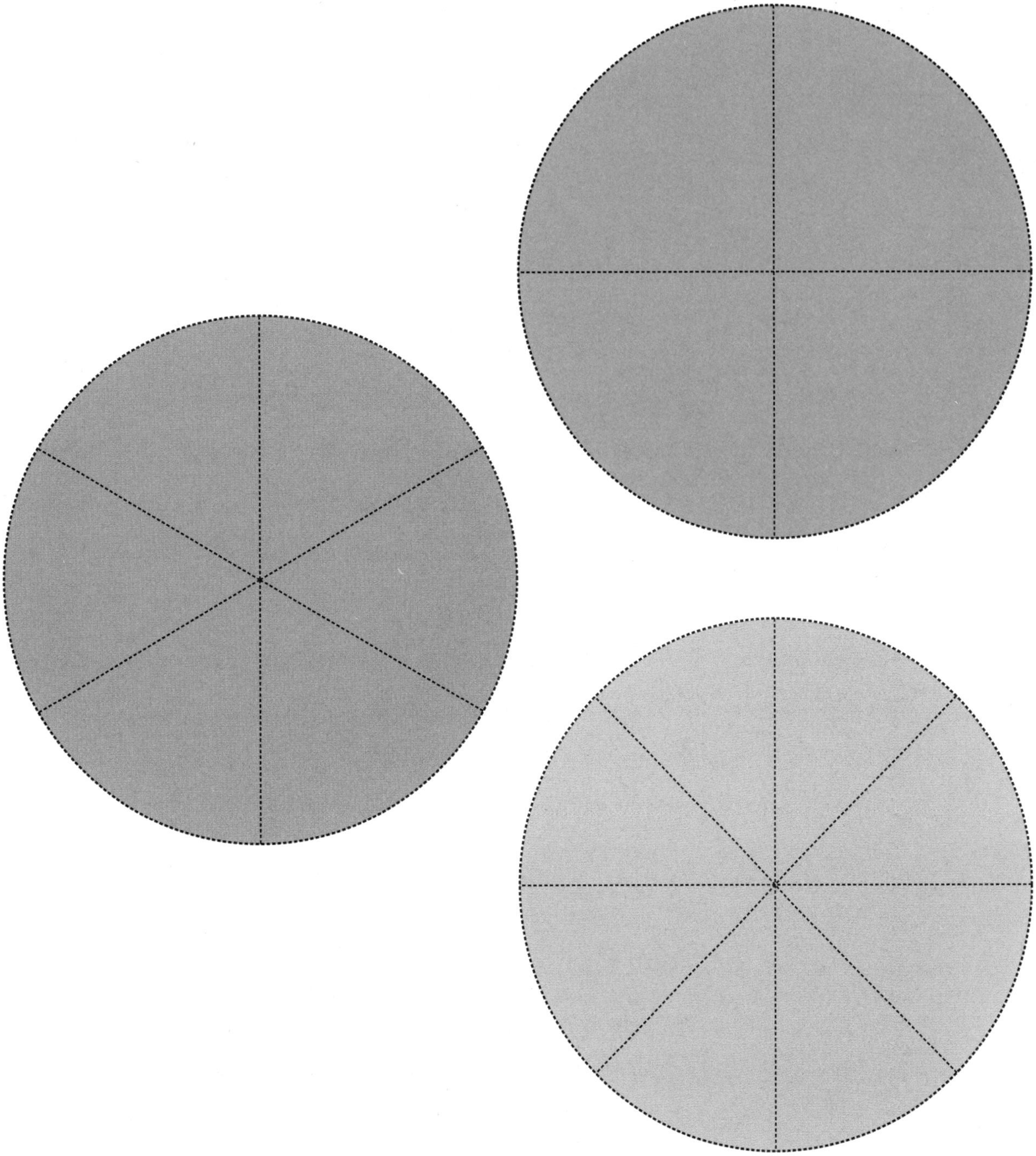

Name ______________________

Compare Fractions

These circles are the same size. They are also the same size as the circles on page 275A. Use each circle as 1 whole.

Work with a partner. Use your fraction circles to compare fractions during the class activity.

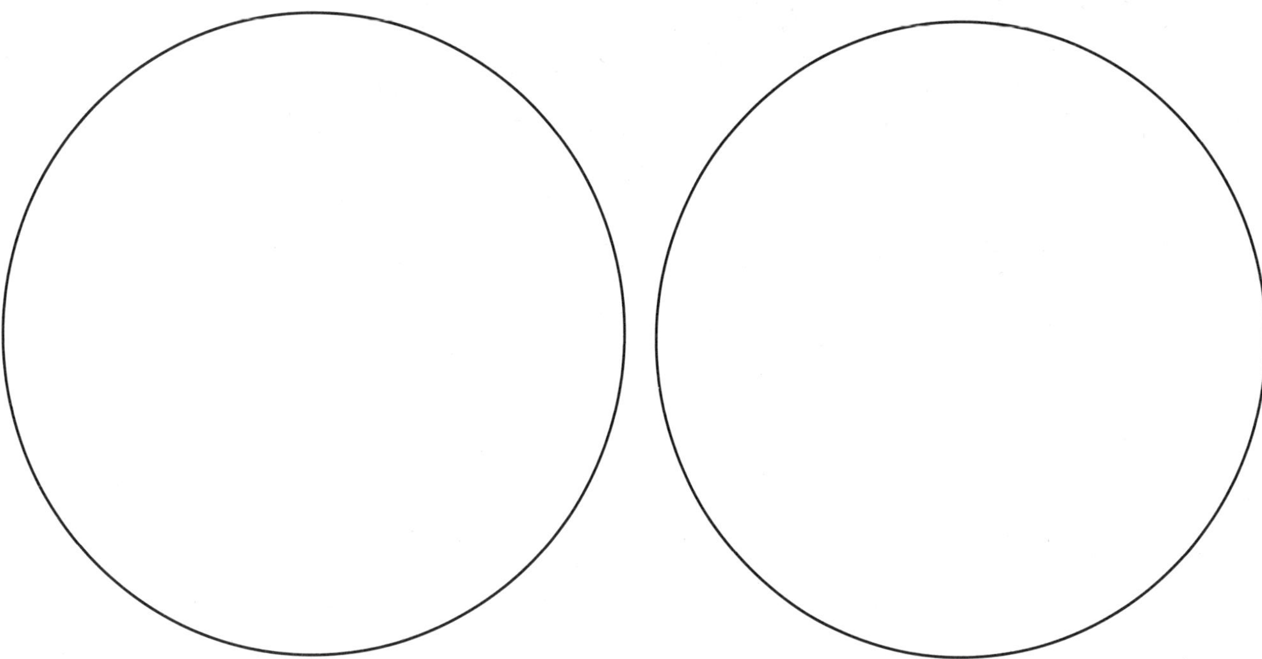

Record your work during the class activity.

1. $\frac{7}{8} \bigcirc \frac{5}{8}$

2. $\frac{3}{6} \bigcirc \frac{5}{6}$

3. Explain how to compare two fractions that have the same denominator.

____

____

4. $\frac{3}{4} \bigcirc \frac{3}{8}$

5. $\frac{5}{8} \bigcirc \frac{5}{6}$

6. Explain how to compare two fractions that have the same numerator.

____

____

Compare and Order Fractions

Compare. Use <, >, or =.

7 $\frac{2}{2} \bigcirc \frac{2}{3}$ 8 $\frac{1}{3} \bigcirc \frac{5}{3}$ 9 $\frac{3}{2} \bigcirc \frac{3}{6}$ 10 $\frac{5}{6} \bigcirc \frac{4}{6}$

Order the fractions from least to greatest.

11 $\frac{5}{8}$ $\frac{3}{8}$ $\frac{7}{8}$

_____, _____, _____

12 $\frac{7}{3}$ $\frac{7}{6}$ $\frac{7}{5}$

_____, _____, _____

13 $\frac{2}{5}$ $\frac{1}{5}$ $\frac{3}{5}$

_____, _____, _____

What's the Error?

Dear Math Students,

Today my teacher asked me to compare $\frac{3}{7}$ and $\frac{3}{9}$ and to explain my thinking.

I wrote $\frac{3}{7} = \frac{3}{9}$. My thinking is that both fractions have 3 unit fractions so they must be equal.

Is my work correct? If not, please correct my work and tell me what I did wrong. How do you know my answer is wrong?

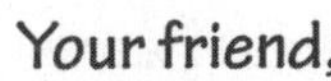

Your friend,
Puzzled Penguin

14 Write an answer to Puzzled Penguin.

____

____

____

Check Understanding

Explain how comparing two fractions with the same denominator is different from comparing two fractions with the same numerator.

Name ____________________

VOCABULARY
line segment

Units of Length

Loop length units and fractions of units to show the length of the line segment. Write the length.

1 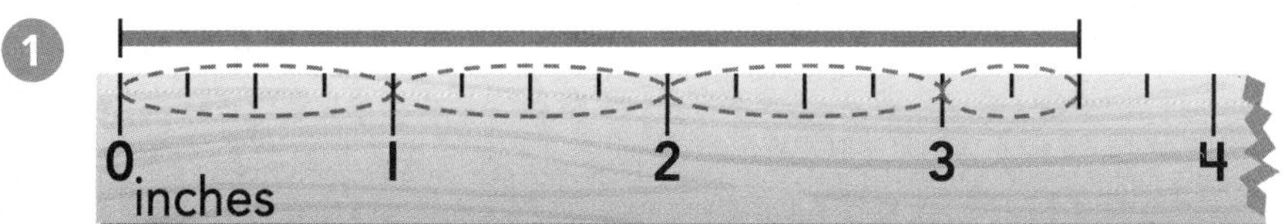

____

2 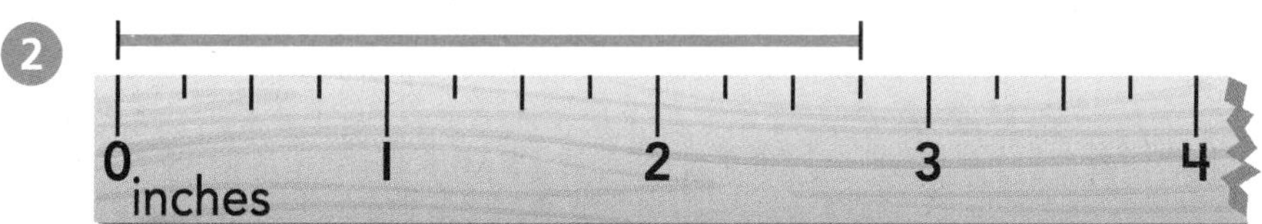

____

3 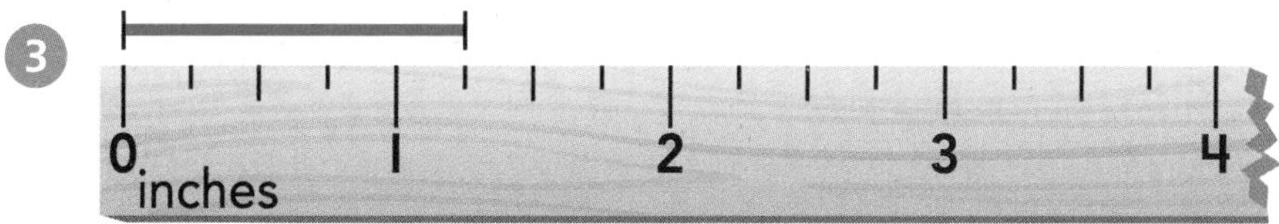

____

4 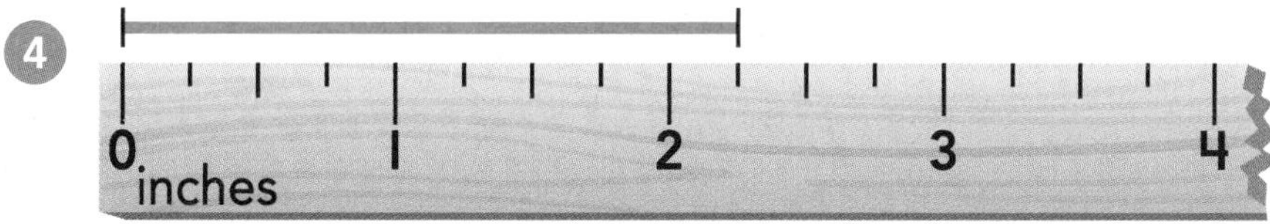

____

5 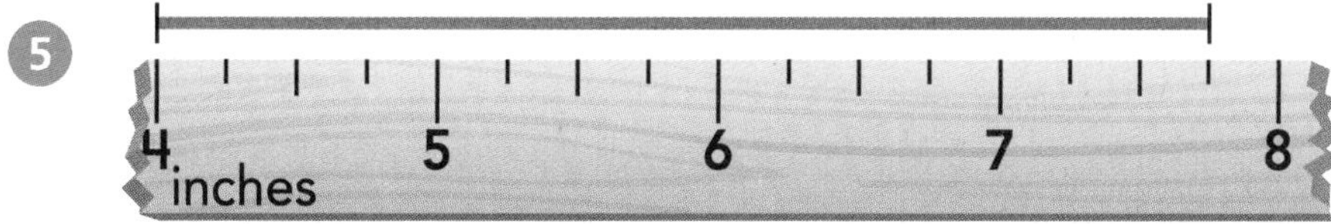

____

6 Why is this ruler wrong?

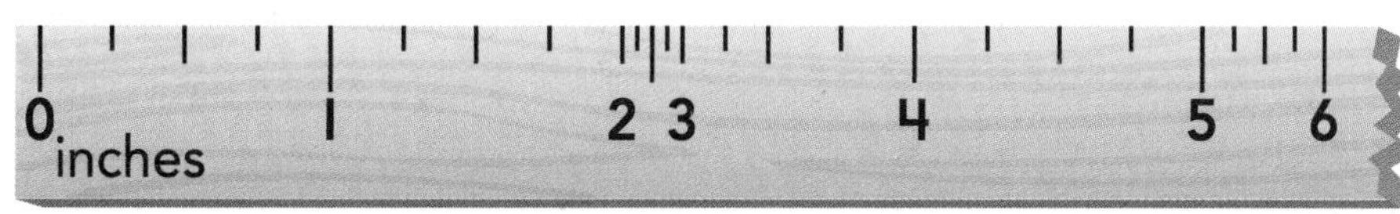

____

Estimate and Measure Length

VOCABULARY
inch (in.)

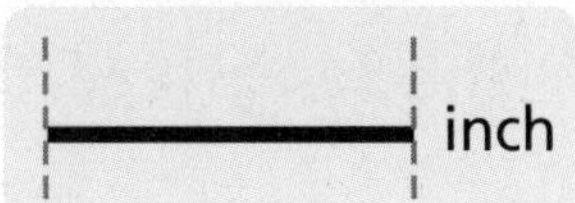

Estimate the length of each line segment in inches. Then measure it to the nearest $\frac{1}{2}$ inch.

7

Estimate: __________ Actual: __________

8

Estimate: __________ Actual: __________

Estimate the length of the line segment in inches. Then measure it to the nearest $\frac{1}{4}$ inch.

9

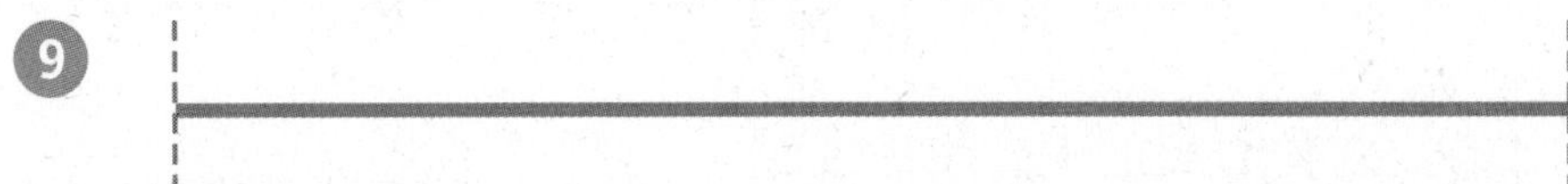

Estimate: __________ Actual: __________

Draw Line Segments

Draw a line segment that has the given length.

10 5 inches

11 $4\frac{1}{2}$ inches

12 $4\frac{3}{4}$ inches

13 Draw a line segment that is between $1\frac{1}{4}$ and $3\frac{3}{4}$ inches long. Trade books with a partner and measure the line segment they drew. __________

Name ______________________________

Line Plots with Fractions

VOCABULARY
line plot

A **line plot** shows the frequency of data on a number line. In science class, students measured the lengths of leaves in a leaf collection. They measured the lengths to the nearest $\frac{1}{4}$ inch. The line plot shows the results.

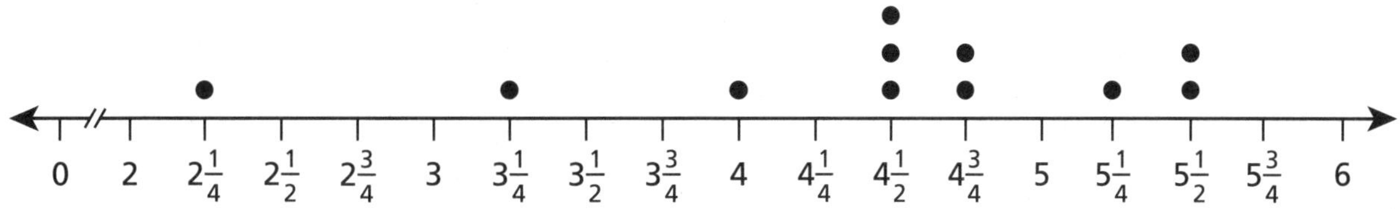

Length of Leaves (in inches)

Use the line plot to answer the questions.

14 How many leaves have a length of $4\frac{1}{2}$ inches? ________

15 How many leaves have a length that is less than 5 inches? ________

16 Write a question that can be answered using the line plot.

____

____

____

____

____

____

Make a Line Plot

Use the box below to record the actual measure for the line segments that each classmate drew on page 278.

17 Use the measurement data from the box above to complete the line plot below.

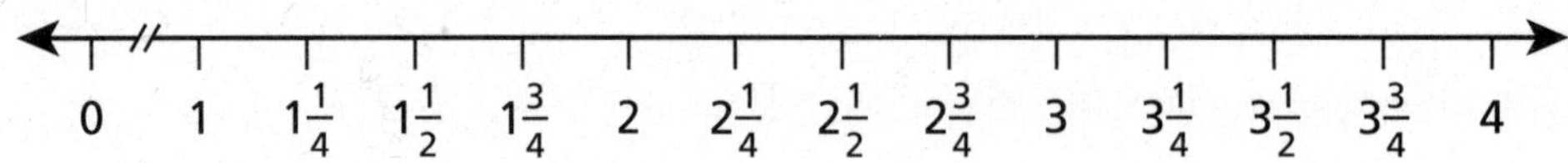

Length of Line Segments (in inches)

18 How many of the line segments have a measure of $2\frac{1}{2}$ inches? ______________________

19 Which length appears the most often on the line plot? ______________________

Check Understanding

Describe how to measure a line segment to the nearest $\frac{1}{4}$ inch.

Unit 4
Quick Quiz 1

Name ______________________ Date ______________

Show the shaded fraction as a sum of unit fractions.

1. 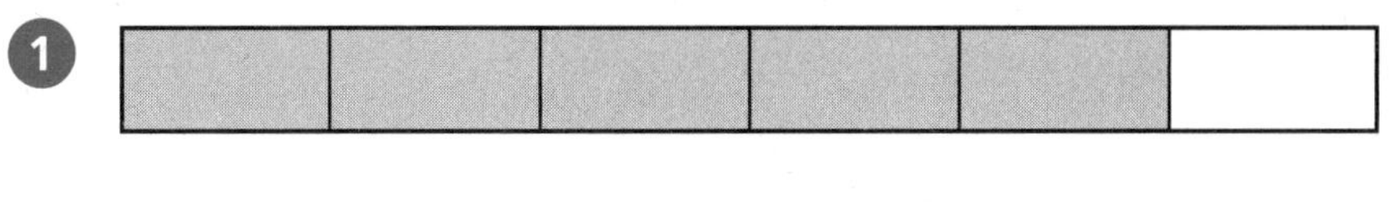

____

Divide the fraction bar into the correct number of equal parts.

2. 8 equal parts

Shade the fraction bar to show the fraction. First divide the fraction bar into the correct unit fractions.

3. $\frac{1}{3}$

1 whole

Mark the number line to show the fraction. First divide the number line into correct unit fractions.

4. $\frac{5}{3}$

0 1 2 3

Compare. Use <, >, or =.

5. $\frac{1}{6}$ ◯ $\frac{1}{2}$

Strategy Check 5

Name ____________________ Date ____________________

1 Flavien uses string in the colors and lengths shown below to create a pattern. Measure the length of each of the strings shown to the nearest $\frac{1}{4}$ inch.

☐ inches

☐ inches

☐ inches

☐ inches

2 Flavien uses 3 green strings, 2 blue strings, 4 red strings, and 2 yellow strings to make his pattern. Use the length measurements from the previous question to complete the line plot below.

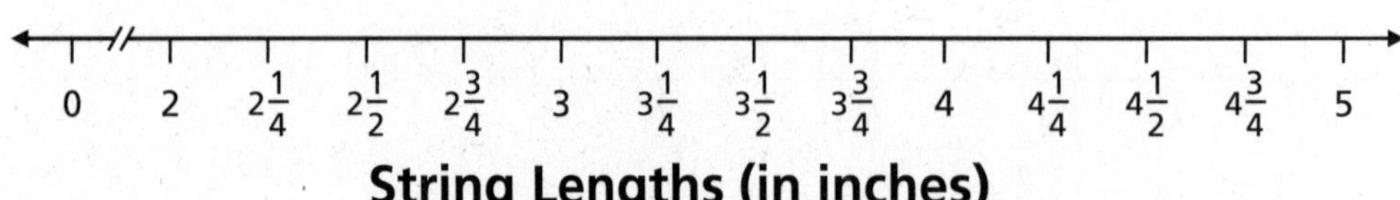

Dear Family:

In math class, your child is beginning lessons about time. This topic is directly connected to home and community and involves skills your child will use often in everyday situations.

Students are reading time to the hour, half-hour, quarter-hour, five minutes, and minute, as well as describing the time before the hour and after the hour.

For example, you can read 3:49 both as minutes after the hour and minutes before the hour.

Forty-nine minutes after three **Eleven minutes before four**

Students will be using clocks to solve problems about elapsed time.

Help your child read time and find elapsed time. Ask your child to estimate how long it takes to do activities such as eating a meal, traveling to the store, or doing homework. Have your child look at the clock when starting an activity and then again at the end of the activity. Ask how long the activity took.

Your child will also learn to add and subtract time on a number line.

If you have any questions or comments, please contact me.

Sincerely,
Your child's teacher

Estimada familia:

En la clase de matemáticas su niño está comenzando lecciones que le enseñan sobre la hora. Este tema se relaciona directamente con la casa y la comunidad, y trata de destrezas que su niño usará a menudo en situaciones de la vida diaria.

Los estudiantes leerán la hora, la media hora, el cuarto de hora, los cinco minutos y el minuto; también describirán la hora antes y después de la hora en punto.

Por ejemplo, 3:49 se puede leer de dos maneras:

Las tres y cuarenta y nueve | **Once para las cuatro**

Los estudiantes usarán relojes para resolver problemas acerca del tiempo transcurrido en diferentes situaciones.

Ayude a su niño a leer la hora y hallar el tiempo transcurrido. Pídale que estime cuánto tiempo tomarán ciertas actividades, tales como comer una comida completa, ir a la tienda o hacer la tarea. Pida a su niño que vea el reloj cuando comience la actividad y cuando la termine. Pregúntele cuánto tiempo tomó la actividad.

Su niño también aprenderá a sumar y restar tiempo en una recta numérica.

Si tiene alguna pregunta o algún comentario, por favor comuníquese conmigo.

Atentamente,
El maestro de su niño

Name ______________________________

Make an Analog Clock

Attach the clock hands to the clock face using a prong fastener.

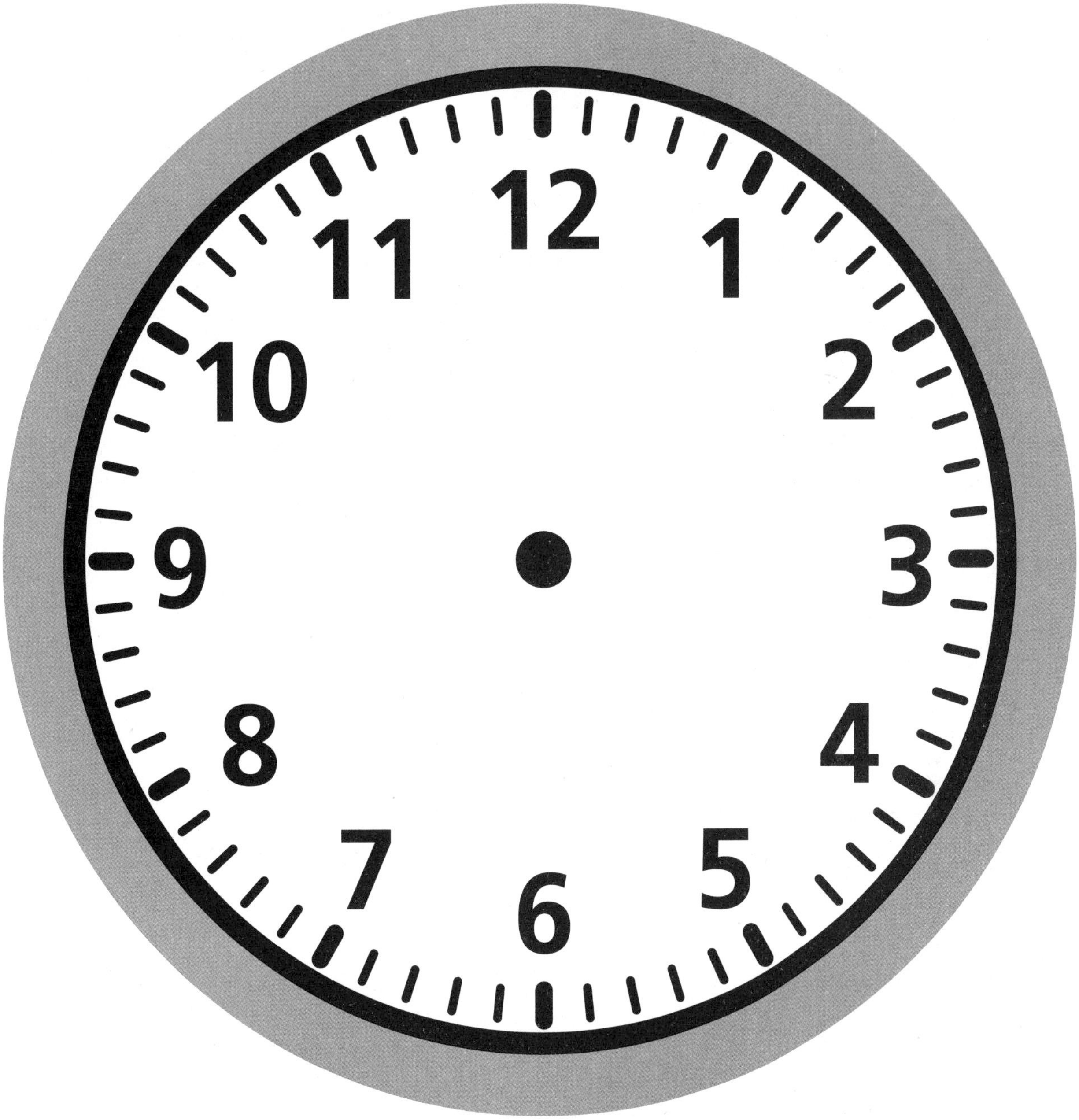

12 1 2 3 4 5 6 7 8 9 10 11

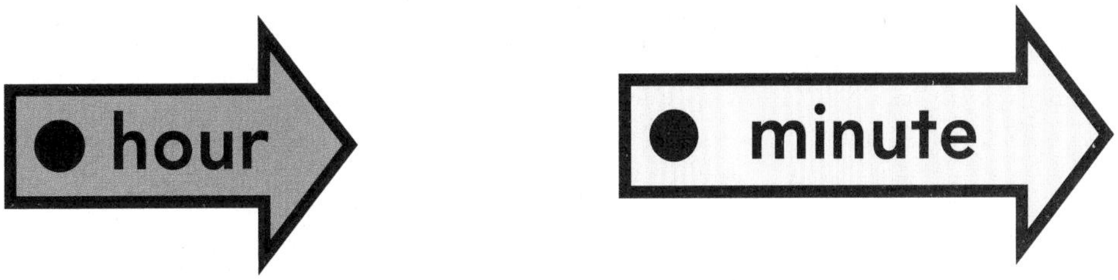

hour

minute

Name ______________________________

Time to 15 Minutes

Write the time on the digital clock. Then write how to say the time.

1 

2 

3 

4 

Write the time on the digital clock. Write two ways to say the time.

5 

6 

7 

8 

9 

10 

11 

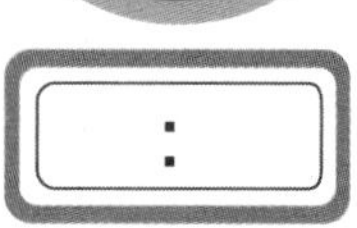

12 

Show Time to 15 Minutes

Draw the hands on the analog clock. Write the time on the digital clock.

13 nine fifteen

:

14 half past seven

:

15 three o'clock

:

16 seven thirty

:

17 one forty-five

:

18 fifteen minutes after two

:

Times of Daily Activities

19 Complete the table.

Time	Light or Dark	Part of the Day	Activity
3:15 A.M.			
8:00 A.M.			
2:30 P.M			
6:15 P.M			
8:45 P.M			

Name ______________________

Time to 5 Minutes

Write the time on the digital clock. Then write how to say the time.

20 

:

____

____

21 

:

____

____

22 

:

____

____

23 

:

____

____

24 

:

____

____

25 

:

____

____

Write the time on the digital clock.

26 ten minutes after eight

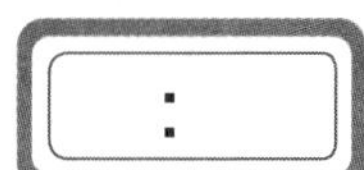

27 seven twenty-five

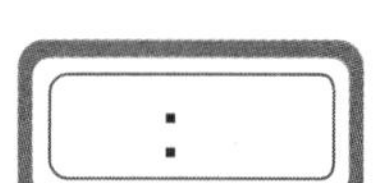

28 eleven fifty

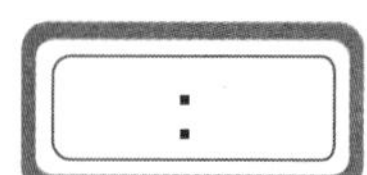

29 six forty

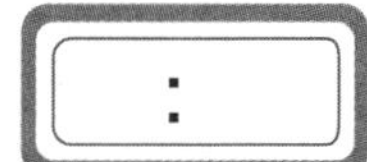

30 five minutes after three

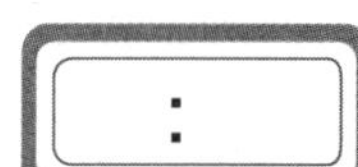

31 four fifty-five

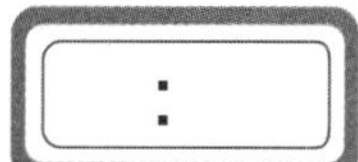

Time to 1 Minute

Write the time on the digital clock. Then write how to say the time.

32 

33 

34 

35 

36 

37 

Write the time on the digital clock.

38 ten fourteen

39 fifty-two minutes after eight

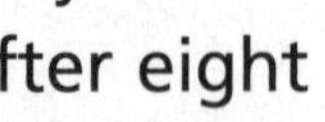

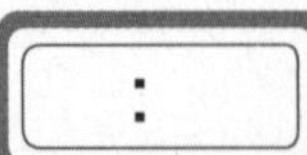

40 seven twenty-eight

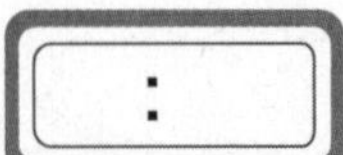

41 nine thirty-one

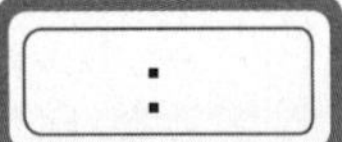

Check Understanding

Use your analog clock to show 1:26 and write the time in word form on your MathBoard.

Name ______________________________

Times Before and After the Hour to 5 Minutes

Write the time as minutes *after* an hour and minutes *before* an hour.

1 

2 

3 

4 

5 

6 

7 

8 

9 

Times Before and After the Hour to 1 Minute

Write the time as minutes *after* an hour and minutes *before* an hour.

10 

11 

12 

13 

14 

15 

Check Understanding

Use the analog clock to show 7:31. Write the time as minutes *after* the hour and minutes *before* the hour.

Name ______________________________

Elapsed Time in Minutes and Hours

1. Find the end time.

Start Time	Elapsed Time	End Time
1:00 P.M.	2 hours	
4:15 A.M.	4 hours	
4:55 P.M.	18 minutes	
2:15 A.M.	1 hour and 55 minutes	
11:55 A.M.	2 hours and 17 minutes	

2. Find the **elapsed time**.

Start Time	Elapsed Time	End Time
2:30 P.M.		4:42 P.M.
7:45 A.M.		8:15 A.M.
2:17 P.M.		7:17 P.M.
11:00 A.M.		2:00 P.M.
11:55 A.M.		4:25 P.M.

3. Find the start time.

Start Time	Elapsed Time	End Time
	3 hours	4:15 P.M.
	15 minutes	2:45 P.M.
	2 hours and 35 minutes	11:55 A.M.
	1 hour and 20 minutes	3:42 A.M.

Solve Problems About Elapsed Time on a Clock

Solve. Use your clock if you need to.

Show your work.

4. Loretta left her friend's house at 3:45 P.M. She had been there for 2 hours and 20 minutes. What time did she get there?

____

5. Berto spent from 3:45 P.M. to 4:15 P.M. doing math homework and from 4:30 P.M. to 5:10 P.M. doing social studies homework. How much time did he spend on his math and social studies homework?

____

6. Ed arrived at a biking trail at 9:00 A.M. He biked for 1 hour and 45 minutes. He spent 20 minutes riding home. What time did he get home?

____

7. Mario finished swimming at 10:45 A.M. He swam for 1 hour and 15 minutes. What time did he start?

____

8. Eric has basketball practice from 3:30 P.M. to 4:15 P.M. He has violin practice at 5:30 P.M. Today basketball practice ended 30 minutes late and it takes Eric 15 minutes to walk to violin practice. Will he be on time? Explain.

____

____

Check Understanding

Explain how you could find the elapsed time between 3:15 P.M. and 4:45 P.M.

Name ______________________________

Add Time

Solve using a number line.

Show your work.

1. Keisha went into a park at 1:30 P.M. She hiked for 1 hour 35 minutes. Then she went to the picnic area for 45 minutes and left the park. What time did Keisha leave the park?

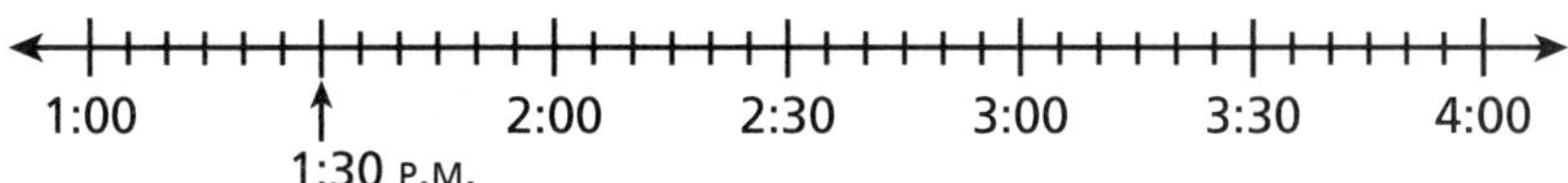

____

2. Loren arrived at the children's museum at 1:15 P.M. First, he spent 30 minutes looking at the dinosaur exhibit. Next, he watched a movie for 20 minutes. Then he spent 15 minutes in the museum gift shop. What time did Loren leave the museum? How long was he in the museum?

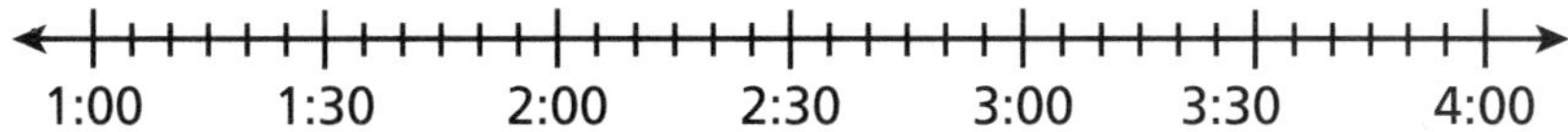

____

3. Caleb started working in the yard at 8:45 A.M. He raked for 1 hour 45 minutes and mowed for 45 minutes. Then he went inside. What time did he go inside? How long did he work in the yard?

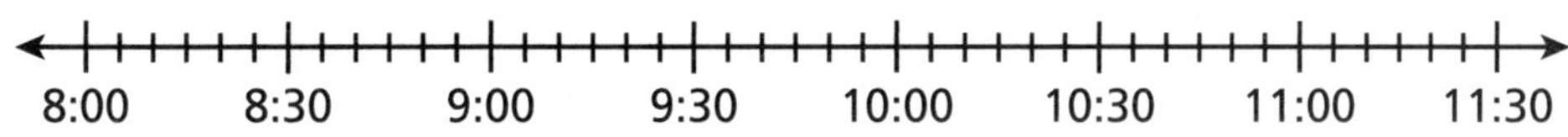

____

Subtract Time

Solve using a number line. *Show your work.*

4 Hank finished bowling at 7:15 P.M. He bowled for 2 hours 35 minutes. At what time did he start bowling?

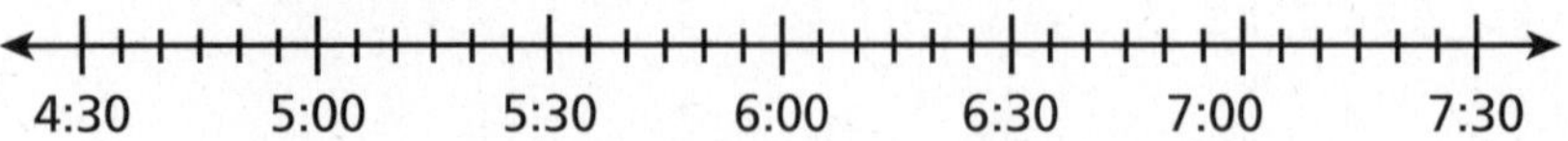

5 The school music program ended at 8:35 P.M. It lasted for 1 hour 50 minutes. What time did the program start?

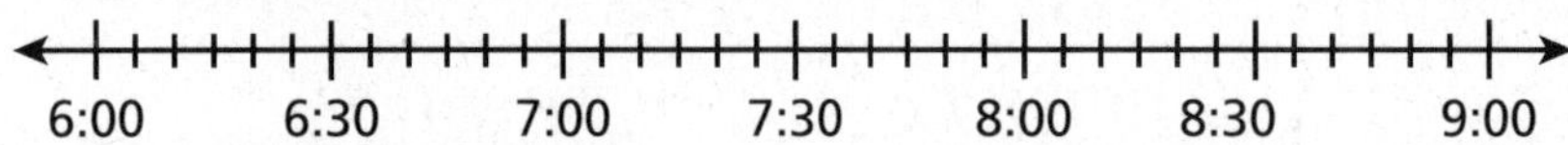

6 Lia served the salad at 3:15 P.M. It cooled in the refrigerator for 35 minutes. She spent 15 minutes gathering the ingredients from the garden and 15 minutes chopping the vegetables. What time did Lia start working on the salad?

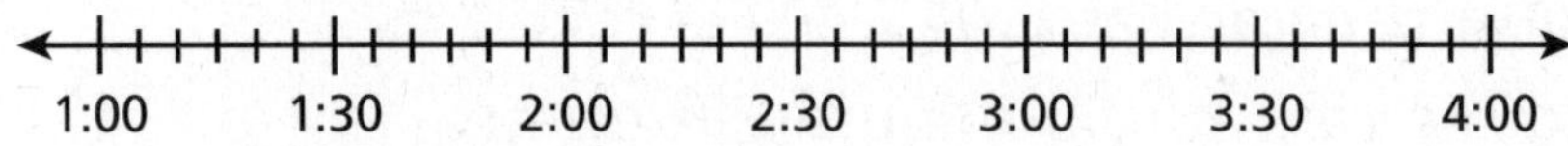

Check Understanding

Explain how you know to jump forward or backward when adding and subtracting on the number line.

Name ______________________________

Make Sense of Word Problems Involving Time Intervals

Solve. Use a clock or sketch a number line diagram if you need to.

Show your work.

1. Mr. Cox caught a train at 1:45 P.M. to visit his grandchildren. The train trip lasted 35 minutes. Then he spent 10 minutes waiting for a cab and another 15 minutes riding in the cab. What time did Mr. Cox get to his grandchildren's house?

   ____

2. Hirva left home at 9:45 A.M. and returned home at 11:20 A.M. She spent 55 minutes at the gym and the rest of the time at the library. How much time did Hirva spend at the library?

   ____

3. Diego arrived at soccer practice at 8:45 A.M. Practice lasted 45 minutes and then it took him 10 minutes to walk home. What time did Diego get home?

   ____

4. Jan started working on her homework at 6:25 P.M. and she finished at 7:30 P.M. She spent 45 minutes on a book report and the rest of the time on math. How long did Jan spend on math?

   ____

5. Shanna finished her chores at 4:25 P.M. She spent 35 minutes cleaning her room, 20 minutes bathing her dog, and 15 minutes folding clothes. What time did Shanna begin her chores?

   ____

What's the Error?

Dear Math Students,

Today I was asked to find the time Jim got to the doctor's office if he woke up at 7:55 A.M., spent 45 minutes getting ready, and then drove 20 minutes to the doctor's office.

Here is how I solved the problem.

From 7:55 on a clock, I counted up 45 minutes to 8:45, then I counted up 20 minutes to 9:05. Jim got to the doctor's office at 9:05 A.M.

Is my answer correct? If not, please correct my work and tell me what I did wrong. How do you know my answer is wrong?

Your friend,
Puzzled Penguin

6 **Write an answer to the Puzzled Penguin.**

___

___

___

Solve.

7 Wayne left home at 3:50 P.M. to go to the park. It took 30 minutes to get to the park. He spent 45 minutes at the park. What time did he leave the park?

___

8 Leslie finished her project at 11:05 A.M. She spent 1 hour 10 minutes making a poster and 35 minutes writing a report. What time did Leslie start her project?

___

Name ______________________________

Parts of an Hour

Use the clocks to help you solve each problem.

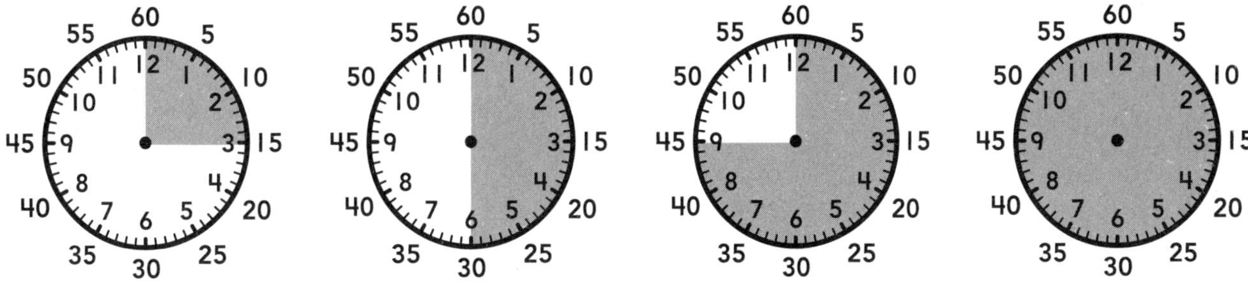

9. Erin jogs for $\frac{1}{4}$ hour. How many minutes does she jog?

____

10. Franklin starts his homework at 4:15 P.M. He does homework for $\frac{3}{4}$ hour. What time does he finish?

____

11. Jason and Amy are painting a fence. Jason paints for 1 hour. Amy paints for $\frac{1}{2}$ hour. How many more minutes does Jason paint than Amy?

____

12. Spencer starts walking home at 3:15 P.M. It takes him $\frac{1}{2}$-hour to get home. What time does he get home?

____

13. Becca walks her dog for $\frac{1}{4}$ hour in the morning and $\frac{1}{2}$ hour in the afternoon. How many minutes does she spend walking her dog?

____

Time Relationships

Use the table to help you solve the problems.

Show your work.

1 year = 12 months
1 year = 365 days
1 week = 7 days
1 day = 24 hours
1 hour = 60 minutes

14 Victor has lived in Albany for 2 years and 3 months. How many months has he lived there?

____

15 Katherine spends 3 weeks visiting her grandparents. How many days does she spend with her grandparents?

____

16 The school field trip was delayed 3 days because of a winter storm. How many hours was the trip delayed?

____

17 Camille spends 2 weeks and 4 days at summer camp. How many days does she spend at summer camp?

____

18 Seth has soccer practice for 2 hours. The team takes a break for 20 minutes. How many minutes did the team practice?

____

Check Understanding

Explain how to find the number of hours in one week.

Unit 4
Quick Quiz 2

Name ______ Date ______

Write the correct answer.

1. Write the time as minutes *after* an hour.

______

2. Write the time as minutes *before* an hour.

______

3. Carol leaves her house at 4:30 P.M. and drives for one hour to the grocery store. She shops for 20 minutes and then drives for one hour to get home. At what time does she get home?

Show your work.

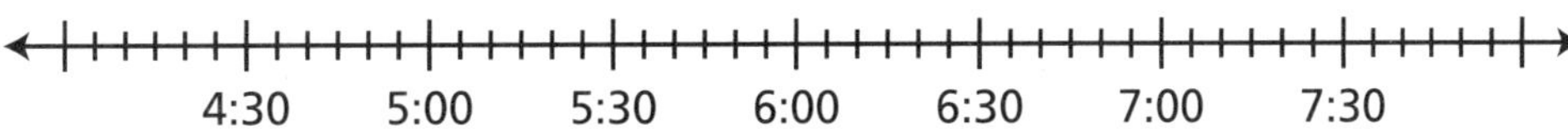

______

4. Stephen leaves the house at 2:00 P.M. to walk the dog to the park. He walks for an hour. He lets the dog run around in the park for 50 minutes and then walks the dog home. He arrives home at 5:30 P.M. How long did it take Stephen to walk home?

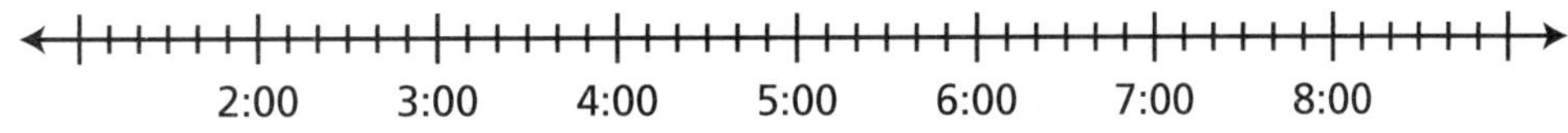

______

5. Band practice starts at 3:15 P.M. and ends at 3:50 P.M. How long does practice last?

______

Fluency Check 7

Name ____________________ Date ____________

PATH to FLUENCY

Add or subtract.

1. $14 + 23 = \square$
2. $48 - 20 = \square$
3. $27 + 11 = \square$
4. $56 - 32 = \square$
5. $30 + 16 = \square$
6. $49 - 43 = \square$
7. $\begin{array}{r} 46 \\ +\ 25 \\ \hline \end{array}$
8. $\begin{array}{r} 42 \\ -\ 19 \\ \hline \end{array}$
9. $\begin{array}{r} 59 \\ +\ 18 \\ \hline \end{array}$
10. $\begin{array}{r} 60 \\ -\ 35 \\ \hline \end{array}$
11. $\begin{array}{r} 44 \\ +\ 38 \\ \hline \end{array}$
12. $\begin{array}{r} 74 \\ -\ 69 \\ \hline \end{array}$
13. $\begin{array}{r} 76 \\ +\ 19 \\ \hline \end{array}$
14. $\begin{array}{r} 91 \\ -\ 58 \\ \hline \end{array}$
15. $\begin{array}{r} 53 \\ +\ 47 \\ \hline \end{array}$

Dear Family:

In the rest of the lessons in this unit, your child will be learning to show information in various ways. Students will learn to read and create pictographs and bar graphs. They will organize and display data in frequency tables and line plots. Students will also learn how to use graphs to solve real world problems.

Examples of pictographs, bar graphs, and line plots are shown below.

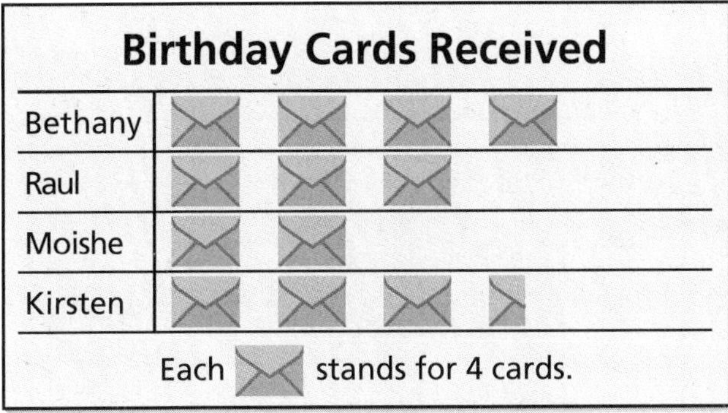

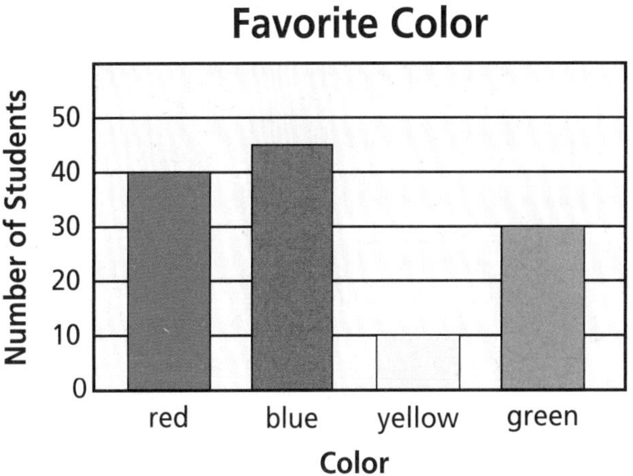

Your child is learning how graphs are used in the world around us. You can help your child learn by sharing graphs that appear in newspapers, magazines, or online.

Thank you for helping your child learn how to read, interpret, and create graphs.

Sincerely,
Your child's teacher

Estimada familia:

Durante el resto de las lecciones de esta unidad, su niño aprenderá a mostrar información de varias maneras. Los estudiantes aprenderán a leer y a crear pictografías y gráficas de barras. Organizarán y mostrarán datos en tablas de frecuencia y en diagramas de puntos. También aprenderán cómo usar las gráficas para resolver problemas cotidianos.

Debajo se muestran ejemplos de pictografías, gráficas de barras y diagramas de puntos.

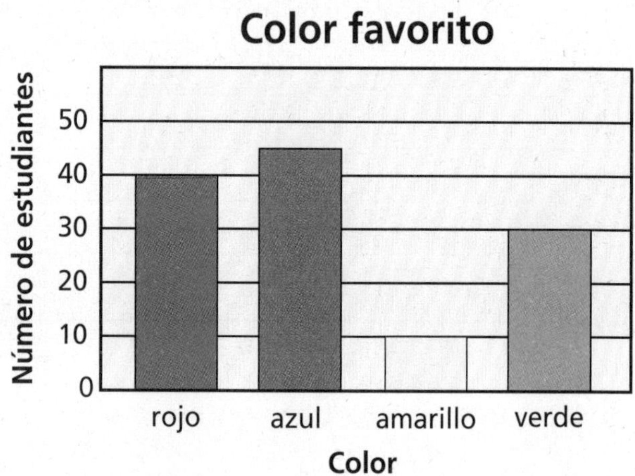

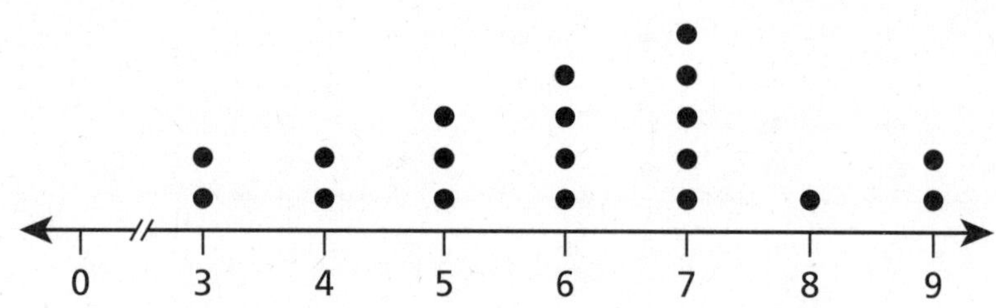

Número de letras en un nombre

Su niño está aprendiendo cómo se usan las gráficas en la vida cotidiana. Puede ayudarlo mostrándole gráficas que aparezcan en periódicos, revistas o Internet.

Gracias por ayudar a su niño a aprender cómo leer, interpretar y crear gráficas.

Atentamente,
El maestro de su niño

Name ______________________

VOCABULARY
key

Read a Pictograph

A pictograph is a graph that uses pictures or symbols to represent data. The pictograph below shows the number of votes for favorite ice cream flavors. The **key** tells that each ice cream cone symbol stands for the way 4 students voted.

Favorite Ice Cream Flavors

Peanut Butter Crunch	🍦 (half)
Cherry Vanilla	🍦 🍦 🍦
Chocolate	🍦 🍦 🍦 🍦 🍦

Each 🍦 stands for 4 votes.

Use the pictograph above to answer the questions.

1. How many votes were there for chocolate?

   ____

2. How many people in all voted for their favorite ice cream flavor?

   ____

3. How many votes were there for Cherry Vanilla?

   ____

4. How many people did not vote for chocolate?

   ____

5. How many fewer votes were there for Peanut Butter Crunch than Chocolate?

   ____

6. How many more people voted for Chocolate than for Peanut Butter Crunch and Cherry Vanilla combined?

   ____

Make a Pictograph

7 **Use the data about Kanye's Playlists to make your own pictograph.**

Kanye's Playlists	
Type	**Number of Playlists**
Jazz	12
Rap	16
Classical	4

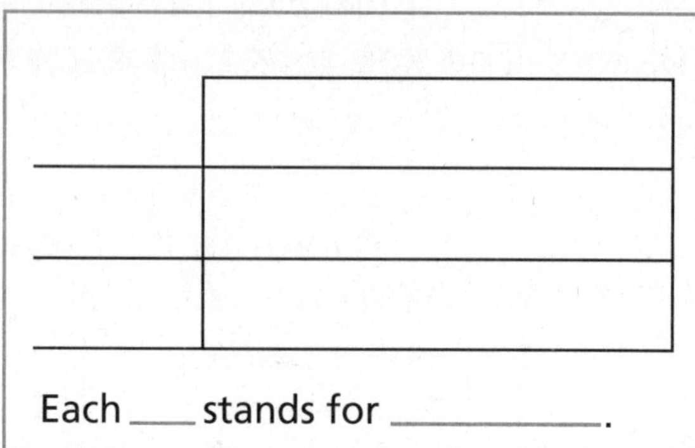

8 How many playlists in all does Kanye have?

____

9 How many more rap playlists does Kanye have than classical?

____

10 How many fewer jazz playlists does Kanye have than rap?

____

11 How many pictures would you draw to show that Kanye has 9 country playlists?

____

Name ______________________

Read Bar Graphs

VOCABULARY
horizontal bar graph
vertical bar graph

Look at this horizontal bar graph and answer the questions.

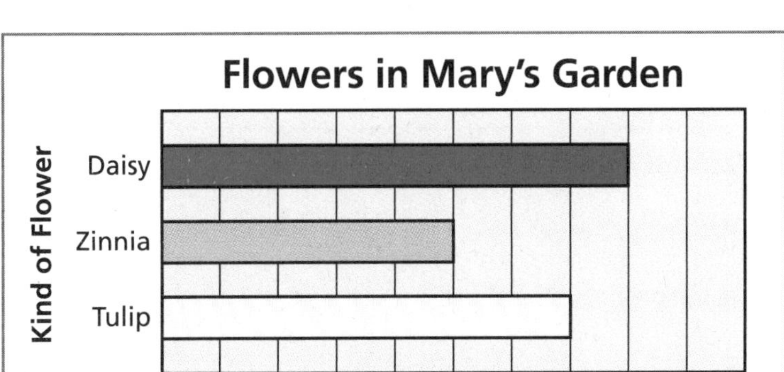

12 What do the bars represent?

____

____

13 How many tulips are in Mary's garden?

____

Look at this vertical bar graph and answer the questions.

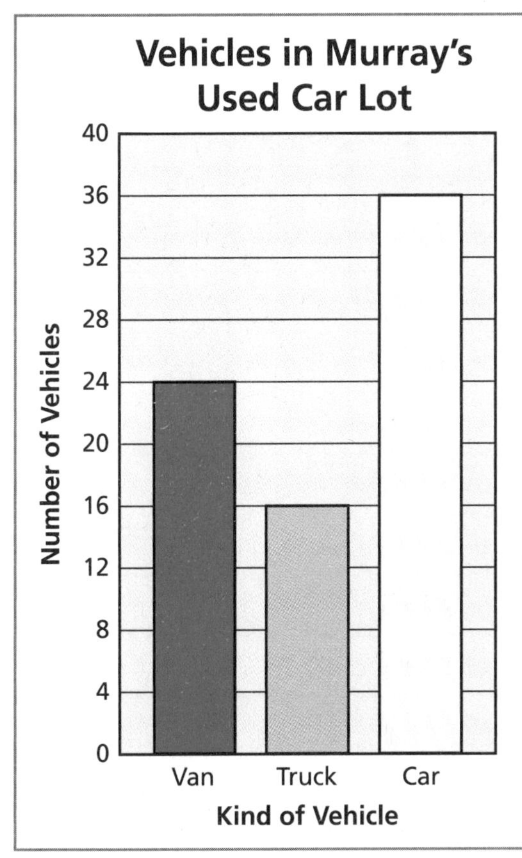

14 What do the bars represent?

____

____

____

15 How many more vans than trucks are on Murray's Used Car Lot?

____

Create Bar Graphs

16 **Use the information in this table to complete the horizontal bar graph.**

Favorite Way to Exercise	
Activity	**Number of Students**
Biking	12
Swimming	14
Walking	10

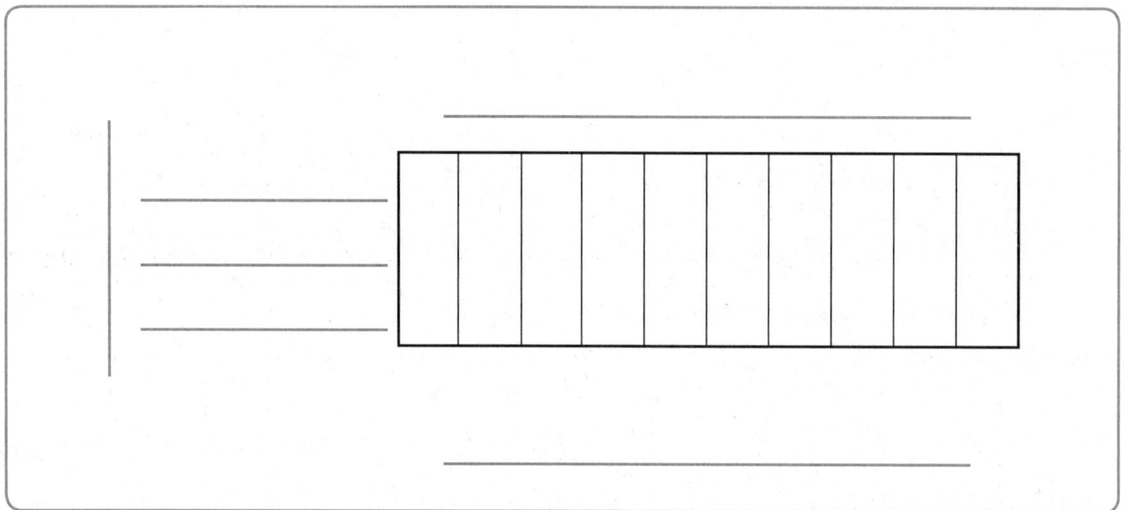

17 **Use the information in this table to complete the vertical bar graph.**

Favorite Team Sport	
Sport	**Number of Students**
Baseball	35
Soccer	60
Basketball	40

Name ______________________________

Solve Comparison Problems Using Data in Pictographs

Use the pictograph below to answer the questions.

What Musical Instrument Do You Play?

Each ♪ = 4 students.

18. How many more students play guitar than violin?

____

19. How many students do not play drums?

____

20. Do more students play drums or guitar and violin combined?

____

21. How many more students play guitar and piano combined than drums?

____

22. Twelve fewer students play this instrument than drums.

____

23. How many students in all were surveyed?

____

Solve Comparison Problems Using Data in Bar Graphs

Use the bar graph below to answer the questions.

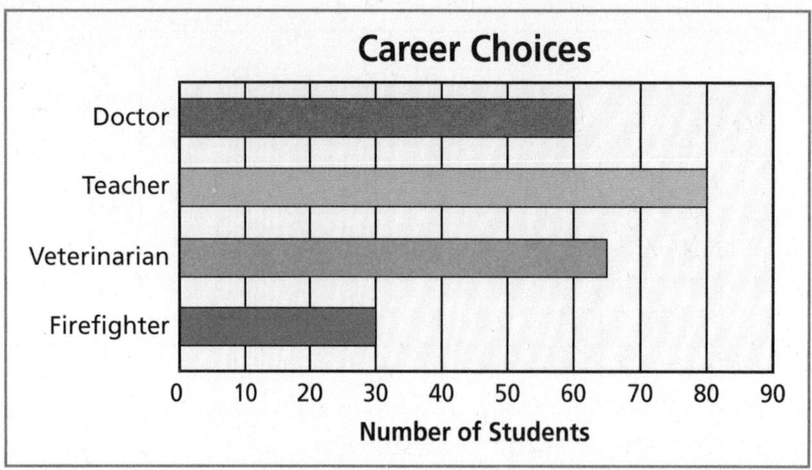

24. Twenty fewer students chose this career than teacher.

25. Did more students choose veterinarian and firefighter combined or teacher?

26. How many more students chose doctor than firefighter?

27. How many students did not choose teacher?

28. How many students in all were surveyed?

29. How many more students chose doctor and firefighter combined than veterinarian?

Check Understanding

What equation can you write to solve Problem 27?

 Name ____________________

Horizontal Bar Graphs with Multidigit Numbers

Use this horizontal bar graph to answer the questions below.

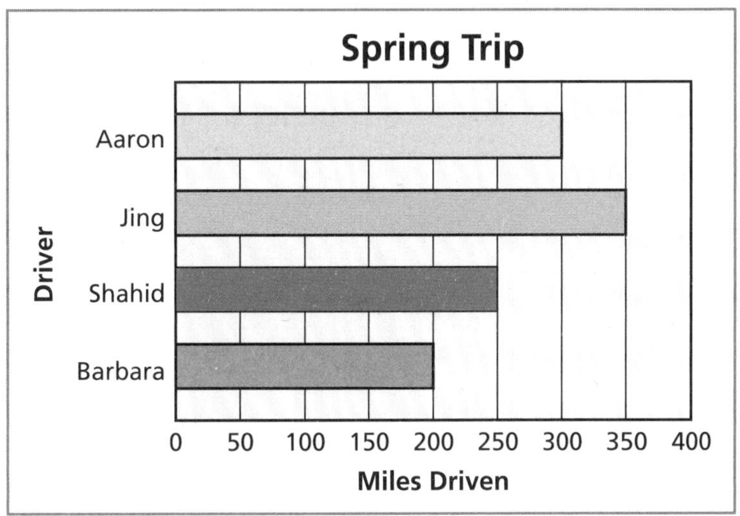

1. How many miles did Shahid drive?

   ____

2. Who drove 100 more miles than Barbara?

   ____

3. How many more miles did Aaron and Barbara combined drive than Jing?

   ____

4. How many more miles did Shahid and Aaron combined drive than Barbara?

   ____

5. How many fewer miles did Barbara drive than Jing?

   ____

6. Write another question that can be answered by using the graph.

   ____

Vertical Bar Graphs with Multidigit Numbers

Use the vertical bar graph at the right to answer the questions below.

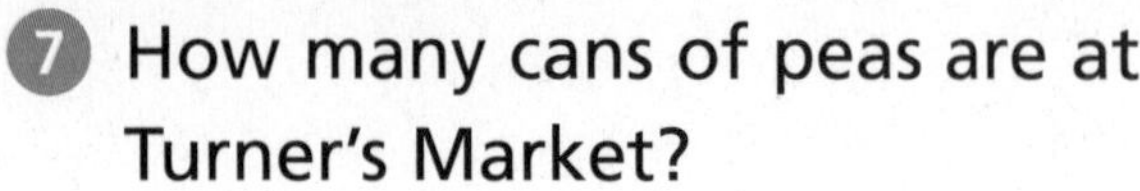

7. How many cans of peas are at Turner's Market?

____

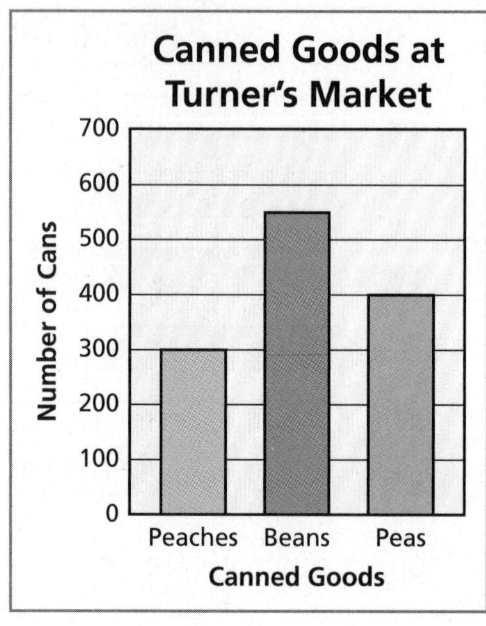

8. Are there more cans of beans or of peas and peaches combined?

____

9. How many cans of beans and peaches are there altogether?

____

10. How many more cans of beans are there than peas?

____

11. How many fewer cans of peaches are there than peas and beans combined?

____

12. Write another question that can be answered by using the graph.

____

____

____

____

____

Name ___

Create Bar Graphs with Multidigit Numbers

13 Use the information in the table on the right to make a horizontal bar graph.

Joe's Cap Collection	
Type	**Caps**
Baseball	60
Basketball	35
Golf	20

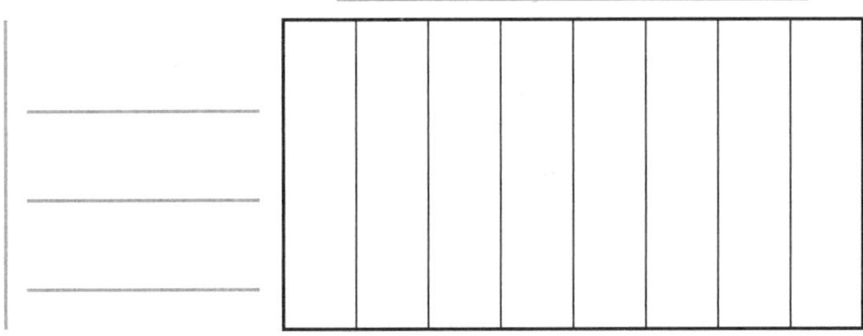

14 Use the information in the table on the right to make a vertical bar graph.

Summer Bike Sales	
Type of Bike	**Number Sold**
Road Bike	200
Mountain Bike	600
Hybrid Bike	450

Solve Problems Using Bar Graphs

Use the horizontal bar graph to answer the questions below.

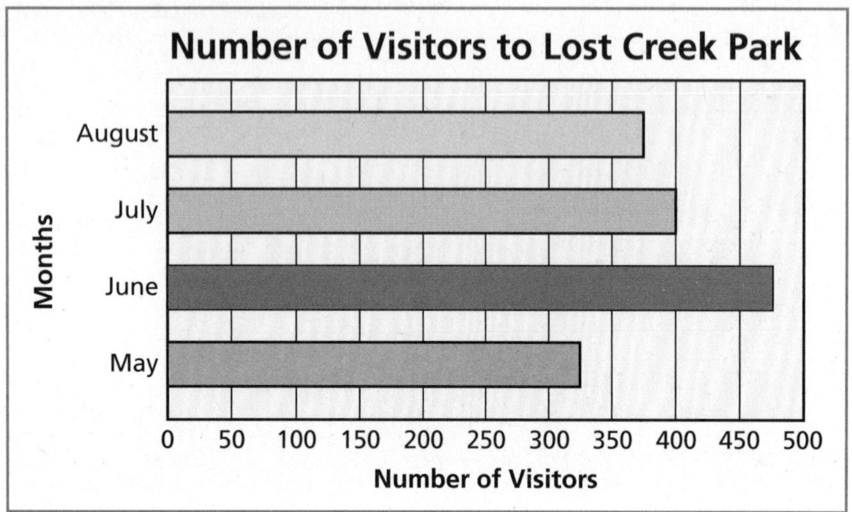

15 How many more visitors went to Lost Creek Park in June than in May?

____

16 How many visitors did the park have during the months of May and June combined?

____

17 How many more visitors went to the park in July than in August?

____

18 Did more visitors go to the park in June or in May and August combined?

____

Check Understanding

Suppose there were 225 visitors in September. Draw a bar graph that includes September.

Name ______________________________

Frequency Tables and Line Plots

VOCABULARY
tally chart
frequency table

The ages of some players on a basketball team can be shown in different ways.

A **tally chart** can be used to record and organize data.

A **frequency table** shows how many times events occur.

A line plot shows the frequency of data on a number line.

Tally Chart	
Age	Tally
7	I
8	III
9	𝍸
10	IIII
11	II

Frequency Table	
Age	Numbers of Players
7	1
8	3
9	5
10	4
11	2

Line Plot

Ages of Basketball Players

Make Sense of Data Displays

Use the data displays above to answer Exercises 1–4.

1. How many basketball players are 10 years old?

____

2. Which age appears the most often?

____

3. Are there more players younger than 9 or more players who are older than 9?

____

4. Write another question that can be answered by using the data displays.

____

____

Create Line Plots with Fractions

5 Have 10 classmates spread their fingers apart as far as possible, and measure from the tip of the thumb to the tip of the little finger to the nearest $\frac{1}{2}$ inch. Record the data in the tally chart below and then make a frequency table.

Tally Chart

Length	Tally

Frequency Table

Length	Number of Classmates

6 Use the data to make a line plot.

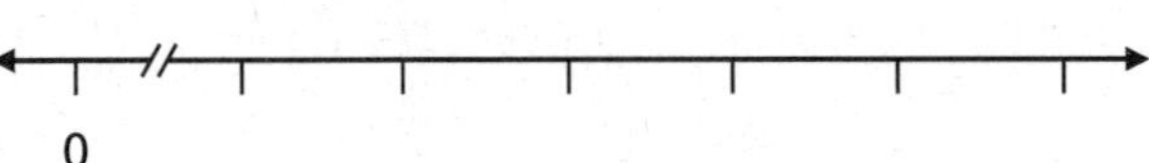

Hand Span Lengths (in inches)

7 Which length occurred the most often? ______________________

8 What is the difference between the greatest length and the least length?

____

9 Write a question that can be answered by using the data in the line plot.

____

____

Name ____________________

Take a Survey and Make a Pictograph

10 Ask 10 classmates to tell whether winter, spring, summer, or fall is their favorite season. Record their answers in the tally chart below and then make a frequency table.

Favorite Season

Tally Chart	
Season	**Tally**
Winter	
Spring	
Summer	
Fall	

Favorite Season

Frequency Table	
Season	**Number of Classmates**
Winter	
Spring	
Summer	
Fall	

11 Use the data from above to make a pictograph.

____________________	
__________	
__________	
__________	
__________	
Key: Each ☺ stands for __________.	

12 Suppose you ask two more students to tell their favorite season and both of them answered, "Winter." How would the pictograph need to change?

____

____

Use Measurement Data to Make a Bar Graph

13 Estimate the distance around 4 classmates' wrists in centimeters. Then measure the distance around their wrists to the nearest centimeter. Complete the table.

Distance Around the Wrist to the Nearest Centimeter		
Student	**Estimate in centimeters**	**Measurement in centimeters**

14 Use the measurement data to make a bar graph.

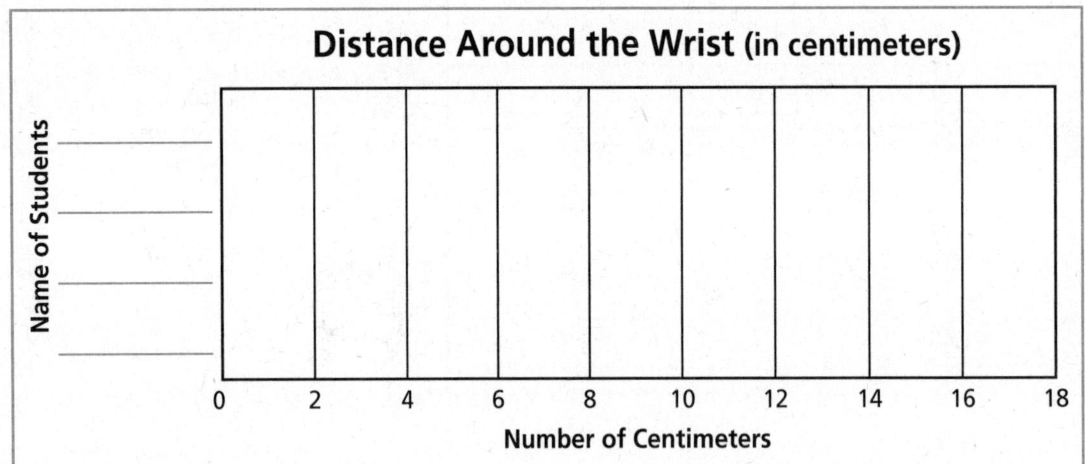

Check Understanding

Complete.

The bar graph above shows that ______ students have a distance around their wrists of less than 14 centimeters.

Name ______________________

Solve Problems Using a Bar Graph

Five teams of students are riding their bikes after school to raise money for the computer lab. Every completed mile will earn the computer lab $2. The bar graph below shows the number of miles completed in one week.

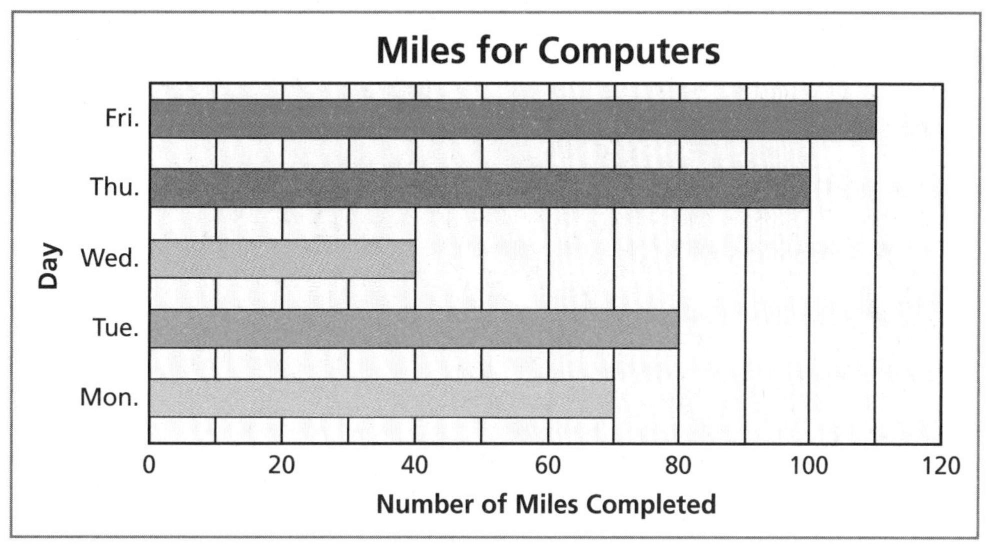

Use the bar graph to solve the problems.

1. How much money was earned for the computer lab on Tuesday?

 ____

2. How many fewer miles were completed on Monday than on Friday?

 ____

3. How many miles in all did the students ride?

 ____

4. How many more miles did students ride on Monday and Tuesday combined than on Friday?

 ____

5. There are 4 riders on each of the 5 teams. If each student completed the same number of miles, how many miles did each student ride on Wednesday?

 ____

6. Did students ride more miles on Monday and Wednesday combined or on Thursday?

 ____

 ____

Solve Problems Using a Line Plot

The physical fitness coach asked her students to walk around a track four times. Four laps equal one mile. She recorded their times on the line plot below.

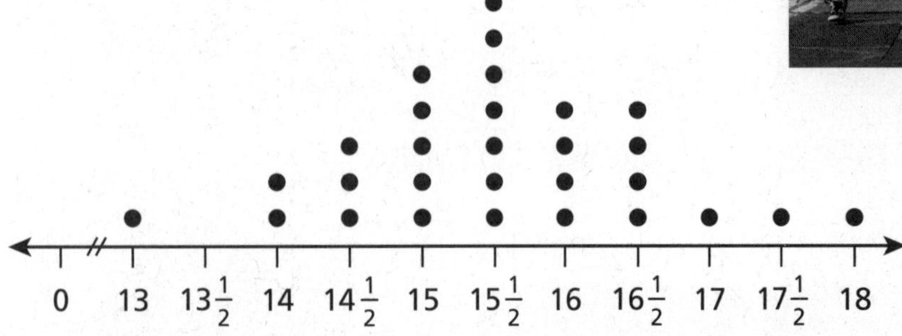

Time to Complete Four Laps (in minutes)

Use the plot to solve the problems.

7. What is the difference between the greatest and the least amount of time students took to walk four laps?

____

8. Did more students complete the laps in 16 minutes or more or in $15\frac{1}{2}$ minutes or fewer?

____

9. How many students completed four laps in 16 minutes?

____

10. The coach recorded the times of how many students?

____

11. How many students completed four laps in fewer than 15 minutes?

____

Check Understanding

Complete the sentences.
Most students completed the laps in ______ minutes. The ______ dots above that time represent ______ students.

Name ____________________

Math and Sports

Many students take part in a track and field day at school each year. One event is the standing broad jump. In the standing broad jump, the jumper stands directly behind a starting line and then jumps. The length of the jump is measured from the starting line to the mark of the first part of the jumper to touch the ground.

Complete.

1. Your teacher will tell you when to do a standing broad jump. Another student should measure the length of your jump to the nearest $\frac{1}{2}$ foot and record it on a slip of paper.

2. Record the lengths of the students' jumps in the box below.

How Far Can a Third Grader Jump?

To analyze how far a third grader can jump, the data needs to be organized and displayed.

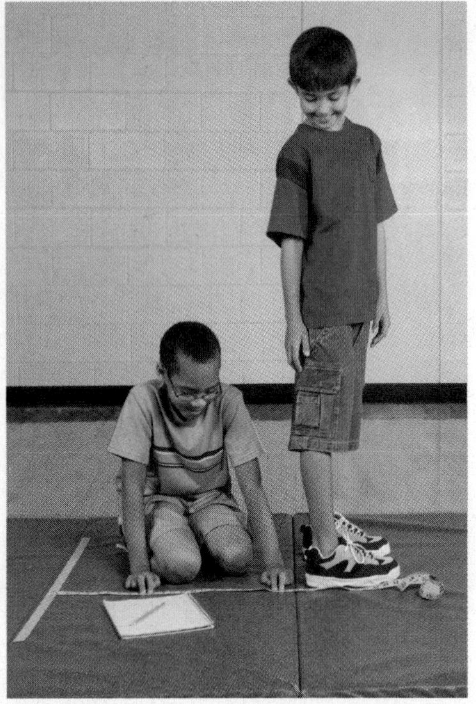

3 Use the lengths of the students' jumps to complete the tally chart and the frequency table.

Tally Chart	
Length	**Tally**

Frequency Table	
Length	**Number of Students**

4 Make a line plot.

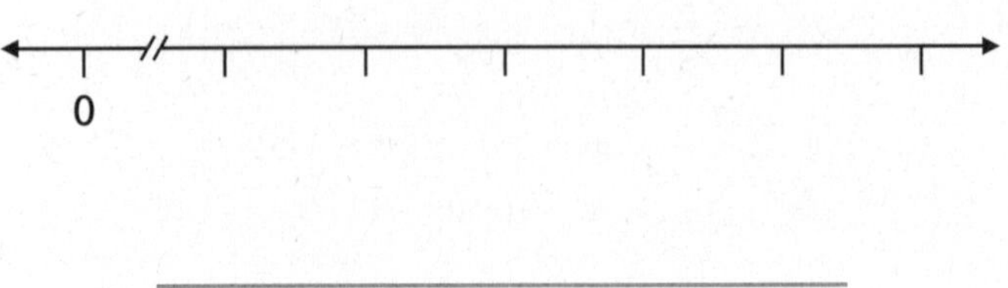

Name Date

1 Use the data in the table to complete the bar graph.

Students	
Grade	**Number of Students**
2nd	25
3rd	40
4th	80
5th	50

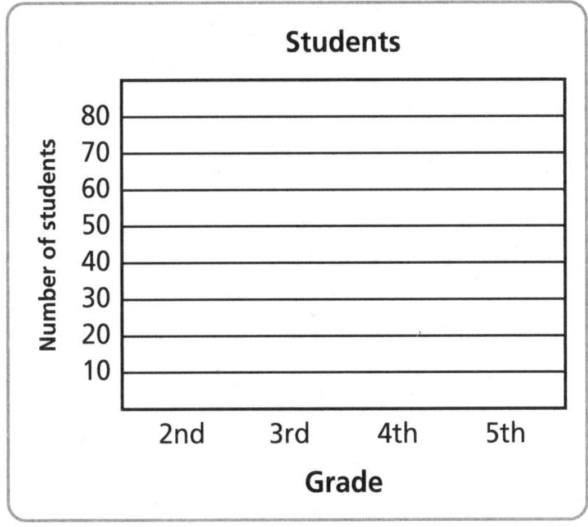

2 Use the data in the table to complete the line plot.

Time Spent at After School Activities	
Hours	**Number of students**
$\frac{1}{2}$	4
1	3
$1\frac{1}{2}$	2
2	1
$2\frac{1}{2}$	3
3	5

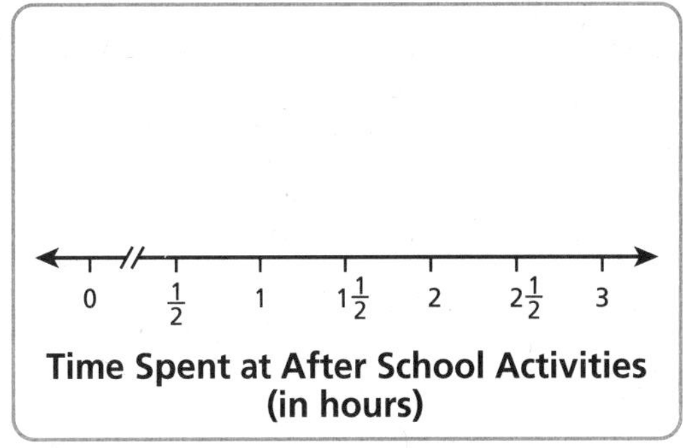

The animals that Gary saw while hiking are shown in the pictograph on the right. Use the pictograph to answer questions 3 and 4.

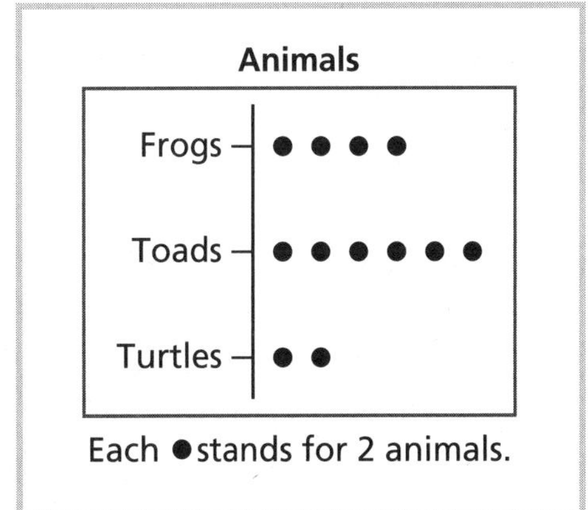

3 How many toads did Gary see?

____

4 How many more frogs than turtles did Gary see?

____

Fluency Check 8

Name ____________________ Date ____________________

PATH to FLUENCY

Multiply or divide.

1. $8 \div 2 = \square$
2. $3 \times 5 = \square$
3. $7 \times 6 = \square$
4. $4 \times 10 = \square$
5. $60 \div 10 = \square$
6. $7 \div 1 = \square$
7. $64 \div 8 = \square$
8. $6 \times 9 = \square$
9. $45 \div 5 = \square$

Add or subtract.

10. $342 + 117$
11. $754 - 342$
12. $263 + 474$
13. $556 - 438$
14. $387 + 476$
15. $803 - 598$

Name ______________________________ Date ______________

1 Select the letter that shows the shaded fraction. Mark all that apply.

Ⓐ $\frac{1}{4}$

Ⓑ $\frac{4}{3}$

Ⓒ $\frac{3}{4}$

Ⓓ $\frac{1}{4} + \frac{1}{4} + \frac{1}{4}$

Ⓔ $\frac{4}{1} + \frac{4}{1} + \frac{4}{1}$

2 For numbers 2a–2d, choose Yes or No to tell whether the words say the time on the clock.

2a. twenty-six minutes before eleven	○ Yes	○ No
2b. thirty-four minutes after twelve	○ Yes	○ No
2c. thirty-four minutes after eleven	○ Yes	○ No
2d. twenty-six minutes before twelve	○ Yes	○ No

3 Use a straightedge to divide the fraction bar into 6 equal parts. Then shade four parts.

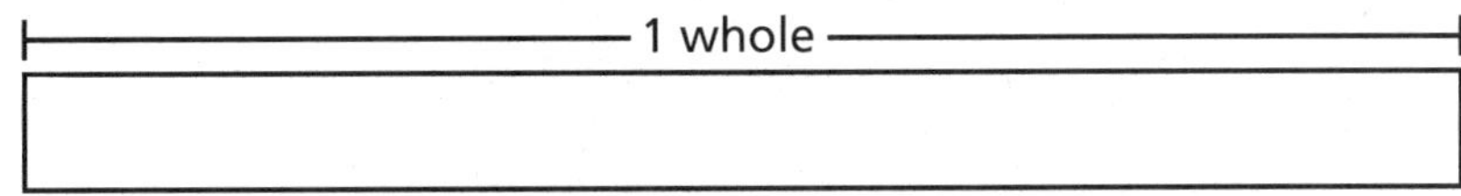

What fraction does the shaded fraction bar represent?

____

Show the fraction as the sum of unit fractions.

____

Name ______________________ Date ______________________

4 Kyle starts his homework at 6:30 P.M. He spends 35 minutes doing math homework and 40 minutes doing science homework. At what time does Kyle finish his homework? How much time does he spend on homework? Use the number line to help you.

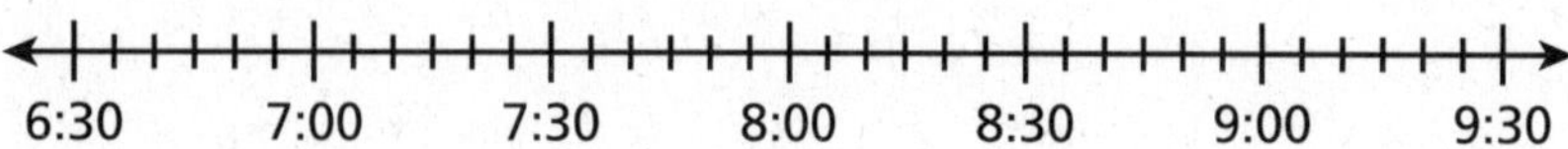

Kyle finishes his homework at ______________ P.M.

He spends [1 hour 5 minutes / 1 hour 15 minutes / 1 hour 25 minutes] on homework.

5 Locate the fraction on the number line.

$\frac{3}{4}$

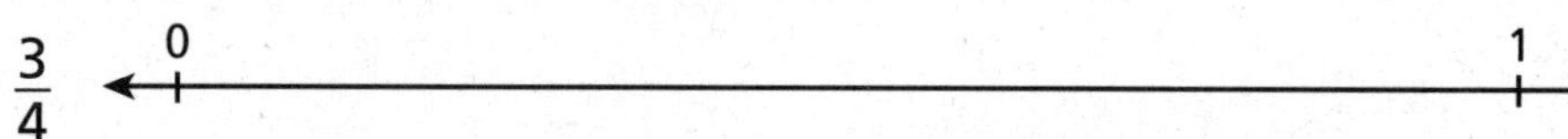

Name ________________________ Date ____________

6. The bar graph shows the number of plants sold at a nursery.

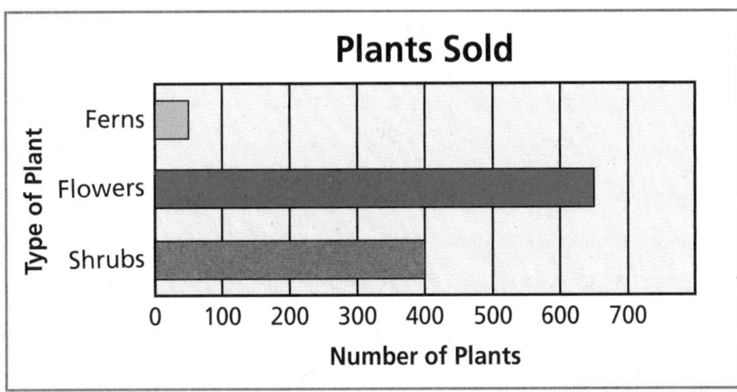

How many more flowers does the nursery sell than ferns and shrubs combined?

__________ more flowers

Write and answer another question using data from the graph.

7. Estimate the length of the marker in inches. Then measure it to the nearest $\frac{1}{4}$ inch.

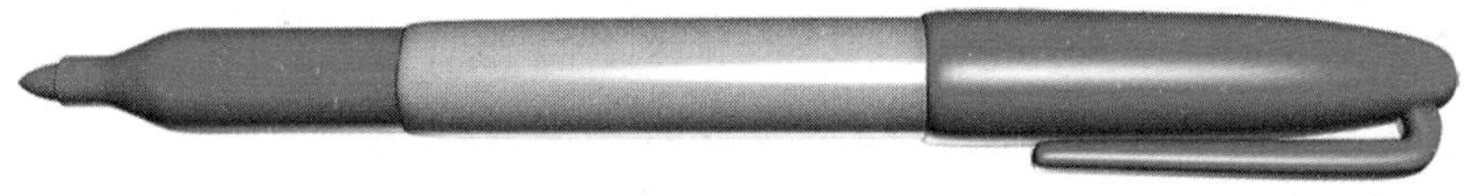

Estimate: ________ in. Actual: ________ in.

Name ______________________ Date ______________

8 Jeff has two shelves. The length of the wood shelf is $\frac{2}{4}$ meter and the length of the metal shelf is $\frac{2}{8}$ meter.

Which shelf is longer? Label and shade the circles to help solve the problem.

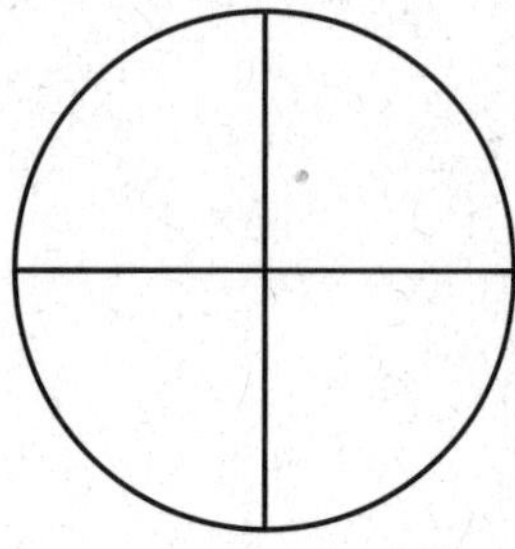

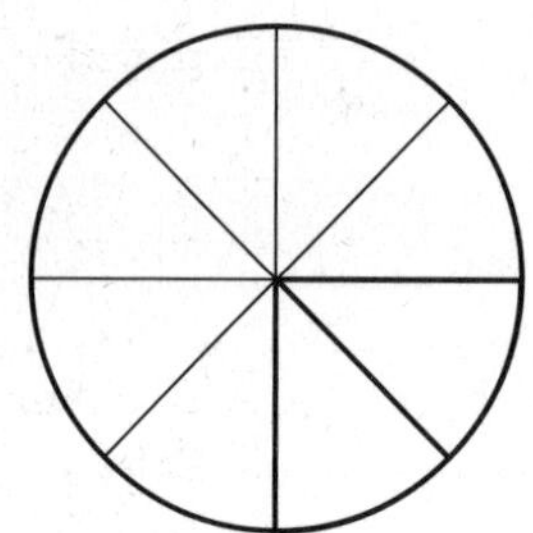

The ______________ shelf is longer.

9 Tom measures the distances some softballs were thrown from home plate. The results are shown in the line plot. For numbers 9a–9d, select True or False for each statement.

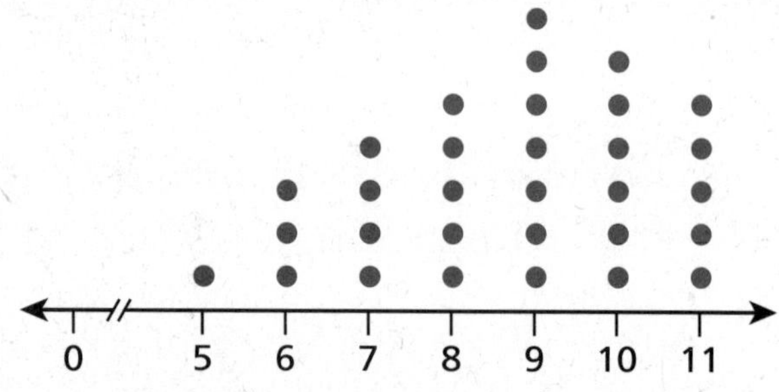

Distance from Home Plate (in feet)

9a. 8 softballs are thrown 5 feet. ○ True ○ False

9b. 13 softballs are thrown less than 9 feet. ○ True ○ False

9c. 11 softballs are thrown farther than 9 feet. ○ True ○ False

9d. 4 feet is the difference between the least and greatest distances thrown. ○ True ○ False

Name ______________________ Date ______________

10 Use the data in the table to complete the pictograph and bar graph.

T-Shirt Sales			
Size	Small	Medium	Large
Number of Shirts	40	70	50

T-Shirt Sales

Small	
Medium	
Large	

Key: ____________

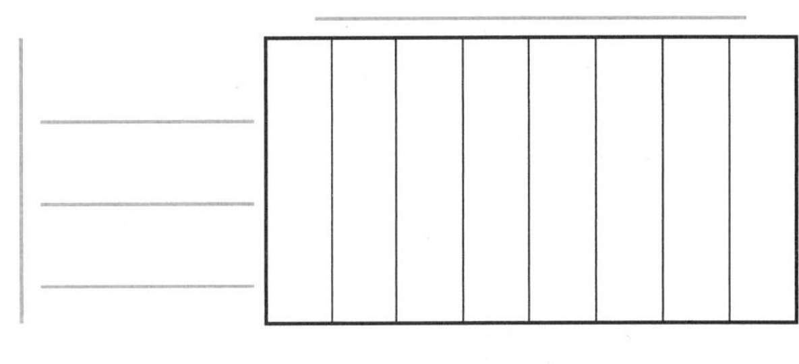

Which graph would you choose to show the data? Why?

11 Write the start time or end time to complete the chart.

8:48 A.M.	3:25 A.M.	12:50 P.M.
8:53 A.M.	3:35 P.M.	1:10 P.M.

Start Time	Elapsed Time	End Time
8:15 A.M.	38 minutes	
	55 minutes	4:20 A.M.
10:45 A.M.	2 hours 25 minutes	

Name _______________ Date _______________

12 Diane has $\frac{5}{4}$ meter of blue ribbon and $\frac{3}{4}$ meter of red ribbon. Write a comparison. Which ribbon is longer?

Comparison: __________

The __________ ribbon is longer.

13 The frequency table shows the lengths of some books in a classroom.

Part A

Use the frequency table to complete the line plot.

Frequency Table	
Length (in inches)	**Number of Books**
5	2
$5\frac{1}{2}$	3
6	6
$6\frac{1}{2}$	5
7	8
$7\frac{1}{2}$	5
8	7

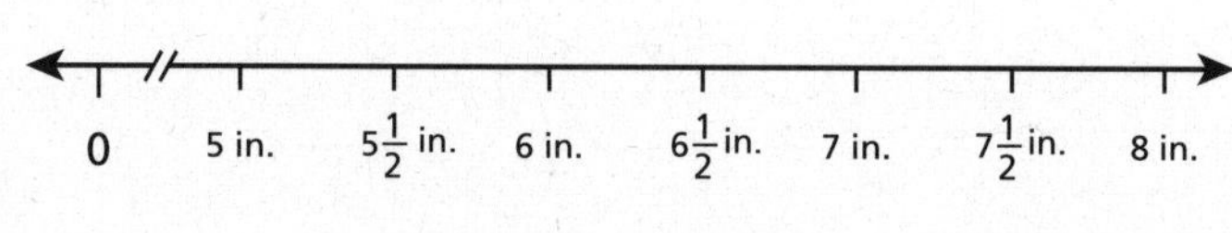

Part B

Most book lengths are between which two measures?

__________ inches and __________ inches

What if you measure three more book lengths at $7\frac{1}{2}$ inches and add the data to the line plot? How would your answer change?

Name ______________________ Date ______________

Plan a Class Craft Fair

Imagine that your class is having a Craft Fair. You will help plan the schedule for all the activities. Use the information in the table and in Steps A–C to find the start time for each event.

1 Complete the table showing the start time for each event and its duration.

Step A Add 10 minutes between activities to prepare for the next craft.

Step B Include a reasonable amount of time for setting up the first activity and for cleaning up at the end of the fair.

Step C Decide on a good time for the Craft Fair to begin.

Craft Fair Schedule		
Event	**Start Time**	**Amount of time**
Set-up		
Make Craft-Stick Towers		35 minutes
Make Puppets		25 minutes
Paint Pictures		20 minutes
Clean-up		

2 Explain how you decided the time the Craft Fair will begin.

____

____

3 The table shows the names of students and the heights of their craft-stick towers. Use the data in the table to complete the bar graph.

Craft-Stick Towers	
Student Name	**Tower Height**
Lee	25 inches
Juan	15 inches
Mei	10 inches

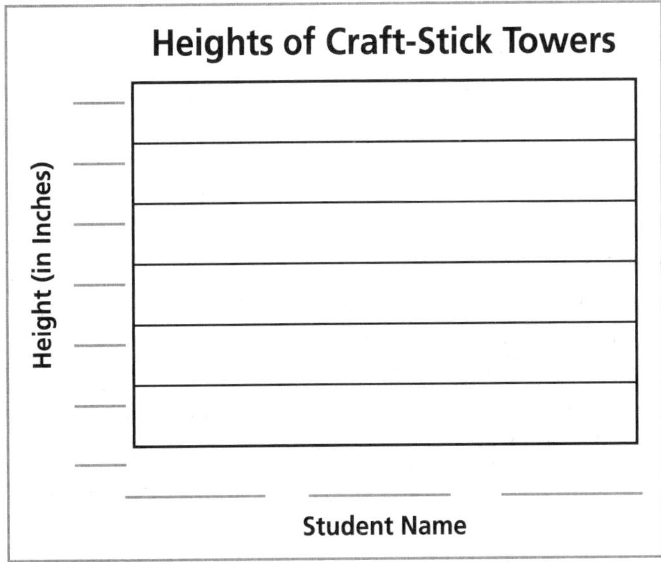

Name ______________________ Date ______________

4 Making puppets took most of the students longer than the 25 minutes that was planned. This table shows the time students spent making puppets.

Make a line plot to show the times.

Frequency Table	
Length of Time (in minutes)	Number of Students
25	2
26	5
27	3
28	7
29	3
30	9
31	1

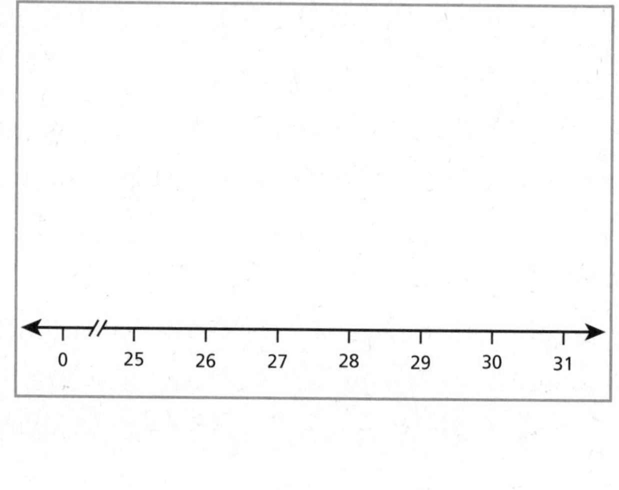

____

Do you think the class should plan more time for puppet making next year? Explain.

____

____

5 The teacher made a table to show the number of each type of painting students painted.

Make a pictograph to show the data from the table.

Frequency Table	
Subject of Painting	Number of Paintings
Animals	12
People	8
Places	7
Designs	3

Types of Paintings	
Animals	
People	
Places	
Designs	
Key: Each = ______.	

Dear Family:

Your child is currently learning about perimeter and area. Students find the area of a rectangle by counting the number of square units inside the figure and find the perimeter of a rectangle by counting linear units around the outside of the figure. They develop methods to find the perimeter and area of a rectangle.

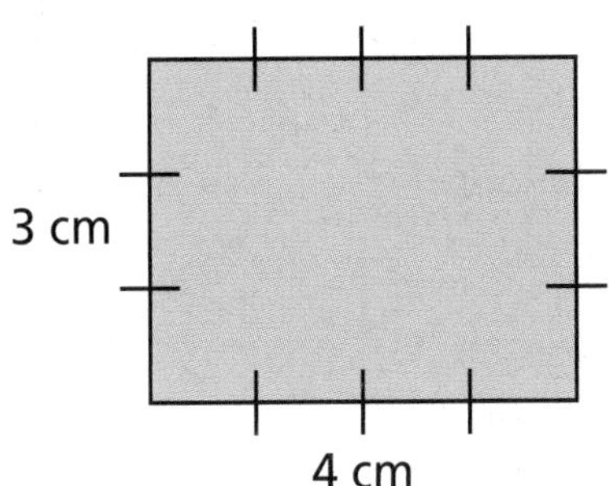

Perimeter = distance around the rectangle

Perimeter = *side length* + *side length* + *side length* + *side length*

$P = 4\text{ cm} + 3\text{ cm} + 4\text{ cm} + 3\text{ cm}$

$P = 14\text{ cm}$

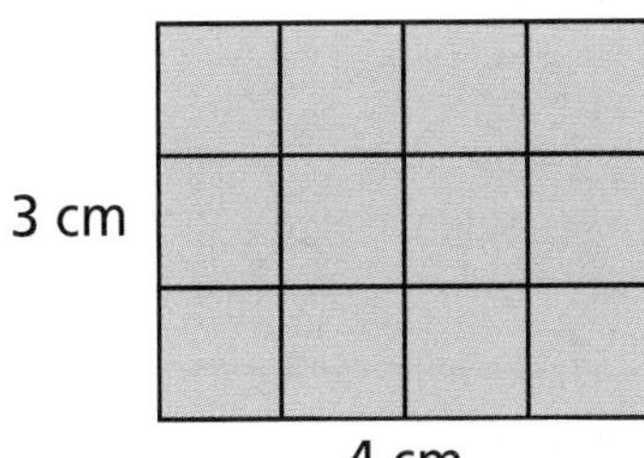

Area = square units inside the rectangle

Area = *side length* × *side length*

$A = 4\text{ cm} \times 3\text{ cm}$

$A = 12\text{ sq cm}$

Students draw rectangles and discover relationships between perimeter and area, such as for a given area, the longest, skinniest rectangle has the greatest perimeter and the rectangle with sides closest to the same length or the same length has the least perimeter.

Students create shapes with tangrams and use the shapes as improvised units to measure area.

In this unit, students use fraction bars and number lines to find equivalent fractions and solve real world problems using their understanding of fraction concepts.

$$\frac{1}{2} = \frac{3}{6}$$

If you have any questions or comments, please contact me.

Thank you.

Sincerely,
Your child's teacher

Estimada familia:

Su niño está aprendiendo acerca de perímetro y área. Los estudiantes encontrarán el área de un rectángulo contando las unidades cuadradas que caben en la figura y hallarán el perímetro de un rectángulo contando las unidades lineales alrededor de la figura. Ellos desarrollarán métodos para hallar el perímetro y el área de un rectángulo.

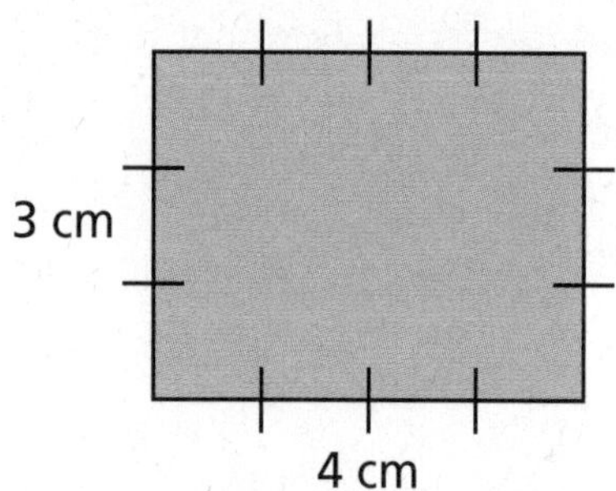

Perímetro = distancia alrededor del rectángulo

Perímetro = largo del lado + largo del lado + largo del lado + largo del lado

$P = 4\text{ cm} + 3\text{ cm} + 4\text{ cm} + 3\text{ cm}$

$P = 14\text{ cm}$

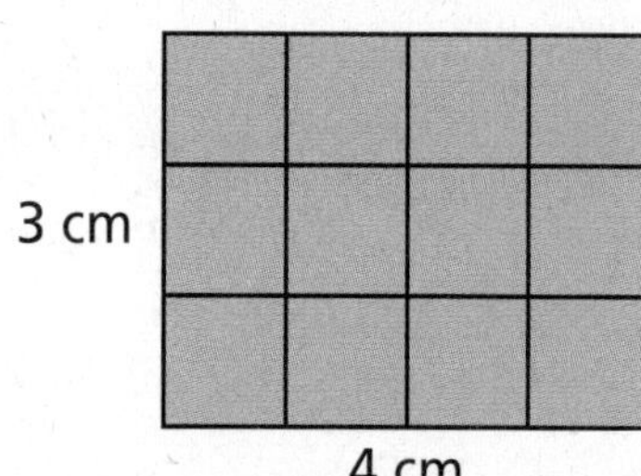

Área = unidades cuadradas dentro del rectángulo

Área = largo del lado × largo del lado

$A = 4\text{ cm} \times 3\text{ cm}$

$A = 12\text{ cm cuad}$

Los estudiantes dibujarán rectángulos y descubrirán cómo se relacionan el perímetro y el área, por ejemplo, para un área determinada, el rectángulo más largo y angosto tiene el perímetro mayor y el rectángulo con lados de igual o casi igual longitud, tiene el perímetro menor.

Los estudiantes crearán figuras con tangramas y las usarán como medidas improvisadas para medir área.

En esta unidad, los estudiantes usarán barras de fracciones y rectas numéricas para hallar fracciones equivalentes y resolver problemas cotidianos usando los conceptos que aprendan sobre fracciones.

$$\frac{1}{2} = \frac{3}{6}$$

Si tiene alguna duda o algún comentario, por favor comuníquese conmigo.

Atentamente,
El maestro de su niño

Celsius (°C)

Fahrenheit (°F)

decompose

perimeter

equivalent fractions

temperature

A scale used to measure temperature.

Examples:

Water freezes at 32°F.

Water boils at 212°F.

A scale used to measure temperature.

Example:

Water freezes at 0°C.

Water boils at 100°C.

The distance around a figure.

Example:

Perimeter = 3 cm + 5 cm + 3 cm + 5 cm

= 16 cm

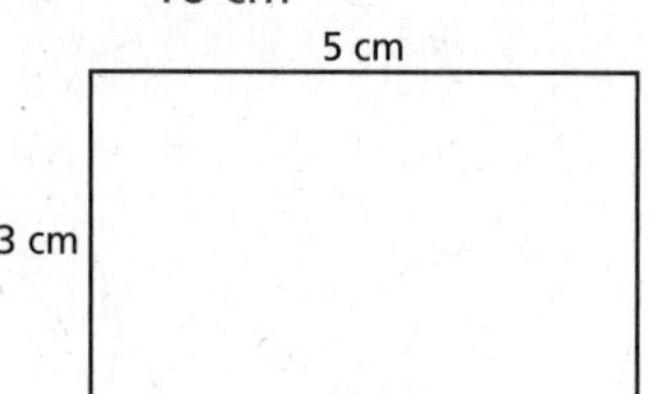

To separate or break apart (a geometric figure or a number) into smaller parts.

The measure of how hot or cold something is.

Fractions that name the same amount.

Example:

$\frac{1}{2}$ and $\frac{2}{4}$

equivalent fractions

thermometer

A tool that is used to measure temperature.

Name ____________________

VOCABULARY
perimeter

Recognize Perimeter and Area

On this page, the dots on the dot paper are 1 cm apart. Use the rectangle for Exercises 1–4.

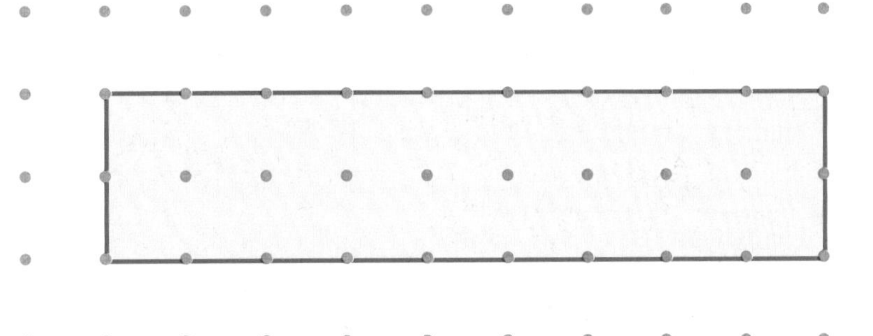

1. What part of the rectangle is its **perimeter**?

____

2. What part of the rectangle is its area?

____

3. Find the perimeter. Draw tick marks to help.

____

4. Find the area. Draw unit squares to help.

____

5. Draw a rectangle 4 cm long and 3 cm wide on the dot paper. Find the perimeter and area.

Perimeter ____________

Area ____________

6. Explain how you found the area of the rectangle in Exercise 5.

____

____

____

____

____

____

Find Perimeter and Area

Find the perimeter and area of each figure.
Remember to include the correct units in your answers.

7

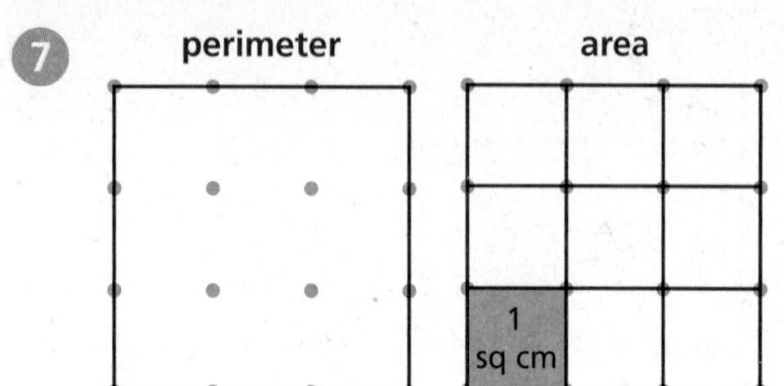

Perimeter = ______________

Area = ______________

8

Perimeter = ______________

Area = ______________

9

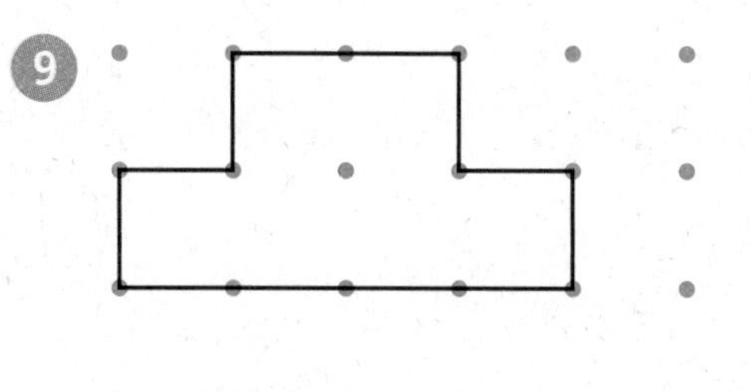

Perimeter = ______________

Area = ______________

10

Perimeter = ______________

Area = ______________

11

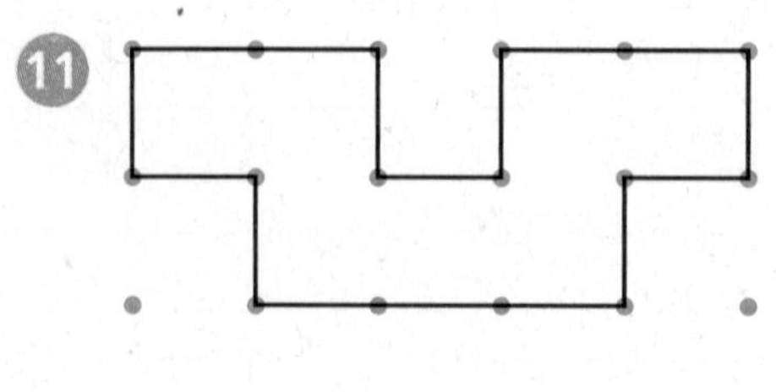

Perimeter = ______________

Area = ______________

12

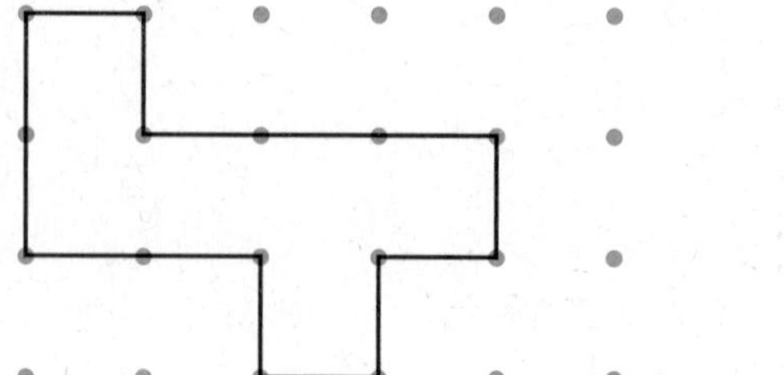

Perimeter = ______________

Area = ______________

Name ______________________________

Tile a Rectangle

Cut out the 1-inch unit squares along the dashed lines. Try to cut as carefully and as straight as you can.

Name ________________

Tile a Rectangle

13 Use the 1-inch unit squares from page 335A to cover the rectangle below.

Be sure there are no gaps between the unit squares.

Be sure no unit squares overlap.

14 Draw lines with a straight edge to show the unit squares. The number of unit squares is the area in square inches. What is the area?

____

15 Use an inch ruler to measure the side lengths of the rectangle. Label the length and the width.

____

____

16 Write a multiplication equation to show the area.

____

Tile a Rectangle (continued)

Cover each rectangle with 1-inch unit squares. Count the squares to find the area. Then write an equation to show the area.

17 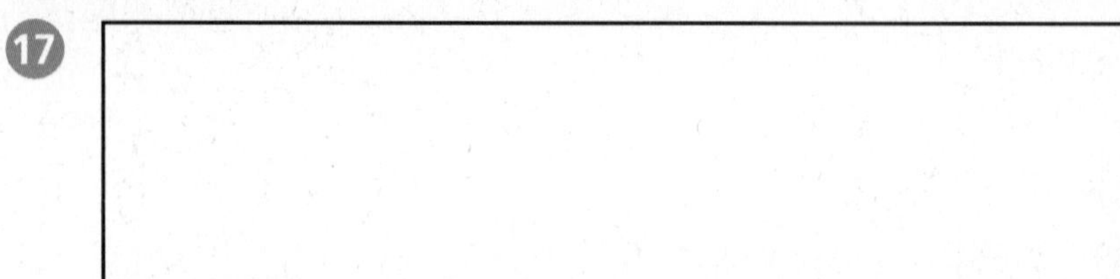

The area is ________. The equation is ________.

18 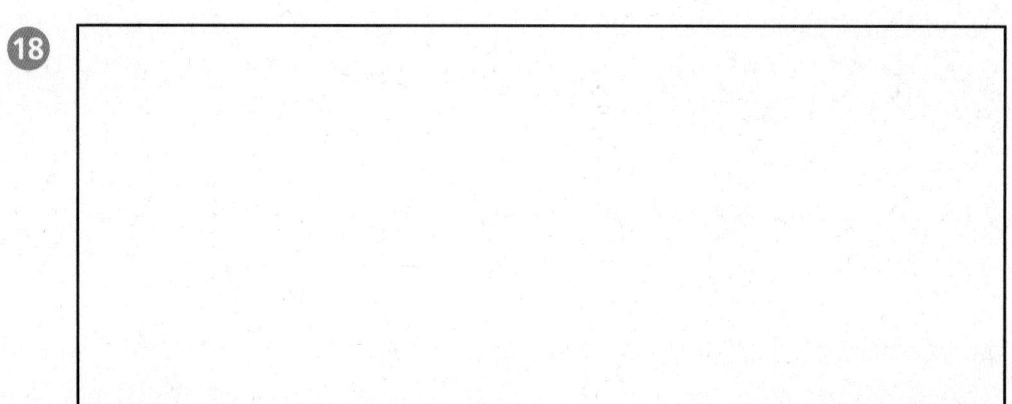

The area is ________. The equation is ________.

19 How many 1-inch unit squares are needed to cover a rectangle that is 7 inches long and 4 inches wide?

____

20 What is the area of a rectangle that is 7 inches long and 4 inches wide?

____

Check Understanding

Complete the sentences.

Perimeter measures ____________________.

Area measures ____________________.

Name ____________________

Write Different Equations for Area

1. Use the drawings. Show two ways to find the area of a rectangle that is 10 units long and 6 units wide.

2. Write equations for your two rectangle drawings.

____________________ ____________________

3. Suppose the rectangle is 10 feet long and 6 feet wide. What is its area?

____

4. Suppose the rectangle is 10 meters long and 6 meters wide. What is its area?

____

5. Use drawings and write equations to show two ways to find the area of a rectangle that is 9 yards long and 5 yards wide.

____________________ ____________________

Rectangle Equations and Drawings

Write an equation for each rectangle.

6

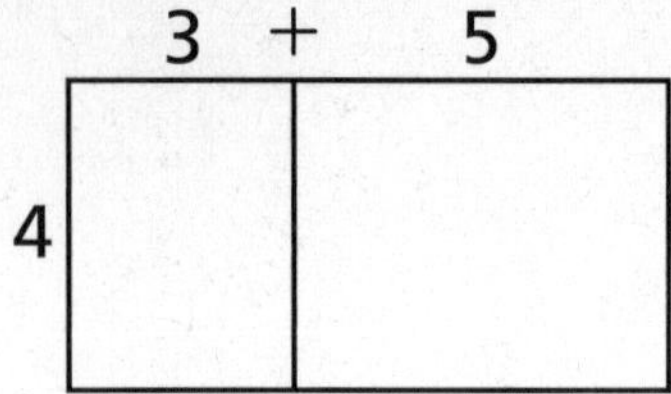

____

7

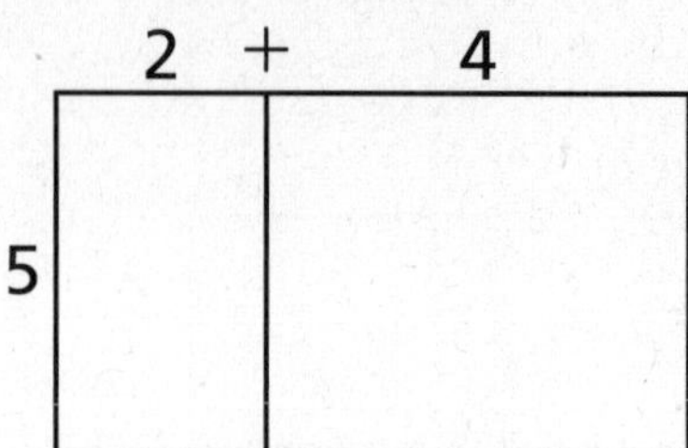

____

8 3 + 6

3

____

9

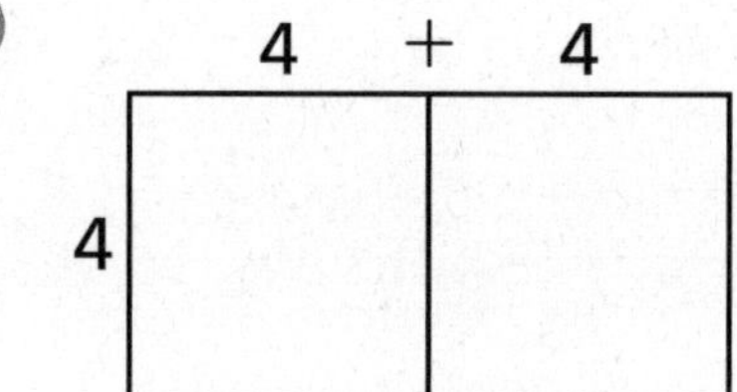

____

Draw a rectangle for each equation.

10 $(3 \times 3) + (3 \times 5) = 3 \times 8$

11 $(4 \times 5) + (4 \times 3) = 4 \times 8$

12 $(5 \times 3) + (5 \times 6) = 5 \times 9$

13 $(4 \times 6) + (4 \times 4) = 4 \times 10$

Name ______________________________

Find Unknown Side Lengths

Find the unknown side length in each rectangle.

14. 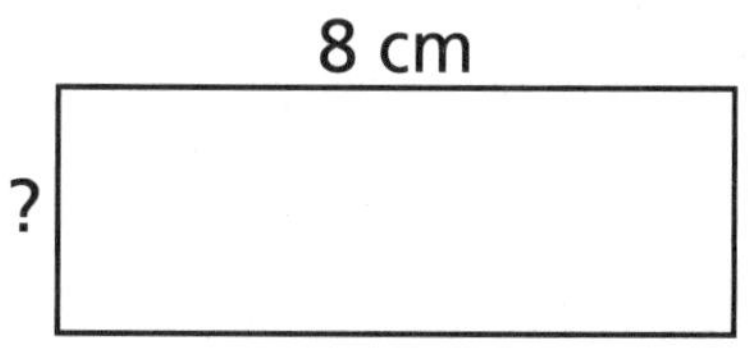

Area = 72 sq cm

____

15. 12 cm

?

Perimeter = 38 cm

____

16. 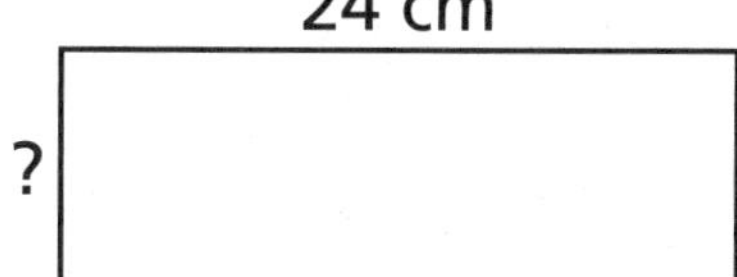

Perimeter = 64 cm

____

17. 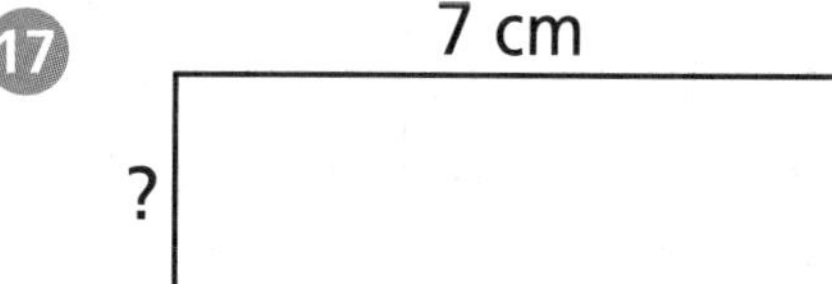

Area = 56 sq cm

____

18. 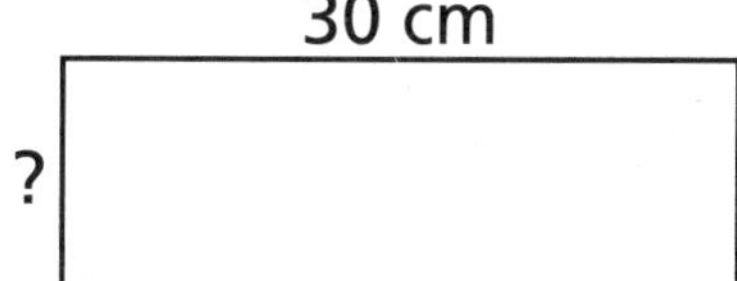

Perimeter = 72 cm

____

19. 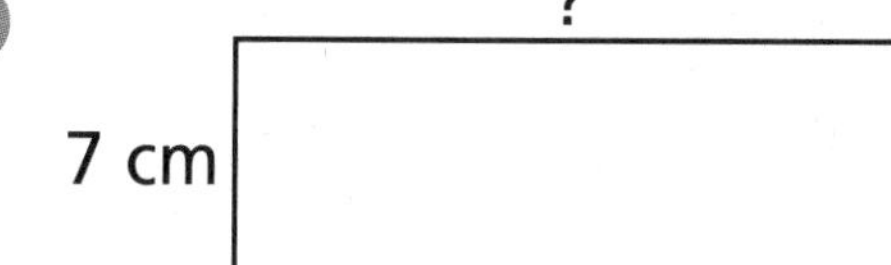

Area = 63 sq cm

____

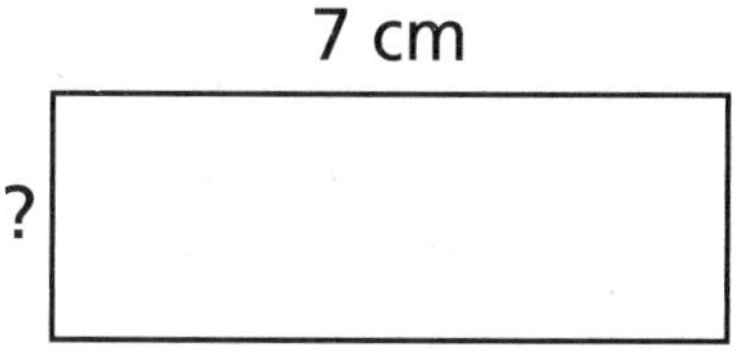

Area = 28 sq cm

____

21. 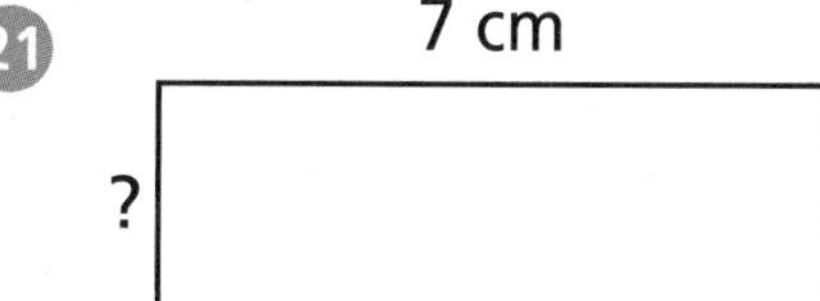

Perimeter = 20 cm

____

Unknown Side Length Problems

Solve. Draw a rectangle to represent the situation.

Show your work.

22 Alexander and his grandfather are tiling their rectangular kitchen floor. They need to use 42 tiles. They are making rows of 7 tiles. How many rows do they make?

____

23 Martha has 63 quilt squares ready to sew together. She wants the quilt to be 9 rows long. How many squares will be in each row?

____

24 Rick is painting a mural of different sizes of rectangles, with no gaps or overlaps of the rectangles. He has enough paint to cover 15 square yards. He wants the mural to be 3 yards long. How wide can the mural be?

____

25 Mr. Baker is making a picture frame using all of a 48-inch strip of oak. The picture frame will be 14 inches wide. How long will the picture frame be?

____

✔ Check Understanding

Draw and label a rectangle with an area of 36 square centimeters and one side length of 4 centimeters. Find the unknown side length. Then find the perimeter.

Name ____________________

Compare Rectangles with the Same Perimeter

Complete.

1. On a centimeter dot grid, draw all possible rectangles with a perimeter of 12 cm and sides whose lengths are whole centimeters. Label the lengths of two adjacent sides of each rectangle.

2. Find and label the area of each rectangle. In the table, record the lengths of the adjacent sides and the area of each rectangle.

3. Compare the shapes of the rectangles with the least area and greatest area.

Rectangles with Perimeter 12 cm	
Lengths of Two Adjacent Sides	Area

____

____

4. On a centimeter dot grid, draw all possible rectangles with a perimeter of 22 cm and sides whose lengths are whole centimeters. Label the lengths of two adjacent sides of each rectangle.

5. Find and label the area of each rectangle. In the table, record the lengths of the adjacent sides and the area of each rectangle.

Rectangles with Perimeter 22 cm	
Lengths of Two Adjacent Sides	Area

6. Compare the shapes of the rectangles with the least area and greatest area.

____

____

Compare Rectangles with the Same Area

7 On a centimeter dot grid, draw all possible rectangles with an area of 12 sq cm and sides whose lengths are whole centimeters. Label the lengths of two adjacent sides of each rectangle.

8 Find and label the perimeter of each rectangle. In the table, record the lengths of the adjacent sides and the perimeter of each rectangle.

Rectangles with Area 12 sq cm	
Lengths of Two Adjacent Sides	**Perimeter**

9 On a centimeter dot grid, draw all possible rectangles with an area of 18 sq cm and sides whose lengths are whole centimeters. Label the lengths of two adjacent sides of each rectangle.

10 Find and label the perimeter of each rectangle. In the table, record the lengths of the adjacent sides and the perimeter of each rectangle.

Rectangles with Area 18 sq cm	
Lengths of Two Adjacent Sides	**Perimeter**

11 Compare the shapes of the rectangles with the least and greatest perimeter.

____

____

____

Check Understanding

Draw and label a rectangle with the greatest area possible for a perimeter of 18 inches. The sides must be whole inches.

Name ______________________

VOCABULARY
decompose

Find Area by Decomposing into Rectangles

Decompose each figure into rectangles.
Then find the area of the figure.

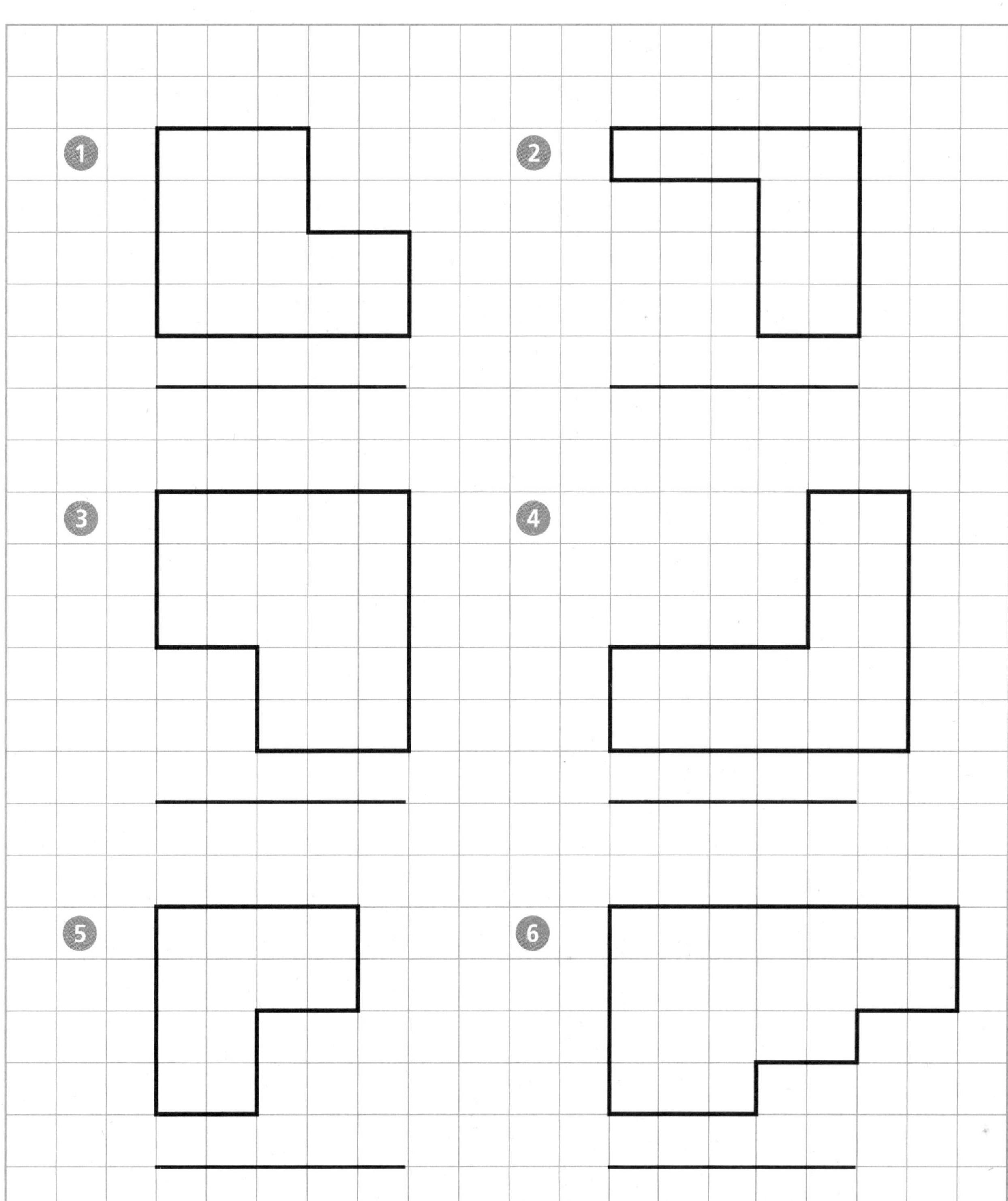

Find Area by Decomposing into Rectangles (continued)

Decompose each figure into rectangles. Then find the area of the figure.

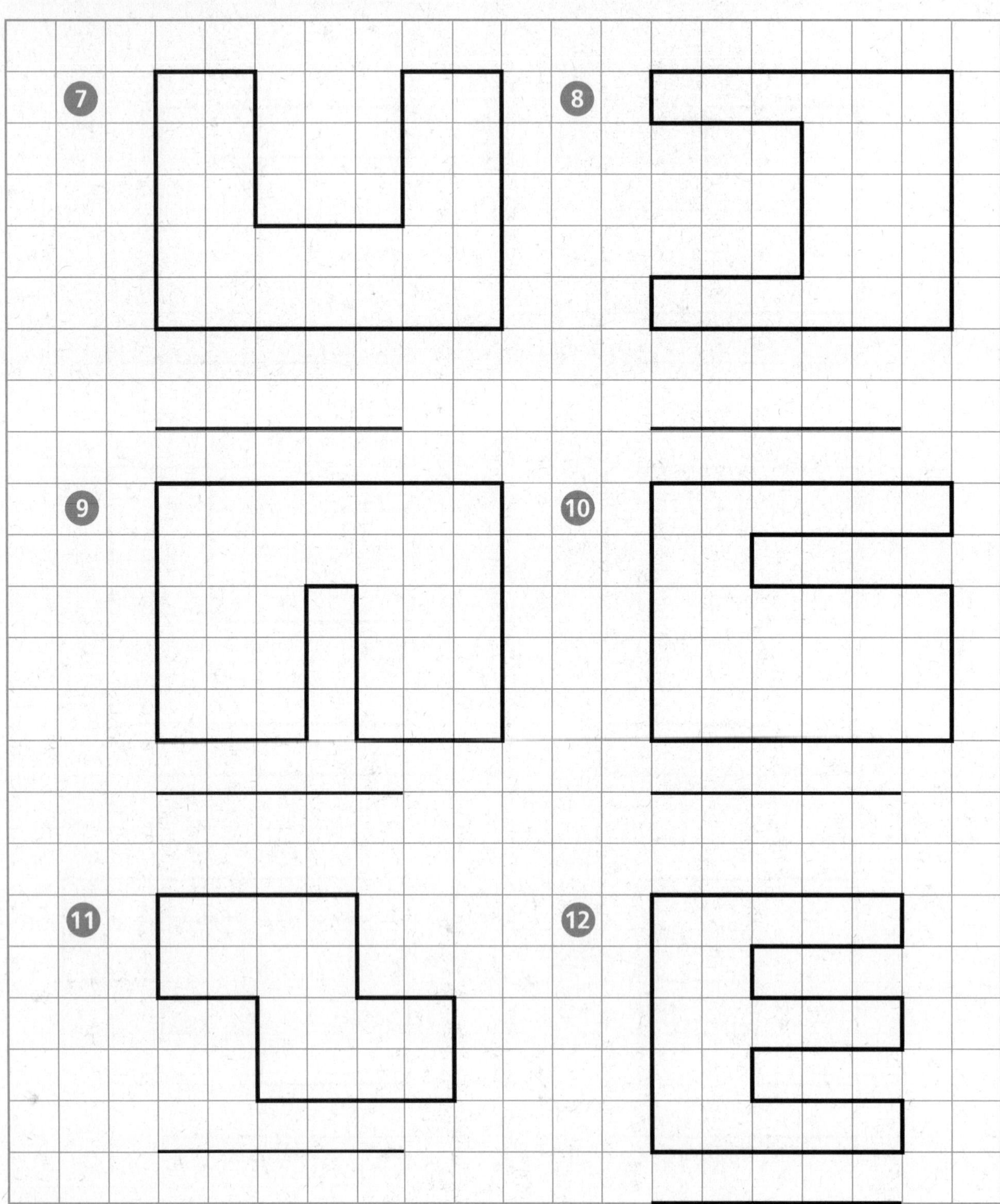

Name ____________________

Find Area by Decomposing into Rectangles (continued)

Decompose each figure into rectangles. Then find the area of the figure.

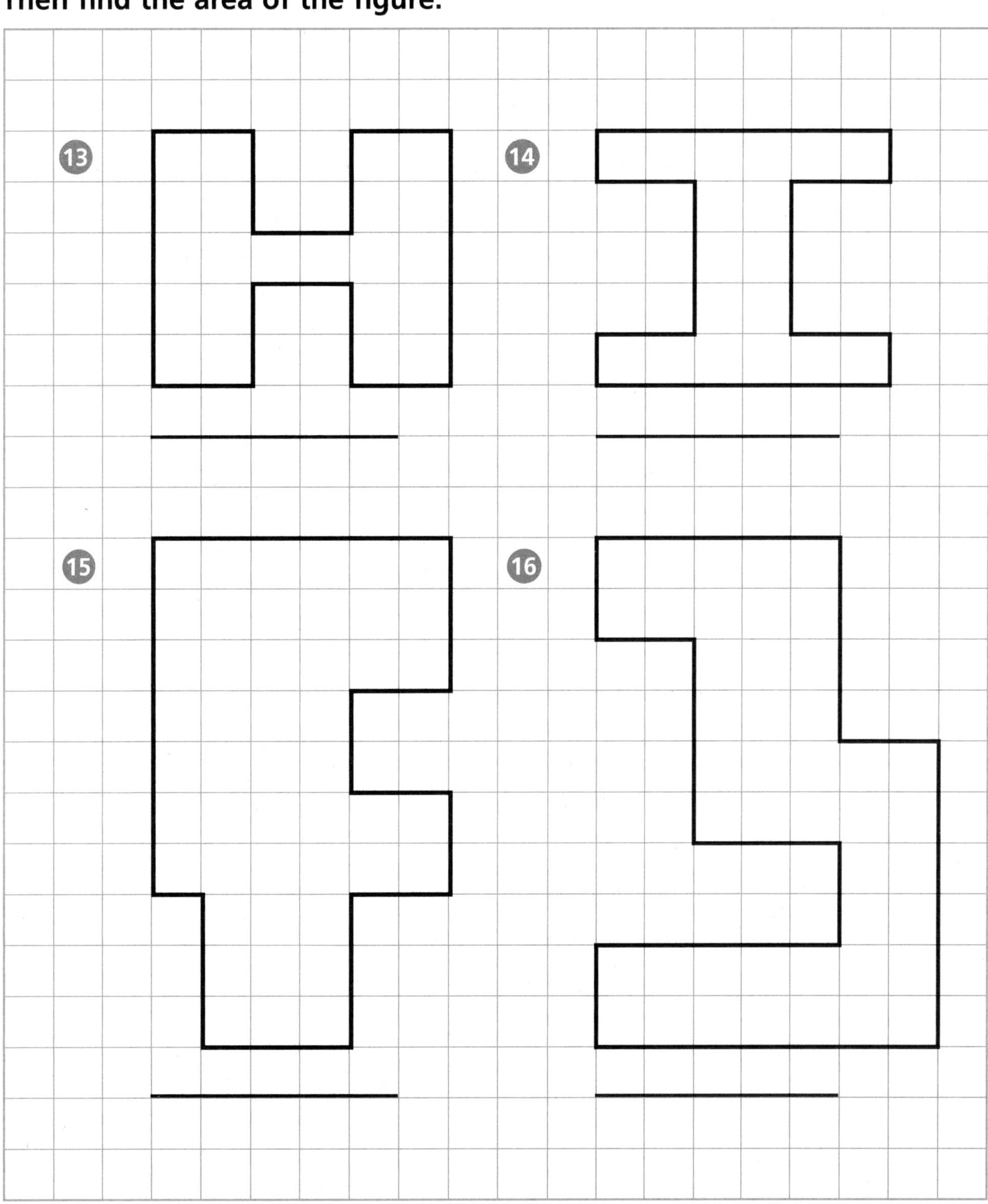

What's the Error?

Dear Math Students,

Today my teacher asked me to find the area of a figure. I knew that I could decompose the figure into rectangles. This is what I did.

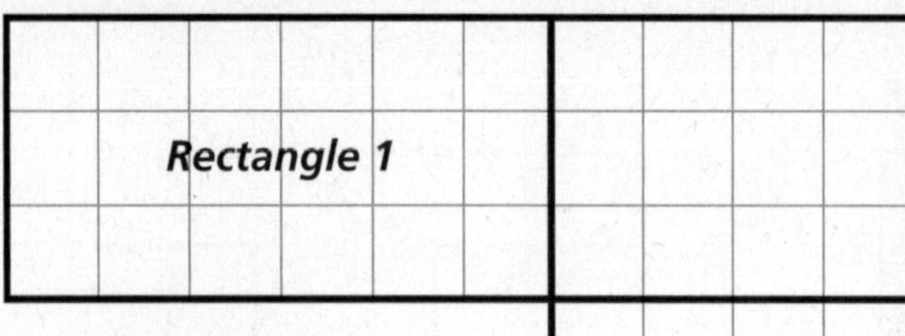

Area of Rectangle 1:
3 × 6 = 18 square units

Area of Rectangle 2:
5 × 4 = 20 square units

Area of Figure:
18 + 20 = 38 square units

Is my work correct? If not, please correct my work and tell me what I did wrong. How do you know my answer is wrong?

Your friend,
Puzzled Penguin

17 Write an answer to Puzzled Penguin.

Check Understanding

Decompose the figure Puzzled Penguin decomposed into rectangles a different way and find the area of the figure.

Name ______________________________

Solve Perimeter and Area Problems

Solve. Circle whether you need to find a perimeter, an area, or an unknown side length. Draw a figure to represent each situation.

Show your work.

1. The dimensions of a rectangular picture frame are 9 inches and 6 inches. What is the greatest size picture that would fit in the frame?

   Perimeter Area Side Length

   ____

2. A garden has the shape of a hexagon. Each side of the garden is 5 feet long. How much fence is needed to go around the garden?

   Perimeter Area Side Length

   ____

3. The length of a water slide is 9 yards. The slide is 2 yards wide. How much of the surface of the slide must be covered with water?

   Perimeter Area Side Length

   ____

4. Mr. Schmidt is installing 32 cubbies in the hallway. He puts 8 cubbies in each row. How many rows of cubbies can he make?

   Perimeter Area Side Length

   ____

Solve Perimeter and Area Problems (continued)

Solve. Circle whether you need to find a perimeter, an area, or an unknown side length. Draw a figure to represent each situation.

Show your work.

5. The floor of a delivery van has an area of 56 square feet and is 8 feet long. How many rows of 8 boxes that measure 1 foot by 1 foot can be put on the floor of the delivery van?

   Perimeter   Area   Side Length

   ____

6. Zack is planning to make a flower garden. He has 24 one-yard sections of fence that he plans to place around the garden. He wants the garden to be as long as possible. What is the longest length he can use for the garden? How wide will the garden be?

   Perimeter   Area   Side Length

   ____

7. An exercise room is 9 yards long and 7 yards wide. A locker room 8 yards long and 6 yards wide is attached to one end of the exercise room. How much floor space do the exercise room and the locker room take up?

   Perimeter   Area   Side Length

   ____

8. Rosa's dog Sparky is 24 inches long. One side of Sparky's doghouse is 36 inches long and the other side is twice as long as Sparky. What is the distance around Sparky's doghouse?

   Perimeter   Area   Side Length

   ____

Name ______________________________

Solve Perimeter and Area Problems (continued)

Solve. Circle whether you need to find a perimeter, an area, or an unknown side length. Draw a figure to represent each situation.

Show your work.

9. Joanne made 16 fruit bars in a square pan. The fruit bars are 2 inches by 2 inches. What are the dimensions of the pan she used to bake the fruit bars?

   Perimeter Area Side Length

   ____

10. A scout troop is making triangular pennants for their tents. Two sides of each pennant are 2 feet long and the third side is 1 foot long. How much binding tape is needed to go around 4 pennants?

    Perimeter Area Side Length

    ____

11. A rectangular quilt is 5 feet wide and 7 feet long. How many feet of lace are needed to cover the edges of the quilt?

    Perimeter Area Side Length

    ____

12. Amy has a piece of fleece fabric that is 4 feet wide and 6 feet long. How many squares of fleece fabric that are 1 foot wide and 1 foot long can she cut from the fabric?

    Perimeter Area Side Length

    ____

Solve Perimeter and Area Problems (continued)

Solve. Circle whether you need to find a perimeter, an area, or an unknown side length. Draw a figure to represent each situation.

Show your work.

13 Vanita has 23 tiles with dimensions of 1 foot by 1 foot. She wants to tile a hallway that is 8 feet long and 3 feet wide. Does she have enough tiles? If not, how many more does she need?

Perimeter Area Side Length

____

14 Mrs. Lee has 48 one-foot pieces of garden fence. What dimensions should she use for a square garden to have as much room as possible?

Perimeter Area Side Length

____

15 Martha has 27 striped squares and 27 dotted squares. She wants a quilt with rows of 6 squares. How many rows will the quilt have?

Perimeter Area Side Length

____

16 A 20-mile bike path is in the shape of a triangle. Don rode 6 miles and 8 miles on the two sides. How long is the third side of the path?

Perimeter Area Side Length

____

Check Understanding

Describe a real-world situation when you would need to find perimeter and another for area.

Name ______________________

Explore Tangrams

Cut one tangram figure into pieces along the dotted lines. Try to cut as carefully and as straight as you can. Save the other figures to use later.

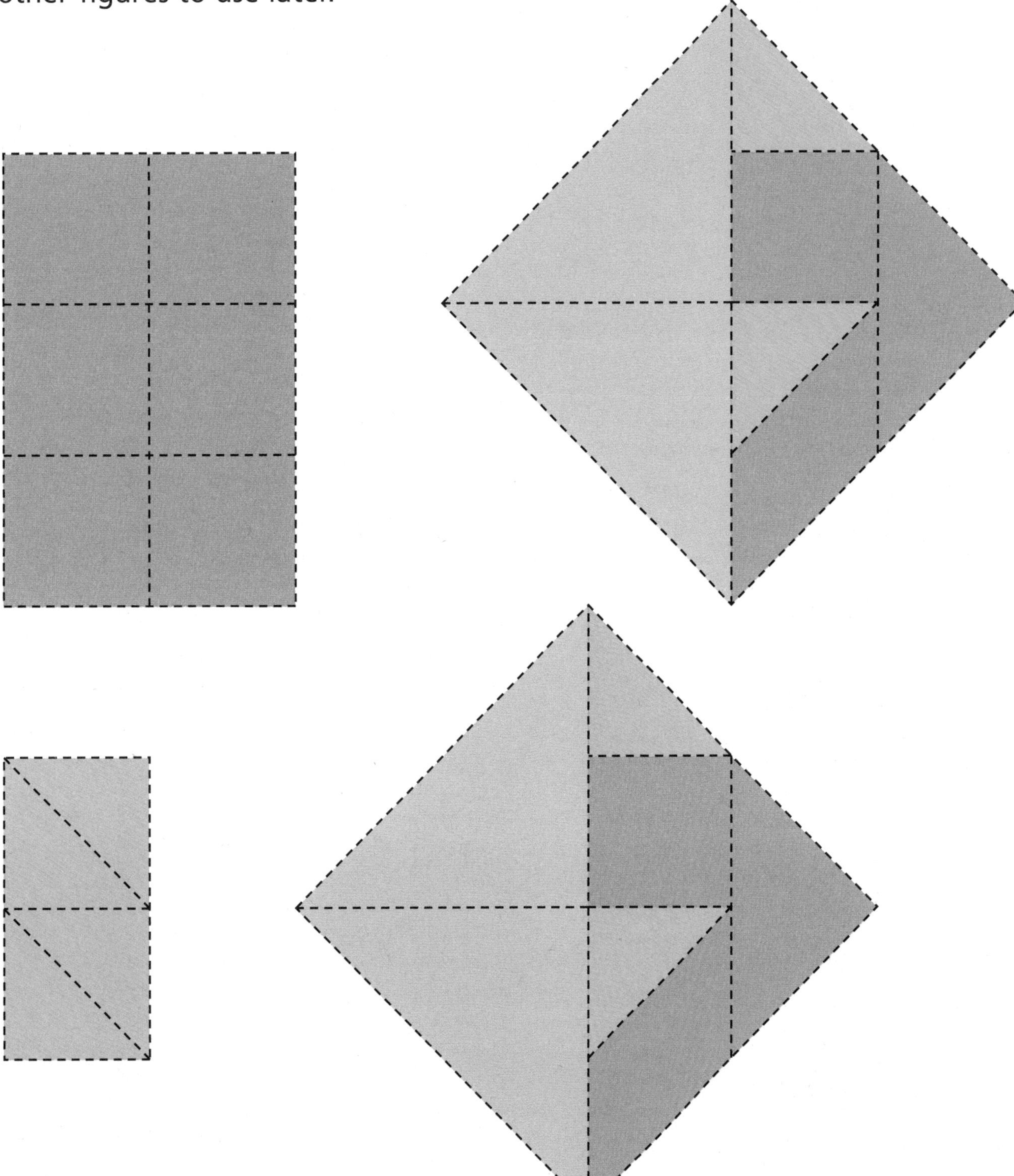

Explore Tangrams (continued)

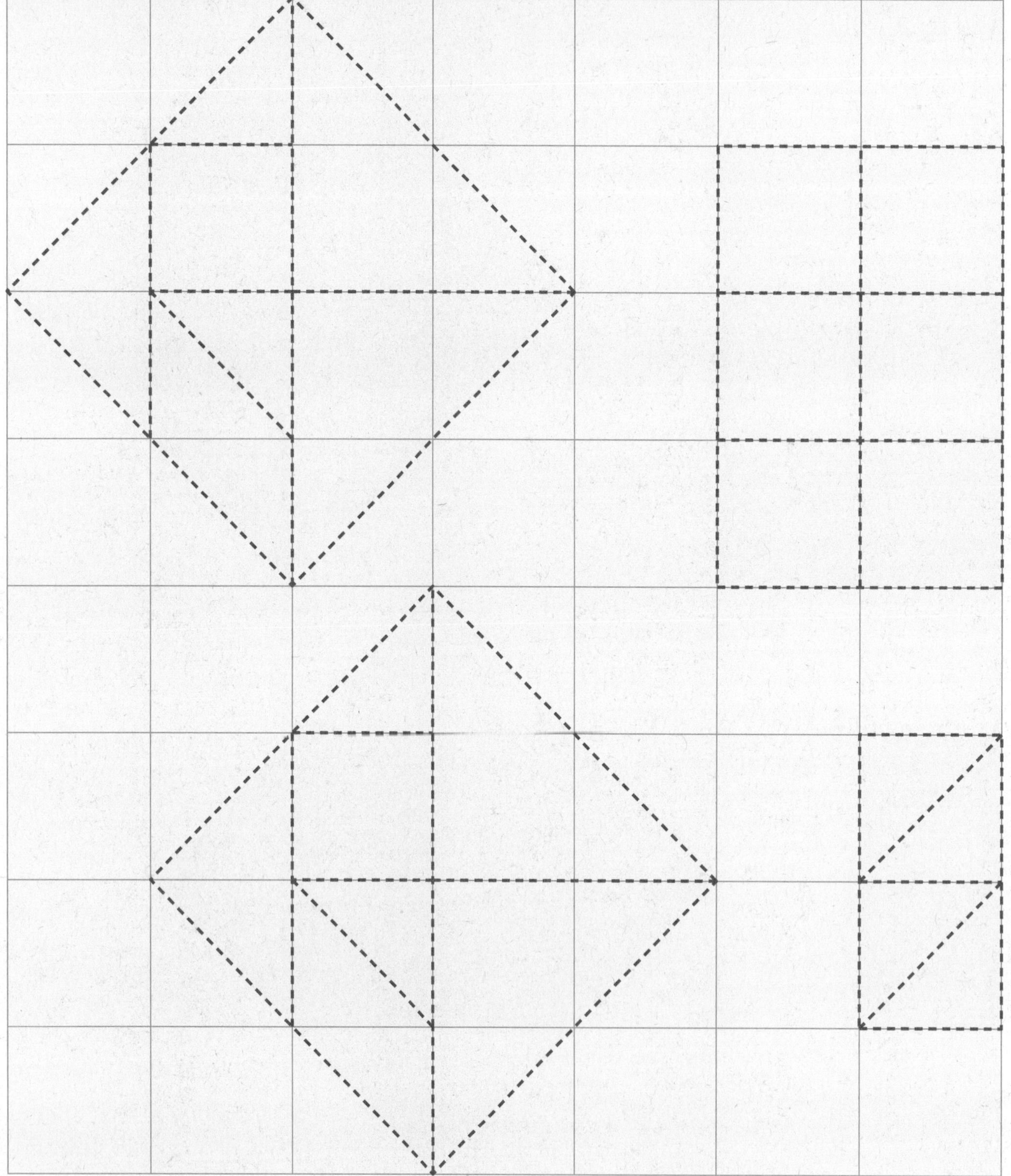

Name

Solve Tangram Puzzles

Use the tangram pieces from page 351A.

1. Make this bird. When you finish, draw lines to show how you placed the pieces.

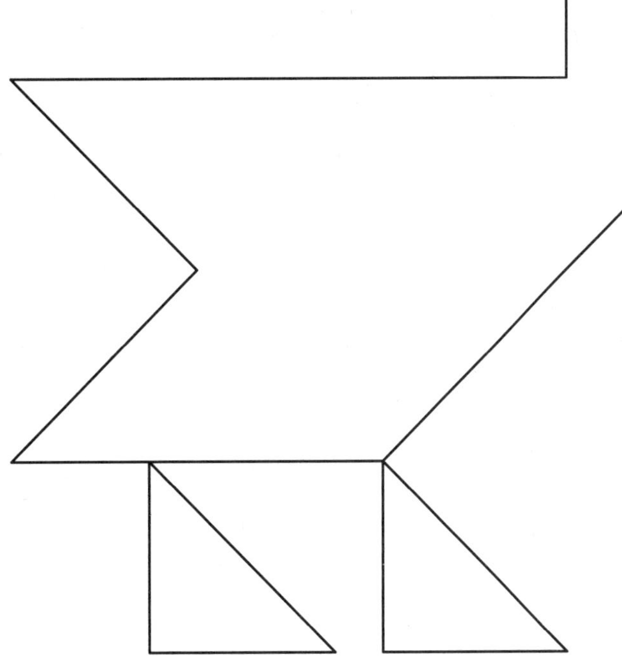

2. Make this rectangle. Draw lines to show how you placed the pieces. Hint: You do not need all the pieces.

Solve Tangram Puzzles (continued)

Use the tangram pieces. Draw lines to show how you placed the pieces.

3 Make this boat.

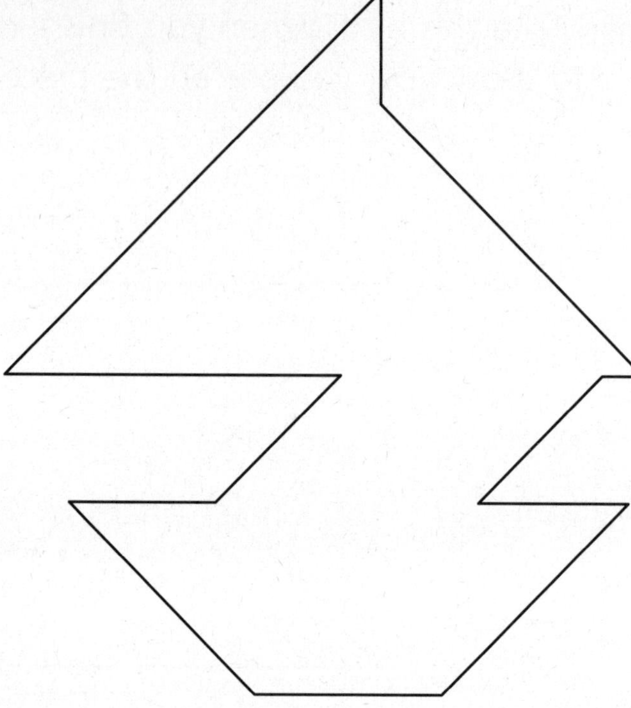

4 Make this tree.

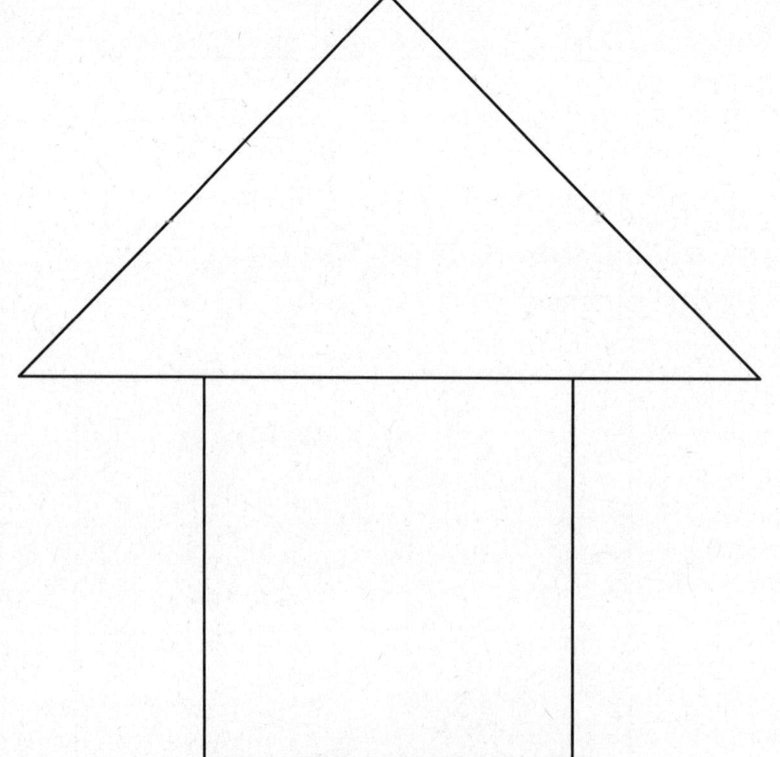

Name ______________________________

Use Tangram Pieces to Find Area

5 Use all seven tangram pieces. Cover this rectangle.

6 What is the area of the rectangle?

____

7 Use any tangram pieces. Cover this rectangle.

8 What is the area of the rectangle?

____

Use Tangram Pieces to Find Area (continued)

Use any tangram pieces. Cover each rectangle.

9

What is the area of the rectangle?

____

10

What is the area of the square?

____

Name ______________________________

Use Tangram Pieces to Find Area (continued)

Use any tangram pieces. Cover each figure.

11 

What is the area of the rectangle?

____

12 

What is the area of the square?

____

13 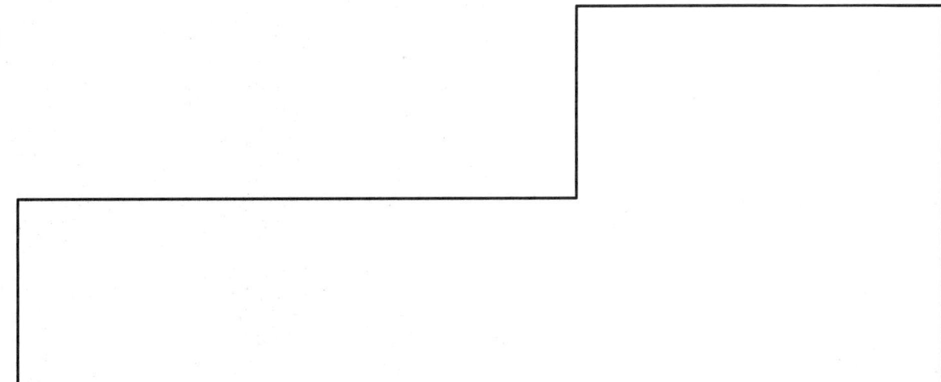

What is the area of the figure?

____

Use Tangram Pieces to Find Area (continued)

Use any tangram pieces. Cover each figure.

14 What is the area of the triangle?

____

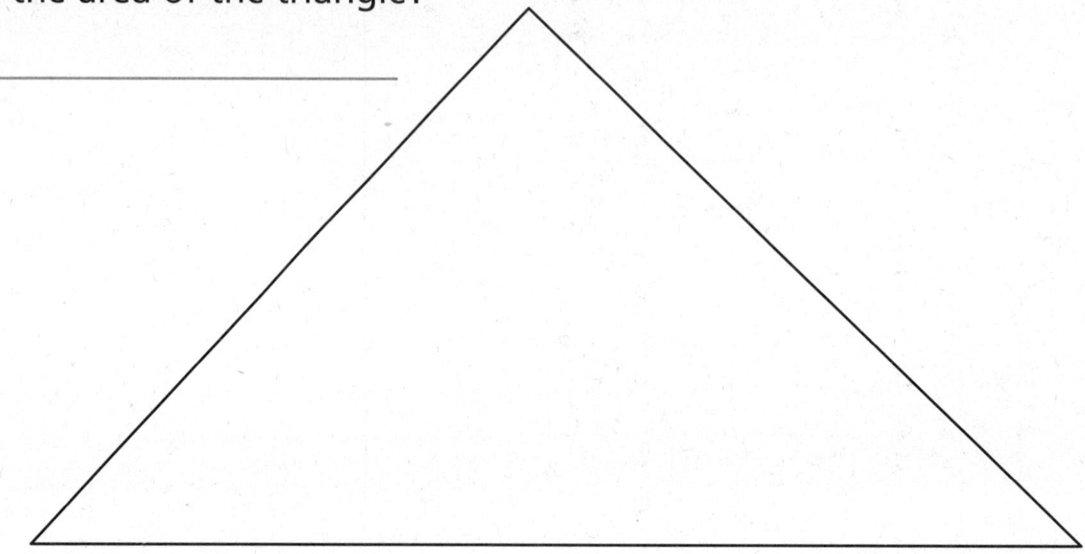

15

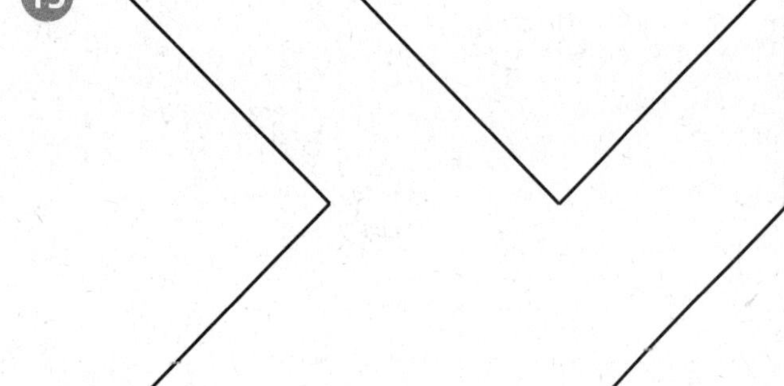

What is the area of the figure?

____

Check Understanding

What is the area of a figure made with all seven tangram pieces? ______________________

Unit 5
Quick Quiz 1

Name ______________________ Date ______________

Write the correct answer.

Show your work.

1. What is the area of the figure?

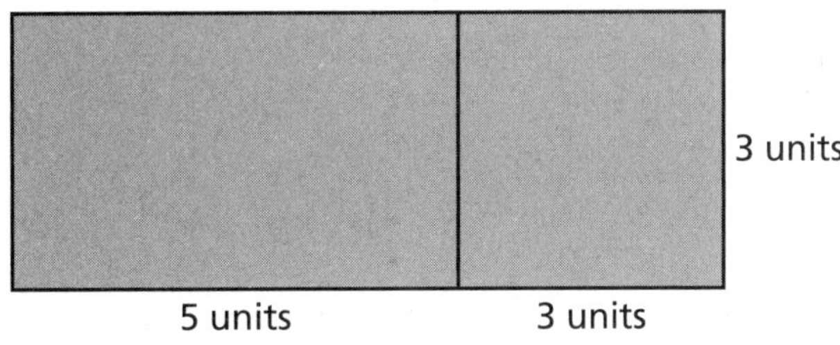

____

2. The area of a rectangle is 80 square units. The length of one of the shorter sides is 8 units. What is the length of one of the longer sides?

____

3. Rectangles *A* and *B* have the same areas. Rectangle *A* is 3 inches wide and 8 inches long. If Rectangle *B* is 4 inches wide, how long is it?

____

Use the centimeter dot grid for Exercises 4–5.

4. Which figure has an area of 18 square centimeters?

____

5. What is the perimeter of each figure?

____

Figure A

Figure B

Figure C

Strategy Check 6

Name ______________________ Date ______________

Solve.

1. Marcy uses 48 inches of ribbon to frame a rectangular picture. The length of the picture is 14 inches. How wide is the picture?

____

2. A rectangular carpet has an area of 110 square feet. The length of the rug is 11 feet. What is the width of the rug?

____

3. On the centimeter grid below, draw two different rectangles with a perimeter of 12 centimeters. Label the area of each figure.

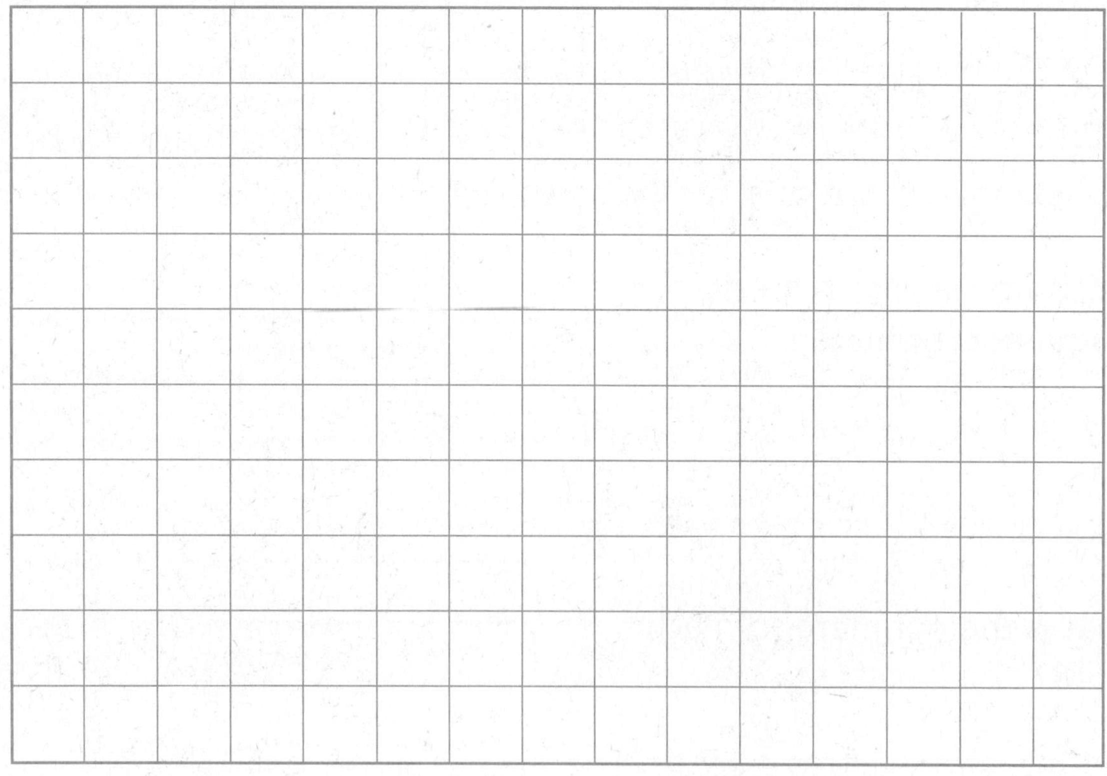

Name ______________________________

Make Fraction Strips

Name ______________________________

Halves, Fourths, and Eighths

VOCABULARY
equivalent fractions

Two fractions are **equivalent fractions** if they name the same part of a whole.

Use your halves, fourths, and eighths strips to complete Exercises 1–4.

$\frac{1}{2}$				$\frac{1}{2}$			
$\frac{1}{4}$		$\frac{1}{4}$		$\frac{1}{4}$		$\frac{1}{4}$	
$\frac{1}{8}$	$\frac{1}{8}$	$\frac{1}{8}$	$\frac{1}{8}$	$\frac{1}{8}$	$\frac{1}{8}$	$\frac{1}{8}$	$\frac{1}{8}$

1. If you compare your halves strip and your fourths strip, you can see that 2 fourths are the same as 1 half.

   Complete these two equations:

   ________ fourths = 1 half $\qquad \frac{\square}{4} = \frac{1}{2}$

2. How many eighths are in one half? ________

   Complete these two equations:

   ________ eighths = 1 half $\qquad \frac{\square}{8} = \frac{1}{2}$

3. What are two fractions that are equivalent to $\frac{1}{2}$?

   ____

4. How many eighths are in one fourth? ________

   Complete these two equations:

   ________ eighths = 1 fourth $\qquad \frac{\square}{8} = \frac{1}{4}$

Thirds and Sixths

Use your thirds and sixths strips to answer Exercises 5–6.

5 How many sixths are in one third? ________

Complete these two equations:

________ sixths = 1 third $\qquad \frac{\square}{6} = \frac{1}{3}$

6 How many sixths are in two thirds? ________

Complete these two equations:

________ sixths = 2 thirds $\qquad \frac{\square}{6} = \frac{2}{3}$

What's the Error?

Dear Math Students,

Today my teacher asked me to name a fraction that is equivalent to $\frac{1}{2}$.

I wrote $\frac{2}{6} = \frac{1}{2}$.

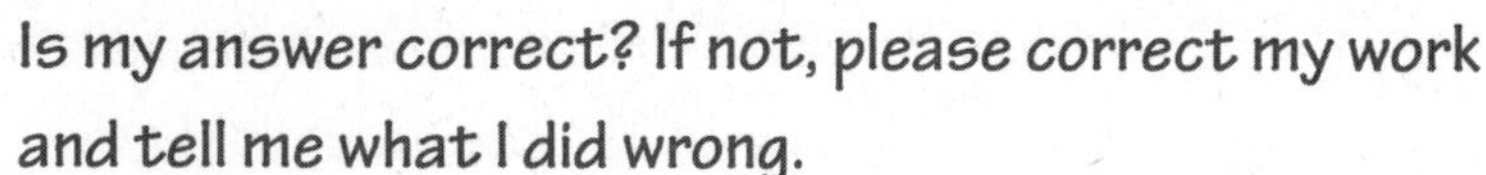
Is my answer correct? If not, please correct my work and tell me what I did wrong.

Your Friend,
Puzzled Penguin

7 Write an answer to Puzzled Penguin.

____

____

____

Check Understanding

Name another fraction equivalent to $\frac{1}{2}$ that Puzzled Penguin could have written. ________

Name ______________________

Equivalent Fractions on Number Lines

1 Complete each number line. Show all fractions including each fraction for 1.

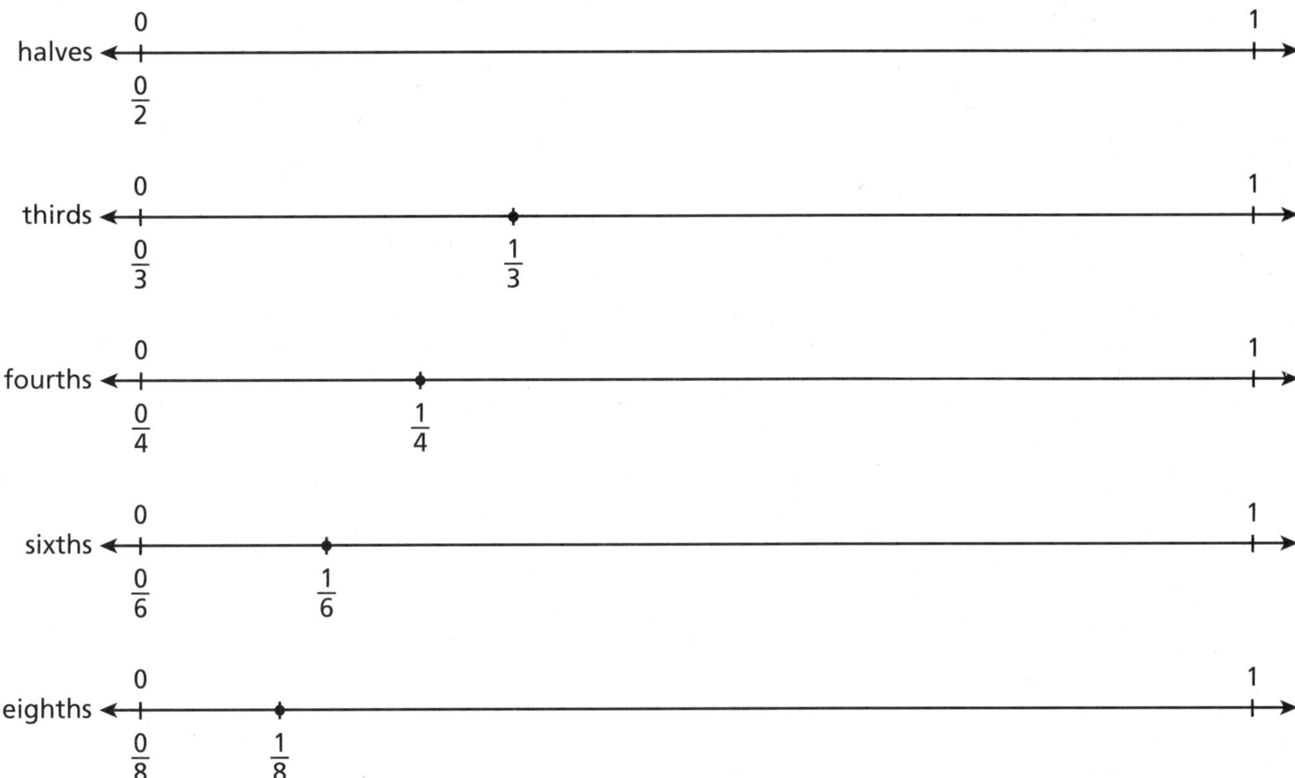

2 Write an equivalence chain with fractions that equal $\frac{2}{2}$.

____

3 Why are the fractions in the equivalence chain for $\frac{2}{2}$ equal?

____

4 Why does the length of unit fractions grow smaller as their denominators get larger?

____

____

Equivalence Chains

Use your number lines from page 361 to write an equivalence chain.

5. With fractions that equal $\frac{1}{2}$ ______

6. With fractions that equal $\frac{1}{3}$ ______

7. With fractions that equal $\frac{2}{3}$ ______

8. With fractions that equal $\frac{1}{4}$ ______

9. With fractions that equal $\frac{3}{4}$ ______

10. With fractions that equal $\frac{8}{8}$ ______

Solve. Use what you have learned about equivalent fractions and about comparing fractions.

Show your work.

11. Jaime has $\frac{1}{2}$ foot of red ribbon and $\frac{4}{8}$ foot of green ribbon. Does he have more red ribbon or green ribbon?

______

12. Chin and Maya collected conch shells at the beach. They both used the same kind of basket. Chin's basket is $\frac{3}{4}$ filled, and Maya's basket is $\frac{3}{3}$ filled. Who collected more shells?

______

______

Check Understanding

Explain how you could use a number line to help you solve Problem 12.

Name ______________________________

Solve Fraction Problems

Solve. Draw diagrams or number lines if you need to.

1. The shelves in Roger's bookcase are $\frac{7}{8}$ yard long. Ana's bookcase has shelves that are $\frac{5}{8}$ yard long. Whose bookcase has longer shelves? How do you know?

____

2. Rosa buys $\frac{3}{4}$ pound of cheese. Lucy buys $\frac{3}{8}$ pound of cheese. Who buys more cheese? Explain your answer.

____

3. Vera has same-size muffin pans. She fills $\frac{8}{4}$ pans with cranberry muffins and $\frac{8}{6}$ pans with banana muffins. Does Vera have fewer cranberry muffins or banana muffins? How do you know?

____

4. Lester walks $\frac{3}{4}$ mile to school. Bert said that he walks farther because he walks $\frac{6}{8}$ mile to school. Is his statement correct? Explain your answer.

____

5. Rusty painted $\frac{5}{6}$ of a mural for a hallway. Has he painted more than half of the mural? Explain your answer.
Hint: Find an equivalent fraction in sixths for $\frac{1}{2}$.

____

Solve Fraction Problems (continued)

Solve. Draw diagrams or number lines if you need to.

6. Pearl used $\frac{3}{3}$ yard of fabric to make a pillow. Julia made her pillow from $\frac{4}{4}$ yard of fabric. They both paid $5 a yard for their fabric. Who paid more for fabric? How do you know?

____

____

7. Deena's pan has a total of $\frac{2}{5}$ liter of water. John's pan has a total of $\frac{5}{2}$ liters of water. Whose pan has more water? How do you know?

____

____

8. Andy, Lu, and Carlos have $\frac{3}{3}$, $\frac{3}{4}$, and $\frac{3}{6}$ dozen pencils, but not in that order. Andy has the fewest pencils and Lu has the most. How many pencils does each boy have? Explain.

____

____

9. At Binata's Bakery, two different recipes are used for wheat bread. For a round loaf, $\frac{5}{2}$ cups of wheat flour are used. For a long loaf, $\frac{7}{2}$ cups of wheat flour are used. For which kind of bread is more wheat flour used? Explain your answer.

____

____

Name ______________________________

Fraction of a Set

Write a fraction to answer each question.

10 What fraction of the buttons are large buttons?

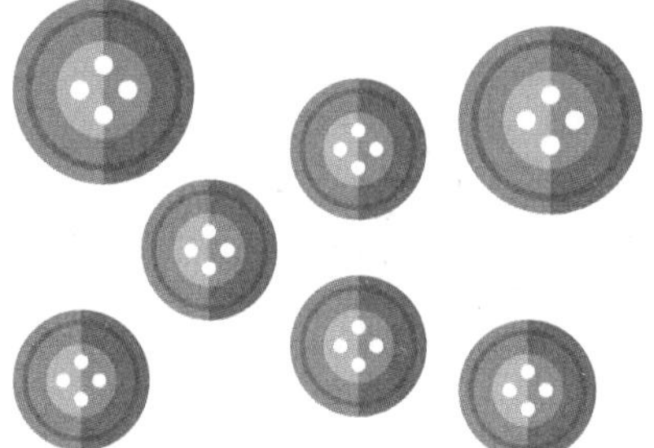

______

11 What fraction of the balls are soccer balls?

______

Write two fractions to answer each question.

12 What fraction of the coins are pennies?

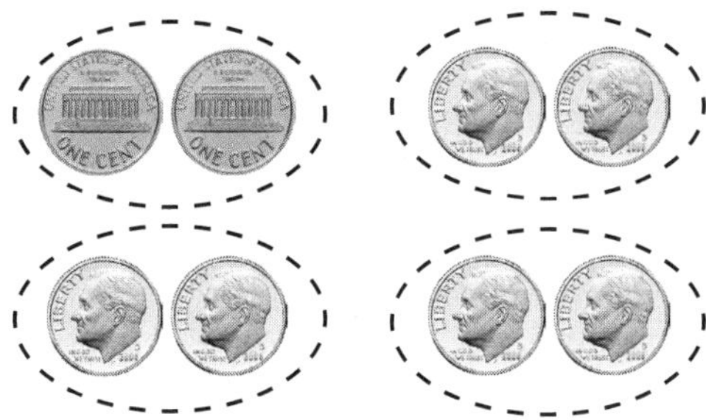

______ ______

13 What fraction of the pieces of fruit are pears?

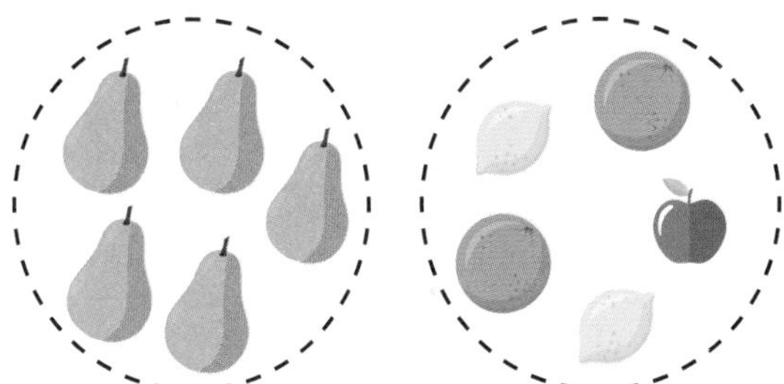

______ ______

Shade the given fraction of each set.

14 $\frac{7}{11}$

15 $\frac{2}{9}$

16 $\frac{1}{5}$

Solve Word Problems Involving Unit Fractions of Sets

Solve each problem.

Show your work.

17 One sixth of Kiera's cousins have red hair. Kiera has 12 cousins. How many cousins have red hair?

____

18 One third of the students on the bus are in the third grade. There are 15 students on the bus. How many students on the bus are in the third grade?

____

19 One half of Angel's crayons are sharp. Angel has 14 crayons. How many crayons are sharp?

____

20 One fourth of the roses in a bouquet are pink. There are 24 roses in the bouquet. How many roses are pink?

____

21 There are 56 seals at the aquarium. One eighth of the seals are swimming. How many seals are swimming?

____

Name ______________________________

Fractions of a Dollar

Equal shares of 1 whole dollar can be written as a fraction or as cents. Each whole dollar below is equal to 100 pennies. Discuss the patterns you see.

22 $\frac{1}{2}$ 1 of 2 equal parts

$\frac{1}{2}$ of one dollar = 50 pennies = 50¢

23 $\frac{1}{2} + \frac{1}{2} = \frac{2}{2}$ 2 of 2 equal parts = 1 whole

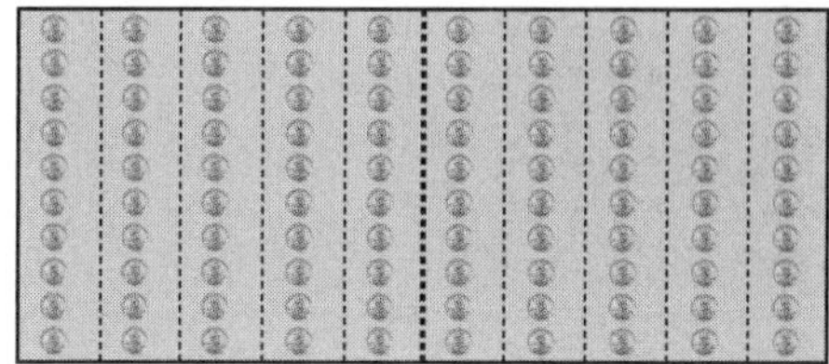

$\frac{2}{2}$ of one dollar = 100 pennies = \$1

24 $\frac{1}{4}$ 1 of 4 equal parts

$\frac{1}{4}$ of one dollar = 25 pennies = 25¢

25 $\frac{1}{4} + \frac{1}{4} = \frac{2}{4}$ 2 of 4 equal parts

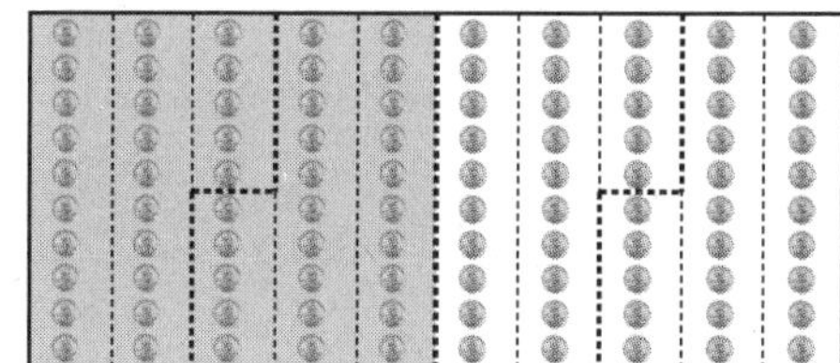

$\frac{2}{4}$ of one dollar = 50 pennies = 50¢

26 $\frac{1}{4} + \frac{1}{4} + \frac{1}{4} = \frac{3}{4}$ 3 of 4 equal parts

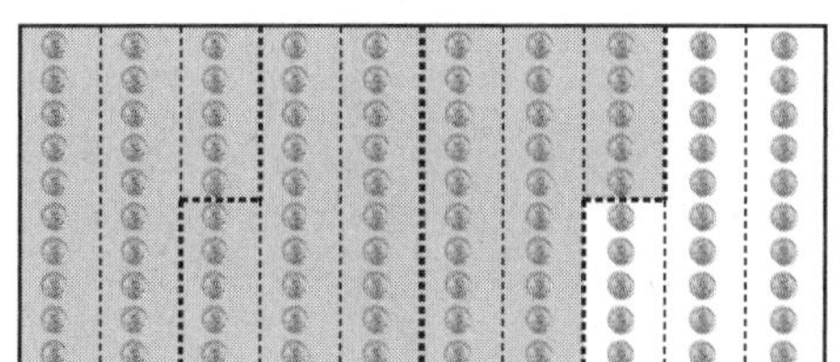

$\frac{3}{4}$ of one dollar = 75 pennies = 75¢

27 $\frac{1}{4} + \frac{1}{4} + \frac{1}{4} + \frac{1}{4} = \frac{4}{4}$ 4 of 4 equal parts = 1 whole

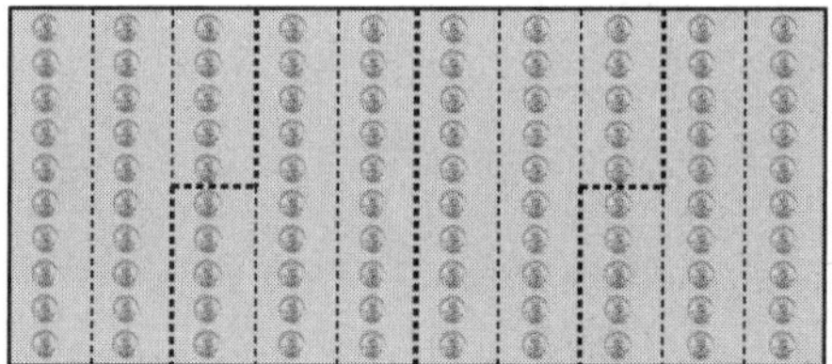

$\frac{4}{4}$ of one dollar = 100 pennies = \$1

Represent Fractions of a Dollar

Shade each whole to show the given fraction and write the money amount.

28 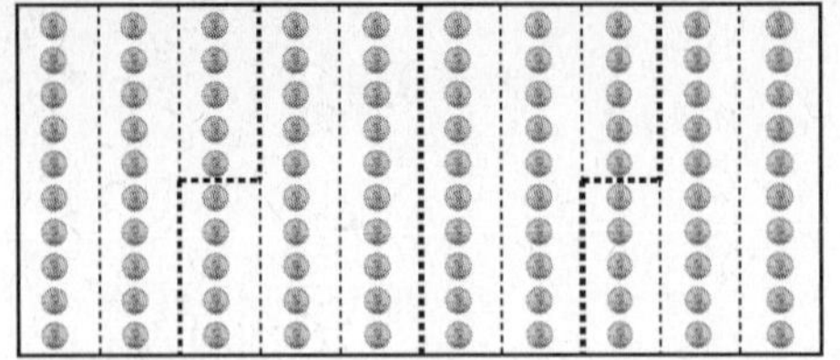

$\frac{2}{4}$ = ____________

29 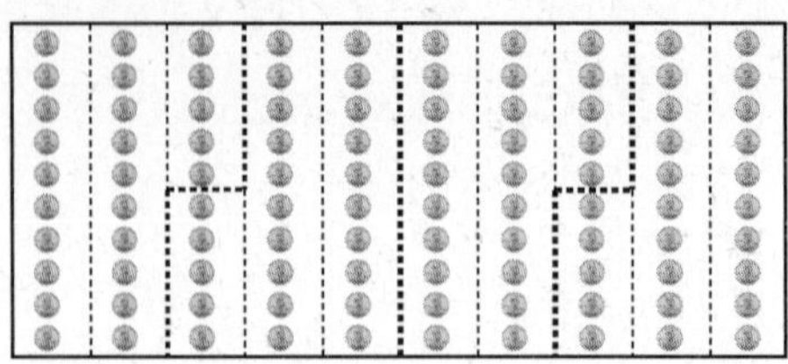

$\frac{1}{4}$ = ____________

30 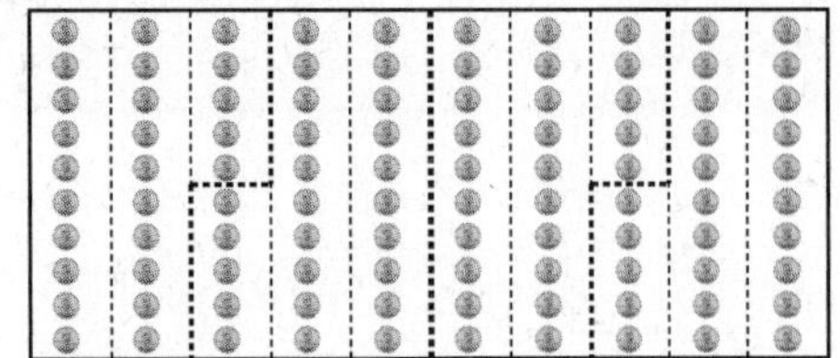

$\frac{4}{4}$ = ____________

31 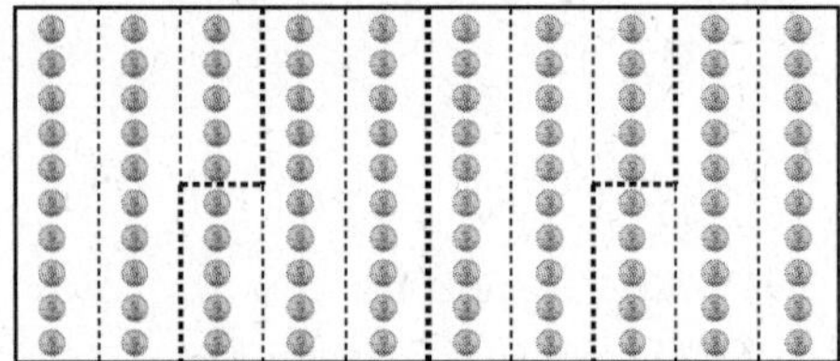

$\frac{3}{4}$ = ____________

Check Understanding

Jenna has 100 pennies. She gives $\frac{3}{4}$ of her pennies to her sister. How many pennies does Jenna give to her sister?

____

Which exercise above models the number of pennies Jenna gave to her sister?

____

 Name ______________________

Fractions and Paper Folding

The art of paper folding began in China. Later, Japan's version of paper folding, called origami, became very popular. Origami sculptures are made by folding and sculpting a flat sheet of square paper without cuts or glue.

Complete.

1. Fold a square sheet of paper in half diagonally. What part of the square is each triangle?

   ____

2. Fold the paper in half again. What part of the square is each triangle?

   ____

3. Fold the paper in half again. Open the paper. What part of the square is each triangle?

   ____

4. Explain how you know the eight parts have the same area.

   ____

   ____

5. Fold four triangles to the center as shown on the right. What part of the square is each triangle? Explain how you know.

   ____

   ____

   ____

This basic origami fold is used for making many objects.

Fractions and Design

Complete.

6. Fold a square sheet of paper in half 3 times. Open the paper. Choose two different colors. Color every other rectangle or triangle one color. Color the other rectangles or triangles the second color.

7. Write 3 equivalent fractions for the part of the square that has the same color.

8. Predict the number of shapes you would make if you folded the square 4 times. Explain.

Name ________________ Date ________________

Complete.

1. How many sixths are in one third? __________

Complete these two equations:

__________ sixths = 1 third

$\frac{\square}{6} = \frac{1}{3}$

2. How many eighths are in one half? __________

Complete these two equations:

__________ eighths = 1 half

$\frac{\square}{8} = \frac{1}{2}$

3. Write an equivalence chain with three fractions that equal $\frac{1}{4}$.

____

Complete the number line. Show the fraction for 1.

4.

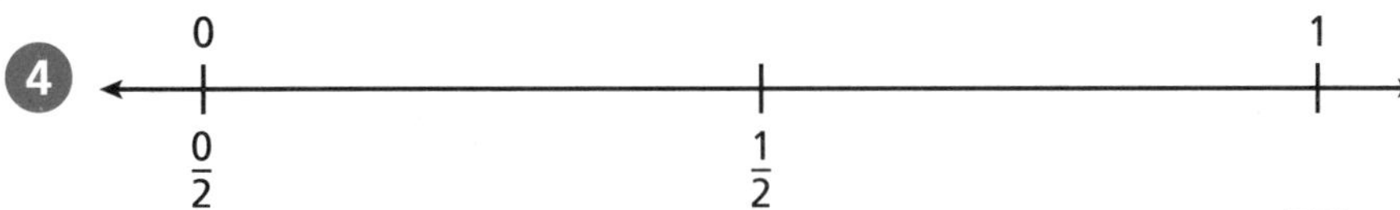

Solve.

Show your work.

5. Monica buys $\frac{2}{3}$ pound of apples. Nicole buys $\frac{5}{6}$ pound of peaches. Do the apples or the peaches weigh more? Explain your answer.

____

____

Fluency Check 9

Name ______________________ Date ______________

PATH to FLUENCY

Multiply or divide.

1. $7 \times 0 = \square$
2. $12 \div 2 = \square$
3. $8 \times 3 = \square$
4. $16 \div 4 = \square$
5. $3 \times 7 = \square$
6. $42 \div 6 = \square$
7. $6 \times 8 = \square$
8. $81 \div 9 = \square$
9. $8 \times 7 = \square$

Add or subtract.

10. $\begin{array}{r} 885 \\ -\ 345 \\ \hline \end{array}$
11. $\begin{array}{r} 326 \\ +\ 421 \\ \hline \end{array}$
12. $\begin{array}{r} 508 \\ -\ 329 \\ \hline \end{array}$
13. $\begin{array}{r} 264 \\ +\ 338 \\ \hline \end{array}$
14. $\begin{array}{r} 623 \\ -\ 365 \\ \hline \end{array}$
15. $\begin{array}{r} 478 \\ +\ 385 \\ \hline \end{array}$

Name

Name ____________________

Count On to Make Change

Imagine you are working at a sandwich shop. A customer pays for a sandwich that costs $4.28 with a $5 bill. Your cash register is broken and you don't have a pencil. How can you figure out how much change to give the customer?

Start with $4.28. Count on until you get to $5.00.

$4.28						
	$4.29	$4.30	$4.40	$4.50	$4.75	$5.00

Add the coins to find the total amount of change, 72¢.

Practice Making Change

Find the amount of change by counting on to the amount paid. Draw the coins you counted.

1. Fernando paid $1.39 for a bottle of juice. He paid with two $1 bills. How much change should he get?

   ____

2. At a book sale, Ana bought a book for $4.53. She paid with a $5 bill. How much change should she get? ____________

3. Valerie bought a nutrition bar for $2.12. She paid with three $1 bills. How much change should she get? ____________

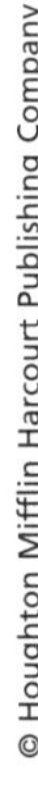

The following items are for sale at the Beach Snack Shop:

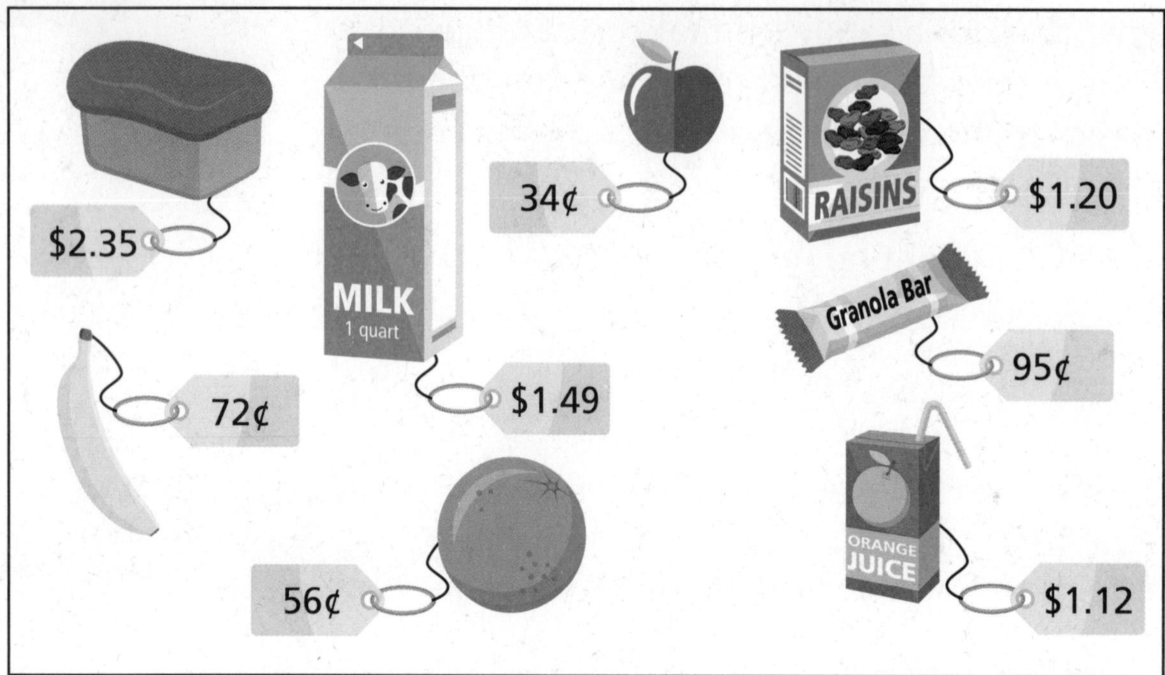

Act Out Using Money

You and your partner can take turns being the customer and the shopkeeper. Here's what to do:

Step 1: The customer chooses two items to buy.

Step 2: The shopkeeper writes down the prices and finds the total cost.

Step 3: The customer pays with bills only.

Step 4: The shopkeeper counts on to find the change. Then the shopkeeper writes down the bills used to pay and the amount of change.

Show your work on a separate sheet of paper.

Check Understanding

Describe how to find the amount of change to give a customer.

Name ______________________________

Temperature in Fahrenheit

Use the thermometer. Circle the better estimate of the temperature in degrees Fahrenheit.

VOCABULARY
thermometer
temperature
Fahrenheit (°F)

HOT 212°F water boils

HOT 104°F very hot day

WARM 70°F room temperature

COOL 50°F day for a jacket

COLD 32°F water freezes

COLD −10°F very cold day

1. 20°F 80°F
2. 32°F 84°F
3. 0°F 53°F

Write the temperature using °F. Then write *hot, warm, cool,* or *cold* to describe the temperature.

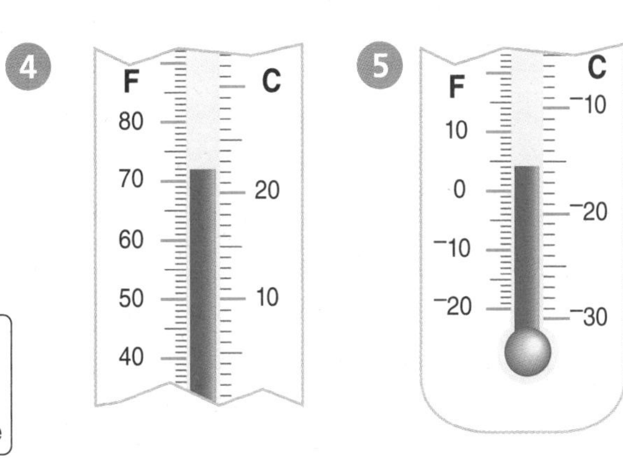

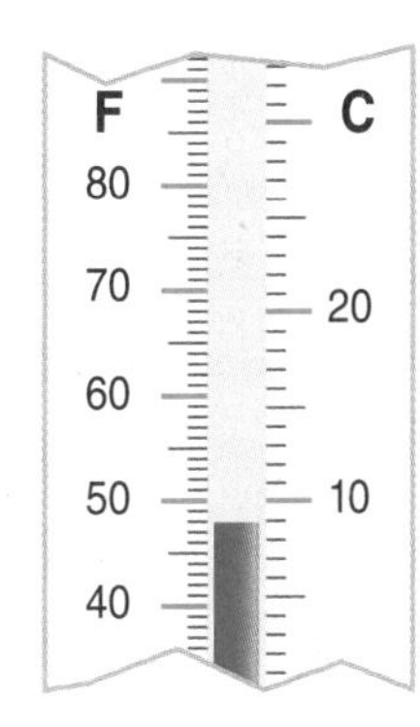

4. ____________
5. ____________
6. ____________

7. The thermometer shows the high temperature on Thursday.

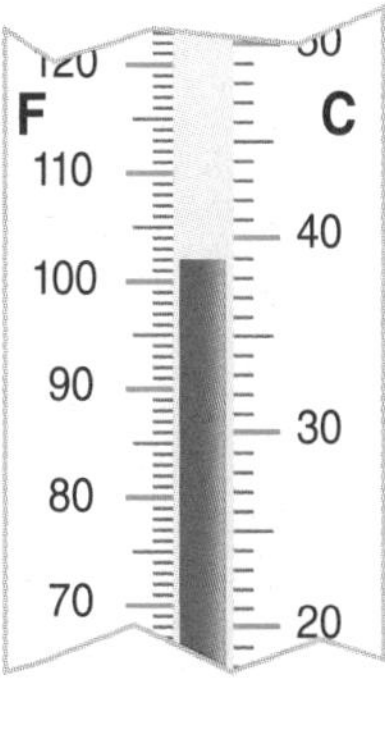

a. What was the temperature in degrees Fahrenheit on Thursday?

____

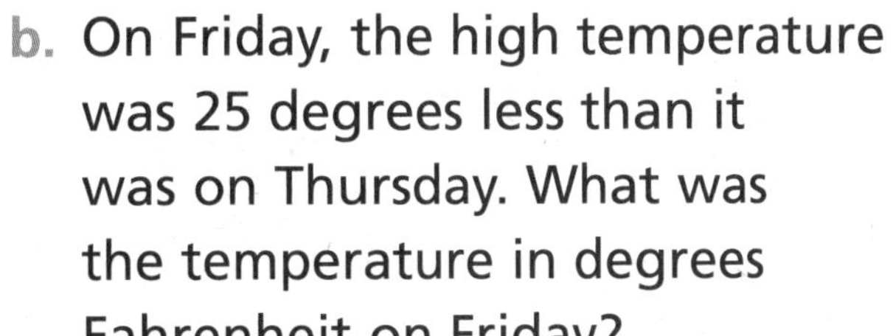

b. On Friday, the high temperature was 25 degrees less than it was on Thursday. What was the temperature in degrees Fahrenheit on Friday? ____________

Temperature in Celsius

VOCABULARY
Celsius (°C)

Use the thermometer. Circle the better estimate of the temperature in degrees Celsius.

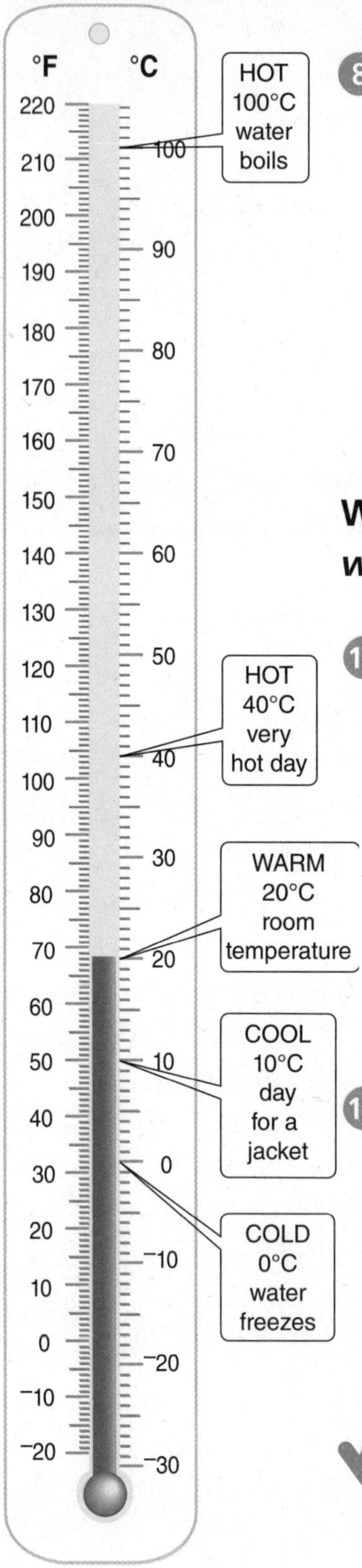

8  50°C 11°C

9 30°C 100°C

10 22°C 0°C

Write the temperature using °C. Then write *hot, warm, cool,* or *cold* to describe the temperature.

11 ______

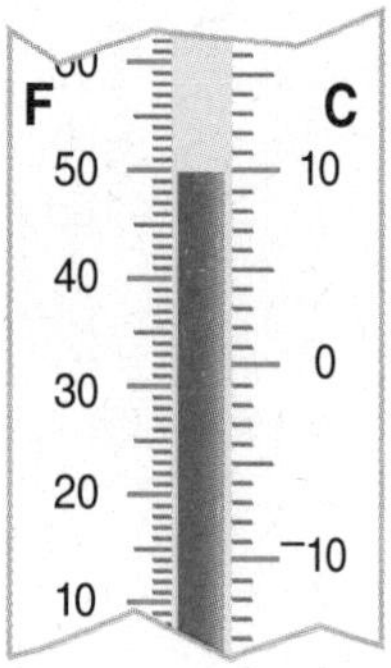

12 ______

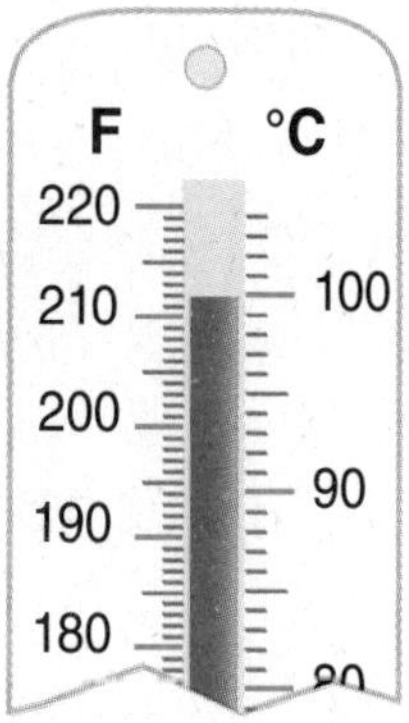

13 ______

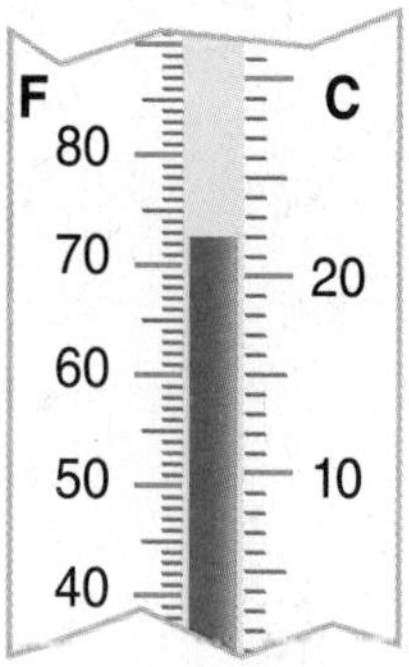

14 The thermometer shows the temperature at 8 A.M. The temperature is 14 degrees higher at 2 P.M. What is the temperature in degrees Celsius at 2 P.M.?

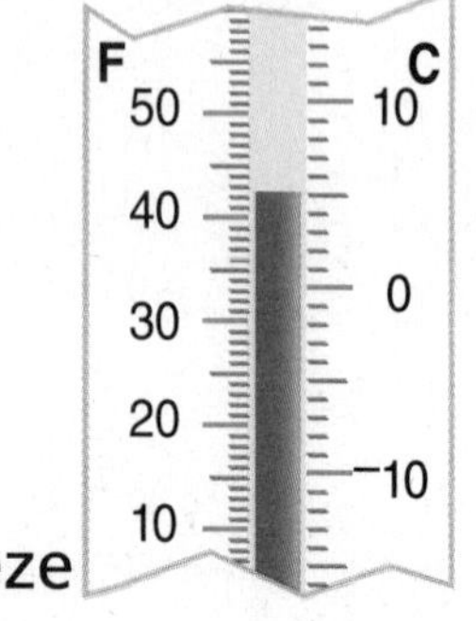

______

Check Understanding

At what temperature does water freeze on the Fahrenheit and Celsius scales?

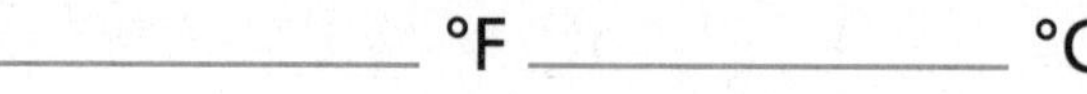

______ °F ______ °C

Unit 5
Quick Quiz 3

Name ____________________ Date ____________________

Use the thermometer for Exercises 1–2.

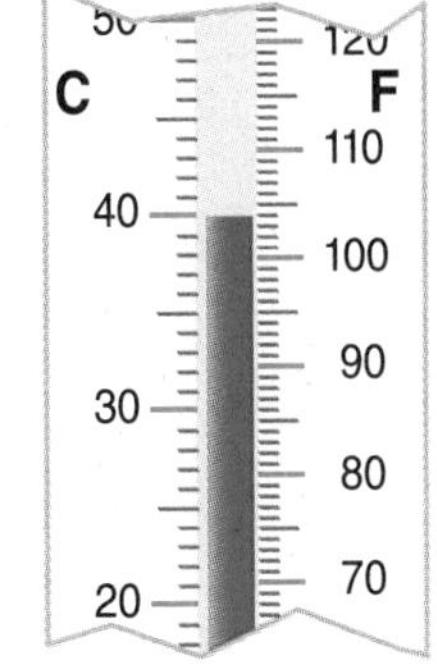

1. Write the temperature using °C.

____

2. It is predicted that the temperature will be lower by 8° C next week. What is the predicted temperature in degrees Celsius?

____

3. Nancy's thermometer shows that the temperature outside is 80° F. Name a possible activity that Nancy could do outdoors?

____

4. Gianni paid for a $1.65 pen with two $1 bills. How much change should he get?

____

5. Abdul buys a sandwich for $4.15. He uses a $5 bill to pay. How much change should he receive?

____

Fluency Check 10

Name ____________________ Date ____________

PATH to FLUENCY

Multiply or divide.

1. $8 \times 0 = \square$
2. $18 \div 3 = \square$
3. $9 \times 3 = \square$
4. $16 \div 8 = \square$
5. $7 \times 7 = \square$
6. $48 \div 6 = \square$
7. $5 \times 9 = \square$
8. $72 \div 9 = \square$
9. $3 \times 7 = \square$

Add or subtract.

10. $\begin{array}{r} 489 \\ -\ 345 \\ \hline \end{array}$
11. $\begin{array}{r} 363 \\ +\ 128 \\ \hline \end{array}$
12. $\begin{array}{r} 208 \\ -\ 192 \\ \hline \end{array}$
13. $\begin{array}{r} 568 \\ +\ 338 \\ \hline \end{array}$
14. $\begin{array}{r} 453 \\ -\ 365 \\ \hline \end{array}$
15. $\begin{array}{r} 406 \\ +\ 314 \\ \hline \end{array}$

Name ______________________________ Date ______________

1 A park ranger has 32 feet of fencing to fence four sides of a rectangular recycling site. What is the greatest area of the recycling site that the ranger can fence? Explain how you know.

2 Use the fractions to label each point on the number line.

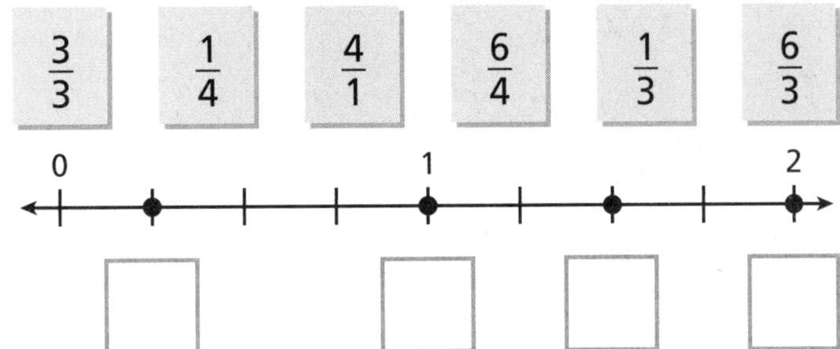

3 Select the fraction that would be included in an equivalence chain for $\frac{6}{6}$. Mark all that apply.

Ⓐ $\frac{3}{3}$

Ⓑ $\frac{3}{6}$

Ⓒ $\frac{4}{4}$

Ⓓ $\frac{5}{5}$

Ⓔ $\frac{6}{1}$

Name ______________________ Date ______________

4 Steve makes a banner with an area of 8 square feet. On the grid, draw all possible rectangles with an area of 8 square feet and whose side lengths are whole feet. Label the lengths of two adjacent sides of each rectangle. Label each rectangle with its perimeter.

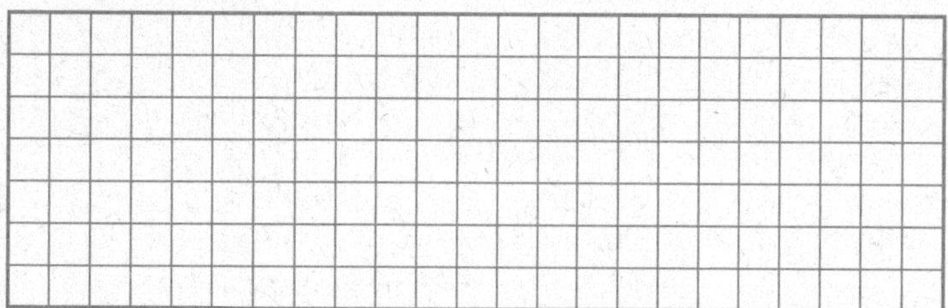

Compare the perimeters of the banners. What do you notice about their shapes?

5 Draw a line from the fraction on the left to match the equivalent fraction or number on the right.

$\frac{4}{6}$ •	• 8
$\frac{8}{1}$ •	• $\frac{2}{3}$
$\frac{3}{4}$ •	• 1
$\frac{2}{8}$ •	• $\frac{6}{8}$
$\frac{2}{2}$ •	• $\frac{1}{4}$

Name ______________________ Date ______________________

6 Mark the number line to show the fractions. First divide the number line into correct unit fractions.

$\frac{1}{8}$ $\frac{5}{8}$ $\frac{8}{8}$ $\frac{3}{4}$

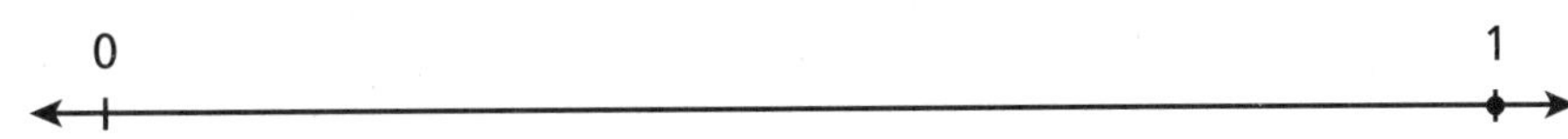

7 What fraction of the coins are pennies?

____

8 Mr. Gomez hangs a mural on the classroom wall. Find the perimeter and area of the mural.

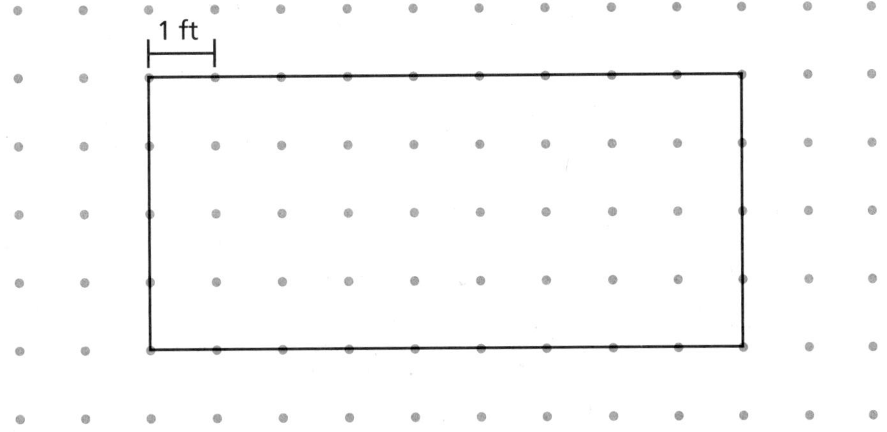

Perimeter: ______________ feet

Area: ______________ square feet

Name ______________________________ Date ______________

9 Liana plants a vegetable garden in two sections. She plants corn in a section that is 5 meters long and 6 meters wide. She plants squash in a section that is 3 meters long and 6 meters wide.

Part A

Describe one way to find the area of the garden. Then find the area.

Area: ________ square meters

Part B

Draw a picture of the garden to show your answer is correct.

Name ______________________ Date ______________

10 Dan walks $\frac{5}{8}$ mile to school. Beth walks $\frac{3}{4}$ mile to school.

Part A

Who walks farther? Label and shade the circles to help solve the problem.

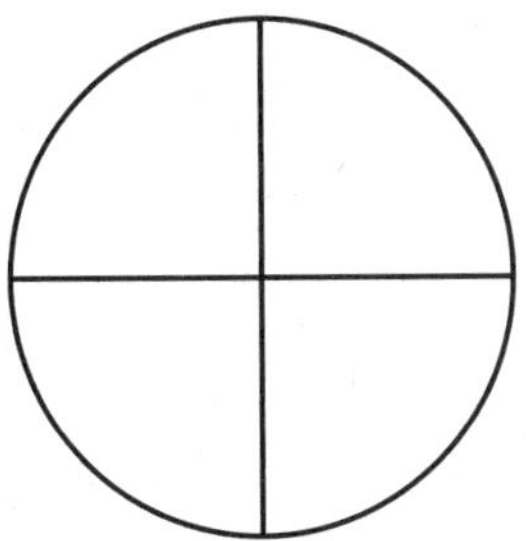

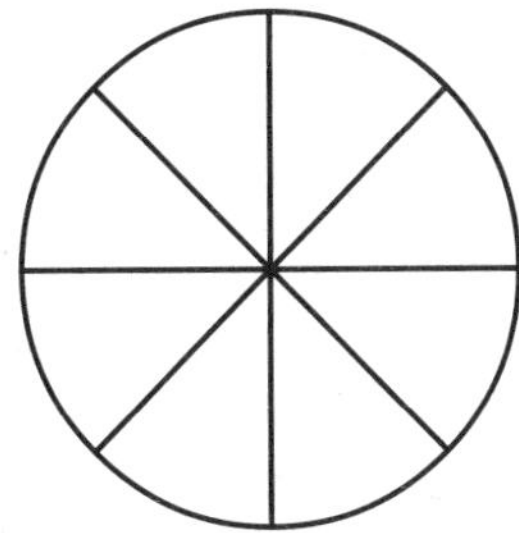

__________ walks farther.

Part B

Suppose Dan walks $\frac{6}{8}$ mile instead of $\frac{5}{8}$ mile. Who walks farther? How do the circles help you decide?

11 The thermometer shows the temperature at 3:00 P.M.

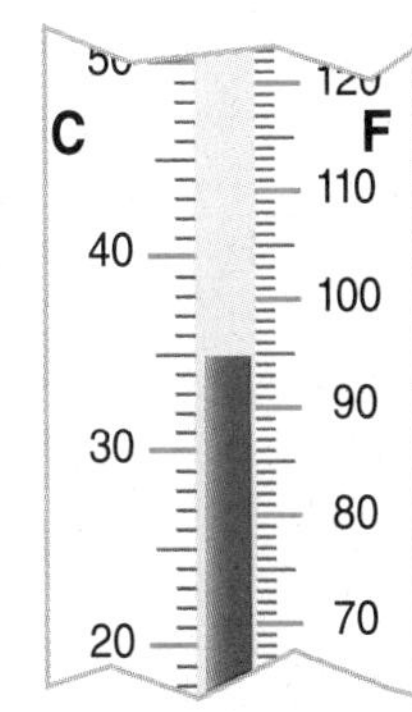

11a What temperature does the thermometer show in degrees Fahrenheit? ______

11b At 2:00 A.M. it is predicted that the temperature will be 16° lower. What is the predicted temperature in degrees Fahrenheit for 2:00 A.M.? ______

Name ____________________ Date ____________

12 Draw a line from the figure to the area of the figure.

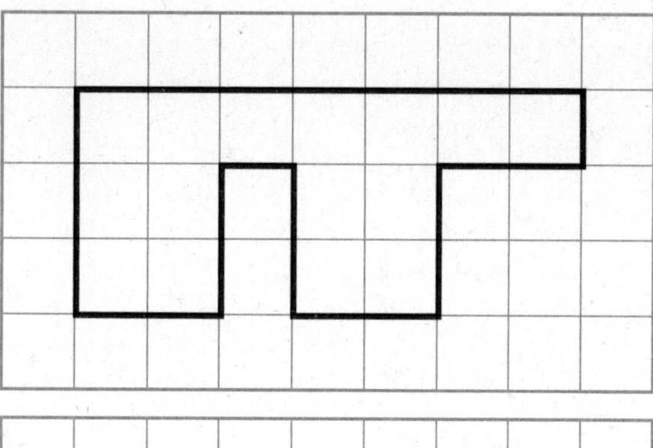

• • 13 square units

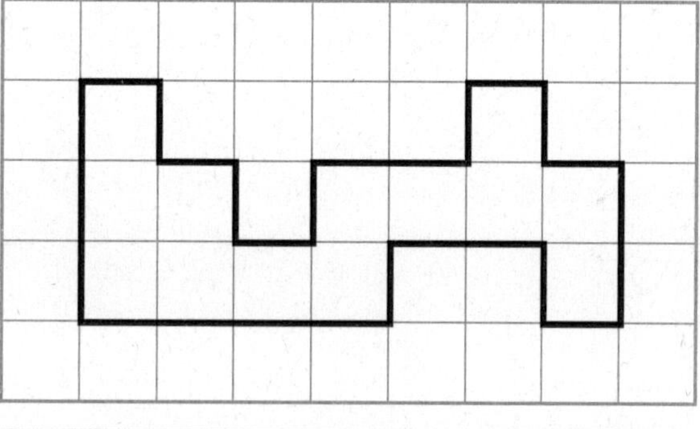

• • 14 square units

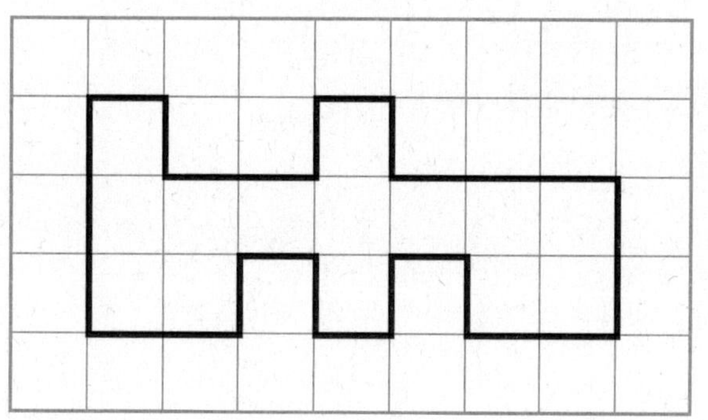

• • 15 square units

13 Riki buys some tomatoes for $2.19. She pays with three $1 bills. How much change should she receive?

____

14 Rino needs $\frac{1}{2}$ cup of pineapple juice for a shake. What are two other fractions equivalent to $\frac{1}{2}$?

____

Name ______________________________ Date ____________

Dog Park

The town of Springfield is planning to create a rectangular dog park. The park will be 8 yards long and 10 yards wide.

1. How much fencing is needed to go around the park?

____

2. What is the area of the planned park?

____

3. Half of the park will have a lawn and one fourth of the park will be covered with gravel. Shade the model below to show the lawn and the part with gravel.

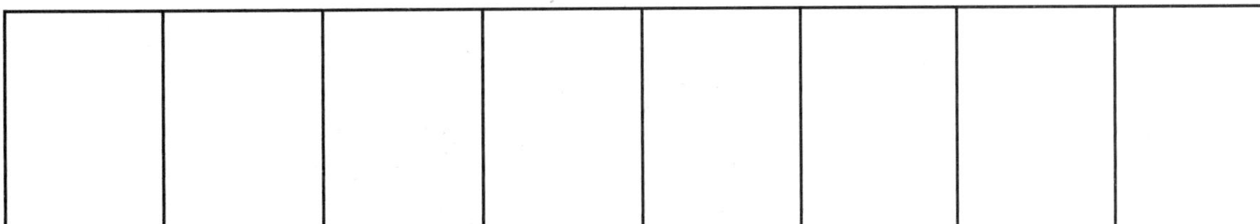

4. The remaining area of the park will have benches. What fraction of the total area will have benches?

____

5. Write two equivalent fractions to represent the area of the park with the lawn.

____

Name ______________________ Date __________

The town of Springfield plans to make the dog park larger.

6. The town will add 20 square yards of land next to the original park. Draw and label the possible dimensions of the addition.

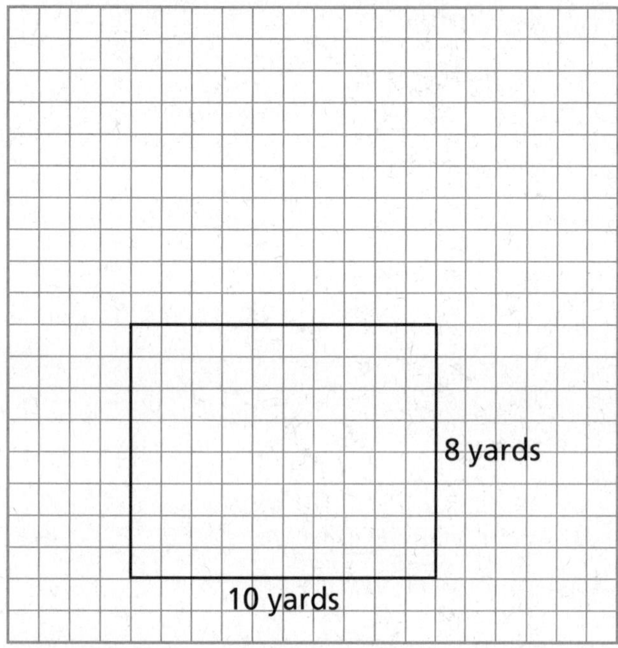

7. How much fencing is needed to go around the outside boundaries of the entire dog park?

____

8. Use the grid below to design your own dog park. Each square represents 1 square unit. The area of your park must be 24 square units. Label the drawing with the perimeter of the park.

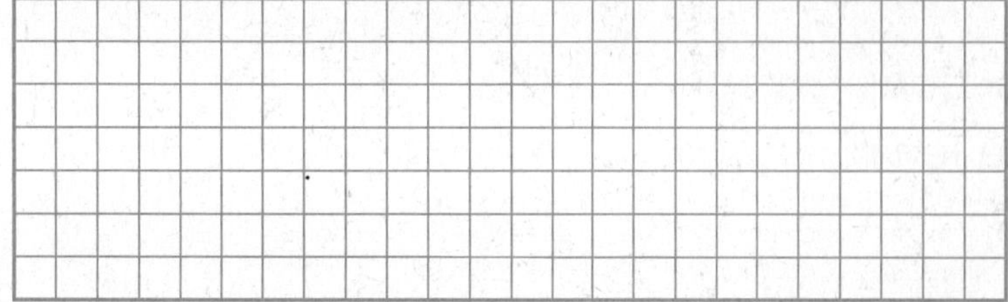

Dear Family:

In this unit, your child will solve addition, subtraction, multiplication, and division problems involving unknown addends and factors.

- If one of the addends is unknown, it can be found by subtracting the known addend from the total or by counting on from the known addend to the total.
- If the total is unknown, it can be found by adding the addends.
- If one of the factors is unknown, it can be found by dividing the product by the other factor.
- If the product is unknown, it can be found by multiplying the factors.

Math Mountains are used to show a total and two addends. Students can use the Math Mountain to write an equation and then solve the equation to find the unknown.

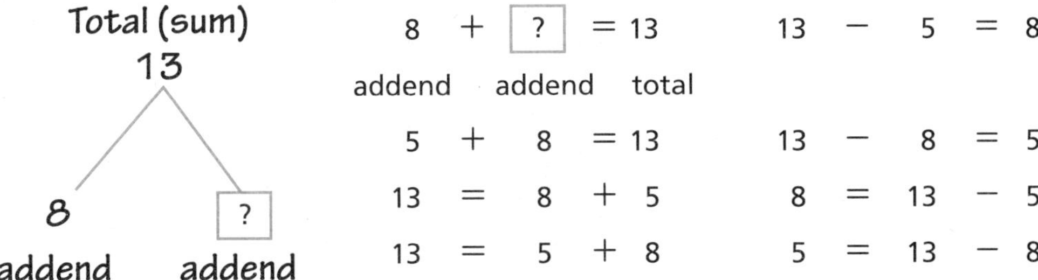

Equations with numbers alone on the left are also emphasized to help with the understanding of algebra.

Comparison Bars are used to solve problems that involve one amount that is more than or less than another amount. Drawing Comparison Bars can help a student organize the information in the problem in order to find the unknown smaller amount, the unknown larger amount, or the difference.

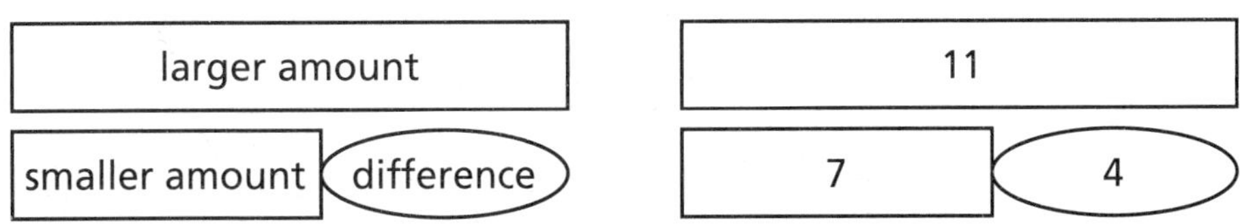

Please contact me if you have any questions or comments.

Sincerely,
Your child's teacher

Estimada familia:

En esta unidad, su niño resolverá sumas, restas, multiplicaciones y divisiones con sumandos o factores desconocidos.

- Si uno de los sumandos se desconoce, puede hallarse restando el sumando conocido del total, o contando hacia adelante desde el sumando conocido hasta llegar al total.
- Si el total se desconoce, puede hallarse sumando los sumandos.
- Si uno de los factores se desconoce, puede hallarse dividiendo el producto entre el otro factor.
- Si el producto se desconoce, puede hallarse multiplicando los factores.

Para mostrar un total y dos sumandos se usan las **Montañas matemáticas**. Los estudiantes puede usarlas para escribir una ecuación, y al resolverla, hallar el elemento desconocido.

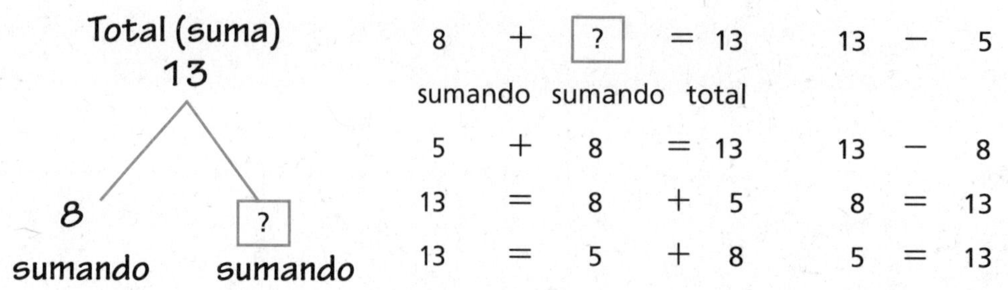

Se hace énfasis en las ecuaciones que tienen números solos en el lado izquierdo, para facilitar la comprensión del álgebra.

Para resolver problemas con una cantidad que es más o menos que otra, se usan **Barras de comparación**. Estas barras sirven para organizar la información del problema, y hallar así, la cantidad desconocida más pequeña, la más grande o la diferencia.

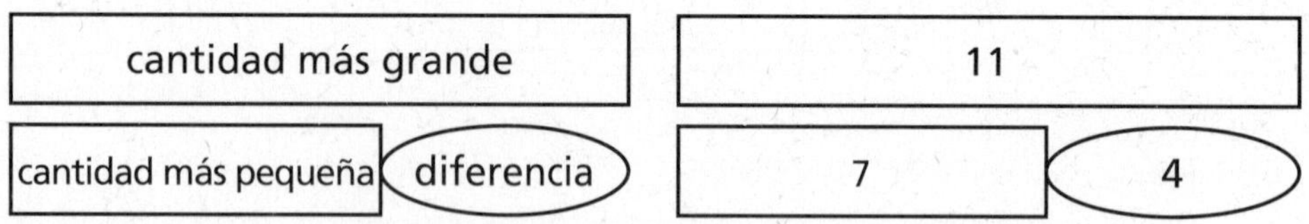

Si tiene alguna pregunta o algún comentario, por favor comuníquese conmigo.

Atentamente,
El maestro de su niño

addend

sum

total

One of two or more numbers to be added together to find a sum.

Example:

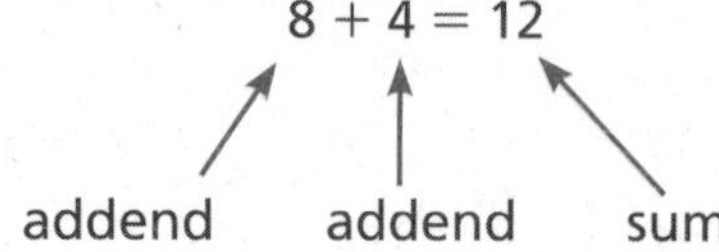

The answer when adding two or more addends.

Example:

37 + 52 = 89

addend addend sum

The answer when adding two or more addends. The sum of two or more numbers.

Example:

672 + 228 = 900

addend addend total or sum

Name ______________________

Math Mountains and Equations

VOCABULARY
total
addend
sum

Complete.

1. Look at the Math Mountain and the 8 equations. What relationships do you see? In each equation, label each number as an **addend** (*A*) or the **total** (*T*).

sum
total
110

70 addend — 40 addend

110	=	70	+	40	70	+	40	=	110
___		___		___	___		___		___
110	=	40	+	70	40	+	70	=	110
___		___		___	___		___		___
40	=	110	−	70	110	−	70	=	40
___		___		___	___		___		___
70	=	110	−	40	110	−	40	=	70
___		___		___	___		___		___

2. Write the 8 equations for this Math Mountain. Label each number as the total (*T*) or an addend (*A*).

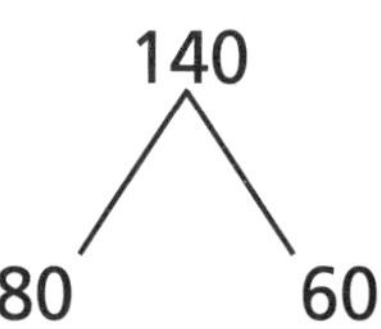

______________________ ______________________

______________________ ______________________

______________________ ______________________

______________________ ______________________

Solve and Discuss

Solve each problem. Label your answers.

Show your work.

3 **Add To** Chris's group picked 80 apples. His mother's group picked 60 more apples. How many apples do they have now?

____

4 **Take From** Chris's group had 140 apples. They ate 80 of them. How many apples do they have now?

____

5 **Put Together/Take Apart** Alison's class brought 70 juice boxes to the picnic. Taylor's class brought 50 juice boxes. How many juice boxes did they bring altogether?

____

6 **Put Together/Take Apart** There are 120 juice boxes at the picnic. Alison puts 70 on tables and leaves the rest in the cooler. How many juice boxes are in the cooler?

____

Name ______________________

Represent Word Problems with Math Tools

The equations and Math Mountains below show the word problems on page 390.

Add To

80	+	60	=	☐
Chris's group		Mom's group		total

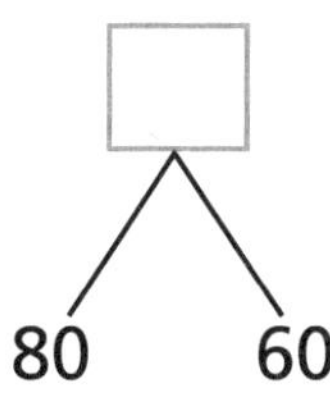

Take From

140	–	80	=	☐
total		ate		now

140

80

Put Together/Take Apart

70	+	50	=	☐
Alison's class		Taylor's class		total

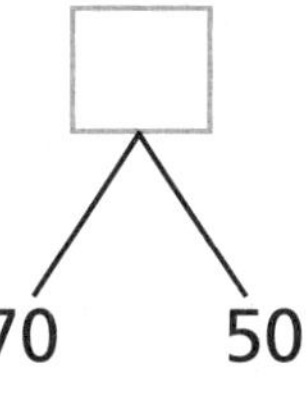

Put Together/Take Apart

120	–	70	=	☐
total		tables		cooler

70	+	☐	=	120
tables		cooler		total

120

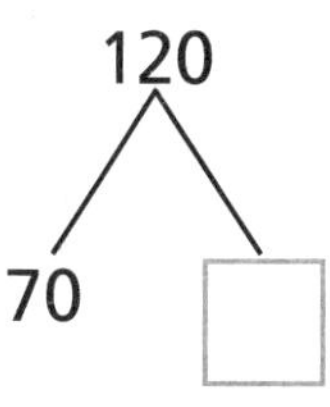

7. Write the unknown numbers in the boxes.

8. How are these math tools the same? How are they different?

____

9. **Math Journal** Write a word problem for this equation: $110 - 40 = \square$. Then solve it.

PATH to FLUENCY Discuss the = and ≠ Signs

An expression is a combination of numbers, variables, and/or operation signs. Expressions do not have an equal sign.

An equation is made up of two equal quantities or expressions. An equal sign (=) is used to show that the two sides are equal.

$8 = 5 + 3$ $4 + 2 = 6$ $7 = 7$ $3 + 2 = 2 + 3$

The "is not equal to" sign (≠) shows that two quantities are not equal.

$7 \neq 5 + 3$ $4 + 2 \neq 8$ $7 \neq 6$ $5 + 2 \neq 1 + 1 + 3$

10 Use the = sign to write three equations. Vary how many numbers you have on each side of the sign.

____

____

____

11 Use the ≠ sign to write three "is not equal to" statements. Vary how many numbers you have on each side of the sign.

____

____

____

Write a number to make the number sentence true.

12 $160 = \square + 90$

13 $30 + \square \neq 120$

14 $150 - \square = 70$

15 $\square \neq 140 - 70$

Write = or ≠ to make a true number sentence.

16 $80 + 20 + 40$ ◯ $90 + 50$

17 80 ◯ $60 - 20$

Check Understanding

Draw a Math Mountain for this problem: Cory had 12 grapes. He ate 4 of them. How many grapes does he have now? Then write an equation for the problem and solve.

Name ____________________

Solve Unknown Addend Word Problems

Draw a Math Mountain and write and label an equation with a variable. Then solve each problem.

Show your work.

1. **Put Together/Take Apart: Unknown Addend**
There were 90 girls and some boys in an after-school program. 160 children were in the program in all. How many boys were in the after-school program?

____

2. **Put Together/Take Apart: Unknown Addend**
There were 150 people at the park. 70 were playing soccer. The others were playing softball. How many people were playing softball?

____

3. **Add To: Unknown Addend** Jan planted 80 tulips last week. Today she planted some roses. Now she has 170 flowers. How many roses did she plant?

____

4. **Take From: Unknown Addend** Tim's team had 140 tennis balls. Then his brother's team borrowed some. Now Tim's team has 60 tennis balls. How many did his brother's team borrow?

____

Represent Unknown Addends with Math Tools

The equations and Math Mountains below show the word problems on page 393.

Put Together/Take Apart: Unknown Addend

90	+	b	=	160
girls		boys		children

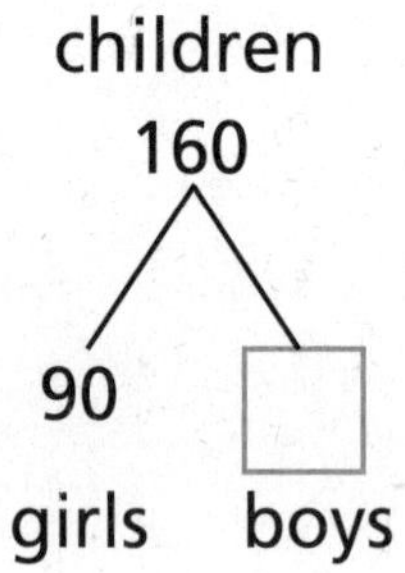

children
160

90 ☐

girls boys

Put Together/Take Apart: Unknown Addend

150	−	s	=	70
park		softball		soccer

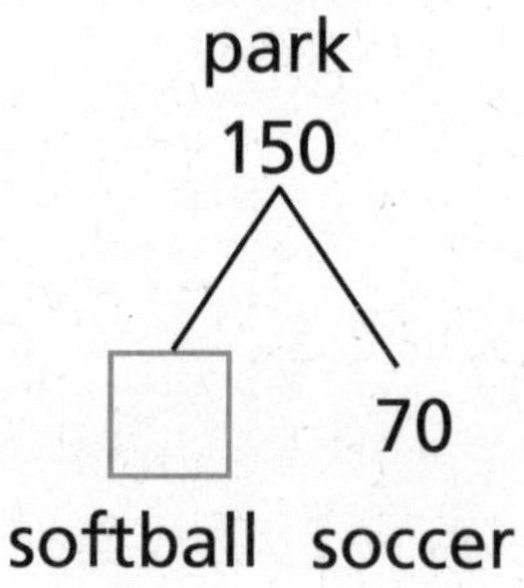

park
150

☐ 70

softball soccer

Add To: Unknown Addend

80	+	r	=	170
tulips		roses		flowers

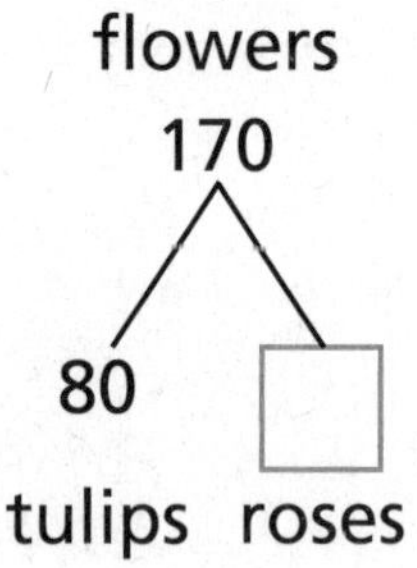

flowers
170

80 ☐

tulips roses

Take From: Unknown Addend

140	−	b	=	60
balls		some		now

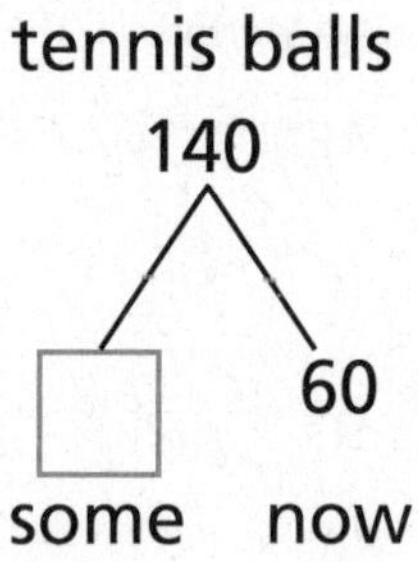

tennis balls
140

☐ 60

some now

5. Write the unknown numbers in the boxes and above the variables.

6. How are these math tools alike? How are they different?

Name ____________________

Solve Unknown Factor Word Problems

Write an equation for each word problem. Use a variable to represent the unknown factor. Then solve the problem.

Show your work.

7. A toymaker has 36 boxes of toy trains to ship to 4 toy shops. Each shop will get the same number of boxes. How many boxes of toy trains will each shop get?

____

8. There are 56 cars in a parking lot. There are 8 rows and the same number of cars is in each row. How many cars are in each row?

____

9. An apartment building has 42 apartments. There are 6 apartments on each floor. How many floors are in the apartment building?

____

10. There are 48 students in the marching band. The students stand in equal rows of 8. How many rows of students are there?

____

Solve Unknown Factor Word Problems (continued)

Write an equation for each word problem. Use a variable to represent the unknown factor. Then solve the problem.

Show your work.

11 Daniel is setting up seats for the third grade play. There are 6 seats in each row. There are 54 seats in all. How many rows of seats are there?

____

12 Mrs. Martinez is sewing buttons on 4 costumes. Each costume has the same number of buttons. There are 32 buttons in all. How many buttons are on each costume?

____

13 The library received 63 new books. The librarian will put 7 books on each shelf of a bookcase. How many shelves are there?

____

14 There are 72 juice boxes for the class picnic. The juice boxes are in packs of 8. How many packs of juice boxes are there?

____

Check Understanding

Draw a picture to represent Problem 14: 72 juice boxes in packs of 8.

Name ______________________________

Solve Unknown Start Problems

Solve each problem. Label your answers.

Show your work.

1. Add To: Unknown Start Greta puts some beads on a string. Then she puts on 70 more beads. Now there are 130 beads on the string. How many beads did she put on the string to start?

____

2. Take From: Unknown Start Greta puts some beads on a string. Then 70 of the beads fell off the string. There are 60 beads still on the string. How many beads were there at first?

____

3. Add To: Unknown Start Patrick was carrying some booklets. His teacher asked him to carry 30 more booklets. Now he has 110 booklets. How many booklets did he start with?

____

4. Take From: Unknown Start Patricia was carrying some pencils. Her friend took 30 of them. Patricia has 80 pencils left. How many pencils was she carrying at first?

____

Represent Unknown Start Problems with Math Tools

The equations and Math Mountains below show the word problems on page 397.

Add To: Unknown Start

Situation Equation:

$\square + 70 = 130$

start more now

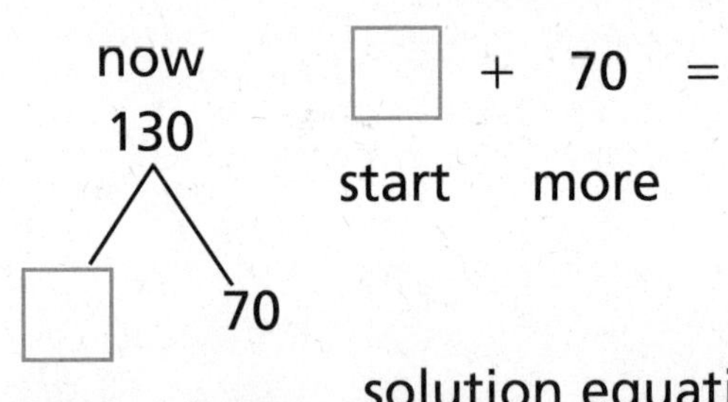

solution equations:

$70 + \square = 130$

$130 - 70 = \square$

Take From: Unknown Start

Situation Equation:

$\square - 70 = 60$

beads fell off on

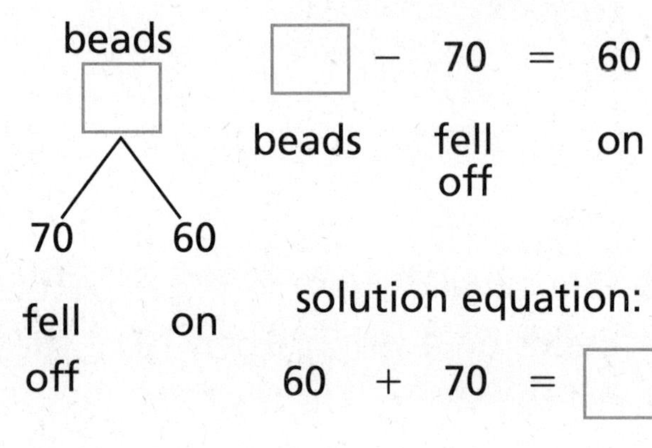

solution equation:

$60 + 70 = \square$

Add To: Unknown Start

Situation Equation:

$\square + 30 = 110$

start more now

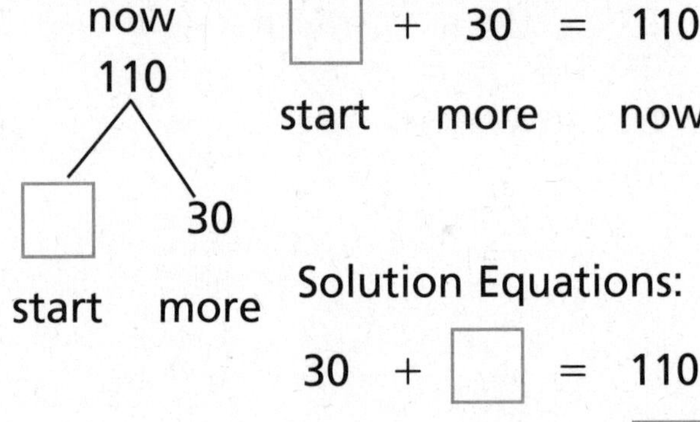

Solution Equations:

$30 + \square = 110$

$110 - 30 = \square$

Take From: Unknown Start

Situation Equation:

$\square - 30 = 80$

start friend now

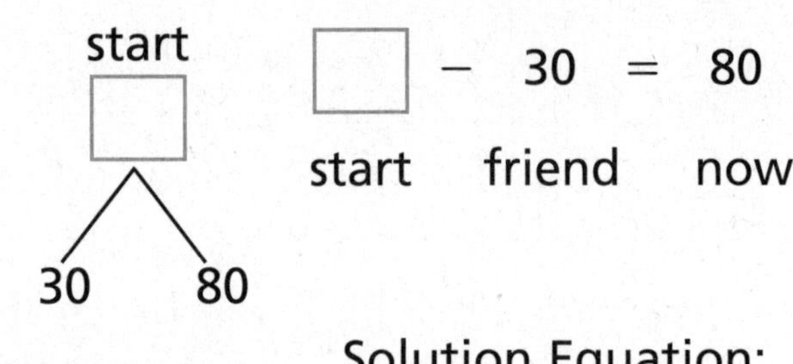

Solution Equation:

$80 + 30 = \square$

5. Write the unknown numbers in the boxes.

6. How are these math tools alike? How are they different?

____

____

Name ____________________

Write Situation and Solution Equations

Write a situation equation and a solution equation. Then solve the problem.

7. Eight vans with the same number of students in each van took 40 students to the science center for a field trip. How many students were in each van?

Situation Equation: ____________________

Solution Equation: ____________________

8. Fiona made some barrettes. She put 9 beads on each barrette. If she used 63 beads, how many barrettes did she make?

Situation Equation: ____________________

Solution Equation: ____________________

9. A bird sanctuary has 81 birds. There are 9 birds in each section. How many section are there?

Situation Equation: ____________________

Solution Equation: ____________________

10. Enrique has 56 miniature cars. He put the same number of cars on 7 shelves in his room. How many cars are on each shelf?

Situation Equation: ____________________

Solution Equation: ____________________

Write Situation and Solution Equations (continued)

Write a situation equation and a solution equation. Then solve the problem.

11 A group of 48 students from 8 schools are competing in the science fair. Each school sends the same number of students. How many students are competing from each school?

Situation Equation: ______________________

Solution Equation: ______________________

12 An array on one wall in an art gallery has 27 photographs. Each row has 9 photographs. How many rows are there?

Situation Equation: ______________________

Solution Equation: ______________________

13 Jody bought 4 bags of lemons. The same number of lemons was in each bag. There were a total of 36 lemons. How many lemons were in each bag?

Situation Equation: ______________________

Solution Equation: ______________________

14 A hardware store sold a number of boxes of furnace filters. There were 6 filters in each box. If they sold 54 furnace filters, how many boxes of filters did the hardware store sell?

Situation Equation: ______________________

Solution Equation: ______________________

Check Understanding

Explain the difference between a situation equation and a solution equation.

Name ______________________________

Compare Numbers

Compare the numbers. Write $>$, $<$, or $=$ in each ◯.

1. 34 ◯ 86
2. 97 ◯ 67
3. 653 ◯ 663
4. 875 ◯ 587
5. 752 ◯ 572
6. 864 ◯ 846
7. 1,932 ◯ 2,951
8. 2,633 ◯ 2,487
9. 3,478 ◯ 3,478
10. 4,786 ◯ 4,876

Order Numbers

Write the numbers in order from greatest to least.

11. 69; 20; 81

    ____

12. 381; 124; 197

    ____

Write the numbers in order from least to greatest.

13. 2,245; 1,642; 787

    ____

14. 1,987; 1,898; 1,789

    ____

Discuss Comparison Problems

Solve each problem. Label your answers.

David has 5 marbles. Ana has 8 marbles.

15. How many more marbles does Ana have than David? ___________

16. How many fewer marbles does David have than Ana? ___________

Here are two ways to represent the comparison situation.

Comparison Drawing

Ana OOOOOOOO

David OOOOO

Comparison Bars

Ana	8	
David	5	?

Claire has 8 marbles. Sasha has 15 marbles.

Show your work.

17. How many more marbles does Sasha have than Claire? ___________

18. How many fewer marbles does Claire have than Sasha? ___________

Rocky has 7 fishing lures. Megan has 12 fishing lures.

19. How many fewer fishing lures does Rocky have than Megan? ___________

Name ______________________________

Comparison Problems With an Unknown Larger or Smaller Amount

Solve each problem. Label your answers.

Show your work.

20 Unknown Larger Amount Maribel has 18 stickers. Arnon has 13 more stickers than Maribel. How many stickers does Arnon have?

____

21 Unknown Smaller Amount Arnon has 31 stickers. Maribel has 13 fewer stickers than Arnon. How many stickers does Maribel have?

____

22 Unknown Larger Amount Ivan has 19 goldfish. Milo has 15 more goldfish than Ivan. How many goldfish does Milo have?

____

23 Unknown Smaller Amount Milo has 34 goldfish. Ivan has 15 fewer goldfish than Milo. How many goldfish does Ivan have?

____

Use Comparison Bars to Represent an Unknown Amount

Solve each problem. Label your answers.

Show your work.

24 **Unknown Smaller Amount** T.J. has 18 fewer miniature cars than Corey. Corey has 32 miniature cars. How many miniature cars does T.J. have?

____

25 **Unknown Larger Amount** Corey has 18 more miniature cars than T.J. T.J. has 14 miniature cars. How many miniature cars does Corey have?

____

26 **Unknown Smaller Amount** Grace has 19 fewer stuffed animals than Sophia. Sophia has 31 stuffed animals. How many stuffed animals does Grace have?

____

27 **Unknown Larger Amount** Sophia has 19 more stuffed animals than Grace. Grace has 12 stuffed animals. How many stuffed animals does Sophia have?

____

Check Understanding

Jen has 14 more dolls than Avery. Avery has 16 dolls. Draw comparison bars to find the number of dolls Jen has.

Name ______________________

What's the Error?

Dear Math Students,

As part of my math homework, I solved this problem:

Carlos has 19 fish. He has 14 fewer fish than Daniel. How many fish does Daniel have?

Here is what I did: 19 − 14 = 5

Daniel has 5 fish.

Carlos	19	
Daniel	?	14

Is my answer right? If not, please correct my work, and tell me what I did wrong.

Your friend,
Puzzled Penguin

1. Write an answer to Puzzled Penguin.

____

____

Solve Comparison Problems with Misleading Language

Solve each problem on a separate piece of paper.

2. **Unknown Smaller Amount**
Daniel has 23 fish. He has 15 more fish than Carlos. How many fish does Carlos have?

____

3. **Unknown Larger Amount**
Gina ran 12 laps. She ran 8 fewer laps than Bettina. How many laps did Bettina run?

____

4. **Unknown Smaller Amount**
Bettina ran 20 laps. She ran 8 more laps than Gina. How many laps did Gina run?

____

5. **Unknown Larger Amount**
Sara read 18 books this year. She read 13 fewer books than Lupe. How many books did Lupe read this year?

____

Solve Comparison Problems Without the Words *More* or *Fewer*

Solve each problem. Label your answers.

Show your work.

6 The coach brought 18 hockey sticks to practice. There were 23 players at practice. How many players didn't get sticks?

____

7 At a meeting, 15 people had to stand because there were not enough chairs. There were 12 chairs. How many people came to the meeting?

____

8 At the park, 4 of the children could not swing because there were not enough swings. There were 20 children at the park. How many swings were on the swing set?

____

9 Maile stepped on 14 tiles along the garden path. There were 13 tiles she did not step on. How many tiles were there along the path?

____

Check Understanding

Rewrite the comparison statement "Pete has 12 fewer tools than Cooper" using the word *more*.

____

Name ____________________

Solve Problems with Extra Information

Read each problem. Cross out any extra information. Then solve.

1. Emma solved 9 math problems and answered 7 reading questions. Her sister solved 8 math problems. How many math problems did they solve in all?

____

2. Mark had 6 shirts and 5 pairs of pants. Today his aunt gave him 4 more shirts and another pair of pants. How many shirts does he have now?

____

3. A parking lot had 179 cars and 95 trucks. Then 85 cars left the lot. How many cars are in the parking lot now?

____

4. Laura had some roses in a vase. From her garden, she picked 7 more roses and 6 daisies. Now she has 12 roses in all. How many roses did she have at first?

____

5. Nikko had 245 pennies and 123 nickels. His brother gave him 89 more pennies and 25 more nickels. How many pennies does Nikko have now?

____

Solve Problems with Hidden Information

Read each problem. Circle the hidden information. Then solve.

6 Samuel had 16 new horseshoes in the shed yesterday. Today, he put a new set of horseshoes on his horse Betsy. How many horseshoes are left in the shed?

____

7 Maya is going on a vacation with her family for a week and 3 days. How many days will she be on vacation?

____

8 Julie bought a dozen eggs at the market. She gave 3 of them to Serge. How many eggs does Julie have left?

____

9 Lisa had 3 quarters and 2 dimes. Then she found 3 nickels and 12 pennies. What is the value of the coins in cents she has now?

____

10 Marissa is moving away. She is going to move back in 1 year and 21 days. How many days will she be gone?

____

Name

Recognize Word Problems with Not Enough Information

Tell what information is needed to solve each problem.

11. Sara bought 8 bananas at the fruit market. She put them in a bowl with some oranges. How many pieces of fruit are in the bowl?

12. Rebecca did 112 dives in competition last summer. This summer, she did many more dives in competition. How many competition dives did she do in the two summers?

13. Meg bought 3 mystery books and put them on the shelf with her other mystery books. How many mystery books are now on the shelf?

14. Our school has 5 soccer balls, 6 basketballs, and 4 footballs. Today, some of the footballs were lost. How many balls does the school have now?

Solve Word Problems with Not Enough Information

If more information is needed, rewrite the problem to include the necessary information. Then solve it.

Show your work.

15. Leah began fishing at 2:00 P.M. She stopped at dinnertime. How many hours did Leah fish?

____

____

16. The train traveled 376 miles on Thursday. It traveled even more miles on Friday. How many miles did the train travel on the two days?

____

____

17. The Kitchen Store sold 532 pans and 294 pots. Then some pans were returned. How many pans were not returned?

____

____

18. Julio and Scott played 6 card games and 4 computer games today. How many hours did they play games?

____

____

✓ Check Understanding

Write extra information from a problem above that is not needed to solve the problem. ________________

____

Name ______________________ Date ______________

Solve the problem. Label your answer.

Show your work.

1. Marie drove 43 miles. Sherry drove 15 miles. How many more miles did Marie drive than Sherry?

____

2. George had some money in his wallet. He spent $35 but still has $27 left. How much money did he have in his wallet before he spent any of it?

____

3. There are 63 potatoes in a sack. There are 29 rotten potatoes in the sack. How many are not rotten?

____

4. Jessica scored 38 points fewer than Elizabeth. Jessica scored 54 points. How many points did Elizabeth score?

____

Read the problem. Circle the hidden information. Then solve.

5. Omar buys a dozen oranges at the market. He uses 5 of them to make juice. How many oranges does Omar have left?

____

Fluency Check 11

Name ____________________ Date ____________________

PATH to FLUENCY

Multiply or divide.

1. $4 \times 1 = \square$
2. $2 \div 1 = \square$
3. $3 \times 2 = \square$
4. $9 \div 3 = \square$
5. $5 \times 6 = \square$
6. $24 \div 4 = \square$
7. $8 \times 5 = \square$
8. $63 \div 7 = \square$
9. $9 \times 9 = \square$

Add or subtract.

10. $\begin{array}{r} 478 \\ -\ 265 \\ \hline \end{array}$
11. $\begin{array}{r} 243 \\ +\ 536 \\ \hline \end{array}$
12. $\begin{array}{r} 562 \\ -\ 348 \\ \hline \end{array}$
13. $\begin{array}{r} 635 \\ +\ 258 \\ \hline \end{array}$
14. $\begin{array}{r} 824 \\ -\ 659 \\ \hline \end{array}$
15. $\begin{array}{r} 579 \\ +\ 323 \\ \hline \end{array}$

 Name ______________________

Write First-Step Questions

Write the first-step question and answer. Then solve the problem.

1. The orchard has 8 rows of apple trees. There are 7 rows with 6 apple trees and one row with 4 apple trees. How many apple trees are in the orchard?

   ____

   ____

2. Ms. Hayes bought 4 packs of pencils with 10 pencils in each pack. She divided the pencils evenly among her 5 children. How many pencils did each child get?

   ____

   ____

3. Kylen made 30 necklaces and gave 6 away. She put the rest in 4 boxes with an equal number in each box. How many necklaces were in each box?

   ____

   ____

4. Libby had 42 vacation pictures and 12 birthday pictures. She put an equal number of pictures in 9 photo folders. How many pictures did she put in each photo folder?

   ____

   ____

5. Mr. Cerda bought 9 boxes of tiles. Each box had 8 tiles. He used all but 5 of the tiles. How many tiles did Mr. Cerda use?

   ____

   ____

Write First-Step Questions (continued)

Write the first-step question and answer. Then solve the problem.

Show your work.

6. A bus has 10 seats that can each hold 2 passengers and another seat that can hold 3 passengers. How many passengers can be seated on the bus?

7. Dana made 6 fruit baskets. She put 4 apples, 2 pears, and 3 oranges in each basket. How many pieces of fruit did Dana use in all?

8. Cecilia ordered 5 pizzas for a group of friends. Each pizza had 8 slices. All but 3 slices were eaten. How many slices were eaten?

9. Randall has 122 coins in his collection. He has 50 coins that are quarters and the rest are nickels. If he fills 9 pages in a coin folder with the same number of nickels, how many nickels are on each page?

Check Understanding

Explain how you know a problem is a two-step problem.

Name ____________________

What's the Error?

Dear Math Students,

My teacher gave me this problem:

Luther had 11 sheets of color paper. There were 6 orange sheets, and the rest were blue. Today he used 2 sheets of blue paper. How many sheets of blue paper does Luther have now?

Here is what I did: 11 − 6 = 5
Luther now has 5 blue sheets.

Is my answer correct? If not, please correct my work and tell me what I did wrong.

Your friend,
Puzzled Penguin

1. Write an answer to Puzzled Penguin.

____

Solve Two-Step Word Problems

Solve each problem. Label your answers.

2. The bus had 14 passengers. When it stopped, 5 people got off and 8 people got on. How many people are riding the bus now?

____

3. There are 15 fish in a tank. 12 have stripes, and the others are do not. How many more striped fish are there than fish without stripes?

____

Solve and Discuss

Solve each problem. Label your answers.

4. Sun Mi picked 14 apricots. Celia picked 5 fewer apricots than Sun Mi. How many apricots did Sun Mi and Celia pick altogether?

___

5. Annie took 8 photographs at home and 7 photographs at school. Her sister Amanda took 6 fewer photographs than Annie. How many photographs did Amanda take?

___

6. There are 5 sheep, 3 goats, and some rabbits in the petting zoo. Altogether there are 15 animals in the petting zoo. How many rabbits are there?

___

7. A new library opened on Saturday. The library lent out 234 books on Saturday. On Sunday, they lent out 138 books. By the end of the weekend, 78 books were returned. How many books were not returned?

___

8. Katie had 8 dimes and some nickels in her duck bank. She had 4 more nickels than dimes. She took out 5 nickels to put in her coin purse. How many nickels are in her duck bank now?

___

9. Tony had 14 color pencils. There were 9 of them that needed to be sharpened, and the rest were sharp. Yesterday, his uncle gave him some new color pencils. Now Tony has 12 sharp color pencils. How many color pencils did his uncle give him?

___

Name ______________________________

Is the Answer Reasonable?

Use rounding or mental math to decide if the answer is reasonable. Write *yes* or *no*. Then write an equation and solve the problem to see if you were correct.

Show your work.

10 Chelsea's class collected cans of food for their local food pantry. They collected 27 cans on Monday and 78 cans on Tuesday. Then on Wednesday they collected 53 cans. How many cans did the class collect on those three days?
Answer: 158 cans

____

11 Barry strings beads. He had 54 beads on a string and he took off 29 beads. Then he took off 5 more. How many beads are on the string now?
Answer: 35 beads

____

12 Dena counted the books on three shelves of the classroom library. She counted 33 books on the top shelf, 52 books on the middle shelf, and 48 books on the bottom shelf. How many books are on the three shelves?
Answer: 163 books

____

13 Ms. Lance bought 6 packages of paper cups. Each package has 20 cups. She used 78 cups for a party. How many cups does Ms. Lance have left?
Answer: 58 cups

____

Reasonable Answers

Use rounding or mental math to decide if the answer is reasonable. Write *yes* or *no*. Then write an equation and solve the problem to see if you were correct.

Show your work.

14 There were 83 students in a spelling contest. First, 9 students were eliminated. Then 29 students were eliminated. How many students were left?
Answer: 24 students

____

15 During one week Tina rode her bicycle 42 miles and Jim rode 9 fewer miles than Tina. How many miles did they ride altogether that week?
Answer: 75 miles

____

16 It costs $10 a day to care for a cat or dog in the animal shelter. The total cost one day was $90. There were 5 dogs at the shelter and the rest were cats. How many cats were at the shelter that day?
Answer: 9 cats

____

17 Jake is saving money for a bike that costs $187. He saved $55 in April and $44 in May. How much more money does Jake need to buy the bike?
Answer: $88

____

Check Understanding

Explain how you decided if $88 for Problem 17 was reasonable.

Name ______________________________

Equations and Two-Step Word Problems

Write an equation and solve the problem.

Show your work.

1. Mrs. Delgado is baking pies and cakes for a school fundraiser. She bought 26 apples, 29 peaches, and a number of bananas at the Farmers' Market. She bought 66 pieces of fruit. How many bananas did she buy?

   ____

2. Abby bought 8 packages of stickers with the same number of stickers in each package. She gave 15 stickers to her sister. Now Abby has 49 stickers. How many stickers were in each package?

   ____

3. Taylor is reading a 340-page book. He read 174 pages of the book on Saturday and 120 pages on Sunday. How many pages does he have left to read?

   ____

4. Lauren had a piece of ribbon that was 36 inches long. She cut a number of 3-inch pieces. She has 15 inches of ribbon left. How many 3-inch pieces did she cut?

   ____

5. There are 47 students in the marching band. There are 5 students in the first row, and the rest are in equal rows of 6. How many students are in each of the 6 rows?

   ____

Solve Two-Step Word Problems

Write an equation and solve the problem. *Show your work.*

6. Sara baked 48 cookies and gave a dozen cookies to her friend. She put the remaining cookies on plates of 9 cookies each. How many plates did she use?

7. Marissa is making floral bouquets. She bought 56 tulips, 73 daisies, and some roses. She bought 153 flowers in all. How many roses did she buy?

8. Tom has 103 photos on his digital camera. He deletes 33 photos. He prints the remaining photos and puts an equal number on each page of an album that has 10 pages. How many photos are on each page?

9. Leo bought 6 sets of books. Each set had the same number of books. He donated 11 books to the school library. Now he has 37 books left. How many books were in each set of books Leo bought?

10. Amber has 5 packages of chalk. Each package has 9 pieces of chalk. She gave a number of pieces of chalk to her brother. Amber has 37 pieces of chalk left. How many pieces did Amber give her brother?

Check Understanding

Describe the strategy you used to solve Problem 10.

 Name ______________________

Write Two-Step Equations

Write an equation and solve the problem.

Show your work.

1. Carrie played a video game and scored 20 points 7 times and 55 points 1 time. How many points did Carrie score?

 ____

2. Darin earns $8 each week doing chores. He is saving his money to buy a game that costs $49 and a cap that costs $15. How many weeks will Darin need to save his money?

 ____

3. A dog trainer is working with 7 dogs. He rewards each dog with the same number of treats. He started with 35 treats and he has 7 left. How many treats did he give each dog?

 ____

4. A truck is carrying a mother elephant and her calf. The mother elephant weighs 6,728 pounds. The elephant calf weighs 205 pounds. The truck can carry a total of 8,900 pounds. How many pounds of feed for the elephants can be loaded on the truck?

 ____

5. Eli has 36 stamps and his brother has 24 stamps. They put their stamps in the same book. They put the same number of stamps on each page. They used 10 pages. How many stamps are on each page?

 ____

Write Two-Step Equations (continued)

Write an equation and solve the problem.

Show your work.

6 There were 9 rows of chairs set up in the school gym. Each row had 20 chairs. After the students were seated, there were 12 empty chairs. How many chairs were filled?

____

7 Eric had 143 baseball cards. His uncle gave him a number more. Then Eric gave 26 cards to a friend. He has 184 cards now. How many cards did Eric's uncle give him?

____

8 Brandi had 8 equal rows of stickers. She bought 5 more and now she has 53 stickers. How many were in each row before she bought more?

____

9 There are 5,280 feet in a mile. In a 1-mile relay race Jessie ran 2,400 feet. Her friend Maddie ran 1,800 feet. How many feet did the third runner run to finish the race?

____

10 A science poster shows 9 insects with 6 legs each and a spider with 8 legs. How many legs is that altogether?

____

Check Understanding

Explain how you decided which operations to use in your equation for Problem 10.

Name ______________________________

Sports Statistics in the News

Little League Baseball Championships: Wheaton Wolves Score Win

Wheaton Wolves win Little League World Series Championship. The chart shows some statistics from the six games the team played.

Wheaton Wolves Statistics	
Times at Bat	155
Hits	47
Base on Balls	25
Runs Scored	36
Strike Outs	36

Use the information in the table to write an equation and solve the problem.

1. How many times at bat did players not strike out or get a base on balls?

____

2. How many hits and base on balls did not result in a run?

____

3. The Wheaton Wolves had 13 triple or double-base hits, 3 homeruns, and the rest were single-base hits. How many single-base hits did the team get?

____

Sports News

Danielle plays on a third grade basketball team in a league. Her team made the news when they scored 47 points, 41 points, and 53 points in a three-game tournament.

Write a two-step equation and solve the problem.

4. How many points did Danielle's team score altogether?

____

5. Describe how you can use mental math to decide if your answer to Problem 4 is reasonable.

____

____

____

6. Danielle's scorecard shows her statistics for the three games. Use the information in the table to write equations to find the unknown numbers. Then complete the table.

____

____

	Number of 1-pt Free Throws	Number of 2-pt Field Goals	Total Points
Game 1	5	7	
Game 2		6	18
Game 3	3		21

Name _______________ Date _______________

Complete.

Show your work.

1. Lila makes bags of stickers that are exactly the same for 5 friends. She uses a total of 45 stickers. Each bag has 2 butterfly stickers and the rest are flower stickers. How many flower stickers are in each bag? Write a first-step question and answer. Then solve the problem.

____

____

2. Troy saves money for a bike that costs $126. He saves $58 one month and $43 the next month. How much more money does Troy need to buy the bike?
   Answer: $15
   Is the answer reasonable? Explain.

____

3. The Downtown bus has 16 passengers. When it stops, 4 people get off and 7 people get on. How many passengers are on the Downtown bus now?

____

Write an equation and solve the problem.

4. Lauren has 109 rare coins. She sells 37 coins. She wants to put the rest of the coins in an album. Each page in the album holds 8 coins. How many pages will she use?

____

____

____

5. Peyton cuts a pipe into two pieces. One piece has a length of 13 feet. The other piece is 9 feet shorter. How long was the pipe Peyton cut?

____

____

____

Name ____________________ Date ____________________

Multiply or divide.

1. $4 \div 2 = \square$
2. $2 \times 4 = \square$
3. $72 \div 8 = \square$
4. $3 \times 8 = \square$
5. $25 \div 5 = \square$
6. $8 \times 4 = \square$
7. $40 \div 8 = \square$
8. $9 \times 6 = \square$
9. $80 \div 8 = \square$

Add or subtract.

10. $\begin{array}{r} 211 \\ +\ 167 \\ \hline \end{array}$
11. $\begin{array}{r} 472 \\ -\ 231 \\ \hline \end{array}$
12. $\begin{array}{r} 527 \\ +\ 268 \\ \hline \end{array}$
13. $\begin{array}{r} 682 \\ -\ 537 \\ \hline \end{array}$
14. $\begin{array}{r} 636 \\ +\ 289 \\ \hline \end{array}$
15. $\begin{array}{r} 911 \\ -\ 685 \\ \hline \end{array}$

Name ____________________ Date ____________

1. Mr. Taylor arranges some chairs in rows. He puts the same number of chairs in each of 7 rows and puts 7 chairs in the last row. He sets up 70 chairs. How many chairs does he put in each of the 7 equal rows?

Choose the equation that can be used to solve the problem.

I can use the equation

- $(7 \times c) + 7 = 70$
- $(70 \div 7) + 7 = c$
- $(7 \times c) - 7 = 70$

.

Solve the problem.

______ chairs

2. Marisol picks 150 flowers. She picks 80 red flowers and the rest are yellow. She sells 45 yellow flowers. How many yellow flowers does she have now?

For numbers 2a–2e, choose Yes or No to tell whether the equation can be used to find the number of yellow flowers Marisol has now.

2a.	$150 - 80 - 45 = y$	○ Yes	○ No
2b.	$150 + 80 - 45 = y$	○ Yes	○ No
2c.	$150 + 80 + 45 = y$	○ Yes	○ No
2d.	$150 = 80 + 45 + y$	○ Yes	○ No
2e.	$150 = 80 - 45 + y$	○ Yes	○ No

Name ________________ Date ________________

3 Mark makes 18 picture frames this month. He makes 7 fewer picture frames than Sara. How many picture frames does Sara make?

Draw comparison bars to represent the problem. Then solve.

______ picture frames.

4 David and Marne pick cucumbers at a farm. David picks 93 cucumbers. How many cucumbers does Marne pick?

What information is not helpful for solving the problem?

Ⓐ how many more cucumbers David picks

Ⓑ how many fewer cucumbers Marne picks

Ⓒ how many cucumbers are grown at the farm each year

Ⓓ how many cucumbers David and Marne pick

Rewrite the problem to include the necessary information. Then solve it.

Name ______________________ Date ______________________

5. There are 240 boys and girls in a soccer league. There are 130 girls. How many boys are there?

Write an equation with a variable to represent the problem. Then draw a Math Mountain to solve the problem.

______________ boys

6. On Wednesday, Jonah sees 30 birds and 4 rabbits. Of the birds, 13 are robins and the rest are pigeons. On Thursday, he sees some more pigeons. He has now seen 21 pigeons. How many pigeons did he see on Thursday?

Part A Write the information in the correct box.

30 birds 4 rabbits 13 robins 21 pigeons

Needed Information	Extra Information

Part B Solve the problem. What strategy did you use? How did it help?

Name ______________________ Date ______________________

7 Susan buys 24 postcards. She sends 6 postcards to friends. She puts the rest in 3 folders, with an equal number in each folder. How many postcards are in each folder?

Write the first step question and answer. Then solve.

______________ postcards

8 Kato uses 56 photos to make online albums. He puts 7 photos in each album. How many albums does Kato make?

For Exercises 8a–8d, select True or False if the equation can be used to solve the problem.

8a. $7 \times a = 56$ ○ True ○ False

8b. $56 \div 7 = a$ ○ True ○ False

8c. $7 \times 56 = a$ ○ True ○ False

8d. $56 \div a = 7$ ○ True ○ False

9 Tara posts 35 flyers for the school carnival. Keisha posts 8 more flyers than Tara. How many flyers did Tara and Keisha post? Choose the number that completes the sentence.

Tara and Keisha post [43 / 62 / 78] flyers.

Name ______________________ Date ______________________

10 Jason packs 54 grapefruit in 9 boxes for shipping. He packs the same number of grapefruit in each box. How many grapefruit does Jason pack into each box?

Use the numbers and symbols to write a situation equation and a solution equation. Then solve.

g 9 54  ÷ 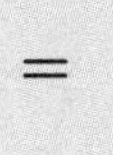

Situation Equation: ______________

Solution Equation: ______________

______________ grapefruit

11 A ship can hold 3,250 cargo containers. There are1,852 containers on the lower deck and 650 containers on the upper deck of the ship. How many more containers can be loaded on the ship? Write an equation and solve the problem.

12 Parker has 452 toy dinosaurs in his collection. His sister gives him 38 more toy dinosaurs. Then he sells some of them online. Parker now has 418 toy dinosaurs. How many did he sell?

Answer: 72 toy dinosaurs

Is the answer reasonable? Tell why or why not. Then write an equation and solve the problem.

Name ________________________________ Date ____________

13 Eva buys some items at the store and pays with pennies and nickels. Use the information in the table to write equations to find the unknown numbers. Then complete the table.

Pencil: ____________________

Eraser: ____________________

Clip: ____________________

	Number of Pennies	Number of Nickels	Total Cost
Pencil	6	8	¢
Eraser		4	24¢
Clip	2		37¢

14 Holly is going to the beach in 2 weeks and 4 days.

Which equation can be used to find the number of days until Holly goes to the beach?

Ⓐ $2 \times 7 + 4 = b$; $b = 18$ days

Ⓑ $2 \times 5 + 4 = b$; $b = 14$ days

Ⓒ $2 + 7 + 4 = b$; $b = 13$ days

Ⓓ $2 \times 7 - 4 = b$; $b = 10$ days

15 Omar has 5 ties and Ryan has 12 ties. How many more ties does Ryan have than Omar?

Make a comparison drawing to represent the problem. Then solve.

____________ more ties

Name ______________________ Date ____________

Planning a Garden

Last year community gardeners planted 8 rows of tomato plants with the same number in each row. Then they planted 10 more plants. There was a total of 58 plants. How many plants were in each row before they planted the additional 10?

1. Write an equation to represent the problem. Solve.

2. Could you write an equation for the problem using other operations than the ones you used? Explain why or why not.

3. Gardeners decided to buy stakes to help support the tomato plants. The stakes are sold in bundles of 12. If the gardeners bought 5 bundles of stakes, did they buy enough stakes? How many more do they need or how many extras do they have? Write an equation to solve. Explain the solution.

Name ______________________________ Date ______________

4 Community gardeners plan to plant pumpkins this year. Write a two-step word problem about planting pumpkins that can be solved using an equation. Solve and explain the solution.

5 The gardeners plan to plant 40 pumpkin plants. They have space for 7 rows. They would like to keep an equal number of pumpkin plants in each row, if possible. Draw a picture to show the number of pumpkin plants they should plant in each row. Write an equation to match your picture.

6 How would the garden change if gardeners planted the pumpkin plants in 8 rows?

Dear Family:

In this unit, students explore ways to measure things using the customary and metric systems of measurement.

The units of measure we will be working with include:

U.S. Customary System

Capacity
1 cup (c) = 8 fluid ounces (oz) 1 pint (pt) = 2 cups (c) 1 quart (qt) = 2 pints (pt) 1 gallon (gal) = 4 quarts (qt)
Weight
1 pound (lb) = 16 ounces (oz)

Metric System

Capacity
1 liter (L) = 1,000 milliliters (mL)
Mass
1 kilogram (kg) = 1,000 grams (g)

Students will solve problems that involve liquid volumes or masses given in the same unit by adding, subtracting, multiplying, or dividing and by using a drawing to represent the problem.

You can help your child become familiar with these units of measure by working with measurements together. For example, you might use a measuring cup to explore how the cup can be used to fill pints, quarts, or gallons of liquid.

Thank you for helping your child learn important math skills. Please contact me, if you have any questions or comments.

Sincerely,
Your child's teacher

Estimada familia:

En esta unidad los niños estudian cómo medir cosas usando el sistema usual de medidas y el sistema métrico decimal.

Las unidades de medida con las que trabajaremos incluirán:

Sistema usual

Capacidad
1 taza (tz) = 8 onzas líquidas (oz)
1 pinta (pt) = 2 tazas (tz)
1 cuarto (ct) = 2 pintas (pt)
1 galón (gal) = 4 cuartos (ct)
Peso
1 libra (lb) = 16 onzas (oz)

Sistema métrico decimal

Capacidad
1 litro (L) = 1,000 mililitros (mL)
Masa
1 kilogramo (kg) = 1,000 gramos (g)

Los estudiantes resolverán problemas relacionados con volúmenes de líquido o masas, que se dan en la misma unidad, sumando, restando o dividiendo, y usando un dibujo para representar el problema.

Puede ayudar a que su niño se familiarice con estas unidades de medida midiendo con él diversas cosas. Por ejemplo, podrían usar una taza de medidas para aprender cómo se pueden llenar pintas, cuartos o galones con líquido.

Gracias por ayudar a su niño a aprender destrezas matemáticas importantes. Si tiene alguna duda o algún comentario, por favor comuníquese conmigo.

Atentamente,
El maestro de su niño

adjacent sides	**convex**
angle	**cup (c)**
concave	**decagon**

A polygon is convex if all of its diagonals are inside it.

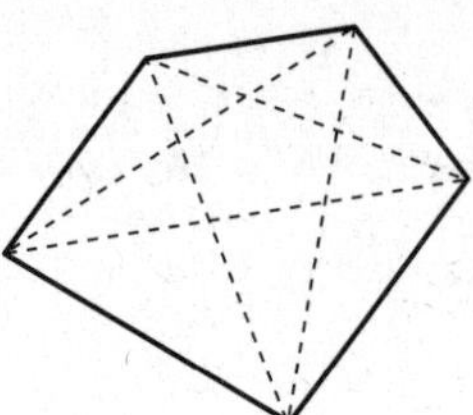

Two sides of a figure that meet at a point.

Example:
Sides *a* and *b* are adjacent.

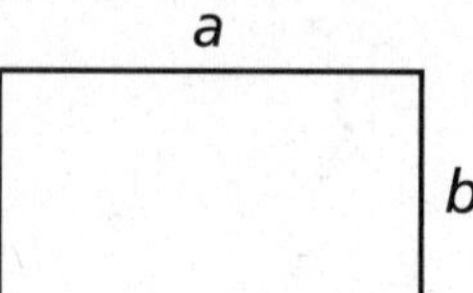

A U.S. customary unit of measure used to measure capacity.

1 cup = 8 fluid ounces
2 cups = 1 pint
4 cups = 1 quart
16 cups = 1 gallon

A figure formed by two rays or two line segments that meet at an endpoint.

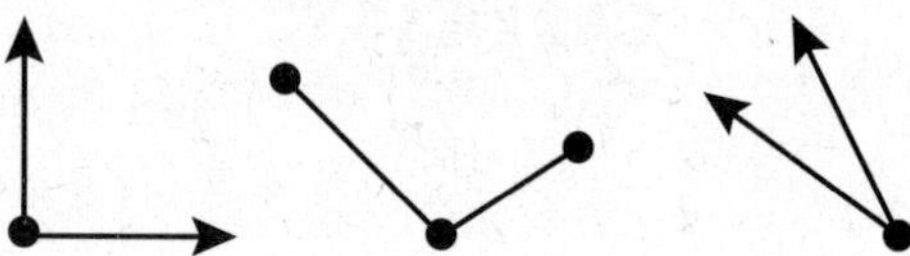

A polygon with 10 sides.

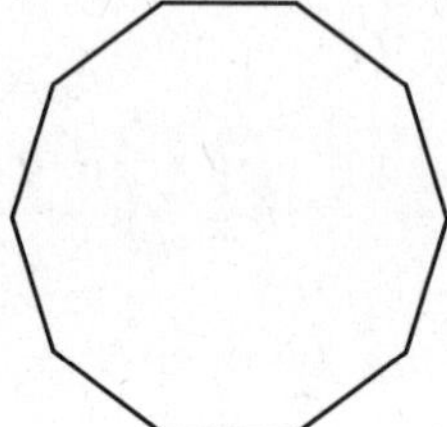

A polygon for which you can connect two points inside the polygon with a segment that passes outside the polygon.

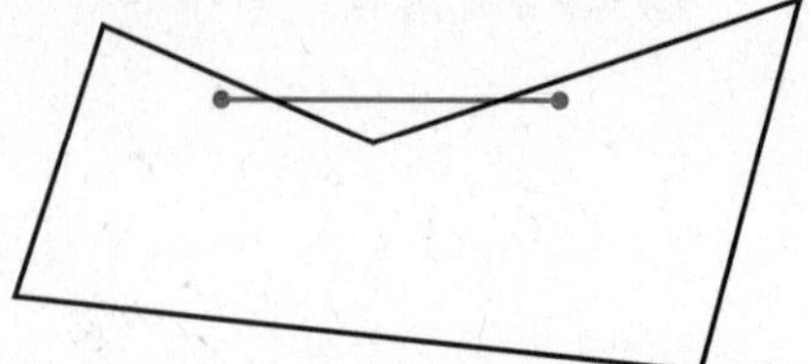

fluid ounce (fl oz)	**hexagon**
gallon (gal)	**kilogram (kg)**
gram (g)	**liquid volume**

A polygon with six sides.

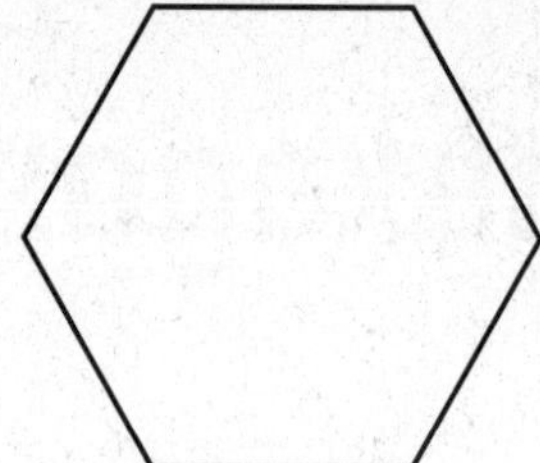

A unit of liquid volume in the U.S. customary system that equals $\frac{1}{8}$ cup or 2 tablespoons.

A metric unit of mass.

1 kilogram = 1,000 grams

A U.S. customary unit used to measure capacity.

1 gallon = 4 quarts = 8 pints = 16 cups

A measure of how much a container can hold. Also called *capacity.*

A metric unit of mass. One paper clip has a mass of about 1 gram.

1,000 grams = 1 kilogram

liter (L)	**octagon**
mass	**opposite sides**
milliliter (mL)	**ounce (oz)**

A polygon with eight sides.

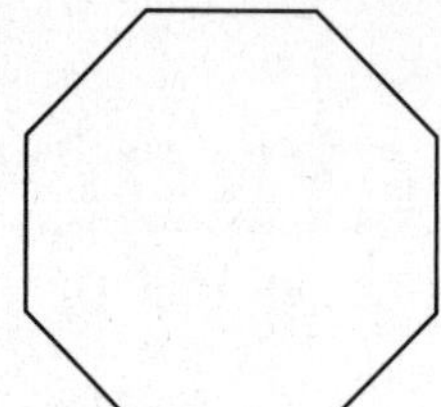

A metric unit used to measure capacity.

1 liter = 1,000 milliliters

Sides of a polygon that are across from each other; they do not meet at a point.

Example:

Sides *a* and *c* are opposite.

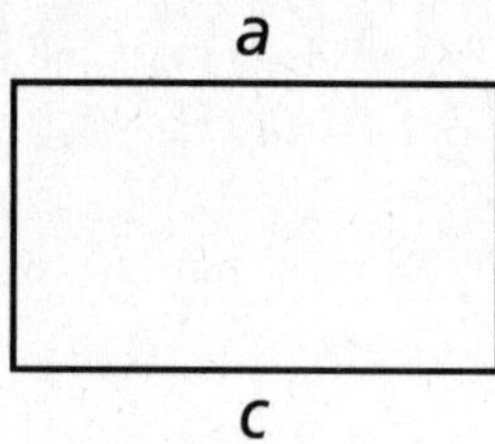

The amount of matter in an object.

A U.S. customary unit used to measure weight.

16 ounces = 1 pound

A metric unit used to measure capacity.

1,000 milliliters = 1 liter

parallel	**perpendicular**
parallelogram	**pint (pt)**
pentagon	**polygon**

Two lines are perpendicular if they cross or meet to form square corners.

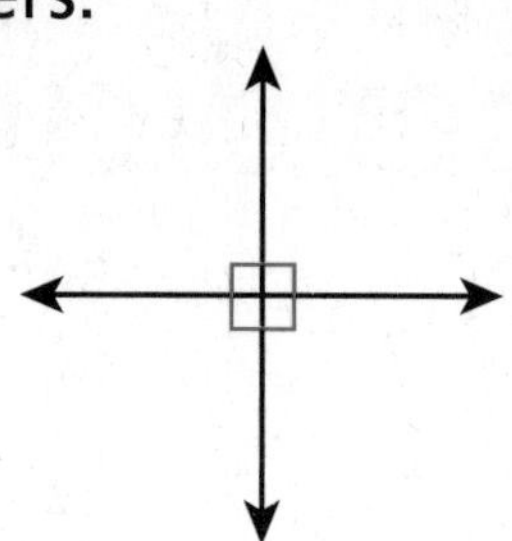

Two lines are parallel if they never cross or meet. They are the same distance apart.

A U.S. customary unit used to measure weight.

1 pint = 2 cups

A quadrilateral with both pairs of opposite sides parallel.

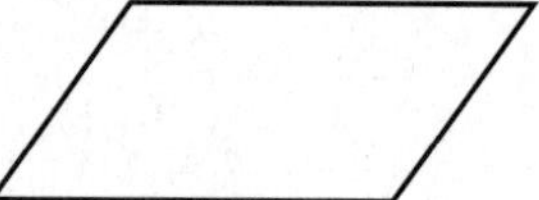

A closed plane figure with sides made up of straight line segments.

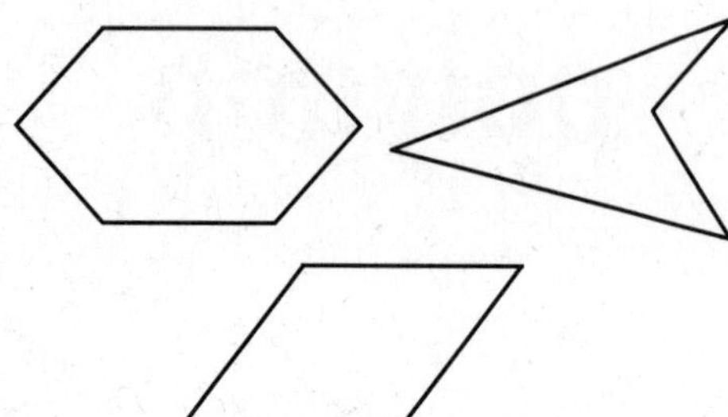

A polygon with five sides.

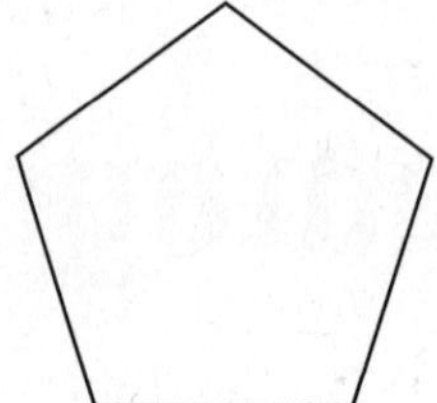

pound	**ray**
quadrilateral	**rectangle**
quart (qt)	**rhombus**

A part of a line that has one endpoint and goes on forever in one direction.

A U.S. customary unit used to measure weight.

1 pound = 16 ounces

A parallelogram that has 4 right angles.

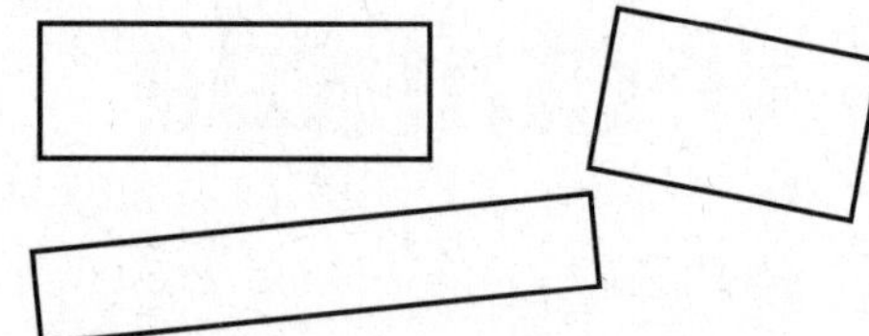

A polygon with four sides.

A parallelogram with equal sides.

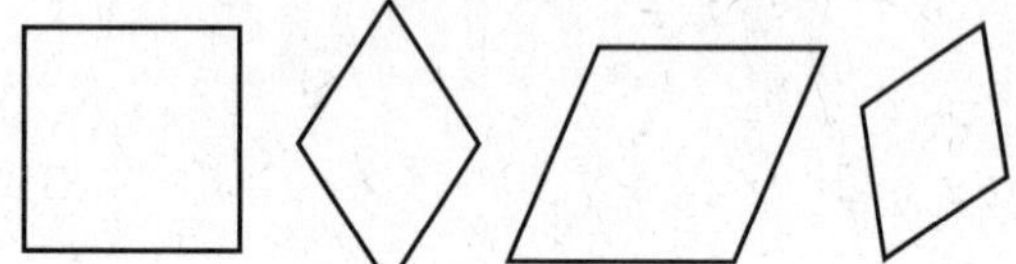

A U.S. customary unit used to measure capacity.

1 quart = 4 cups

right angle	triangle
square	vertex
trapezoid	weight

A polygon with three sides.

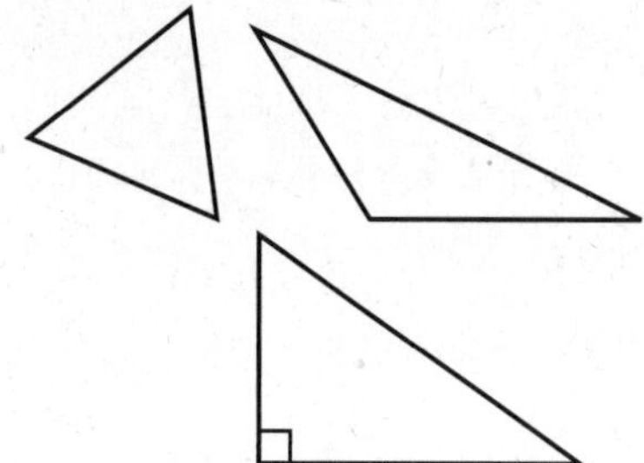

An angle that measures 90°.

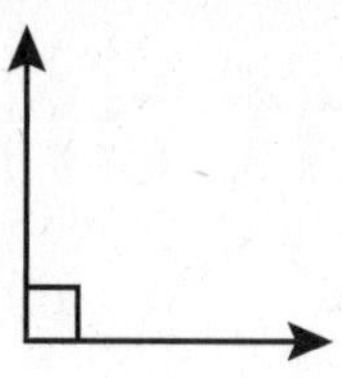

A point where sides, rays, or edges meet.

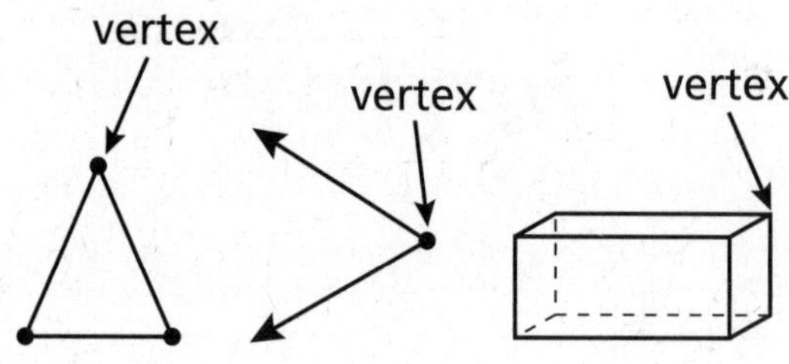

A rectangle with four sides of the same length.

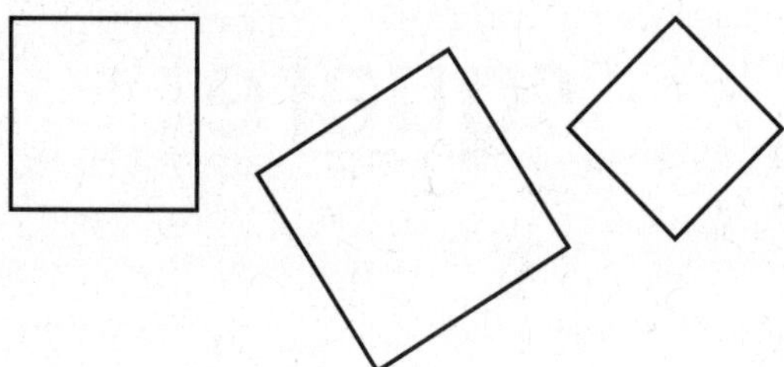

The measure of how heavy something is.

A quadrilateral with exactly one pair of parallel sides.

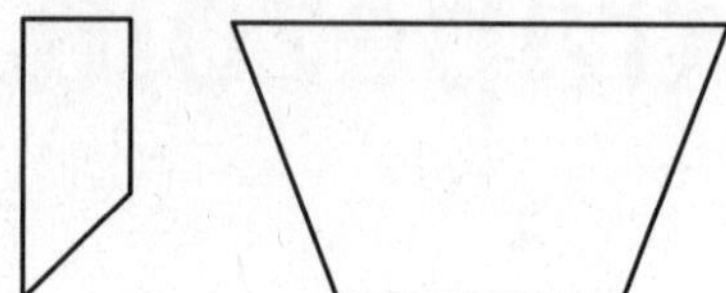

Name

Choose the Unit

VOCABULARY

liquid volume	quart (qt)
cup (c)	gallon (gal)
pint (pt)	fluid ounce (fl oz)

Choose the best unit to use to measure the liquid volume. Write *fluid ounce, cup, pint, quart,* or *gallon*.

1. a carton of heavy cream

2. a flower vase

3. a swimming pool

4. a wash tub

What's the Error?

Dear Math Students,

Today I had to choose the best unit to use to measure how much water is needed to fill a kitchen sink. I said the best unit to use is cups. Is my answer correct? If not, please correct my work and tell me what I did wrong.

Your friend,
Puzzled Penguin

5. Write an answer to Puzzled Penguin.

6. Math Journal Think of a container. Choose the unit you would use to measure its capacity. Draw the container and write the name of the unit you chose. Explain why you chose that unit.

Estimate Customary Units of Liquid Volume

Ring the better estimate.

2 cups

2 quarts

8 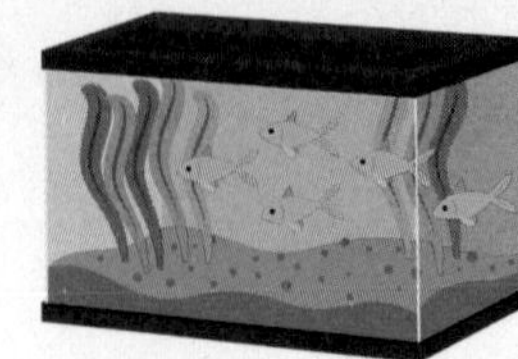

5 cups

5 gallons

1 pint

1 gallon

10 

1 cup

1 pint

1 cup

1 gallon

12 

30 cups

30 gallons

Solve.

13 Jamie makes a shopping list for a picnic with his four friends. He estimates that he'll need 5 quarts of lemonade for the group to drink. Do you think his estimate is reasonable? Explain.

___

___

___

Name ______________________________

Use Drawings to Solve Problems

Use the drawing to represent and solve the problem.

14 A painter mixes 5 pints of yellow and 3 pints of blue paint to make green paint. How many pints of green paint does he make?

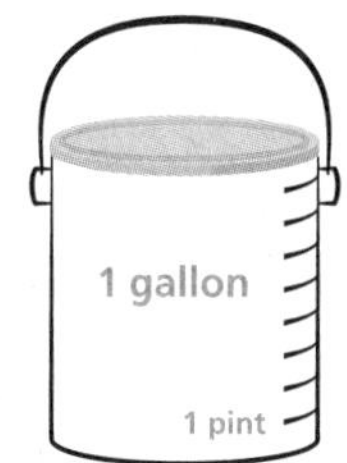

____

15 Ryan has a bottle of orange juice with 16 fluid ounces. He pours 6 fluid ounces in a cup. How many fluid ounces are left in the bottle?

____

16 A restaurant makes 8 quarts of tea. They use all the tea to fill pitchers that hold 2 quarts each. How many pitchers are filled with tea?

____

17 An ice cream machine makes 5 pints of ice cream in a batch. If 3 batches are made, how many pints of ice cream are made?

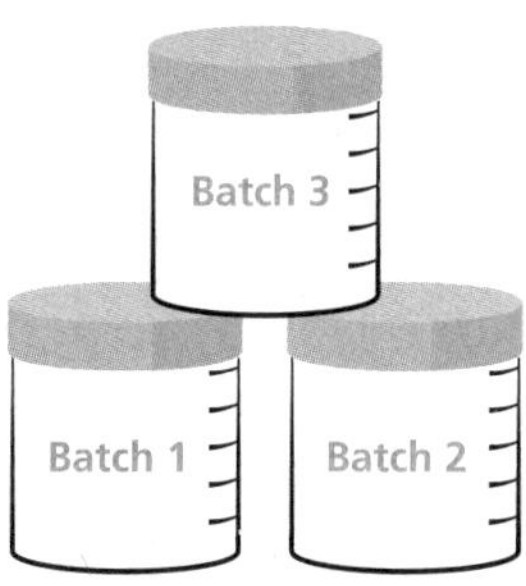

____

18 Fran has a water jug that holds 24 quarts of water. She fills it with a container that holds 4 quarts. How many times must she fill the 4-quart container and pour it into the jug to fill the jug with 24 quarts?

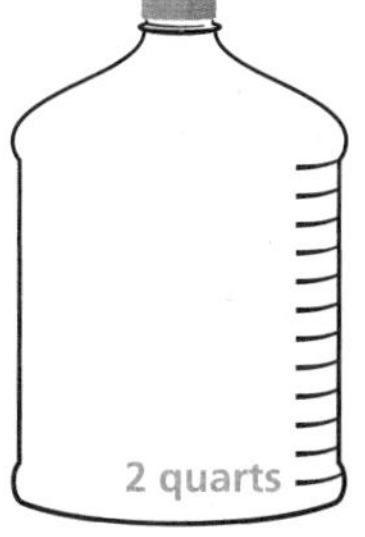

____

Solve Problems

Use the drawing to represent and solve the problem.

Show your work.

19 Shanna bought 8 juice boxes filled with her favorite juice. Each box holds 10 fluid ounces. How many fluid ounces of her favorite juice did Shanna buy?

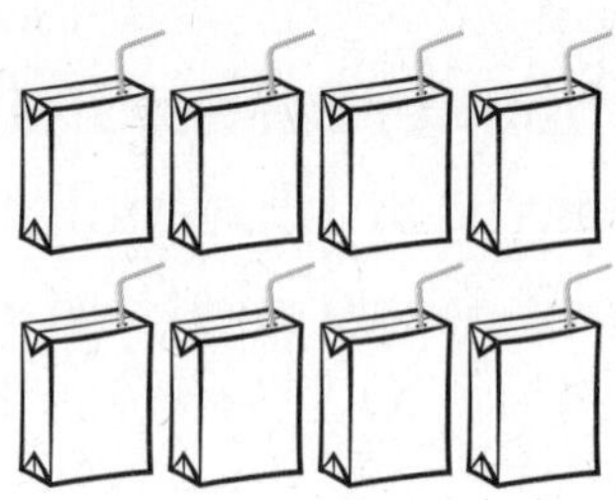

____

20 Juana filled her punch bowl with 12 cups of punch. She gave some of her friends each a cup of punch. There are 7 cups of punch left in the bowl. How many cups did she give to friends?

____

21 Mrs. Chavez made 20 quarts of pickles. She made 4 quarts each day. How many days did it take her to make the pickles?

____

22 A mid-sized aquarium holds 25 gallons of water and a large aquarium holds 35 gallons of water. How many gallons of water is needed to fill both aquariums?

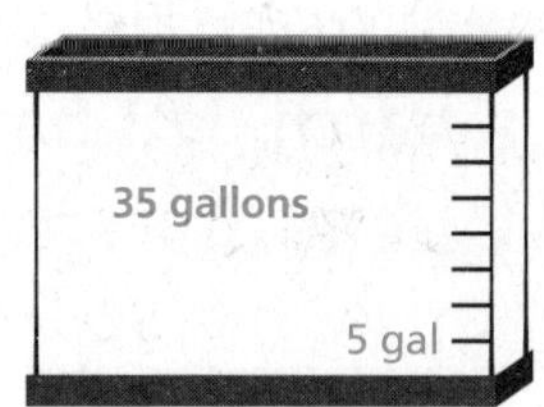

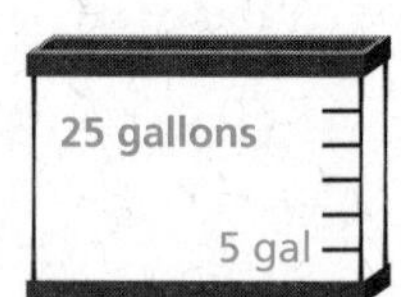

____

Check Understanding

Name the 5 units of liquid volume in this lesson from largest to smallest.

_______________, _______________, _______________,

_______________, _______________

Name ____________________

VOCABULARY
milliliter (mL)
liter (L)

Choose the Appropriate Unit

Choose the unit you would use to measure the liquid volume of each. Write *mL* or *L*.

1. a kitchen sink ______
2. a soup spoon ______
3. a teacup ______
4. a washing machine ______

Circle the better estimate.

5. a juice container 1 L 1 mL
6. a bowl of soup 500 L 500 mL

Use Drawings to Represent Problems

Use the drawing to represent and solve the problem.

7. There are 900 milliliters of water in a pitcher. Terri pours 500 milliliters of water into a bowl. How many milliliters of water are left in the pitcher?

____

8. Mr. Rojo put 6 liters of fuel into a gas can that can hold 10 liters. Then he added more liters to fill the can. How many liters of fuel did he add to the can?

____

9. Shelby needs to water each of her 3 plants with 200 milliliters of water. How many milliliters of water does she need?

____

Make Sense of Problems Involving Liquid Volume

Use the drawing to represent and solve the problem.

10 The deli sold 24 liters of juice in 3 days. The same amount was sold each day. How many liters of juice did the deli sell each day?

____

11 Tim has a bucket filled with 12 liters of water and a bucket filled with 20 liters of water. What is the total liquid volume of the buckets?

____

12 Sara made a smoothie and gave her friend 250 milliliters. There are 550 milliliters left. How many milliliters of smoothie did Sara make?

____

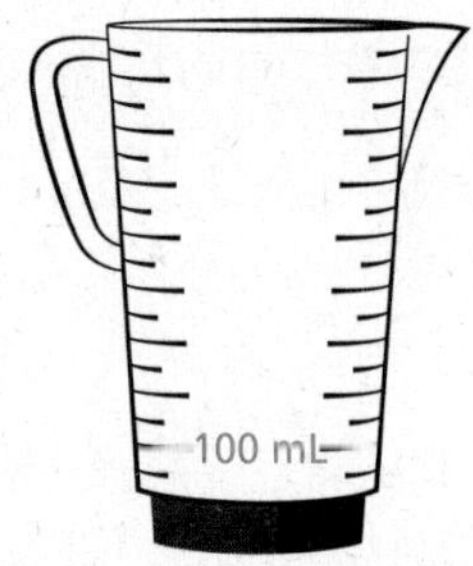

Solve. Use a drawing if you need to.

13 Diane has 12 liters of iced tea to divide equally among 4 tables. How many liters should she put at each table?

____

14 Mr. Valle filled 7 jars with his famous barbeque sauce. Each jar holds 500 milliliters. How many milliliters of sauce did he have?

____

Check Understanding

Describe the relationship between a liter and a milliliter.

Name ______________________________

VOCABULARY
weight
pound (lb)
ounce (oz)

Choose the Appropriate Unit

Choose the unit you would use to measure the weight of each. Write *pound or ounce*.

1. a backpack full of books ______________
2. a couch ______________
3. a peanut ______________
4. a pencil ______________

Circle the better estimate.

5. a student desk	3 lb	30 lb
6. a television	20 oz	20 lb
7. a hamster	5 oz	5 lb
8. a slice of cheese	1 lb	1 oz

Use Drawings to Represent Problems

Use the drawing to represent and solve the problem.

9. Selma filled each of 3 bags with 5 ounces of her favorite nuts. How many ounces of nuts did she use altogether to fill the bags?

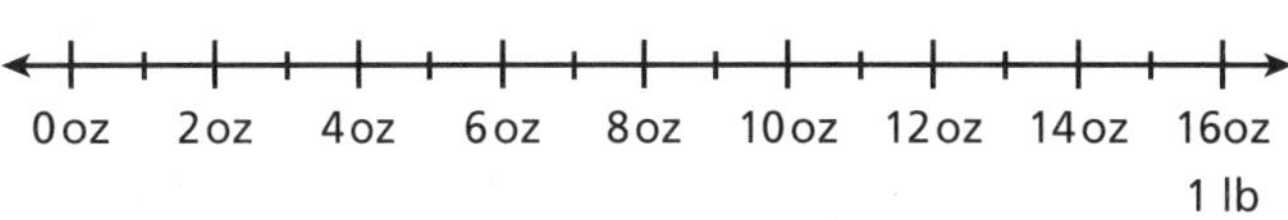

____

10. Two apples together weigh 16 ounces. If one apple weighs 9 ounces, how much does the other apple weigh?

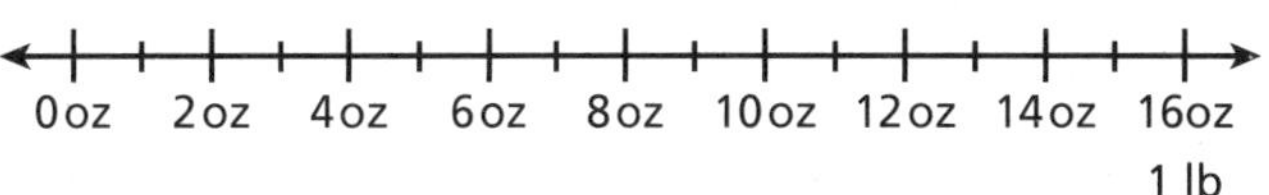

____

Use Drawings to Represent Problems (continued)

Use the drawing to represent and solve the problem.

11 Noah bought 16 ounces of turkey meat. If he uses 4 ounces to make a turkey patty, how many patties can he make?

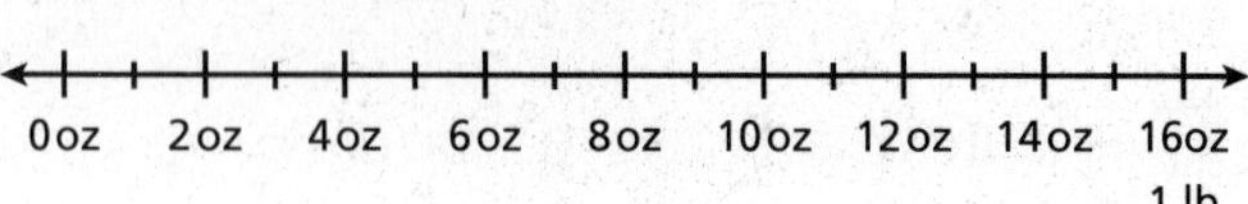

12 A package of silver beads weighs 6 ounces and a package of wooden beads weighs 7 ounces more. How much does the package of wooden beads weigh?

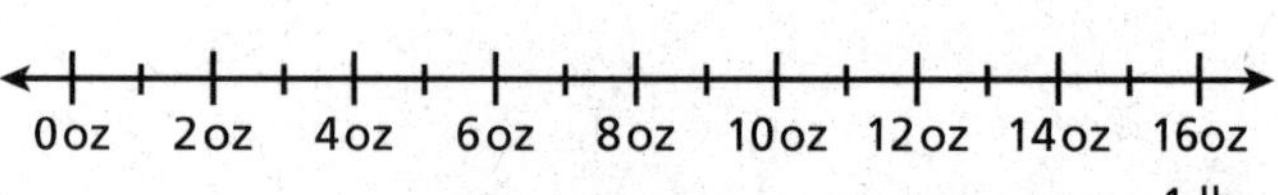

Solve Word Problems

Solve. Use a drawing if you need to.

13 Ted has two dogs. Together they weigh 88 pounds. If one dog weighs 70 pounds, how much does the other dog weigh?

14 Emma has 20 ounces of popcorn kernels in a bag. If she pops 4 ounces of kernels at a time, how many times can Emma pop corn?

15 Susan mailed 3 packages. Each package weighed 20 ounces. What was the total weight of the 3 packages?

16 Bailey caught two fish. The smaller fish weighs 14 ounces and the larger fish weighs 6 ounces more. How much does the larger fish weigh?

Name ______________________

Choose the Appropriate Unit

VOCABULARY
mass
gram (g)
kilogram (kg)

Choose the unit you would use to measure the mass of each. Write *gram* or *kilogram*.

17 an elephant ______________

18 a crayon ______________

19 a stamp ______________

20 a dog ______________

Circle the better estimate.

21	a pair of sunglasses	150 g	150 kg
22	a horse	6 kg	600 kg
23	a watermelon	40 g	4 kg
24	a quarter	500 g	5 g

Use Drawings to Represent Problems

Use the drawing to represent and solve the problem.

25 Zach wants to buy 900 grams of pumpkin seed. The scale shows 400 grams. How many more grams does he need?

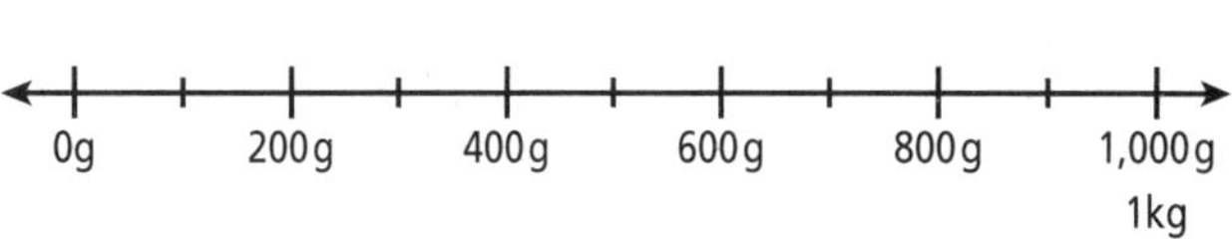

____

26 Laura had 800 grams of fruit snacks. She put an equal amount into each of 4 containers. How many grams did she put in each container?

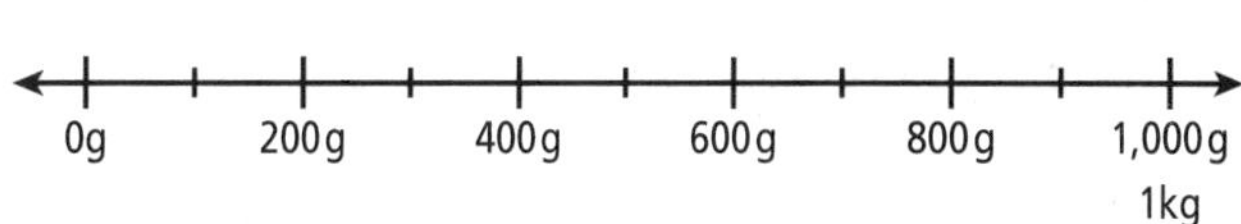

____

Solve Word Problems

Use the drawing to represent and solve the problem.

27 Nancy used 30 grams of strawberries and 45 grams of apples in her salad. How many grams of fruit altogether did she put in her salad?

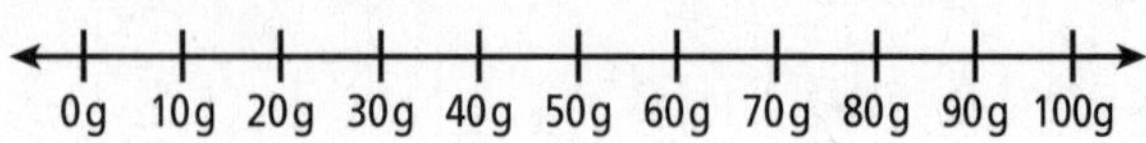

____

28 Three people each donated a 20-kilogram bag of dog food to the animal shelter. How many kilograms of dog food was donated altogether?

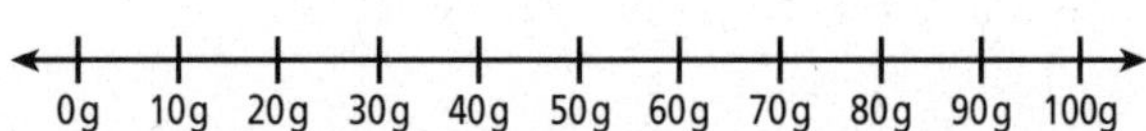

____

Solve. Use a drawing if you need to.

29 A male leopard has a mass of 40 kilograms and a female leopard has a mass of 25 kilograms. How much greater is the mass of the male?

____

30 Jolie made 3 necklaces that have a total mass of 180 grams. If each necklace has the same mass, what is the mass of each necklace?

____

31 Dan bought 6 small bags of treats for his dog. Each bag has a mass of 40 grams. What is the total mass of all the bags?

____

32 Carrie has a dog and a cat. Together they have a mass of 21 kilograms. If the cat has a mass of 9 kilograms, what is the mass of Carrie's dog?

____

Name ______________________________

What's the Error?

Dear Math Students,

Today I had to solve this problem: Toby bought 3 bags of chips. Each bag of chips has a mass of 50 grams. What is the mass of all 3 bags of chips? Here is how I solved the problem.

50 + 3 = 53; 53 grams

Is my answer correct? If not, please correct my work and tell me what I did wrong. How do you know my answer is wrong?

Your friend,
Puzzled Penguin

33 Write an answer to the Puzzled Penguin.

____

____

____

____

Solve. Show your work on a separate sheet of paper.

34 A tennis ball has a mass of 60 grams. A golf ball has a mass of 45 grams. What is the total mass of the two ball?

____

35 How many more grams is the mass of the tennis ball than the mass of the golf ball?

____

36 Gary bought 10 slices of ham at the deli. Each slice weighed 2 ounces. How many ounces of ham did Gary buy?

____

37 Sadie had 40 grams of sunflower seeds. She divided the seeds evenly among her 5 friends. How many grams did each friend get?

____

Choose the Better Estimate

Circle the better estimate.

 38

90 grams

90 kilograms

39

100 pounds

10 ounces

40

3 ounces

3 pounds

41

10 kilograms

10 grams

42

100 kilograms

1,000 kilograms

43

1 pound

10 pounds

Solve.

 44 Suzie explained that smaller objects weigh the least and larger objects weigh the most. Do you agree with Suzie?

____

____

Check Understanding

Explain the strategies you used to estimate mass in Problem 38.

Name ____________________

Make Sense of Problems About Liquid Volume

Solve. Use drawings if you need to.

Show your work.

1. Fran works in a science lab. She pours 80 milliliters of liquid into each of 4 test tubes. How many milliliters of liquid does Fran pour into the test tubes altogether?

   ____

2. Nicholas wants to buy a bottle of shampoo. A large bottle has 375 milliliters of shampoo and a small bottle has 250 milliliters of shampoo. How many more milliliters of shampoo is in the larger bottle?

   ____

3. Allison uses two containers of water to fill her aquarium. She uses a container filled with 18 liters of water and another with 12 liters of water. What is the total liquid volume of the aquarium?

   ____

4. The coffee shop made 28 liters of hot chocolate. If the same amount is poured into 4 different containers, how many liters of hot chocolate are in each container?

   ____

5. A recipe calls for 50 milliliters of milk. Eva has a spoon that holds 10 milliliters. How many times will Eva need to fill the spoon to follow the recipe?

   ____

Make Sense of Problems About Masses

Solve. Use drawings if you need to.

Show your work.

6 A bag of green beans has a mass of 335 grams. A bag of peas has a mass of 424 grams. What is the total mass of both bags?

____

7 An average sized chicken egg has a mass of 60 grams. What would be the total mass of a half dozen eggs?

____

8 A kangaroo and her joey together have a mass of 75 kilograms. If the mother kangaroo has a mass of 69 kilograms, what is the mass of the joey?

____

9 Liam and 2 of his friends have backpacks. The backpacks have masses of 6 kilograms, 4 kilograms, and 5 kilograms. What is the total mass of the 3 backpacks?

____

10 Grady bought 4 bags of sunflower seeds. Each bag has 60 grams of seeds. Luke bought 3 bags of pumpkin seeds. Each bag has 80 grams of seeds. Who bought more grams of seeds, Grady or Luke? Explain.

____

Check Understanding

Write and solve an equation for Problem 8.

____

Name ______________________ Date ______________

Write the correct answer.

1. What would be the better unit to use to specify the mass of a large truck, grams or kilograms?

____

2. What would be the better unit to use to specify the volume of water you can hold in your hand, liters or milliliters?

____

Solve.

Show your work.

3. A pack of 6 markers weighs 48 grams. How much does 1 marker weigh?

____

4. It takes 15 liters of paint to paint the shed. I have used 8 liters so far. How many more liters of paint will I need to finish painting the shed?

____

5. A boy with a mass of 50 kilograms is riding on a surfboard with a mass of 7 kilograms. What is the mass of the boy and surfboard altogether?

____

Fluency Check 13

Name ______________________ Date ______________

PATH to FLUENCY

Multiply or divide.

1. $3 \div 1 = \square$
2. $2 \times 6 = \square$
3. $18 \div 3 = \square$
4. $6 \times 8 = \square$
5. $32 \div 4 = \square$
6. $7 \times 10 = \square$
7. $42 \div 7 = \square$
8. $7 \times 9 = \square$
9. $72 \div 8 = \square$

Add or subtract.

10. $\begin{array}{r} 112 \\ +\ 834 \\ \hline \end{array}$
11. $\begin{array}{r} 650 \\ -\ 300 \\ \hline \end{array}$
12. $\begin{array}{r} 534 \\ +\ 307 \\ \hline \end{array}$
13. $\begin{array}{r} 843 \\ -\ 478 \\ \hline \end{array}$
14. $\begin{array}{r} 354 \\ +\ 618 \\ \hline \end{array}$
15. $\begin{array}{r} 903 \\ -\ 648 \\ \hline \end{array}$

Dear Family:

Your student has been learning about geometry and measurement during this school year. The second part of Unit 7 is about angles, triangles, and other polygons, including the geometric figures called quadrilaterals. These polygons get their name because they have four (*quad-*) sides (*-lateral*).

Here are some examples of quadrilaterals students will be learning about in this unit.

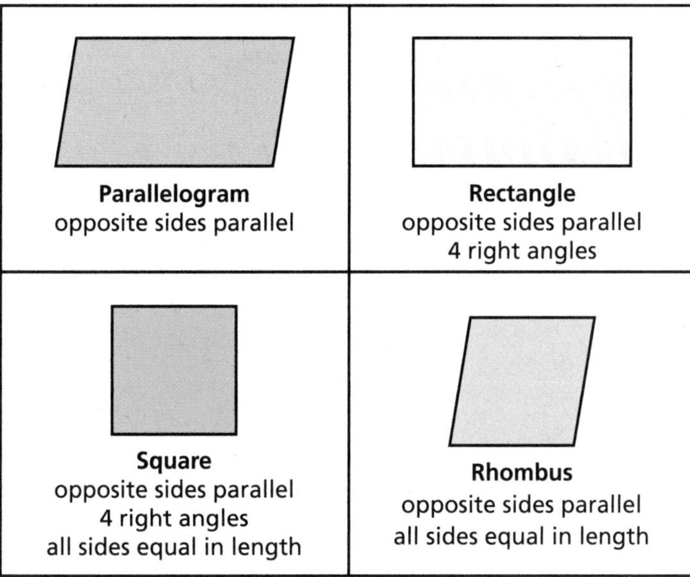

Students will be able to recognize and describe different quadrilaterals by their sides angles, and vertices. Some sides may be of equal length. Some sides may be parallel; they do not meet no matter how far they are extended. Some sides may be perpendicular; where they meet is like the corner of a square.

If you have any questions, please contact me.

Thank you.

Sincerely,
Your child's teacher

Estimada familia:

Su niño ha estado aprendiendo acerca de geometría y medición. La segunda parte de la Unidad 7 trata sobre ángulos, triángulos y otros polígonos incluyendo las figuras geométricas llamadas cuadriláteros. Se llaman así porque tienen cuatro (*quadri-*) lados (*-lateris*).

Aquí se muestran algunos ejemplos de cuadriláteros que los estudiantes estudiarán en esta unidad.

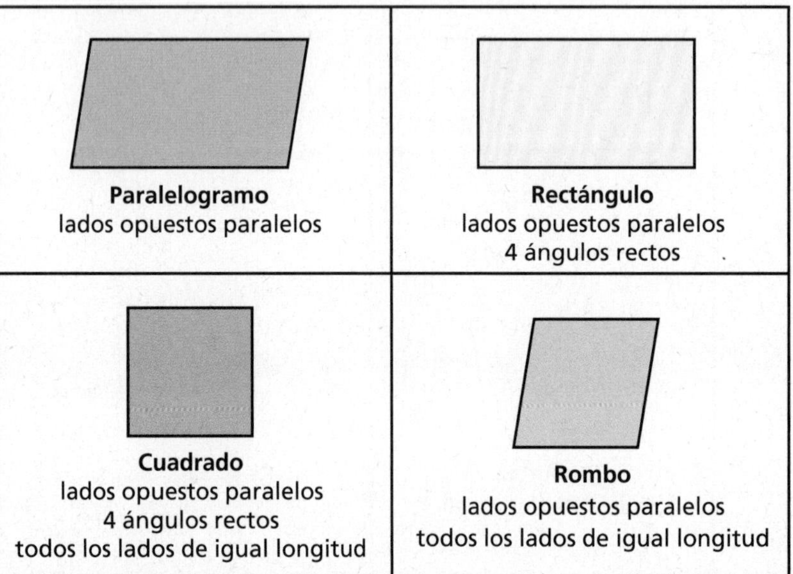

Los estudiantes podrán reconocer y describir diferentes cuadriláteros según sus lados, ángulos y vértices. Algunos lados pueden tener la misma longitud. Algunos lados pueden ser paralelos; nunca se juntan, no importa cuánto se extiendan. Algunos lados pueden ser perpendiculares; donde se juntan es como el vértice de un cuadrado.

Si tiene alguna pregunta o algún comentario, por favor comuníquese conmigo.

Gracias.

Atentamente,
El maestro de su niño

Name ______________________________

Types of Lines

VOCABULARY
parallel
perpendicular

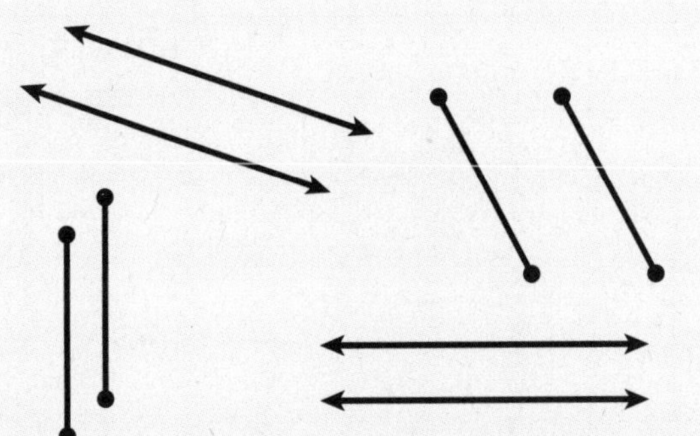

The lines or line segments in these pairs are **parallel**.

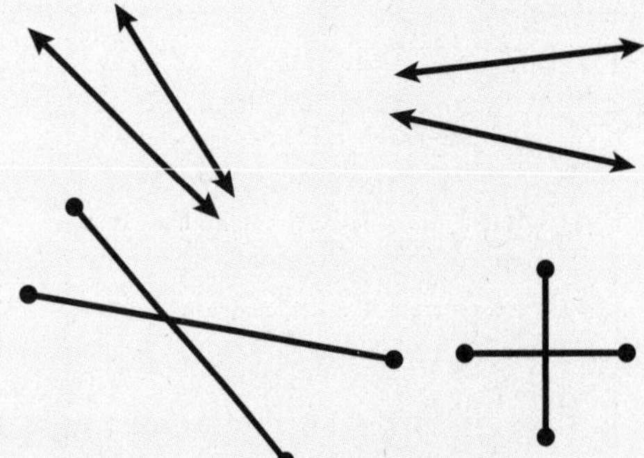

The lines or line segments in these pairs are not parallel.

1. Write a description of parallel line segments.

____

____

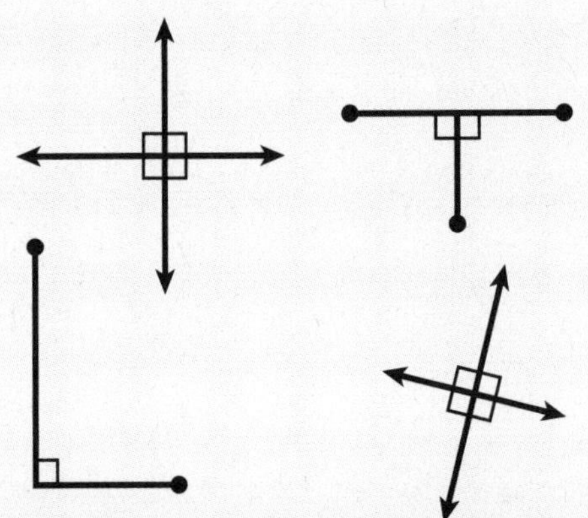

The lines or line segments in these pairs are **perpendicular**.

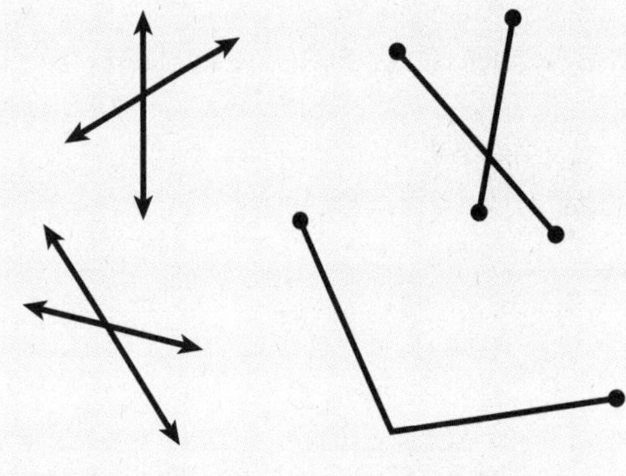

The lines or line segments in these pairs are not perpendicular.

2. Write a description of perpendicular line segments.

____

____

Types of Angles

VOCABULARY
ray
angle
vertex
right angle

A **ray** is part of a line that has one endpoint and continues forever in one direction. To draw a ray, make an arrow to show that it goes on forever.

Two line segments or two rays that meet at an endpoint form an **angle**. The point is called the **vertex**.

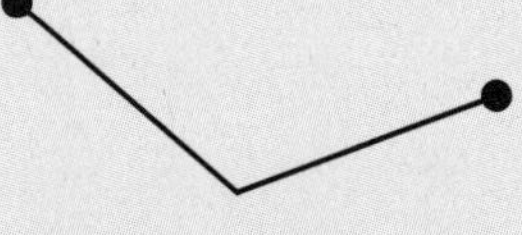
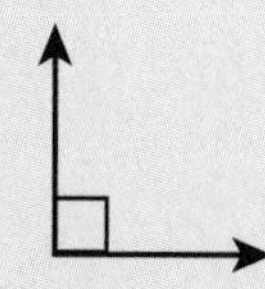
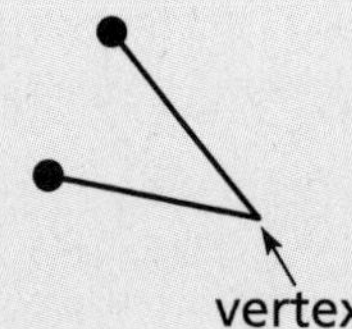

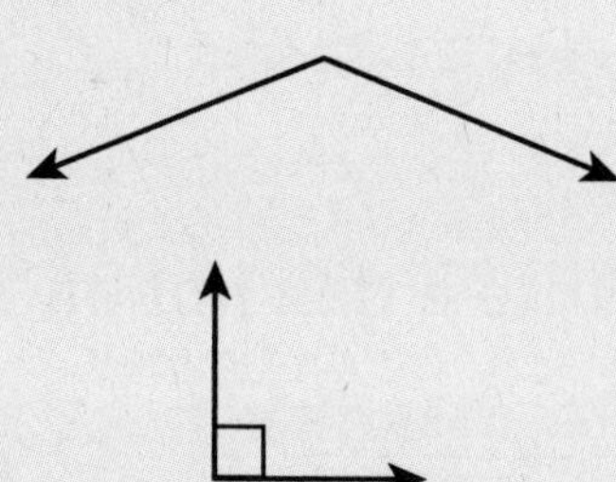

An angle that forms a square corner is called a **right angle**.

right angle

Some angles are smaller than a right angle.

Some angles are larger than a right angle.

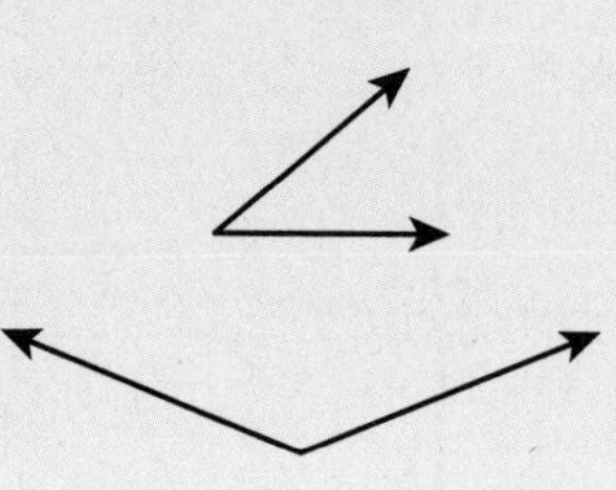

These angles are named with a letter in the corner.

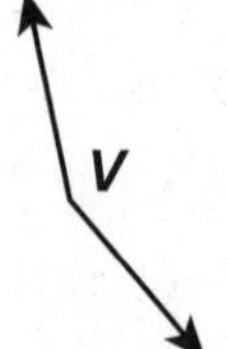

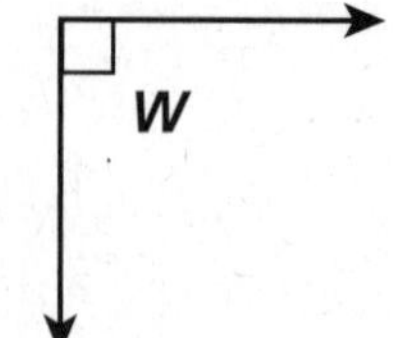

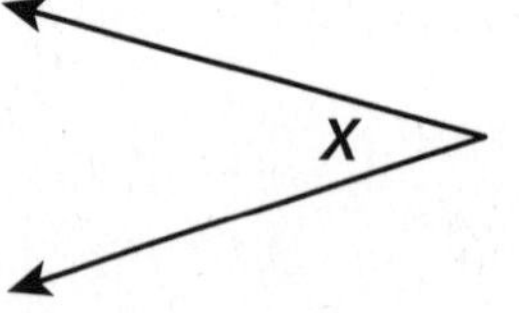

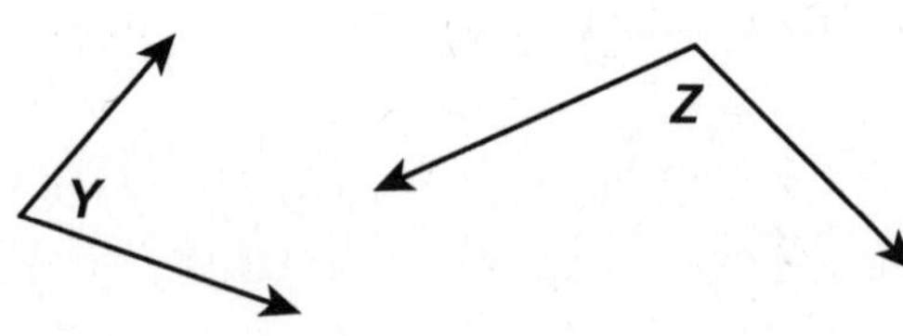

3. Which of the angles are right angles? ____________

4. Which of the angles are smaller than a right angle? ____________

5. Which of the angles are larger than a right angle? ____________

Name ___________________________

VOCABULARY
triangle

Describe Triangles by Types of Angles

Triangles can be described by the types of angles they have.

In these triangles, two perpendicular line segments meet to form one angle that is a right angle.

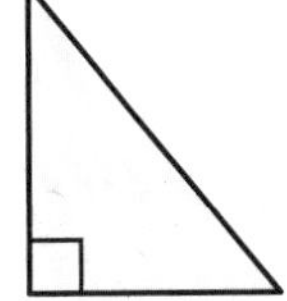
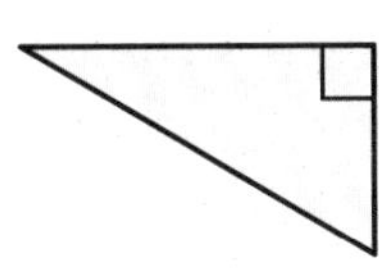
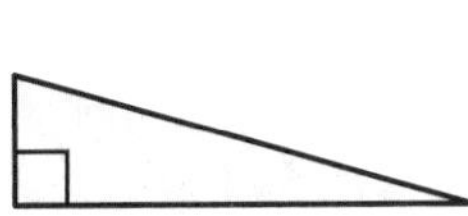
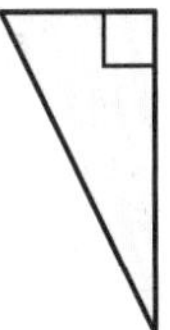

In these triangles, three angles are smaller than a right angle.

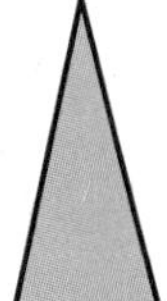

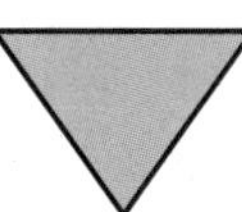
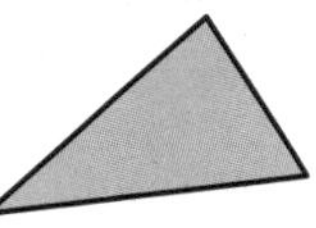

In these triangles, one angle is larger than a right angle.

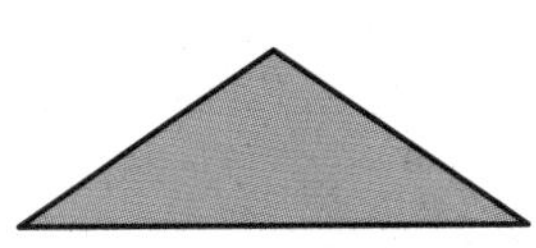
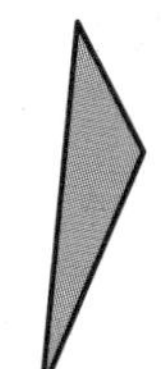
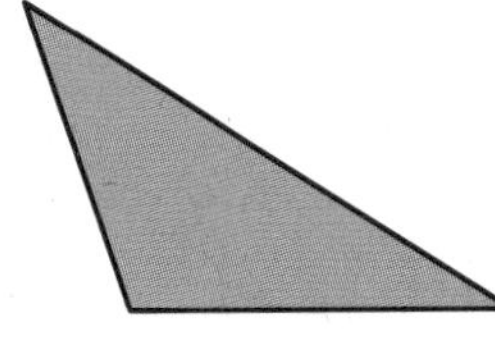

Use Triangles *K*, *L*, and *M* for Exercises 6–8.

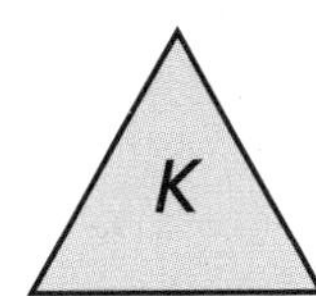

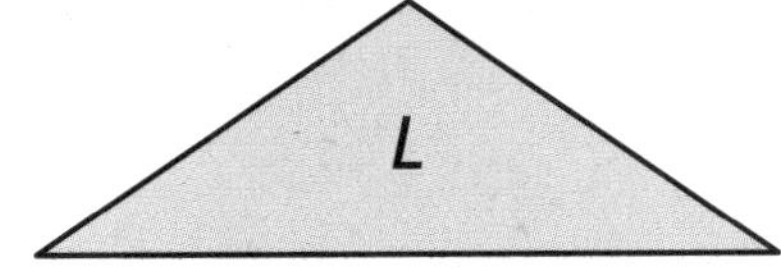

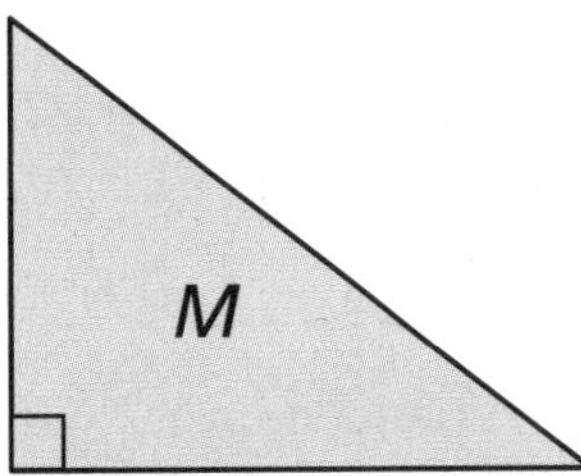

6. Which triangle has one right angle?

____

7. Which triangle has three angles smaller than a right angle?

____

8. Which triangle has one angle larger than a right angle?

____

Describe Triangles by the Number of Sides of Equal Length

You can also describe triangles by the number of sides that are of equal length.

In these triangles, three sides are equal in length.

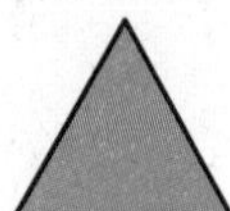

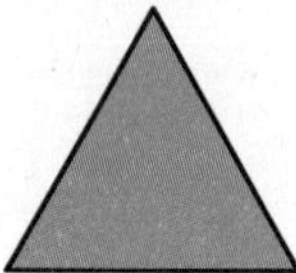

In these triangles, two sides are equal in length.

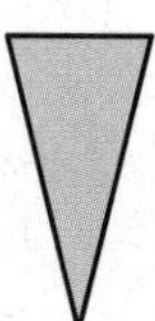
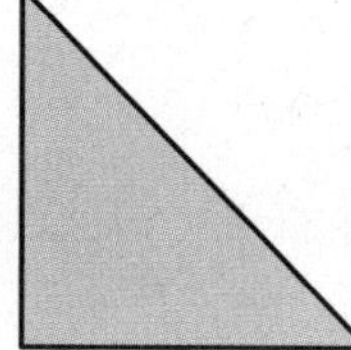
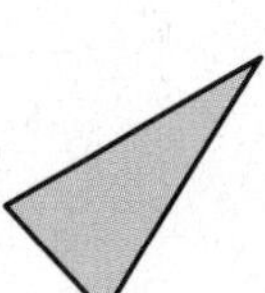
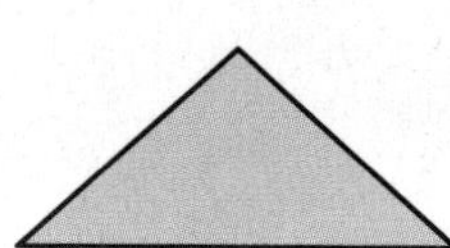

In these triangles, no sides are equal in length.

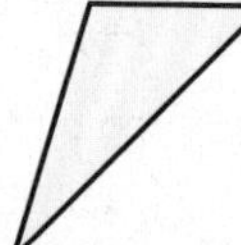
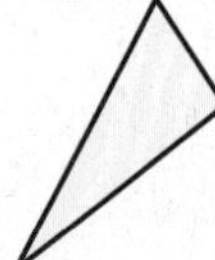
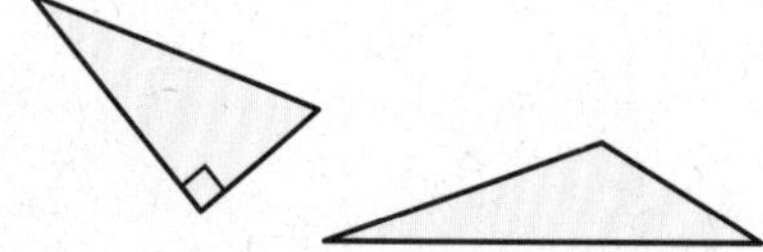

Use Triangles *B*, *C*, and *D* for Exercises 9–11.

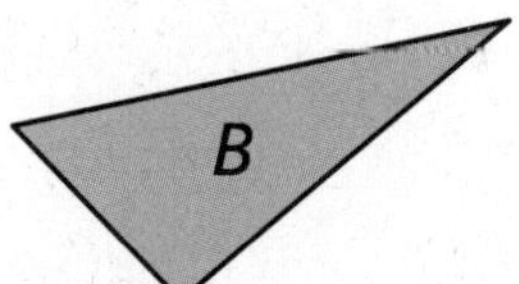

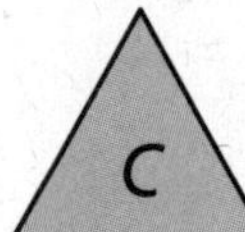

9 Which triangle has 3 sides of equal length?

____

10 Which triangle has 2 sides of equal length?

____

11 Which triangle has 0 sides of equal length?

____

Name ______________________________

Describe Triangles by Types of Angles and Number of Sides of Equal Length

Use Triangles *M*, *N*, and *O* for 12–14. Write *M*, *N*, or *O*. Then complete the sentences.

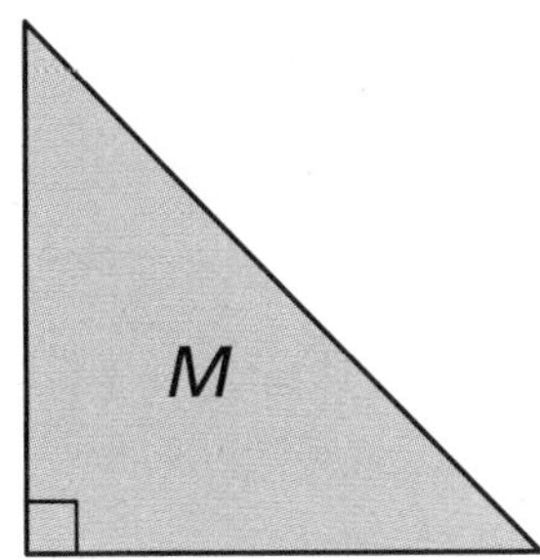

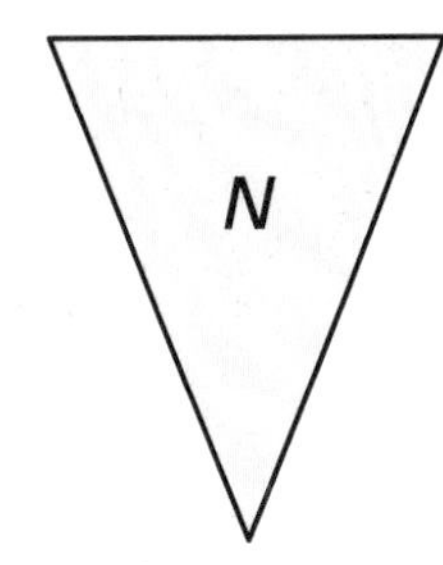

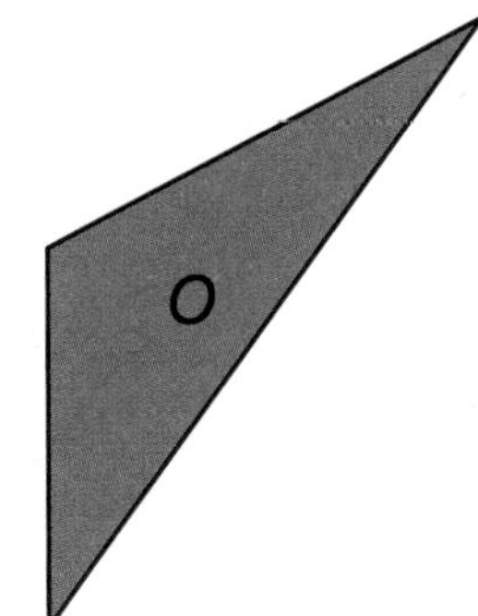

12. Triangle ________ has 1 angle larger than a right angle and has ________ sides of equal length.

13. Triangle ________ has 1 right angle and has ________ sides of equal length.

14. Triangle ________ has 3 angles smaller than a right angle and has ________ sides of equal length.

Use Triangles *P*, *Q*, and *R* for 15–17. Write *P*, *Q*, or *R*. Then complete the sentences.

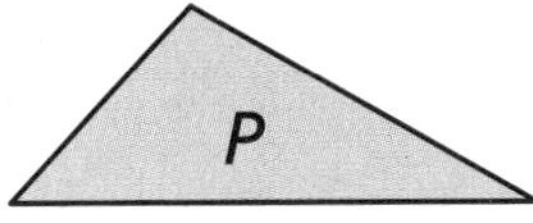

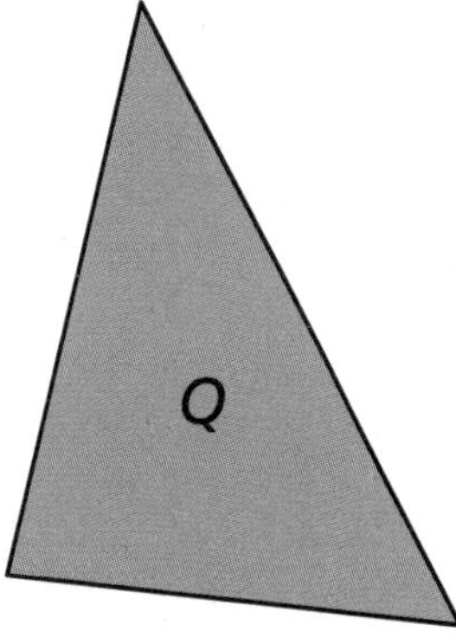

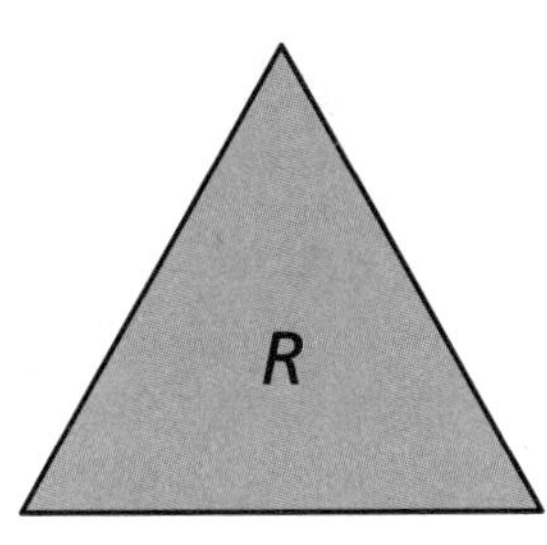

15. Triangle ________ has 3 angles smaller than a right angle and has ________ sides of equal length.

16. Triangle ________ has 3 angles smaller than a right angle and has ________ sides of equal length.

17. Triangle ________ has 1 angle larger than a right angle and has ________ sides of equal length.

Polygons

VOCABULARY
polygon
concave
convex

A **polygon** is a flat, closed figure made up of line segments that do not cross each other.

Circle the figures that are polygons.

18 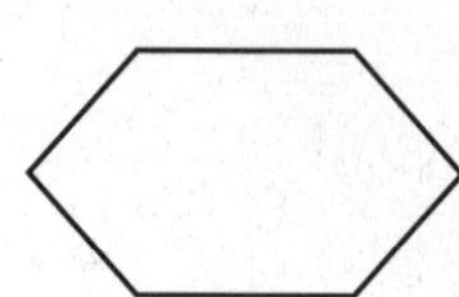

19 

20 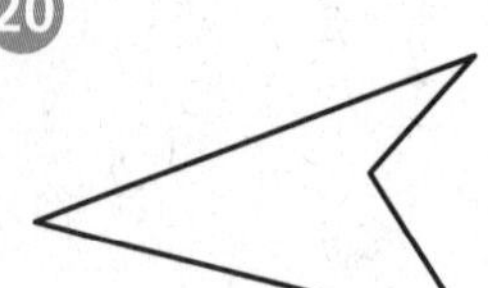

21 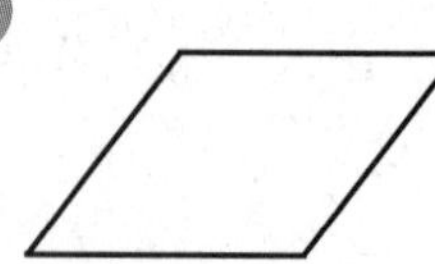

22 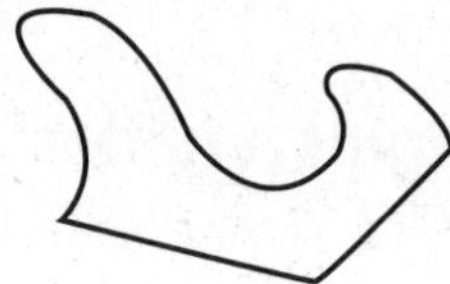

23 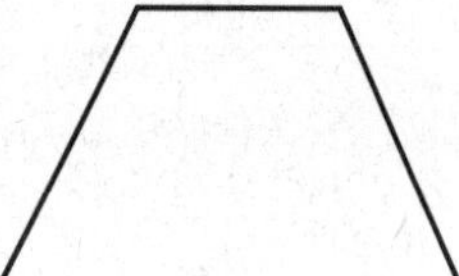

24 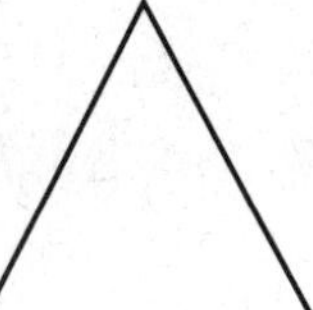

25 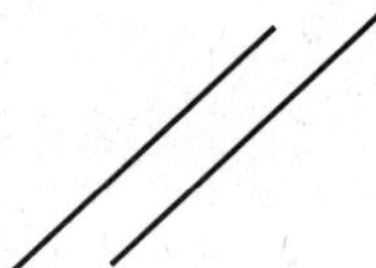

A figure can be **concave** or **convex**. In concave polygons, there exists a line segment with endpoints inside the polygon and a point on the line segment that is outside the polygon. A convex figure has no such line segment.

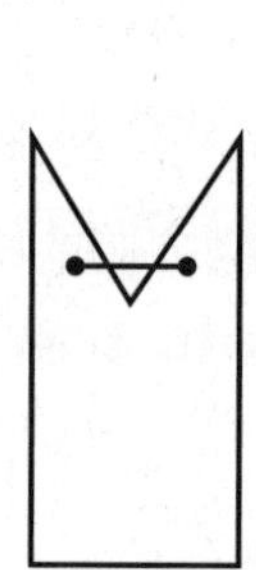

concave

convex

Which figures are convex and which are concave?

26 

____

27 

____

28 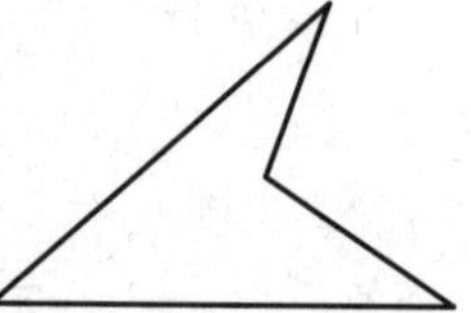

____

29 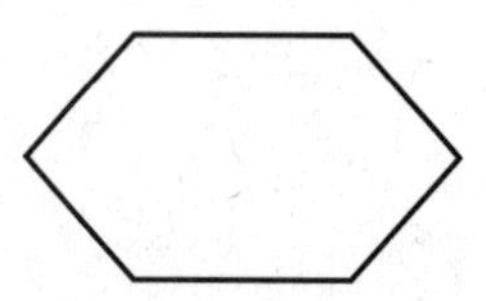

____

Name ____________________

Name Polygons

Polygons are named according to how many sides and vertices they have.

VOCABULARY
quadrilateral
pentagon **hexagon**
octagon **decagon**

triangle	**quadrilateral**	**pentagon**	**hexagon**	**octagon**	**decagon**
3 sides	4 sides	5 sides	6 sides	8 sides	10 sides
3 vertices	4 vertices	5 vertices	6 vertices	8 vertices	10 vertices

Write the number of sides and vertices. Then name each figure.

30

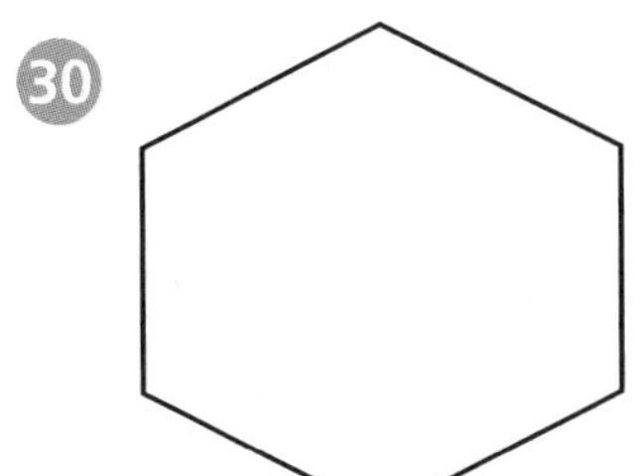

________ sides

________ vertices

____

31

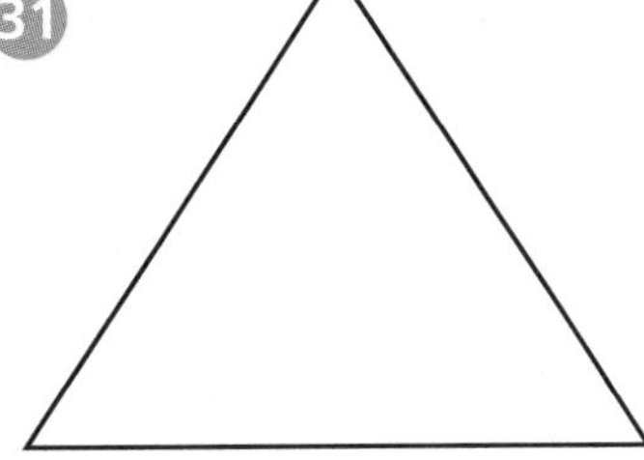

________ sides

________ vertices

____

32

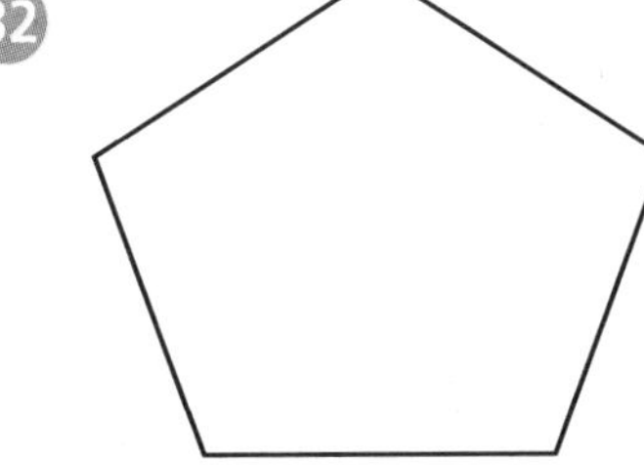

________ sides

________ vertices

____

33

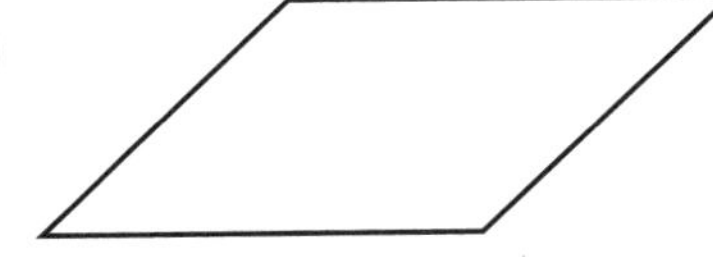

________ sides

________ vertices

____

34

________ sides

________ vertices

____

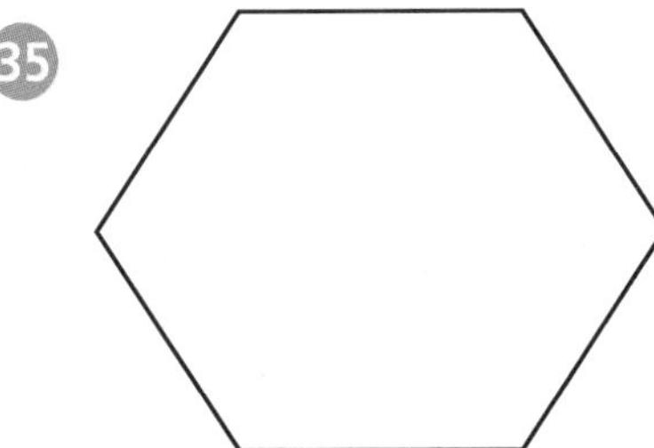

________ sides

________ vertices

____

Name Polygons (continued)

Write the number of sides and vertices. Then name each figure.

36 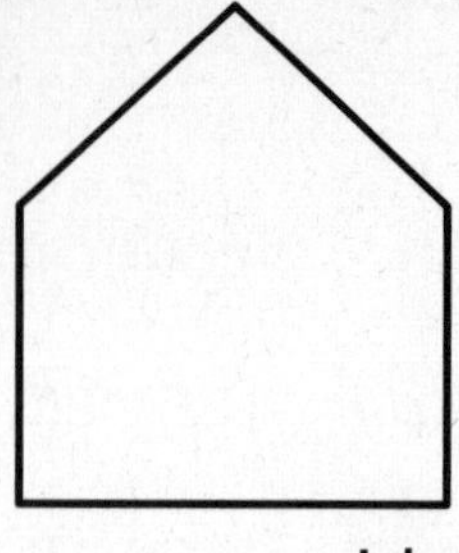

______ sides

______ vertices

____

37 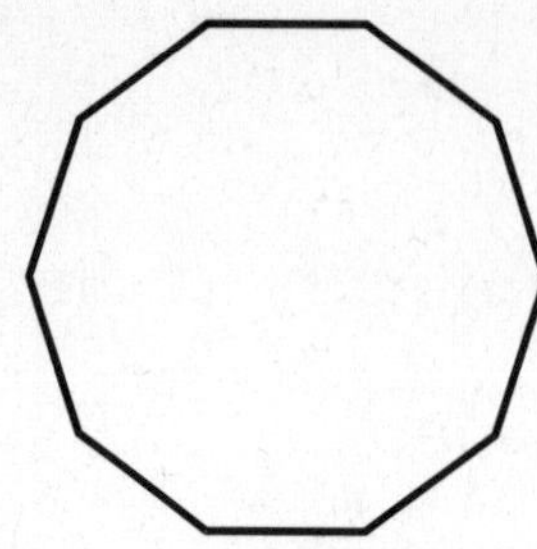

______ sides

______ vertices

____

38 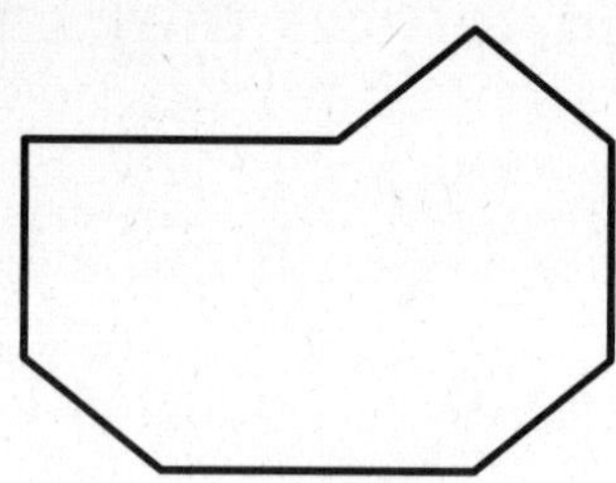

______ sides

______ vertices

____

Classify Polygons

39 Frans drew two different polygons in art class that will be displayed during his school's art show. Use the clues below to identify the polygons he drew.

- The polygons have fewer sides than a decagon.
- Each polygon has an odd number of sides.
- Neither polygon can be classified as one of the figures listed on page 461.

Draw each polygon that Frans drew. Identify the number of sides and vertices.

______ sides

______ vertices

______ sides

______ vertices

Check Understanding

Draw and describe three different triangles.

Name ______________________________

Build Quadrilaterals from Triangles

A quadrilateral is a figure with 4 sides.

Cut out each pair of triangles. Use each pair to make as many different quadrilaterals as you can. You may flip a triangle and use the back. On a separate piece of paper, trace each quadrilateral that you make.

Triangles with One Angle Larger Than a Right Angle

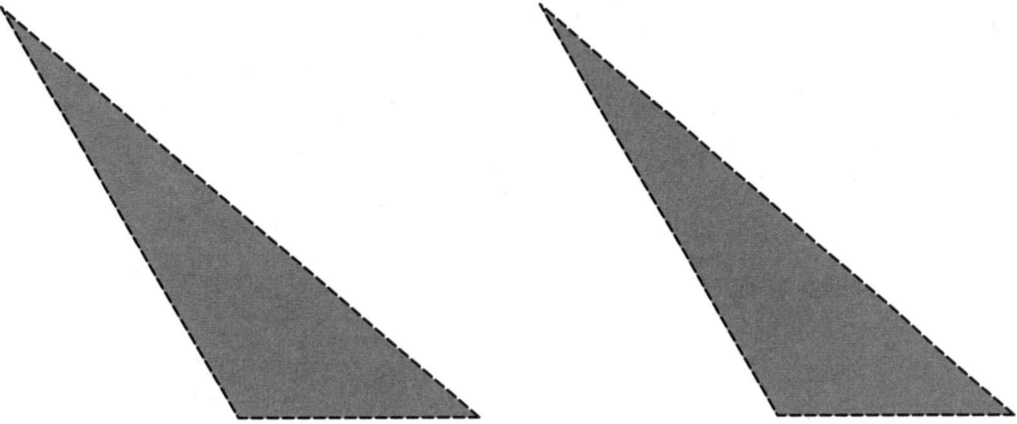

Triangles with Three Angles Smaller Than a Right Angle

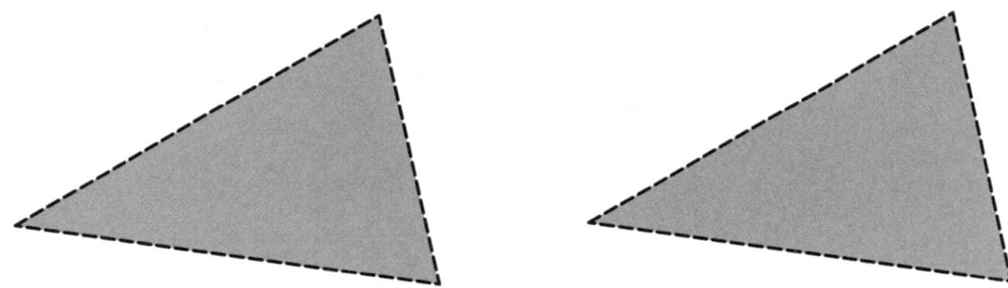

Triangles with One Right Angle

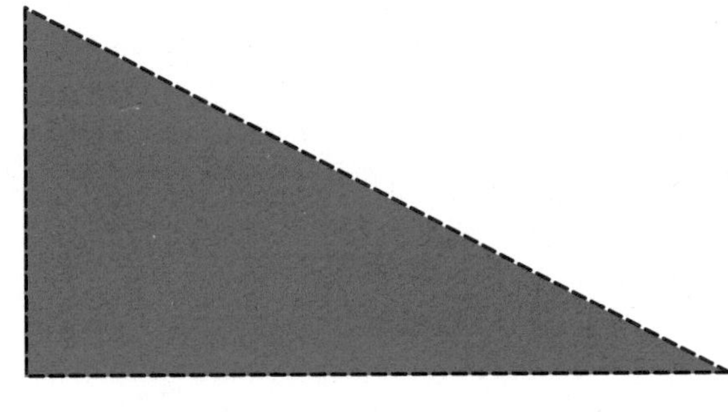

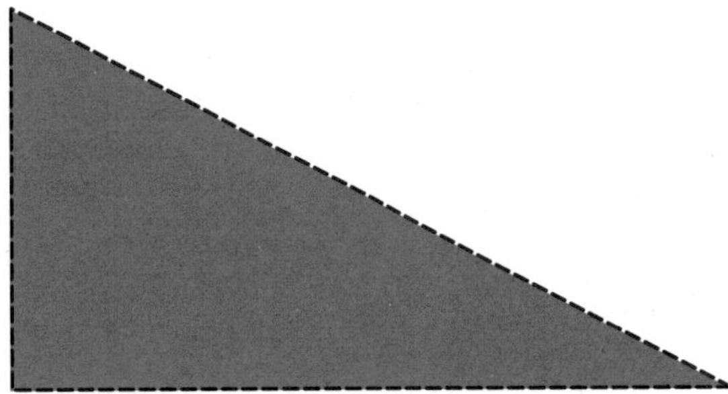

Name ______________________________

Build Polygons from Triangles

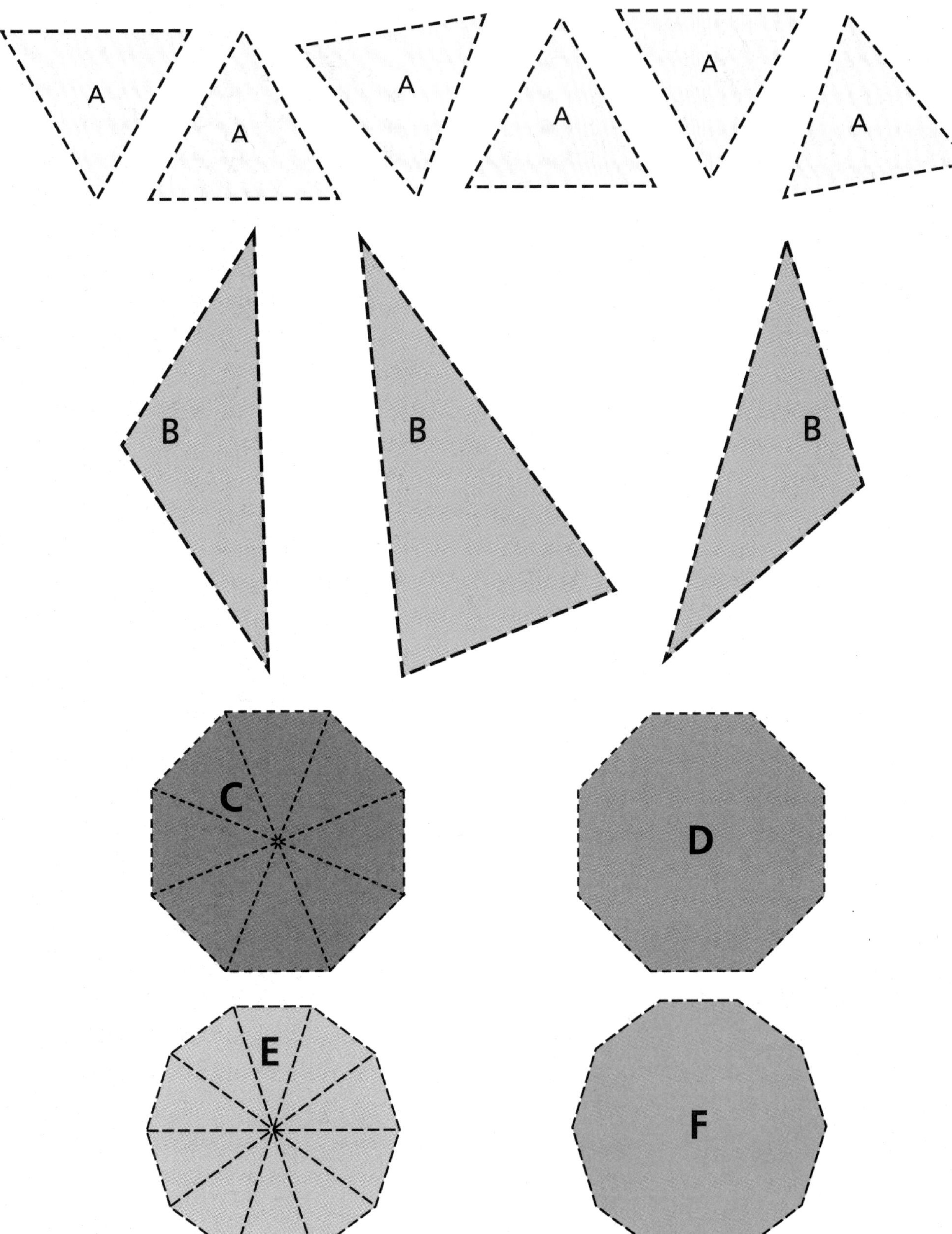

Name ______________________________

VOCABULARY
parallelogram

Describe Parallelograms

All of these figures are **parallelograms**. Both pairs of opposite sides are parallel.

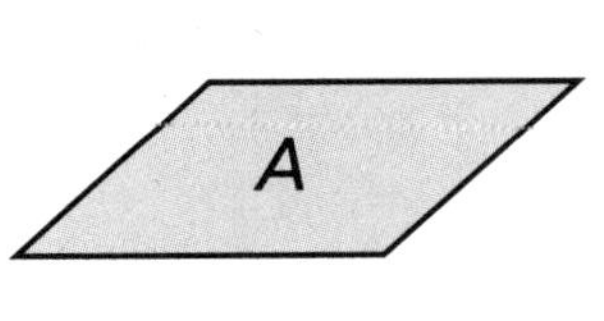

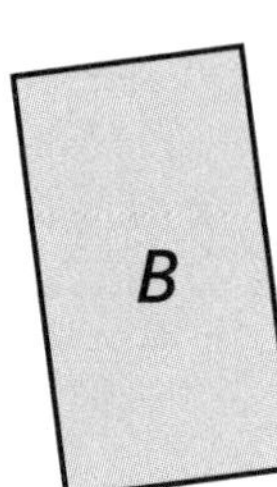

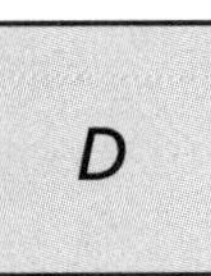

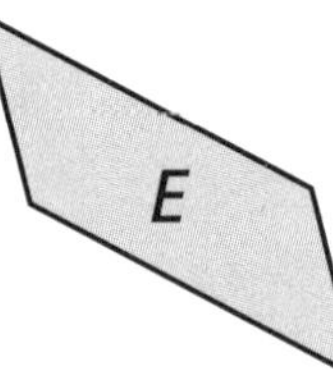

These figures are not parallelograms.

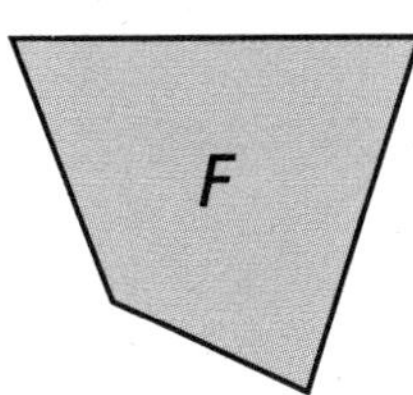

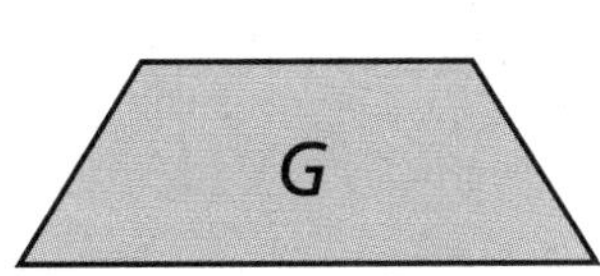

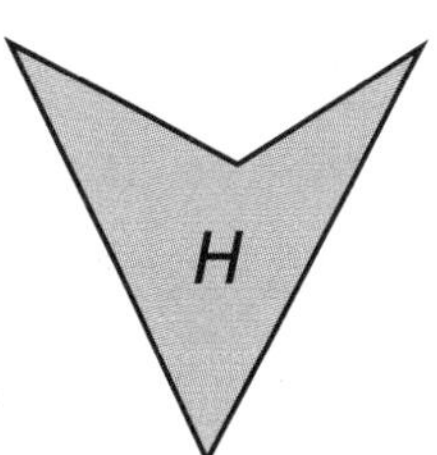

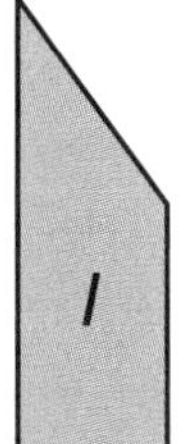

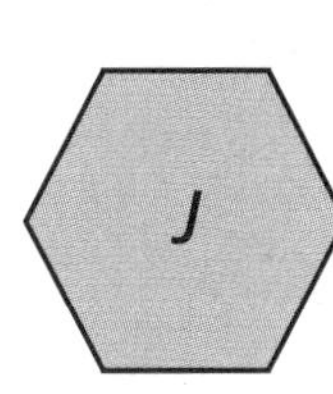

Complete the sentence.

1. A parallelogram is a quadrilateral with ______________________________

____

Measure Sides of Parallelograms

For each parallelogram, measure the sides to the nearest centimeter and label them with their lengths.

2. 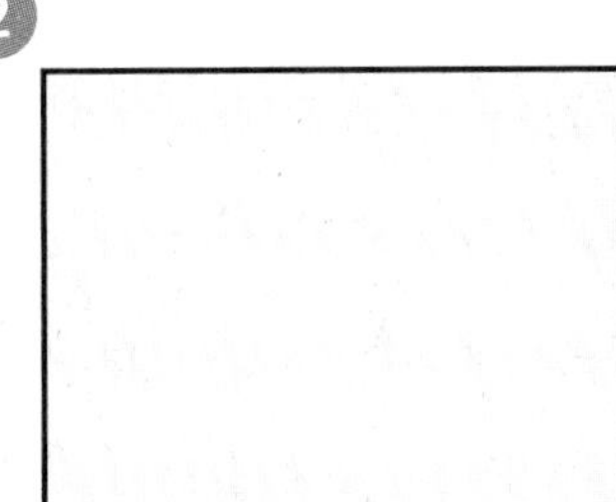

3. 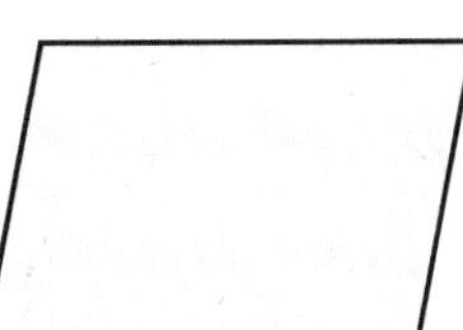

4. 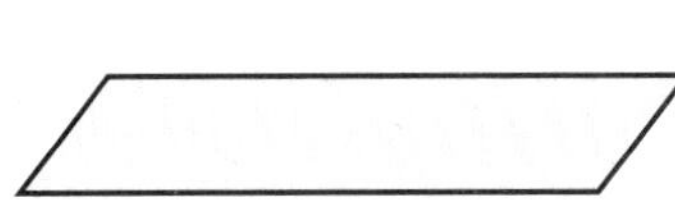

5. Look at the lengths of the sides. What patterns do you notice? ______________________________

Describe Rectangles

VOCABULARY
rectangle
square
rhombus

All of these figures are **rectangles**. Rectangles have adjacent sides that are perpendicular.

Adel said, "Rectangles are special kinds of parallelograms."

Complete the sentence.

6 A rectangle is a parallelogram with ______________________________

____

Explore Squares and Rhombuses

These figures are **squares**.

  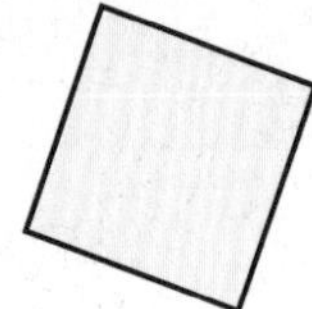

These figures are **rhombuses**.

 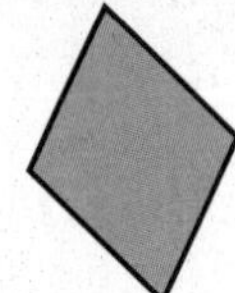 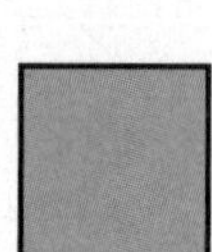

Takeshi said, "Squares are special kinds of rectangles."

Cora said, "Rhombuses are special kinds of parallelograms."

Complete the sentence.

7 A square is a rectangle with ______________________________

____

8 A rhombus is a parallelogram with ______________________________

____

Name ____________________

Describe Quadrilaterals

Use as many words below as possible to describe each figure.

quadrilateral **parallelogram** **rectangle** **square**

9 ____________________

10 ____________________

11 ____________________

12 ____________________

Describe Trapezoids

VOCABULARY
trapezoid
opposite sides

The quadrilaterals below are **trapezoids**.

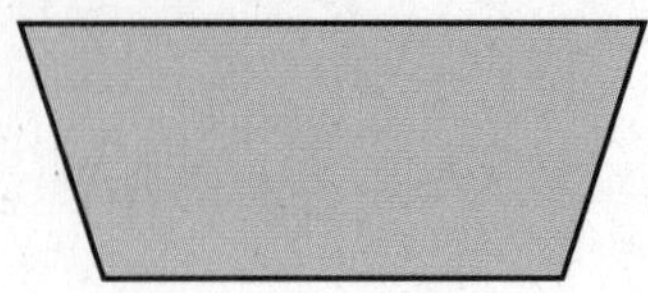
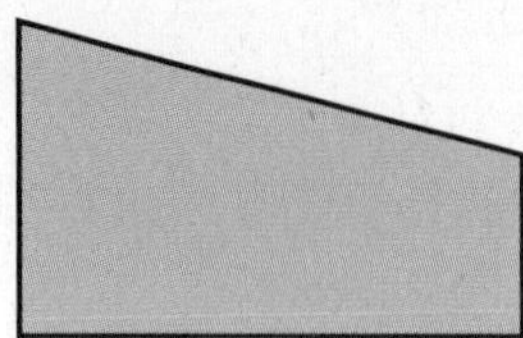
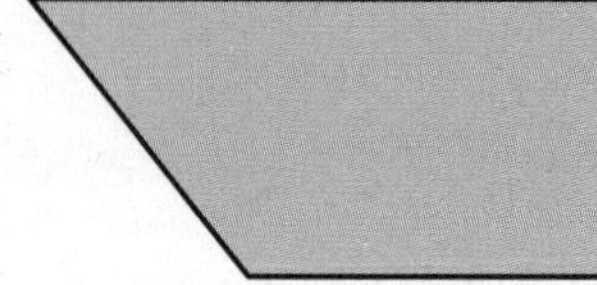

13 Write what you know about the **opposite sides** of a trapezoid.

____

____

14 Circle the quadrilaterals that are trapezoids.

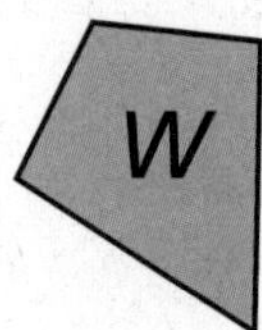

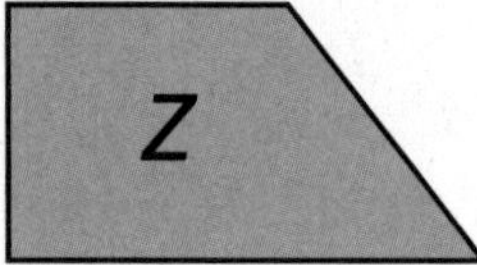

15 Explain why the figures you did not circle are not trapezoids.

____

____

____

Check Understanding
Draw a quadrilateral and describe it.

Name ______________________

Draw Parallelograms

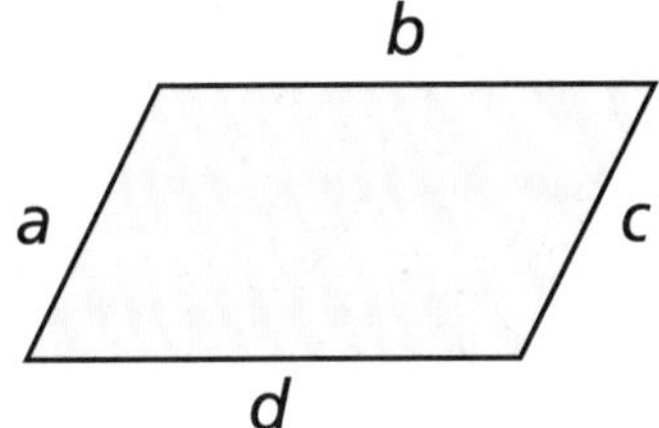

1. Write what you know about the opposite sides of a parallelogram.

____

____

2. Draw three different parallelograms.

Draw Rectangles

VOCABULARY
adjacent sides

3 Write everything you know about the opposite sides of a rectangle.

____

4 What do you know about the **adjacent sides** of a rectangle?

____

5 Draw three different rectangles.

Name ______________________

Draw Squares and Rhombuses

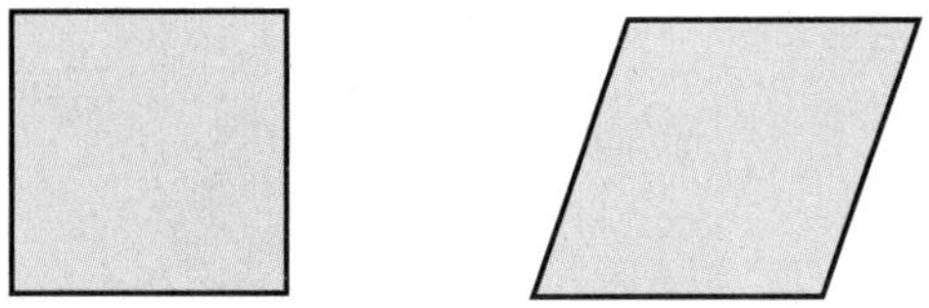

6 Write everything you know about squares.

____

7 Write all you know about rhombuses.

____

____

8 Draw two different squares and two different rhombuses.

Draw Quadrilaterals That Are Not Squares, Rectangles, or Rhombuses

 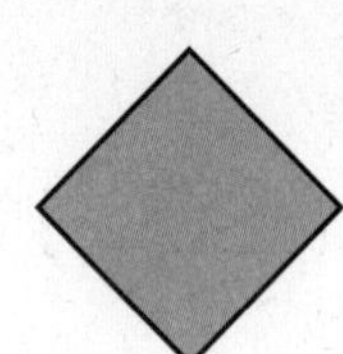 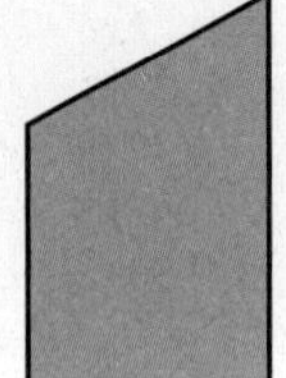 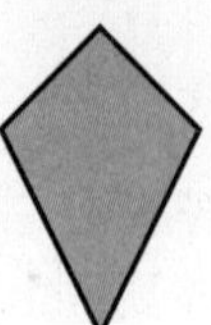  

9 What is a quadrilateral?

____

10 Name all the quadrilaterals that have at least one pair of parallel sides.

____

11 Draw three different quadrilaterals that are not squares, rectangles, or rhombuses.

Check Understanding

Draw a quadrilateral that is not a parallelogram.

Name ____________________

Name Quadrilaterals

Place a check mark beside every name that describes the figure.

1
- ☐ quadrilateral
- ☐ parallelogram
- ☐ rhombus
- ☐ rectangle
- ☐ square

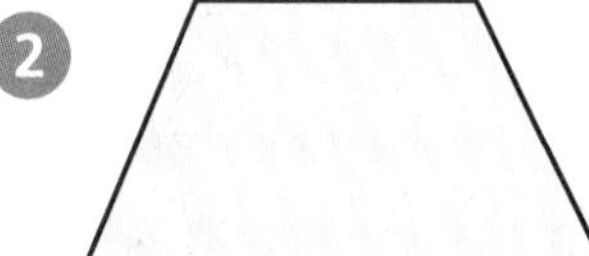

2
- ☐ quadrilateral
- ☐ parallelogram
- ☐ rhombus
- ☐ rectangle
- ☐ trapezoid

3
- ☐ quadrilateral
- ☐ parallelogram
- ☐ rhombus
- ☐ rectangle
- ☐ square

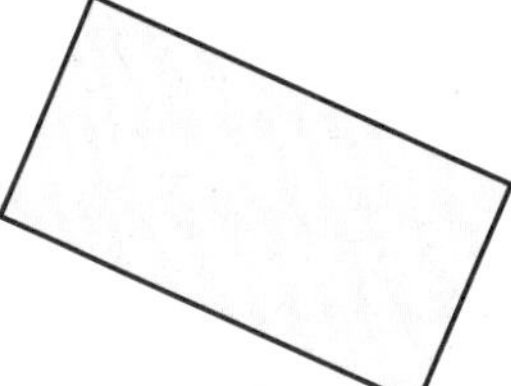

4
- ☐ quadrilateral
- ☐ parallelogram
- ☐ rhombus
- ☐ rectangle
- ☐ square

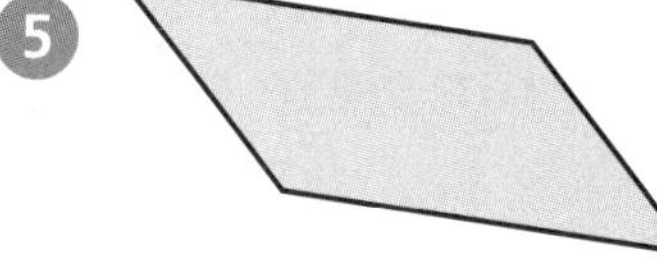

5
- ☐ quadrilateral
- ☐ parallelogram
- ☐ rhombus
- ☐ rectangle
- ☐ square

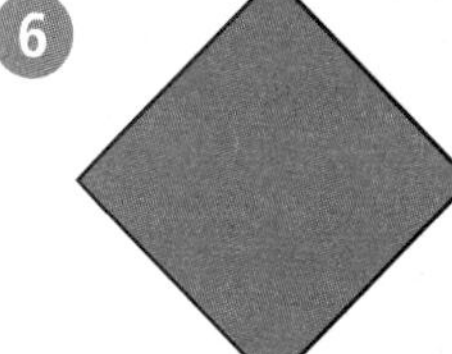

6
- ☐ quadrilateral
- ☐ parallelogram
- ☐ rhombus
- ☐ rectangle
- ☐ square

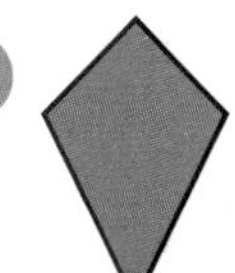

7
- ☐ quadrilateral
- ☐ parallelogram
- ☐ rhombus
- ☐ rectangle
- ☐ square

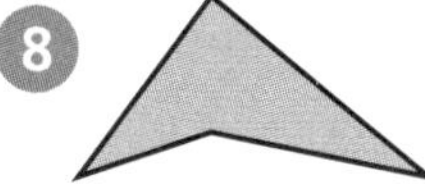

8
- ☐ quadrilateral
- ☐ parallelogram
- ☐ rhombus
- ☐ rectangle
- ☐ square

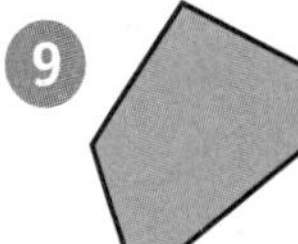

9
- ☐ quadrilateral
- ☐ parallelogram
- ☐ rhombus
- ☐ rectangle
- ☐ square

Analyze Quadrilaterals

10 For each figure, put Xs under the descriptions that are always true.

	Four sides	Both pairs of opposite sides parallel	Both pairs of opposite sides the same length	Four right angles	All sides the same length
Quadrilateral					
Trapezoid					
Parallelogram					
Rhombus					
Rectangle					
Square					

Use the finished chart above to complete each statement.

11 Parallelograms have all the features of quadrilaterals *plus*

____

____

12 Rectangles have all the features of parallelograms *plus*

____

13 Squares have all the features of quadrilaterals *plus*

____

____

14 Rhombuses have all the features of quadrilaterals *plus*

____

____

Name ______________________________

Draw Quadrilaterals from a Description

Draw each figure.

15. Draw a quadrilateral that is *not* a parallelogram.
16. Draw a parallelogram that is *not* a rectangle.
17. Draw a rectangle that is *not* a square.

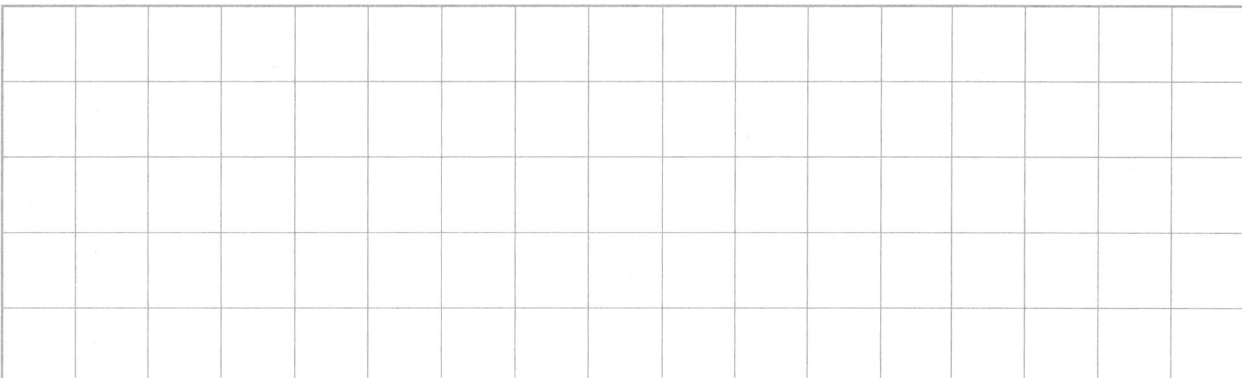

What's the Error?

Dear Math Students,

Today I had to draw a quadrilateral with parallel sides that is not a rectangle, square, or rhombus.
This is my drawing.

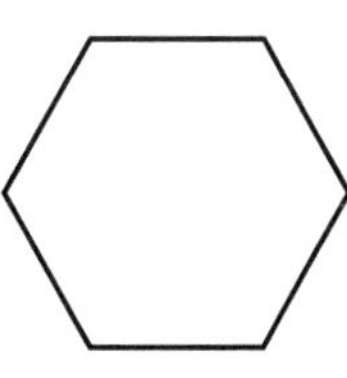

Is my drawing correct?
If not, please help me understand why it is wrong.

Your friend,
Puzzled Penguin

18. Write an answer to Puzzled Penguin.

____

____

Sort and Classify Quadrilaterals

Use the category diagram to sort the figures you cut out from Student Activity Book page 475A. Write the letter of the figure in the diagram to record your work.

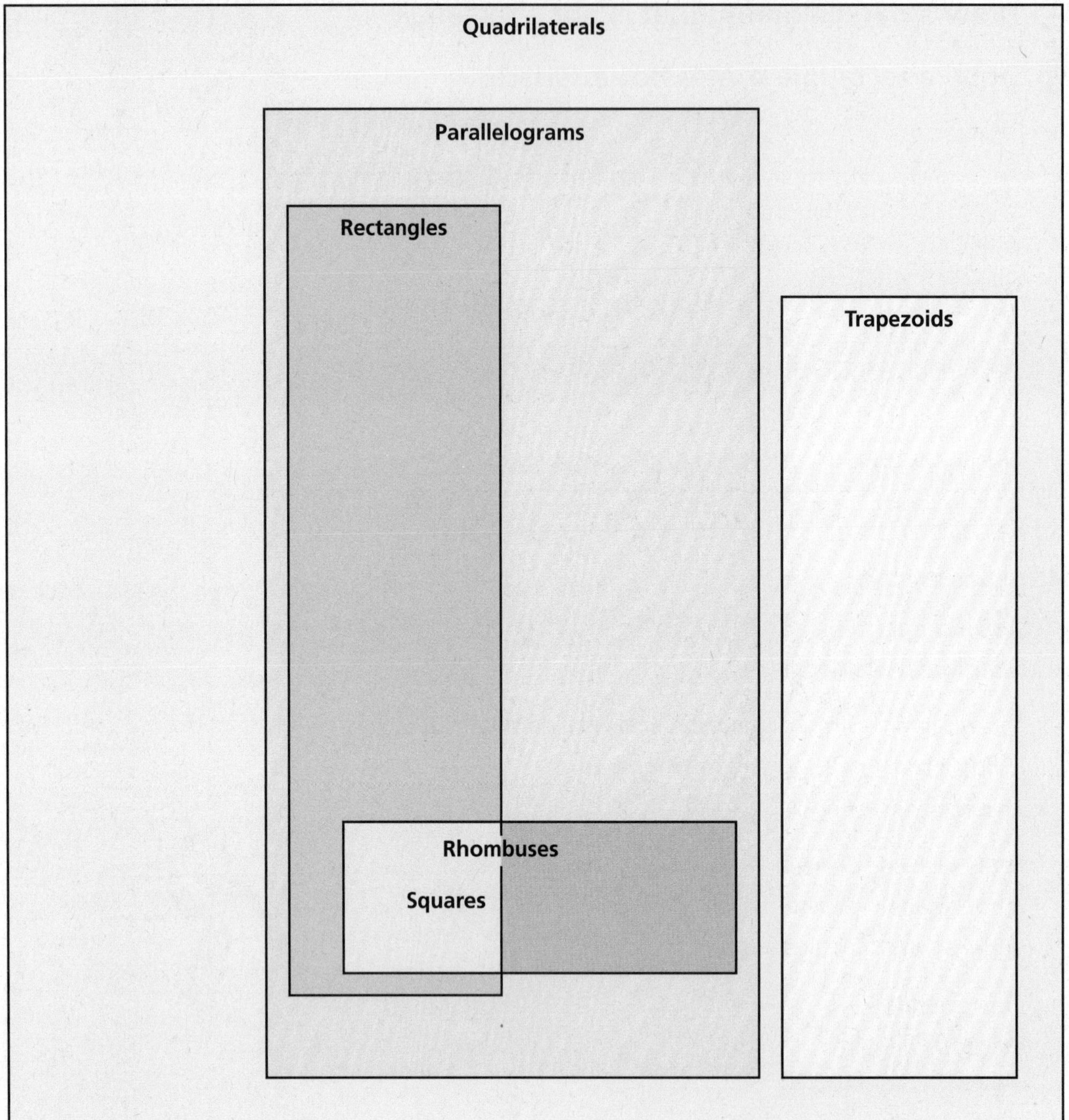

Check Understanding

Complete the sentence. A rhombus is always a ________________ and a ________________.

Name ______________________

Quadrilaterals for Sorting

Cut along the dashed lines.

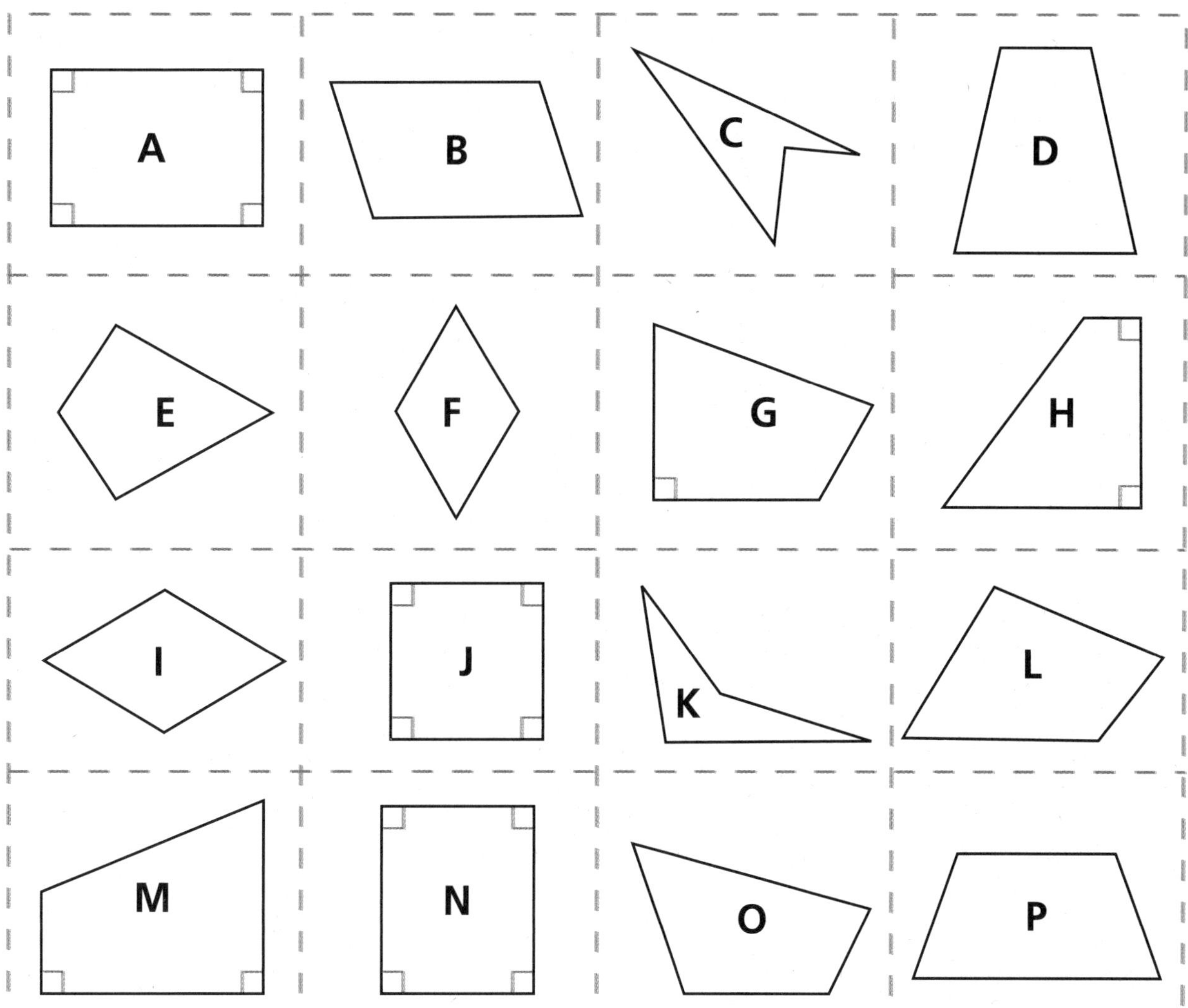

Name ____________________

Area and Gardening

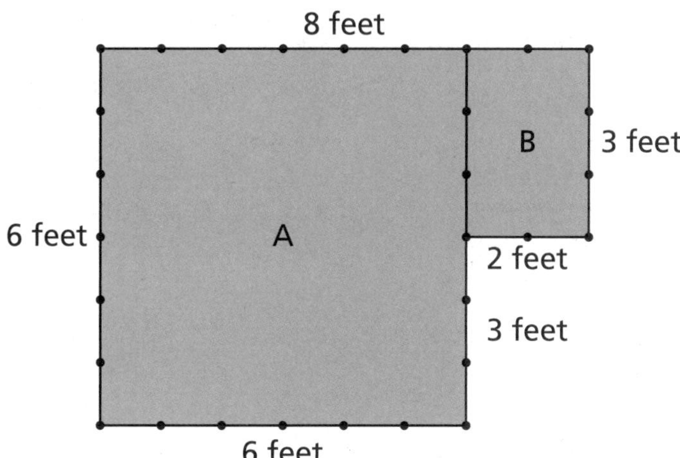

Look at the drawing of Yoakim's garden.
It is divided into two quadrilaterals.

1. What is the perimeter of part A? ____________

   What is the perimeter of part B? ____________

2. What is the perimeter of the combined garden? ____________

3. Will Yoakim need more fencing to enclose the two parts of his garden separately or to enclose the combined garden? ____________

   ____

4. What is the area of part A? ____________

   What is the area of part B? ____________

5. What is the area of the combined garden?

   ____

6. How does the total area of the two parts of the garden compare with the area of the combined garden?

   ____

Design a Garden

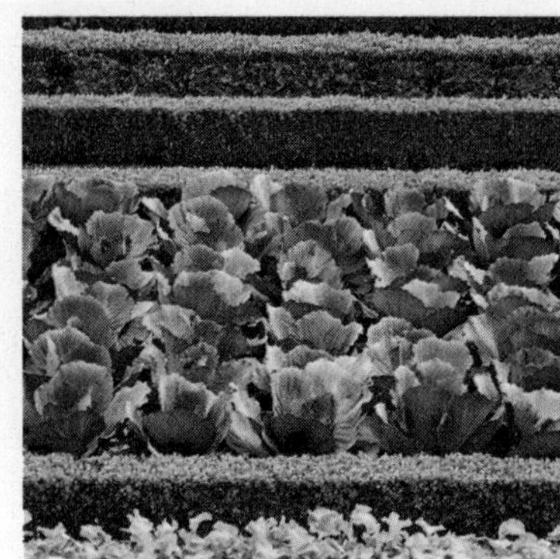

Use the dot paper below to draw a different garden that has the same perimeter as Yoakim's combined garden. Beside it, draw a different garden that has the same area as Yoakim's garden.

1 ft

7 What is the area of your garden that has the same perimeter as Yoakim's garden?

____

8 What is the perimeter of your garden that has the same area as Yoakim's garden?

____

9 Use the centimeter dot paper at the right to draw separate areas within a garden where you would plant corn, beans, and tomatoes.

The area for corn is 12 square feet.
The area for beans is 25 square feet.
The area for tomatoes is 20 square feet.

Unit 7
Quick Quiz 2

Name ______________________ Date ______________

Write the correct answer.

1. What do a rhombus and a square have in common?

____

2. Put a check mark beside every name that describes the figure.

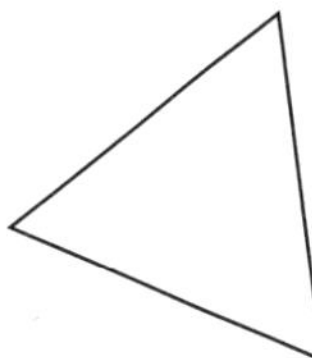

- ☐ quadrilateral
- ☐ not a quadrilateral
- ☐ rectangle
- ☐ rhombus
- ☐ trapezoid
- ☐ square

3. Which triangle has a right angle?

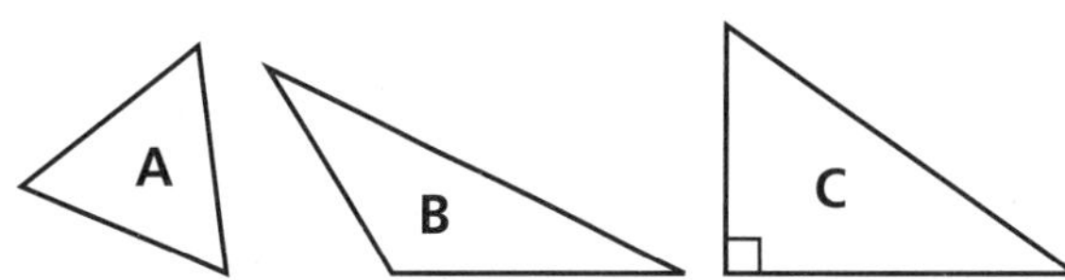

____

4. List the figures that are quadrilaterals.

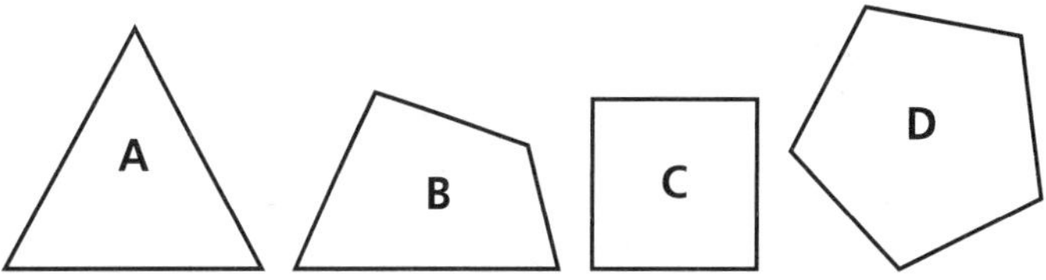

____

5. What do the figures have in common?

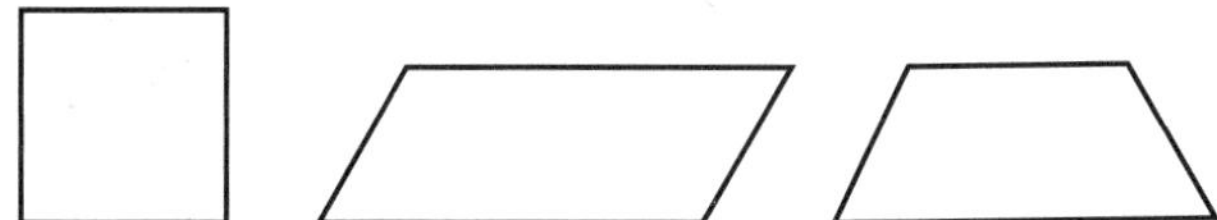

____

Fluency Check 14

Name ________________________________ Date ________________

PATH to FLUENCY

Multiply or divide.

1. $2 \times 4 = \square$
2. $9 \div 3 = \square$
3. $6 \times 6 = \square$
4. $30 \div 6 = \square$
5. $6 \times 9 = \square$
6. $48 \div 8 = \square$
7. $4 \times 9 = \square$
8. $72 \div 9 = \square$
9. $8 \times 7 = \square$

Add or subtract.

10. $\begin{array}{r} 563 \\ -\ 240 \\ \hline \end{array}$
11. $\begin{array}{r} 300 \\ +\ 620 \\ \hline \end{array}$
12. $\begin{array}{r} 562 \\ -\ 428 \\ \hline \end{array}$
13. $\begin{array}{r} 529 \\ +\ 386 \\ \hline \end{array}$
14. $\begin{array}{r} 338 \\ -\ 189 \\ \hline \end{array}$
15. $\begin{array}{r} 482 \\ +\ 379 \\ \hline \end{array}$

Name ____________________ Date ____________

1 Write the letter for each shape in the box that describes the shape.

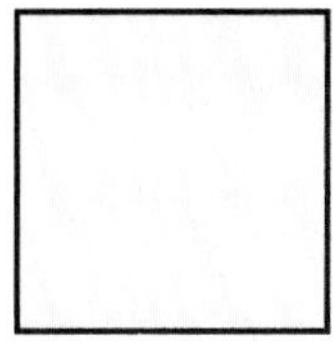
A

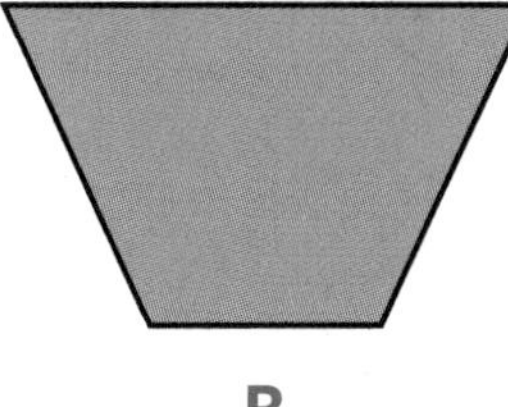
B

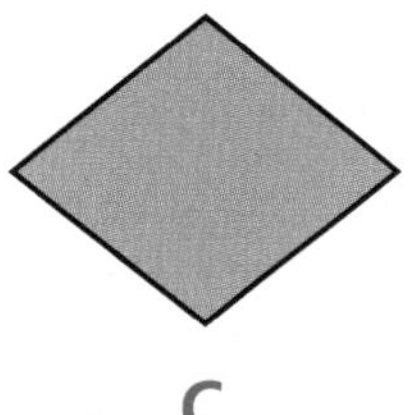
C

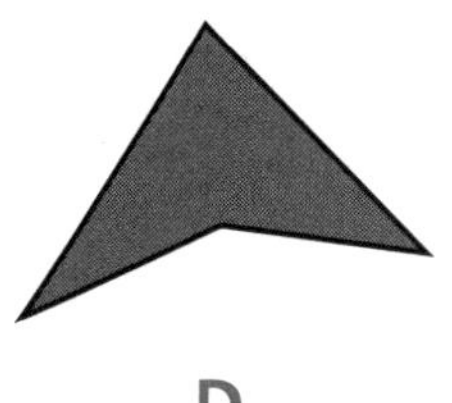
D

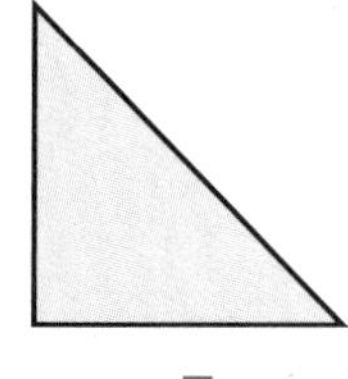
E

Quadrilateral	Parallelogram	Perpendicular sides	All sides the same length

2 Draw two different parallelograms that are not squares or rhombuses.

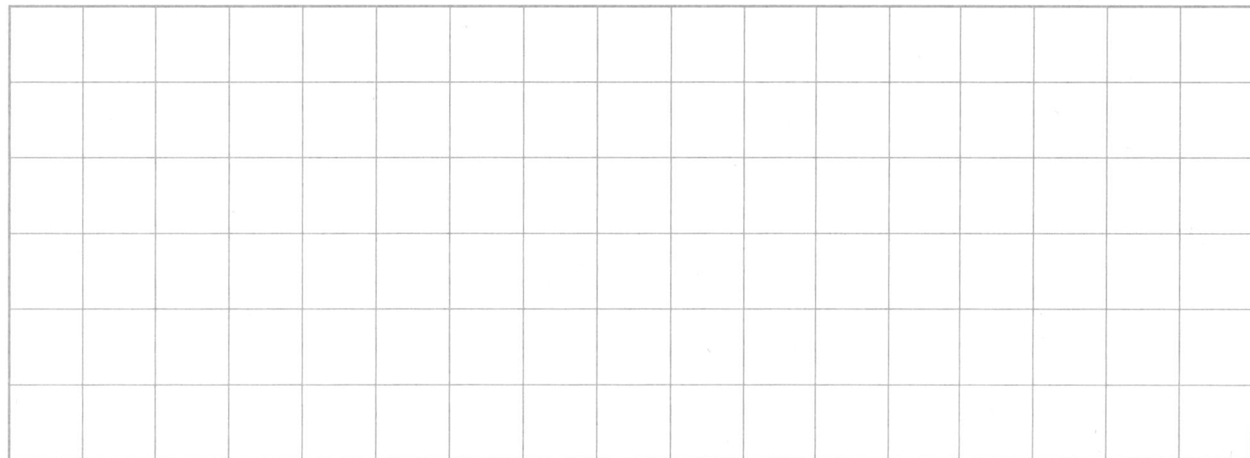

How did you decide which figures to draw?

Name Date

3 Emily draws this figure.

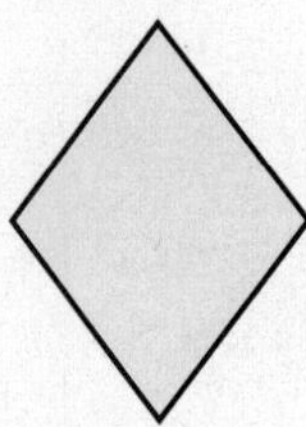

For Exercises 3a–3e, choose Yes or No to tell whether the name describes the figure.

3a. quadrilateral ○ Yes ○ No

3b. rectangle ○ Yes ○ No

3c. parallelogram ○ Yes ○ No

3d. rhombus ○ Yes ○ No

3e. square ○ Yes ○ No

4 Emma is eating a bowl of soup for dinner. She estimates the bowl holds 2 quarts of soup. Do you think Emma's estimate is reasonable? Why or why not?

Name ________________________ Date ____________

5 Draw a figure with 8 sides and 8 vertices.
Name the figure.

____

6 Write the name of the object in the box that shows the unit you would use to measure the mass of the object.

loaf of bread	watermelon	person
house key	lion	comb

gram	kilogram

7 Estimate the liquid volume of each object.
Draw a line from the estimate to the object.

100 liters • 3 liters • 300 milliliters •

Name ______________________________ Date ______________

8. Billy needs 200 milliliters of lemonade to fill a small jar. How many milliliters of lemonade does he need to fill 6 jars of the same size?

Choose the measure to complete the sentence.

Billy needs [600 / 800 / 1,200] milliliters of lemonade.

9. Draw a quadrilateral that is both a square and a rhombus.

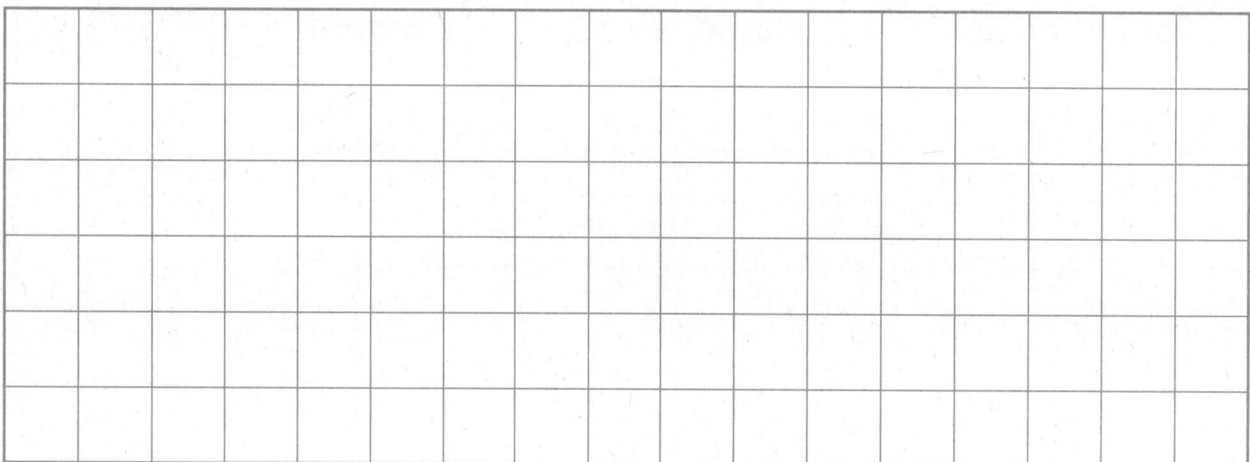

Is every rhombus also a square? Explain.

10. Mia uses 40 liters of water for her garden. That is 12 more liters than Rob. How many liters of water does Rob use?

______________ liters

Name ______________________ Date ______________

11 Rani uses a container that can hold 2 liters of water to fill a fish tank. The fish tank can hold 8 liters of water. How many times must she fill the smaller container to fill the fish tank?

______________ times

12 Sam uses 28 grams of chopped onions in his sauce. There are 6 grams of onions left. How many grams of onions did Sam start with?

______________ grams

13 Mei has 80 kilograms of firewood to divide equally into 10 bundles. How many kilograms of firewood should be in each bundle?

______________ kilograms

14 Chaseedah thinks this shape is a square. Anaya thinks the shape is a rectangle.

Who is correct? Explain your answer.

Name ______________________ Date ______________

15 Roy uses 6 grams of corn in each veggie burger. How many grams of corn does he need to make 20 veggie burgers?

_______________ grams

16 Janie has three dogs. The dogs have masses of 4 kilograms, 8 kilograms, and 7 kilograms. What is the total mass of the three dogs?

_______________ kilograms

17 If each bag contains 185 grams of apple chips, how many grams of apple chips are in 3 bags?

_______________ grams

18 Select all the figures that have at least one set of parallel sides.

○ 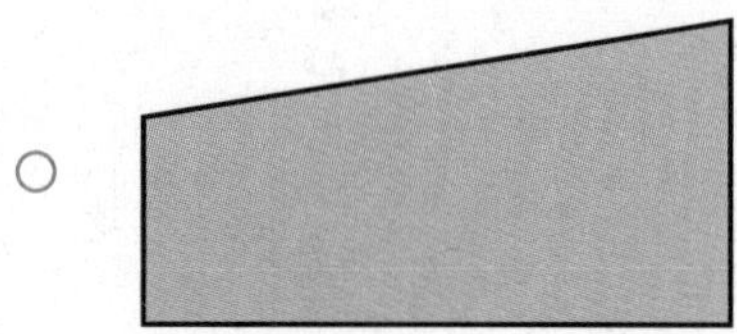

○ 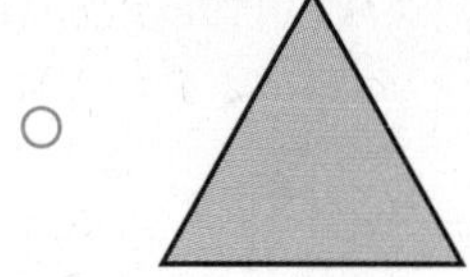

○ 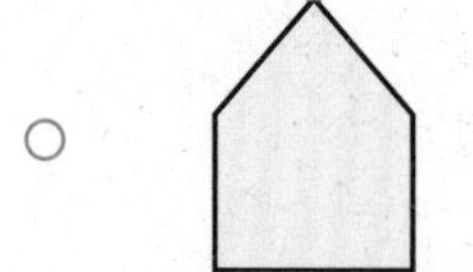

○ 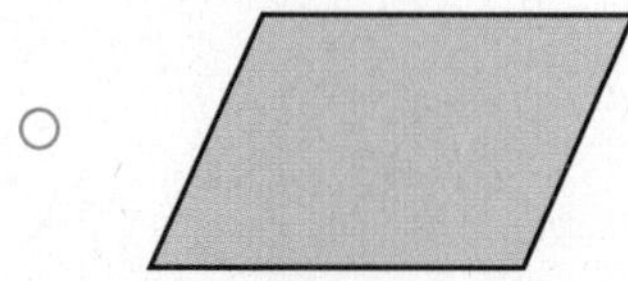

○ 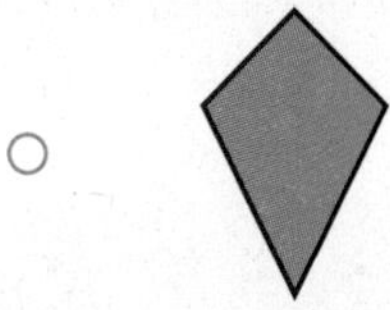

Name _______________ Date _______________

Can You Cut It?

Lucia's class is making sandwiches for a math fair. Lucia will cut the sandwiches into these three different shapes.

Shape A: a quadrilateral that is not a square

Shape B: a triangle with one right angle

Shape C: a parallelogram that is not a rectangle

1. Use your ruler to help you draw Lucia's shapes.

2. Label the shapes **Shape A, Shape B,** and **Shape C**.

3. Combine 2 or more of the above shapes to create a different quadrilateral that Lucia can use for the sandwiches.

Name ____________________ Date ____________

Lucia's class is also making fruit salad for the fair.
Use the chart to help plan the fruit salad.

1 apple............150 grams	**1 pear......150 grams**
1 tangerine........75 grams	**1 plum.......65 grams**
1 banana.........160 grams	**1 peach....100 grams**

Directions for Making Fruit Salad

- The fruit salad should have a total of 8 servings.
- Each serving should be between 90 and 100 grams.
- The fruit salad should include at least 3 different types of fruit.

4 Complete the table to show the ingredients of the fruit salad.

Fruit	Number	Total Mass

Total mass of the fruit salad: ____________

5 Explain the method you used to decide how many of each fruit to include.

____

____

____

____

____

____

Halves and Fourths in Measurement

Fractions in Measurement

Halves	Quarters
Length	
0 1 2 3	0 1 2 3
Money	
50¢ 50¢ Half-Dollar Half-Dollar	25¢ 25¢ 25¢ 25¢ 4 Quarters
Time 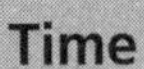	
 30 minutes + 30 minutes = 60 minutes = 1 hour	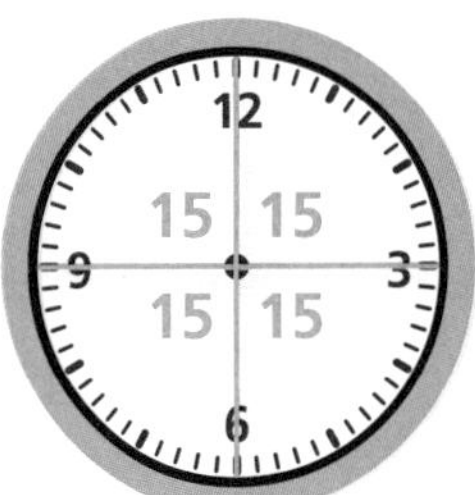 15 minutes + 15 minutes + 15 minutes + 15 minutes = 60 minutes = 1 hour
Liquid Capacity	
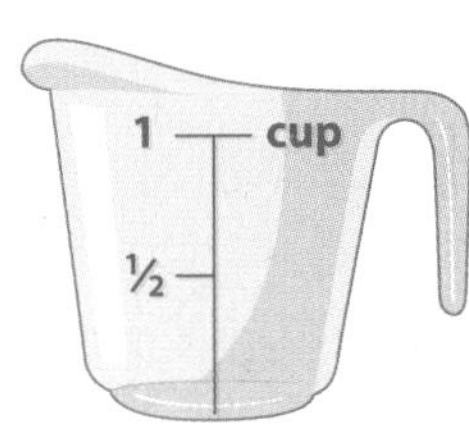 	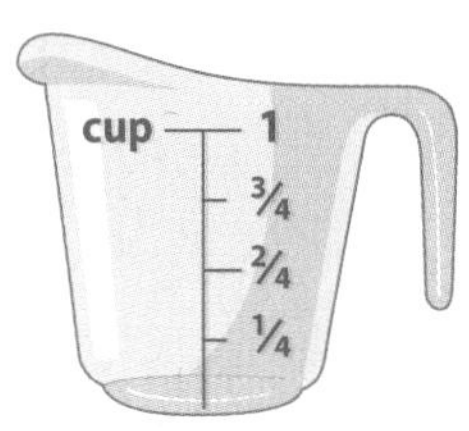

Measures and Units of Time

Table of Measures

Metric	Customary
Length/Area	
1 meter (m) = 10 decimeters (dm) 1 meter (m) = 100 centimeters (cm) 1 decimeter (dm) = 10 centimeters (cm) 1 square centimeter = 1 cm^2 A metric unit for measuring area. It is the area of a square that is one centimeter on each side.	1 foot (ft) = 12 inches (in.) 1 yard (yd) = 3 feet (ft) 1 mile (mi) = 5,280 feet (ft) 1 square inch = 1 in^2 A customary unit for measuring area. It is the area of a square that is one inch on each side.
Liquid Volume	
1 liter (L) = 1,000 milliliters (mL)	1 tablespoon (tbsp) = $\frac{1}{2}$ fluid ounce (fl oz) 1 cup (c) = 8 fluid ounces (fl oz) 1 pint (pt) = 2 cups (c) 1 quart (qt) = 2 pints (pt) 1 gallon (gal) = 4 quarts (qt)

Table of Units of Time

Time	
1 minute (min) = 60 seconds (sec) 1 hour (hr) = 60 minutes 1 day = 24 hours 1 week (wk) = 7 days 1 month, about 30 days 1 year (yr) = 12 months (mo) or about 52 weeks	1 year = 365 days 1 leap year = 366 days

Properties of Operations

Property	Algebraic form	Example
Associative Property of Addition	$(a + b) + c = a + (b + c)$	$(2 + 5) + 3 = 2 + (5 + 3)$
Commutative Property of Addition	$a + b = b + a$	$4 + 6 = 6 + 4$
Identity Property of Addition	$a + 0 = 0 + a = a$	$3 + 0 = 0 + 3 = 3$
Associative Property of Multiplication	$(a \cdot b) \cdot c = a \cdot (b \cdot c)$	$(3 \cdot 5) \cdot 7 = 3 \cdot (5 \cdot 7)$
Commutative Property of Multiplication	$a \cdot b = b \cdot a$	$6 \cdot 3 = 3 \cdot 6$
Identity Property of Multiplication	$a \cdot 1 = 1 \cdot a = a$	$8 \cdot 1 = 1 \cdot 8 = 8$
Zero Property of Multiplication	$a \cdot 0 = 0 \cdot a = 0$	$5 \cdot 0 = 0 \cdot 5 = 0$
Distributive Property of Multiplication over Addition	$a \cdot (b + c) = (a \cdot b) + (a \cdot c)$	$2 \cdot (4 + 3) = (2 \cdot 4) + (2 \cdot 3)$

Problem Types

Addition and Subtraction Problem Types

	Result Unknown	Change Unknown	Start Unknown
Add to	Aisha had 274 stamps in her collection. Then her grandfather gave her 65 stamps. How many stamps does she have now? *Situation and solution equation:*[1] $274 + 65 = s$	Aisha had 274 stamps in her collection. Then her grandfather gave her some stamps. Now she has 339 stamps. How many stamps did her grandfather give her? *Situation equation:* $274 + s = 339$ *Solution equation:* $s = 339 - 274$	Aisha had some stamps in her collection. Then her grandfather gave her 65 stamps. Now she has 339 stamps. How many stamps did she have to start? *Situation equation* $s + 65 = 339$ *Solution equation:* $s = 339 - 65$
Take from	A store had 750 bottles of water at the start of the day. During the day, the store sold 490 bottles. How many bottles did they have at the end of the day? *Situation and solution equation:* $750 - 490 = b$	A store had 750 bottles of water at the start of the day. The store had 260 bottles left at the end of the day. How many bottles did the store sell? *Situation equation:* $750 - b = 260$ *Solution equation:* $b = 750 - 260$	A store had a number of bottles of water at the start of the day. The store sold 490 bottles of water. At the end of the day 260 bottles were left. How many bottles did the store have to start with? *Situation equation:* $b - 490 = 260$ *Solution equation:* $b = 260 + 490$

[1]A situation equation represents the structure (action) in the problem situation. A solution equation shows the operation used to find the answer.

Addition and Subtraction Problem Types (continued)

	Total Unknown	Addend Unknown	Other Addends Unknown
Put Together/ Take Apart	A clothing store has 375 shirts with short sleeves and 148 shirts with long sleeves. How many shirts does the store have in all? *Math drawing:*[1]  *Situation and solution equation:* $375 + 148 = s$	Of the 523 shirts in a clothing store, 375 have short sleeves. The rest have long sleeves. How many shirts have long sleeves? *Math drawing:*  *Situation equation:* $523 = 375 + s$ *Solution equation:* $s = 523 - 375$	A clothing store has 523 shirts. Some have short sleeves and 148 have long sleeves. How many of the shirts have short sleeves? *Math drawing:*  *Situation equation* $523 = s + 148$ *Solution equation:* $s = 523 - 148$
	Both Addends Unknown is a productive extension of this basic situation, especially for small numbers less than or equal to 10. Such take apart situations can be used to show all the decompositions of a given number. The associated equations, which have the total on the left of the equal sign, help students understand that the = sign does not always mean makes or results in but always does mean is the same number as.		**Both Addends Unknown** A clothing store has 523 shirts. Some have short sleeves and some have long sleeves. Write a situation equation for how many shirts with long sleeves and how many shirts with short sleeves the store could have. *Math Drawing:*  *Situation Equation:* $523 = \square + \square$

[1]These math drawings are called math mountains in Grades 1–3 and break apart drawings in Grades 4 and 5.

Addition and Subtraction Problem Types (continued)

	Difference Unknown	Greater Unknown	Smaller Unknown
Compare	At a zoo, the female black bear weighs 175 pounds. The male black bear weighs 260 pounds. How much more does the male black bear weigh than the female black bear? At a zoo, the female black bear weighs 175 pounds. The male black bear weighs 260 pounds. How much less does the female black bear weigh than the male black bear? *Math drawing:* 260 175 d *Situation equation:* $175 + d = 260$, or $d = 260 - 175$ *Solution equation:* $d = 260 - 175$	**Leading Language** At a zoo, the female black bear weighs 175 pounds. The male black bear weighs 85 pounds more than the female black bear. How much does the male black bear weigh? **Misleading Language** At a zoo, the female black bear weighs 175 pounds. The female black bear weighs 85 pounds less than the male black bear. How much does the male black bear weigh? *Math drawing:* m 175 85 *Situation and solution equation:* $175 + 85 = m$	**Leading Language** At a zoo, the male black bear weighs 260 pounds. The female black bear weighs 85 pounds less than the male black bear. How much does the female black bear weigh? **Misleading Language** At a zoo, the male black bear weighs 260 pounds. The male black bear weighs 85 pounds more than the female black bear. How much does the female black bear weigh? *Math drawing:* 260 f 85 *Situation equation* $f + 85 = 260$, or $f = 260 - 85$ *Solution equation:* $f = 260 - 85$

A comparison sentence can always be said in two ways. One way uses *more*, and the other uses *fewer* or *less*. Misleading language suggests the wrong operation. For example, it says *the female black bear weighs 85 pounds less than the male*, but you have to add 85 pounds to the female's weight to get the male's weight.

Multiplication and Division Problem Types

	Product Unknown	Group Size Unknown	Number of Groups Unknown
Equal Groups	A teacher bought 5 boxes of markers. There are 8 markers in each box. How many markers did the teacher buy? *Math drawing:* n; $5\times$; 8 8 8 8 8 *Situation and solution equation:* $n = 5 \cdot 8$	A teacher bought 5 boxes of markers. She bought 40 markers in all. How many markers are in each box? *Math drawing:* 40; $5\times$; n n n n n *Situation equation:* $5 \cdot n = 40$ *Solution equation:* $n = 40 \div 5$	A teacher bought boxes of 8 markers. She bought 40 markers in all. How many boxes of markers did she buy? *Math drawing:* 40; $n\times$; 8 8 8 8 8 *Situation equation* $n \cdot 8 = 40$ *Solution equation:* $n = 40 \div 8$

Multiplication and Division Problem Types (continued)

	Product Unknown	Factor Unknown	Factor Unknown
Arrays	For the yearbook photo, the drama club stood in 3 rows of 7 students. How many students were in the photo in all? *Math drawing:* 7 OOOOOOO 3 OOOOOOO OOOOOOO *Situation and solution equation:* $n = 3 \cdot 7$	For the yearbook photo, the 21 students in drama club stood in 3 equal rows. How many students were in each row? *Math drawing:* n, n, n → Total: 21 *Situation equation:* $3 \cdot n = 21$ *Solution equation:* $n = 21 \div 3$	For the yearbook photo, the 21 students in drama club stood in rows of 7 students. How many rows were there? *Math drawing:* 7, 7, 7 → Total: 21 *Situation equation* $n \cdot 7 = 21$ *Solution equation:* $n = 21 \div 7$
Area	The floor of the kitchen is 2 meters by 5 meters. What is the area of the floor? *Math drawing:* 5 (top), 2 (side), A (inside) *Situation and solution equation:* $A = 5 \cdot 2$	The floor of the kitchen is 5 meters long. The area of the floor is 10 square meters. What is the width of the floor? *Math drawing:* 5 (top), w (side), 10 (inside) *Situation equation:* $5 \cdot w = 10$ *Solution equation:* $w = 10 \div 5$	The floor of the kitchen is 2 meters wide. The area of the floor is 10 square meters. What is the length of the floor? *Math drawing:* l (top), 2 (side), 10 (inside) *Situation equation* $l \cdot 2 = 10$ *Solution equation:* $l = 10 \div 2$

MathWord **Power**

Word Review 

Work with a partner. Choose a word from a current unit or a review word from a previous unit. Use the word to complete one of the activities listed on the right. Then ask your partner if they have any edits to your work or questions about what you described. Repeat, having your partner choose a word.

Activities

- Give the meaning in words or gestures.
- Use the word in a sentence.
- Give another word that is related to the word in some way and explain the relationship.

Crossword Puzzle 

Create a crossword puzzle similar to the example below. Use vocabulary words from the unit. You can add other related words, too. Challenge your partner to solve the puzzle.

				1 s	u	m	
	2 a			u			
	d			b			
3 a	d	d	i	t	i	o	4 n
	e			r			u
	n			a			m
5 a	d	d		c			b
				t			e
				i			r
6 r	e	g	r	o	u	p	
				n			

Across

1. The answer to an addition problem
3. ___________ and subtraction are operations that undo each other.
5. To put amounts together
6. When you trade 10 ones for 1 ten, you ___________.

Down

1. The operation that you can use to find out how much more one number is than another
2. In 24 + 65 = 89, 24 is an _____.
4. A combination of the digits 0, 1, 2, 3, 4, 5, 6, 7, 8, and 9

Vocabulary Activities

Word Wall

With your teacher's permission, start a word wall in your classroom. As you work through each lesson, put the math vocabulary words on index cards and place them on the word wall. You can work with a partner or a small group choosing a word and giving the definition.

Word Web 

Make a word web for a word or words you do not understand in a unit. Fill in the web with words or phrases that are related to the vocabulary word.

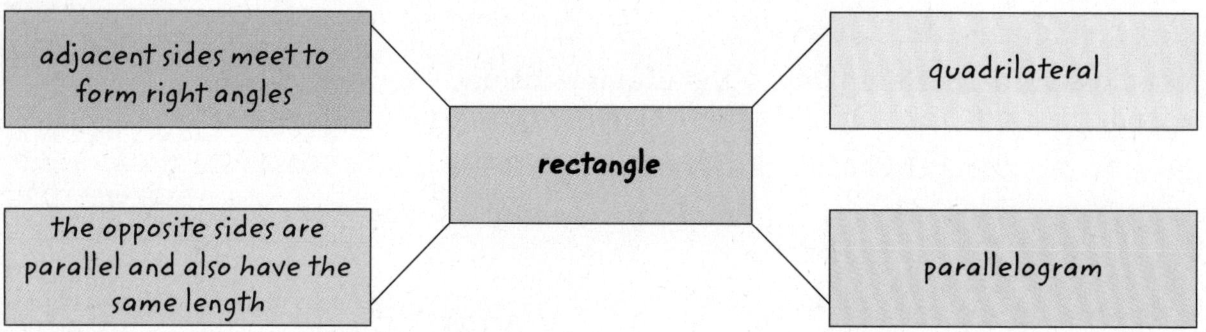

Alphabet Challenge 

Take an alphabet challenge. Choose three letters from the alphabet. Think of three vocabulary words for each letter. Then write the definition or draw an example for each word.

A	D	L
addition	data	liter
array	denominator	line segment
area	divide	line plot

Concentration 

Write the vocabulary words and related words from a unit on index cards. Write the definitions on a different set of index cards. Choose 3 to 6 pairs of vocabulary words and definitions. Mix up the set of pairs. Then place the cards facedown on a table. Take turns turning over two cards. If one card is a word and one card is a definition that matches the word, take the pair. Continue until each word has been matched with its definition.

Math Journal 

As you learn new words, write them in your Math Journal. Write the definition of the word and include a sketch or an example. As you learn new information about the word, add notes to your definition.

polygon: a closed plane figure with sides made of straight line segments.

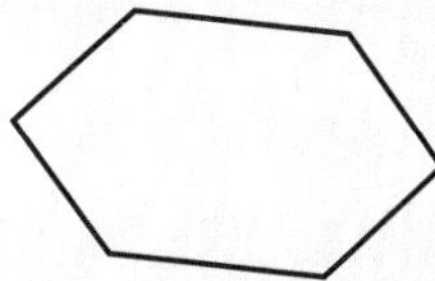

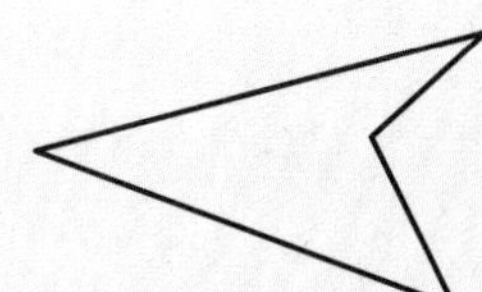

In concave polygons, there exists a line segment with endpoints inside the polygon and a point on the line segment that is outside the polygon.

What's the Word? 

Work together to make a poster or bulletin board display of the words in a unit. Write definitions on a set of index cards. Mix up the cards. Work with a partner, choosing a definition from the index cards. Have your partner point to the word on the poster and name the matching math vocabulary word. Switch roles and try the activity again.

the bottom number in a fraction that shows the total number of equal parts in the whole

fraction
unit fraction
denominator
numerator
equivalent
equivalent fractions
equivalence chain
thirds
fourths
eighths
halves
sixths

A

addend
One of two or more numbers to be added together to find a sum.

Example:

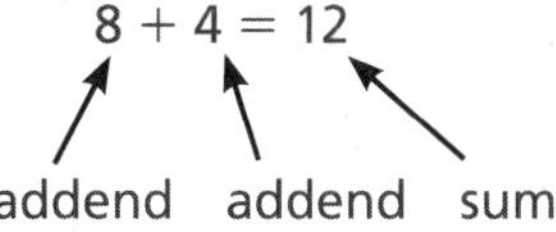

addition
A mathematical operation that combines two or more numbers.

Example:

$23 + 52 = 75$

addend addend sum

adjacent sides
Two sides of a figure that meet at a point.

Example:

Sides *a* and *b* are adjacent.

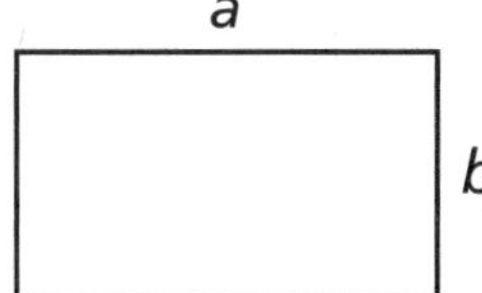

A.M.
The time period between midnight and noon.

analog clock
A clock with a face and hands.

angle
A figure formed by two rays or two line segments that meet at an endpoint.

area
The total number of square units that cover a figure.

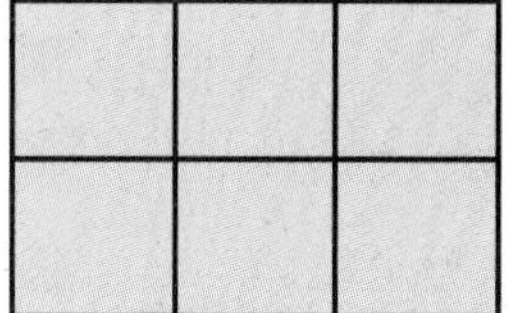

Example:

The area of the rectangle is 6 square units.

array
An arrangement of objects, pictures, or numbers in columns and rows.

Associative Property of Addition (Grouping Property of Addition)
The property that states that changing the way in which addends are grouped does not change the sum.

Example:

$(2 + 3) + 1 = 2 + (3 + 1)$

$5 + 1 = 2 + 4$

$6 = 6$

Associative Property of Multiplication (Grouping Property of Multiplication)

The property that states that changing the way in which factors are grouped does not change the product.

Example:

$(2 \times 3) \times 4 = 2 \times (3 \times 4)$

$6 \times 4 = 2 \times 12$

$24 = 24$

axis (plural: axes)

A reference line for a graph. A graph has two axes; one is horizontal and the other is vertical.

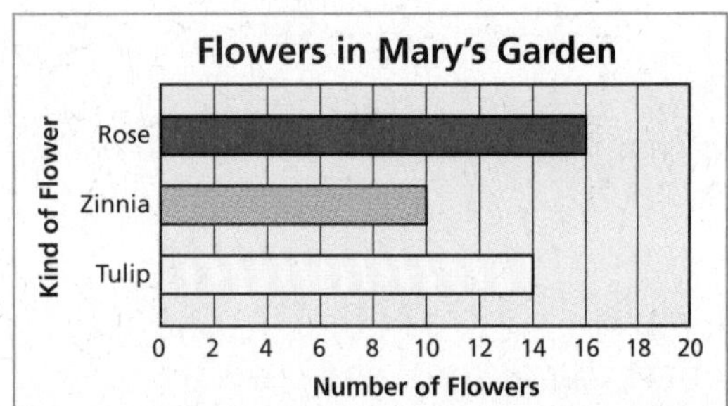

B

bar graph

A graph that uses bars to show data. The bars may be horizontal, as in the graph above, or vertical, as in the graph below.

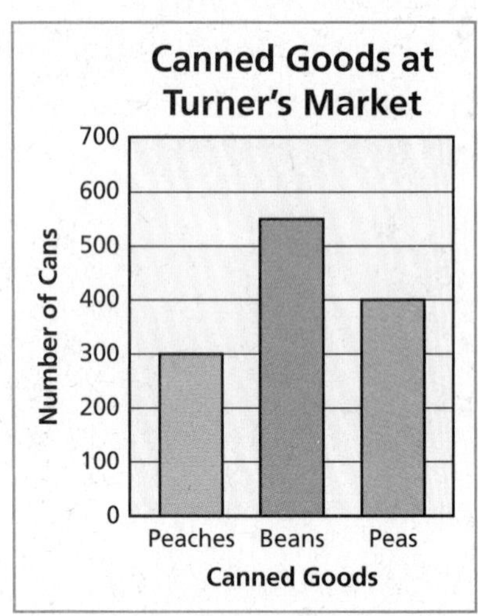

C

capacity

The amount a container can hold.

Celsius (°C)

A scale used to measure temperature.

Examples:

Water freezes at 0°C.

Water boils at 100°C.

centimeter (cm)

A metric unit used to measure length.

100 centimeters = 1 meter

column

A part of a table or array that contains items arranged vertically.

Commutative Property of Addition (Order Property of Addition)

The property that states that changing the order of addends does not change the sum.

Example:

$3 + 7 = 7 + 3$

$10 = 10$

Commutative Property of Multiplication (Order Property of Multiplication)

The property that states that changing the order of factors does not change the product.

Example:

$5 \times 4 = 4 \times 5$

$20 = 20$

comparison bars*

Bars that represent the greater amount, lesser amount, and difference in a comparison problem.

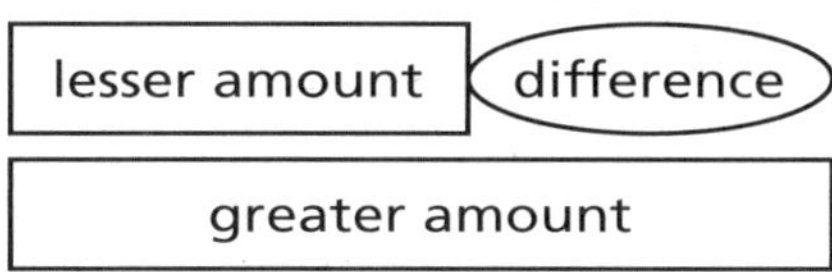

compatible numbers

Numbers that are easy to compute mentally. Compatible numbers can be used to check if answers are reasonable.

Example:

692 + 234

Some compatible numbers for the addends are 700 and 200 or 700 and 234.

concave

A polygon for which you can connect two points inside the polygon with a segment that passes outside the polygon.

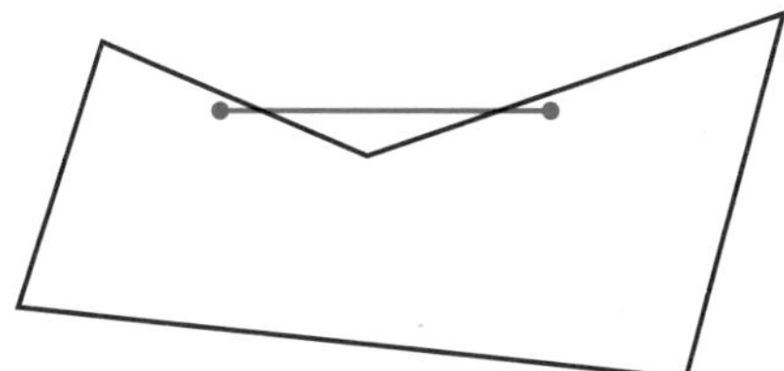

convex

A polygon is convex if all of its diagonals are inside it.

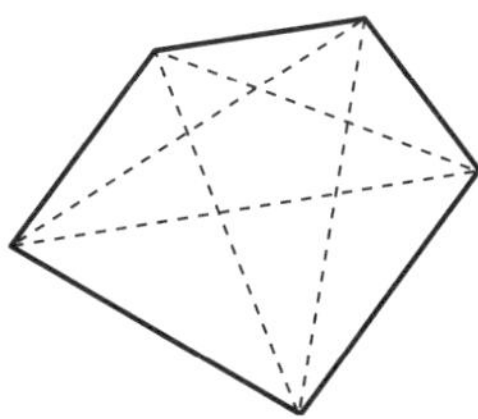

cup (c)

A U.S. customary unit of measure used to measure capacity.

1 cup = 8 fluid ounces

2 cups = 1 pint

4 cups = 1 quart

16 cups = 1 gallon

D

data

A collection of information about people or things.

decagon

A polygon with 10 sides.

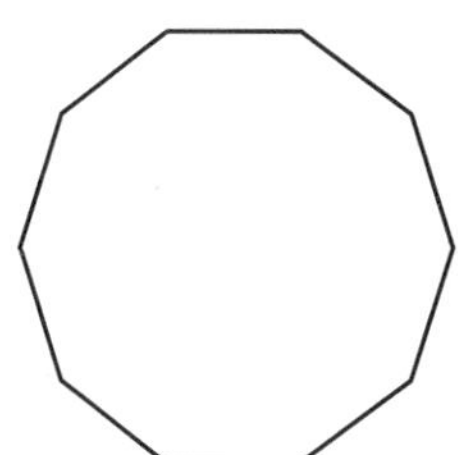

decimeter (dm)

A metric unit used to measure length.

1 decimeter = 10 centimeters

decompose

To separate or break apart (a geometric figure or a number) into smaller parts.

denominator

The bottom number in a fraction that shows the total number of equal parts in the whole.

Example:

$\frac{1}{3}$ ← denominator

diagonal

A line segment that connects two corners of a figure and is not a side of the figure.

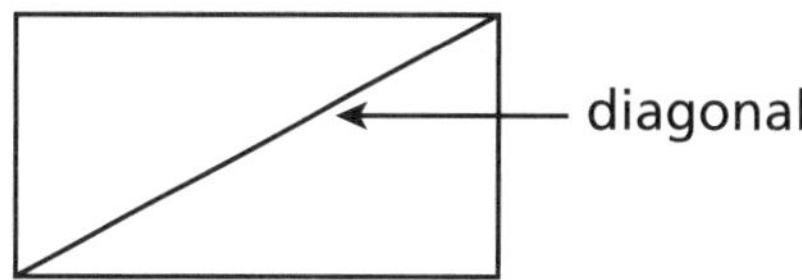

difference

The result of subtraction or of comparing.

*A classroom research-based term developed for *Math Expressions*

digit
Any of the symbols 0, 1, 2, 3, 4, 5, 6, 7, 8, 9.

digital clock
A clock that displays the hour and minutes with numbers.

Distributive Property
You can multiply a sum by a number, or multiply each addend by the number and add the products; the result is the same.

Example:
$3 \times (2 + 4) = (3 \times 2) + (3 \times 4)$
$3 \times 6 = 6 + 12$
$18 = 18$

dividend
The number that is divided in division.

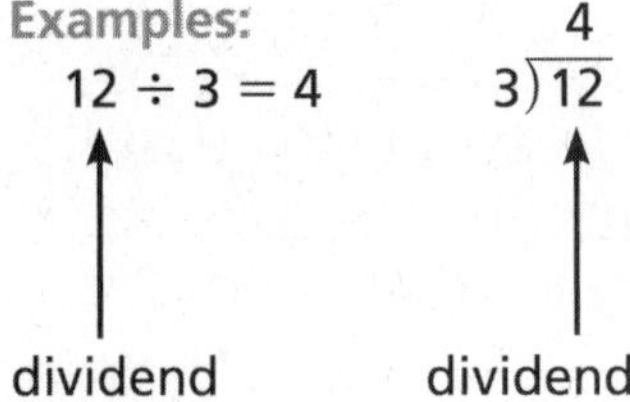

division
The mathematical operation that separates an amount into smaller equal groups to find the number of groups or the number in each group.

Example:
$12 \div 3 = 4$ is a division number sentence.

divisor
The number that you divide by in division.

Example:
$12 \div 3 = 4$ $\quad 3\overline{)12}$ with quotient 4

divisor divisor

E

elapsed time
The time that passes between the beginning and the end of an activity.

endpoint
The point at either end of a line segment or the beginning point of a ray.

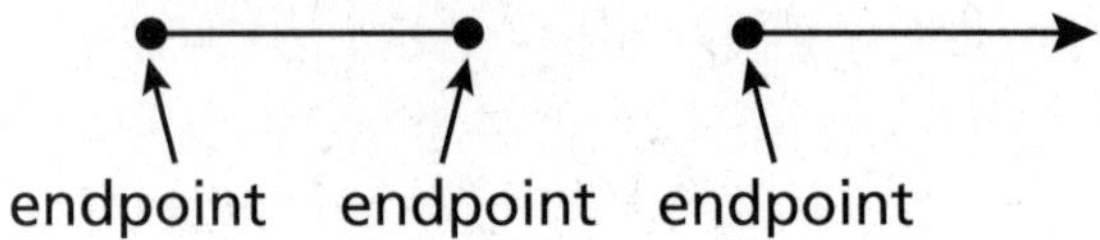

equal (=)
A symbol used to compare two amounts or values. It shows that what is on the left of the sign is equal to or the same value as what is on the right of the sign.

Example:
$3{,}756 = 3{,}756$

3,756 *is equal to* 3,756.

equal groups
Two or more groups with the same number of items in each group.

equation
A mathematical sentence with an equals sign.

Examples:
$11 + 22 = 33$
$75 - 25 = 50$

equivalent
Equal, or naming the same amount.

equivalent fractions
Fractions that name the same amount.

Example:

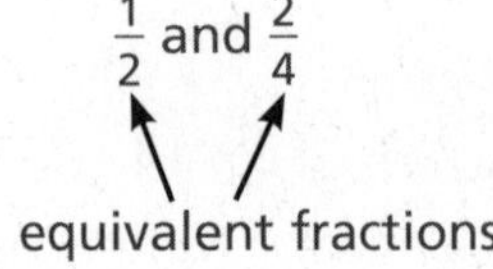

estimate
A reasonable guess about how many or about how much.

even number
A whole number that is a multiple of 2. The ones digit in an even number is 0, 2, 4, 6, or 8.

expanded form
A number written to show the value of each of its digits.

Examples:
347 = 300 + 40 + 7
347 = 3 hundreds + 4 tens + 7 ones

expression
A combination of numbers, variables, and/or operation signs. An expression does not have an equal sign.

Examples:
$4 + 7$ $a - 3$

F

factor
Any of the numbers that are multiplied to give a product.

Example:
$4 \times 5 = 20$

factor factor product

Fahrenheit (°F)
A scale used to measure temperature.

Examples:
Water freezes at 32°F.
Water boils at 212°F.

fluid ounce (fl oz)
A unit of liquid volume in the U.S. customary system that equals $\frac{1}{8}$ cup or 2 tablespoons.

foot (ft)
A U.S. customary unit used to measure length.

1 foot = 12 inches

fraction
A number that names part of a whole or part of a set.

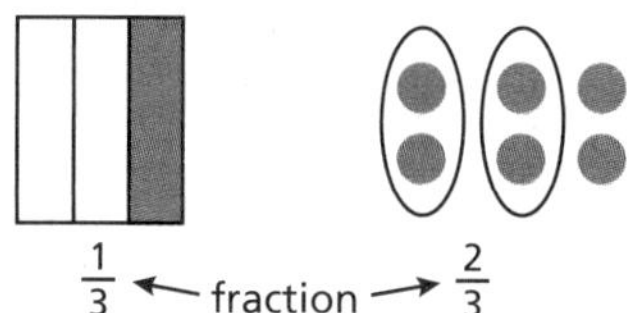

frequency table
A table that shows how many times each event, item, or category occurs.

Frequency Table	
Age	Number of Players
7	1
8	3
9	5
10	4
11	2

function table
A table of ordered pairs that shows a function.

For every input number, there is only one possible output number.

Rule: Add 2	
Input	Output
1	3
2	4
3	5
4	6

G

gallon (gal)
A U.S. customary unit used to measure capacity.

1 gallon = 4 quarts = 8 pints = 16 cups

gram (g)
A metric unit of mass. One paper clip has a mass of about 1 gram.

1,000 grams = 1 kilogram

greatest
56 29 64

64 is the greatest number.

group
To combine numbers to form new tens, hundreds, thousands, and so on.

H

height
A vertical distance, or how tall something is.

hexagon
A polygon with six sides.

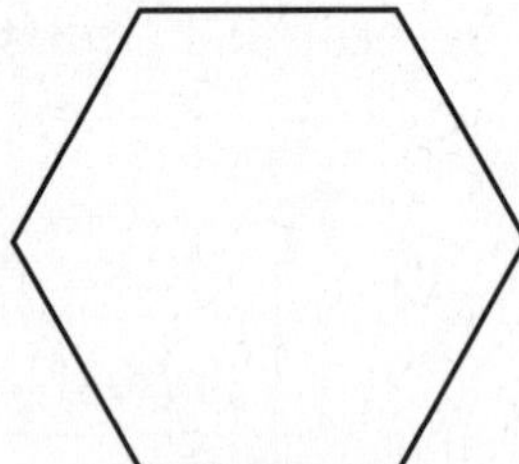

horizontal
Extending in two directions, left and right.

horizontal bar graph
A bar graph with horizontal bars.

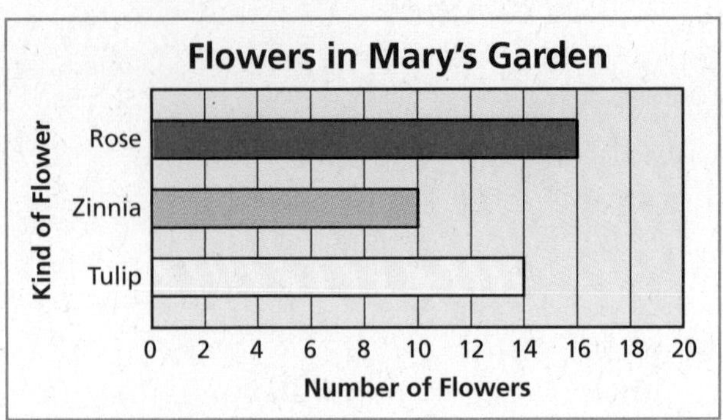

hundred thousands

Hundred Thousands	Ten Thousands	Thousands	Hundreds	Tens	Ones
5	4	6	7	8	2

There are 5 hundred thousands in 546,782.

hundreds

3 hundreds

347 has 3 hundreds.

hundreds

I

Identity Property of Addition
If 0 is added to a number, the sum equals that number.

Example:
$3 + 0 = 3$

Identity Property of Multiplication
The product of 1 and any number equals that number.

Example:
$10 \times 1 = 10$

improper fraction
A fraction in which the numerator is equal to or is greater than the denominator. Improper fractions are equal to or greater than 1.

$\frac{5}{5}$ and $\frac{8}{3}$ are improper fractions.

inch (in.)
A U.S. customary unit used to measure length.

12 inches = 1 foot

input-output table
A table that displays ordered pairs of numbers that follow a specific rule.

Rule: Add 4	
Input	**Output**
3	7
5	9
9	13
11	15
15	19

is greater than ($>$)
A symbol used to compare two numbers.

Example:

$6 > 5$

6 *is greater than* 5.

is less than ($<$)
A symbol used to compare two numbers.

Example:

$5 < 6$

5 *is less than* 6.

K

key
A part of a map, graph, or chart that explains what symbols mean.

kilogram (kg)
A metric unit of mass.

1 kilogram = 1,000 grams

kilometer (km)
A metric unit of length.

1 kilometer = 1,000 meters

L

least
72   41   89

41 is the least number.

line
A straight path that goes on forever in opposite directions.

line plot
A diagram that shows frequency of data on a number line. Also called a *dot plot*.

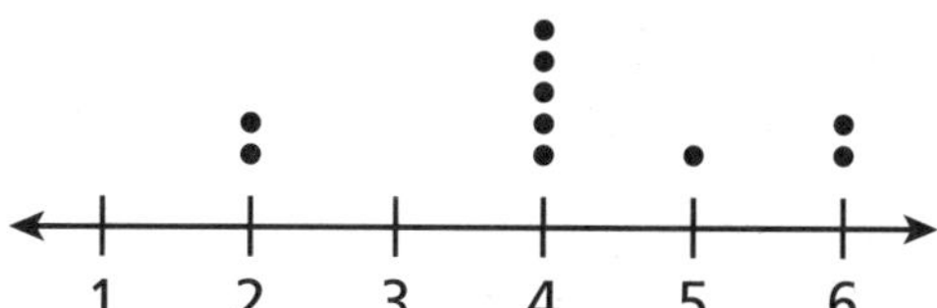

line segment
A part of a line. A line segment has two endpoints.

liquid volume
A measure of how much a container can hold. Also called *capacity*.

liter (L)
A metric unit used to measure capacity.

1 liter = 1,000 milliliters

M

mass
The amount of matter in an object.

mental math
A way to solve problems without using pencil and paper or a calculator.

meter (m)
A metric unit used to measure length.

1 meter = 100 centimeters

method
A procedure, or way, of doing something.

mile (mi)
A U.S. customary unit of length.

1 mile = 5,280 feet

milliliter (mL)
A metric unit used to measure capacity.

1,000 milliliters = 1 liter

mixed number
A whole number and a fraction.

$1\frac{3}{4}$ is a mixed number.

multiple
A number that is the product of the given number and any whole number.

multiplication
A mathematical operation that combines equal groups.

Example:

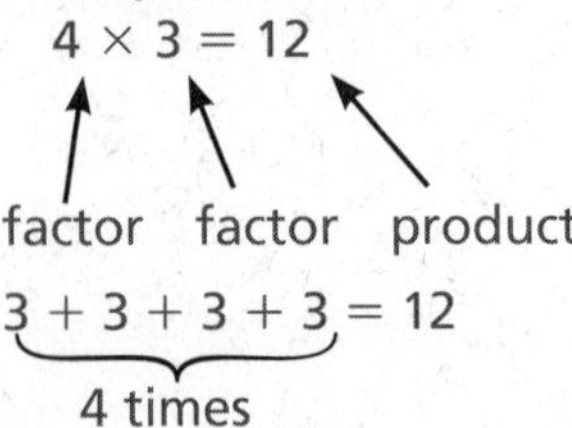

N

number line
A line on which numbers are assigned to lengths.

numerator
The top number in a fraction that shows the number of equal parts counted.

Example:

$\frac{1}{3}$ ← numerator

O

octagon
A polygon with eight sides.

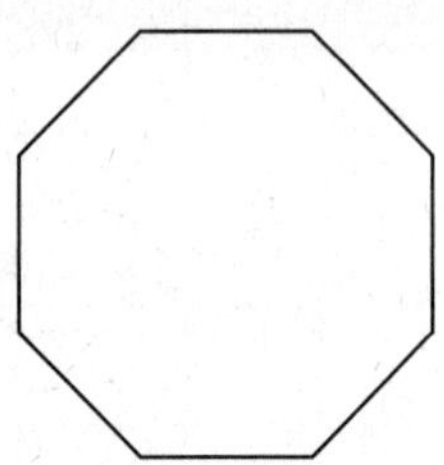

odd number
A whole number that is not a multiple of 2. The ones digit in an odd number is 1, 3, 5, 7, or 9.

ones

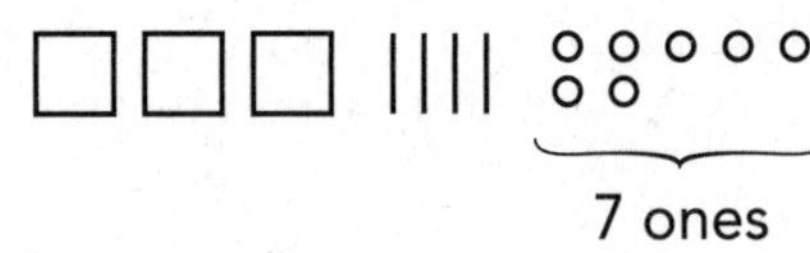

347 has 7 ones.

↑

ones

opposite sides
Sides of a polygon that are across from each other; they do not meet at a point.

Example:
Sides *a* and *c* are opposite.

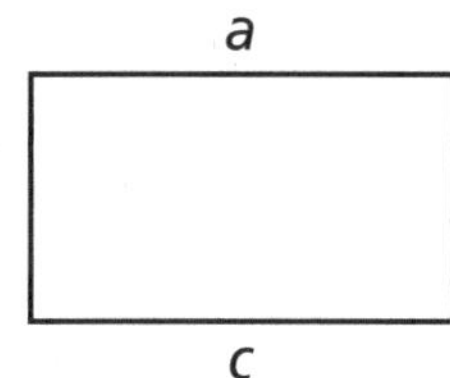

Order of Operations
A set of rules that state the order in which the operations in an expression should be done.

STEP 1: Perform operations inside parentheses first.

STEP 2: Multiply and divide from left to right.

STEP 3: Add and subtract from left to right.

ounce (oz)
A U.S. customary unit used to measure weight.
16 ounces = 1 pound

P

parallel
Two lines are parallel if they never cross or meet. They are the same distance apart.

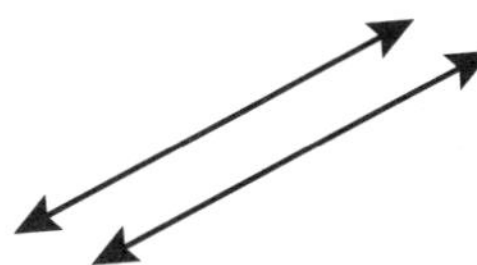

parallelogram
A quadrilateral with both pairs of opposite sides parallel.

pentagon
A polygon with five sides.

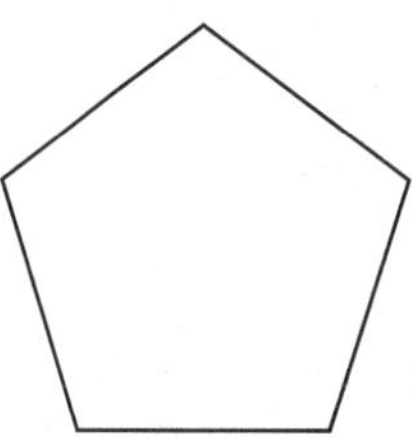

perimeter
The distance around a figure.

Example:
Perimeter = 3 cm + 5 cm + 3 cm + 5 cm = 16 cm

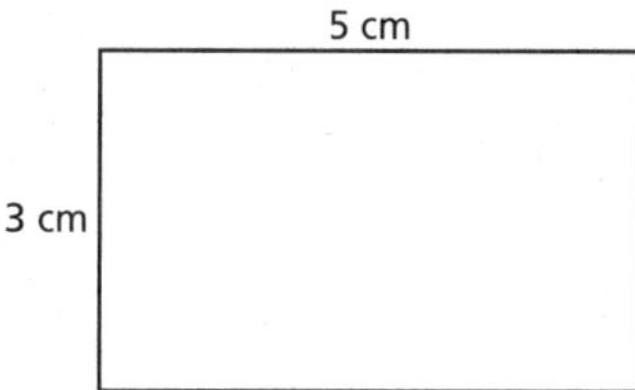

perpendicular
Two lines are perpendicular if they cross or meet to form square corners.

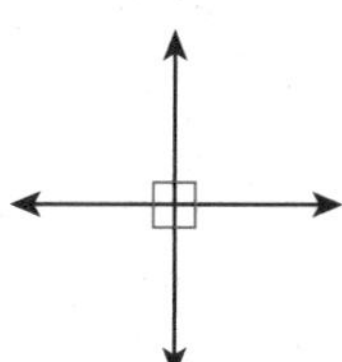

pictograph
A graph that uses pictures or symbols to represent data.

Favorite Ice Cream Flavors

Flavor	Votes
Peanut Butter Crunch	🍦 ½🍦
Cherry Vanilla	🍦 🍦 🍦
Chocolate	🍦 🍦 🍦 🍦 🍦

Each 🍦 stands for 4 votes.

pint (pt)
A U.S. customary unit used to measure capacity.
1 pint = 2 cups

place value

The value assigned to the place that a digit occupies in a number.

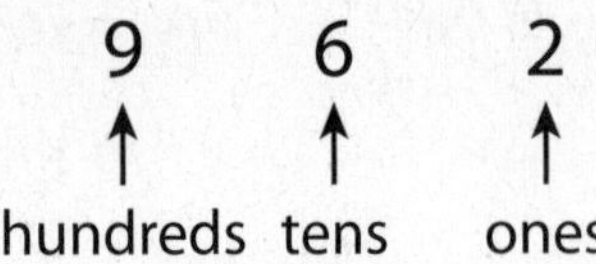

place value drawing

A drawing that represents a number. Hundreds are represented by boxes, tens by vertical lines, and ones by small circles.

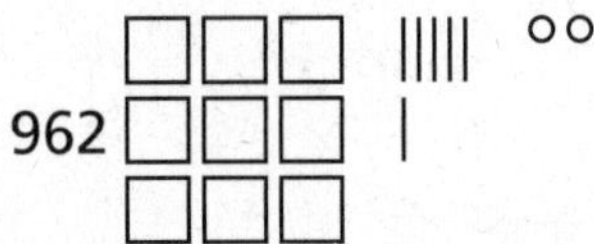

P.M.

The time period between noon and midnight.

polygon

A closed plane figure with sides made up of straight line segments.

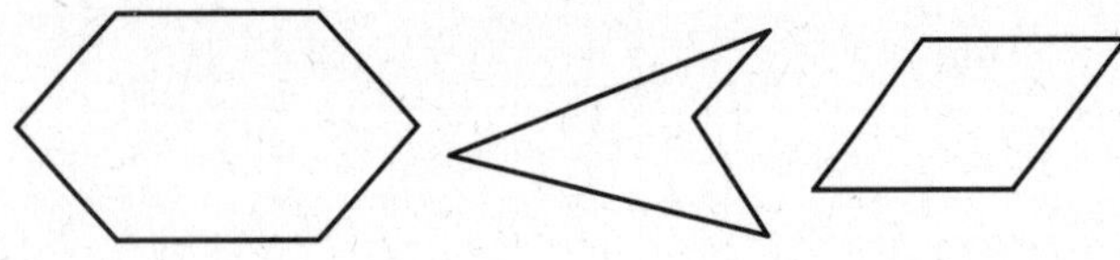

pound (lb)

A U.S. customary unit used to measure weight.

1 pound = 16 ounces

product

The answer when you multiply numbers.

Example:

$4 \times 7 = 28$

factor factor product

proof drawing*

A drawing used to show that an answer is correct.

$$\begin{array}{r} 249 \\ +\ 386 \\ \hline 635 \end{array}$$

(carry marks: 11)

Q

quadrilateral

A polygon with four sides.

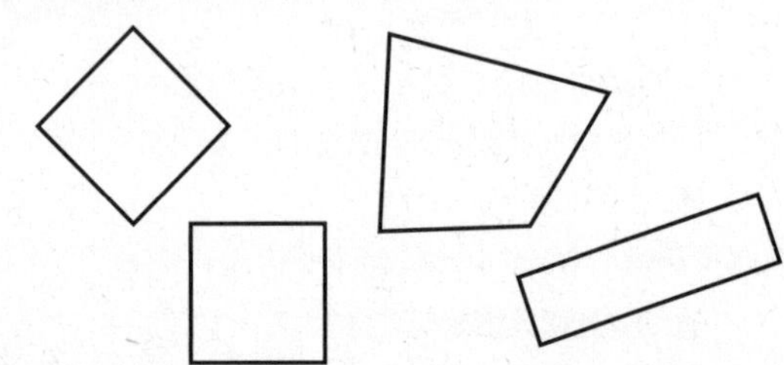

quart (qt)

A U.S. customary unit used to measure capacity.

1 quart = 4 cups

quotient

The answer when you divide numbers.

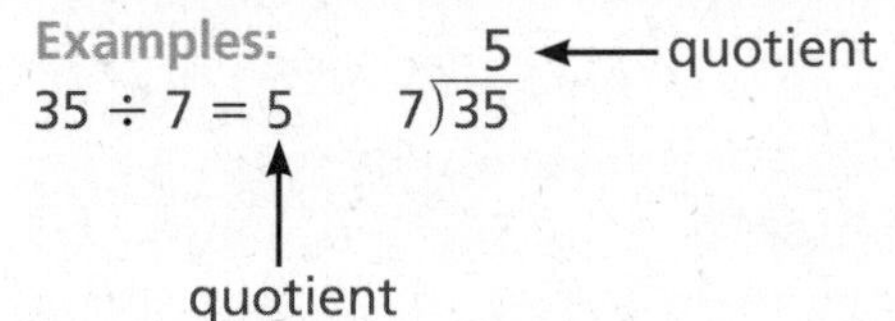

R

ray

A part of a line that has one endpoint and goes on forever in one direction.

*A classroom research-based term developed for *Math Expressions*

rectangle
A parallelogram that has four right angles.

rhombus
A parallelogram with equal sides.

right angle
An angle that measures 90°.

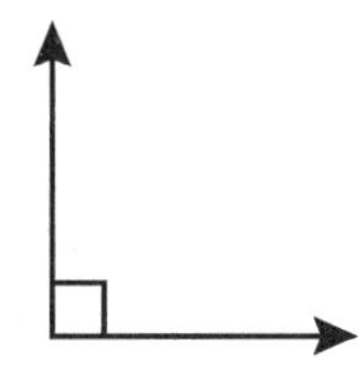

round
To find about how many or how much by expressing a number to the nearest ten, hundred, thousand, and so on.

row
A part of a table or array that contains items arranged horizontally.

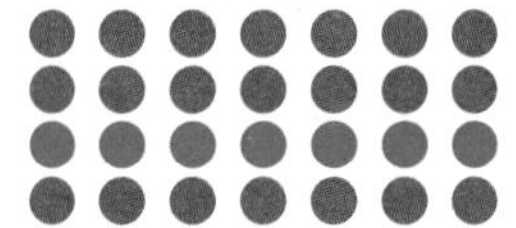

rule
For an input-output table, a *rule* is applied to the input to find the output.

Rule: Add 4	
Input	**Output**
3	7
5	9
9	13
11	15
15	19

S

scale
An arrangement of numbers in order with equal intervals.

side (of a figure)
One of the line segments that make up a polygon.

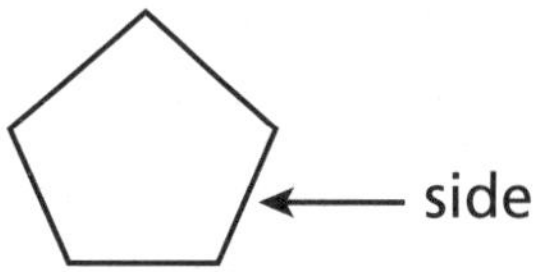

simplify
To write an equivalent fraction with a smaller numerator and denominator.

situation equation*
An equation that shows the action or the relationship in a problem.

Example:
$35 + n = 40$

solution equation*
An equation that shows the operation to perform in order to solve the problem.

Example:
$n = 40 - 35$

square
A rectangle with four sides of the same length.

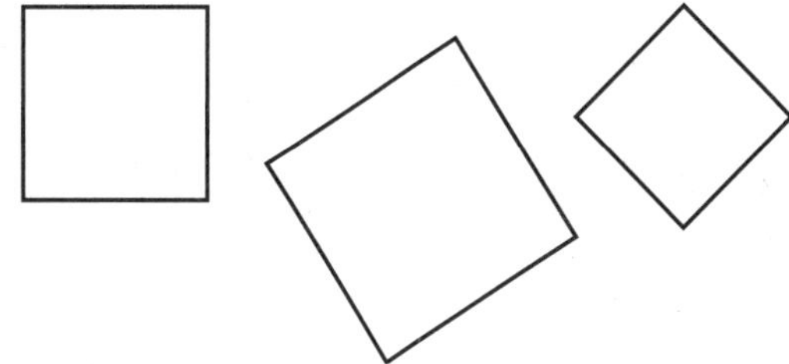

*A classroom research-based term developed for *Math Expressions*

square number
The product of a whole number and itself.

Example:
4 × 4 = 16

square number

square unit
A unit of area equal to the area of a square with one-unit sides.

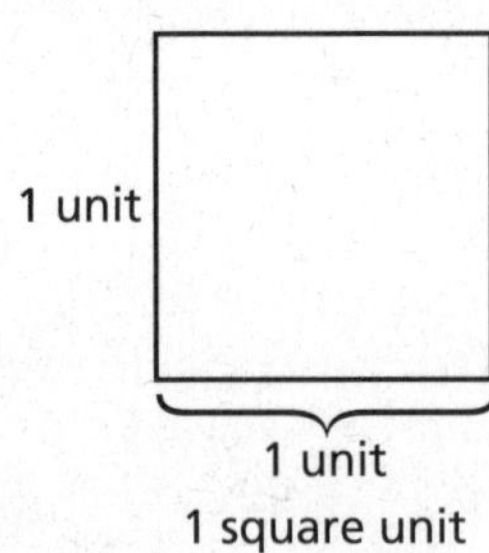

1 square unit

standard form
The name of a number written using digits.

Example:
1,829

subtract
To find the difference of two numbers.

Example:
18 − 11 = 7

subtraction
A mathematical operation on two numbers that gives the difference.

Example:
43 − 40 = 3

sum
The answer when adding two or more addends.

Example:
37 + 52 = 89

addend addend sum

T

table
An easy-to-read arrangement of data, usually in rows and columns.

Favorite Team Sport	
Sport	**Number of Students**
Baseball	35
Soccer	60
Basketball	40

tally chart
A chart used to record and organize data with tally marks.

Tally Chart	
Age	**Tally**
7	I
8	III
9	~~IIII~~

tally marks
Short line segments drawn in groups of 5. Each mark, including the slanted mark, stands for 1 unit.

~~IIII~~ ~~IIII~~ III means 13
5 5 3

temperature
The measure of how hot or cold something is.

ten thousands

Hundred Thousands	Ten Thousands	Thousands	Hundreds	Tens	Ones
5	4	6	7	8	2

There are 4 ten thousands in 546,782.

tens

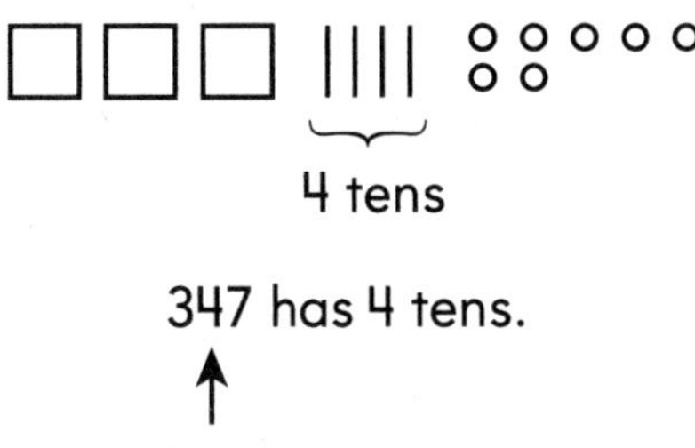

thermometer

A tool that is used to measure temperature.

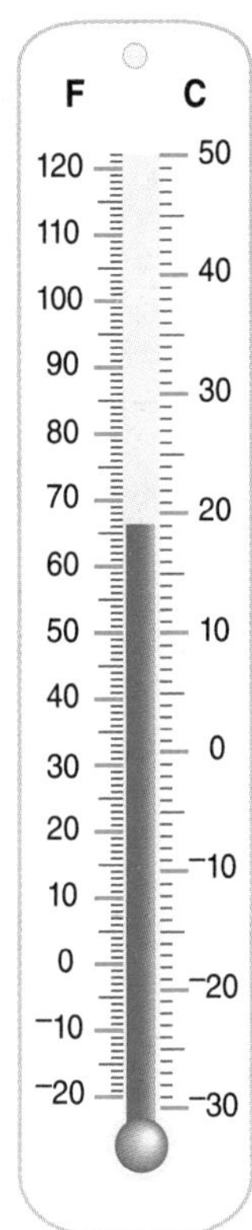

thousands

Hundred Thousands	Ten Thousands	Thousands	Hundreds	Tens	Ones
5	4	6	7	8	2

There are 6 thousands in 546,782.

total

The answer when adding two or more addends. The sum of two or more numbers.

Example:

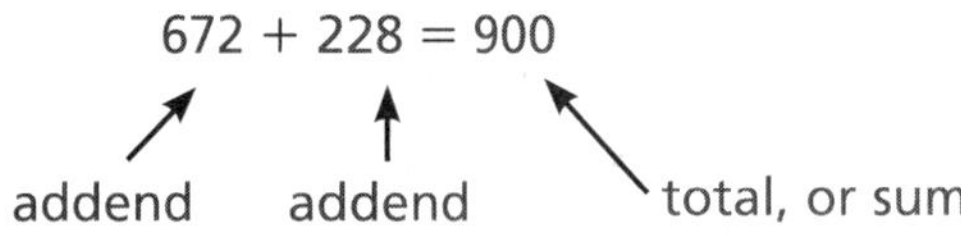

trapezoid

A quadrilateral with exactly one pair of parallel sides.

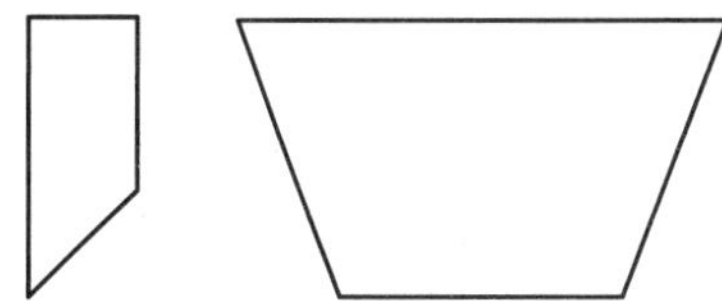

triangle

A polygon with three sides.

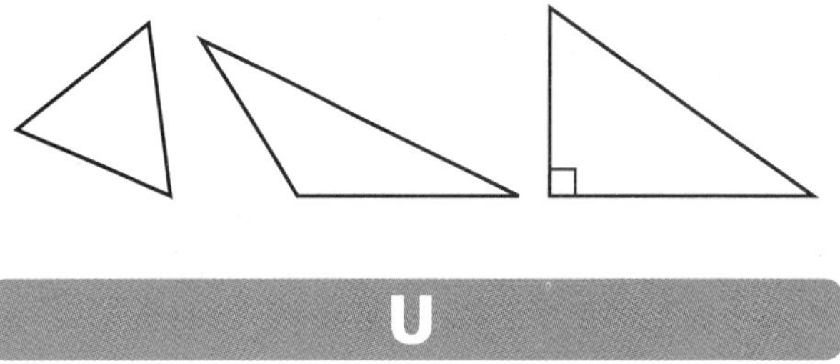

U

ungroup*

To open up 1 in a given place to make 10 of the next smaller place value in order to subtract.

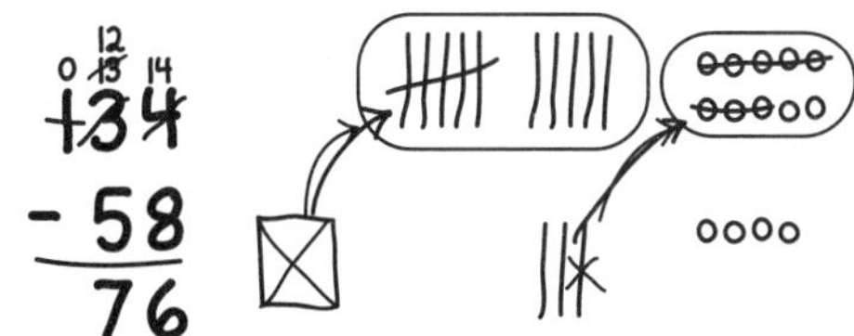

unit fraction

A fraction whose numerator is 1. It shows one equal part of a whole.

Example:

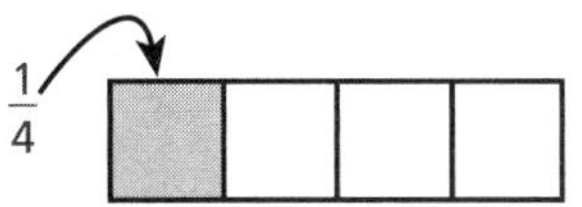

*A classroom research-based term developed for *Math Expressions*

unit square
A square whose area is 1 square unit.

V

variable
A letter or symbol used to represent an unknown number in an algebraic expression or equation.

Example:
$2 + n$
n is a variable.

Venn diagram
A diagram that uses circles to show the relationship among sets of objects.

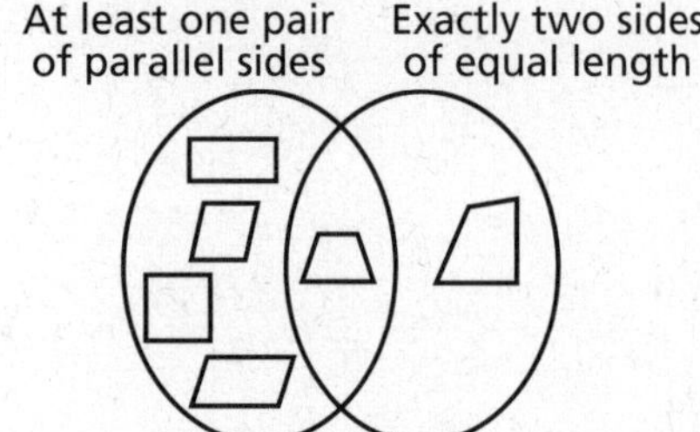

vertex
A point where sides, rays, or edges meet.

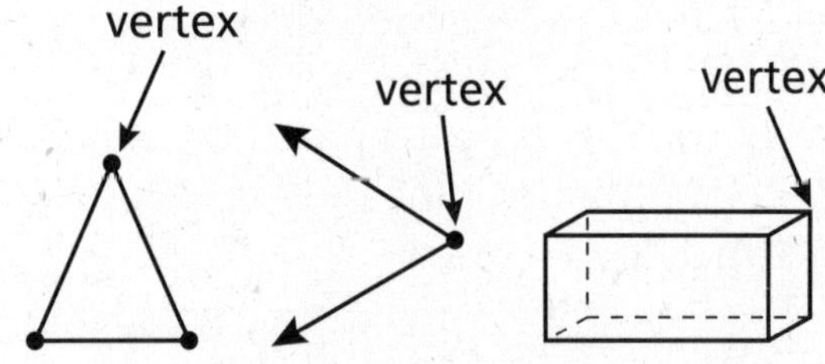

vertical
Extending in two directions, up and down.

vertical bar graph
A bar graph with vertical bars.

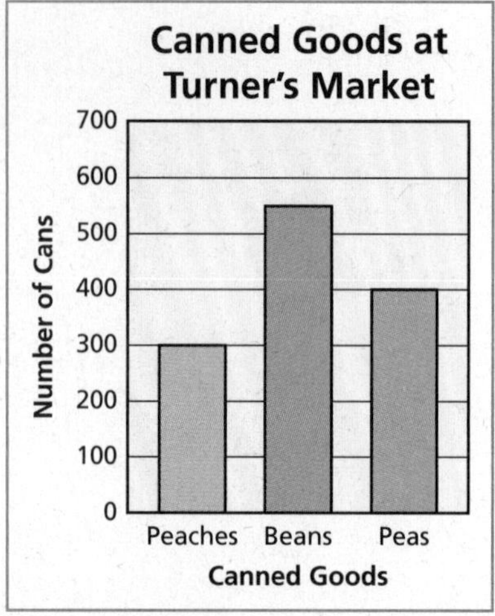

W

weight
The measure of how heavy something is.

word form
A name of a number written using words instead of digits.

Example:
Nine hundred eighty-four

Y

yard (yd)
A U.S. customary unit used to measure length.

1 yard = 3 feet = 36 inches

Z

Zero Property of Multiplication
If 0 is multiplied by a number, the product is 0.

Example:
$3 \times 0 = 0$

3.ARO Algebraic Reasoning and Operations

3.ARO.1	Given an expression such as 3×8, describe the product as the total number of objects in 3 groups of 8 objects.	Unit 1 Lessons 1, 2, 3, 4, 5, 6, 7, 8, 9, 10, 12, 13, 14, 16, 18, 19; Unit 2 Lessons 2, 4, 7, 9, 10, 11, 13, 15
3.ARO.2	Given an expression such as $35 \div 7$, describe the quotient as the *number of objects in a group* when 35 objects are separated into equal shares, or the *number of equal shares* when 35 objects are separated into equal groups of 7 objects.	Unit 1 Lessons 4, 5, 6, 7, 9, 10, 12, 13, 14, 16, 17, 18, 19; Unit 2 Lessons 2, 4, 7, 9, 10, 11, 13, 15
3.ARO.3	Solve multiplication and division word problems through 100 involving arrays, equal groups, and measurements (example: area model); represent the problem using for example, pictures and equations that have symbols for the unknown quantity.	Unit 1 Lessons 2, 3, 4, 5, 6, 7, 9, 10, 12, 13, 14, 16, 17, 18, 19; Unit 2 Lessons 2, 4, 7, 9, 10, 11, 13, 15; Unit 3 Lessons 20, 21; Unit 4 Lesson 15; Unit 5 Lesson 5; Unit 6 Lessons 2, 3, 8, 9, 10, 11; Unit 7 Lessons 1, 2, 3, 4
3.ARO.4	Given a multiplication or division equation involving 3 whole numbers, find the unknown quantity that makes the equation true.	Unit 1 Lessons 1, 4, 5, 6, 7, 8, 9, 10, 12, 13, 14, 16, 17, 18, 19; Unit 2 Lessons 1, 2, 3, 4, 5, 6, 7, 8, 9, 10, 11, 13, 14, 15; Unit 5 Lesson 2; Unit 6 Lessons 2, 3
3.ARO.5	Use properties of operations as strategies for multiplying and dividing.	Unit 1 Lessons 3, 6, 11, 12, 14, 15, 19; Unit 2 Lessons 1, 8, 12, 15; Unit 5 Lesson 2
3.ARO.6	Use multiplication knowledge to recognize that division can be thought of as an unknown factor problem.	Unit 1 Lessons 4, 5, 6, 7, 8, 9, 10, 11, 12, 13, 14, 15, 16, 17, 18; Unit 2 Lessons 1, 2, 3, 4, 5, 6, 7, 8, 9, 10, 11, 12, 13, 14; Unit 5 Lesson 2
3.ARO.7	Demonstrate fluency in multiplying and dividing through 100 by using strategies like the properties of operations or the relationship between multiplication and division (example: if you know $4 \times 7 = 28$ then you know $28 \div 4 = 7$). Know the products of two 1-digit numbers from memory by the end of Grade 3.	Unit 1 Lessons 1, 2, 3, 4, 5, 6, 7, 8, 9, 10, 11, 12, 13, 14, 15, 16, 17, 18, 19; Unit 2 Lessons 1, 2, 3, 4, 5, 6, 7, 8, 9, 10, 11, 12, 13, 14, 15

3.ARO.8	Use the four operations to solve two-step word problems; represent the problems with equations using a letter for an unknown quantity. Determine if an answer is reasonable by estimating (example: round to estimate the answer) and using mental math.	Unit 2 Lessons 9, 10, 11, 13; Unit 3 Lessons 17, 19; Unit 6 Lessons 7, 8, 9, 10, 11
3.ARO.9	Find arithmetic patterns (example: find patterns in addition and multiplication tables). Use properties of operations to explain the patterns.	Unit 1 Lessons 1, 5, 6, 7, 8, 10, 12, 15, 19; Unit 2 Lessons 1, 3, 5, 6, 8, 14, 15; Unit 3 Lesson 17
3.ARO.10	Create, describe, and apply single-operation input-output rules involving addition, subtraction and multiplication to solve problems in various contexts.	Unit 3 Lesson 22

3.PVO Place Value and Operations

3.PVO.1	Understand how to use place value when rounding whole numbers to the nearest 10, 100, 1,000, and 10,000.	Unit 3 Lessons 1, 2, 3, 4, 5, 6, 10, 18, 19; Unit 6 Lessons 4, 8
3.PVO.2	Use strategies and algorithms reflecting properties of operations, place value, and/or the fact that addition and subtraction are related, to fluently add and subtract through 1,000.	Unit 3 Lessons 2, 3, 4, 5, 6, 7, 8, 9, 10, 11, 12, 13, 14, 15, 16, 18; Unit 4 Lessons 12, 13; Unit 6 Lessons 1, 2, 3, 4, 5, 6, 8, 9, 10, 11; Unit 7 Lessons 1, 2, 3
3.PVO.3	Use place value and properties of operations to multiply a 1-digit number and a multiple of 10 through 90 (example: 6×40 and 9×70).	Unit 2 Lesson 12; Unit 3 Lessons 20, 21
3.PVO.4	Read, write and demonstrate multiple equivalent representations for numbers up to 100,000 using objects, visual representations, including standard form, word form, expanded form, and expanded notation.	Unit 3 Lesson 19
3.PVO.5	Compare whole numbers through the hundred thousands and represent the comparisons using the symbols $>$, $<$, or $=$.	Unit 3 Lesson 19
3.PVO.6	Find 10,000 more or 10,000 less than a given five-digit number. Find 1,000 more or 1,000 less than a given four- or five-digit. Find 100 more or 100 less than a given four- or five-digit number.	Unit 3 Lesson 19
3.PVO.7	Use strategies and algorithms based on knowledge of place value, equality and properties of addition and multiplication to multiply a two- or three-digit number by a one-digit number.	Unit 3 Lessons 20, 21

3.FO Fractions and Operations		
3.FO.1	Understand that a unit fraction, $\frac{1}{b}$, represents one part of a whole that has been separated into b equal parts (example: $\frac{1}{3}$ is one of 3 equal parts) and the fraction $\frac{a}{b}$ is formed by $\frac{1}{b}$-size parts (example: $\frac{2}{3}$ can be thought of as putting together two $\frac{1}{3}$ parts). Find parts of a set using visual representations.	Unit 4 Lessons 1, 2, 4, 5; Unit 5 Lessons 9, 10
3.FO.2	Recognize that fractions can be indicated on a number line. Use a number line to represent fractions.	Unit 4 Lessons 2, 3, 4
3.FO.2.a	Use a number line to show a unit fraction $\frac{1}{b}$. Know that the interval from 0 to 1 represents the whole; to show $\frac{1}{b}$ the whole must be separated into b equal parts. Understand that from 0 to the first endpoint of the partitioned whole is where the fraction $\frac{1}{b}$ is located.	Unit 4 Lessons 2, 3; Unit 5 Lesson 8
3.FO.2.b	Draw a number line to locate fractions; starting at 0 and ending at 1, separate the whole into a equal-size parts, $\frac{1}{b}$. Understand that the length of the interval created is $\frac{a}{b}$, and the endpoint of the interval locates $\frac{a}{b}$.	Unit 4 Lessons 2, 3, 4; Unit 5 Lesson 8
3.FO.3	Understand special cases of equivalent fractions and explain why such fractions are equivalent. Reason about size to compare and order fractions.	Unit 4 Lessons 2, 3, 4, 5; Unit 5 Lessons 7, 9, 10
3.FO.3.a	Given two fractions, understand that they are equivalent if their size is the same, or if they are located at the same point on the number line.	Unit 4 Lesson 3; Unit 5 Lessons 8, 9
3.FO.3.b	Recognize and find equivalent fractions less than 1 (example: $\frac{1}{3} = \frac{3}{6}$ and $\frac{1}{4} = \frac{2}{8}$). Use methods such as, making models, to explain why the fractions are equivalent.	Unit 5 Lessons 7, 8, 9, 10
3.FO.3.c	Write a whole number as a fraction; identify fractions equivalent to whole numbers.	Unit 4 Lessons 2, 3; Unit 5 Lessons 8, 9
3.FO.3.d	Use reasoning about size to compare and order fractions with the same numerator but different denominators, or with the same denominator. Understand that to make an accurate comparison, the two fractions must refer to the same whole. Record the comparison with symbols >, <, or =, and justify the results (example: use a picture or other model).	Unit 4 Lessons 4, 5; Unit 5 Lessons 9, 10
3.FO.4	Explain and demonstrate how fractions $\frac{1}{4}$, $\frac{1}{2}$, $\frac{3}{4}$ and a whole relate to time, measurement, and money, and demonstrate using visual representation.	Unit 4 Lesson 11; Unit 5 Lesson 9

3.MDA Measurement and Data Analysis		
3.MDA.1	Know how to tell and write time to the nearest minute and measure time in minutes. Use a number line, or other methods, to solve word problems that involve adding and subtracting time in minutes. Know relationships among units of time.	Unit 4 Lessons 7, 8, 9, 10, 11
3.MDA.2	Use the standard units, liter (L), grams (g), and kilograms (kg) to measure and estimate liquid volume and mass. Solve one-step problems about mass or volume given in the same units and that involve the four operations. Represent the problem by using a diagram (example: a number line) or other methods.	Unit 7 Lessons 1, 2, 3, 4
3.MDA.2.a	Solve problems and make change involving money using a combination of coins and bills.	Unit 5 Lessons 11, 12
3.MDA.2.b	Solve problems involving estimating of temperature and use an analog thermometer to determine temperature to the nearest degree in Fahrenheit and Celsius.	Unit 4 Lesson 14; Unit 5 Lessons 11, 12
3.MDA.3	Given a collection of data in several categories, make a picture graph and bar graph with labeled scales. Use information from bar graphs to solve one- and two-step problems to answer *how many more* and *how many less* questions. Collect data through observations, surveys, and experiments.	Unit 4 Lessons 12, 13, 14, 15
3.MDA.4	Create a group of data by estimating and measuring lengths with customary units (inch, half-inch, quarter-inch) or the metric unit, centimeter. Use a line plot to display the data, labeling the horizontal scale with the correct units (example: whole inches, half-inches, or quarter-inches).	Unit 4 Lessons 6, 14, 15, 16
3.MDA.5	Know that area is an attribute of two-dimensional (plane) figures; understand concepts of area measurement.	Unit 1 Lesson 11; Unit 2 Lesson 2; Unit 4 Lesson 6; Unit 5 Lessons 1, 3, 5, 6
3.MDA.5.a	Recognize that a *unit square* has a side length of *1 unit* and an area of *1 square unit* and can be used to measure area of plane figures.	Unit 1 Lesson 11; Unit 2 Lesson 2; Unit 5 Lessons 1, 3
3.MDA.5.b	Understand that if a plane figure can be covered by *n* unit squares without having gaps or overlaps, then the figure has an area of *n* square units.	Unit 1 Lesson 11; Unit 2 Lesson 2; Unit 5 Lessons 1, 3, 6
3.MDA.6	Count unit squares to find the area of a figure; use standard units (square inch, square foot, square centimeter, square meter) and non-standard units (example: tiles) to measure area.	Unit 1 Lesson 11; Unit 5 Lessons 1, 2, 4, 6

3.MDA.7	Understand the relationship between area and the operations of multiplication and addition.	Unit 1 Lessons 11, 12; Unit 2 Lesson 1; Unit 3 Lessons 20, 21; Unit 5 Lessons 1, 2, 3; Unit Lesson 9
3.MDA.7.a	Use tiling to find the area of rectangles with given side lengths; show that the resulting area can also be found by multiplying the two side lengths.	Unit 1 Lesson 11; Unit 2 Lesson 2; Unit 5 Lessons 1, 2
3.MDA.7.b	Solve real-world and other mathematical problems that involve finding the area of rectangles by multiplying the side lengths (given in whole-numbers); use reasoning to illustrate the products as rectangular areas.	Unit 1 Lessons 11,12; Unit 2 Lessons 2, 6; Unit 5 Lessons 1, 2, 3, 4, 5; Unit 7 Lesson 9
3.MDA.7.c	Use reasoning and area models to represent the Distributive Property: given a rectangle that has side lengths a and $b + c$ use tiles to illustrate understanding that the area is the sum of $a \times b$ and $a \times c$.	Unit 1 Lessons 11, 12, 14; Unit 2 Lesson 1; Unit 5 Lesson 2
3.MDA.7.d	Recognize that addition can be used to find area. Partition rectilinear figures (example: composite rectangular figures) into rectangles having no overlaps, then find the area of the original figure by adding the areas of the parts; use this approach to solve real-world problems.	Unit 1 Lessons 11, 12; Unit 5 Lessons 2, 4, 5, 6
3.MDA.8	Solve problems (real world and other mathematical contexts) that involve perimeters of polygons in the following situations: given side lengths, find perimeter; given perimeter and a side length, find the unknown length; find rectangles with the same perimeter and different areas or same area and different perimeters.	Unit 5 Lessons 1, 2, 3, 5; Unit 7 Lesson 9
3.MDA.9	Measure distances around objects.	Unit 4 Lesson 14

3.GSR Geometry and Spatial Reasoning

3.GSR.1	Recognize that geometric figures belonging to different categories may have attributes in common and these shared attributes can form a larger category (example: although squares, rectangles, and rhombuses belong to different categories they share the attributes four sides, four angles, and four vertices and belong to the larger category, quadrilaterals.) Know that squares, rectangles, and rhombuses are quadrilaterals; sketch quadrilaterals that are not in those categories.	Unit 7 Lessons 5, 6, 7, 8, 9
3.GSR.2	Separate geometric figures into parts with equal areas. Represent the area of a part as a unit fraction of the whole.	Unit 4 Lessons 1, 2, 4, 5; Unit 5 Lesson 10; Unit 7 Lesson 5
3.GSR.3	Identify parallel and perpendicular lines in various contexts, and use them to describe and create geometric figures such as right triangles, rectangles, parallelograms and trapezoids.	Unit 7 Lessons 5, 6, 7, 8

MPP1	
Problem Solving	Unit 1 Lessons 3, 4, 5, 6, 7, 9, 10, 12, 13, 14, 16, 18, 19 Unit 2 Lessons 1, 2, 4, 7, 9, 10, 13, 15 Unit 3 Lessons 3, 4, 5, 6, 7, 8, 9, 10, 11, 12, 14, 15, 16, 17, 18, 20, 21 Unit 4 Lessons 9, 10, 11, 12, 13, 14, 15, 16 Unit 5 Lessons 2, 5, 9, 10, 11 Unit 6 Lessons 1, 2, 3, 4, 5, 6, 7, 8, 9, 10, 11 Unit 7 Lessons 1, 2, 3, 4, 5, 9
MPP2	
Abstract and Quantitative Reasoning	Unit 1 Lessons 1, 3, 5, 7, 8, 10, 11, 12, 19 Unit 2 Lessons 1, 2, 3, 5, 6, 8, 13, 15 Unit 3 Lessons 1, 2, 5, 6, 8, 9, 11, 12, 13, 14, 15, 16, 17, 18, 19, 20, 22 Unit 4 Lessons 1, 2, 3, 4, 5, 6, 9, 11, 12, 16 Unit 5 Lessons 1, 2, 3, 4, 5, 7, 8, 9, 10 Unit 6 Lessons 1, 2, 3, 4, 8, 11 Unit 7 Lessons 1, 2, 3, 5, 9
MPP3	
Use and Evaluate Logical Reasoning	Unit 1 Lessons 1, 2, 3, 4, 5, 6, 7, 8, 9, 10, 11, 12, 13, 14, 15, 16, 18, 19 Unit 2 Lessons 1, 2, 3, 4, 5, 6, 8, 9, 10, 11, 12, 13, 14, 15 Unit 3 Lessons 1, 2, 3, 4, 5, 6, 7, 8, 9, 10, 11, 12, 13, 14, 15, 16, 17, 18, 20, 21, 22 Unit 4 Lessons 1, 2, 3, 4, 5, 6, 7, 8, 9, 10, 11, 12, 13, 14, 15, 16 Unit 5 Lessons 1, 2, 3, 4, 5, 7, 8, 9, 10, 11, 12 Unit 6 Lessons 1, 2, 3, 4, 5, 6, 7, 8, 9, 10, 11 Unit 7 Lessons 1, 2, 3, 4, 5, 6, 8, 9
MPP4	
Mathematical Modeling	Unit 1 Lessons 1, 2, 3, 4, 5, 6, 7, 9, 10, 12, 13, 14, 15, 16, 17, 18, 19 Unit 2 Lessons 2, 4, 7, 9, 11, 13, 15 Unit 3 Lessons 3, 4, 8, 9, 10, 11, 12, 14, 16, 17, 18, 20, 21, 22 Unit 4 Lessons 9, 10, 11, 12, 13, 14, 16 Unit 5 Lessons 2, 5, 9, 10, 11 Unit 6 Lessons 1, 2, 3, 4, 8, 9, 10, 11 Unit 7 Lessons 1, 2, 3, 4, 5, 9

MPP5	
Use Mathematical Tools	Unit 1 Lessons 1, 2, 3, 4, 5, 6, 7, 8, 9, 10, 11, 12, 13, 14, 15, 16, 17, 18 Unit 2 Lessons 1, 2, 3, 4, 5, 6, 7, 8, 9, 10, 11, 12, 13, 14, 15 Unit 3 Lessons 1, 2, 3, 4, 5, 6, 7, 8, 13, 17, 18, 19, 20, 21 Unit 4 Lessons 1, 2, 3, 5, 6, 7, 8, 9, 10, 11, 14, 16 Unit 5 Lessons 1, 2, 6, 7, 8, 11, 12 Unit 6 Lessons 4, 11 Unit 7 Lessons 2, 3, 5, 7, 8, 9
MPP6	
Use Precise Mathematical Language	Unit 1 Lessons 1, 2, 3, 4, 5, 6, 7, 8, 9, 10, 11, 12, 13, 14, 15, 16, 18, 19 Unit 2 Lessons 1, 2, 3, 4, 5, 6, 7, 8, 9, 10, 11, 12, 13, 14, 15 Unit 3 Lessons 1, 2, 3, 4, 5, 6, 7, 8, 9, 10, 11, 12, 13, 14, 15, 16, 17, 18, 19, 20, 21, 22 Unit 4 Lessons 1, 2, 3, 4, 5, 6, 7, 8, 9, 10, 11, 12, 13, 14, 15, 16 Unit 5 Lessons 1, 2, 3, 4, 5, 7, 8, 9, 11 Unit 6 Lessons 1, 2, 3, 4, 5, 6, 7, 8, 9, 10, 11 Unit 7 Lessons 1, 2, 3, 4, 5, 6, 7, 8, 9
MPP7	
See Structure	Unit 1 Lessons 1, 2, 4, 5, 6, 7, 8, 10, 11, 12, 13, 15, 17, 18, 19 Unit 2 Lessons 1, 3, 5, 6, 14, 15 Unit 3 Lessons 1, 2, 3, 4, 11, 14, 16, 17, 18, 19, 21, 22 Unit 4 Lessons 1, 2, 3, 13, 16 Unit 5 Lessons 1, 4, 6, 7, 10 Unit 6 Lessons 1, 2, 3, 5, 8, 11 Unit 7 Lessons 1, 5, 6, 7, 8, 9
MPP8	
Generalize	Unit 1 Lessons 1, 3, 5, 7, 8, 10, 11, 13, 15, 19 Unit 2 Lessons 1, 3, 5, 6, 10, 12, 14, 15 Unit 3 Lessons 5, 6, 14, 17, 18, 19, 20 Unit 4 Lessons 1, 2, 3, 4, 5, 6, 15, 16 Unit 5 Lessons 3, 6, 7, 8, 9, 10, 11 Unit 6 Lessons 1, 2, 4, 11 Unit 7 Lessons 3, 5, 8, 9

A

B

C

D

E

F

G

H

I

K

L

M

N

O

P

Q

R

Number Tables

Scrambled Tables (Volume 2)

E

×	4	2	5	1	3	8	10	7	9	6
4	16	8	20	4	12	32	40	28	36	24
1	4	2	5	1	3	8	10	7	9	6
2	8	4	10	2	6	16	20	14	18	12
5	20	10	25	5	15	40	50	35	45	30
3	12	6	15	3	9	24	30	21	27	18
9	36	18	45	9	27	72	90	63	81	54
6	24	12	30	6	18	48	60	42	54	36
10	40	20	50	10	30	80	100	70	90	60
7	28	14	35	7	21	56	70	49	63	42
8	32	16	40	8	24	64	80	56	72	48

F

×	9	8	6	7	4	6	8	7	4	9
2	18	16	12	14	8	12	16	14	8	18
3	27	24	18	21	12	18	24	21	12	27
5	45	40	30	35	20	30	40	35	20	45
3	27	24	18	21	12	18	24	21	12	27
5	45	40	30	35	20	30	40	35	20	45
9	81	72	54	63	36	54	72	63	36	81
7	63	56	42	49	28	42	56	49	28	63
6	54	48	36	42	24	36	48	42	24	54
8	72	64	48	56	32	48	64	56	32	72
4	36	32	24	28	16	24	32	28	16	36

G

×	7	6	8	7	8	6	8	7	6	8
5	35	30	40	35	40	30	40	35	30	40
4	28	24	32	28	32	24	32	28	24	32
3	21	18	24	21	24	18	24	21	18	24
2	14	12	16	14	16	12	16	14	12	16
8	56	48	64	56	64	48	64	56	48	64
9	63	54	72	63	72	54	72	63	54	72
7	49	42	56	49	56	42	56	49	42	56
6	42	36	48	42	48	36	48	42	36	48
8	56	48	64	56	64	48	64	56	48	64
6	42	36	48	42	48	36	48	42	36	48

H

×	4	6	7	8	9	6	9	8	7	4
4	16	24	28	32	36	24	36	32	28	16
6	24	36	42	48	54	36	54	48	42	24
7	28	42	49	56	63	42	63	56	49	28
8	32	48	56	64	72	48	72	64	56	32
9	36	54	63	72	81	54	81	72	63	36
8	32	48	56	64	72	48	72	64	56	32
9	36	54	63	72	81	54	81	72	63	36
4	16	24	28	32	36	24	36	32	28	16
7	28	42	49	56	63	42	63	56	49	28
6	24	36	42	48	54	36	54	48	42	24

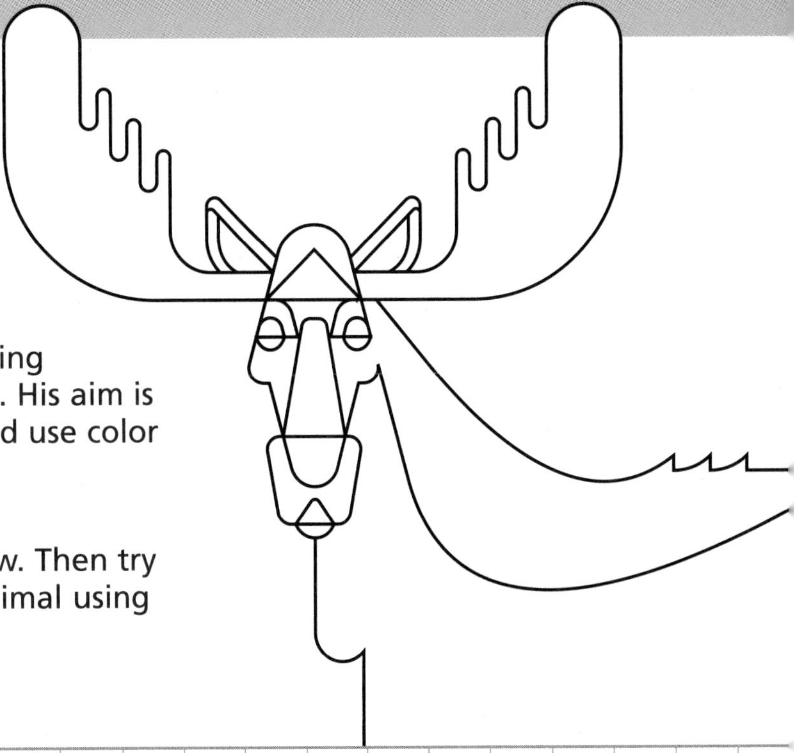

Illustrator: Josh Brill

Did you ever try to use shapes to draw animals like the moose on the cover?

Over the last 10 years Josh has been using geometric shapes to design his animals. His aim is to keep the animal drawings simple and use color to make them appealing.

Add some color to the moose Josh drew. Then try drawing a cat or dog or some other animal using the shapes below.

Shape Toolbox

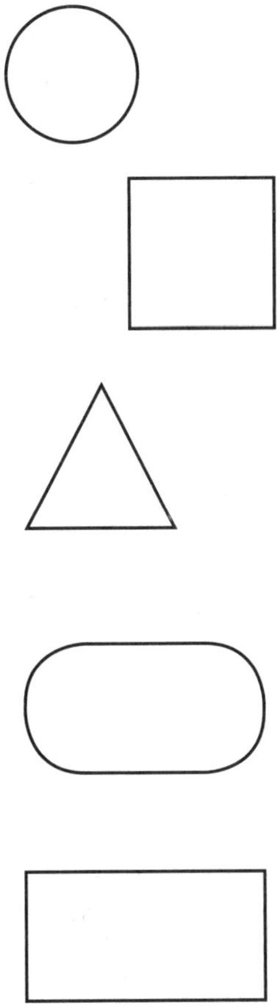